Lords of Life

A History of the Kings of Thailand

HRH Prince Chula Chakrabongse

RIVER BOOKS

Printed and distributed in 2019 by River Books
396 Maharaj Road, Tatien, Bangkok 10200
Tel. (66 2) 224 6686, 225 0139, 622 1900
Fax. (66 2) 225 3861
E-mail: order@riverbooksbk.com
www.riverbooksbk.com

Editor: Narisa Chakrabongse
Production supervision: Paisarn Piemmettawat
Design: Narisa Chakrabongse

ISBN 978 616 451 030 2

Printed and bound by Sirivatana Interprint Public Co., Ltd.

Contents

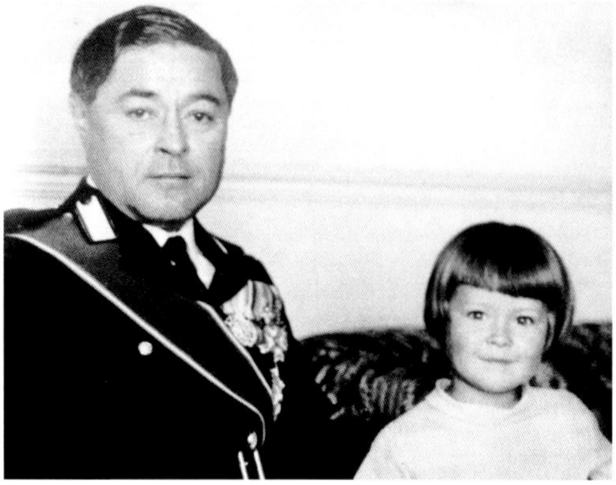

To Narisara Chakrabongse

Darling Daughter,
It will be a long time before you can read this book. It will be even longer before you can understand and appreciate it. But as it is the history of our Chakri Family, I can only dedicate it to you, a very junior and humble member of that great family, for amongst their members, high or low in rank, you are naturally the one closest to my heart.

I hope that when you come to read and understand this book, you will be truly and rightly proud of your Chakri ancestry and your direct descent from five kings and five queens, as well as from your grandfather who did not live long enough to complete his work for the country he loved so well. In all your actions I ask you always to try to cherish and honour their sacred memory. With my very best love and wishes for your happiness above all else.

Papa.
Tredethy, near Bodmin, Cornwall.

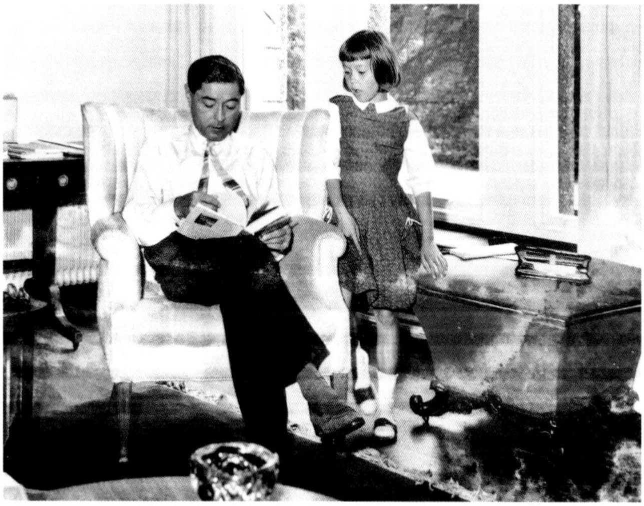

Foreword

It is now 60 years since my father dedicated this book to me in moving words that for years have made me cry. Sadly, he died when I was only seven and so we never had the chance to discuss his work together and I never got to tell him how much I enjoyed this book and also his Thai autobiography *Born in Paruskavan Palace.*

Years after his death, when I talked to some people about the book and read some reviews, I learned that it has been criticised by some Western and Thai scholars for being too reverential towards the Chakri dynasty. Of course, this is true, and there are not many authors who include themselves in the narrative of what was intended as a general history. Nevertheless, I can also see that my father sought to counter various accounts which, for example, credited the reforms enacted by King Mongkut and his successor King Chulalongkorn to the influence of Anna Leonowens, the infamous governess whose memoirs inspired the Broadway musical *The King and I.* Thus he devotes several pages to showing how her account contained many untruths and that subsequent retellings resulted in almost complete fantasy.

Having been to Trinity College Cambridge and written numerous history books, which were not about his family, I am sure my father would have been fascinated by new approaches in the historiography of Southeast Asia in general and Thailand in particular. On the other hand, having put a positive slant on the changes from an absolute to a constitutional monarchy, I'm also sure he would be surprised to see how little democracy has advanced in Thailand and, as someone who lived through the Second World War and for whom being in the British Home Guard was one of his proudest accomplishments, I feel certain he would be shocked by the recent rise of right-wing nativism across the world including in his adopted home of Great Britain.

As my father is no longer here to make any changes to this book, I and my colleagues at River Books have decided to leave his text and footnotes unchanged except for Thai place names and the names of some individuals. Transliterating Thai into English remains difficult and it was decided to choose the most commonly-used version of a particular name. If someone's name has been spelt incorrectly, the fault is mine and not my father's.

In 1995, my colleague Paisarn Piemmettawat and I republished the Thai version of this book with many additional photographs. In preparing this 60th anniversary version of *Lords of Life*, we decided to do the same. I also asked Barend J. Terwiel, a River Books author and distinguished scholar of Thai history, to write a short essay bringing Thai history up to date, as far as that is possible.

Although I was only seven when my father died, his life and his words have been a great influence on me. I have always loved books and thirty years ago decided to found River Books to publish on the history, art and culture of Thailand and Southeast Asia, attempting in a small way to continue my father's inspiring example. Sixty years on, two of my father's books in Thai remain among the River Books bestsellers.

Narisa Chakrabongse

Author's Preface

This is an attempt to write a History of Thailand (or Siam) in English, a task not accomplished since W. A. R. Wood's book was first published in 1924. There have been many different works in which some parts of Thai history have been included, and some excellent monographs on certain personages and aspects of that history. Also an English book by a Thai, Phra Sarasas, was published first in Japan, in December, 1940, which dealt partly with History, Geography, and Thai Civilization.

I have chosen to concentrate on the Absolute, or rather Paternal Monarchy of Bangkok (1782 to 1932) for three reasons. Firstly because it is the most fully documentated period, secondly because it leads directly to Thailand today and her relations with the rest of the world, and thirdly because Wood barely touched on it at all. Also I feel that the House of Chakri, judged by any standards, has been an outstanding dynasty.

As there has been no general history of Thailand in English since Wood's, which may not be so universally available now, I have added a preceding chapter dealing briefly with the history of the Thai race since they were first known until the fall of Ayutthaya in 1767. Without knowing something of the earlier periods, it would be difficult to measure the work of the Chakri monarchs of Bangkok. For students of present-day Thai affairs, I have closed this book with a chapter on Thailand after December 10th, 1932, which is really a catalogue of events and dates down to the end of 1959.

The book is mainly based on Thai sources, published and unpublished, as well as contemporary sources in English and French. I have also drawn upon and freely quoted modern works in these two languages, largely because Thai sources and early English and French sources may not be so readily available to the general reader for consultation. I gratefully acknowledge with thanks my indebtedness to these later and living authors, but wherever I have had to disagree with their interpretation of Thai history, I have clearly said so, and I trust, with supporting evidence or justifiable surmise.

I have tried to write this book objectively and not from the Thai point of view. I wished especially to avoid references to myself, but as my father held a prominent position and was involved in dynastic problems, and I myself have been an eye-witness of certain events, as well as being the recipient of important information and letters, my wish has not proved possible. It has also been necessary almost to over-stress the importance of the rank of Chao Fa, which I have followed King Mongkut in translating as celestial prince, for without understanding its importance or difference, it would be impossible to comprehend the dynastic problems or the very fabric of ranks in the Chakri Family.

No rule has yet been definitely laid down for the writing of Thai or Thai-Sanskrit names in Roman characters, as to whether it should be phonetic or by transliteration. I have chosen to compromise on what is nearest in writing or in sound. As the word written as Thai should be pronounced as tie rather than thigh, I have followed the other custom of writing it as Thai. The reason for the usual existence of the "h" is to show that the "t" is not aspirated. In the Thai language we have both aspirated and unaspirated "t" and "p".

I have used the name Siam for the country as it was so universally accepted, until I come to the time when it was officially changed to Thailand, as accepted by the United Nations and all the countries with which Thailand has diplomatic relations. As I maintain that the equivalent of the name or adjective Siamese does not exist in our language, I have used the term Thai throughout.

I have acknowledged at appropriate places the valuable help I have received from so many kind and interested persons. I want to pay a tribute of gratitude especially to my cousin, Prince Dhani, for his help in the form of information, advice, and clarifying some of my doubts. I should like here to thank Professor H. R. Trevor-Roper for his preface, my wife for her constant interest and inspiration, Captain Bisdar Chulasewok and Captain R. W. Potts for their assistance to me in writing this book, in Thailand and in England respectively. I also wish to pay a sincere tribute to Alvin Redman for his encouragement in urging me to write this history which has for so long been in my thoughts.

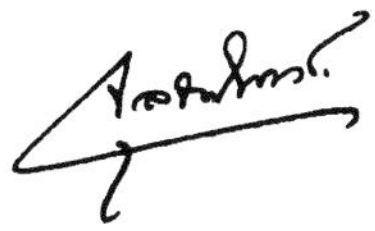

Chula Chakrabongse.

Tredethy, near Bodmin, Cornwall.

INTRODUCTION

by H. R. Trevor-Roper

Regius Professor of Modern History in the University of Oxford

In the nineteenth century the ancient monarchies of the Far East surrendered one by one to the power of Europe. For three centuries they had known Europe and felt its touch; they had realized, or been made to realize, its technical superiority; but they had still preserved their independence and their pride. The Emperor of China regarded George III as an outer barbarian whose emissary could only come to pay tribute. The King of Burma insisted on treating George IV as one of his 'vassals'. These rulers were prepared to use Europeans: they did not expect to be used by them. But then, as the nineteenth century wore on, the cascade began. The 'Opium War' in China was the warning signal. By the end of the century, what was left of ancient Asia? China, the Celestial Empire, the symbol and pillar of tradition and stability, was humbled, cantoned, garrisoned. The British, from India, had imposed their rule on Burma and Malaya, the French on Indo-China. Indonesia had long been Dutch. In South-East Asia only one historic kingdom preserved its independence: Siam, or, as we should now call it, Thailand. Like Japan, Siam stood out as an island, circled but not swamped by the imperialist flood.

How did Siam survive? We have compared it with Japan, but in fact it is not comparable. Japan is an insular power, protected by its insularity. It also protected itself by a revolution : it resisted Europe by imitating Europe and becoming an industrial, military power. But Siam had no such advantages. It is accessible by land on all sides. It was not an industrial or even a commercial power. Its occupation was agriculture. At that time it did not even, as now, export rice. Its only export was a trickle of elephants. Its trade was passive, carried on by Chinese settlers and merely taxed or skimmed by Thai rulers and courtiers. And yet it was not, like Tibet, ignored by the West as unimportant. Successive missions and treaties showed the interest of Europe. Siam offered opportunities: it could be a consumer of British goods; it also offered dangers; it could be a focus of resistance to the French in Indo-China. Its survival among all these dangers is therefore all the more remarkable.

Partly, of course, it was due to good luck. In their imperialist expansion the European powers sought to avoid expensive conflict with each other. To do so, sometimes they agreed on equitable division - a free hand in Morocco to the French in exchange for a free hand in Egypt to the British. But sometimes they found it more convenient to maintain buffer-states between them. Thus, in the Middle East, Britain and Russia agreed to preserve Persia and Afghanistan. Thus, in the Far East, Britain and France agreed to preserve Siam. Between them, they had destroyed its traditional enemy, Burma, and had pared away its vassal states in the Malay Peninsula, in Laos and Cambodia. They had ensured an open market for their goods. They had even, indirectly, fostered its prosperity: for to pay for those goods they had stimulated rice-growing not merely for consumption but for export. Having done all this they could afford to leave the country politically independent, a comfortable poultice between their otherwise raw frontiers.

To British readers this diplomatic history is the most obvious and most accessible explanation. And yet it is only part of the story: the external part. If the internal history of Siam had been different – if the country had been unskilfully ruled, or divided, like so many Asiatic monarchies, by social unrest or courtly or tribal or religious quarrels, how much easier it would have been, or seemed, for the colonizing powers to invade and conquer rather than to spare and cultivate it. A buffer-state loses its purpose unless it is also a stable state: an unstable state is a standing danger, and better partitioned. As the only buffer-state which European imperialism left in East Asia, Siam must have given evidence of extraordinary stability.

That stability, all historians agree, was the achievement of an extraordinary line of kings, the Chakri dynasty, which ruled, as absolute monarchs, 'Lords of Life', for 150 years from 1782 until 1932, and which still reigns under a new middle-class constitution. The work of this dynasty was so important, and made such an impact on British history in Asia, that it deserves to be better known in Britain. If it is not known, that is largely because it must depend upon Siamese as well as upon British sources. To be understood, it must also be written from a Siamese, not a British, point of view. After all, we can easily see 19th century Siam through British eyes – through the eyes of the government of India, of Rajah Brooke, of Sir John Bowring, of that English woman who was for five years the governess of the Siamese crown, Mrs. Leonowens. But this is an external view. To see how the problems of Siam were faced and solved from within, by the Siamese rulers, requires a different perspective. We must put ourselves in the place of men who, with their own ancient traditions behind and around them, found themselves suddenly face to face with a new force – a force which was dissolving the whole world around them and might easily, if they failed in understanding, or nerve, or tact, or duty, dissolve theirs. To do this requires, on our part, an effort of imagination. We can be helped if the historian who interprets this history to us comes himself from the society which faced, instead of posed, the problem.

For this reason, we could hardly have a better guide than Prince Chula Chakrabongse, himself a member of the Chakri dynasty, the grandson of its greatest, most revolutionary king, Chulalongkorn. Prince Chula, like so many of his family in the last century, is an anglophil prince, educated in England, resident partly in England, married to an English wife. At the same time he remains devoted to his own country which he here interprets to us as he has previously, by his writings and his translations, interpreted us to them. As a member of the dynasty, his history is necessarily a family history. A family history, in this sense, like a family biography, has its special charm, as it also has its special difficulties. But Prince Chula, while displaying this charm, is fortified against the difficulties. He has studied history at Cambridge and has written 'objective', 'professional' history before turning his industry and talent to this tempting but intimate and therefore difficult subject. He is therefore, in many ways, the ideal biographer of his line of kings.

Introductions should be brief, and I do not wish to forestall Prince Chula's narrative. I shall only say something about what the reader may expect to learn from it. In the first chapter he will find eighteenth century Siam placed in its long historical perspective. He will see it, as it were, developing out of the past, out of itself, out of contact with its immediate neighbours. He will learn the terms of its existence, the basis of its nineteenth century problems. And he will see the state to which it was reduced just before the accession of the new dynasty. After a century of anarchy and isolation, the ancient capital of Ayutthya had been sacked by the Burmese, its buildings and records destroyed, its life and government and culture dislocated. A successful usurper for a time restored order, only to lapse into whimsical megalomania, on one hand unfrocking the clergy by the thousands, on the other hand seeking, by concentrated private devotion, 'to enable himself to fly in the air'. It was a palace revolt against this interesting *dévot* which brought his most successful general in haste from Cambodia to accept the throne and become the first Chakri king. Such was the inauspicious beginning of the dynasty which, from its new capital of Bangkok, would soon have to face the mounting pressure of imperialist Europe throughout the Far East.

Through the rest of the book we can follow the fortunes of this new dynasty : a dynasty which ruled absolutely, taking its ministers largely from its own numerous members, but which nevertheless first rebuilt and reformed the fabric of the state and then, by understanding the realities of power – by study, imitation, adaptation, and occasional timely surrender – carried its country independently through the nineteenth, the colonial, into the twentieth, the ex-colonial century. The greatest of these kings, without doubt, were the two who faced the colonial thrust at its heaviest : King Mongkut, who, after 27 years as a reforming Buddhist abbot, ruled over Siam from 1851 to 1868, and who, by learning the English language, and through it, the sciences of the West, enabled his country to keep its independence; and his son, King Chulalongkorn, the widely-travelled 'revolutionary on the throne', whose reign, from 1868 to 1910, saw the peaceful abolition of slavery, the creation of a modem administration, and the beginning of that tradition, which Prince Chula himself illustrates, of sending all the royal princes to Europe for their education.

These are undoubtedly the greatest of the Chakri kings; but the others also, though less famous, are equally essential to the story. And running through it all, besides the great work of construction and adaptation, there are certain family characteristics which it is pleasant to detect: an unbounded intellectual curiosity, and a natural gentleness which extends even to the revolutions by which the absolute rule of the dynasty was both installed and ended.

This intellectual curiosity, which Prince Chula describes as a typical Siamese trait, finds many forms among the Chakri kings. One of them wrote poems, another reformed historical study, another the ballet, a fourth pained his subjects by performing on the stage. King Mongkut, among his many attainments, studied astronomy and confounded the old believers by predicting a total eclipse of the sun. He learned from everyone, including Christian missionaries, whose virtues he so shrewdly summarized: 4 what you teach us to *do* is admirable, but what you teach us to *believe* is foolish. Most Chakri kings were lovers of elephants : one even had a doctorate in the abstruse science of elephantotrophy; another, King Mongkut himself, wrote a book on the points of a good elephant, which includes, apparently, 'a beautiful snore'; and a third removed the white elephant from the national flag because, in that setting, the noble animal too often resembled a pig. Later members of the family have moved on from elephants; King Chulalongkorn's widow, we read, turned night into day sitting up in bed reading *The Motor* and *The Autocar*, and a younger prince has more recently distinguished himself in Europe as a racing motorist. King Chulalongkorn himself had his literary interests: in the intervals of revolution from above he wrote a cookery book. As for gentleness – how pleasant to read the language of King Mongkut's edicts : 'the absolute monarch's advice against the inelegant practice of throwing dead animals into the waterways', or his insistence that the electors of judges should not hesitate, 'thinking that perhaps their choice would not meet with His Majesty's approval'. And then there are the amiable traits of Mongkut's half-brother and predecessor, King Chesda (Rama III), who – much to the annoyance of Catholic missionaries, who declared it a useless superstition – bought up animals from the slaughterhouse and set them free; and of their father, King Isarasuntom (Rama II), who commuted the death penalty for unchaste monks to the more agreeable fate of cutting grass for the royal elephants.

Altogether it is easy to fall in love with these Siamese kings, with their boat-races and ballets, elephants and astronomy, recipes and poems. But let us not be seduced by these engaging foibles. They enliven Prince Chula's narrative, but are not the substance of it. These rulers were not dilettanti. Their work was a solid work of social construction and reform which deserves commemoration. Thanks to it, they carried their country successfully through the nineteenth century revolution, in which all their neighbours foundered. If they were not able to carry it through the twentieth century revolution, which is still in progress, at least they have enabled themselves, as the reward of such service, to preside over it, and, in Prince Chula's narrative, to record it.

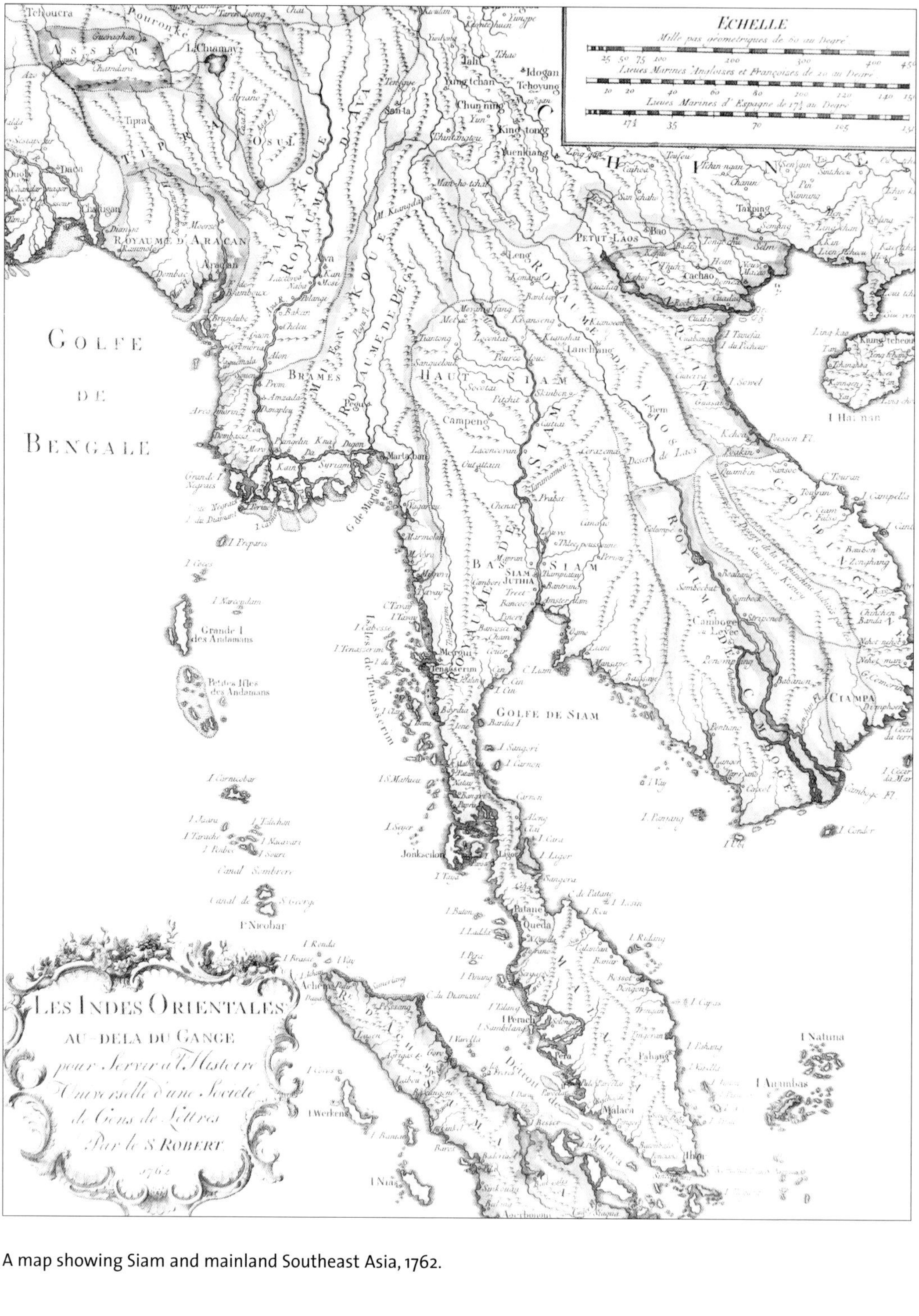

A map showing Siam and mainland Southeast Asia, 1762.

Before

(Circa 4000 B.C. To A.D. 1767)

Lord of Life, or *Chao Jivit*, was the title given to their King by the Thais especially in the latter part of the Paternal Monarchy of Bangkok. It was a colloquial, affectionate, yet awesome title; suggesting that the sovereign had the absolute power of life and death ewer his subjects and enjoyed complete ownership of all the land and resources of the country. Whether or not the first seven monarchs of the Chakri Dynasty uring the years of their absolute rule, from 1782 to 1932, deserved or justified this title is left to the opinion of the reader.

The people over whom they ruled, and of whom their direct descendant is today King, are known in the Western World mostly as Siamese. But in their own language they have for centuries called themselves Thai. There is in fact no such thing as a Siamese language, and in Thai one refers only to Thai people, (*Khon Thai*), Thai food, Thai silk and so on. As for Siam or Thailand, these are both comparatively modern names, as the conception of a nation is of recent date.

The Siamese form a branch of the ancient Thai race who themselves were a branch of a still older race-group – the Mongols, believed to have originated thousands of years ago along the Altai range of mountains now forming the western border of Outer Mongolia. The first semi-historical traces of the Thais were along a strip of land in China, now known as Kiangsu-Shantung, which lies between the Hwang (or Yellow) River and the Yangtse River, where they appeared about 4,500 years ago.[1] Some authorities even say that it was as much as 6,000 years ago, but all early Thai history is lost, and the little that is known is from Chinese history. The Thais first called themselves Ai Lao, while the Chinese called them Mung.

The Thais had been well established for some hundreds of years before the Chinese themselves came on the scene.[2] The Chinese were nomadic tribes who had migrated from the Caspian Sea, and they made the long trail to the Yellow River some 4,000 to 5,000 years ago. Having penetrated peacefully into the area occupied by the Thais, they began to encroach on Thai livelihood, for the Chinese were more industrious and highly gifted in all trades, whereas the Thais preferred simple agriculture. Later the Chinese changed to warlike action and were so successful that they gained full access to the Yellow River. An uneasy peace followed for some time between the Thais along the banks of the Yangtse and the Chinese on the Yellow River, and there were even many marriages between Thai ruling princes and Chinese daughters. Thus the Chinese methods were similar to those used by the Normans in England before the Conquest.

1 Luang Vichitra Vadhkarn: *Siam and the Golden Land* (in Thai), page 39, Bangkok, 1936.

2 *Ibid.*, page 39.

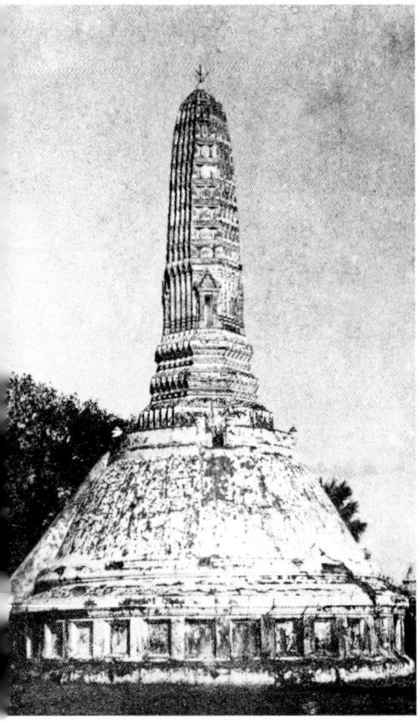

One of the stupa at Nakhon Pathom centre of the Dvaravati kingdom before King Rama IV's renovation. (National Archives Bangkok)

By 2,208 B.C. or roughly 4,000 years ago, the Chinese had already been properly organized as an empire with powerful and autocratic emperors, whilst the Thais still had the disadvantage of being ruled by minor princes or chieftains and were divided into small groups. It became increasingly difficult to live alongside the Chinese without being fully integrated, and many of the Thais must have been absorbed by them. To make matters worse, the ruthless and hardy Tartar horsemen now arrived to harass them further. The obvious way of escape was by mass migration, and the great trek began in the beginning of the Christian era.[3] It was during this long march when they met indigenous peoples who had been living under foreign domination that they came to call themselves Thai – the Free.

They followed the rivers and valleys which ran south, and once started, they never ceased to move slowly – very slowly – down towards the great plains of Indo-China. The "long walk" took hundreds of years and the Thais marched in small groups under their separate chieftains. Some are believed to have paused in the present Chinese province of Yunnan and in the seventh century A.D. founded the Thai Kingdom of Nan Chao. But another theory has recently been put forward that Nan Chao was founded by a Tibeto-Burman race which had ousted the Thais from the Yangtse valley.[4] Prince Dhani, the distinguished Thai scholar, declares that "I have to be convinced by more definite details before I accept the new theory."[5] In any case Nanchao was in A.D. 1254 totally destroyed by the Mongol Emperor Kublai Khan – grandson of Genghis Khan, thus putting an end to any Thai state existing as such in China. A few of the Thais might have escaped to join others in the south, but the majority must have been absorbed into the Chinese race. It is nevertheless claimed that Thai speaking people can still be found in Yunnan to this day.

The land into which various groups of Thais were continually though slowly seeping through – Indo-China – had for long been known to the Indians by the Sanskrit name of *Suvarnabhumi* – Golden Land. This was because gold was plentiful in that area now comprising the modern countries of Burma, Thailand, Laos, Vietnam, Cambodia, and Malaya. The early inhabitants of Golden Land were negroid – some still remain as aboriginal jungle tribes – but they had been largely replaced by more civilized peoples before the Thais arrived. The Mons were the first, coming from the mountains of China, and they set themselves up by the River Salween. The Khmers – later to be such great builders – were a branch of the Mon race. Other early migrants were the Burmese who came from Tibet and they settled along the River Irrawaddy. The central plain and the narrow neck of the Malay peninsula in the south were occupied by the Lawas. The full history of the origins of the Lawas are not exactly known. That they were an artistic and civilized people leaves no doubt, testified by the ruins of their buildings and their utensils which have been found. There was their kingdom of Dvaravati whose actual extent, or even that it was of

3 *Ibid.*, page 50.

4 *The 9th Pacific Science Congress*, Section on Anthropology. Nov., 1957.

5 Prince Dhani in his review of Prince Chula's *The Twain Have Met*, etc. in *Journal of the Siam Society*, Vol. XLVI, Part I, page 77, June, 1958.

the Lawas, is still of some doubt, and is an object of intense research through the method of combining archaeology with geography and topography. The greatest monument to the period is the immense chedi (stupa). Phra Pathom *Chedi*, meaning the first *chedi*, which was built over a thousand years ago, and still stands in its restored form about 40 miles west of Bangkok by the main road and railway line. Although this great *chedi* was built as a Buddhist shrine, it is, however, certain that Dvaravati had been Hinduized and had accepted Brahmanism before the arrival of Buddhist missionaries sent by the Emperor Asoka in the first century of the Christian era.

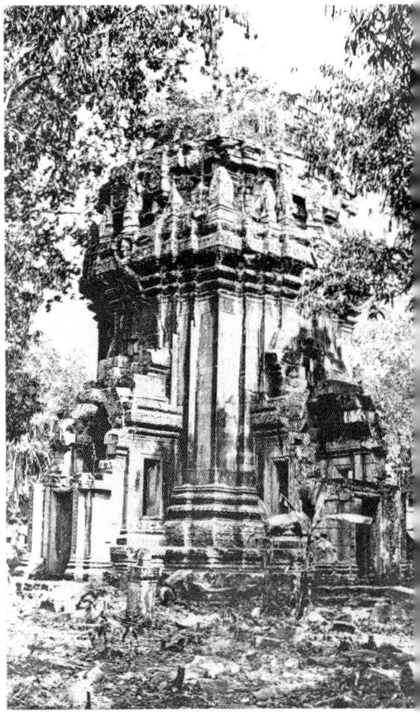

Khmer ruins at Phimai before renovation. (National Archives Bangkok)

It was down the length of the four great river valleys that the Thais made their trails. The western group came to the River Salween and settling down north of the Mons, they became Shans (their states now form part of the Republic of Burma). The eastern tribes descended along the River Mekong or halted around the four sources of the Chao Phraya River, and all of those tribes became collectively known as Laos. The middle groups chose the basin of the Chao Phraya River (incorrectly known in western geography as the Menam. The Thai word *Menam* literally means "mother of water" and is the term used for a river). These middle Thais never had any other name except that of the whole race – Thai – and it was only after they had welded themselves into a country, which would take hundreds of years, that they would be called Siamese after the land they had adopted.

When the Thais arrived in Golden Land they first met with the Lawas. They appeared to have passed through Lawa land in their own groups, owing allegiance to the Lawas only when it was necessary. By the time they reached the large plain, however, the Lawas had been replaced by the Khmer as the new power in Indo-China. Migrations in Asia generally took the lines north to south or west to east, and the Khmers took the latter. They left their old race group – the Mons – and going east and crossing the Chao Phraya basin, they went to settle along the southern reaches of the Mekong in the land which is now modern Cambodia. When exactly the Khmers' power replaced the Lawas is not known, but Khorat was clearly one of the first cities taken, and the beautiful ruins of a Khmer temple can still be seen at nearby Phimai. This was probably built even before the Khmers' own great city of Angkor Thom, begun in A.D. 894, which, with the later but enormous and grandiose temple of Angkor Wat and numerous other fine stone buildings, is one of the greatest sights still to be seen in the world. These incomparable buildings stand near the present Cambodian town of Siem Reap, and after seeing them one cannot be surprised at the great power wielded by the Khmers. They did once lose their power temporarily over the Lawas which was when the land was invaded by the legendary hero King of Burma – Anurudh – in A.D. 1010. But after the death of Anurudh, Burma, as was often the case, became disunited and all the Lawa lands were back firmly in the hands of the Khmer at the appearance of the Thais on the scene.

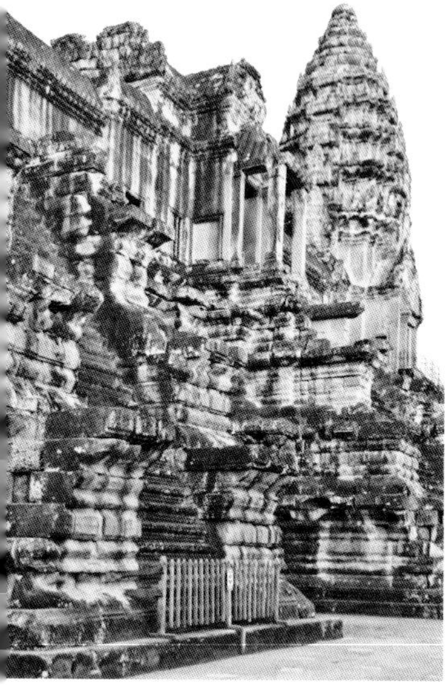

Angkor Wat, built by King Suryavarman II in the mid 12th century. (Paisarn Piemmettawat)

The Thais were originally animists, believing in the countless benevolent and malevolent spirits who existed everywhere in their midst. They had to be constantly placated with offerings of flowers, candles with joss sticks, food and wine, and from them favour could be asked. Every tree, hill, or house had a spirit. Hence near every house there must be a little tiny house for the spirit whom one has displaced. Little spirit houses can still be seen all over Thailand today. The Thais are some of the most adaptable people on earth, mentally as well as physically. Once moved south into Golden Land they were soon accustomed to tropical conditions. It has been well said of them that "They were as remarkable as assimilators as the Normans in Europe."[6] When they were still living in China the Thais had made contact with the Buddhism of the Mahayana sect. Buddhism was divided into two sects at the end of the first century A.D. when a grand council was held at the instigation of a powerful Indian monarch. On this occasion the more aristocratic Sanskrit language was used instead of the vernacular Pali. The Buddha, who was a prince by birth, must have spoken Sanskrit, but after his enlightenment he preached to the masses in Pali, and all of the Buddhist doctrine, when it came to be written, was written in Pali. Furthermore at this council many beliefs of a miraculous and legendary kind as well as new ceremonial practices were merged into the canons. This new doctrine was accepted largely in the north and became known as the Mahayana school, or Larger Vehicle. Those who adhered to the original doctrine as propagated in Pali, who were mostly in the south, became known as the Hinayana school or Smaller Vehicle, which is also called Theravada, namely, the way of the Theras (Teachers). Despite the splitting up of the religion into two sects, there have been no quarrels or warlike action between them. Buddhists can, and do, attend services with either of the two sects.[7]

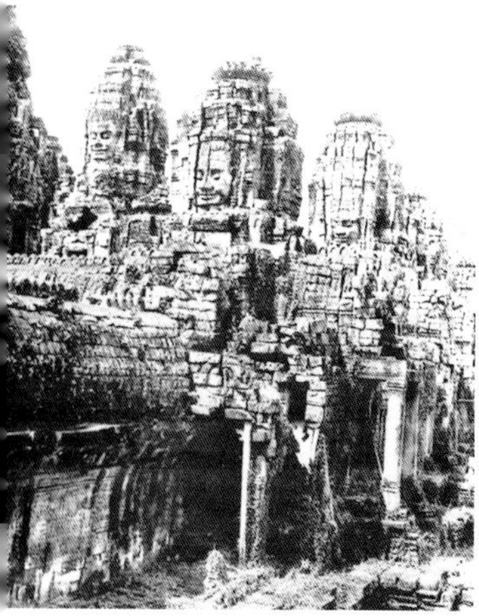

Angkor Thom. (River Books)

The Khmers for a long time followed the practices of Brahmanism (commonly known as Hinduism) to which they had been converted by Brahmin priests from India who came by sea across the Bay of Bengal, then by land across the narrow Siamese peninsula, and once again by sea across the Gulf of Siam to Cambodia. The magnificent stone buildings of the Khmers, including the colossal temple of Angkor Wat, were originally dedicated to Brahmanic deities. The titles of the kings and the forms of ceremonies and etiquette at the Khmer court were all of Brahmanic style. This was to be of the utmost importance to the Thais, for as easy assimilators, having come into contact with Khmer culture, they adopted certain Brahmanic ceremonial practices.

There were numerous Thai settlements known as Mueng, each ruled by their own Chao (Ruling Prince), all were under Khmer suzerainty, but Khmer rule was not at all times so strict or rigid. Communication was difficult and the *muengs* were scattered over a wide area and interspersed by thick tropical jungle. The vassals had at stated times to send tributes, often in the form of water which was scarce at

Angkor. The greatest hardship was the supply of forced labour to build the stone temples and palaces, both large and small. Under this loose-knit Khmer domination, the Thai *chaos* came to realize that it was in their interest to unite and mould themselves into large principalities, and finally into a kingdom. Before that object was achieved the Khmers had been converted to Buddhism, which might have begun during the invasion of King Anurudh of Burma, who was a Buddhist, and partly by later Buddhist missionaries from Ceylon, then the metropolis of Hinayana Buddhism. The Thais had left their Mahayana Buddhism behind when they started on the long trail from China. Now when they followed their overlords and accepted the religion of the yellow robe for the second time, it was the Hinayana school which has remained with them to this day.

The Thais, maintained some Brahmanic practices alongside Buddhism, especially after their chief had become a king, for the Thais then followed the Khmers by adorning their king and his family with the pomp and ceremonies of the Brahmanic cult. At the same time the belief in thousands of local spirits of every sort persisted. Even today except for the intellectual few it can be said that the Thais follow their own particular religion which is a mixture of all three with Buddhism the most predominant. Thus even the least educated and most superstitious among them have always understood the basic principles of Buddhism, namely, that from birth and existence came different degrees of misery, and to escape from these one had to escape from birth itself. This could not be easily achieved, and it was only through rebirth from countless lives, each life ruled by one's own *Karma,* the result of past deeds or the law of cause and effect, that the soul could be gradually purified until it was able to enter into Nibhana or eternal bliss. Each one had to walk his or her own way which the Enlightened Buddha could only show by his teaching. The most seemingly ignorant villager has always understood the simple maxim: "Do good, receive good. Do evil, receive evil."

Thai unification in the north came in the beginning of the thirteenth century A.D. with the Kingdom of Sukhothai, successful over all nearby principalities. The name thus spelt is the phonetic form of the Pali Sukhodaya which means the Dawn of Happiness.[8] One of the greatest Thai scholars, Prince Naris, once wrote to ask his half-brother, Prince Damrong, the renowned historian, whether the name could not in simple Thai – *Sukho-Thai* just mean : Happy Thai.[9] Prince Damrong insisted that it must have been a Pali name and Udaya was Dawn, as the name of the city had been written down by former occupants in Pali before the Thais had arrived there, although he admitted that the happiness which dawned there was Thai happiness.[10] Prince Naris retorted that it was impossible to know for certain when the name was first written down.[11]

Whatever meaning the city's name might have, it was from Sukhothai that a Thai King first defied the Khmers by refusing to send

6 D.G.E Hall: *A History af S.E Asia,* page 146, London, 1955.

7 Today Mahayana is practised largely in China (where permitted), Japan, Tibet, and Vietnam; while Hinayana is followed in Ceylon, Burma, Thailand, Laos, and Cambodia.

8 Prince Dhani: Review of Prince Chula's *The Twain Have Met,* etc. *J.O.S.S.,* Vol. XIVI. Part I, page 78.

9 *Letters of Princes.* Part 49, page 57 (in Thai), Bangkok, 1959.

10 *Ibid.,* page 68.

11 *Ibid.,* page 113.

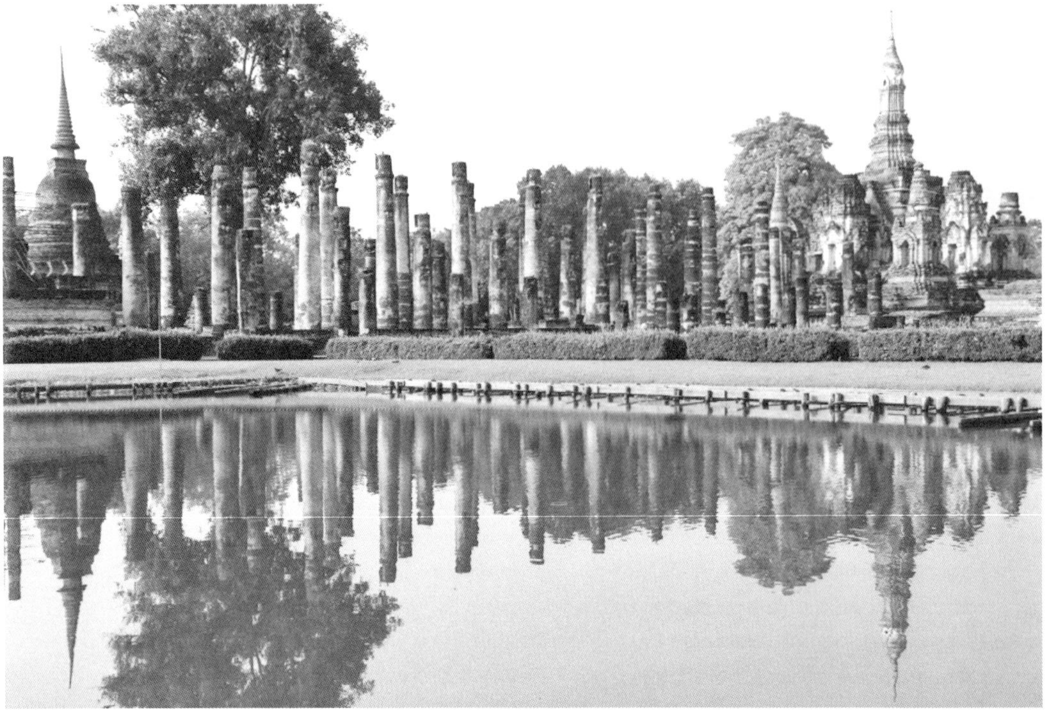

A view within the historical park of Sukhothai. (River Books)

any further tributes, which was after the Khmers had weakened themselves in trying to maintain their hold over Champa, one of the older states then occupying the west coast of present-day south Vietnam. In the battle against the Khmers the Thais won a conclusive victory, and from then on the Thai Kingdom of Sukhothai became independent.

There has been much curiosity about the origins of the name Sayam which became Siam in European languages. Luang Vichitra suggests that when the Lawas lived in Sukhothai the name of the city was *Sayam*,[12] and it was the Thais who changed the name. But the Chinese, who had been trading in Indo-China before the thirteenth century called the country of the Thais : *Hsien* which might have turned into *Sayam*.[13] Some authorities say that *Sayam* was the name given by the Khmers to the savage tribes who lived in the Chao Phraya basin before the Thais came there.[14] From all this it seems certain that *Sayam* or *Siam* did not apply to the Thai people themselves. The Thais preferred to call their country by the name of the current capital, and *Sayam* did not become the official name of the country until the reign of the fourth monarch of the Chakri Dynasty – King Mongkut (1851).

Independent Sukhothai was ruled by the Phra Ruang Dynasty which had six kings. The success of the king in freeing his people from Khmer domination attracted the Thai princes from nearby *muengs* who then came to submit to him which made Sukhothai the cornerstone of the Kingdom of Siam or Thailand of the future. If the place had been called *Sayam* and was changed to Sukhothai by the

12 Luang Vichitra Vadhkarn, *op cit.*, page 101.

13 G. William Skinner: *Chinese Society in Thailand,* page 3, New York, 1957.

14 D. G. E. Hall, *op cit.*, page 150.

15 Mgr. Pallegoix: *Description du Royaume Thai ou Siam,* page 64, Paris, 1854. Vol. II.

Thais, then Bishop Pallegoix was right in 1854 when he wrote : "It was at this epoch that *Sayam* took the name of Thai."[15]

The Kingdom of Sukhothai was founded in A.D. 1238 by King Sri Inthratit, but its zenith was reached in the reign of the third king – his younger son – Ramkhamhaeng or Rama the Valiant (A.D. 1275 - 1317). His name indicates the strong influence at the court. The Brahmin priests who converted the Thais were of the Vishnu cult, and Rama was one of the Avatars of Vishnu – his birth into human form to save humanity. The life of Rama was told in the epic Sanskrit poem, *Ramayana* which was later given a Thai version, the *Ramakien*.

The economy of Sukhothai was agriculture, growing both rice and fruit, which, together with fish, formed the staple food of the people. Occasionally meat or game might be seen in the royal or aristocratic kitchens. The capital city and other towns were market centres, military headquarters or seats of the administration as well as the localities of the more important Buddhist temples. The country was loosely governed through the towns in a kind of feudalism, but if the king was as able and strong as Ramkamhaeng, then he held them all with a tight rein. All the high officials in the capitals were courtiers, soldiers and civil servants simultaneously, and the royal palace itself was the seat of government. The nearer provincial towns were ruled directly by the king through officials sent from the palace. The outlying towns were ruled as feudal fiefs by royal princes or great officers as viceroys, but none of these had hereditary claims. They could be replaced at death by anyone of the king's choice as they could be recalled at will in their lifetime. Then there were also the real vassals, usually not of Thai race, who, unless guilty of grave misconduct, held their fiefs by hereditary rights, subject to the king approving the heir. This was how Siam was governed until about 1868, regardless of where the capital was or which dynasty was on the throne.

Ramkhamhaeng was a brilliant diplomat. By the pact of Blood Brother Friendship in A.D. 1287 with Prince Mangrai, the founder of Chiang Rai-Chiang Mai, and Chao Ngam Mueng, Prince of the Thai state of Phayao, which had existed since A.D. 1096, and both of whom were highly powerful rulers, Ramkhamhaeng safeguarded his country from all dangers in the north, and he was free to concentrate on consolidating his own patrimony and extending its territories to the south. He also established friendly relations with the Emperor of China. Sino-Thai trade soon developed, first by the overland route and later by sea to and from ports on the Gulf of Siam. Ramkhamhaeng sent many diplomatic missions to China with suitable presents which were interpreted by the Chinese courts as tributes from a vassal. Although China from then on claimed suzerainty

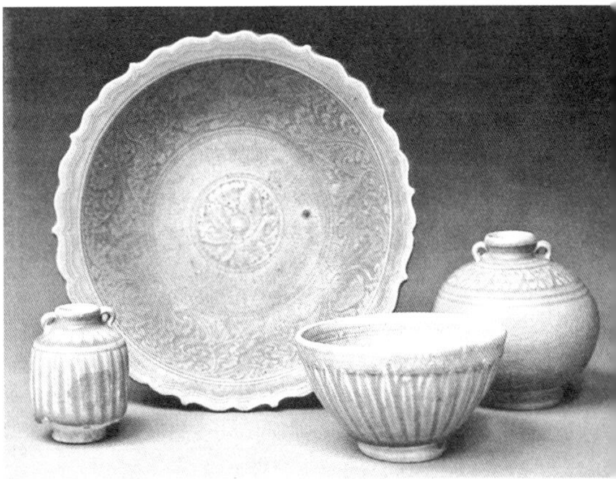

Examples of Sawankhalok ceramics produced in the twin city of the same name, adjacent with Sukhothai. (National Archives Bangkok)

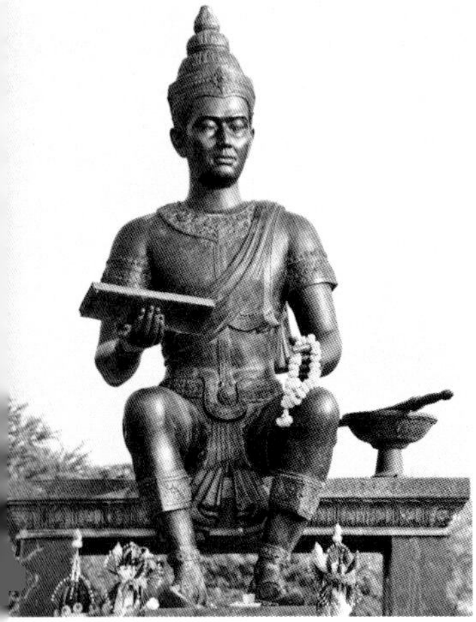

Memorial to King Ramkhamhaeng. (River Books)

over Siam for hundreds of years, she never attempted to exercise an external or internal control. According to Thai traditions King Ramkhamhaeng himself visited Peking twice, and in A.D. 1300 brought back Chinese artisans to set up the production of pottery ware at Sukhothai and other towns, and their kilns can today still be seen among the city ruins.

Ramkhamhaeng had already been renowned as a warrior in his father's reign, and in his own he brought under control nearly the whole of present-day Thailand after the Thais had been in Indo-China for barely three centuries. Besides being a devout Buddhist, he was also a scholar of Pali and neighbouring languages. By using the Mon and Khmer scripts as a basis, and some earlier primitive forms of Thai writings,[16] he created the first complete Thai alphabet, in A.D. 1283, which, with some changes, is in use to the present day. It consists of 44 consonants, 30 vowels, and five tonal signs. One of the most highly prized possessions of the National Museum in Bangkok is an ancient stone with an inscription attributed to King Ramkamhaeng dating from A.D. 1292. According to Prince Damrong[17] it is the first stone on which Thai characters were inscribed. Sukhothai is described in a simple and charming way as a land of plenty : "This Sukhothai is good. In the water there is fish, in the field there is rice. The king takes no advantage of the people. Who wants to trade, trades. The faces of the people shine bright with happiness."[18]

The monarch also concluded a treaty with Ceylon, the great metropolis of Hinayana Buddhism. Many priests came from that island to reside in Siam and preached the pure doctrine which resulted in the revival of the religion to a still greater degree. A bronze image – Phra Buddha Sihing – was sent from Ceylon which probably inspired the creation of many bronze and gilt images during that period. Many of them were enormous and fortunately some of them have been preserved despite the violent times which Siam has passed through, and can still be seen and worshipped today. There is the exquisite image at Phitsanulok – Phra Buddha Chinnarat – which has often been copied. In Bangkok there is the colossal image at Wat Suthat, brought down by the first king of the Bangkok period, which measures six feet from knee to knee in a sitting position with legs crossed. People have been surprised at the size of these immense bronze statues and wondered how they were ever cast. According to Professor Silpa Bhirasri (C. Feroci),[19] the material used for the mould for casting cannot be known with certainty and it was probably a mixture of husk, cow dung, and clay, as such mixtures would not expand or shrink under the high temperatures which the mould would have to undergo before the metal is poured in. A large all-gold image found in 1957 may well belong to this epoch. It is now at Wat Traimit in Bangkok. Its height is 11 ft. 1 ins., the width is 10 ft. 2 ins. and the image weighs 5 tons. As Professor Bhirasri said, it is sad that no name is ever recorded of these great Thai artists and only their art itself is their name. But

16 J. Burney and G. Coedès: *The Origins of the Sukhodaya Script. J.O.S.S.*, Vol. XXI, Part 2.

17 Prince Damrong: *Records of Siamese History. J.O.S.S.* Vol. XI, Part 2.

18 My own translation from the original Thai.

19 Professor Silpa Bhirasri (C. Feroci), *The Buddhist Sculpture. Thailand Culture Series* No. 17, Bangkok, 1954.

20 Luang Vichitra Vadhkarn: *op. cit.*, page 166.

21 D. G. E. Hall, *op. cit.*, page 146.

22 Prince Damrong: *Tales of Ancient Times* (in Thai). pages 530-541, Bangkok, 1954.

23 Prince Dhani: Review of Prince Chula's *The Twain Have Met*, etc. *J.O.S.S.*, Vol. XIVI, Part I, page 78.

they did not work for fame or riches, but like men of holy inspiration they felt a sense of mission in their work, which was to glorify their teacher, the Buddha. When one really gets down to it, the names of artists are merely reference signs and it is only their production which matters and forms immortal reality.

Despite their devout belief in Buddhism the Thais of Sukhothai, as indeed of any time, did not abandon an age-old belief in spirits. On the south side of the city a royal hill was where the most important spirits were believed to dwell, and to them the king and his court paid regular homage. Most of what one knows about this great monarch may make him seem a paragon of morality and somewhat unreal. But according to Luang Vichitra he had at least one lapse from virtue when he had a love affair with the wife of his friend and blood-brother, Chao Ngam Mueng of Phayao. But such was the bond between the two friends, that through the intervention of the third friend, Prince Mangrai, the wrong was forgiven when Ramkamhaeng showed himself truly penitent.[20] When Ramkamhaeng died in A.D. 1317, he had indeed "made Sukhothai the cradle of Siamese civilisation."[21]

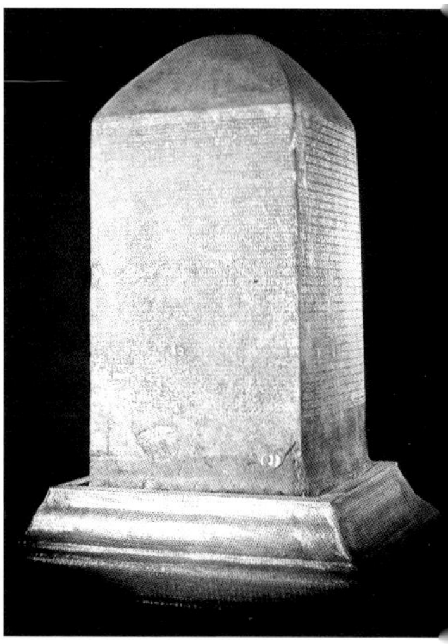

Inscription No. I created by King Ramkhamhaeng in 1292. (River Books)

His son and grandson were cast in a lesser mould, and the kingdom which he had created might have perished soon after his death, and there might not have been another Thai kingdom to replace it in the Golden Land. Happily another group of Thais in the south-west who had been outside his rule, had won many victories against the Mons or Lawas, whichever race ruled in ancient Dvaravati, and these Thais extended their territories westward until they took over an old city with the legendary name of U Thong or "Golden Cradle." The site of U Thong were unknown until Prince Damrong, late in the nineteenth century, found the ruins of a large city near Suphan Buri which answered in every way to the various descriptions.[22] He suggested that U Thong did not refer to the golden cradle in which a heroic prince had slept as a child according to one of the legends, but to the fact that gold was found in plenty in the vicinity which had led him to look for such ruins near Suphan Buri – town of gold. All sources, however, agree that a prince from U Thong, his personal name being unknown[23] led the survivors of a cholera scourge away from U Thong to found a new city which we now know as Ayutthaya, built on an island along the main stream of the Chao Phraya River, 45 miles due north of modern Bangkok. Once again the influence of the Vishnu cult is seen, for the name Ayutthaya derived from Ayodhya (now Oudh in India) the city of Prince Rama, the *avatar* of Vishnu. After founding Ayutthaya in A.D. 1350, the prince from U Thong had himself appropriately proclaimed as King Rama Tibodi. Probably to remind people that his ancestors had once conquered a city of ancient Dvaravati, the full name which he gave to his new city was *Krung* (Thai for capital city) *Thep* (Sanskrit – of Deva – Divine) *Dvaravati Sri* (Blessed) *Ayutthaya*, which was to remain the capital of Siam for 419 years.

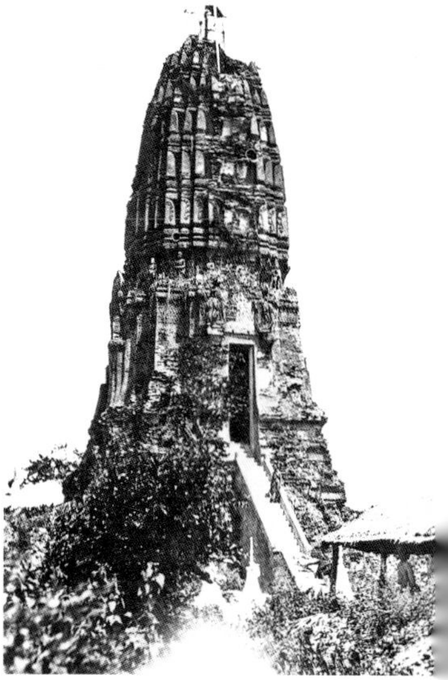

The *prang* of Wat Phra Si Rattana Mahathat, Suphan Buri province. Early Ayutthaya period probably constructed by King Boromma Rachathirat II. (National Archives Bangkok)

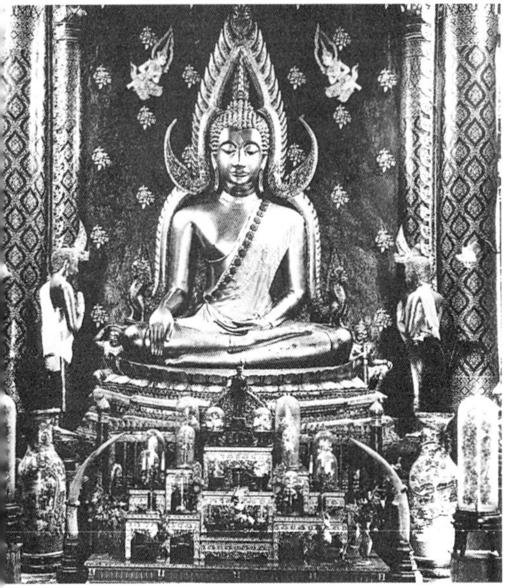

The Phra Buddha Chinnarat Buddha image, housed in Wat Phra Si Rattana Mahathat, Phitsanulok. (River Books)

Little is known about King Rama Tibodi himself, but it is thought by some that he was somehow descended from Prince Mangrai, the founder of Chiang Rai-Chiang Mai – one of the blood-brothers of Ramkhamhaeng of Sukhothai. Once Ayutthaya had been founded, Rama Tibodi set about making a kingdom for it. When he had succeeded, the kingdom was not called Siam, but, in the usual Thai manner, the Kingdom of Ayutthaya. In a little time he acquired control over the whole of the Chao Phraya basin. He fought a successful war against the Khmers in A.D. 1352 and brought Khorat in the east and Chantaburi in the south-east into his kingdom. His rule spread west as far as Tavoy and Tenasserim on the Bay of Bengal (now in Burma), and south as far as Malacca which meant that he had control of a large part of Malaya.[24]

He was an accomplished ruler and legislator and most of his system of government was to survive in Siam until nearly the end of the nineteenth century A.D. – over 600 years. The main structure was similar to that of Ramkhamhaeng, but Rama Tibodi regulated the services more definitely into different branches. He established the offices of the four Great Officers of State – foreshadowing cabinet ministers of the future. The Thai word *mueang* can, as has been said, mean town or city. It can also mean country or land. Today the Thais colloquially refer to their country as Mueang Thai and Thailand does not seem such a bad translation. But in the northern dialect the word *wieng* can be substituted for *mueang* and the former term was also used in the centre in the old days. The four ministries of Rama Tibodi were as follows:The Ministry of Wieng. As the capital city represented the whole country, it was in fact the Ministry of the Interior. The Ministry of Klang (which is pronounced as sung in a song) was the Treasury. The Ministry of Wang (pronounced likewise) was in charge of the King's Household. The Ministry of Na (pronounced as car) was in charge of the rice fields which meant all forms of agriculture. As legislator he codified the Thai laws both contemporary and ancient, including the laws and customs said to have dated back to the Thai Kingdom of Nanchao. All were examined, with the good retained and the bad discarded. A form of divorce was already known in his legal system. He was also successful in diplomacy and he arranged an alliance with the powerful Chinese Emperors of the Ming Dynasty, who had by then

Painting imagining how King Rama Thibodi I began building Ayutthaya. (National Gallery Bangkok)

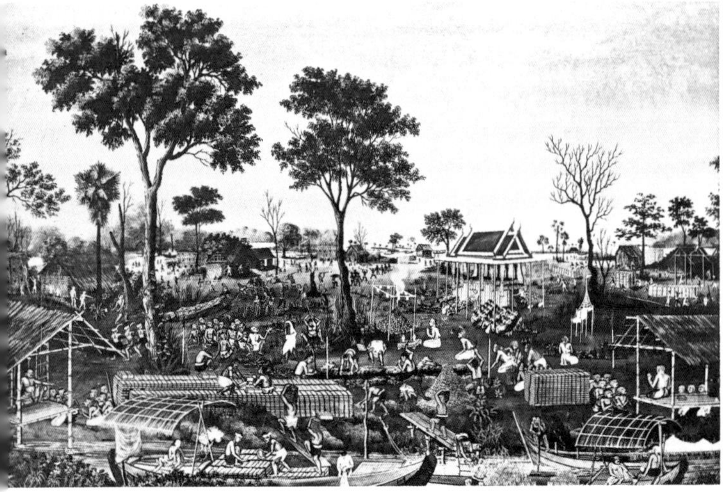

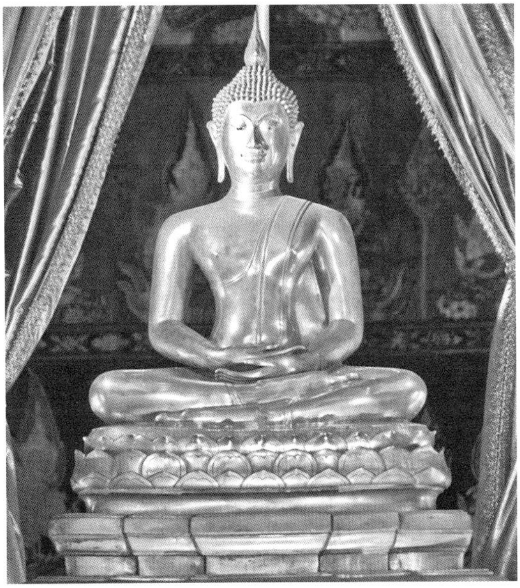

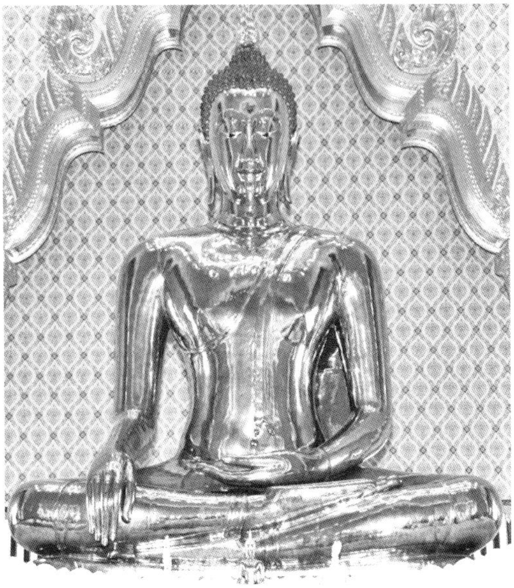

replaced the Mongols, and as Hall says, as diplomatists the Thais have never been surpassed".[25]

In contrast to the power and glory of Ayutthaya, so newly founded, the Kingdom of Sukhothai began to fade away after the death of Ramkhamhaeng in 1317. His son and grandson were not of his calibre and they were more interested in the arts and letters than in being rulers and warriors, and in a short time Sukhothai would find it difficult to withstand the rivalry of the southern kingdom. But such was the fame left behind by Ramkhamhaeng that his son was able to rule an independent kingdom for 30 years. His grandson, King Maha Thammaraja Lithai was the author of the first complete Thai book, known later as Traiphumi Phra Ruang (Three Worlds by Phra Ruang), a religious work in which the Ten Virtues of a sovereign were set down and these have ever remained the guiding principles of all Thai monarchs.

When Rama Tibodi of Ayutthaya died in 1369 he left to his son a powerful and prosperous kingdom, but the new king's position was weakened from the beginning by the rivalry for the throne on the part of his uncle, who was successful and became King Boromarachathirat I.[26] This was the first of many occasions in Ayutthaya when an uncle would seize his nephew's inheritance. Indeed, the history of Ayutthaya in the following years was one of endless struggles for the throne by the different claimants as no definite rule of succession was laid down. The most dramatic of these was after the death of King Intharacha (1408-1424) when his two elder sons fought a duel to the death from the necks of their elephants. This has always been considered in South-East Asia as the most noble form of single combat. On this occasion as they charged each other, each prince knocked the other off the elephants simultaneously, and both were killed. The

LEFT: The Phra Buddha Sihing image installed in the Buddhaisawan Throne Hall within the grounds of the National Museum. (River Books)

ABOVE: The Sukhothai-period image within Wat Traimit in Bangkok. (River Books)

24 Sir Josiah Crsboy: *Siam: The Crossroads*, page 15, London, 1945.

25 D. G. E. Hall, *op. cit.*, page 152.

26 D. G. E. Hall calls him Boromoraja, and uses "O" for "A" for Thai-Sanskrit names in many places, *op. cit.*, page 153. The Thai practice for the short or invisible "A" is to use "A". (It is the same for the present writer's name which the Thais spell as Chula Chakrabongse and not Chulo-chakrabongse. The "a" of Chula is also short or invisible).

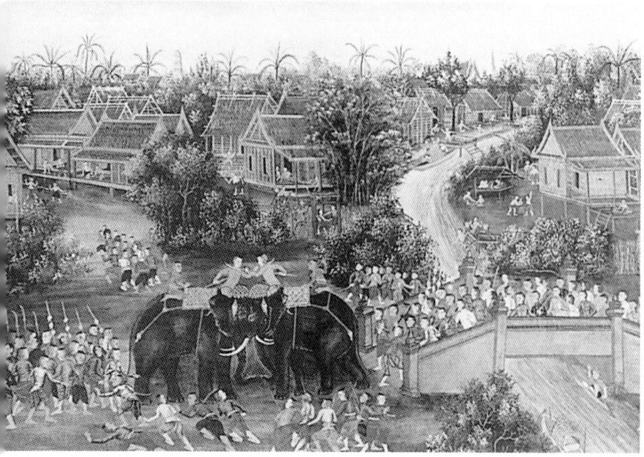

Chao Ai and Chao Yi engaged in a duel on elephant back resulting in their simultaneous deaths. (National Gallery Bangkok)

youngest brother came to the throne as King Borommarachathirat II (1424-1448). He is noted as the conqueror of the Khmers, sacking their great capital of Angkor Thom, but he failed to keep the Khmers in subjection. It was then that the Khmers left Angkor and went south-east, and it was also about then that their country became known as Cambodia and the people Cambodians.

Meanwhile Sukhothai had been easily taken, almost without a fight, by Ayutthaya in 1378. It was fortunate that the northern people had become so weak as it spared the Thai people the horrors of a long fratricidal war. Thus Siam or Thailand became one single kingdom ruled from Ayutthaya. Sukhothai became a vassal state after 121 years of independence, but the descendants of the Phra Ruang were permitted to rule at Phitsanulok for some time, while the city of Sukhothai itself was neglected.

The new kingdom of Ayutthaya was surrounded in the north by states which were sometimes her vassals, sometimes independent, or sometimes vassals of Burma, such as Chiang Mai, Luang Prabang, and Lan Xang. These states would frequently change sides during the struggles to come between Siam and Burma. These principalities were collectively known to Ayutthaya as Laos. The people spoke Thai but with different accents and dialects, and had different customs and food.

The new, large, and seemingly united kingdom must not be thought of in terms of modern nations. In days of poor communication and delayed news, no clearly defined frontiers existed, and the size and extent of the kingdom depended on the prestige and vigilance of the reigning king and the power which he was actually able to wield over the many cities and towns far and near. Otherwise the state of affairs could change from day to day without his knowledge. The sense of nationhood did not exist in South-East Asia then any more than it did in Europe, and the people were the liegemen of the king rather than citizens of any state. The king was the absolute all-powerful monarch, the *Chao Jivit* – the Lord of Life – restrained only by the Ten Virtues, and he was responsible to no one but himself – not even to God as was the case of the medieval sovereigns of Europe. As the succession to the throne was not clearly defined by any rules, it has been well said[27] that "the man is not king by divine right, it is the monarchy which is divine". It is with the control of the whole length of the Chao Phraya River that the Ayutthaya kings were able to rule nearly all of what was to be modem Siam, and it was equally true that "this great river explains this country ".[28]

There then came a great change, namely, an attempt to regulate the succession and to tighten up administrative rules. Borommaracha II's son had been Viceroy at Phitsanulok following the troubles with

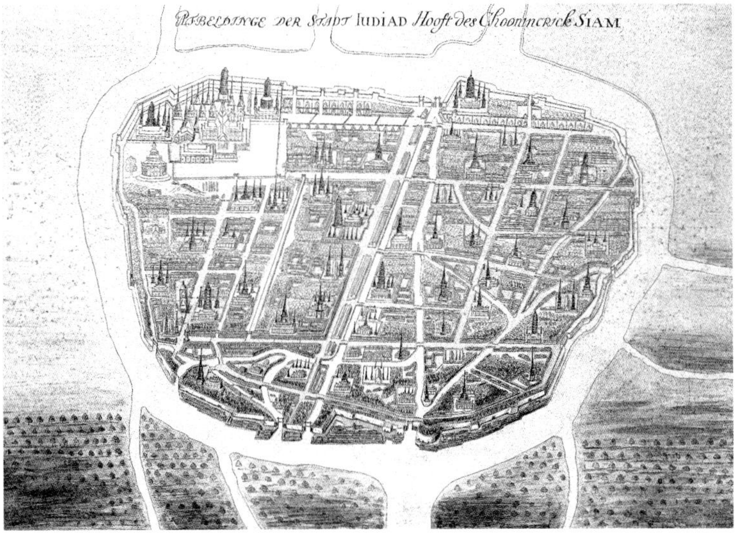

A map of the island of Ayutthaya by Johannes Wingboons in 1665. (Nationaal Archief, The Hague)

Chiang Mai, before he succeeded his father as king in 1448 with the title of Boromma Trailokanat[29] who can be called King Trailok for short. His long reign of forty years marked an important step in Thai history. King Trailok was fortunate in being the first Thai monarch to have in his veins the blood of both the kings of Ayutthaya and the kings of Sukhothai for his father had taken to wife the daughter of the vassal Prince of Sukhothai, Maha Thammaraja IV, a direct descendant of Ramkhamhaeng, thus Trailok's accession ended all possible rivalry between the two capitals.[30] He therefore terminated the appointment of one of the Phra Ruang family as a Viceroy of the north which naturally was displeasing to them. Trailok either resided at Phitsanulok himself or sent his son there. His reign saw an almost continuous struggle with the Prince of Chiang Mai, encouraged by the heirs of the Phra Ruang line. Also the northern princes took heart from the fact that at the beginning of the reign Trailok tarried so long at Ayutthaya.

The capital was further embellished by nearly all her kings. Hundreds of *wats* (monasteries) abounded in the island city, and in one of them was erected a huge image of the Buddha, 48ft. high with a 25ft. pedestal, the whole of which was covered with 600 lbs. of gold.[31] The colossal statue can still be seen, and it was for a long time in a roofless building, although the gold had disappeared long ago. The importance in those days of the *wats* cannot be overestimated. There were merit-making festivals when offerings were made to the monks, which were followed by much revelry, sports of all sorts including boat-racing and side-shows. It was then that the young men and women met one another – there has never been a system of purdah in Siam – and these meetings generally led to marriage. The *wats* were the only places of education, and they were schools and colleges for both the monks and laymen. Girls were taught at home, or, if they were highly born or had good connections with ladies of the

27 Leopold Robert-Martignan: *La Monarchie Absolue Siamoise de 1350 à 1925*, page 18, Paris, undated, but sometime after 1926.

28 *Ibid.*, page 28.

29 Here again D. G. E. Hall calls him Boromo Trailokanat, *op. cit.*, page 54.

30 Prince Damrong: *Tales of Ancient Times, op. cit.*, page 358.

31 Robert-Martignan: *op. cit.*, page 26. W. A. R. Wood: *A History of Siam*, page 96, Bangkok, 1933 Edition.

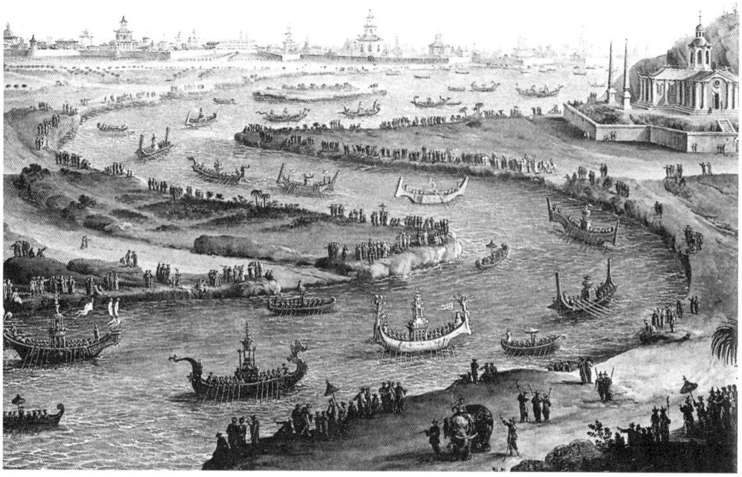

An imagined scene of when the French embassy arrived in Ayutthaya in 1675.

Court, were sent to live in the Royal Palace, which for girls was nothing less than a university. There they studied the Buddhist religion, Thai history and customs, and also learned the refined domestic arts and crafts. It was generally from these young women that polygamous kings and princes chose their wives.

Thai polygamy, which did not end legally until 1935, did not imply the equality of all the wives, the number of whom varied from house to house. There was nearly always a chief wife – two sisters might sometimes be first equal – who presided over the household composed of minor wives, her own children and step-children, and the usually vast domestic staff. Amongst the peasants the number of wives were far less owing to expense, and more often it was a case of bigamy. If the householder was the king, then the chief wife would be the queen, who was usually of royal blood either of the king's family or a vassal state. Even so the present style for queen which is *Somdech Phra Baroma Rajini* was unknown and was only created in the fifth reign of Bangkok. The early queens were known by their own names after the title Phra such as Phra Suriyothai, the heroic queen of King Maha Chakrapat who will be mentioned later. Other wives of the king were known as *Chao Chom* which can be roughly translated as Royal Lady Companions. Their children, if recognized by the king as his, were all legitimate, but they had lower ranks than the queen's children. This accounts for, and will do so for some years to come, the enormous size of the Thai royal family, which is puzzling to foreigners who do not know precisely the different ranks and relevant importance of the seemingly numerous members.

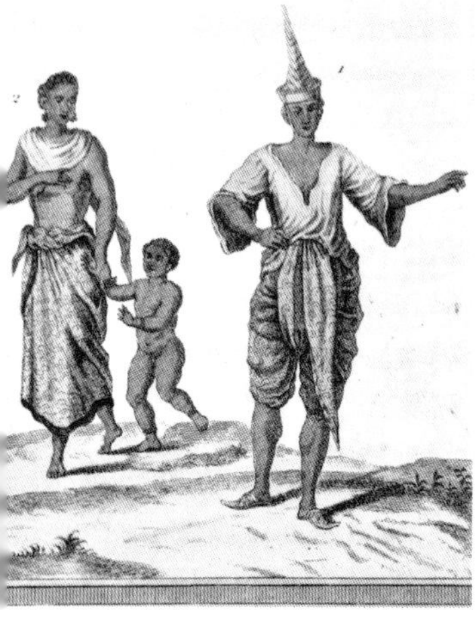

A drawing showing a courtier and villager in the time of Ayutthaya. From Simon de la Loubère *Royaume de Siam*.

The forward step taken by King Trailok in 1450 was the creation of the *Uparaja* (pronounced in Thai Uparart) who was the Deputy-King and his likely successor. It was an *attempt* to regulate the succession, but as the king was still all-powerful the Uparaja did not attain his position by primogeniture. The king could appoint anybody, and the conception of a legitimist line had always been vague in Siam until recent years. In actual fact the kings of Ayutthaya nearly always created their next full brothers or the sons of their queens as Uparaja. The position of the Uparaja has led many foreign writers to think that there had always been two kings in Siam at the same time. This was not so except in a few reigns when a Second King was appointed for some specific reason. The Uparaja, let it be strongly stressed, was not king – but the Deputy-King. Although comparisons are odious, his position was in some ways similar to the Vice-President of the United States of America. Strangely enough the first king to appoint a Second King was the creator of the Uparaja title himself – King Trailok. Deciding that he had to move back to Phitsanulok to keep Chiang Mai and the north in order, he appointed his eldest son King to rule in Ayutthaya at the same time. Later on he created a younger son Uparaja in Phitsanulok, who was junior to the Second King in Ayutthaya. That this is confusing to western writers is understandable.

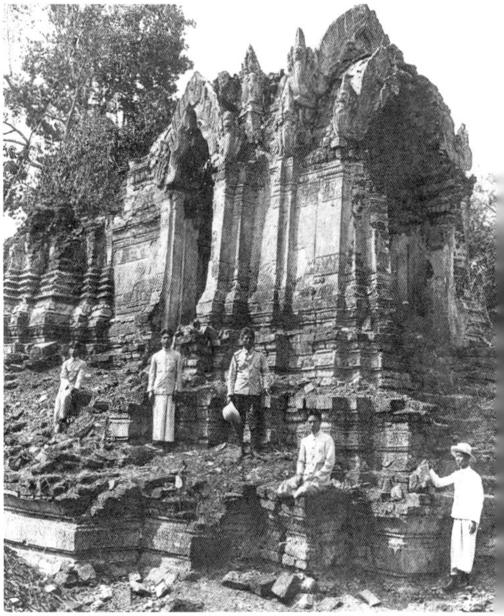

The ruins of Wat Chulamani in Phitsanulok. This was where King Trailok stayed when he was in the monkhood. (National Archives Bangkok)

King Trailok remained in Phitsanulok for twenty-five years and successfully thwarted all attempts by Chiang Mai to annex his northern provinces. Before he resided there Phitsanulok had a simple Thai name which he changed for a Sanskrit one. The name chosen proves the persistent influence of the Brahmanic Vishnu cult. In Sanskrit V and B/Ph are interchangeable, thus Phitsanulok means the abode of Vishnu. Although successful in the north, King Trailok was less successful in the extreme south and lost control over Malacca, and his Thai officials left shortly before the arrival of the Portuguese.

During his long sojourn in Phitsanulok, the king was not only busy directing operations there, but he even found time to become a monk for a period, and the *wat* where he stayed still has monks and can today be visited. In addition, he also managed to send to Ayutthaya a large number of edicts affecting many reforms. He tightened the administration by bringing the provincial towns more closely under central control by creating the offices of the two Greater Officers of State, namely, the Kalahom in charge of the north, and the Mahad Thai in charge of the south. Because in later years the Kalahom became purely military, and the Mahad Thai the civilian Minister of the Interior, there has since grown up an idea that it had always been so. But in the time of Ayutthaya until early Bangkok, all the king's ministers were military and civil simultaneously.[32] These two Greater Officers, in addition to their civil work, were G.O.C.-in-C. of the North and South respectively.

It was the same with the Governors of the provincial towns which were divided into four classes. A system of baronial titles was then created. The highest, *Chao Phraya,* was for the Governor of first class towns; the second title, *Phraya* for the second class towns; *Phra* for third class, and *Luang* for fourth class towns. Officials in the capital were

32 MSS. Notes by General Prince Alongkot for his unpublished book.

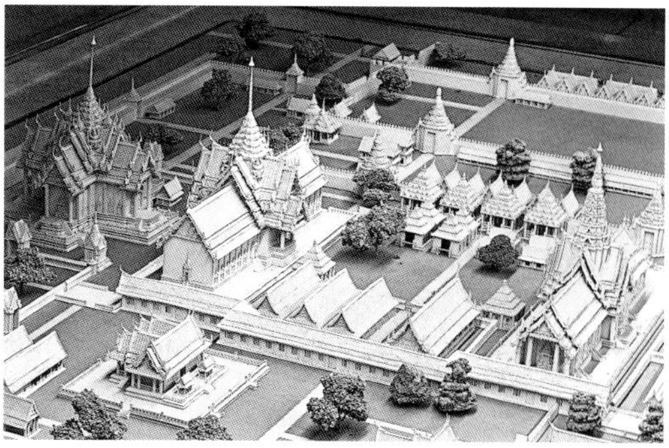

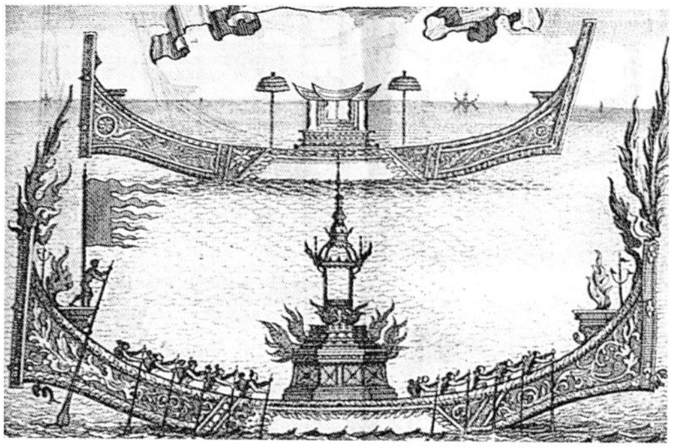

A model of the palace in Ayutthaya and Phra Sri Sanphet temple. (River Books)

ABOVE RIGHT: A drawing by a foreign artist of one of the processional boats. (River Books)

given the same grades of titles for similar responsibilities. Below Luang there were also fifth and sixth grades, *Khun*[33] and *Muen* respectively. As the titles were not hereditary, it would be profitless to compare them to the European aristocracy. It should, however, be noticed that the name of the great river was the same as the highest title – *Chao Phraya.*

Attention must especially be drawn to the title *Phra.* This is as loosely used as the English term, Lord. Besides being the third grade amongst the titles of nobility as stated above, it could be applied to the Buddha himself who was always called *Phra Buddha Chao* in the same way the English refer to the Saviour as Our Lord. It was further used to call all Buddhist monks – *Phra.* It could refer to the King, the *Uparaja,* or important princes. The word *Phra* set before any noun or adjective would mean "royal". Thus the word *Phra* is indeed an important Thai word, and if not properly appreciated or understood by those who aspire to understand the Thai language or Thai ways, could lead to a good deal of confusion.

Without a hereditary aristocracy the all-powerful king created life-nobles from the sons of nobles or commoners according to his whims. Some of the titles continued for hundreds of years, but they did not pass down from father to son. Often the titles went with certain posts, such as Chao Phraya Chakri was the Commander-in-Chief, and Chao Phraya Phra Klang was the Lord High Treasurer. Occasionally a brilliant son, nephew or grandson might be given the same post as his forbear and would thus receive the same title. The above procedure would be applied to the life-nobility of Bangkok until the granting of titles ceased in 1932.

Although the ranks of the life-nobility were carefully regulated, any grade or order of precedence in the Royal Family would remain in a confused state for some time. From ancient times the Thai princes or chieftains were called *Chao* which was used for rulers only. Later this title of *Chao* was extended to members of the ruling families, so as to become hereditary. In the Laos principalities which were vassals of Siam such as Chiang Mai or Lampang, descendants of *Chao* were always *Chao ad infinitum,* and they all call themselves thus to this day. But in the Ayutthaya royal family, despite the promulgation of the *Kot Montian Barn* or Palace Law in 1450, different ranks of royalty were not

33 Pronounced in a high tone, and not to be confused with the modern *Khun*, pronounced in an even tone by which everybody is now called, which is equivalent to the French: *Monsieur, Madame,* or *Mademoiselle.*

yet defined. The Palace Law, however, laid down complicated rules and regulations regarding palace government as well as religious and royal ceremonies, many of which have never been repealed. It was decreed that princes could only be executed for treason by being hit on the back of the neck with a club of sandalwood. It was believed that this method was devised to avoid the shedding of royal blood, if beheaded with a sword which was the lot of other traitors. An English pathologist, Dr. F. D. M. Hocking, of Cornwall, has recently confirmed that it was also a more humane way, for death would be instantaneous and painless with no blood being shed.

Another of King Trailok's measures, which would last for centuries, was the regulation of the *Sakdi Na* grades or honours by the granting of rice fields. The Thai people had always possessed a certain amount of land according to their positions. King Trailok put the whole system into a defined order and made clear how many *rais* (2 ½ *rais* equal 1 acre) a person of a certain rank could hold. For example, a *Chao Phraya* could have 4,000 acres, whilst a peasant of the humblest class could have ten acres. The *Sakdi Na* also served as a salary for officials, by providing an income from their land; and in a court of law, fines were based on the *Sakdi Na* of the accused. This system survived until comparatively recent times.

When he died in 1488, King Trailok left to his two sons, who succeeded him one after the other, a united and prosperous Siam with the arts and literature well to the fore. The religious poem *Maha Jati* and the romantic tragedy *Phra Law* were both written in his reign and have greatly influenced the literature of the Bangkok era.

His elder son, Baromaraja III survived him by three years and was peacefully succeeded by his brother in 1491, known as Rama Tibodi II, whose long reign of 38 years saw the first sign of that stupendous change which was to sweep over Siam and indeed all of South-East Asia – the advent of the European.

Following the successful voyage of Vasco da Gama to Asia round the Cape of Good Hope, the Portuguese were the first Europeans to appear in Asia as missionaries and traders. An attempt to preach and to trade often meant clashes with the local people which would lead to war and finally to European conquest. In the reign of Rama Tibodi II the Portuguese had gained a firm foothold in Malaya at Malacca after defeating the Muslim Malay princes.

In 1518, just over 160 years after its foundation, the Portuguese arrived in Ayutthaya with an embassy from their Governor of Malacca, the great Alburquerque, and its leader, Duarte Fernandez, can be considered the first European to set foot in Siam. The Portuguese met with a friendly reception which might well have been a surprise for them. Rama Tibodi II signed a treaty with Albuquerque and allowed the Portuguese complete commercial freedom and they were given facilities to trade at Ayutthaya and Nakhon Si Thammarat, called in early European books Ligor, Pattani, and on the Gulf of Bengal at

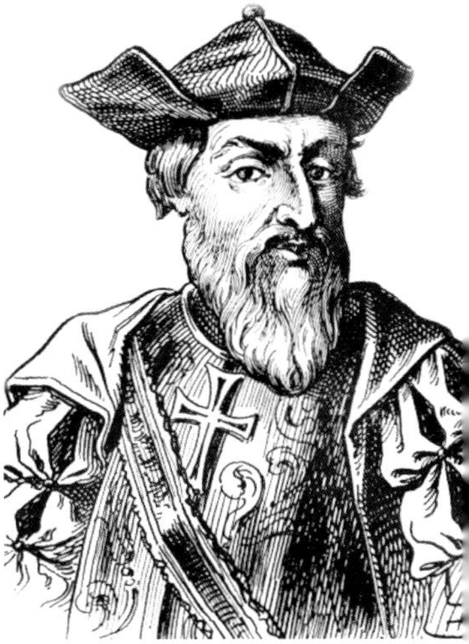

An engraving of the Portuguese explorer Vasco da Gama (1460-1525). (*The Career and Legend of Vasco da Gama* by Sanjay Subrahmanyam, 1998)

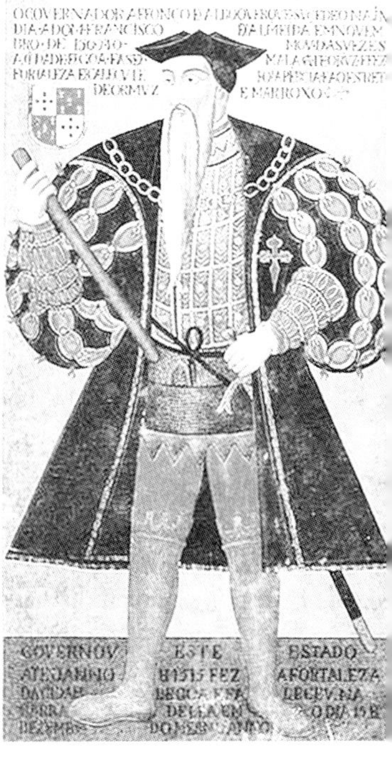

The explorer, general and empire builder, Afonso de Alburquerque (1453-1515). (Instituto de Investigação Científica Tropical, Lisboa)

Tenasserim and Mergui, then belonging to Siam. The Portuguese were permitted to open their Christian mission, and so tolerant were the Buddhist Thais that the king himself gave a large donation to build the first Christian church in the country. This typical forbearance would, with rare exceptions, be the case in Siam until the present day.

As the first Europeans to come to Siam were the Portuguese, it may seem rather surprising that all people of the white races have always been known to the Thais as *farang* which might be a shortening of the word *français*. The word *farang* came from the fact that the Indians had first called the French *feringhi*. The Indians brought that term to Ayutthaya before the Portuguese appeared, and the Thais thought that it applied to all of the white races. Thus when the Portuguese arrived they were automatically called *farang* and the mistake has survived long enough now for *farang* to have become an established Thai word. It is convenient and so generally understood that, in Thailand today it is readily used by the *farangs* even amongst themselves.[34]

In prosperous Ayutthaya there were already people of other races and the largest number were the Chinese, who, as traders, had reached the Golden Land before the Thais had settled there. On the Bayon temple in the middle of Angkor Thom, built by the Khmers between the ninth and thirteenth centuries A.D., there is a bas-relief showing an early Chinese junk. The Chinese, while trading by sea with India, stopped in Siam and Malaya, first along the seaports of the Gulf of Siam and later in the capital.[35] The kings of Ayutthaya continued the Sukhothai custom of sending presents to the Chinese emperors who still regarded them as tributes from a vassal. But the Chinese emperors never attempted at any time to interfere with Thai affairs. The Emperor of China had recognized Rama Tibodi I as the King of Hsien-Lo. Hsien was what the Chinese had called Sukhothai, while Lo was part of Louvo or Lawa. Thus as King of Hsien-Lo, he was recognized as King of all Siam.[36]

After 81 years of prosperity and progress during the two long reigns, the death of Rama Tibodi II ushered in a period of confusion and wars which was to last for almost the same time – 76 years. His son succeeded him but he only lived five years. The grandson, who ascended the throne as a minor, was killed by an elder relative after only five months. The relationship of the usurper, who became King Phra Chai, to the Royal Family is not exactly known, but he must have been a prince of some standing to have succeeded in his plot.[37] He was probably the son of Rama Tibodi II by a minor wife.[38] It was early in this reign – 1538, that 100 Portuguese artillerymen went to assist the Thai army in the war against Chiang Mai and Burma. It was the time of the Portuguese adventurer and writer, Ferñao Mendes Pinto, whose accounts of life in those parts were graphic and informative, if sometimes extravagant especially when relating to his own exploits.

King Phra Chai was on the throne for 21 years, but was absent from the capital most of the time on campaign. He had no sons by a queen, but he did have one by one of his favourite *Chao Choms* – the Lady Sudachan, who was secretly in love with a distant relative of hers – an officer of the guards by the name of Khun Worawongsa. Soon after one of his returns from the north King Phra Chai became ill and died in mysterious circumstances. Thai history of this period is confusing and it seems that Lady Sudachan was suspected of having poisoned the king, so as to hasten the accession of her little boy, who succeeded as King Yodfa in 1546 at the tender age of eleven. Prince Tien, probably a half-brother of King Phra Chai, became Regent and there was a struggle for real power between him and Sudachan who was now Queen Mother. She was apparently as amorous as she was ambitious, and she soon hinted to Prince Tien that she was in love with him, and that they could be happy together as king and queen. Deeply shocked by these suggestions and wishing to remain faithful to his wife, Suriyothai, who was by birth a princess, Prince Tien was also fearful of the consequences of Sudachan's wrath. He took the line of escape which is usual in Thai history namely giving up the Regency and entering the monastery as a Buddhist monk.

Thwarted in this direction, Sudachan meanwhile continued her love affair with Khun Worawongsa, and in due course she became pregnant. Little King Yodfa apparently had some inkling as to what was going on as he was in constant conference with one of his equerries, Khun Piren, a descendant of the Phra Ruangs of Sukhothai. Khun Worawongsa, who now had a great deal of power since Prince Tien's disappearance from the capital, was told of these talks. He therefore found some excuse to have Khun Piren, and other officers known to be loyal to the king, dismissed from service. Thus isolated, the helpless young king was quietly murdered. It is probable that it was done without his mother's knowledge, but once it was achieved, she, who was now too deep in all these plots, had no choice but to condone. Khun Worawongsa was now bold enough to have himself proclaimed king, but his power probably did not extend far beyond the palace walls. It was now time for Khun Piren to take action. He had gathered together a band of brothers – all retired officers who had men loyal to them – but he still lacked sufficient force to storm the palace. Then he heard that Khun Worawongsa and Queen Sudachan were travelling by boat to an elephant hunt outside the city. Khun Piren and his friends laid a successful ambush at a bend in the river. The surprised lovers were taken from the boat and quickly executed.[39]

Prince Tien, who had shared their secret from the first, was induced to discard the yellow robe, as Buddhist monks are at liberty to do at any time. He was invited to ascend the throne – in 1549 – and was proclaimed as Maha Chakrapat – meaning Great Emperor. The attempt met with no opposition, but on the contrary, the new king was acclaimed on all sides and obviously Khun Worawongsa's usurpation had met with silent antagonism. Outside the palace and the capital, the life of the people continued as before with hard work but on the whole full liberty to enjoy the fruits of their labour. Except when they were

34 Information kindly supplied by Prince Dhani in 1958.

35 G. William Skinner, *op. cit.*, pages 1 and 2.

36 *Ibid., page 3.*

37 Prince Damrong: *Tales of Ancient Times, op cit.*, page 364.

38 D. G. E. Hall, *op. cit.*, Appendix, page 750.

39 As surmised by Prince Damrong: *Tales of Ancient Times, op. cit.*, pages 365-368.

conscripted in time of war or for some special work of construction in peace time, the free people of Siam were left very much to themselves. The state demanded little from them and thereby gave them little in return except a plot of land.

Khun Piren and his friends were richly rewarded. He himself was made a prince with the old Sukhothai title of Maha Thammaracha, and a daughter of the king and Queen Suriyothai was given to him as a bride. He was sent to Phitsanulok as the Viceroy of the North, and was to be the father of one of the greatest men in Thai history.

With such an auspicious title as the Great Emperor, Maha Chakrapat should have enjoyed a long and glorious reign. It was certainly long – twenty years – but it was one of almost incessant war and misery, which was brought about by what should have been objects of good fortune. According to Brahmanic belief, if a monarch possessed one or more "white" elephants, it was a glorious and happy sign. The first Thai king recorded in history to have owned one was King Trailok. These noble animals were not exactly white and in the Thai language they are not called white but albino. They had pale yellow eyes and white nails, any hair on the head or body was white, and the hard rough skin was either pink all over or had pink patches on the head, trunk, or forelegs. The king never rode on them and they were not used for anything. However, they were not worshipped for themselves and were regarded as an appendage to the king's majesty. King Chakrapat quite early in his reign had as many as seven "white" elephants, an unprecedented number, but they were to drag the country into a prolonged war which went on intermittently for twenty years.

Up till then war between Siam and Burma, despite the presence of Portuguese gunners, had been more like skirmishes, the result of the rivalry for the control of Chiang Mai and other north-eastern Laos principalities. The real reason for the great war was because the Burmese were a martial race. Fortunately the Burmese most of the time were fighting amongst themselves. Whenever they were united under some strong king, then they would usually launch an attack eastward towards the Thais. In King Maha Chakrapat's reign Burma was under the strong rule of King Tabinshwehti,[40] and the conquest of Siam was his next logical objective. The Thai king's possession of seven "white" elephants was a romantic and knightly pretext. He sent a royal message that he himself had no "white" elephants at all, could not his dear brother, the King of Ayutthaya, spare him just two when he had so many. King Maha Chakrapat gracefully but firmly refused, explaining that these special beasts were appendages of a king's majesty, and, haying been found in one kingdom, they could not be transferred to another.

Using that refusal as a pretext King Tabinshwehti invaded Siam with a vast army. The Thai strategy was to pull all defensive resources into the capital, thus the Burmese met with very little or no opposition until they reached the walls of the city. Ayutthaya was

40 The Burmese form of the name is Tabinschweti. D. G. E. Hall, *op cit.*, page 140.

surrounded not only by tall and massive walls, with forts and ramparts, but it was also bounded on all sides by rivers and canals which acted as formidable moats. During the siege the Thais, who were often more redoubtable in defence than in aggression into another country, made several brave sorties against the enemy. One of these was led by the king in person, riding astride the neck of his combat elephant, although of course this was not a "white" one. A combat elephant was one of the usual grey colour, very large and strong, with especially long and pointed tusks, and all were thoroughly well trained for the purpose. The king or a general, who rode on the elephant's neck, carried a sabre attached to a long pole which also had a metal hook to control the animal. From that height he could direct the movements of his army through his signaller, sitting on a howdah behind him and waving a pair of peacock feathers. Above the signaller's seat was placed the *chatras* – circular canopies – whose number, one on top of another, varied according to his master's rank. Behind the howdah, and on the elephant's back sat the steerer who had a long pole to control the elephant with. Later, in the days of firearms he would have a short musket slung behind his back and a sword to defend himself.

This particular sortie had a special feature, for, besides the king and his son, Prince Mahin, Queen Suriyothai, well versed in the art of elephant-craft and dressed in the warlike garb of a warrior, went out with her husband on another elephant. When the king became involved in single combat with a Burmese general, the Prince of Phrae, and seemed in danger of being cut down, Queen Suriyothai drove her animal in between them and herself received the mortal blow. Her husband and son, together with their troops, succeeded in disengaging themselves from the enemy and escorted her body back into Ayutthaya. She has since been regarded as one of the greatest heroines of Thai history. Countless pictures have been painted of the incident and many poems extol her heroic virtues. One of the most beautiful is that by Prince Naradhip (the First, born in 1861) published in Bangkok in 1919.

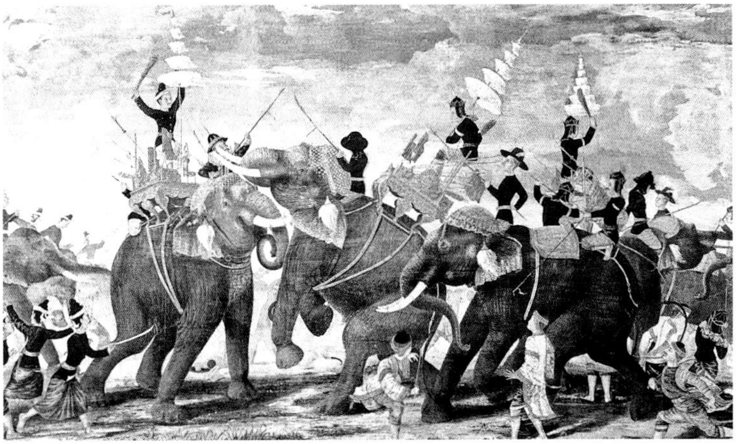

A painting by Prince Narisara Nuvattiwongse recording the daring exploits of Queen Sri Suriyothai. (National Gallery Bangkok)

The Thai defenders fought so well that after four months' siege the Burmese could make no headway. The relieving force, under command of the king's son-in-law, Maha Thammaracha, then arrived from Phitsanulok. The exhausted Burmese did not stay to fight two Thai armies, and Tabinshwehti went home without any "white" elephants. This break in actual hostilities was followed by a "cold war." Maha Chakrapat became ill off and on most of the time, while Prince Mahin did not have the making of an absolute ruler, so the central power in Ayutthaya dwindled. During those years Maha Thammaracha was virtually independent in the north, setting up his own government at Phitsanulok. Two sons had been born to him and his wife, Chakrapat's daughter, and in their veins ran the blood of both the Phra Ruang and U Thong lines of kings.

As the king's condition worsened, the reins of affairs at Ayutthaya were centred in the hands of the incompetent Prince Mahin. Maha Thammaracha had heard that there was discord between the prince and the nobles, so he became truculent and refused many summonses to the capital. Once when Maha Thammaracha was away from Phitsanulok on an inspection tour, Prince Mahin arranged to have his sister, who was Maha Tam – Maharacha's wife, and their two sons abducted to Ayutthaya in the hope of bringing his brother-in-law to heel. The result was the opposite for the other knew full well that no harm would come to his family in Ayutthaya, and the kidnap only turned him into an enemy.

There was the usual confusion in Burma towards the close of Tabinshwehti's reign and Siam was left in peace. Soon after the succession of his brother-in-law, Bayinnaung[41] Burma once again became united under one strong king who was later to become known as The Victor in Ten Directions. Popular Thai legend had it that he had a black tongue. Having put his country in order he set up his capital at Hanthawaddy or Pep which was in the Mon country. If Tabinshwehti had "sought to become a Chakravartin, the world conqueror . . . "[42] it was "Bayinnaung's" dearest ambition to force the most powerful of all the Thai states to submit to his authority.[43] When he invaded Siam with an army even more numerous in number, things were still worse for Siam for the embittered Maha Thammaracha marched alongside with a Thai army of 70,000 men from Phitsanulok. King Maha Chakrapat died during the enemy's advance. The new king, Mahin, followed the usual routine of abandoning the rest of the country and concentrating on the defence of Ayutthaya. Once again the valour of Thai troops and the formidable walls and ramparts of the city kept the enemy at bay for eight months. It was only through discord amongst the Thai generals, the unpopularity of King Mahin, and the propaganda work of Maha Thammaracha, that the capital fell through treachery from within. Thus it was on August 30th, 1569, that Ayutthaya fell for the first time – 219 years after its foundation.

41 The Burmese form of the name is Bayinnaung. *Ibid.*, page 140.

42 *Ibid.*, page 211.

43 *Ibid.*, page 213.

44 The Burmese form of the name is Nanda Bayin. *Ibid.*, page 217.

No doubt Bayinnaung had some previous understanding with Maha Thammaracha as the capital was spared total pillage which was the usual order of the day. Nevertheless many valuable and artistic objects were removed to Burma, this being the first serious loss of Thai heritage. He also carried out the customary method of disarming the enemy country. One was to order the strongly resisting walls of Ayutthaya to be dismantled. The other was the more effective way – the removal to Burma of thousands of Thai families, especially the young and healthy. They were compelled to migrate to Burma in the wake of his victorious troops returning to their homeland. Amongst them was King Mahin who died in captivity on the way. This method was humane in those harsher times, but its adverse influence on the speed of the development of the Thai race cannot be estimated. It appeared that Bayinnaung remained at Ayutthaya for only two months and ten days. Before he departed for Hanthawaddy, he appointed his Thai ally, Maha Thammaracha, King of Siam, which was to be a vassal state. To make certain of his complete loyalty, the new king's eldest son, Prince Naresuan, was taken along to Burma as a hostage. It was because his skin was darker than his younger brother's – Ekatotsarot – that he received the nickname of "The Black Prince" in contrast to the other who was "The White Prince". In the retinue of the Burmese king there also marched four "white" elephants, more than half of Maha Chakrapat's prized stables. Thus ended the U Thong Dynasty of sixteen kings. The usurper, Khun Worawongsa (1548), alone, has not been accepted as a predecessor by the Chakri Dynasty of Bangkok.

The exile of Naresuan as a hostage in Burma turned out to be a blessing in disguise. He followed the best of Burmese military training which was then probably pre-eminent in South-east Asia. He was conscientious in studying the art of war at which the Burmese were supreme, which he did with the elite of Burmese youth, sons of princes and nobles. That he was allowed to do this demonstrated not only the nobility of Bayinnaung's character, but also that he now had no fear whatever as far as Siam was concerned. Besides being gifted in military prowess, Naresuan, who was highly intelligent, gained a great deal of general knowledge of the times. Living in the Burmese Court and being at the centre of affairs, he was able to size up the strengths and weaknesses of the Burmese and had certainly absorbed a good deal of such knowledge by the time he was permitted to return home in 1571. Although he was only sixteen he was created Uparaja and sent to Phitsanulok as Viceroy of the North like his father before him, but young men grew up quicker in those days, especially in adversity.

A statue of Bayinnaung. (River Books)

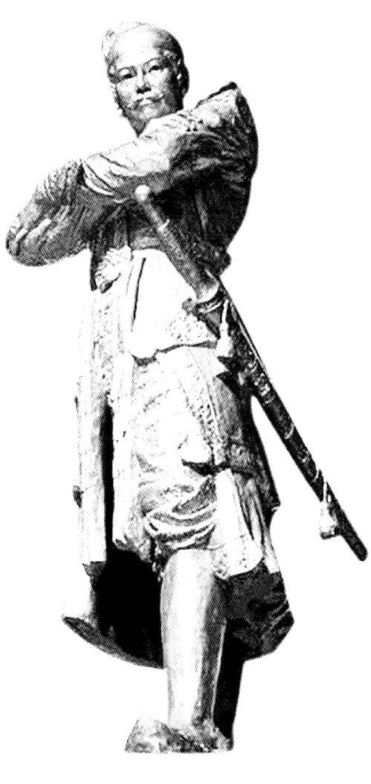

Bayinnaung died ten years later in 1581. He had been so successful and powerful that no confusion occurred at his death and he was succeeded peacefully by his son, Nanda Bhureng.[44] The latter's son, now the Uparaja of Burma, was a fellow student of Naresuan. The Black Prince knew that Nanda Bhureng was not of the same calibre as his father, but, as was shown by his easy accession, Burma was still

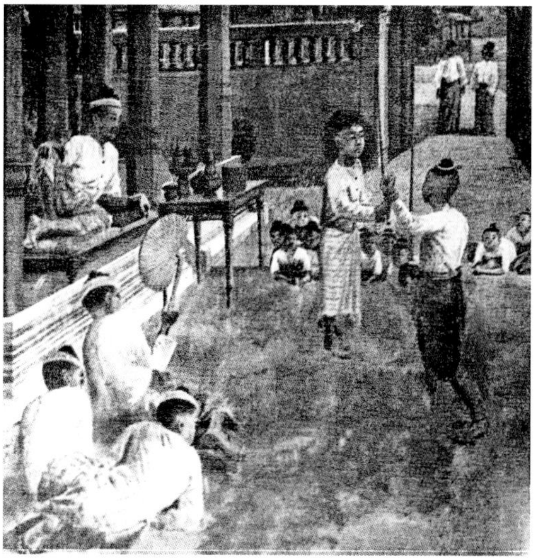

strong and united, and her trained soldiers were far in excess of Siam's. Not only had the victorious Bayinnaung taken thousands of healthy young Thais to Burma, but whenever Ayutthaya was facing a Burmese invasion, the Cambodian king sent strong raiding parties into the eastern provinces and took away many families too. That was the system of those days which explains why the Golden Land today has people combining many diverse ethnicities. Such continuing external threats gave the Thais an excuse to start rebuilding the city walls.

But it seems certain that from the moment he was back in Siam and at Phitsanulok, Naresuan's one burning wish and zealous aim was to free Siam from Burmese bondage. Fully aware that his people could not match the Burmese in numbers and military equipment, that for their lines of communication the Burmese had the support of Chiang Mai and her associated Laos princes, and that perhaps time was on his side, Naresuan decided to raise and train a small compact force of volunteers who were to be taught novel methods of warfare. He would rely on the tactics of ambush and surprise attacks by small highly trained and fully mobile combat teams, who were to be aided by local guerillas who later became known as Wild Tigers and Peeping Cats. The former name would return to Thai history in the early part of the twentieth century.

Mural painting from Wat Suwandararam showing Prince Naresuan in Hanthawaddy. (River Books)

As Nanda Bhureng lacked the great qualities of his father, Burma, as always when there was not a mighty king, began to disintegrate; but so tremendous had Bayinnaung been, that this time the process, though sure, was very slow. Local rebellions flared up here and there. On one of these occasions, Naresuan, as a vassal prince, was required to take his small Thai force to Burma to help the king, his father's overlord. In this way he and his men had practical and valuable experience of real warlike operations. It was also a splendid reconnaissance visit for himself when he could examine the exact situation in Burma. In this particular campaign he was once asked to capture a rebellious town by assault in the most unfavourable conditions. Although he and his men were successful, Naresuan sensed that the Burmese had hoped that they would fail, or even that the brave young prince himself might have been killed in the battle. He realized that the Burmese probably suspected or knew his ulterior motives, and they were no more friends of his than he was a friend of theirs.

Mural painting from Wat showing Prince Naresuan shooting a gun across the Sadong river killing Surakama the general of the Burmese army in 1584. (National Gallery Bangkok)

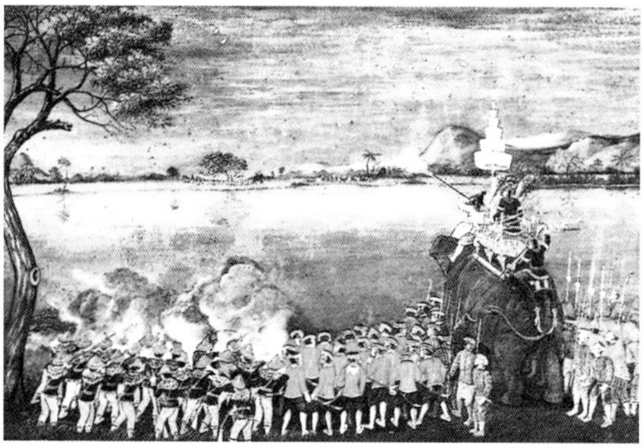

By 1584 Naresuan, who was back in Siam, felt full confidence in the strength of his little army.

With his father's consent and in his name he declared the Thai vassalage to be at an end, and proclaimed the independence of Siam. With characteristic boldness he did this on the very border of Burma. It is believed that a few dissatisfied Mon officers, in the service of Burma, then came over to Siam to serve under Naresuan, and that their descendants would one day serve Siam in a similar way.

Such a gesture could not possibly be accepted by King Nandha Bhureng, or he would not have been able to maintain any prestige in his own country amongst his brave and martial subjects, and another war with Siam was inevitable.

Of Naresuan, Robert-Martignan writes[45] that "it is a constant fortune for Siam never to despair of her destiny. When all seems lost the right man comes along. The Siamese have found a new chief."

Naresuan did not have to wait long to join in battle with the Burmese. In December of that year Nanda Bhureng invaded with two armies, one in the west by the Three Pagoda Pass, and the other from the north-west through Chiang Mai whose prince helped to transport the heavy supplies by boats down the rivers. By the lightning movements of his mobile columns, consisting mostly of cavalry, Naresuan in several successful skirmishes much weakened both of the two Burmese forces before they could form a junction. By then his own personal daring and deeds of bravery had become a legend, and it helped to inspire his troops to emulate him and know no fear. In fact King Maha Thammaracha had once to rebuke his son for being too intrepid. This was when he heard that Naresuan had led the assault on a Burmese camp by climbing the wooden ramparts with the blunt side of a sabre held in his mouth. The Burmese came again in November, 1586, and tried to besiege the capital in January and again in May, 1587, but they were unable to get close enough because their lines of communications were so harassed by Naresuan's little groups of fast-moving horsemen, and the Burmese knew that a serious siege was not possible unless supplies were coming in regularly. On each occasion that Burma invaded Siam in the west, the Cambodians ravaged the Thai eastern border, again and again taking away many Thai families, who were forcibly settled in the Cambodian provinces of Srisophon, Siem Reap, and Battambang. These raids were a source of annoyance and rage to Naresuan who was not yet strong enough to do anything about it.

In July, 1590, King Maha Thammaracha died aged 75, and Naresuan, who had been king in fact, now became king in name also at the age of 35. The new monarch so loved his brother that he was not content with appointing him Uparaja, and Ekatotsarot was made the Second King, and was, in accordance with custom, responsible for the northern provinces. But such was the close bond between the two brothers that they were inseparable and Ekatotsarot resided in Ayutthaya instead of at Phitsanulok. His decrees concerning the government of the north, written in and sent from Ayutthaya, have

45 Robert-Martignan: *op. cit.*, pages 36, 37.

been found. Fortunately Naresuan had a breathing space until the end of 1590 to prepare for the Burmese onslaught which he knew for certain was coming.

Burma and Siam were separated by many ranges of mountains, and either side could only enter the other's territory through mountain passes close to some streams. The closest pass to the Thai capital was the Three Pagoda Pass which the Burmese would have to cross quickly in order to seize the first town in the plain – Kanchanaburi – as their base. But this was a difficult route and it was not possible to bring heavy supplies. Thus as always it was essential for Burma to hold Chiang Mai. Then the large army marching south from there could be supplied by boats along the rivers. Both Burma and Naresuan knew that to conquer Siam completely, Burma must take Ayutthaya. For the Thais to concentrate only on the defence of the capital as in the past was dangerous. If the city should fall, it would again be the final end. It was necessary therefore to bar their way, but Naresuan knew that this time the Burmese armies would be bigger than before. Although no spies appeared to have been used, there were good listening posts along the frontiers which were constantly being crossed. People living on the other side were often Thais who had been taken away by force. Although hostilities began at the end of 1590, the Burmese only came as reconnaissance forces which were easily repulsed. All the time Naresuan was increasing the number of his well trained men.

The big war can be said to have begun in December, 1592. News came that the Burmese had assembled two large forces, both of them together totalling 250,000 men. One was at Tavoy aiming at the Three Pagoda Pass and the other was at Chiang Mai. To fight the Burmese everywhere with fewer numbers would mean facing total defeat at every point and leaving the way open to Ayutthaya. Naresuan therefore decided on a scorched earth policy by sacrificing northern towns such as Tak. These were evacuated of everyone, their protective forts and ramparts dismantled, and the population and food supplies removed to Ayutthaya. As the rice harvest had been gathered, everything of value to the enemy on his way south was destroyed. The defences of these towns were dismantled so that the Burmese themselves could not retreat and use them as bases for any possible counter attacks. The people of these towns, either in Ayutthaya or in camps close to the city were trained as soldiers to defend the capital, and generally to act as the mass of reserves. In every part of Siam where his rule held sway, all men from the ages of 18 to 60 were called up. In those days of simple warfare, they brought with them their own weapons which they knew how to use, and they only needed a little training in discipline and in co-ordinated fighting. In time there would be a large reserve army east of the city.

The king's elite force was placed to the west of the capital, poised to advance in any direction. These preparations had taken two years and were barely completed in time. They reveal this king as not merely a bold and valiant knight, or foolhardy fighter, but a great commander with sound strategic and tactical knowledge.[46]

As Naresuan had expected, war broke out seriously in December 1592, with the approaching march of two formidable Burmese armies. The one commanded by his erstwhile fellow student, the Crown Prince of Burma, came by the short and direct route of the Three Pagoda Pass. It was this enemy force that Naresuan hurried to meet with his own field army in the direction of Suphan Buri. Patrols and other forward elements clashed, and in the ensuing battle Naresuan prepared a feint retreat which was an uncommon tactic at that time. He sent ahead a forward force under his favourite cavalry leader, Phra Rajamanu, who then received an order to fall back on the main army which was commanded by the king in person. This army was divided in half and lay in ambush on both sides of a narrow jungle defile. But Rajamanu, once he came to grips with the Burmese, met with such success that he forgot to retreat. He even sent back a message to say that he thought he could hold the enemy and urged the king to follow up with his own men. Naresuan knew that his men would then be crowded together in the narrow passage. He handed his own sword to an equerry, saying, "Go to Rajamanu. Tell him to fall back on me instantly. If he wavers, cut off his head with this sword and bring it back to me." The general knew that in carrying the king's sword the equerry had full powers. He was electrified by the message and the retreat was made rapidly. The Burmese, believing themselves victorious, poured into the defile as into a funnel. The hidden Thai soldiers charged them from all sides and cut them to pieces, inflicting severe losses. His officers and men finally understood that they would often fight with tactics which they might not at first understand. Naresuan was again and again successful and in this way he eventually, and in a short time, achieved parity or almost superiority in numbers which was required for the decisive battle.

This battle Naresuan forced on his opponent soon afterwards. As the two armies were locked in furious combat, Naresuan and Ekatotsarot were closely encouraging their men. They themselves were riding on the necks of their combat elephants which were at the time in musk. This made them more ferocious than usual. Hearing the tumult of the shouting, the shots fired, the clashing of naked weapons, the animals went mad and ran off in the direction of the Crown Prince of Burma, setting up such a curtain of dust in that dry season that none could see where they were going. When the elephants did come to a halt and the dust cleared, the two brothers saw that, but for a

46 MSS Notes by General Alongkot.

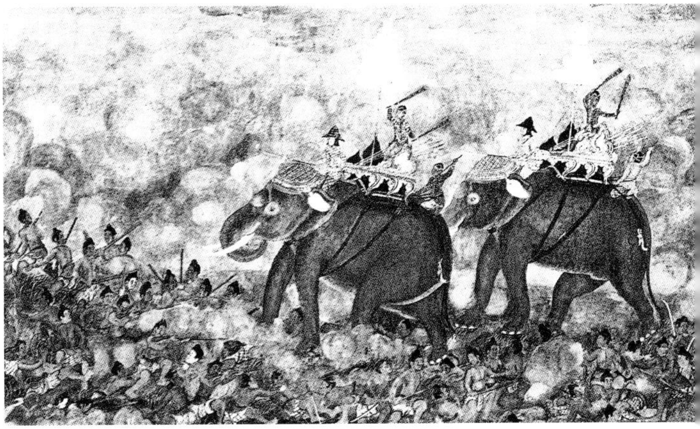

An imaginative portrayal of Prince Naresuan attacking the army of Hinthawaddy. (National Gallery Bangkok)

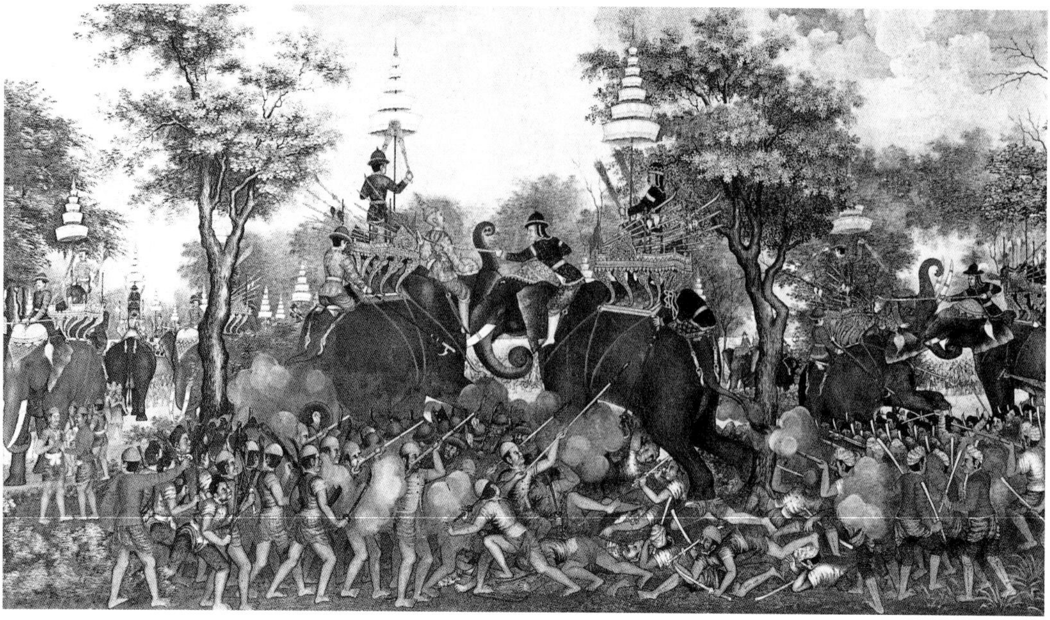

An imaginative portrayal of Prince Naresuan engaged in single elephant combat with the Crown Prince of Burma. (National Gallery Bangkok)

handful of their personal guards in their red coats,[47] who had managed somehow to follow them on foot, they were alone in the midst of the enemy. Furthermore, they were in mortal peril, the steerer of one elephant and the signaller of the other had been shot dead, but Naresuan never flinched. He saw the Crown Prince sitting on his elephant in the shade of a large tree, and he hailed him in a loud voice : "Elder Brother, why do you sit thus under that tree. Drive your elephant out, and let us join in single combat as we used to do in practice when we were students. Let it be a sight for our troops to see, so that it will be known that brave deeds have not yet deserted princes, nor have they lost their skill, and they can still perform the noble art of single combat on elephants."

The Crown Prince could have ordered his troops to kill or capture the Thai king and his brother, but he had the noble and royal blood of Burmese warriors in his veins, so he drove his elephant out into the open. In this type of personal battle the trained beasts charged one another like the horses of European knights. The rider must hook the elephant at the right time so that its tusks would catch the opponent's elephant and lift him up so that the other rider would be exposed and unable to use his weapon. On this memorable occasion the Burmese timed his hooking splendidly which made Naresuan appear to be helpless. As the Crown Prince swept with his sabre attached to the long pole, the Black Prince ducked and only the brim of his leather hat was cut off in the shape of a crescent moon. After the two elephants disengaged, they charged one another again and this time it was the Thai animal which got in below, and the hapless Crown Prince was cut in half from his shoulder to his waist. The bulk of Thai troops now arrived and a confused melee followed, but Naresuan gave an order to

47 The First Infantry Regiment, King Chulalongkorn's Own Bodyguard, wear scarlet coats for full-dress today.

48 Of this personal combat D. G. E. Hall's comment was, "according to the Siamese," *op. cit.,* page 221. Later, when he wrote of Naresuan's defeat in Burma, he did not add, "according to the Burmese", page 223. Contemporary history was vague on both sides, and very little, if any, original documents survive.

permit the enemy to carry the body of their valiant prince off the field. This tragic end to the personal duel – the last on elephants between royal princes – brought the war to an end with both Burmese armies retiring to their country. Naresuan had a *chedi* (pagoda) erected on the spot to commemorate the event which is believed to have occurred on the 25th January, 1593. The *chedi* was lost to the ever-growing tropical jungle for hundreds of years until it was found by Prince Damrong early in the twentieth century when it was a barely recognizable ruin. It has now been restored and a monument set up close by which was unveiled by His Majesty King Bhumibol, the ninth king of the Chakri Dynasty of Bangkok, on January 25th, 1959 – and that date is still commemorated as Army Day in Thailand to the present time.[48]

Having disposed of the danger from Burma, King Naresuan, who had been much annoyed by the Cambodian habit of sending marauding parties into his eastern provinces, now turned his attention to that country. He invaded Cambodia later in 1593 with a strong force, decisively defeated their king, and turned his south-eastern neighbour into a vassal. Attacks from Burma did not only cease because of Naresuan's victory over their prince and armies, but also because Burma had again entered into one of her many periods of internal strife, and Nanda Bhureng was barely able to maintain himself on his throne. When he died in 1599 without a direct heir, every part of Burma was in rebellion against the rest, and there was an interregnum of six years. In order to make sure that the leaders whom he favoured should be successful and therefore his ally, Naresuan undertook many expeditions to help one side or another. On one of these expeditions and on April 1st, 1605, he crossed the River Salween, but had not marched much further when he fell seriously ill with a carbuncle on the neck. For once his brother was not by his side, and Ekatotsarot hurried to meet Naresuan, but only to be in time for a last farewell. Naresuan died on May 16th and was duly succeeded by Ekatotsarot, already the Second King, who brought the hero's body back to Ayutthaya. Naresuan was one of the very few Thai monarchs to have had no children at all, and it is not definitely known that he ever had a wife. Is it possible that during his exile in Burma he had fallen in love with a Burmese princess, and, knowing that enmity between the two royal families was unavoidable, he sacrificed his love and personal happiness for his country? To put things in a chronological context, his death occurred two years after that of Queen Elizabeth I of England.

Naresuan is generally known and revered in Thailand today as a great commander, but he was not only a warrior, and was equally interested in agriculture and commerce. That his defensive wars were so successful was largely because everything was planned to harmonize with rice-farming and the harvest. He helped foreign merchants to improve their trade, and it was he who signal the first treaty with Spain. He would have done even more for the peaceful progress of his

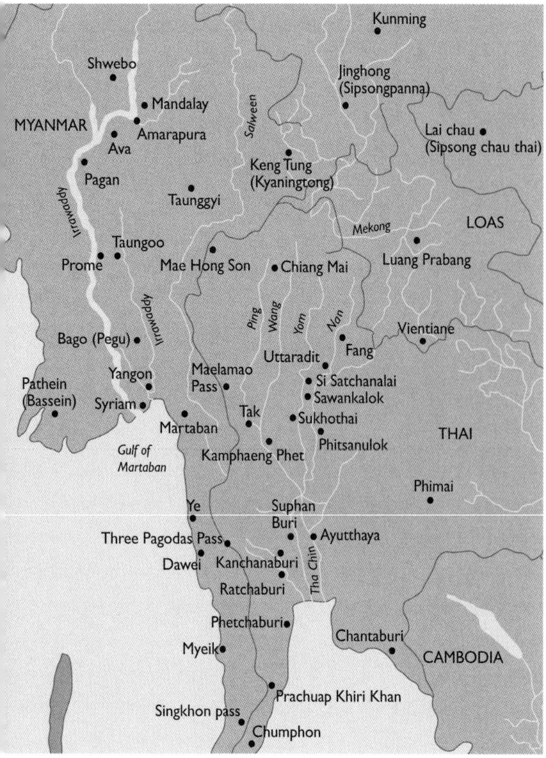

Siam and Burma in the Ayutthaya period.

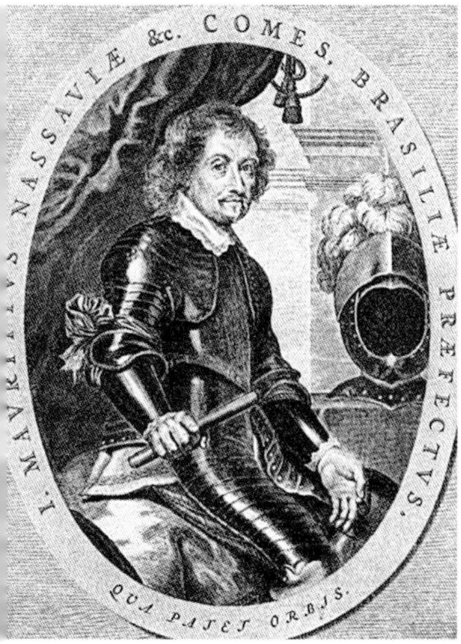

Prince Maurice of Nassau. (*Encyclopedia Britannica*)

country, but most of the time the problems of Burma and the dangers therefrom dominated his thoughts. Yet in tackling these he showed a constant regard for his own kingdom rather than a lust for power, as Professor Hall has pointed out: "He did not seek to inflict a knock-out blow, which would merely have brought plunder and might have involved him in exhausting attempts to hold the turbulent Burmese in subjection . . . Siam was a trading state and had urgent need of ports on the Indian Ocean. Southern Burma had useful ones within easy reach of Ayutthaya. It was on these that Naresuan concentrated his attention."[49] These ports were Mergui, Tavoy, and Tenassarim, which Naresuan's generals obtained for him to atone for their failure to keep up with the two royal brothers when their elephants rushed off with them into the midst of the enemy. Thus the later Ayutthayan traders of the seventeenth and eighteenth centuries would owe the useful possession of these ports on the Gulf of Bengal to King Naresuan the Great.

Despite having been a brother-in-arms of Naresuan, the reign of Ekatotsarot was a peaceful one, and Ayutthaya and her provincial towns gained in prosperity. The capital was further embellished with new palace buildings, temples, and monuments. Under Ekatotsarot, the Japanese came to trade in Siam and were granted a settlement in Ayutthaya. The king soon had a regiment of professional Japanese guards, whose commander, Yamada by name, was created a *Phraya*, and the Japanese gradually increased their influence at court. Complimentary letters were exchanged between the king of Siam and the powerful shogun in Japan, yet the Dutch were gaining in influence too. A Thai embassy was received at The Hague by Prince Maurice of Nassau, which was the first recorded visit of any Thais to Europe.[50]

However, the White Prince's reign was but a short one of fifteen years, the king becoming insane before he died in 1620. His younger son, who had killed the elder brother when their father was alive but helpless, now seized the throne. As he later showed abject repentance for this act, and his life was one of goodness and piety, ironically enough he became known in history as King Songtham – "The Pious" or "The Just". By then royal ranks had become more stabilised, and the higher rank of princes – son of a queen – was confirmed with a title borrowed from that north-western race of Thais – the Shans. This title was *Chao Fa*, Celestial Prince or Princess. The Shans, however, had used this title for their kings or ruling chiefs only, whereas at Ayutthaya, and subsequently in Bangkok, it was used mostly for the sovereign's children who had mothers of royal birth, and

49 *Ibid.*, page 222.
50 *Ibid.*, page 297.
51 *Ibid.*, page 299.

were thus in a higher grade than the king's children by minor wives, even if these were noble ladies. This distinction undoubtedly led Westerners to the misunderstanding that the King's children who were not *chao fas* were *illegitimate*. This difference in rank between the two kinds of princes would have a profound influence on the history of the Chakri Dynasty of Bangkok.

Below the members of the Royal Family, who were few in the Ayutthaya period, and the "life" nobility – also not a very large number since it was not hereditary – were the free men and the word was synonymous with the name of the race – Thai. They had their land of at least ten acres, and apart from occasional military service – from 18 to 60 years of age, and generally only in times of war – they had but to pay minor indirect taxes, mostly in kind such as rice and other produce, and at stated periods they were called upon for some manual work of construction, such services being known to the Europeans as corvée. Otherwise such men appeared to have been free to live their own lives.

As in all countries of South-East Asia at that time, there was a system of slavery in Siam. The slaves or serfs were of two kinds: firstly, slaves by birth, namely the offspring of slaves; secondly, those who were sold by free parents when they were children; or thirdly, others who sold themselves to pay off debt. Another kind of slaves, were the foreign prisoners of war. These would belong to the king or their own captors, and could be given away or sold. The life of a slave was probably not as bad as one might imagine. Obviously it did not pay an owner to maltreat slaves or he would not get the best service, and slaves were seldom re-sold to other owners without their consent.

King Songtham's reign saw the arrival of the English in Ayutthaya. The voyage of the ship *Globe* in 1611 opened up a new route for the East India Company, and the result was that the company established a factory on the Coromandel coast on which Madras and Pondicherry lay, which meant direct trade relations with Siam and indirectly with Burma. The *Globe* arrived in Ayutthaya in 1612 and the captain delivered an amicable letter from King James I of England and Scotland to the King of Siam.[51] Both the Dutch and English were well treated and the English were given a cantonment between the Japanese and the Dutch, who had been in Ayutthaya four years before.

The English followed the Dutch in building a factory in Ayutthaya itself, and they also set up another at Pattani, a Malay state under Thai rule. Ayutthaya was already an important centre for the

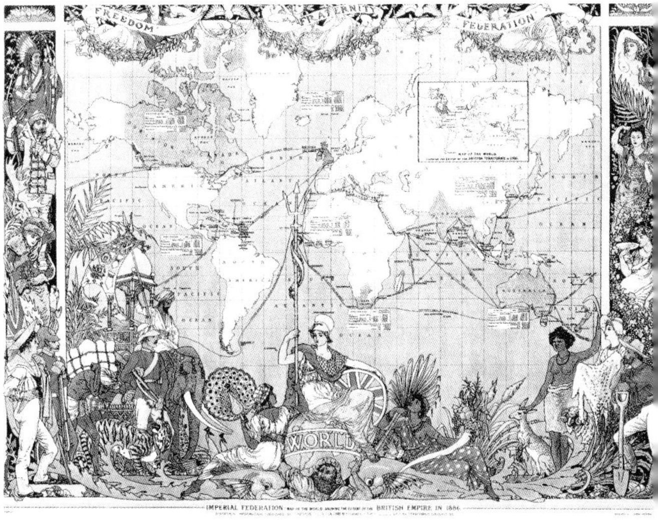

The extent of British overseas territories in the 17th century. (Norman B. Leventhal Map Center Collection, USA)

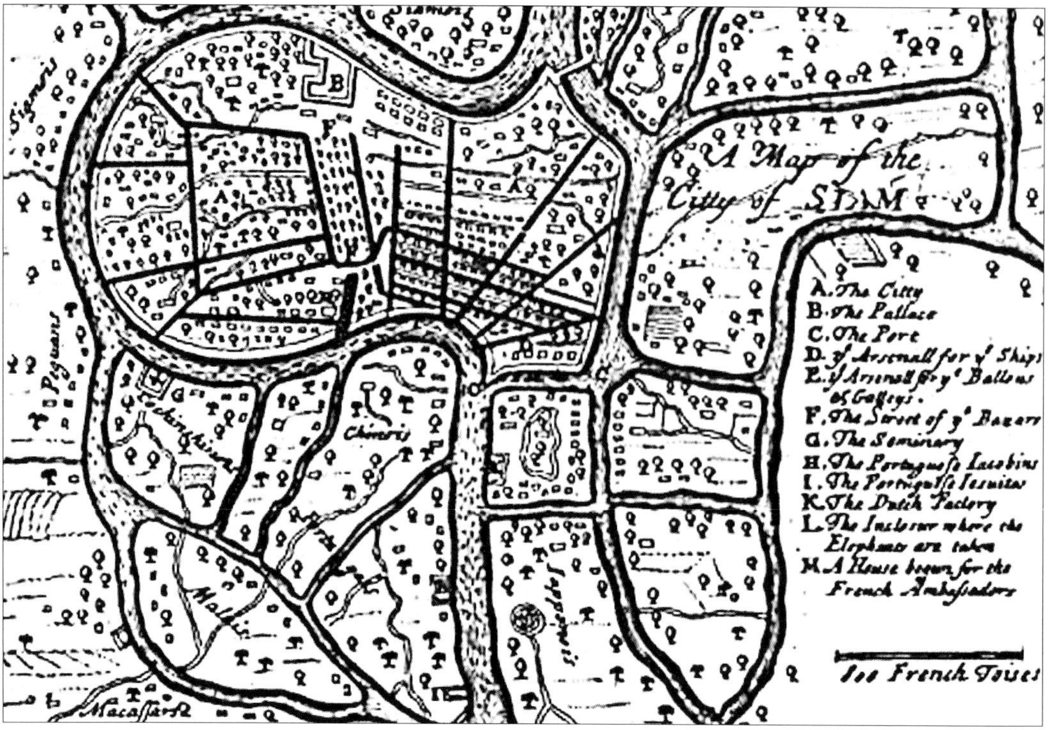

A plan of Ayutthaya showing the various foreign cantonments. (River Books)

overland route from China, the chief trades then being silk and porcelain. But without Naresuan's victories, which ended the long series of "great wars" with Burma, peaceful trading at Ayutthaya would have been impossible. Thus not only the city, but all the foreign merchants trading there, owed him an immense debt for their prosperity.

The English and Dutch merchants obtained hides and skin from the capital, and of these products the Dutch would for a time have a monopoly. They both derived the valuable trade in spices from Pattani. The dye-wood known as "Brazil", aloes-wood, benzoin and tin were also available. What was later to be such an important Thai export, namely rice, was then only sufficient for home consumption. From Ayutthaya, European factors were sent to do business in Chiang Mai, then vassal in turn of Siam and Burma. All trading at Ayutthaya had to be done through the king's government. The king was pleased to have traders of as many nationalities as possible, for they competed with one another and all courted his favour. In King Songtham's reign – on June 12th, 1617 – Siam signed her first treaty with the Dutch.[52] It was not only the royal welcome accorded to them which prevented the Europeans from having designs on Thai independence as they had had elsewhere. It was also because the Thais were as nearly united into one real country as conditions of those days would permit. In what has become modem Indonesia, India, or Pakistan there were at that time many states contending against one another, and the Europeans first took sides and then gradually obtained control over the side they had helped to win. Rival Europeans then encouraged the

52 E. W. Hutchinson: *Adventurers in Siam in the 17th Century,* page 34, London, 1940.

53 D. G. E. Hall, *op. cit.,* pages 239-249.

54 Robert-Martignan, *op. cit.,* page 20.

55 Mgr. Pallegoix, *op. cit.,* Vol. II, page 123.

natives to rebel against their new western rulers which usually meant the exchange of one set of masters for another.[53] Neither tactic would work with the Thais at the time.

The general occupation of the Thai themselves was still agriculture, mostly growing rice. Trade was in the hands of foreigners, European and Asian, with the Thai royal court supervising over all. The foreign communities, who lived in their separate cantonments, were ruled by their own chiefs approved of or even chosen by the Thai monarch. He was also benevolent towards colonies of Chinese, Malays, Japanese, Burmese, Cambodians, Laos, and Vietnamese amongst the Asians. As Robert-Martignan writes,[54] "The Thais are ingenious at making others work for them and themselves remain to direct."

The English, Dutch, and sometime afterwards, French East India Companies had factories at Ayutthaya, all of which were fortified, not against the Thais but to protect themselves against fellow Europeans, and the continuous violent squabbles between the "white men" throughout South-East Asia could hardly have been an edifying spectacle to the Asians themselves. A later French writer quotes a contemporary French traveller as saying of Ayutthaya at the time : "It was a city of all the different peoples and the commercial centre of the universe where all the languages were spoken."[55] But the spirit of Buddhism was all pervading. There were hundreds of temples which were also monasteries into which many men retired as monks for life, while others might for once in their lives don the yellow robe for a period of three months in the rainy season. They kept many strict rules such as celibacy, the shaving of the hair on their heads, and no eating of meals after midday, and they learned to live a good life and study the doctrine of Buddhism. It was a doctrine which preached right living, compassion, and self-reliance for this life. As for the hereafter there was an almost limitless vista of future incarnations, with the hope of finally achieving spiritual bliss known as *Nibhana* or *Nirvarna*.

However, the structure of the Ayutthaya monarchy declined instead of keeping pace with the progress of the city, and the dynasty of Maha Thammaracha, known as the Sukhothai Dynasty because of his descent from the Phra Ruangs, did not last more than 61 years. When King Songtham died in 1628, he was succeeded by a weakling of a son who further had the stupidity to provoke and annoy without reason the Military Commander-in-Chief, Chao Phraya Kalahom. Soon enough the latter lost patience and, revolting against the misguided king, had him done away with. At first the general acted as a "king-maker" by raising a younger son of King Songtham to the throne, but he did not remain on it for more than 36 days. He had the temerity to mistrust Chao Phraya Kalahom and was plotting to arrest him. The king-maker now turned into a double-regicide, and it was the young king who was eliminated. The general seized the throne for himself in 1630. He and his dynasty, also of short duration, were known as Prasat Thong or the Golden Palace.

Ever since the death of Ekatotsarot, Yamada and his Japanese guards had been turbulent, had revolted and been forgiven more than once. Having also helped Prasat Thong to become king, the Japanese were now dissatisfied with the measure of their rewards and they turned against the new monarch. Prasat Thong, however, was a match for them, and he suppressed the revolt with a massacre of most of the Japanese, by first removing their leader – Yamada – by poisoning, and the expulsion of the rest. As a result, the Japanese lost any influence in Siam for over 300 years.

The Dutch took advantage of the Japanese eclipse by gaining more prestige and increasing their trade as a result of giving Prasat Thong naval help against his restive vassals such as Cambodia and Pattani. In 1632 Prince Frederick Henry of the Netherlands sent a letter of congratulations to Prasat Thong on his accession.[56] But his was an unhappy reign full of revolts and murders, although he did add some beautiful new buildings to the Royal Palace. His death in 1659 was followed by a further period of shame for the Ayutthaya kingship, unhappily not the only or the last one. Prasat Thong was succeeded by two monarchs who were both murdered within barely a year. First, it was his elder son, who, after only one year as king, was put to death by an uncle with the help of his own younger brother, Chao Fa Narai. The uncle, who then became king, was both a feeble and an immoderately amorous man, and showed that he had desires for his own niece, who was Narai's sister. Using that as one excuse and the unpopularity of the uncle as a further pretext, Narai, who was by now well versed in the art of conspiracy and had many followers, had him done away with and installed himself on the throne. One of his chief virtues was his devoted love for his old nurse, said to be a princess called Amphai, who later became devout and lived near a temple, causing her to be known as the Mother-Princess of Wat Dusit. Her name will re-appear in the history of the Chakri Dynasty of Bangkok.

Although King Narai himself had a long, and prosperous reign of 32 years (1656-88), it cannot be said that it began or ended auspiciously. Despite the continued struggle with the Burmese over Chiang Mai, with himself going on more than one campaign, most events in Narai's reign were dwarfed by one important feature – his relations with European powers. A French contemporary said of Narai that "few sovereigns of the East had as many foreign friends as he did."[57] By the time he came to the throne the Dutch had successfully fought the Portuguese and English elsewhere in Asia and had become the most powerful and richest European traders at Ayutthaya. The English East India Company had closed their factory there since 1622, and because of troubles at home – the Civil War – did not trade in Siam for 37 years. Instead, it was the newly-arrived French who became the rivals to the Dutch. The Dutch had truly achieved wonders all over the world, with their discoveries of Tasmania and New Zealand, their full control over Java and other Indonesian islands. The redoubtable governor, J. P. Coen, had founded Batavia (now Jakarta) which his successor, Van Diemen, further enlarged and beautified. The Dutch had also founded the first real colony in Africa round the Cape of Good Hope. But the French under Louis XIV, despite prolonged and costly wars in Europe, were beginning to expand their power and influence in Asia. The English had suffered a setback in Siam owing to England herself being occupied with more internal troubles, and the uncertain throne of James II.

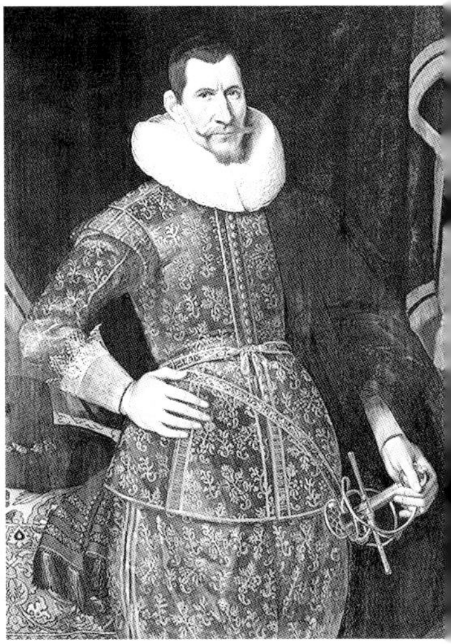

Jan Pieterszoon Coen, Governor-General of the Dutch East Indies and founder of Batavia (present-day Jakarta). (Westfriesmuseum, The Netherlands)

The other highly important foreign traders in Siam were the Chinese. But they differed from the Europeans by being unobtrusive, following the customs of the country easily, and they were humble and submissive in their dealings with Thai princes and nobles. Hence they always had the full privileges enjoyed by the Thais themselves. After King Prasat Thong's expulsion of the Japanese, the trade between Siam and Japan, especially the copper trade, passed into Chinese hands. King Prasat Thong had further developed the policy, initiated by Songtham, that the King of Siam should himself be the biggest merchant and made full use of royal monopolies. Most of the King's goods were despatched abroad in Chinese junks or Thai-owned junks manned by Chinese sailors. Furthermore, it was easy to treat the Chinese as natives of the country because most of them came to Siam without wives and they married Thai women in their thousands. Their children, grandchildren, and further generations, were largely absorbed into the Thai race, which was in turn infused with Chinese blood. This combination of these two races would be of the greatest influence in Thai history, especially in the Bangkok period. Moreover, there was little more than occasional contact with the Imperial Chinese Court, apart from the sending of tributes from time to time, with the result that the Chinese in Siam had no protection from their own country, and they had to submit meekly to Thai rule while trading there. The Chinese claim of suzerainty over Siam, which has recently been extensively treated in a learned work in English,[58] was not so seriously regarded by the Thais, and the tributes sent were really a ruse to get through the formalities and restrictions imposed by Chinese authorities at the ports of entry of Thai goods. The proof lies in the fact that, despite the so-called Chinese suzerainty lasting from the Sukhothai period to 1854, China never once interfered with the internal or external affairs of Siam.

King Narai, who ascended the throne at the age of twenty-five, followed his father's footsteps in being a King-Merchant. With the Dutch being so supreme in trade, he immediately began to look round for their rivals. When the English East India Company arrived in Siam again in 1659 – after a lapse of 37 years – he asked the agents to re-open their branches in his country. The company was by then extremely rich and powerful, paying the English Government £400,000 a year for the monopoly of trading in Asia, having an annual profit of one million, and possessing civil and military power in India.[59]

57 Nicolas Gervaise: *Histoire naturelle et politique du Royaume de Siam*, page 312, Paris, 1688.

58 G. William Skinner, *op. cit.*, New York, 1957.

59 E. W. Hutchinson, *op. cit.*, page 38.

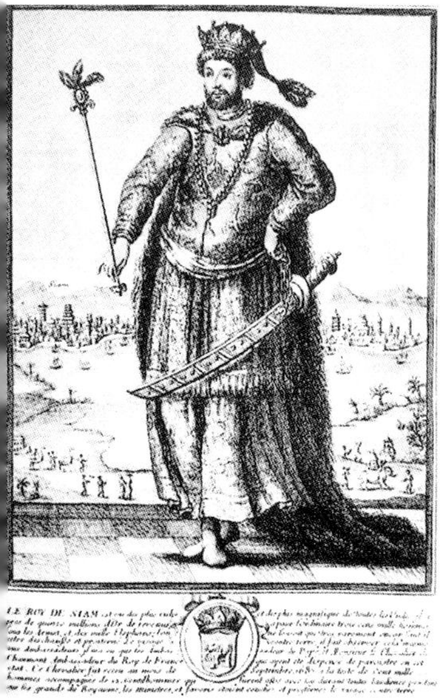

ABOVE: King Narai as envisaged by a western artist. (River Books)

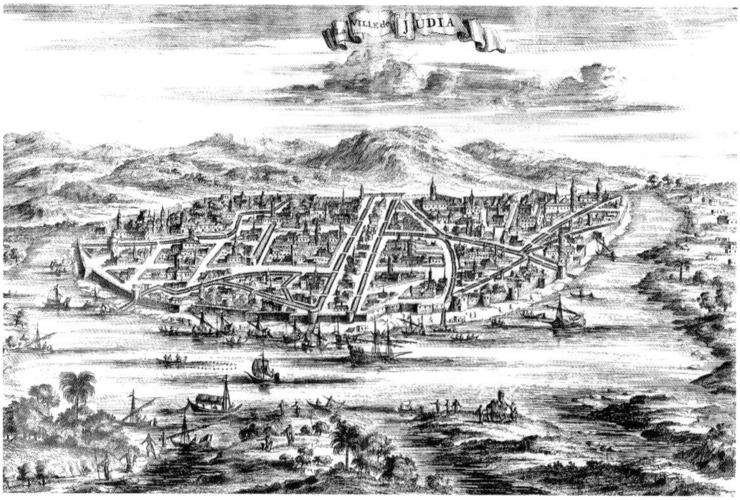

ABOVE RIGHT: Engraving of the city of Ayutthaya. (River Books)

The King-Merchant exercised strict control over foreign traders. All ships had to stop at the mouth of the Chao Phraya River, known as Paknam, and submit to an examination and the paying of duties which were not onerous. What the foreign traders resented, and was to cause serious troubles in the Bangkok period, was the fact that the Thai Treasury had an option on all of the cargo, which it could obtain cheaply and then re-sell at a good profit. The traders themselves could sell on the open market only the cargo which had been rejected by the king, and naturally their profits were much reduced. Yet the trade must still have been good enough to justify the number of foreign ships crossing the bar at Paknam and sailing 45 miles up the twisty river to Ayutthaya. That the King had to trade himself was a necessity as otherwise all trade would have been entirely in foreign hands owing to the attitude of the Thais towards trade and business. As Hutchinson says, they have "a repugnance of an essentially agricultural people for commerce."[60] The minister with whom the foreign traders had to deal was the Minister of the Treasury – Chao Phraya Phra Klang, whose title became known amongst the foreigners as the *Barcalon.*

The most remarkable feature of King Narai's reign was his employment of a European as Chief Minister in the latter part. As this individual might have altered the whole course of Thai history, his origins and his life should be fully told, as has been done admirably by Hutchinson.[61] He was a Greek by the name of Constant Gerakis or Jerakis (which in Modem Greek means Falcon), born in Cephalonia. As a young boy, calling himself Constant Phaulkon, and with his mother's consent, he had joined English merchant ships. Although he grew to maturity in them as they plied European and Asian waters, and was shipwrecked more than once, he apparently never gained officers' rank. In 1656, which was the very year Narai became king, Phaulkon, at the age of thirty, went to Ayutthaya with Richard Burnaby, an agent of the English East India Company, and was first employed by Burnaby and George White, brother of Samuel White, a pilot.

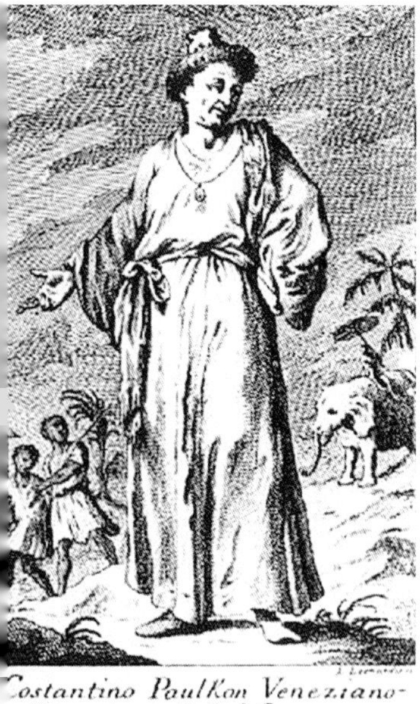

Chao Phraya Vichayen (Constantine Phaulkon). (River Books)

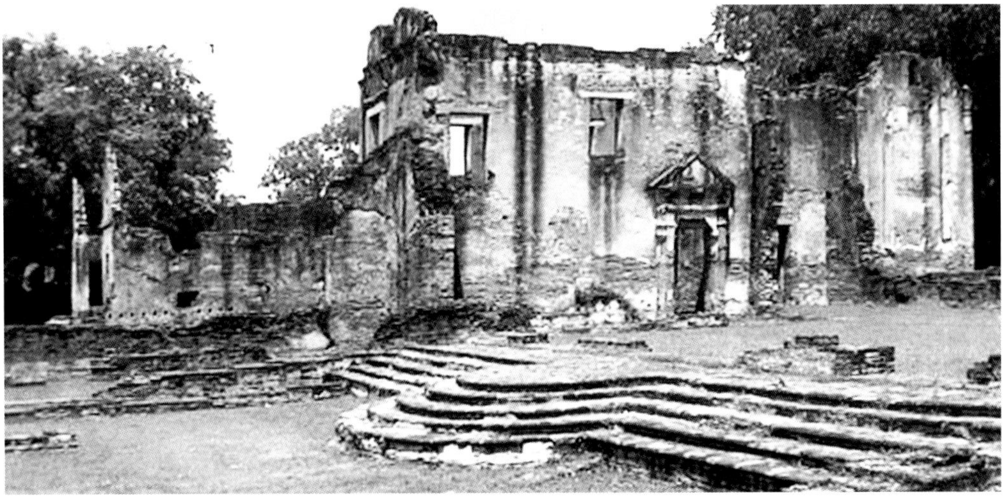

The house built for Chao Phraya Vichayen by King Narai. (National Archives Bangkok)

Through their help Phaulkon entered the service of the king as an interpreter in the Royal Treasury. Besides Thai, an extremely difficult language for Europeans to speak, which he mastered in two years, the Greek was equally fluent in Malay and Portuguese, the latter being then the foremost commercial language in the Far East.

Having made his way into royal service, Phaulkon lost little time in attracting the notice of the king, who, like one of his great successors in Bangkok, had an inquisitive and scientific turn of mind, and he talked to Phaulkon for hours on end. Thai history relates Phaulkon's different exploits such as his ability to get a large and newly-built ship out of the dock easily, or how he weighed a heavy siege gun by placing it in a boat.[62] Once he was in the king's favour, he gained rapid promotion and became Narai's chief counsellor, especially in foreign affairs. In due course he was ennobled as Chao Phraya Vichayen – Lord of Cool Knowledge. When the English East India Company sent William Strangh to negotiate with Siam, it was with Phaulkon, who only seven years before had been a humble employee of the Company. Strangh was the guest of Phaulkon, who lived in great state in a brick house, most rare in Ayutthaya where even royal buildings were made of wood. It was probably through Phaulkon's suggestion that Narai built his summer palace at Lopburi in brick and mortar, and the ruins of Phaulkon's own home there stand extant to this day. He became so rich and powerful that naturally he was the envy of other Europeans, several of whom were employed by the King in lesser capacities, such as the brothers George and Samuel White.[63]

Unfortunately for Phaulkon the aims of the English East India Company did not suit the Thai authorities, and he was blamed by his former employers for being ungrateful and unhelpful. The English company wanted the Thais to promise to buy a specified quota of English goods, but the Thais disliked long-term concessions. They were still smarting under the Dutch threats of force before obtaining the monopoly of the hides trade in 1664-1665. The Thais preferred

60 *Ibid.*, page 38.

61 *Ibid.*, Chapter III, pages 55-66.

62 *History of Ayutthaya* (in Thai), pages 243-244, Bangkok, 1958 version.

63 Maurice Collis: *Siamese White*, London, 1936.

military help against the Dutch rather than to buy English goods for re-sale to their own people. Thus a deadlock was reached, and the company threatened to leave Siam again. Despite every effort at intrigue and sending many costly presents to London, for which he received an autographed letter of thanks from James II, Phaulkon failed to come to terms with the English. War between Siam and the East India Company was narrowly averted, but some desultory threats about taking Mergui persisted for a while. Soon, however, the English would be far too busy at home with their approaching "Glorious Revolution" and they lost contact with Siam for roughly 150 years.

All the above had, of course, taken some years to develop, and as he realized that he would not succeed in getting English help for his Thai king, Phaulkon gradually turned to the idea of a French alliance to counter further Dutch encroachments. According to Thai custom, French missionaries who came to Ayutthaya in 1662 had been as well treated as the Portuguese missionaries before and since. Narai helped them to build both a church and a school. Taking advantage of a letter to Narai which two French bishops had brought from Louis XIV in 1673 to thank the Thai king for his kindness to French missionaries, Phaulkon persuaded Narai to send an embassy to France. At first the French could not provide a ship as they were at war with the Dutch, who held command of the eastern seas. Finally, when a French vessel did arrive in Ayutthaya in 1680, the first Thai embassy went with the ship on its return. Tragically, the ship and the embassy were lost at sea in 1681 and never heard of again.

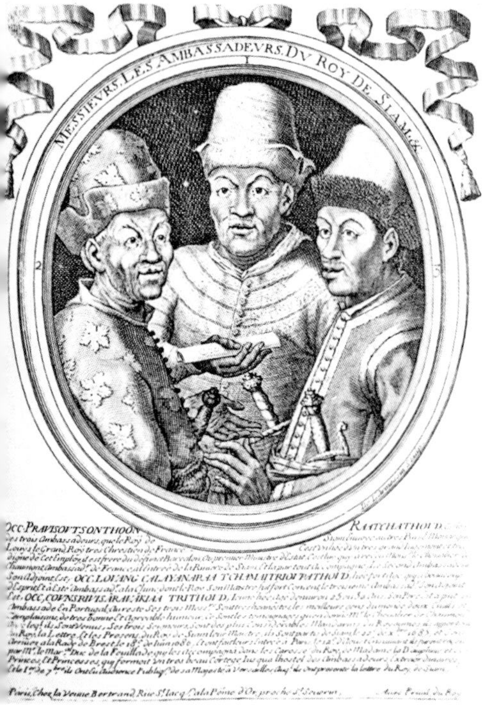

The members of the third Siamese embassy sent to the court of Louis XIV in 1868. Kosa Pan was the ambassador. (River Books)

Both Narai and Phaulkon were undaunted. The second Thai embassy, which left Ayutthaya in 1684, arrived safely, taking with them the first group of Thai students ever to go to Europe. They formed the first trickle of that stream which in years to come would swell into a mighty river. The Thai ambassador and his mission stayed a few days in England as they had gone up the English Channel from the Bay of Biscay. Their interpreter, Brother Vachet, was received by Charles II but the English king did not see the Thais themselves. When they arrived in Paris the Thai diplomats, who had a splendid reception, were themselves unsuccessful, and the French found them rude and unappreciative of everything done for them. That they were bored and yawned at the opera or refused to kneel in Notre Dame during mass might well meet with sympathy from many Thais today. At the audience Louis XIV was gracious to them, saying to the interpreter, Brother Vachet, "Assure these gentlemen that I am delighted to see them, and that I will do for the King of Siam, my brother, always with much pleasure, all that he will desire of me."[64]

Meanwhile as the diplomats indulged in sightseeing or attending functions they did not care for, Brother Vachet and the other French

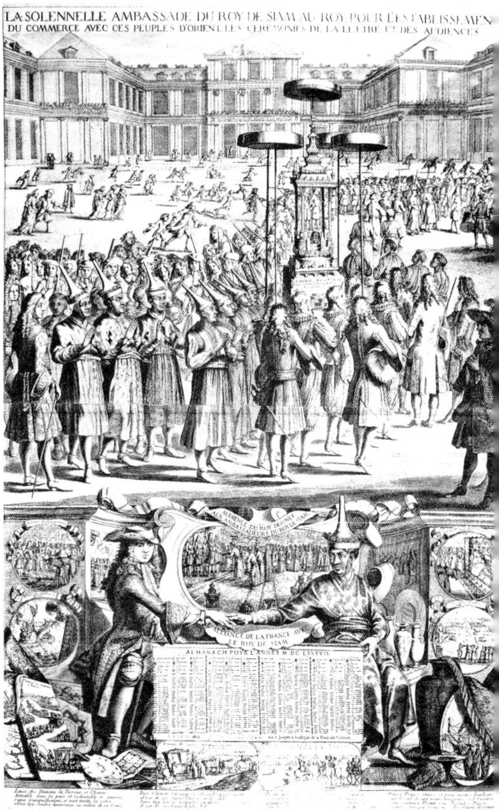

The procession bearing gifts and King Narai's letter to the French king. (River Books)

priests who accompanied them were most active behind the scene. They told the Jesuit confessor of Louis XIV – Père de la Chaise – that Phaulkon had been converted to the Roman Catholic faith by the French Jesuits in Siam. Phaulkon was born in the Greek Orthodox religion, but he had become a Protestant while serving in English ships. In Ayutthaya he married a Japanese, descendant of the Japanese Catholic converts who came there in the reign of Ekatotsarot, and he followed her faith. Brother Vachet suggested that Narai too was ready, through Phaulkon's influence, to be converted if only he was asked to do so by Louis XIV himself, and that the Thai people would then follow their sovereign. After that it was not difficult for the Jesuit confessor to fire His Most Christian Majesty's imagination with the glowing vision of bringing a non-Christian monarch into the true doctrine. The French king therefore agreed to send an embassy to Siam for that express purpose. Thus it was more of an embassy sent by the Jesuits than by the French Foreign Office, and Narai and Louis XIV were at cross purposes from the start, one desiring an alliance and the other a conversion. The ambassador chosen was the Chevalier de Chaumont, himself a recently converted Huguenot and thus a religious zealot. The priest who accompanied him was one of the strangest characters of the seventeenth century, the Abbé de Choisy, better known as a female impersonator, who has since appeared in many works on sexual psychology.[65] It is from Choisy's own book that we get an entertaining picture of the experiences of the mission.[66]

The embassy left Brest in March, 1685, in two men-of-war and the voyage took 204 days. It was magnificently received at Paknam and conducted to Ayutthaya in regal comfort, passing by Bangkok, then a little trading station halfway up the river. They were well accommodated and fed, all in European style, during their entire stay.

King Narai received them in State on October 18th. Louis XIV's letter was laid on a gold salver, deposited first in a gilded royal barge propelled by sixty oarsmen in scarlet, then placed on a gold palanquin carried by ten men, also garbed in red. The king was wearing his crown and golden robes and sat on a throne six foot high. The French Ambassador walked in, bowed, and sat down in the French manner but with the appropriate respectful demeanour. Phaulkon, who acted as interpreter, followed Thai custom by crouching on the floor with the rest of the courtiers. Yet despite the splendour of the reception and the friendly atmosphere, things went wrong from the beginning. The Ambassador of the Shah of Persia was in Ayutthaya at the same time and there was a rumour that he was there to convert the King to Islam. This might have so alarmed de Chaumont that he discarded

64 Vachet as recorded in Adrian Launey *Histoire de la Mission de Siam, Documents Historiques,* pages 142-143, Paris. Vol. I.

65 O. P. Gilbert: *Men in Women's Clothes* (English translation from the French by R. B. Douglas), London, 1926. Havelock Ellis: *Eonism.*

66 L'Abbé de Choisy: *Journal du Voyage de Siam fait en 1685-1686,* Paris, 1687.

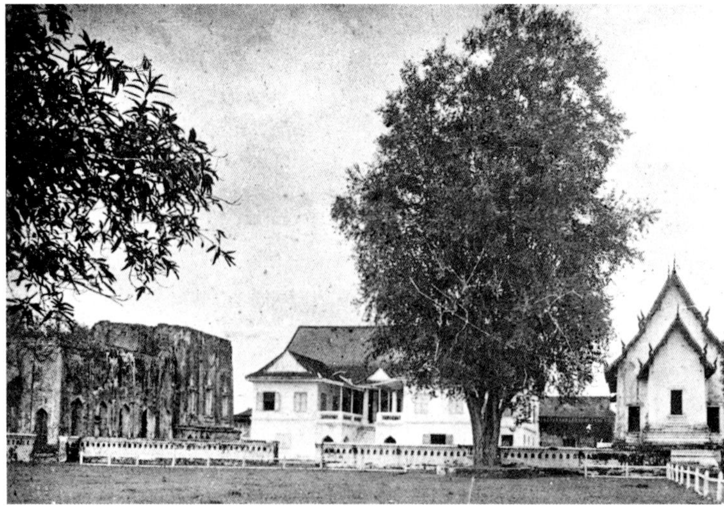

The Chantorn Phisan throne hall within the former palace of King Narai in Lopburi was where he received his officials. It was restored in the reign of King Rama IV. (National Archives Bangkok)

Phaulkon's pleas for caution, and he made Narai's conversion the principle aim of his mission. At less formal meetings he flatly refused to discuss anything else until the conversion question was cleared up. King Narai prevaricated in the hope of discussing the alliance first, but the Ambassador was adamant. The king then ordered Phaulkon to tell de Chaumont that "no king had ever been known to adopt a new faith which had no following amongst his subjects."[67] The French priests should try to convert large numbers of Thais first and popularize the Catholic religion, then the king could follow. Phaulkon clearly believed that in time this was possible and he suggested devious ways. One was that more Jesuit priests should come to Siam and would at first dress as laymen and serve in other more immediately useful capacities.

Despite his long service in Siam, and his prodigious knowledge of conditions in Asia from Bombay to Japan, the Greek failed to appreciate the deep devotion the Thais had for Buddhism – the ancient religion of their ancestors. This might have been due to the usual zeal of a new convert, as much as to the fact that he had become over-confident and arrogant. The Abbé de Choisy was the first to realize that conversion was impossible, and his task as a religious instructor to the king was hopeless.

Phaulkon, as the favourite of Narai, had not only earned the envy of fellow Europeans but of Thai noblemen also. Now that they knew he was intriguing with the French to achieve the king's conversion, he incurred the enmity of a group which would today be called "nationalists." This group was led by Phra Phetracha, Commander of the Royal Regiment of Elephants, who was an old and close friend of the king. Not only had they gone on the Chiang Mai campaigns together, but Narai was a most keen follower of the noble sport of elephant hunting. This was not to kill them, but to capture them for training and future use. Narai loved to chase such elephants by

67 E. W. Hutchinson, *op. cit.*, page 108.

68 Prince Damrong: *Tales of Ancient Times, op cit.*, pages 289-90.

lassooing their hind legs while he himself rode on a tame and well-trained animal. This was considered the most difficult and daring way of catching wild elephants. Friendship grows fast when brave men share a love for a dangerous sport. Narai and Phra Phetracha together compiled a manual on the art of elephant craft which was the basis of all other training manuals on the same subject.[68]

In his silent opposition to the Greek, Phra Phetracha was supported by his son, Luang Surasak, a gallant young officer of the Guards. There was a rumour that Luang Surasak was a natural son of the king, conceived with a common Laos woman during a campaign in the north. It was said that the king was ashamed of the fact, and his good friend, Phetracha, agreed to accept the boy as his own. If that was so, then Surasak has the unique distinction of being the only "natural son" known in Thai history. The nationalists' strong objection to the conversion plan went beyond any religious scruples. They feared that conversion of the king would not only lead to the power of the French priests, but they would be followed by French troops and French domination.

In this fear they were not far wrong. Once he thought that the conversion would fail, and when he knew that he was facing a rising Thai opposition, Phaulkon contemplated a coup d'état with the help of French troops. Such was the religious zeal of a recent convert, he was not deterred by the fact that he was planning treason against King Narai, who had been like a father to him, although Phaulkon was the elder of the two. With such extravagant ideas in his head, Phaulkon the statesman once again became the Greek adventurer, and from that moment his fate was sealed. Having now embarked on treason, Phaulkon persuaded de Chaumont to an alliance without conversion, while Narai would accept French troops with the avowed purposes of defending Mergui against the English and Bangkok against the Dutch. Following this agreement Narai would send with de Chaumont a third embassy to Paris. This was led by a nobleman who was later to be known as Phraya Kosa, whose proper name was Pan, and who, according to King Mongkut, was one of the direct ancestors of the Chakri monarchs of Bangkok.

De Chaumont was granted his farewell audience on December 12th, 1685, before leaving with Phraya Kosa (Pan), his Thai colleagues, and some French priests who were this time led by Father Tachard and the Abbé de Lionne. They were received on their arrival early in 1686 with even more magnificence. Louis XIV gave them an audience in the Gallery of Mirrors at Versailles, and he rose from his throne to receive Narai's letter. Thai history gives full rein to highly amusing stories about the activities of Kosa (Pan) and his highly successful diplomats during their stay in Paris. The Abbé de Lionne

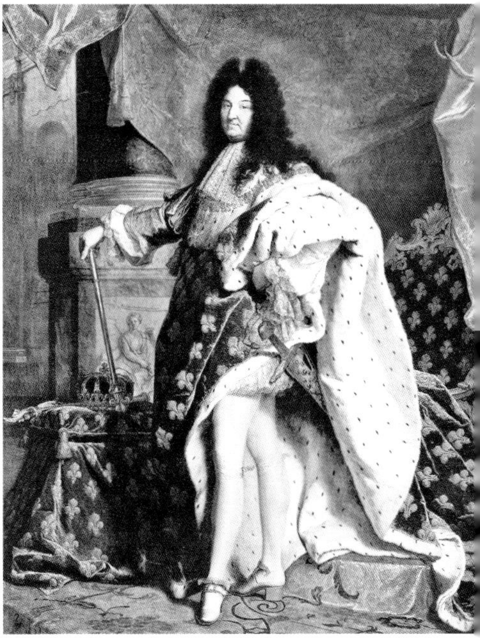

King Louis XIV, reigned 1643-1715. (Louvre Museum)

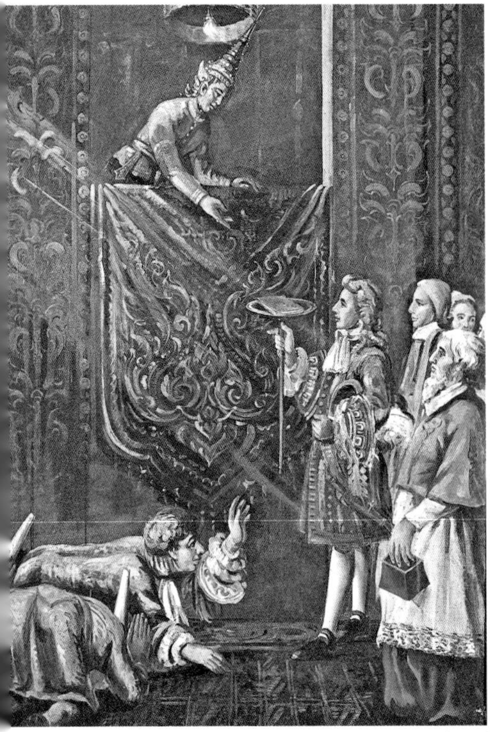

An illustration of King Narai receiving Chevalier de Chaumont, the French ambassador sent by Louis XIV. The Abbé de Choisy stands beside the ambassador while Chao Phraya Vichayen is crouched down on the floor. (King Narai National Museum)

wrote back: "It is beyond my power to tell you how pleased everyone in France is with our (Thai) Ambassador. They are nice people, well-mannered and polite; in fact, the complete reverse in every way of their predecessors, who gave so much trouble."[69]

With them on their return to Siam, Louis XIV sent his second embassy led by M. Simon de La Loubère, who wrote the best French book about the people of Siam and their customs in the seventeenth century.[70] They left Brest on March 1st, 1687, and travelled in five or six ships which had French troops in them according to the agreement, and they were under the command of General Desfarges. They reached Paknam on September 27th, but the embassy was not given an audience until November 2nd. By this time the picture was greatly changed. Narai was ill and sinking, he had become an old man even though he was barely 55, and it was even hinted that he was being slowly poisoned. Opposition to Phaulkon and the official policy was mounting; the Thai people generally did not like the presence of French troops, even though they were left to build and occupy two forts at Bangkok, which were already being constructed by the Thais. These forts were on either side of the river, and the one on the west bank can still be seen today at the entrance of Klong Bang Luang near Wat Arun – the Temple of Dawn.

Louis XIV remained insistent on conversion, but de Chaumont had talked so much about it that with La Loubère Narai avoided the subject altogether. The Ambassador found the situation so hopeless that he took his departure on January 3rd, 1688, leaving behind a small French garrison under General Desfarges which had been depleted by illness, both during the long voyage and since its arrival in Siam.

By spring 1688 Narai was so seriously ill that he lost control of all government. He asked his French doctor to advise Phaulkon to resign and leave the country, but it was of no avail. Now Phra Phetracha and Luang Surasak struck a decisive blow. Phaulkon was sent a false summons from the king, who was there in his summer palace, and lured away from his almost impregnable house in Lopburi. On May 8th Phaulkon was arrested at the palace gate and sent to Surasak's house. He had hoped for help from the remaining French troops, but none was forthcoming. He was accused of high treason in conspiring with the French, and neither General Desfarges nor the Abbé de Lionne, both in Lopburi, said a word in his favour to Phra Phetracha, now in complete control. Phaulkon was condemned to death, his property was confiscated, but his Japanese wife and children were spared. Early in June, after declaring his firm faith in the Roman Catholic religion, Phaulkon was beheaded by the banks of Tale Chupsorn, a natural lake not far from Lopburi. Thus ended the career of one of the most remarkable Europeans to have appeared on the historical scene of South-East Asia.

69 E. W. Hutchinson quotes French Foreign Office MSS. *op. cit.*, page 119.

70 Simon de la Loubère: *Description du Royaume de Siam*. 2 Vols. Paris, 1691.

71 *History of Ayutthaya* (in Thai), *op. cit.*, pages 341-342.

The ailing king was now completely isolated. Phra Phetracha sent for the king's legitimate heirs and summarily had them put to death. He then summoned the Council of Ministers to a meeting, when some of them proposed that, in the event of the king's death, there were none so suitable to succeed him as Phra Phetracha himself. A few amongst them had the audacity to dissent, and they were faced with threats of violence. King Narai died on July 11th, 1688, when Phra Phetracha was able to unsurp the throne without difficulty. Narai's long reign of 32 years saw great progress and prosperity for Ayutthaya, yet it ended as inauspiciously as it had begun, with rebellion and murders. Although Narai is the best-known in the West amongst the Kings of Ayutthaya, the benefits which he conferred on his country were lost by his disastrous foreign policy which ushered in the reign and dynasty of Phra Phetracha. These kings were to turn the glories of Ayutthaya into a twilight end, which might have spelt the final doom for Thai art and culture of six centuries.

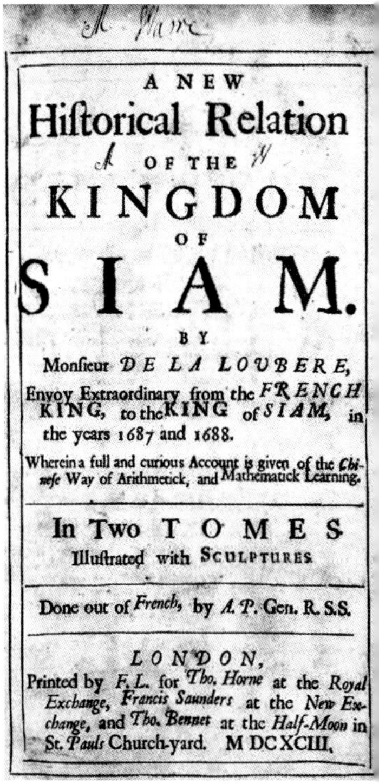
A NEW
Hiſtorical Relation
OF THE
KINGDOM
OF
SIAM.
BY
Monſieur DE LA LOUBERE,
Envoy Extraordinary from the FRENCH KING, to the KING of SIAM, in the years 1687 and 1688.
Wherein a full and curious Account is given of the Chineſe Way of Arithmetick, and Mathematick Learning.
In Two TOMES
Illuſtrated with SCULPTURES.
Done out of French, by A. P. Gen. R. S. S.
LONDON,
Printed by F. L. for Tho. Horne at the Royal Exchange, Francis Saunders at the New Exchange, and Tho. Bennet at the Half-Moon in St. Pauls Church-yard. M DCXCIII.

Title page of English edition of the book by Simon de la Loubère, printed in 1693. (River Books)

After some desultory fighting, with sieges of French forts, exchanges of hostages, mutual betrayals, and some ill-treatment, the French and other Europeans were gradually evacuated from Siam, and the door was to remain shut against them for 130 years. The story of the last Ayutthaya Dynasty, that of Phra Phetracha, which remained for 79 years, is indeed an unhappy one. His own reign was turbulent and full of rebellions, generally by young men who claimed to be heirs of King Narai. They were all suppressed and it was as king that he died at the age of 71. He was succeeded by Surasak, his son or the natural son of Narai, who is known in Thai history as Phra Chao Suea – The Tiger King. Stories abound of his appalling private life and his acts of cruelty. Once he had his two sons flogged almost to death for some trivial offence. There are only two creditable tales about him. One is that he was a keen boxer and sometimes appeared in disguise at public matches and did not mind being beaten, although more often he won. The other was when he wished to spare the life of his favourite coxswain, Norasingh. According to King Trailok's Palace Law of 1450 a coxswain of the king's barge, who allowed the barge to hit the bank, had to forfeit his life. Once when the Tiger King was on an expedition during the flooding season, the current was running so fast and the river was winding with the bank not clearly visible. Norasingh made a mistake and the barge touched the bank. The coxswain jumped on to the grass, and in begging the king's pardon, asked to be executed according to the law. The Tiger King wished to spare him as it was a slight and unavoidable accident, but Norasingh insisted on the law taking its course for the honour of his profession.[71] The king was so deeply upset at the loss of his valiant coxswain that he ordered that bend in the river to be made straight by cutting a canal through, which required the work of 30,000 conscripts.

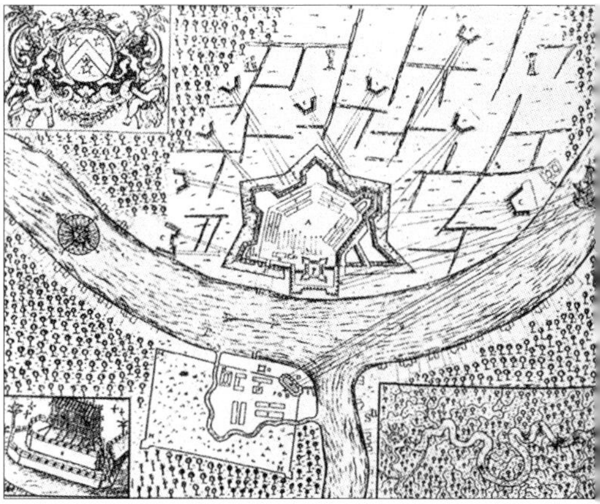

Plan of the fort at Thonburi during the battle with the French at the beginning of the reign of King Phetracha in 1687. (Museum Siam)

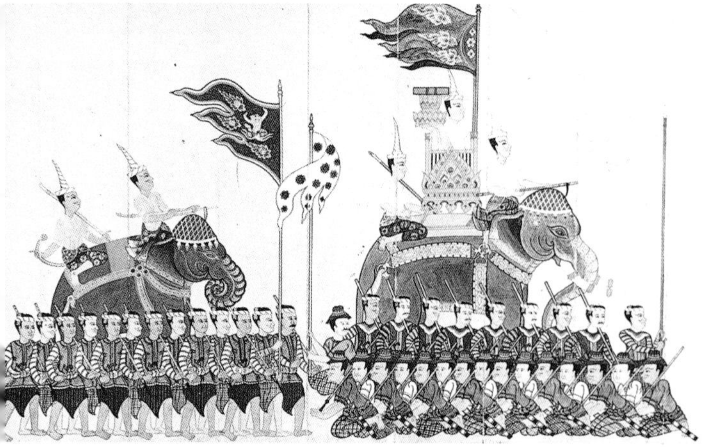

Watercolour showing the uniforms worn by Siamese and foreign soldiers towards the end of the Ayutthaya period. (National Museum Bangkok)

When Phra Chao Suea died in 1709 at the age of 45, the next king was his eldest son, Thai Sra (1709-33) who had a peaceful reign of 24 years, during which time many more canals were constructed, large sea-going vessels built, and there was a big export of live elephants. His quiet reign was but a lull in the turbulent storm of this dynasty. His death was swiftly followed by a ferocious war of succession amongst his sons and his brother, who together with him had survived their father's merciless sentence of flogging. Both the two sons perished in the struggle and the brother became king and was known as Borommakot. His reign of 25 years is important for being the last peaceful period of Ayutthaya during which literature, the arts and crafts flourished. When Siam had again to be re-created in Bangkok, it was the fragments left behind from the reign of Borommakot which served as models. It was in the second year of this reign – 1734 – that a half Chinese boy called Sin was born. This boy was one day going to join the royal service and become an outstanding cavalry officer. In the same reign four years later – 1737 – another boy by the name of Thong Duang was born. He too was to grow up to be a great soldier and finally the founder of the Chakri Dynasty of Bangkok.

King Borommakot himself is known mainly for his cruelty to people and animals alike. Seven of his own sons died violent deaths at his bidding, so afraid was he that they would plot to deprive him of his crown. When his reign closed in 1758 he left the kingdom to his youngest surviving son, Prince Uthumphon, declaring that the elder brother was not so well endowed with such fine qualities.

By then the walls of Ayutthaya had not been reached by any enemy for a century and a half, and there had been no foreign invasion of any kind within the borders of Siam for forty-five years, so that a state of peace was taken for granted – a danger for any country. Moreover, the pious King Uthumphon was distressed by his brother's envy of the throne, and he ceded the crown to him and himself retired into a monastery. The new king, known after the name of his favourite building – Suriyat Amarin – was incompetent and only interested in the diverse pleasures of the flesh.

Burma under King Alaungpaya of Shwebo (1752-60) was united and strong, and as always a united and strong Burma meant an attack against a weak and divided Ayutthaya. But if the king was effete, the Thai people themselves still had plenty of fighting qualities left. The Burmese attack, which began in 1758, endured for nine long years, and it was Alaungpaya's son who carried on the war when he died in 1760. At one juncture the Prince-Priest Uthumphon was invited to leave the monastery to assume control, and he inflicted a severe defeat on the enemy. The king's reward for his brother was to receive him while sitting with a naked sword on his own lap. Prince Uthumphon took the hint and returned to his monastery, refusing to help a second time.

The Burmese then reached the walls of Ayutthaya, but even with the poor leadership shown by the king and his generals, the Thais could still defend their city, and the siege continued for two more years. However, it was not possible, after suffering so much privation, for the people to hold out indefinitely, so Ayutthaya for the second time had to succumb. The enemy entered the capital during the night of April 7-8th, 1767. They were naturally enraged by the relentless resistance which the Thais had shown. The Burmese put Ayutthaya to the fire and sword. The unfortunate monarch escaped to the precincts of a monastery outside the city walls, but he was caught by some Burmese troops and killed. The princes, including the Prince-Priest Uthumphon, the nobility, and those who had survived the massacre, were driven off to Burma as prisoners, as was the custom. Most of the northern towns such as Phitsanulok had already been destroyed, some by the enemy and others by the Thais themselves as part of the scorched-earth policy. After the sack of Ayutthaya, a great city of over a million people was left in ruins with a population of barely 10,000. The history, literature, arts, and history of the Thais seemed lost for ever. In all, Ayutthaya had been the capital of Siam for 417 years under 33 monarchs.

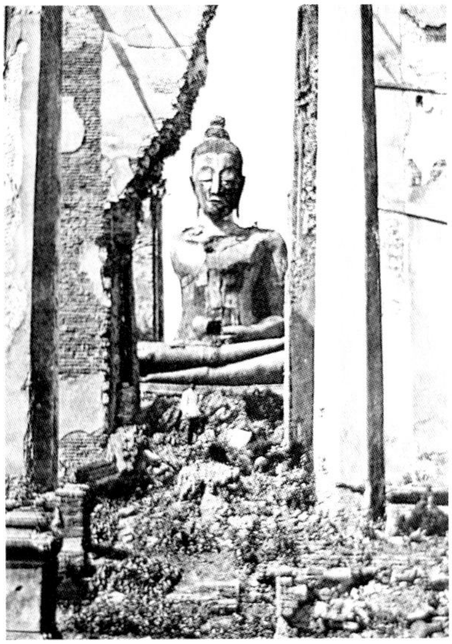

The Phra Mongkol Bophit Buddha image and the *viharn* which was destroyed by the Burmese in 1767. (National Archives Bangkok)

The state of Wat Phra Sri Sanphet after the sacking and having been left more or less untouched for over 150 years. (National Archives Bangkok)

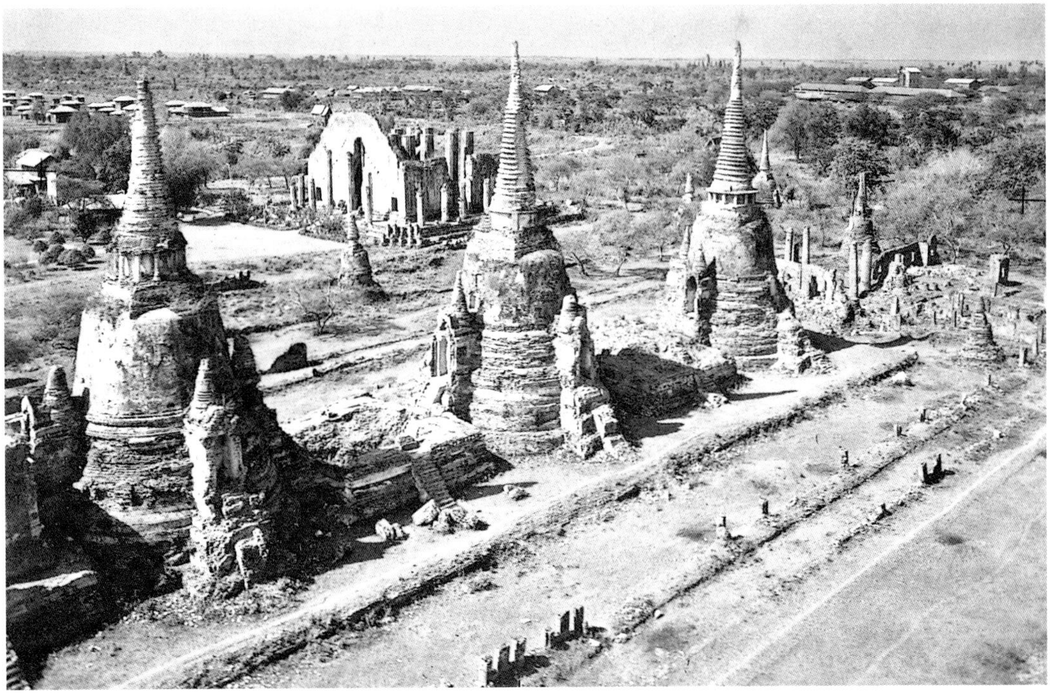

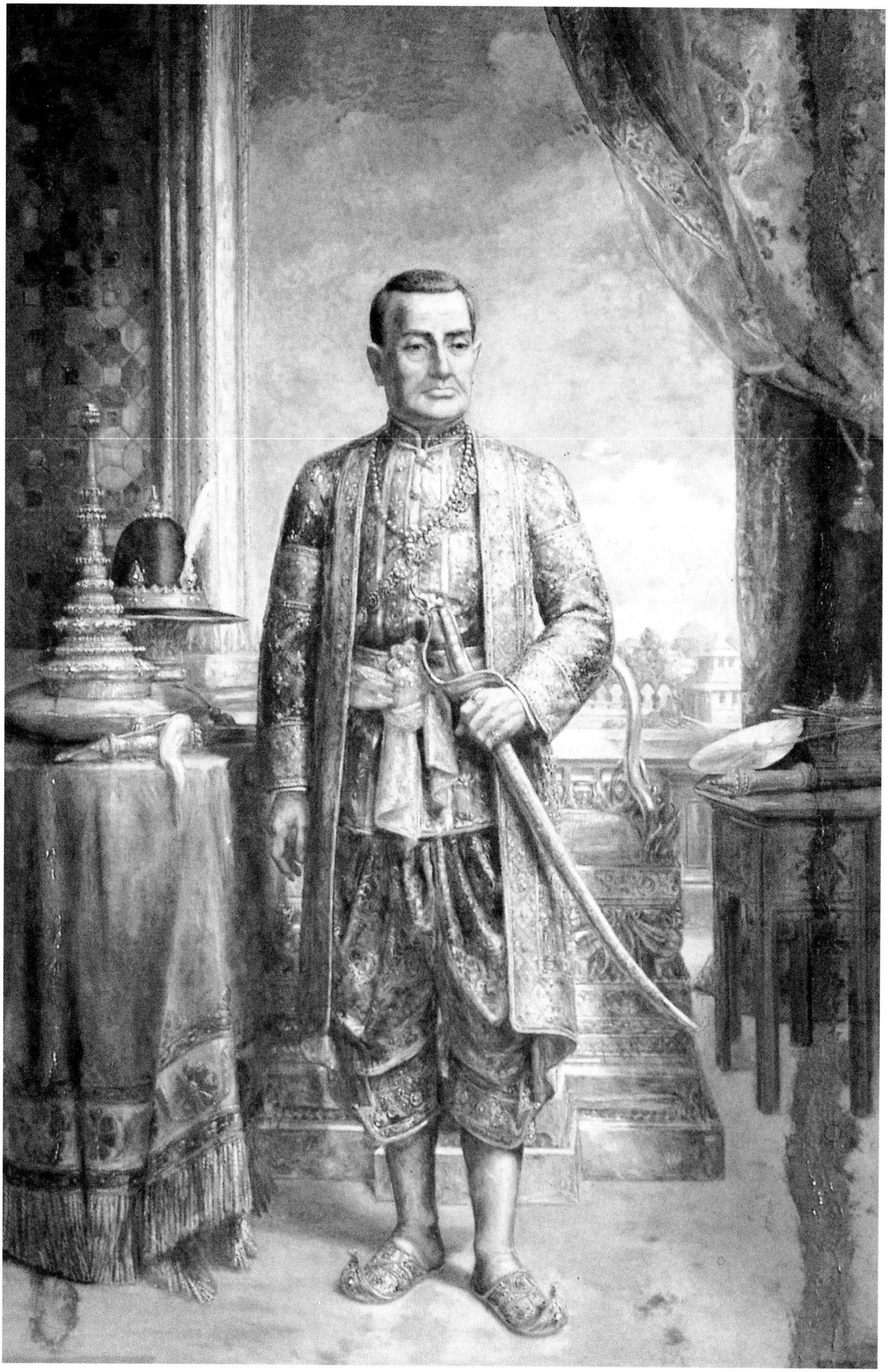

Chapter One
THE FOUNDER
(A.D. 1769 to 1809)

An English friend of the Thais once wrote: "We see them humbled to the dust again and again by a more powerful neighbour, yet always rising up and regaining their freedom ... Those who believe in the survival of the fittest will admit that the Siamese, whatever their faults, must possess some special qualities ."[1]

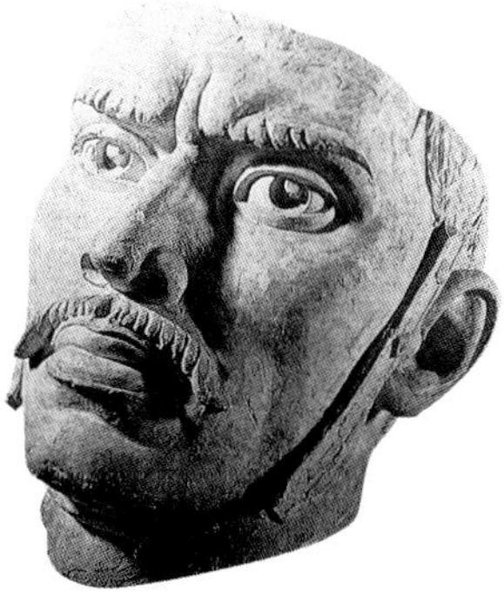

A plaster head of King Taksin by Silpa Bhirasi when preparing the large mounted statue of the king for Wong Wian Yai, Thonburi. (Hall of Sculpture, Bangkok)

Even before the fall of Ayutthaya there was a general, Phraya Tak, with the personal name of Sin (pronounced in the high tone), who felt that all was lost in the capital but there was much to be gained elsewhere, and he left Ayutthaya with a band of five followers. These six Thai horsemen fell into the midst of a Burmese troop of cavalry of 30 men, but they successfully fought their way through to safety. This general is usually known in history as Phraya Taksin, and he was none other than the half-Chinese boy who was born in 1734 in the reign of King Borommakot. His Chinese father had migrated to Ayutthaya and was by then prosperous enough to hold from the state a gambling monopoly in the city. He married a Thai woman, and when the son was born, they were living close to the residence of a nobleman, who took a liking to the boy and finally adopted him. Through the nobleman's help the boy entered the royal service in which he rose rapidly, and by the time he was thirty had been made Governor of Tak, an important garrison town in the west-midlands, and was ennobled as a *Phraya*.[2] When Ayutthaya was being besieged, he and his men had already been withdrawn into the capital to assist in its defence according to custom.

OPPOSITE: An imagined portrait of King. (Chakri Maha Prasat Throne Hall)

Soon after the fall of Ayutthaya some five Thai resistance groups came into existence and were active against the Burmese in different parts of the country. Prominent leaders were the following: The Governor of Phitsanulok in the northern region, the Governor of Sri Thammarat in the south, who asserted his independence as a king, Prince Pipit, who was holding out in the east at Phimai and who was a surviving member of the royal family, and Phraya Taksin, who based himself on Chantaburi in the south-east. This last was by far the most successful and was more aggressive in his actions against the Burmese.

The Burmese, once they had sacked the city and taken away much booty, together with a vast number of the population, did not seem seriously interested in holding down Siam. They probably thought that what seemed an empty shell of a country was not worth any further sacrifice and it was better to go home and enjoy the spoils. Hall has suggested that the Burmese incursions into the Laos-Shan country bordering on Yunnan had forced China to intervene, and that by 1768

1 W. A. R. Wood, *op. cit.*, pages 7-8.

2 G. William Skinner, *op. cit.*, page 20.

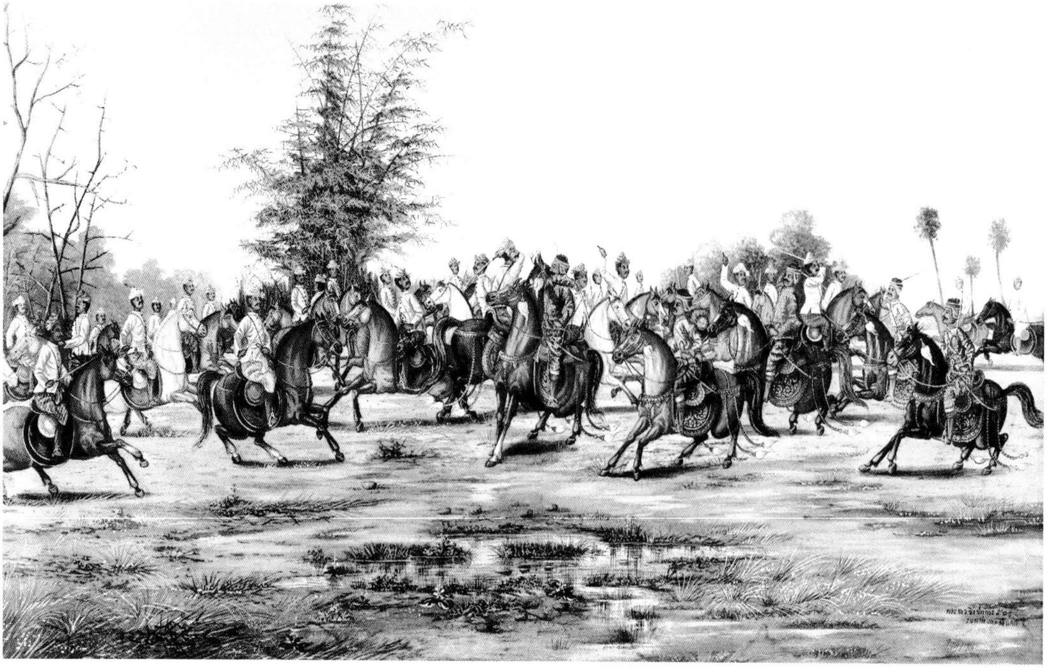

A painting showing the legendary battle in which King Taksin and his small band of men defeated 30 Burmese. (River Books)

Burma herself was on the defensive against Chinese invasion in the north. This weakened their hold on Siam and enabled Phraya Taksin to stage such a rapid recovery.[3] This suggestion has never been put forward before and deserves examination. If it is correct, the fact remains that there were Thai officers and men willing to follow Phraya Taksin so soon after such a crushing defeat which ended the long period of Ayutthaya. This surely tends to show the Thais' "special qualities" mentioned by Wood. Moreover, the Burmese left several garrisons in Siam as Hall himself says of Phraya Taksin: "... he began systematically to exterminate their garrisons, and by the end of 1768 had regained Ayutthaya."[4] This was accomplished by his decisive victory against the Burmese, under General Suki, encamped at Posamton, near Ayutthaya, and it was a victory which broke the back of the Burmese forces which had been left in Siam.

Amongst the young men who flocked to join Phraya Taksin were two brothers, sons of an official of the old regime, who, as King Mongkut later related to Sir John Bowring in his own particular style of English, had obviously served in the Royal Secretariat as he was "the preparers of royal letters and communications for northern regions (i.e. for all states or regions of both dependencies and independency of Siam at northern direction) and protector of the great royal seal for that purpose being; his title being Phra Acksorn Sundorn Smiantra."[5] According to the same source, he "became married with a beautiful daughter of a Chinese richest family."[6] Although King Mongkut did not clearly say that this Chinese lady was the mother of the future king of Siam, he did say that the five children, of whom the future king was one, were of the first wife. A later Thai authority gave the name of the first wife of Phra Ackson Sundorn Smiantra as Yok[7] which in Cantonese Chinese means jade. This is a usual Chinese name, but not at all a common Thai name. It is safe to assume that Yok and the Chinese lady mentioned by King Mongkut was one and the same person. G. William Skinner was cautious when he wrote : "If, as *probable* (my italics), this woman was the mother of Rama I, then the founder of the dynasty was half Chinese."[8]

Comparing King Mongkut's letter to Sir John Bowring with the Thai authority cited, there seems to be no room for any doubt. This only goes to show the importance of the mingling of Thai and Chinese blood throughout the centuries, and that a fine new stock has been made out of them.

Phra Ackson himself had the personal name of Thong Dee, and both of his sons, the two brothers who joined Phraya Tak, were born within the walls of Ayutthaya. The elder called Thong Duang (or sometimes just plain Duang) was born in 1737, and the younger, Boonma, in 1743, so he was six years younger. Besides these two their parents had another son and two daughters, all born before the two. The elder son died in the Ayutthaya period, whereas the two sisters would live to see the glory of their family.

Like most Thai young men Thong Duang entered the priesthood at the age of 21 for the usual three months. Soon after he came out, he married a young woman of a well-to-do family in the province of Rajburi, and he moved there to live with his wife's family. He joined the royal service under the Governor of Rajburi which naturally was military and civil combined. Through his proficiency he was made a *Luang* (4th class) at the age of 25 with the title of Luang Yokrabat.[9] He was therefore not in Ayutthaya at its fall, and nor for that matter was his father. After the death of his first wife, Yok, Thong Dee, who had followed the not uncommon Thai custom of also marrying her younger sister, moved to Phitsanulok. He had had a daughter by her and a son by a minor wife. At Phitsanulok he served under the governor who became one of the resistance leaders after the Burmese victory. Self-appointed as king, he is said to have created Thong Dee Chao Phraya Chakri, but both master and protegé died of illness shortly afterwards. It was Thong Dee's youngest son who arranged his father's cremation and carefully kept his relics. These he later presented to his illustrious half-brother and they now repose in a golden urn in the older of the two mausoleums of the Grand Palace in Bangkok. After his son's accession to the throne in 1782, Thong Dee was reverently given the posthumous title of "The Royal Premier and Supreme Ancestor". But we are anticipating events.

During the confusion of the siege and fall of Ayutthaya the exact whereabouts of Boonma are not known, but obviously he must have been an officer before he joined Phraya Taksin as he immediately became so prominent. He was so brave and able that he soon became a favourite of his chief. As Bowring later related of Phraya Taksin: "His

3 D. G. E. Hall, *op. cit.*, page 352.

4 *Ibid.*

5 King Mongkut (undated) to Sir John Bowring, who misspelt the name as "Acksorn Sundorn". Sir John Bowring: *The Kingdom and People of Siam,* pages 67-69, London, 1857. Vol. I.

6 *Ibid.*

7 *List of Names of Princes and Princesses of the Chakri House* (in Thai), Bangkok, 6th Ed., 1938.

8 G. William Skinner, *op. cit.*, page 26.

9 Chao Phraya Dibakarawongse: *History of the First Reign,* page 316, 1869. Edited by Prince Damrong in 1901. Reprinted 1933 (in Thai).

confidence in his favourite knew no bounds. He insisted upon knowing all his kindred . . . the general told him that he had an elder brother superior to himself in every noble quality, brave, bold, and wise."[10] Soon both brothers were in Phraya Taksin's service and they fought by his side in almost every campaign until Phraya Taksin had himself proclaimed king of all Siam.

The new monarch did not attempt to rebuild Ayutthaya and instead established his capital at Thonburi, a town on the west or opposite bank to present day Bangkok, and he is known in Thai history as the King of Thonburi or King Taksin. He never had time to devote to a grand building scheme, either of his own palace in Thonburi which was merely adequate, or any great temples. His reign of fifteen years was one of incessant strife both internal and external. It took him another seven years before he could quell all his opponents and unite the country as one. In this big task the two brothers were his most staunch henchmen, and they rose quickly through the different ranks of the nobility. At the early age of 35 the elder brother reached the very high rank and position of Chao Phraya Chakri.[11] He was as rapidly followed by his brother who became Chao Phraya Sura Singhanat. King Taksin's armies were successful everywhere. The self-made King of Sri Thammarat agreed to be reduced to the rank of a first class governor and was forgiven. Often General Chakri was sent off on his own, but seldom without his brother as his deputy. The most important occasion was the suppression of Prince Pipit, a scion of the Royal House of Ayutthaya at Phimai near Khorat, and the taking of the town of Siem Reap in Cambodia.

Although the Burmese had been quickly expelled in 1768, they did not give up their idea of conquest but returned again and again, and there was still much fighting to be done. In the first seven years of his reign, King Taksin himself went on campaign with his troops, accompanied always by Generals Chakri and Sura Singhanat. But after seven years as King and Commander-in-Chief, he must have found the strain too great, and he decided to remain in Thonburi and rule his kingdom.[12] Thus from 1775 General Chakri always had independent command, usually supported by his brother in charge of the forward elements. General Sura Singhanath was so bold and decisive that the Burmese gave him the nickname of "The Tiger". He supplied the necessary "push," but the elder brother often had to apply the "brakes".

King Taksin attacking the Burmese Camp at the Three Bodhi trees (Posamton). (National Gallery Bangkok)

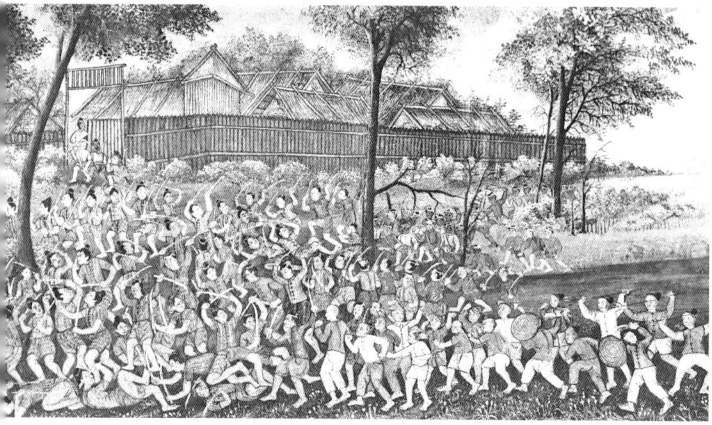

Four serious Burmese invasions were repelled, and besides Chiang Mai and her associates, the two generals also subdued the Laotian principalities of Luang Prabang and

Vientiane, and all of these principalities became vassals of King Taksin. It was in 1778 that General Chakri brought the Emerald Buddha from Vientiane to Thonburi. This is the renowned image, carved from an enormous green nephrite stone or jade, and it does seem appropriate that it was acquired by the son of the Lady Yok (Jade). The origin of this unique image is lost in obscure and ancient myths, and as King Mongkut wrote, "the evidence of these persons cannot be trusted, as they exceed the bounds of truth and they do not agree with each other."[13] The first historically known appearance of the Emerald Buddha was at the northern town, Chiang Rai, in A.D. 1436, when it was found in a *chedi* which had been struck by lightning, yet the image was undamaged. After that it was moved from one Laos capital to another, depending on the power and prosperity of each. Judging by the facial features and the folds of the robe, it was most likely carved in northern India by the Greeks, who had been left behind by Alexander the Great, and the nephrite stone itself was probably brought originally from the Caucasus. The carved image must have taken well over one thousand years to travel from Northern India via Ceylon and Burma to the Golden Land.

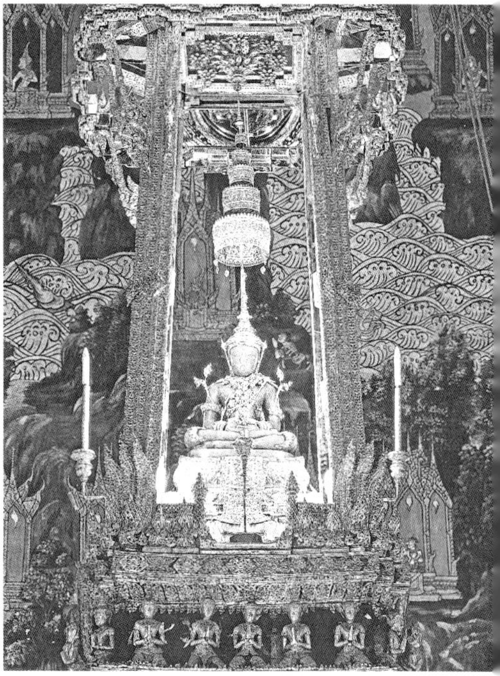

The Emerald Buddha image was brought to Bangkok by Chao Phraya Chakri and when he was king was installed in the Emerald Buddha Temple.

An important incident occurred in 1776 when General Chakri was sent to meet a strong Burmese army encamped to the west of Phitsanulok, and more than one pitched battle took place. Although the Burmese army, under the aged commander – Maha Thihathura – was heavily defeated in the field, it was always able to regain its well fortified camp which General Chakri lacked sufficient forces to take by assault. One day Maha Thirathura asked for a personal meeting with the much younger Thai general, then thirty-nine. A truce was arranged and the two opposing armies were drawn up facing one another with the two commanders on horseback. After an exchange of presents, they approached each other half-way across the gap in the field. Maha Thirathura said that the days were over when the Burmese could conquer the Thais. After lauding the generalship of his opponent, the Burmese general prophesied that General Chakri had high qualities which would one day lead him to become king. It has been been suggested that this was deliberately done to sow discord between General Chakri and King Taksin. It has even been accepted that General Chakri left the meeting with a new and lofty ambition, but no evidence exists to support this conjecture. There is, however, one important fact, after this campaign the Burmese did not invade Siam again for the rest of King Taksin's reign. Having obtained full suzerainty over the Laotian principalities in the north and north-east and Sri Thammarat, King Taksin was determined to get Cambodia to become his vassal as she had previously been to the kings of Ayutthaya. To achieve this end, General Chakri made many expeditions to that country. It was suggested

10 Sir John Bowring, *op. cit.*, Vol. II, page 354.

11 Dibakarawongse: *History of the First Reign*, page 316, *op. cit.*,

12 Prince Dhani: *The Reconstruction of Rama I of the Chakri Dynasty*. *J.O.S.S.*, Vol. XLIII, Part I. August, 1955.

13 King Mongkut to Sir John Bowring. August 7th, 1854.

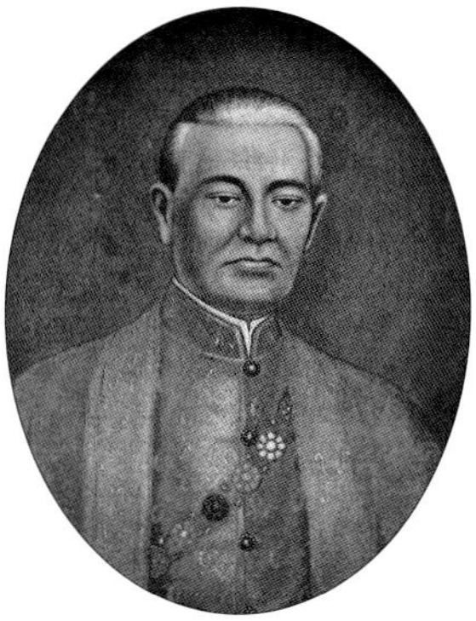

Chao Phraya Chakri,
later King Rama I.
(National Gallery Bangkok)

by others and accepted by King Mongkut,[14] that after the prophecy of Maha Thirathura about General Chakri being likely to reach kingship, King Taksin gave him a higher title still, namely, Somdech Chao Phraya Maha Kasat Suek, meaning The King of War so as to confirm that he was "king" already. Although supported by one of them who looked upon the new title as Generalissimo,[15] those Thai writers, who have shown themselves against General Chakri, have denied its possibility, especially on the ground that no title higher than Chao *Phraya* was in existence. This higher title, however, was to be found more than once during the Chakri Dynasty, so could it not have been first created by King Taksin for its future founder?

Cambodia as a vassal was always in a turbulent state, with frequent internecine strife among the princes or with some of the nobility in revolt, and sometimes the rebels were helped by Vietnam. In 1781 things went as far as the rebels capturing the Cambodian king, Rama Raja. Having put him into a cage, the cage was thrown into the river, and the king was drowned.[16] King Taksin thereupon decided to send General Chakri with strong forces to put matters right and to see that a king approved by the King of Thonburi was installed on the throne. Besides his brother, Chakri was accompanied by a son of King Taksin, whom, it was believed, he intended to make his heir. No Uparaja had by then been appointed. It was while he was in the middle of this campaign that General Chakri heard that a serious revolt had broken out in the capital against the king.

It was alleged that the strain of seven years' campaigning and eight years as the absolute ruler of a large country had driven King Taksin insane. He was said to have indulged in several instances of cruelty, including flogging monks who had refused to make obeisance to him when he claimed to be an incarnation of the Buddha. Unlike priests of some other religions, Buddhist monks paid homage to no one except the Buddha and their elders in the order. Since the change of regime in Bangkok in 1932 there have been not a few suggestions that the whole story of King Taksin's insanity was invented to get him deposed, and for General Chakri to usurp the throne. One author wrote in English: "The proofs were pure fabrication produced to justify Chao Phraya Chakri,"[17] and " King Taksin was no more no less than the pitiful victim of a diabolical plot."[18] None of these writers have produced any evidence in support of their theory. Neither has anyone ever been able to show that in King Taksin's reign of 15 years, General Chakri had ever shown any sign of disloyalty to his king, had ever disobeyed a single order, or made a single complaint about his master.

Here are some extracts from the journals of French missionaries which were written in Thonburi at the time. M. Coudé[19] wrote (in French) to the Directeurs du Seminaire des Missions-Étrangères in 1780 as follows: "Until the month of July 1779, we have had it quiet enough in Siam; the king, however, was angry with us from time to time, but that was temporary. For more than a year now he has not asked us to his

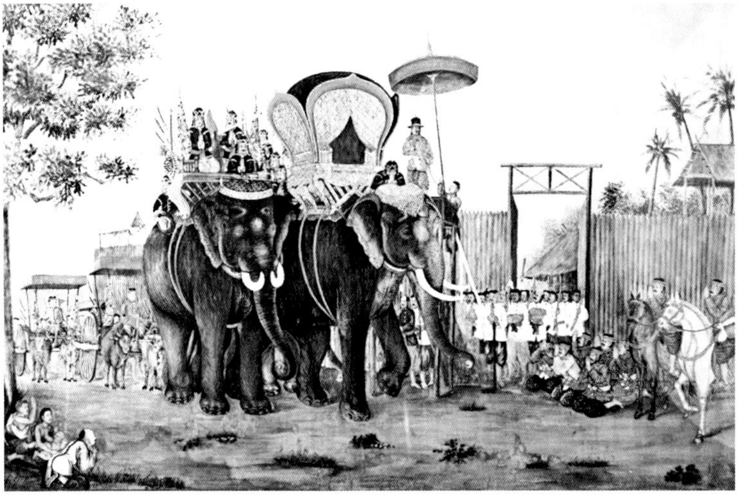

The arrival of Chao Phraya Chakri into the capital to assume the throne. (National Gallery Bangkok)

audiences, and he spent his time in prayers, fasting and meditation, in order by these means to enable himself to fly in the air." He added that they had complained to a son of King Taksin that the king was depriving them of privileges previously granted, and he was expelling them from the country. They reminded the prince of the religious freedom which the king had granted to them and the Thai Christians under their care, and had himself helped them to build their church. M. Coude wrote: "That is true," replied the prince, "but my father has changed."

M. Descrouvrières later wrote on December 21st, 1782, eight months after the revolt was over: "For some years, the king of Siam (Taksin) has tremendously upset his subjects and the foreigners who lived in or came to trade in his kingdom. Last year the Chinese, who were accustomed to trade (here), found it necessary to give up almost altogether. This last year the annoyances caused by this king, more than half-mad, have become more frequent and more cruel than before; he had had imprisoned, tortured, and flogged, according to his mood, his wife, his sons – even the heir presumptive, and his high officials. He wanted to make them confess to crimes of which they were innocent. . ."[20]

The revolt was led by a general called Phraya Sanka and it met with no apparent resistance, which means that King Taksin could not have had much support. By the time General Chakri, far off in Cambodia, heard the news the king had probably been deposed and placed under detention. Phraya Sanka had full control of the capital, and what plans he had in mind for the future have never been divulged. It is known that when he heard that General Chakri was hurrying back as fast as his elephant and his men could march, he was already prepared to give over the power to him. When General Chakri arrived outside the city walls it was obvious that he had the army behind him, and Phraya Sanka quickly went to meet him and paid homage. This was followed by the Officers of State without a dissenting voice, all agreeing to offer General Chakri the throne which he accepted on April 6th, 1782. Obviously the senior officers could not offer the throne to him unless

14 Sir John Bowring, *op. cit.*, pages 67-69.

15 Phra Sarasas: *My Country: Thailand*, pages 112-114. First published in Japan in 1940. Bangkok Edition, 1950.

16 Dibakarawongse. *History of the First Reign*, page 34.

17 Phra Sarasas, *op. cit.*, page 114.

18 *Idib.*, page 115.

19 *A.M.-E.*, Vol. 891, page 1187.

20 *A.M.-E.*, Vol. 891, pages 1239-1245. All quoted in Adrien Launay: *Histoire de la Mission de Siam, 1662-1811*, Vol. II. Extracts were kindly supplied by Prince Dhani, in 1958.

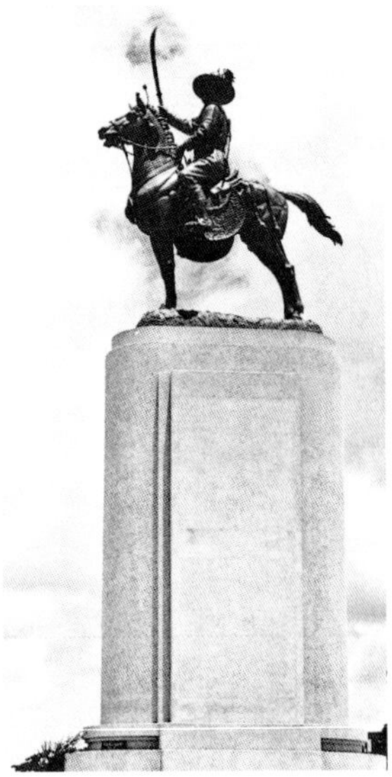

The memorial to King Taksin Maharaj. (River Books)

they knew that they had the backing of the junior officers and the rank and file. The people then were voiceless, and all they asked for was a stable and just government. If, as is generally believed, that is what occurred, General Chakri can hardly be described as having "seized the throne of Siam".[21] It would be more accurate to say that he mounted the proffered throne which was empty.

The problem was what to do with ex-King Taksin? According to Thai sources he had surrendered peacefully and only wished to take up the yellow robe. In eighteenth century South- East Asia, or in Europe for that matter, the idea of an abdicated monarch living in peaceful retirement in his own country was unknown. It has not even been easy in Europe in the twentieth century. For King Taksin to enter a monaster was no guarantee for the future as Buddhist monks could leave the order at any time, and in Ayutthaya two princes had done so to mount the throne. Exile would be no better as the dethroned king could become a useful pawn in the hands of hostile neighbours. The new dynasty had not only to provide security for itself but for the country too. After consulting his council of generals, the new king knew that there was only one answer, Taksin had to forfeit his life. It is said that as he was being carried off on a litter to the place of execution, his last wish was to take personal leave of his favourite general. The new monarch was watching from a pavilion, and when told of the request, tears filled his eyes. Unable to speak for emotion, he waved the messenger away.

King Taksin was executed as a prince – being hit on the back of the neck by a club of sandlewood as decreed by King Trailok in 1450. His body was buried, probably without his successor's knowledge. Later in the new reign when the king heard of it, he had the body exhumed and given a proper cremation according to Buddhist rites and with suitable honours, both the king and his brother personally attending the funeral of their old chief.[22] "Thus perished at the age of 49 one of the most remarkable men who ever wore the crown of Siam (sic)."[23] It was a tragic end for the man who inspired so many to help him expel the Burmese from the country, and the equestrian statue which stands in modem Thonburi is but a small recognition of his great deeds. Whatever the necessities of the time, it cannot be denied that King Taksin's execution has been an asset to those who wished to discredit the Chakri Dynasty, but they did not give tongue to their thoughts until after June 24th, 1932.

One of the earliest ideas in General Chakri's mind was that Thonburi was not a suitable capital because it was on the west bank and open to the traditional enemy from the west – the Burmese. True, Thonburi was on higher ground whereas the east bank was low-lying and liable to flooding. But the General thought in terms of strategy, and what could be a better natural moat than the wide and deep Chao Phraya River itself?

He therefore decided to move the capital to the east bank where there was already a little town – once a flourishing trading centre in

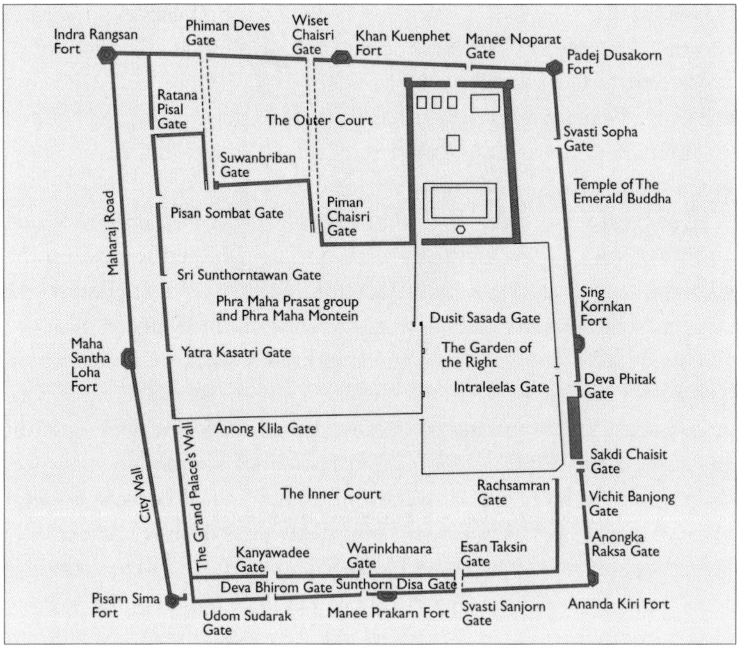

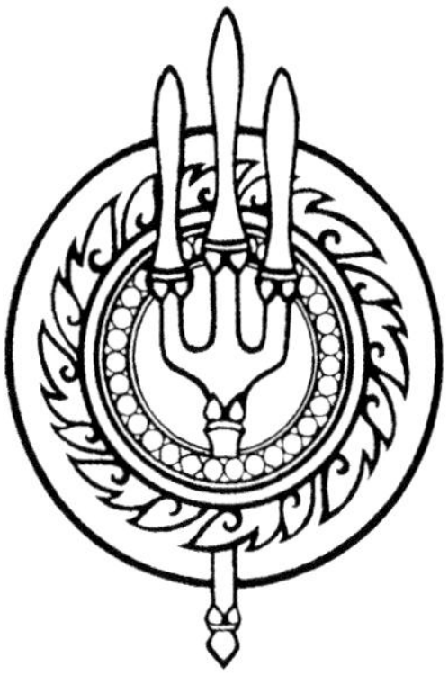

The discus and *trisula*, emblem of Chakri dynasty.

Plan of the Grand Palace during the First Reign.

King Narai's time – with the name of Bangkok. The name meant the village of wild plums or in botanical terminology : *Spondias pinnata*.[24]

The area chosen for the Royal Palace was the Chinatown of old Bangkok, ruled as was then the custom by a rich Chinese merchant with the noble rank of *Phraya*. With suitable compensation, he was asked to move the Chinese community to Sampeng which is still the main Chinatown of modern Bangkok. The vacant ground was first marked out with a wooden fence, and wooden pavilions richly appointed were put up quickly so that the new monarch could have an early and provisional coronation on the chosen site for the new palace and capital city.[25] At the age of 45, General Chakri was enthroned and crowned in June, 1782, taking a lengthy series of titles amongst which was Rama Tibodi, as the first king of Ayutthaya had been called. Years later he was given the posthumous title of Phra Buddha Yod Fa by his grandson, and later still that of Rama I by his great-great-grandson, and that is how he is mostly known in the western tongue. In Thai it is even simpler for they refer to the kings of Bangkok as the First Reign, Second Reign and so on. A reign in Thai is *rajakala*, so the kings are called shortly R I, R II, etc.

As he had been Chao Phraya Chakri for ten years, and his father was allegedly Chao Phraya Chakri at Phitsanulok for a while, the new royal family became known henceforth as the House of Chakri. Many European authors have agreed with Robert-Martignan[26] that "modern Siam dates from the House of Chakri," thus the origins of this family should be of some interest. In the absence of any hereditary titles and there being no surnames until 1916, the Thais had not taken much interest in their distant forbears. Now that more interest is taken,

21 D. G. E. Hall, *op. cit.*, page 381.

22 Dibakarawongse: *History of the First Reign, op. cit.*, page 77.

23 W. A. R. Wood, *op. cit.*, 272. No coronation of King Taksin was ever recorded, and if there was one, his crown and regalia did not survive him.

24 Dr. Malcolm Smith: *A Physician at the Court of Siam*, page 13, London, 1947.

25 Dibakarawongse: *History of the First Reign, op. cit.*, pages 7 and 8.

26 Robert-Martignan, *op. cit.*, page 182.

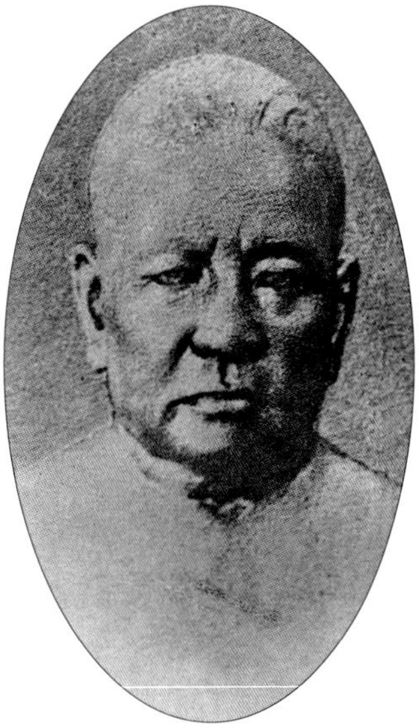

Chao Phraya Akara Mahasena (Bunnag) was an important military officer who fought alongside King Rama I and was made Minister of Defence. (River Books)

only a few, if any, families can trace their ancestry back beyond 1782. King Mongkut stated that his ancestors were Mon officers who chose to come from Burma to serve in Ayutthaya with Prince Naresuan when the latter returned from exile in 1571.

After that they vanished into obscurity until one of their alleged descendants, Phraya Kosa (Pan), in the reign of King Narai, was sent as Ambassador to Louis XIV. It is from him that three generations of direct ancestors can be traced, and the fourth generation was Thongdee, the father of Rama I.[27] It has also been put forward that the mother of Phraya Kosa (Pan) was Princess Amphai,[28] known as the Mother-Princess of Wat Dusit, where she resided in the latter years of her life, after having been King Narai's nurse. If that is true, and judging by her probable age, she must have been a descendant of King Ekatotsarot, as was indeed King Narai's mother, for we know that the usurper had married into the previous dynasty. In that case it would seem that the Chakri family are descended from both the Phra Ruang Dynasty of Sukhothai and the U Thong Dynasty of Ayutthaya through the female line of Princess Amphai. Unfortunately no satisfactory contemporary documents exist as proofs, but one must remember that so much was destroyed in the fires of Ayutthaya in 1767. In any case members of the Chakri family have had little interest in their ancestry beyond the pride they share in their descent from Rama I.

Although he had always recognised his first wife as such, and now that her children were celestial princes and princesses she was clearly the queen, she did not seem to receive a new name or title during his reign. She must have lived a retired life until she died at the age of 89 in 1826 in the reign of her grandson, Rama III. She had one brother and three sisters from whom three families have descended. The brother was the head of the Xuto family. The first sister had no male issue. The second sister married Nai (Mr.) Bunnag, who became an important nobleman and high official with the title of Chao Phraya Akara Mahasena. He was the sixth generation descendant of a Persian, Sheik Ahmed, who had settled in Ayutthaya in the seventeenth century, had seen royal service, and had been made Phraya by King Songtham. All the descendants of the former Nai Bunnag are members of the great Bunnag family, which next to the Chakris, has been the most important in this era, and several members have served in the highest positions in the land.[29] The issue of her third sister form the family of Na Bangchang.

Being the founder of a new line, Rama I had the pleasant task of raising his children and relatives to royal rank. He had nine children with his principal wife who was to be created Queen Amarindra by her son, Rama II. All had been born before his accession by which time five had died. However, the remaining four were created Celestial Princes and Princesses. The elder son, called Chim and born in 1768, became Prince Isarasuntorn. His younger brother, Chuy, born in 1773, was made Prince Senanurak. The two daughters never married and therefore left no issue. Amongst the daughters who died before the accession one was of definite importance, for she had been a wife of King Taksin and had left a son whom Rama I recognised as a celestial prince. He was first called Supantuwongse, but was later given the title of Kasatra. Besides his children, he also created in celestial ranks his brother, two sisters, and eleven nephews and nieces. One of his nephews had just returned from an embassy sent by King Taksin to Peking.[30] Although he had been king for 14 years Taksin was not recognized as such by the Emperor of China until 1781. The most important of Rama I's nieces was Boonrod, born in 1767, who was a daughter of his second sister, and her father was a wealthy Chinese merchant. Her importance lies in the fact that she later married Prince Isarasuntorn (Rama II), thus bringing more Chinese blood into the Chakri line.

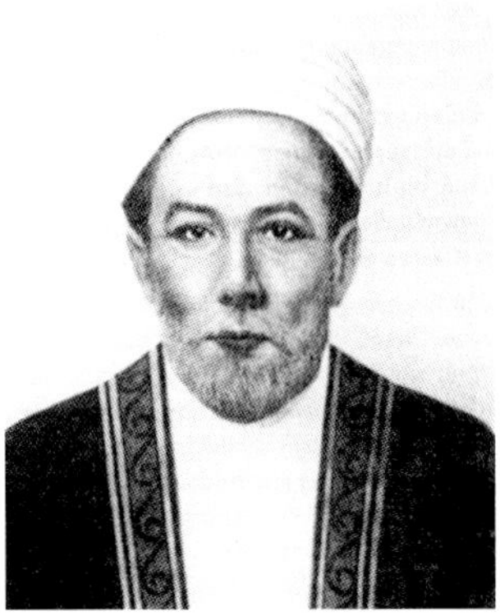

A drawing of Sheik Ahmed. (From *History of Muslim leaders from Ayutthaya to Thaksin Era*, 2008)

Rama I also had children with his *Chao Choms* (minor wives) and these children were given the rank of *Phra Ong Chao* (literally: Royal body prince). All those princes who were created then, other than the direct successor to the throne, in due course became heads of the different branches of the main Chakri family whose surnames were chosen by King Rama VI in 1916, but to all these surnames was added: Na (of) Ayutthaya, to show that they had a common ancestor in the former Thong Dee, the father of Rama I. Rama I had 42 children, 17 sons and 25 daughters. None of the daughters ever married and they left no issue. Now that they were royal, it was considered *infra dig* for them to marry the king's subjects, and all neighbouring royal families were either considered inferior vassals or enemies. Royal princesses of the Chakri Dynasty were to suffer from this handicap for generations. It is here that one finds a disadvantage in the lack of a hereditary aristocracy for in such a society the king would be the *primus inter pares*, and his daughters could have married their sons.

It was clear that primogeniture was not yet considered as a qualification for the succession to the throne, and it was not Prince Isarasuntorn who was designated Uparaja (Deputy King) but the King's only brother, formerly Boonma or Chao Phraya Sura Singhanath. The Uparaja was colloquially known as the *Wang Na* – the Prince of the Front Palace – probably because in war he commanded the forward troops, and this nomenclature was used for the Uparaja in subsequent reigns until the position was finally abolished.

Besides being made *Chao Fa* or *Phra Ong Chao*, most of the princes received the extra rank of *Krom*, an honour begun towards the close of the Ayutthaya period, the complications of which, as it has survived until today, should be explained without further delay. In those days of simultaneous military-civil service, some of the senior princes had command of their regiments-departments which could be used by the king in war or peace and these were called *kroms*. The major-domo of a prince acted as the chief of staff or adjutant, and he was given the title of *Khun*, *Luang*, *Phra*, according to the importance of the *krom*.

27 Sir John Bowring, *op. cit.*, pages 67-69.

28 M. R. S. Navaratana: *Thai Heroes* (in Thai). Undated.

29 Prince Dhani. *The Reconstruction of Rama I*, *op cit.*

30 Dibakarawongse: *History of the First Reign*, *op. cit.*, pages 10-12.

Instead of the *Krom* being known by the name of the prince, it was known by the title of the major-domo. Thus, if the major-domo was Phra Supat, the *Krom* would be known as Krom Phra Supat. It was the custom amongst the Thais not to call their superiors by name, so the prince himself would then be called by his *krom*, e.g., Krom Phra Supat, and he became associated with it as if he had been given a dukedom.[31] In later years when princes no longer commanded their individual regiments-departments, being made a *krom* became an additional way of giving princes further honours. But a prince of a higher rank who is not a *krom* would still remain higher than one of lower rank who was a *krom*.[32] Furthermore it must be remembered that a *krom* was not a hereditary honour, although one of his sons might become worthy of being a *krom* and would get the same title by the king's choice. One of the princes given a *krom* at the beginning of Rama I's reign was his eldest son, Chim, who became Krom Luang Isarasuntorn.

Rama I's next pleasant task was to reward numerous officers who had served with him for many years on different campaigns, and a large number were given appropriate titles. There was one nobleman who had waited in vain for a reward, and that was Phraya Sanka, who had deposed King Taksin and paved the way for Rama I. The Royal Council declared that to depose a reigning monarch was treason and such a man could not be trusted. As would often happen later, Rama I followed the advice of his council and Phraya Sanka was duly executed. For his government Rama I retained the well-tried system of Ayutthaya since the reigns of Rama Tibodi I and Trailok, namely the departments of Defence, Interior, Finance, Palace and Agriculture. With the increasing trade of Bangkok, the Harbour Authorities had become more important, but they were still under Finance. It was from these Harbour Authorities that the modern Foreign Office was to grow, but meanwhile the Finance Minister, Chao Phraya Phra Klang, acted as Foreign Minister. As the king himself had been Chao Phraya Chakri for ten years, he did not give that title to anyone, and it has not been conferred again.

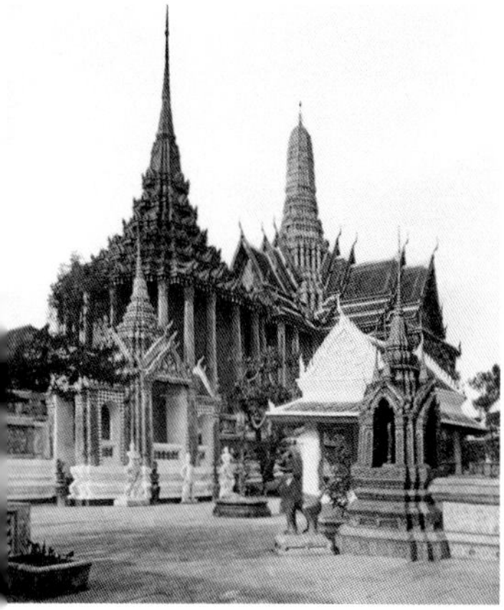

The Mondop housing the Tripitaka, revised and rewritten in the reign of King Rama I (A photograph from the Fifth Reign). (River Books)

Almost everything of artistic or historical value had been lost in the complete destruction of Ayutthaya,[33] and hardly a building, secular or religious, survived. There was a general breakdown of the state, spiritual and moral. The political creed of the Thais was bound together with an individual loyalty to the sovereign, and now the monarch had disappeared with his capital. Rama I found himself the absolute king – the Lord of Life – of a land in a chaotic state, and he set himself two tasks. One was to make the country safe from future invasions, and the other was to revive the Thai heritage of Sukhothai and Ayutthaya. Thus although he was the Founder of the Dynasty for his family, for the Thai people at large he was more the Restorer of what they should have inherited from their ancestors. In briefly describing this stupendous task, the best way is broadly to follow Prince Dhani.[34]

Rama I accepted without question the familiar pattern of Ayutthaya. His rule was not to be what the Europeans in the seventeenth and eighteenth centuries knew as an absolute monarchy based on the Divine Right of Kings. The monarchy of Rama I was a *Paternal* Monarchy with the Ten Virtues as expounded in the *Tammasat*. In this way a truly Buddhistic monarchy was neither absolute nor divine, and the King was inspired and unchangeable, thus limited in his legislative capacity. The Ten Virtues were[35] as follows: 1. Charity. 2. Moral living according to the known code – *sila*. 3. Support for Religion. 4. Honesty. 5. Compassion. 6. Free from wrongful ambition. 7. Free from thoughts of revenge. 8. Loving the people as their father. 9. Moderate with punishment. 10. Constant care for the people's welfare and happiness.

In order to achieve this revival, Rama I's overall policy of reconstruction was three-fold, namely, moral, legal, and artistic. The first required the revision of the Buddhist canon, and before this could be accomplished, the Buddhist hierarchy had to be reorganized. Strictly speaking Buddhist monks should be ruled by their abbots in the different monasteries, but the king (which meant the State) was the Protector of Religion, and he could not be expected to deal with each of the tens of thousands of abbots individually. Some kind of hierachy and a number of prelates was necessary, and that had been accepted since Ayutthaya. From the fall of that capital to the end of Thonburi the hierarchy had gone into a muddled state. King Taksin had "unfrocked" prelates who had refused to bow before him, and some unworthy sycophantic monks had been appointed in their places. These had to be removed and the good men reinstated, thus the whole hierarchy was overhauled.

When it actually came to the revision of the canon, Rama I discovered that the Buddhist Scripture – the Tripitaka – the new edition produced at his expense, was made from unreliable texts, for most of the authoritative books had perished in the flames. He summoned a Council of the Church in 1788 and their object was to collate reliable texts in neighbouring countries. Fortunately all the Hinayana Buddhist texts were in Pali which the learned Thai monks could understand. The Council sat at the seat of the Supreme Patriach who then resided at Wat Mahathat, now rather hidden from view behind the National Library. The Council consisted of 250 learned monks and laymen, and during the five months of their pious and enthusiastic labour, they were fed at the royal expense. This revised and *written* canon can now be read in its latest *printed* edition of 1925-1928 in 46 volumes, each of 500 octavo pages, produced by King Prajadhipok in memory of his brother and predecessor, King Rama VI, both of them great-great-grandsons of Rama I.

Side by side with the production of the new canon, the king issued innumerable decrees to ensure that monks and laymen alike conducted themselves as good Buddhists. The king was not a kind of High Priest, he was, and still is, the Protector of Religion, which meant all the recognized faiths of his subjects. As a Buddhist he showed tolerance for all

31 Such as Prince Henry, Duke of Gloucester.

32 It may simplify the complicated system if the present order of precedence for some of the princes (as at January 1st, 1959) is given:
H.R.H. Prince (*Chao Fa*) Vajiralongkorn (only son of H.M. King Bhumipol).
H.R.H. Prince Chumbhot, *Krom Muen* Nakorn Sawan. (Died September 15th, 1959).
H.R.H. Prince Chula Chakrabongse. (Both two and three are cousins and sons of First Class *Chao Fas*).
H.R.H. Prince Bhanubhand.
H.R.H. Prince Chalermbol.
H.R.H. Prince Anusorn. (All three are brothers and sons of a Second Class *Chao Fa*).
H.R.H. Prince Wanwaitayakorn, *Krom Muen* Naradhip. (Son of a *Phra Ong Chao* and was created a Royal Highness for meritorious service).
Here there are some sons of *Chao Fas* who are in the rank of H.H. Then comes H.H. Prince Dhani, *Krom Muen* Bidhyalap.

33 Prince Dhani: *The Reconstruction of Rama I, op. cit.*

34 *Ibid.*

35 Taken from the poem by King Rama VI: *Phra Nala Kamluang* (in Thai), Bangkok, 1917.

faiths and was not Defender of *the* Faith, but rather the Defender of the *Faiths.* Rama I himself went even beyond tolerance, for he gave material support to Brahmanism, Christianity and Islam without discrimination.

In order to protect such a large number of Buddhist monks, he had to keep them from external evil influence as much as from their own failings – for they were but human. Within two years he issued seven out of the ten decrees designed to clean up some of the moral depravity which had followed the appalling tumult. There were to be identification papers for monks, and each abbot was required to keep a register of his monastery. In the tenth decree issued later, he "unfrocked" 128 profligate monks for "drinking intoxicants, wandering out at night to see entertainments, rubbing shoulders with women, engaging in loose talk . . . boarding Chinese junks in order to obtain fanciful objects of merchandise". Long before his reign was over the canon had been revised and observed for preaching, and the standard of behaviour amongst the monks was well raised to the desired level.[36]

The destruction of Ayutthaya was equally disastrous for the law, only a ninth or tenth of the written legislation survived. Rama I had contemplated revision from the beginning, but he had the more urgent business of Burmese invasions to contend with. According to Prince Dhani the King's attention was drawn to an appeal by Nai Bunsri against the divorce decree which had been granted to his wife by the Court of Justice, for according to the old law a wife could obtain a divorce at any time, and any property she had before marriage would revert to her. On the other hand if the husband had sued for the divorce on the ground of the wife's adultery, she would be punished and her property forfeited to the husband. Nai Bunsri appealed that his wife had been adulterous, and, although he had not tried to divorce her, she should not have been allowed to divorce him who was innocent of any misconduct. Rama I felt that there was injustice, and besides his own copy, he consulted two other texts of the law.

In the days before printing there were three hand-written texts of the statutes. One was in the Court of Justice, another in the official Royal Library under the care of the Secretariat, and a third was kept in the Royal Bedchamber which was the one the King first consulted. He now found that they all agreed that women could obtain a divorce at any time even against an impeccable husband. This made the King doubt the correctness of the statutes which had been written from memory by survivors of Ayutthaya who were judges or lawyers, for he did not believe that past kings could make such unjust laws. He set up a commission to revise the laws and the result of their work was the Law Code of 1805-1808. The Commission, consisting of eleven lawyers, royal scribes, and other learned men, began their work in the year that Nelson won the battle of Trafalgar and Napoleon won Austerlitz. The magnitude of the work is seen in the modern printing in which there are 1,637 pages of octavo size. The rough texts used to devise the new code were destroyed, and the original hand-written new version, also done in three copies for the same three places, can still be seen. Some of it has been published by R. Lingat and J. Burney in the *Journal of the Siam Society.*

The new code began with the *Tammasat* as given in *The Three Worlds of Phra Ruang* which was derived from the genesis theory of Buddhism – some 2,500 years old. In it one may well be surprised to find some modern scientific and astronomical theories. It was written that the earth was developed from a great fire ball which gradually cooled down. Then we had the Brahmanic conception that celestial beings or *deva* were attracted by aromatic vapours and they came to the earth to partake of earthly products, thereby losing their divine nature and became humans. The first leader was elected, and from him were descended all the royal rulers of the earth, and this first leader found the book of the *Tammasat* on a high mountain. All the kings must therefore follow the *Tammasat* with its ten royal virtues. Then in company with his subjects he should maintain every day the five basic Buddhist precepts – the *Pancha Sila* – 1. Not to kill. 2. Not to steal. 3. Not to commit wrongful sexual acts. 4. Not to tell untruths. 5. Not to partake of intoxicants which were the basis of wrongful temptation. All the kings were believed for a long time to have sprung from this mythical leader, and have since had to pretend to be, as can be seen in the Thai coronation ceremony which is largely Brahmanic in origin and form.

Having respected the procedure and decorum of the old order, Rama I's new code now embarked on a series of reforms of the law, and, like Rama Tibodi I of Ayutthaya 455 years before, he decreed that any laws or customs which differed from his were invalid, and he commanded the judges not to deviate from his new code. There were rules for the *guidance* of the Judicature such as court procedure, the reception of plaints, the law of evidence, the law of ordeal by fire and water, the process of appeal, the law for husband and wife, the law for serfdom (e.g., a serf once sold in one place could not be resold at another place). There were the laws of abduction, of inheritance, of debt, of quarrels, of robbery, of offences against the State, of offences against private individuals, of treason, and of many miscellaneous subjects.[37]

In the second year of the reign – 1783 – the king had already issued many practical edicts which were later incorporated into the code. In edict No. 2 he forbade public servants from gambling or consuming intoxicants. Edict No. 34 decreed that if the king promised monetary gifts to anyone they could not go and claim them from the Treasury without reliable witnesses. Although Brahmanism was permitted alongside Buddhism, according to edict No. 35 it should be observed within reason and good sense, and a *deva* was to be regarded as a friend and never to be revered above the Triple Gem of Buddhism. All images of the *lingam* were to be destroyed by burning. Edict No. 37 placed husband and wife on an equal footing for faults of adultery –

36 Prince Dhani in *The Reconstruction of Rama I, op. cit.*, quotes from *Khot Mai Phra Songh*. (Copy of Three Seals). *University of Moral and Political Sciences Publications*. 3 Volumes. Bangkok (in Thai), 1938.

37 Prince Dhani. *Ibid*, page 47, an enlarged version in Thai. Bangkok, 1957.

and this was decreed in 1785. Edict No. 6 required all litigants to attend Court in person, which was designed to prevent clever professional writers – in days of illiteracy – helping to prepare false claims. In the next edict, No. 7, he increased penalties for false witnesses. Also he examined and further tightened the Palace Law of King Trailok.

The Court of Law which carried out the administration of the system so revised was a simple one, and in Bangkok it was in the Grand Palace, close to the building where the King himself daily presided over his council. The judges of those days were known as *Lukh Khun* (pronounced rather like "look" and "bull"). They had learned the art of reading and writing in a monastery either as a lay pupil or a *samnera* (novice), and then entered the service between the ages of 16 and 18 as junior clerks. Their law studies consisted of reading and practice, and they were raised in rank according to their experience and ability. There was no age limit for retirement and some of the *Lukh Khun* might go on working until they were eighty.[38]

The work of the commissioners was simply to report on the devious and contradictory texts and not to be their critics. Rama I himself read all their copious notes, and it was he alone who decided all the changes. This tremendous work took three years before completion in 1808 when he had but one more year to live.[39] His aim was to inculcate a high moral standard amongst the people, and especially his courtiers and officials. The revision of the Law Code of 1805-1808 and that of the Buddhist canon of 1788 formed two of the brightest jewels in the new crown of Rama I, of whom Prince Dhani writes, "(he) had thus set a standard for the spiritual and temporal government of the Kingdom. It singled him out as a broad minded reformer, who was nevertheless a staunch traditionalist, a combination of ideals which has hardly ever failed in the world's history."[40]

On the artistic side the king's most important task was also the most practical and urgent, the construction of Bangkok which was centred on the Grand Palace, already gradually taking shape. As in everything else, Rama I's wish was not to create a new type of city, but as far as possible to restore Ayutthaya. Experts who had known the details of the old capital were called in, so that all the traditions of the monasteries and palaces would be preserved. For reasons of economy and to save unnecessary labour, what was left of the walls and buildings of Ayutthaya were pulled down and the fine old bricks brought down the river for rebuilding. Ayutthaya had been surrounded by water, so Rama I had canals cut in the east so as to surround the city with the wide river. As an extra precaution, the low-lying land, round the present-day new shopping centre of Middle Ratchadamnoen Avenue and the Rattanakosin Hotel, was left as a large swamp which the Burmese would find difficult to cross, had they swung their army round to the east of the city. Like King Naresuan and King Narai of Ayutthaya, Rama I was fond of elephants and was an enthusiast of elephant craft, so much so that he had his sons and grandsons taught the noble art,

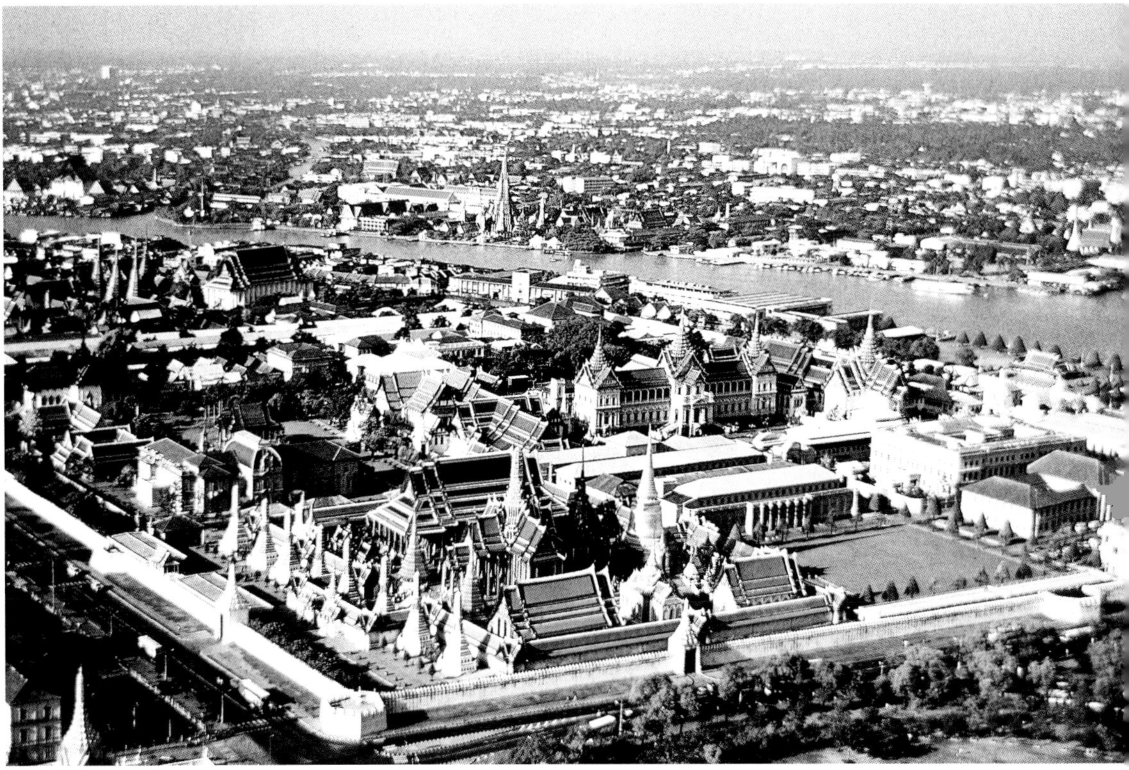

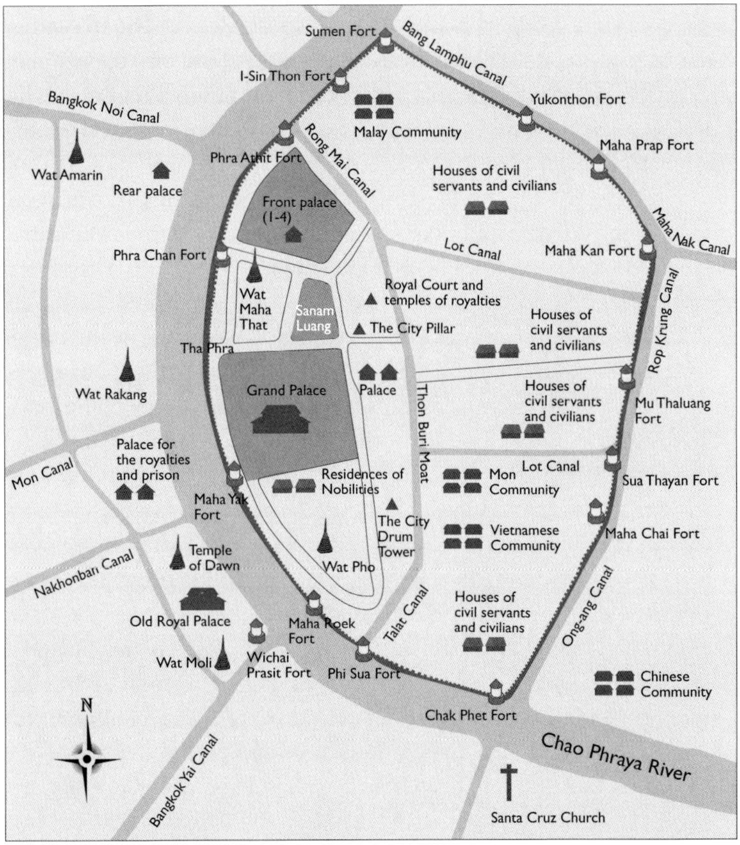

The Grand Palace as it has developed over the years.

Plan of early Bangkok showing the area around the Grand Palace.

38 From notes kindly supplied by Prince Dhani in 1958.

39 R. Lingat: *Note sur la revision des lois Siamoises en 1808, J.O.S.S*, Vol. XIII, Part I.

40 Prince Dhani: *The Reconstruction of Rama I, op. cit.*

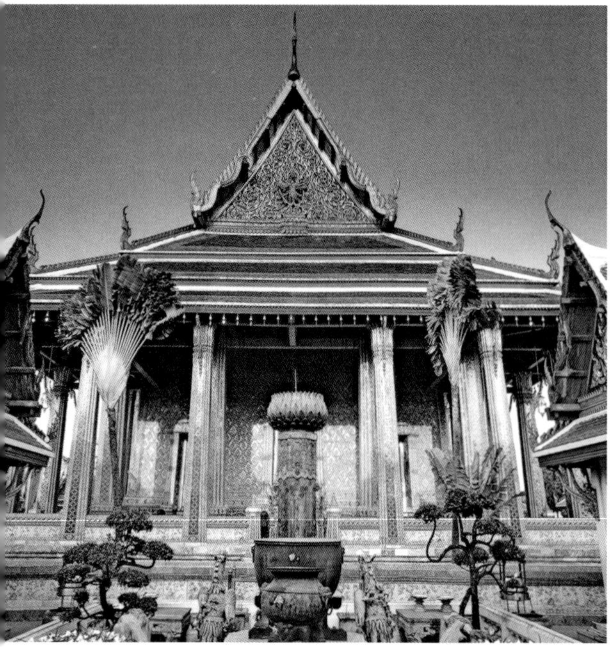

and one of his sons obtained a doctorate in the science. At one time, therefore, he contemplated making a causeway over this swamp so that the royal elephants could enter and leave the capital comfortably. He was advised against this for military reasons, and as always, Rama I took wise counsel. The swamp was left as it was and later became fruit orchards for the people until King Chulalongkorn built his wide avenues to connect the old city with his new garden city of Dusit.[41]

The Emerald Buddha Temple. (River Books)

The concentration of work on the royal palaces was not due to the whims of a selfish man wishing to make for himself a beautiful and comfortable home. The palace was the very core and centre of the capital and indeed of the whole country. In it lived and worked the king, who was his own Prime Minister, with his all-important Royal Secretariat, the Court of Justice, the Ministries – using *salas* (pavilions) close to the King's Council Chamber, the Treasury, the Regiment of Guards, the stables of the horses and elephants, the Regiment of Artillery, the Art Studios and School, all of which formed the Outside. Then within another set of walls was the Inside where no men were permitted except the king himself and his young sons or relatives, other than for essential business when they could only enter with his permission and under the supervision of the female palace police. The Inside contained the King's private residence, his flower gardens, the villas of the queen and the *chao choms* with their children. All these ladies had enormous retinues of women and girls. For the latter it was like attending a high school or university as in the old days of Ayutthaya. Thus the Grand Palace, its area exactly one square mile enclosed within the massive, white crenellated walls, was veritably a city within a city, and in time of war would act as the keep of the city fortress.

The real building task began in 1783. So intent was Rama I on reviving Ayutthaya that one of the new canals round the city had to be sufficiently wide for the people to enjoy having their boat races as in Ayutthaya. Both the king and deputy-king went about closely inspecting the work of construction, and the Palace of the Front – now the National Museum – was being built at the same time. Rama I also caused to be built a temple within the Grand Palace where he wished to house the sacred Emerald Buddha which he had brought from Vientiane in 1778. The Amarindra Audience Hall, now used for religious services and the king's birthday, and the group of residential buildings behind it, together with the temple, were completed in 1785.[42] The nephrite image was brought from Thonburi in a grand procession and it was placed in the oblong building with its walls of old gold mosaic, lofty red and gold ceilings, and high roofs of bluish purple and orange glass tiles with the two richly carved gold gables surmounted by the graceful gold *nagas* – the traditional sacred snakes. From the eaves hung gold bells with pendants shaped like leaves of the *bodhi* tree which to this day still tinkle sweetly when gently touched by the breeze from the river. In this superb and graceful building the Emerald Buddha was placed with great reverence on a canopied throne atop a high altar. Surrounding this chief building in the compound of the temple were many others, the golden chedi, the square-built scripture house with the crownlike spire in which the books of the canon were placed in a gorgeous black wood case decorated with mother- of-pearl designs, and standing on a silver floor. Then there were myriads of other buildings and charming *salas*, all surrounded by cloisters with some 170 large panels of mural paintings from Rama I's favourite story, the *Ramakien*. Bishop Pallegoix, the French prelate, who came to Bangkok in February, 1830 – forty-five years after its completion, wrote: "What is the most remarkable in Bangkok is the palace and the royal pagodas. The royal pagodas (by which he meant the temples) are of a magnificence of which we have no idea in Europe."[43]

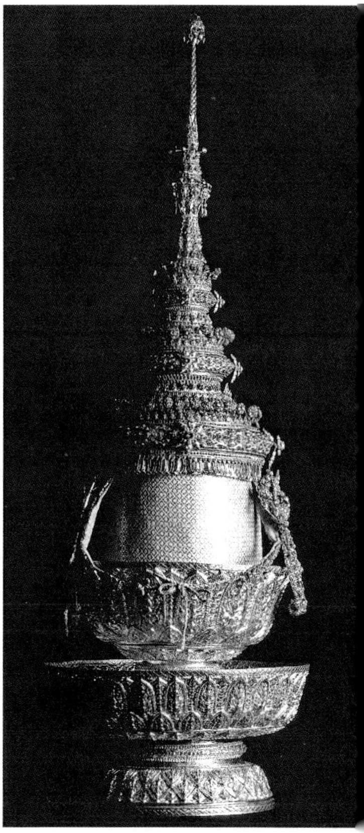

The crown worn by King Rama I at his coronation. (Royal Household)

When in 1785-86 the new palace was near enough completed and the city itself in fair shape, the king held a celebration for the blessing of the capital, and himself underwent another and more grandiose coronation. Before this sacred ceremony he had set up a commission under a high official of Ayutthaya to examine and collate all the old traditions so that the full and lengthy ceremonies would be accurately carried out. The form of the ceremony was that the Brahmin priests presented the king with the crown and other royal regalia. All of these had been lost, and the crown and the accompanying regalia had to be made. Then the high officers of state presented him with the royal possessions, such as the great gold coaches, palanquins both covered and uncovered, the royal palace buildings, the weapons and arms of all kinds, and finally the rice fields and forests of Siam. Rama I said to them: "All of these things will you take good care of. Together we will govern the State, together we will defend and prosper the Buddhist religion, and together we will defend the Kingdom."[44] He gave his city its name as *Krung* (capital city) *Thep* (Divine) *Rattanakosindra* (Jewel Abode of the God Indra). This was a reference to the Emerald Buddha, which, according to ancient tradition, a *deva* had carved for Indra. This legend arose when Buddhism was truly flourishing in India, and the Brahmins for a time accepted the Buddha as the ninth *avatar* of Vishnu who was superior to Indra. Bangkok is still the name used by most western foreigners, but Thais generally call their capital Krungthep.

Architecture indeed formed a large part of Rama I's artistic revival, with a profusion of decoration within and without the buildings, masses of mural frescoes, plaster moulding, and wood carving. Most of the buildings were religious, such as the Emerald Buddha precincts, the vast Wat Pho, which took seven years and five months to construct, and Wat Suthat near the Brahmanic giant swing. The palace buildings still

41 Prince Damrong: *Tales of Ancient Times,* 9, in Thai, *op. cit.*, pages 397 and 401.

42 Dibakarawongse: *History of Rama I, op. cit.*, pages 63-70.

43 Mgr. Pallegoix, *op. cit.*, Vol. II, page 64.

44 Dibakarawongse: *History of Rama I, op. cit.*, page 89.

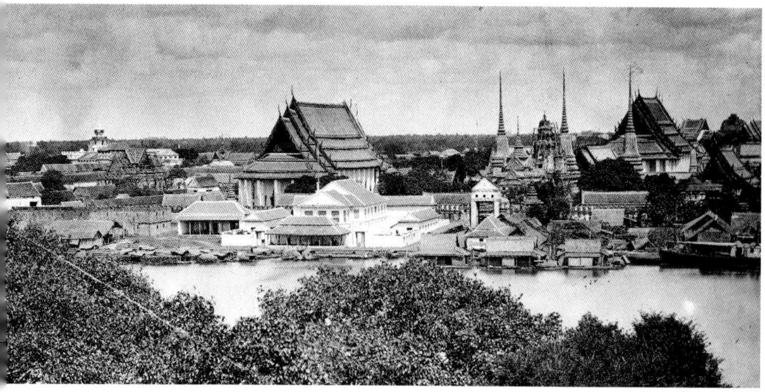

Wat Pho photographed from Wat Arun on the Thonburi side of the river. (Wellcome Collection)

extant from his time are the Amarindra group and the Dusit Maha Prasat. The original building of the latter caught fire in 1789 when the king and the *uparaja* supervised the work of the firemen, and Rama I himself helped to carry to safety the beautiful black wood and mother-of-pearl throne.[45]

The labour used for the building scheme was conscript or corvée, but it is unlikely that they suffered great hardship. Naturally those men would have preferred to remain at home and till their fields, as we today in any country would prefer to spend our money as we please rather than pay taxes. They accepted the work as we accept the taxes, and naturally with some grumbling. They were fed at the royal expense by a communal kitchen, and some might have had better and more food than at home. If there was much hardship, some of the stories would have survived. But even if we grant that forced labour, with threats of punishment, was employed for building the new capital, architects, artists, craftsmen, and skilled artisans, who embellished these buildings, could not be coerced by fear into producing such beautiful works of art. Judging by what we can still see today, even if a lot of it has been restored, these men must have been profoundly inspired and stirred by love for Rama I himself as much as for the glory of Thai culture, to have accomplished so much of it in the space of three years.

Rama I's interest in literature was a strong impetus to all who loved writing. There were the long epic poems such as the *Ramakien* of 1798 based on the ancient Hindu epic poem, the *Ramayana*. These long poems were called *Phra Raja Nibondn* – royal writings –, although Rama I did not write all of it. He and his intimates met and agreed on their version and then split up the parts they would each write, which was done in their spare time by dictating to scribes. The completed parts were then read to the assembled company at later meetings. It is probable that Rama I himself composed most of his own parts as relaxation in camp when he was away on campaign. It is generally agreed that he was a moderate poet,[46] and the best of his own writings were scenes of battle. In the *Ramakien* the hero, Prince Rama, was often called Phra Chakri (the *chakra* or discus was one of Vishnu's weapons) and the poem helped to glorify the new dynasty of that name. The frescoes of the cloisters in the Emerald Buddha Temple were pictures of the *Ramakien* and the figures were based on ballet costumes and poses. They have been restored many times and are a delight to grown-ups and children, for whom they are probably the world's oldest and largest "comic strips."

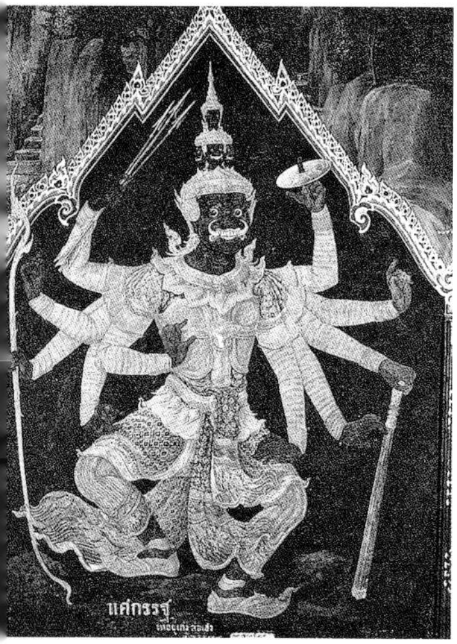

A cartouche showing Tosakan (Ravana) from the Ramakien murals.

Rama I influenced and inspired many authors to translate foreign masterpieces into Thai. They were from Persian, Chinese, as well as

Pali texts from Ceylon. The finest of these Thai authors was also a great minister, Chao Phraya Phra Klang (personal name Hon), and his *Sam Kok* from the Chinese history of the Three Kingdoms is the best known and still popular. He also wrote poetry and his best work, *Rajadhiraj*, is from a Mon original. He died in 1806 – three years before his master. A point to be noticed about these writers is that they all had regular work to perform, and they only wrote in their spare time. In 1796 the king ordered the examination of Thai history, which survived Ayutthaya, by a commission presided over by Chao Phraya Bibidhabijai, an elderly official who had assisted him on the traditions of the coronation and other ceremonies. Each time an ancient ceremony was revived and performed for the first time, the king issued a proclamation explaining its origins and meaning.

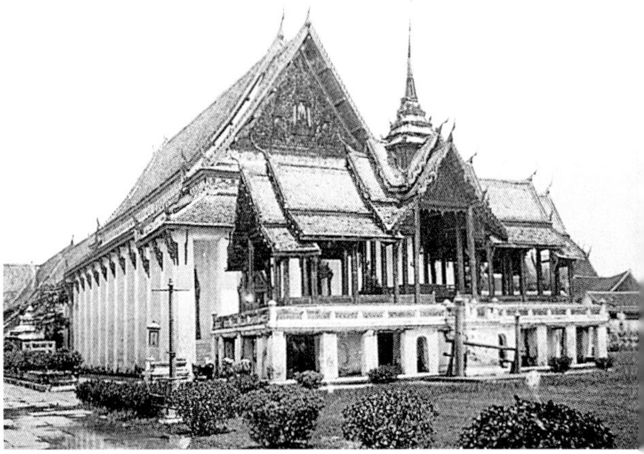

Throne halls in the Front Palace now serve as galleries for the National Museum. (River Books)

While on the subject of literature the Thai language itself should be briefly explained, and it is proposed to follow Phraya Anuman Rajadhon.[47] According to him the Thai language is known in philology as an isolating language because each word is independent, there being no change of case, gender, mood, or tense.[48] Originally it was completely monosyllabic, but later two or more syllabic words were formed into compound words, two good examples being electricity, which is "heaven fire", and matches, which is "wood strikes fire". The arrangement of the sentence is invariably subject – verb – object, with adjectives always following nouns. The Thai language has five tones which startle and puzzle all foreigners a great deal, more so as they are inclined to make the mistake of thinking that the same word alters its meaning by the change of tone, but to the Thais they are completely different words, even if they have exactly the same consonant and vowel parts and differ only in the tone sign. The grammar is simple and much depends on the syntax. Thais say : "I go to Bangkok yesterday" without altering the tense of the verb. Another characteristic is that there is no way of adding the equivalent of an "S" to turn a noun into the plural. Instead they add the word "body" (a quantifier), as for example, "three tables" is "table three bodies". Unfortunately for the foreigner, the word for "body" varies with different groups of objects, and there are exceptions.

Other scholars[49] regard the Thai language as a "priceless tool of communication in the imaginative and creative side of life . . . there is therefore rich ground for the poet and for the imaginative writer to exercise his talents. The little he says can mean a great deal. This makes for great subtlety in literary and poetic expression." There is a large variety of different types and metres in Thai poetry.

Music and the dance were not neglected. The movements of Thai dancing had originally come from India, but already by the

45 *Ibid.*, pages 172-175.

46 Prince Dhani: *The Reconstruction of Rama I, op. cit.*

47 Phya Anuman Rajadhon: *Thai Language, Thailand Culture Series,* No. 47, 1954.

48 The language is now spoken in Thailand, the Shan States (part of Burma), the Kingdom of Laos, and by groups of Thais in Tonkin (part of Vietnam), and in Yunnan (part of Southern China), but with some difference in each region.

49 M. L. Boonlua Kunjara and Dr. Bunchob Bandhumedha in a paper presented at the Round Table Conference of South-East Asian Language Experts at Chulalongkorn University. *Bangkok Post,* November 18th, 1957.

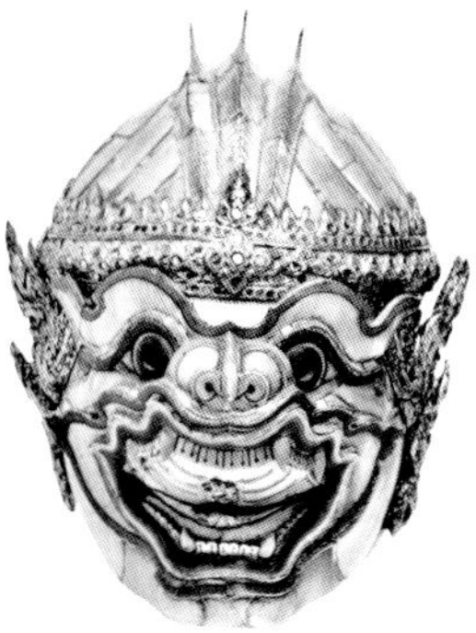

The Thai masked drama of *khon* was revived in the reign of King Rama I. (National Museum Bangkok)

mid-Ayutthaya period it had been made into a classical form for the Royal Ballet. There were many long poems to which the ballet was danced, although usually it was cut into individual scenes. The dancers performed in silence to the chanting and singing of the poem telling the story and dialogue which was accompanied by an orchestra. Very rarely the entire story was performed right through by the ballet, scene after scene, night after night, which would take a month or even more.[50] But even one full scene as performed in those days would be found too long or tedious for the modern Thais, and even more so by visiting foreigners. To them the action would seem slow and repetitive because the action had to suit the words which were sung or chanted, and if the words were not understood and their beauty appreciated, much of the pleasure would be lost. There were two principal kinds of royal ballet. The *khon* was danced by men and it was invariably the *Ramakien* with the dancers taking the parts of the *yaksha* (demons) or monkeys wearing masks. The *Lakorn* was danced by women and girls, often the King's young wives, and the stories were varied and more romantic. The *khon* companies were owned by the king and the deputy king and the competition was keen. Once for a great joyful celebration the two companies performed together in the open air on the royal lawn (sometimes called Phra Mane ground as important cremations took place there), and the principal scene was a battle between Prince Rama and his monkey army against Ravana, King of Lanka, and his demons. Although Rama I and the Uparaja were devoted brothers, often there were clashes of temperament which led to their entourages also being unfriendly rivals, and the joint ballet was the scene of such unhealthy wrangling. In the story Rama and his monkeys won, but in the ballet, Ravana and his demons who were played by the troupe of the Uparaja, refused to be beaten by the monkeys from the royal ballet. This failure to follow the script led to the unedifying spectacle of a free fight between the gentlemen of the two ballets.[51] Fortunately

Lakhon photographed by Feder Jagor, 1861. (Staatliche Museen zu Berlin)

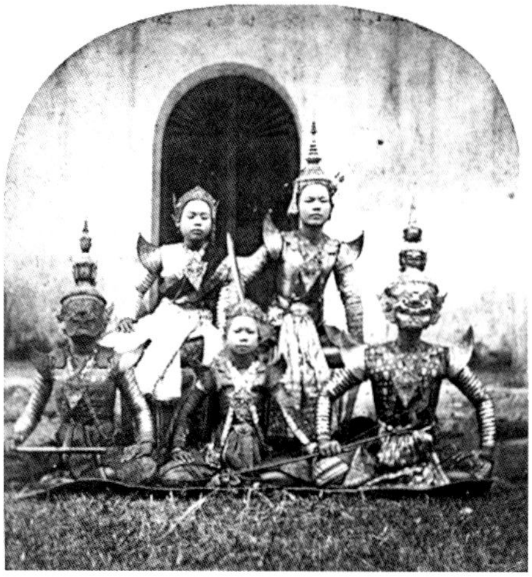

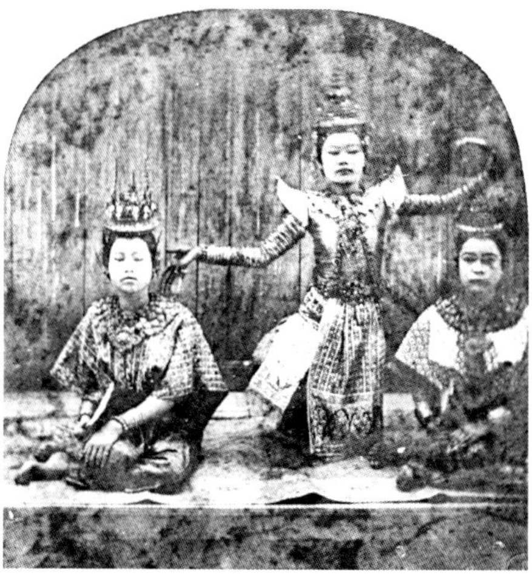

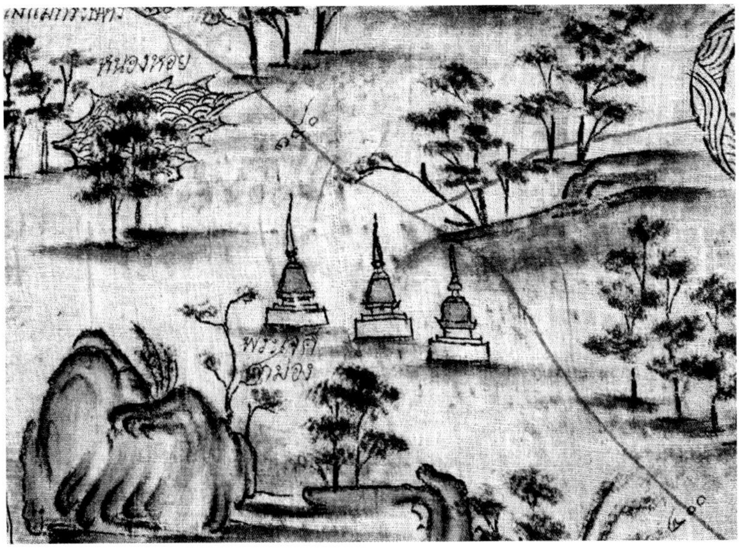

Section of an ancient Thai map dating from the reign of King Rama I discovered in the 1990s. (From *Royal Siamese Maps*, River Books)

these public displays of disunity were relatively rare. There were also other ballet companies outside the royal palaces owned by the high nobles which were called *Lakorn Nok* (outside).

One can but marvel at the tremendous scope of the reconstruction projects, which as Prince Dhani has pointed out, were achieved out of almost nothing. A large part of it was due to the personality and indomitable will of Rama I himself, well supported by his magnificent physical constitution. He possessed in his character sagacity, farsightedness, moderation, and honesty. One can only admire him all the more when it is remembered that there were many other problems facing him besides the work of reconstruction, and he was often interrupted in this pleasant task, for there were many calls of war.

The Burmese, thinking that the change of reign and dynasty would mean confusion in Siam, invaded the country in 1785, just after the building of most of Bangkok was completed. Although unsuccessful they made further invasions in 1786, 1787, 1796, and 1802. The Thai armies which drove them back were more than once personally commanded by the king accompanied by his brother, like Naresuan and Ekatotsarot. As the king was first and foremost a commander of armies, this particular aspect of his life cannot be ignored. Rama I knew Burma well, and, like Naresuan he knew that invasion was a certainty, and that the Burmese could come in four directions

1. Chiang Mai was, as always, the easiest way, but the town was in ruins, and, as a state, Chiang Mai was now a firm vassal, and could be counted upon to defend herself and at least delay the enemy's advance. Other Laotian states such as Luang Prabang and Vientiane had been subdued by Rama I already as King Taksin's Commander-in-Chief.

2. Another favourite way was from Tavoy across the Three Pagoda Pass to Kanchanaburi.

50 The writer once saw the whole story right through put on by the ballet for his grandmother sometime between 1914 and 1919. See Prince Chula: *The Twain Have Met*, etc., page 107, London, 1956.

51 Prince Dhani in *The Reconstruction of Rama I*, Thai version, quotes T'anit Yubodi: *The Khone* (in Thai), Bangkok, 1957.

3. From Mergui to the south to cut off the peninsula and make it a base for future operations.

4. A new way, namely, through Mehlamao pass which Rama I regarded as the most likely and therefore the greatest danger. It would lead easily through flat ground to Tak, Kampaeng Phet, and Nakhon Sawan. If the Burmese came this way and could form a junction with their other army at Kanchanaburi, they would find a terrain of plentiful supplies. Rama I therefore concentrated on these two dangers.

His strategic plan was as follows:

1. His brother, the Uparaja, was to defend Kanchanaburi without giving an inch, and beyond Kanchanaburi the enemy were not to pass.

2. An army under a general was placed at Nakhon Sawan as the king felt that the lines of communication with Kamphaeng Phet and Tak were too long, and around Nakhon Sawan formidable defences were constructed. The enemy must not be permitted to advance beyond the junction of rivers at Paknam Po. The main mobile reserves he held in his own hands, between these two vital points and west of the Chao Phraya River, with which mobile forces he could move to crush the enemy at either point. Should the Burmese army from Tavoy withdraw after their initial failure, the Uparaja was to turn south and attack the enemy coming from Mergui to the south. Anyone who has planned a big military operation with good modern maps may perhaps even admire Rama I all the more, for any maps he had would have been somewhat primitive. Practically the whole of his plan rested on the most brilliant appreciation of verbal reports of accurate reconnaisance.

Rama I organized his reconnaisance parties perfectly. In the Ayutthaya period the Thais had had to wait until after the Burmese crossed the frontier before they knew which way the enemy were coming, but Rama I knew even before they moved. This was because, once he had correctly guessed the four assembly points of the enemy, he organised his reconnaisance personnel around these points, then there were regular signal stations from these points to Bangkok so that all the news could be transmitted rapidly.[52]

For the first invasion the Burmese king, Bodawpaya, assembled a force of over 100,000 men, whilst the Thai could not muster more than 50,000 first-class troops, the Uparaja having 30,000, with the king's general reserves only amounting to 20,000, all wearing bright scarlet uniforms. The troops at Nakhon Sawan were probably second line soldiers.[53] There was severe fighting west of Karnburi and in time both sides had fortified camps pitched close together.[54] The Uparaja was showing himself to be the real Tiger that the Burmese called him, for any subordinate commander who lacked keenness for the attack was put under arrest and under sentence of death as an example to others. Like Frederick the Great of Prussia only a little time before, the Uparaja believed that it paid to make his officers more afraid of him than the enemy. Luckily for those generals, Rama I arrived on the scene in time to plead for their lives, and being saved, they had to promise to

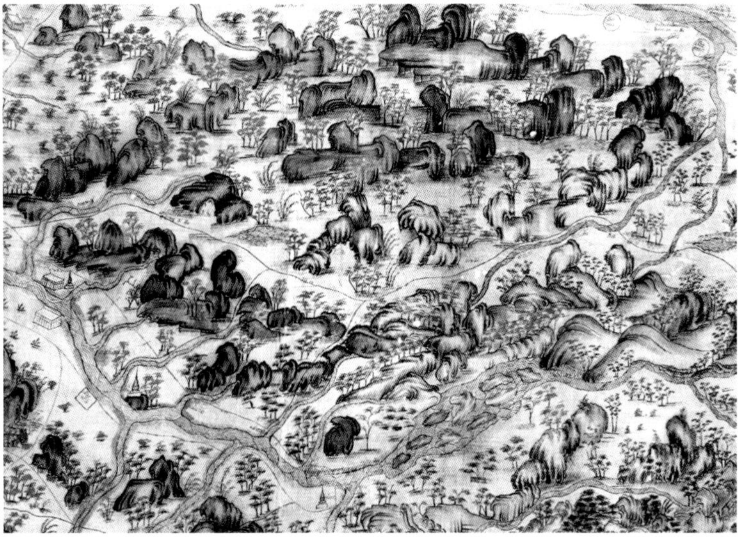

Another section from the royal map showing the area near Kanchanaburi. (From *Royal Siamese Maps*, River Books)

do better next time. But the Uparaja Sura Singhanat was not just a dare-devil fierce leader, he was also a clever general and often employed different ruses against an enemy superior in numbers. One such tactic was to send troops with their horses and baggage elephants back to Kanchanaburi every night under cover of darkness only to return to the front line camps every morning. The Burmese mistook them for daily reinforcements, and did not dare to make sorties out of their camps. The Uparaja had the advantage in heavy artillery for the Thais had never forgotten the art of casting cannon which they had first learned from the Portuguese in Ayutthaya. They brought their siege artillery up right close to the Burmese camps and poured such devastating fire into them that the enemy, despite his numerical superiority, met with crushing losses in the narrow confines of the camp. After that it was not so difficult for the Thai soldiers to take those camps by assault. The king's main force arrived in good time for the final blow, and together the two brothers inflicted a severe defeat on the invaders. King Bodawpaya, who had also ascended the Burmese throne in 1782, was commanding the Burmese army in person, and according to Hall[55] he was nearly captured. The Thais took nearly all the Burmese artillery, but did not have enough men to follow through into Burma. The French missionaries in Siam said that if there had been a proper pursuit, Rama I would have taken the Burmese capital – then Ava.

The Burmese armies in the north, such as the one besieging Lampang, were then attacked by Thai troops released by this victory. The enemy retreated when they heard that their brethren under the command of their own king had been routed. Rama I was well pleased and he returned to Bangkok to carry on his work as the King-Prime Minister. The Uparaja took his force by boats to Chumporn to deal with the Burmese who had invaded in the south and made some headway against weak defences. Once the Uparaja arrived, his vigorous leadership soon whipped up the defenders and all the

52 MSS. Notes by General Prince Alongkot.

53 Dibakarawongse: *History of Rama I, op. cit.*, page 93.

54 *Ibid.*, page 98.

55 D. G. E. Hall, *op. cit.*, Chapter 31.

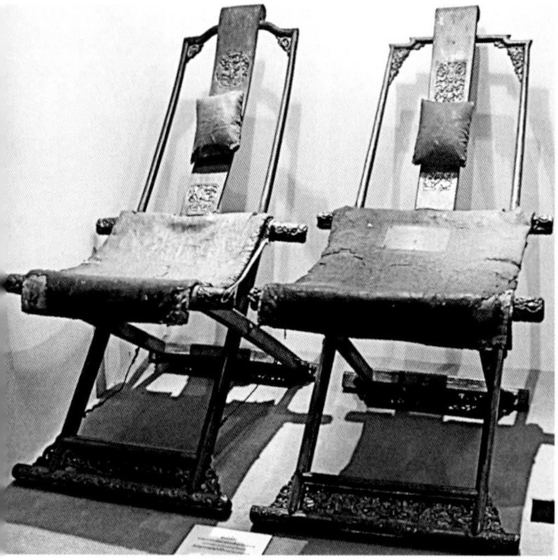

Two folding field chairs used by King Rama I and his brother the Uparaja when campaigning. (National Museum Bangkok)

invaders were defeated. By these victories in the south, the Uparaja regained for his brother control over the Malay provinces of Pattani, Kedah, Kelantan, and Terengganu. King Rama I now had a vast kingdom, if one also counted all the loosely held vassal states, north, east and south.

At Pattani the Uparaja captured a siege gun nine-foot long which he brought to Bangkok. The king was delighted and ordered another gun to be cast to make a pair. Aware of the ever increasing importance of artillery, he had many more large cannon made, and some of these enormous pieces can still be seen on the lawns in front of the Ministry of Defence.[56]

Although the second Burmese invasion of 1786 was well prepared from Moulmein, the Governor of Kanchanaburi was so swift with his warning to Bangkok that the Thai army, under the personal command of the king and the Uparaja, was able to go to Kanchanaburi by boats along the rivers and canals, and thereby take a lot of artillery pieces with them. When the Burmese arrived they found the Thais ready. The campaign was largely fought between pitched camps, and the Thai superiority in heavy guns told in the end, with the Burmese retreating home before it was too late. It was in the middle of these wars that Rama I took an unprecedented step, never imitated by another monarch of the same dynasty, and created his nephew, the son of his eldest sister, Deputy Uparaja, who became known as the Prince of the Rear Palace (Wang Lang). His palace was on the west bank of the river, and the site is now the Nursing School of Siriraj Hospital. This prince died, aged 61, later in the reign and no successor was appointed.

In the same year of 1787 after his victory near Kanchanaburi, Rama I decided that it would accord with the tenets of psychological warfare to advance into Burma. This would demonstrate that Siam now had the strength to attack as well as defend and Tavoy was chosen for that purpose. The first part of the journey was covered easily by boats, but close to Tavoy they had to cross high mountains covered with thick jungle. The mountains were so steep that the elephants were unable to carry people on their backs, and the large beasts themselves could only get up the mountain side by coiling their trunks round the trees and pulling themselves up. Many of them fell off the mountain and were killed. The king himself, then over 49, had to climb on foot and use ropes like the rest of his soldiers. He was distressed and said that he did not know the way was so difficult, or he would not have brought his son and nephews to face such hardship. His eldest son, Prince Isarasuntorn, had his first real taste of war –

The gun brought back from Pattani by the Uparaja Sura Singhanat today stands outside the Ministry of Defence. (River Books)

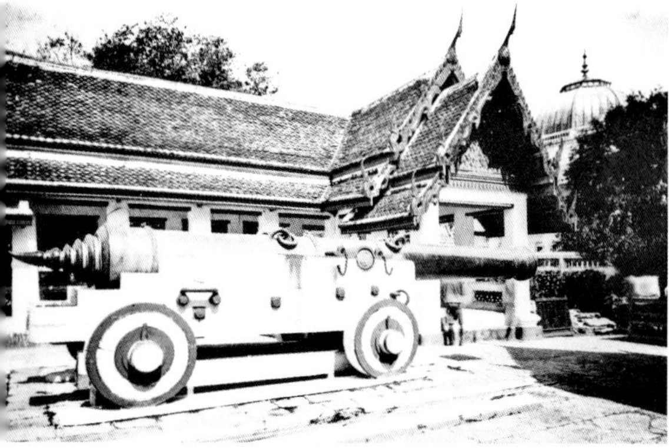

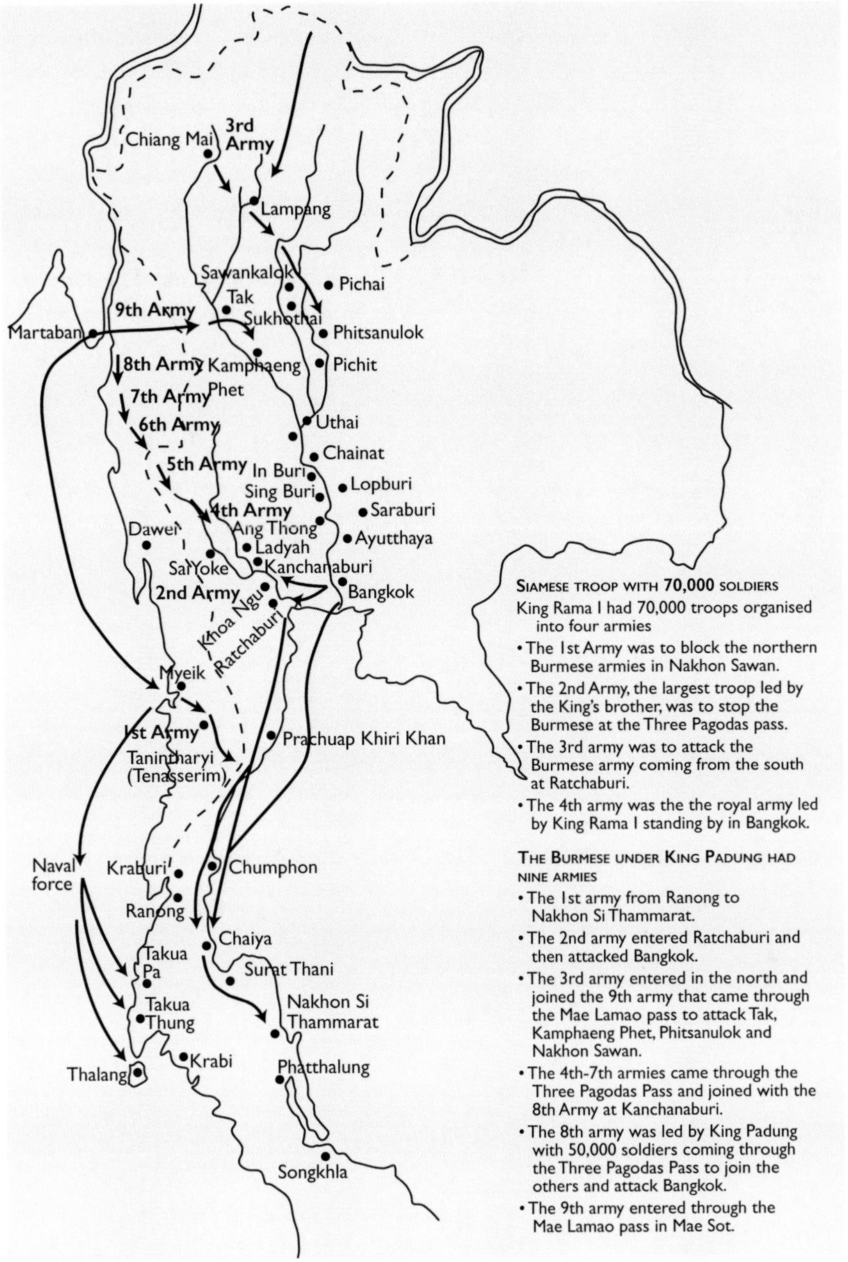

Map showing the invasion routes of the Burmese army in 1785.

despite having been on campaign with his father since he was a little boy of eight – for this time he acted as Quartermaster-General, but being only eighteen, he had a highly experienced deputy.

The Burmese army had left Tavoy as a feint, intending to lure the Thais into the city where they knew there was a scarcity of provisions. After the Thais had requisitioned some of the supplies, the citizens would rise up against them, then the Burmese would return to recapture the city, destroy the Thai army, and with luck capture the king and his brother. As Rama I saw no defenders on the ramparts, he

56 Dibakarawongse: *History of Rama I, op. cit.*, pages 124, 125.

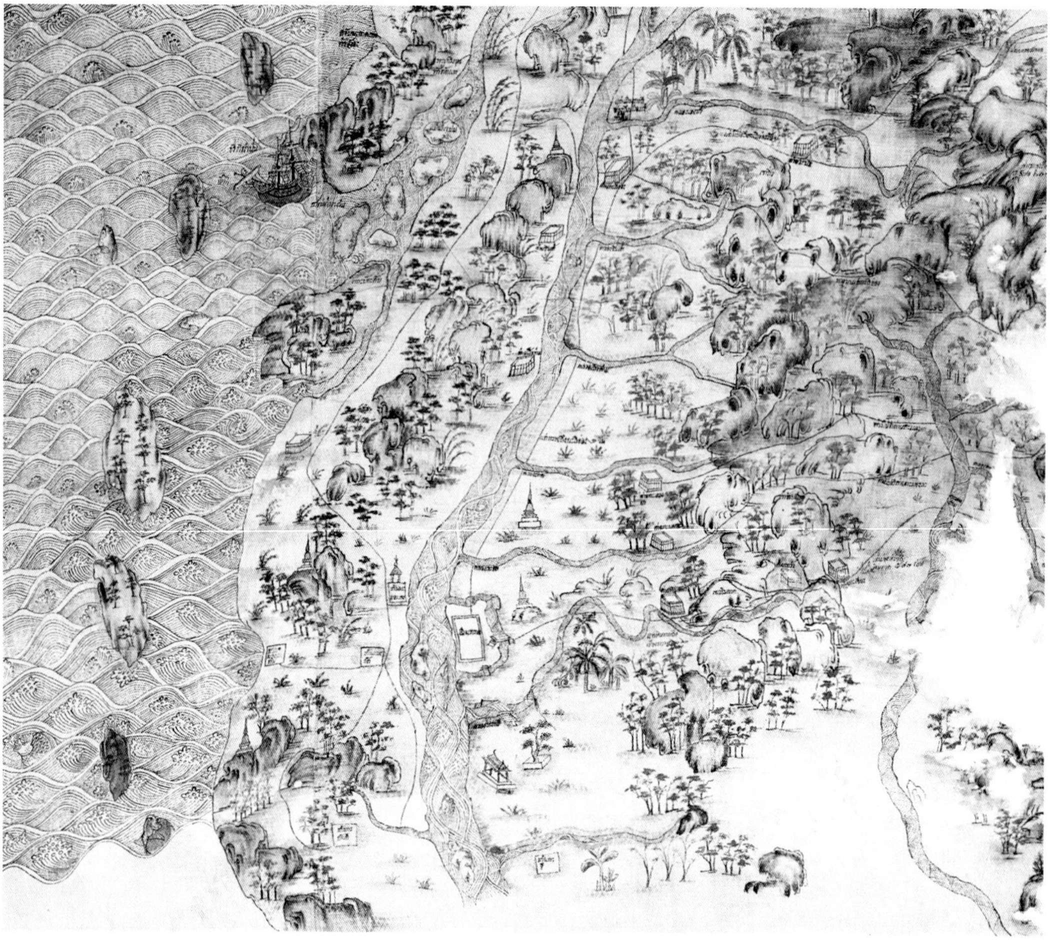

An ancient map from the time of King Rama I showing the area around Tavoy and Kanchanaburi. (From *Royal Siamese Maps*, River Books)

became suspicious, and ordered that Tavoy be investigated first. It was during this siege that his favourite elephant – the companion of many a campaign – became ill and would not eat any grass for three days. The king was deeply upset, but, happily, after Rama I himself spent hours persuading it to eat, the elephant recovered. The troops must have shown signs of boredom, for many generals begged leave to lead their men into taking the city by assault, but the king remained cautious. Feeling that provisions might not be sufficient to take the city and remain there longer, the king decided to raise the siege and return home.[57] The Uparaja was asked to remain with a detached force and watch events by the river. Tavoy was to be a thorn in the flesh for the Thais for some time, with the Burmese Governor wavering between submission and defiance, which caused more than one disagreement between the royal brothers. One happy outcome was when the Governor of Tavoy announced that he had found a niece of the king, who had been removed to Burma in 1767, and who was living in Tavoy as a Buddhist nun. There was a happy reunion between her and her uncles on the bank of the River Kwae, before the king took her back to Bangkok.[58] Finally the brothers agreed that Tavoy, even when submissive, could not be trusted, so the Uparaja went back there to dismantle the defences. On this occasion some of the Thai soldiers committed the usual offences against the women of the town. When news of this reached the king, he ordered an enquiry, and the culprits were punished as examples to others. This shows that Rama I required his soldiers to be *sans peur et sans reproche*.[59]

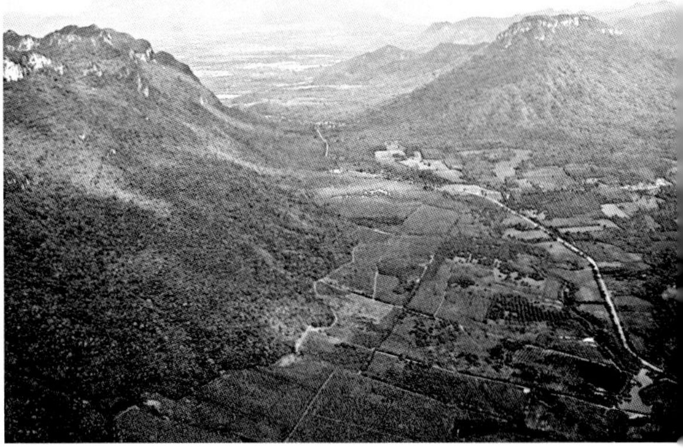

Aerial view showing the route taken by King Rama I towards Tavoy from Kanchanaburi. (River Books)

The Burmese war of 1787 took place only in the north. The most northern town, Chiang Saen, was still in Burmese hands. With the help of Prince Kawila of Lampang, the Burmese in Chiang Saen were now defeated and expelled. As a reward Prince Kawila was given Chiang Mai, which, having changed hands so often in the last thirty years, now lay mostly in ruins. The king sent the Uparaja Sura Singhanat to re-establish it as an important vassal city. A younger brother of Kawila was made prince of Lampang, and their descendants ruled Chiang Mai and Lampang as vassals until the status of ruling princes was suspended in the reign of King Prajadhipok. Although these princes were hereditary, the ruling princes did not succeeed one another automatically, and the heirs had to be approved or chosen by the king of Bangkok. These two families are now called Na Chiang Mai and Na Lampang.

The Burmese had plans to carry out another big campaign against Chiang Mai in 1796, but the Uparaja Sura Singhanat arrived promptly on the scene and helped to drive them back across the border after they had been decisively defeated. It was then that Prince Kawila of Chiang Mai presented the Uparaja with the ancient Buddha image brought from Ceylon long ago, the Phra Buddha Sihing, which is still in the throne room of the Front Palace, now part of the National Museum.

In 1802 the Burmese made their last bid for Chiang Mai and came right up to the city walls. Prince Kawila and the men in whom he had instilled his sense of patriotism for the House of Chakri, hotly defended their newly acquired city. The Burmese closely besieged them on all sides but they held out, and both sides were still fighting when the relieving army arrived under the Uparaja. Unfortunately he was seriously ill with prostate trouble and unable to direct operations with his usual vigour, and the king sent the Deputy Uparaja to help him. The Burmese now formed themselves into a ring of camps, all round Chiang Mai, which the Thais in turn besieged intending to take all of them by simultaneous assault. An order was issued to all ranks that the assaults had to succeed that night, and that they would all have breakfast inside Chiang Mai. During the night the Burmese, having dug themselves into trenches outside their camps, put up a hot barrage of fire, but the assaults were all successful and Chiang Mai was relieved. The Thai army, with Prince Kawila's troops, and the army of the Prince of Vientiane, which had just arrived, followed the enemy in

57 *Ibid.*, pages 146-154.
58 *Ibid.*, pages 185-190.
59 *Ibid.*, page 193.

pursuit and drove them out of the kingdom of Rama I, which was from then on free of the Burmese for the rest of his reign. Prince Kawila was created Phra Chao Chiang Mai – a great vassal prince – and thenceforth he ruled over fifty-seven subordinate Laos towns.

Besides the important enemy – the Burmese – there were many complications amongst the vassals, especially in Cambodia. Rama I had been in Cambodia, carrying out King Taksin's policy of setting up his candidate on the throne, when he was suddenly recalled to Thonburi because of the revolt against King Taksin. Up till then there had been rivalry between Siam and Vietnam for the control of Cambodia. Now at the beginning of Rama I's reign the Cambodian prince on the throne was Ang Eng, the infant son of the former candidate of Vietnam. The boy had replaced King Taksin's protege, Ang Nhon, who had been executed by his rival with the help of Vietnam. By 1784, however, a most serious rebellion had broken out in Vietnam, and the rightful heir, Nguyen Anh, could make no headway against the rebels who held sway in the south – Cochin China. He had a friend in a French missionary priest, Father Pigneau, who tried to get help from the French. However, this was not forthcoming as Louis XVI was heavily preoccupied with his own troubles on the eve of the French Revolution.

In 1785 Nguyen Anh went to Bangkok and sought the protection of Rama I, then in the third year of his reign, which was immediately granted. The Vietnamese prince had already been preceded to Bangkok by Ang Eng of Cambodia, who had been removed thither by Thai sympathisers when the Vietnamese rebels were advancing on Phnom Penh. Thus for some years Rama I had under his protection the potential rulers of Cambodia and Vietnam. Both were set up in suitable houses with their own officials and domestics. While the boy Ang Eng was being educated as a Thai, Nguyen Anh was invited to attend the royal court every day and permitted to sit in the Vietnamese fashion. His Vietnamese followers were allowed sailing ships and were able to go out to sea freely for fishing, trading, or even to make some reconnaisance about affairs in their own country. Rama I hoped to put them both back on their thrones, but so far he was still too busy defending Siam herself against Burmese invasions. Nguyen Anh and his men accompanied the king to the Burmese war in 1785 and he and they distinguished themselves in the fighting.

The successful Vietnamese rebels were now fully occupied in the north and had left weak remnants of their forces in Cochin China. By 1787 Nguyen Anh felt that a good opportunity was presenting itself for the recovery of some of his lands, yet he did not dare to ask Rama I outright for permission to leave Bangkok. Instead, one day in August he escaped by boat and set sail down the river towards the sea. The Uparaja Sura Singhanat, upon hearing the news, was extremely angry, saying that the Vietnamese was ungrateful. He at once followed him in his river boat and caught up with Nguyen Anh at Paknam, when there was no wind to take the latter's junk out to sea. Nguyen Anh was so desperate, he wanted to kill himself, but his followers dissuaded him and then the wind came. The Uparaja was about to change into a sailing junk when a royal messenger arrived in a fast rowing boat with a letter from the king. It said: "Do not try to catch him. He felt that we could not help him get back his lands because we were still busy with our own war. We have given him our kindness with our hands, let us not eradicate the picture with our feet."[60] The Uparaja did not agree as in his view Nguyen Anh knew too much about the Thais and in the future "he would be a danger to our children and grandchildren".

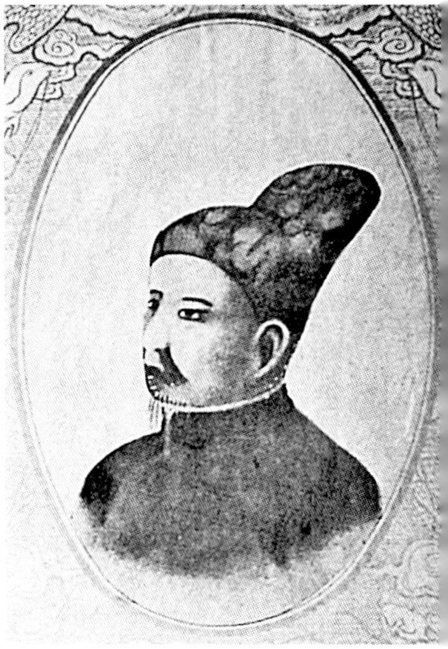

Emperor Gia-Long of Vietnam. (From *Royal Hue*, River Books)

Once he had a foothold in Cochin China, Nguyen Anh found loyalists gathering around him, and soon he was making slow but certain progress. The Vietnamese rebels, seeing danger to their cause, offered Rama I their friendship on the most favourable terms, if he would have Nguyen Anh captured and delivered to them. Rama I firmly refused as it would contravene his principles of the Ten Virtues. On the contrary, he was now in alliance with Nguyen Anh, helping with the supply of arms, clothing, food, and even elephants. Rama I did not know that Nguyen Anh's son, Prince Canh, with the help of Father Pigneau, had concluded an alliance with Louis XVI in Paris, but the French Revolution nullified its effects. By Rama I's help and his own stout efforts, Nguyen Anh captured Saigon in July, 1789 – the year Louis XVI recalled the States-General thereby paving the way to the Revolution. When Nguyen Anh was in possession of Cochin China, he conducted himself towards Rama I as a vassal, namely, regularly sending him tributes in the form of gold and silver trees. In fact, Rama I was receiving so many of these from every direction that he could have had a forest of them. Nguyen Anh went from strength to strength, and in 1802, when Siam was finally cleared of Burmese attacks he was able to establish himself over all of Vietnam and set up his capital again at Hue, ruling from there as the Emperor Gia Long. He no longer regarded himself as a vassal and did not pay customary tributes, but he constantly sent Rama I rich presents and offered him the equal hand of friendship which was gladly accepted. This shows the wisdom of Rama I in allowing Gia Long, when he was Prince Nguyen Anh, to escape from Bangkok and to help him thereafter.

Prince Isarasuntorn, the king's eldest son, took the yellow robe for the customary period in 1789, and the king arranged it as a grandiose affair because he was the first celestial son of the king to undergo the initiation ceremony. After that his other sons entered the order at regular intervals. In 1794 he arranged for Prince Ang Eng of Cambodia to take the yellow robe with them and accorded him equal honours. The Cambodian prince then received his crown from Rama I and was styled King Narai Rama Tibodi, after which he went back to rule his country, accompanied by a Thai army. Meanwhile Chao Phraya Abhaipubet, formerly an opponent of Ang Eng's father, had done well as Regent of Cambodia when Ang Eng was in Bangkok. Rama I wanted to reward him with the vice-royalty of the Siem Reap-Battambang

60 *Ibid.*, page 132.

region. With the new King of Cambodia's agreement made from gratitude for past help, these two provinces were incorporated into the Kingdom of Siam, and placed in the charge of the new Viceroy.

The restoration of the unfortunate Ang Eng was of short duration for he died in 1796 – only two years later. Rama I, who had come to love him like a son, was deeply grieved and wished to give him a last high honour, that of bringing his body to be cremated in great state in Bangkok. The Council of Nobles strongly objected on the ground that the Thais were still preoccupied with the danger of war with Burma. No vassal king or prince had ever been cremated in the Thai capital, and the event might be an ill omen. As had been the case before with Rama I, such wise counsel prevailed. Ang Eng left five young sons, but not one of them was immediately recognised by Rama I as king of Cambodia. Instead he appointed one of their adult relatives as Regent, declaring that when they grew up he would choose the best of them to be king. In this way he emphasized the principle that the Thai king accepted the hereditary rights of a vassal's family, but reserved to himself the right to designate the successor, which shows that this system of vassalage was different from European feudalism.

The difference went further and was more fundamental. In 1802 Ang Chan – eleven-year-old son of Ang Eng – was appointed by Rama I as king of Cambodia, and as Hall surmised,[61] this was probably to steal a march on Emperor Gia Long of Vietnam who had regained the imperial throne that year. In 1806, at the age of fifteen, the young king of Cambodia went to Bangkok to be crowned by his overlord. His Cambodian advisers were determined to prevent Cambodia becoming the battleground of a possible rivalry between Siam and Vietnam, and they wished to be on good terms with both. Accordingly, in 1807 the Cambodian monarch sent tribute to the Emperor Gia Long, and after that he regularly sent tributes to both Bangkok and Hue. Rama I either did not know of this or he did not object, but it was to lead to a great deal of trouble for his grandsons and great-grandson. Whilst Gia Long was Emperor, there was no danger of war between Siam and Vietnam, as Gia Long was sincerely grateful to Rama I for his past help, and he turned down Burmese overtures for an alliance against Siam. Another time when the Raja of Pattani contemplated rebellion against Bangkok, he first told Gia Long who quickly passed the news to Rama I who had the rebellion nipped in the bud and the Raja was taken to Bangkok and given life-imprisonment.

Since 1707 the old Laotian Kingdom of Lan Xang had been divided up between Luang Prabang and Vientiane which became capitals of two separate Laotian principalities riven by bitter rivalry. Both were weak and Vientiane defeated Luang Prabang with Burmese help, before Vientiane herself was taken by General Chakri for King Taksin. Thus both cities were vassals of Siam when he became King Rama I. In 1792 the Vientiane prince, Chao Nan, was accused of planning a rebellion and had indeed attacked Luang Prabang. He was summoned to Bangkok to face treason charges in a special court, and when found guilty, was condemned to death.

The Uparaja Sura Singhanat, alternately severe and compassionate, pleaded for his life which the king granted. Chao Nan was nevertheless deposed and imprisoned, and his brother, Chao In, installed in his place. He proved a loyal vassal, and with his brother, Chao Anou, helped Siam in many campaigns against the Burmese. When Chao In died in 1805, Chao Anou was appointed ruling prince of Vientiane. Although this prince had been popular and much admired in Bangkok, he was planning from the first to free his country from Thai control.

It can thus be seen that although the vassal states were loosely governed as far as their people and internal affairs were concerned, Rama I kept a tight rein on their rulers. By 1804, as Hall wrote,[62] Rama I had made "Siam more powerful than at any time in her history." He held all the Laotian principalities, most of the Malay states, together with Tavoy, Mergui, and Tenasserim.

In King Taksin's time foreign trade was only with China and there were no relations with other far-off countries. In the fifth year of Rama I's reign a Portuguese envoy arrived in a sloop, but it was not known for certain whether he came from Macao only or from Lisbon itself. Rama I gave orders that the embassy was to be well received, the letter from the king of Portugal to be royally treated, and all the Thai officials concerned were to be properly dressed. Rama I received the envoy and the letter in the Amarindra Hall, and his reply was conveyed to the sloop in a procession of royal barges.[63] This was the only European envoy in the first Chakri reign.

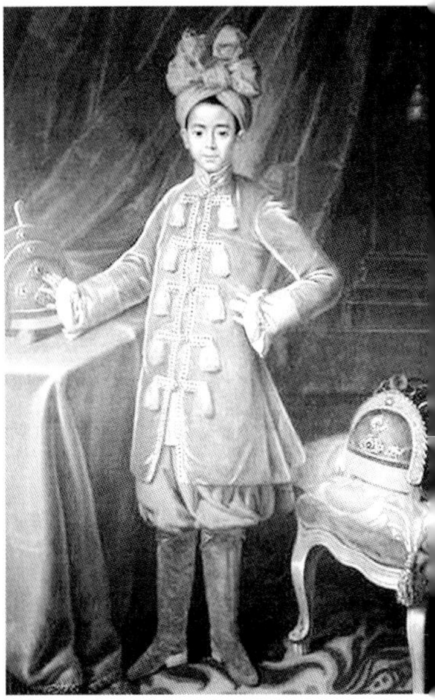

Ang Chieng Seu (Prince Cauk). (The Paris Foreign Missions Society, 1787)

Tributes, however, were as before sent to China with Thai ambassadors. The Thais' principal trade by sea was still with China, and the Chinese only permitted foreign ships at certain ports, and to obtain permission the heads of the trading states had to send a letter and tributes to the Chinese emperor or they were not given any facilities whatsoever. Thus all the nations which traded with China followed this custom including Portugal. Hence there arose the Chinese misunderstanding that all countries which sent ambassadors really considered themselves vassals of China.[64]

The British agent, Francis Light, on August 11th, 1786, took Penang Island from the Sultan of Kedah with the provisional understanding that the British East India Company would help to maintain Kedah's independence from Siam. In 1787 the Government of India repudiated the alliance and so upset the Sultan that he in 1791 threatened to expel the British from Penang, but it is not known how he proposed to accomplish this. Having stated this sequence of events, Hall[65] has speculated as to whether Kedah was independent in 1786 when Siam claimed overlordship over all of Malaya. He cited the Chinese claim of overlordship over South-East Asia including Siam, but it is here submitted that the claim arose out of the special cause just explained, and the Chinese had never at any time made any attempt to put their claim into practice. If, as Hall also said, Burma had the same claim over Siam following the conquest of 1767, this claim was

61 D. G. E. Hall, *op. cit.*, page 373.

62 *Ibid.*, page 444.

63 *Collected History*, Part 62 – Farang Envoys to Bangkok (in Thai), Bangkok, 1937.

64 Prince Damrong's footnotes to his *History of Rama II* (in Thai), Bangkok, 1916.

65 D. G. E. Hall, *op cit.*, pages 434-435.

repudiated by feats of arms when the Burmese forces were expelled by King Taksin, and was further repudiated by the victories of Rama I. Be that as it may, the Thai King was so busy still fighting the Burmese in 1786 that he did not yet have time to press his claims on the Malay states. Vows of fealty such as William the Conqueror extracted from Harold after the latter's shipwreck did not have quite the same value in South-East Asia where vassalage had to be imposed by force of arms. Rama I took no notice when Penang was ceded to the British most probably because he did not know, and if he did he was not in a position to do anything about it. Throughout his life he clearly demonstrated that he understood that politics was "the art of the possible". Whatever might have *de jure* been the status of Kedah, she was obviously *de facto* independent in 1786. It was the East India Company and the Government of India which recognized the suzerainty of Rama I by repudiating the alliance with Kedah arranged by Light. This naturally much upset those British who were actually in Penang and looking forward to extending their trade and influence in Malaya which was halted for a while. Instead, they feared that the whole Malay peninsula would fall under the Thai "yoke".[66]

As Rama I and his only surviving brother had been together for so long, had faced common adversaries, fought side by side and shared in great joy and glory, it is sad to record that they fell out so seriously towards the close of the Uparaja's life. One possible explanation is that his was a schizophrenic nature, one moment violently severe, at another kindly and compassionate. As an example of the latter quality, when he entered the monastery for seven days in 1796, he asked his brother to release from prison thirty-two political prisoners so that they could take up the yellow robe with him.[67] Once in 1788 a French pugilist came to Bangkok and challenged the Thais to a free-for-all bout. The Uparaja put up a Thai opponent whom he ordered to be rubbed all over with oil. As the Frenchman tried to get close and wrestle with him, he could not get a hold, while the Thai hit out at the Frenchman as he himself retreated. The Frenchman's elder brother jumped into the ring to prevent the Thai man from retreating. The Uparaja, who was watching the fight with the king, leapt into the ring and seriously injured the elder Frenchman with a well-placed and accurate kick. This was followed by a free-for-all amongst followers of both sides until the king could intervene to have the fight stopped. The king sent a doctor and a masseur to look after the Frenchmen in their ship.[68]

Another famous quarrel concerned a boat race. Each brother had a boat and a crew, and during practices the king's crew was definitely the faster. However, all the time the Uparaja had had another crew in hiding which was training secretly and was far superior. On the race day he put this secret crew into his boat which beat the king's boat easily. It is not surprising that the king was exceedingly put out.

A more serious issue occurred when the Uparaja complained that he did not get sufficient allowance from the Civil List The king endeavoured to explain that the money collected in taxes from the people must first be used to run the country for their benefit, and only what was left over should be shared amongst the family. If the family needed more money then they had to buy and fit out junks for the trade with China. The Uparaja was deeply hurt and would not come to see the king for many days. The entourages of both sides became so alarmed that extra guards were mounted on the parapets of the Grand Palace as well as the Palace of the Front. The trouble was finally settled through the good offices of the two elder sisters as all troubles between the brothers always were.

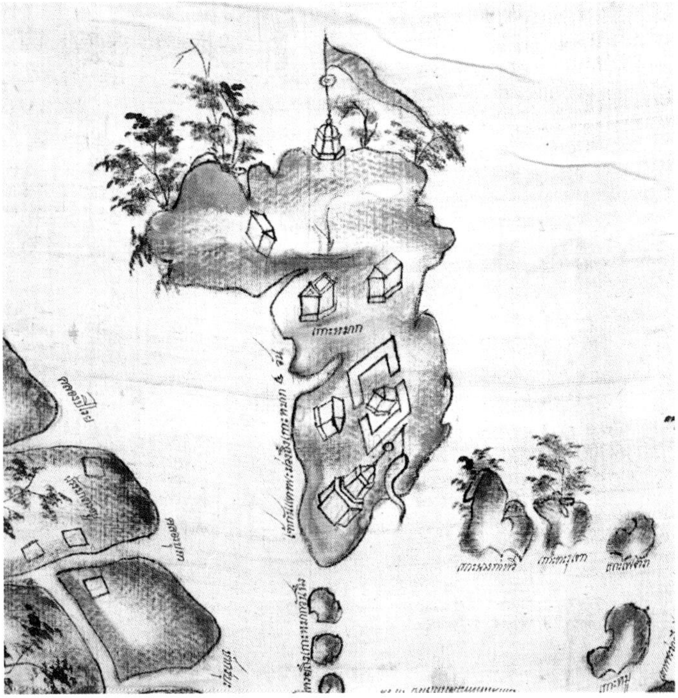

Penang as shown on one of the old Siamese maps. (From *Royal Siamese Maps*, River Books)

Both of the princesses died in 1799. The king had two new golden urns made for their bodies. It must be explained that amongst the Thais, the bodies of royalty and high nobility were kept sitting in urns and not lying in coffins, and the cremation usually took place long after death when many different funeral rites had been held. The origins of the urn are not exactly known, and Prince Naris told the present writer that it probably dated back to the time when the Thais were nomadic and sometimes had to carry the body of their chief for some time in a cart before the funeral could be held. In 1808, Rama I had had constructed a highly decorated great golden urn, known as the *Thong Yai* (Big Golden One), which was intended for the king and queen, or some exceptionally high celestial prince or princess. There was also an inner silver urn in which the body actually rested, while the outerdecorative urn could be broken down into eight pieces and then re-assembled. Other royalty, besides the king and queen, had inner urns made of copper. Rama I was so delighted with the great new golden urn and the plain silver inner urn that he had both of them placed in his bedroom for several days. One of his wives burst into tears saying that it was an ill omen. The king laughed and said he did not mind, adding the equivalent of: "If I don't see them from the outside when I'm still alive, how the hell d'you think I can ever see them?"[69]

They were intended to be used first for his own body.

In 1803 the Uparaja was seriously ill which made him more morose and despondent. As he knew full well that the position of Uparaja or Deputy King was not hereditary, and none of his sons were likely to be appointed on merit as they had not distinguished themselves in any way, he

66 *Ibid.*, page 444.

67 Dibakarawongse: *History of Rama I, op. cit.*, pages 220-221.

68 *Ibid.*, page 154.

69 From the information given by King Chulalongkorn to Prince Damrong who repeated it in his notes in his *History of Rama II, op. cit.*, pages 2-4. The same information was given by King Chulalongkorn to his son, Prince Chakrabongse, who transmitted it to the present writer.

began to regret his palace and all the embellishments which he had made. He decided to present his favourite sword to Wat Mahatat to be made into a candle rail. Already declining in health, he had himself carried to that temple on a litter. Once within the precincts he bemoaned the fact that having done as much as his brother to save the country, his personal possessions would fall to his nephews and their future descendants, and not to his own children and theirs. Having made that statement, he tried to stab himself but was prevented from doing so by his courtiers. He was then ill enough in body and spirit to exclaim that if anyone desired to plot on his behalf, let them do it soon. Clearly his mind was going or already gone, and it was a tragedy that his two elder sons and some of his senior officers took the remark seriously and began immediately to make preparations.

When he heard that his brother was dying, Rama I was most upset and went across to the Palace of the Front to nurse him personally for six days. The Front Palace Guards gave threatening looks to the Grand Palace Guards who accompanied the king, so the king's eldest son, Prince Isarasuntorn, went along to supervise his father's security. It was at midnight on November 3rd, 1803 that the Uparaja's great heart became still as he departed this life at the age of 60. The king was so moved by sorrow that he gave his brother's body another new urn made from the gold taken from the urns of his two sisters. This new urn became known as the *Thong Noi* – lesser golden one. He also ordered general mourning throughout the Kingdom.

Once the death had finally occurred, news of the abortive plot leaked out and reached the royal ears, leading Rama I to order an enquiry. The two elder sons of the Uparaja, Prince Lamuan and Prince Intapat, together with other nobles, were found guilty of high treason. After being disgraced and deprived of their ranks, all were executed. The knowledge that the attempt was supported by his brother hurt the king most deeply, and when it was time for the cremation in 1804, at first he would not attend, as he felt his brother had loved his own family more than the State. But, as always, he accepted the wise counsel of his great officers, and presided in person at the cremation which was arranged as a very great State occasion.[70]

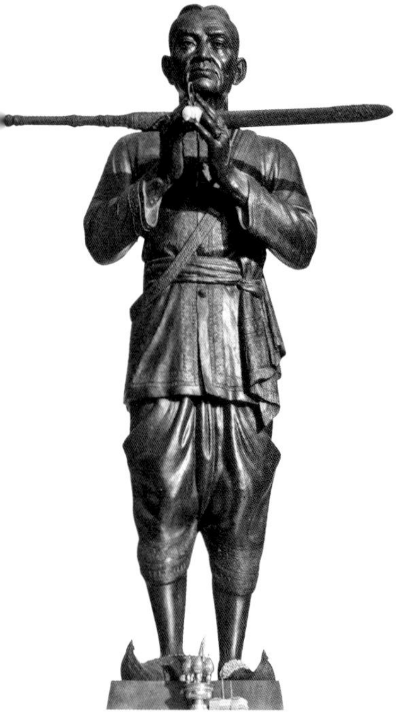

A statue of the Uparaja Maha Sura Singhanat within Wat Mahathat. (River Books)

Some little time after the death of the Uparaja and seeing that a successor had not been appointed, Emperor Gia Long of Vietnam, considering himself a grateful friend, wrote to Rama I saying it was dangerous to leave this important position unfilled. Many of the senior princes had by then died, including the Deputy-Uparaja in 1806 at the age of 61. Most of the princes were now equal in rank and age which might lead to jealousy and competition for the throne, and Gia Long pointed out that Rama I had to realise that he was now an old man.[71] Good advice was the one thing which the king never ignored, and in 1807 he appointed Prince Isarasuntorn as the *Wang Na* or *Uparaja*. This was the only time in the dynasty that the eldest son of the monarch was appointed *Uparaja*, and Rama I held a very big ceremony. Normally the new *Uparaja* should move to live in the *Wang Na*, but that was something Rama I did not desire. It had been built by Uparaja Sura Singhanat, and the king remembered how upset that prince had been that his family might no longer live there after his death. Accordingly, the king allowed them to go on living there, and asked Prince Isarasuntorn to remain at King Taksin's old palace where he had been living for some time. The excuse he gave was that he was now getting old, and it was not worthwhile for his son to move twice as he did not have long to wait before moving into the Grand Palace itself.

Towards the end of his reign Rama I ordered many elaborate, long golden barges, and they are still some of the most popular sights for foreign tourists in present-day Bangkok. At the end of the wet season, during which time the monks were required to remain in their monasteries, and when the temporary young monks took up their abode, there was a ceremony called *Kathin,* when the people went to the temples and gave the monks all kinds of presents. The king yearly presented such gifts to some of the special monasteries associated with the Royal family, journeying to them in state processions. In 1807 he arranged an especially large but informal *Kathin* procession. The king asked the princes and the nobles to join him in decorating boats as water creatures, such as crocodiles, shells, lobsters, crabs, and all kinds of fish. It was a great success and much enjoyed by the general public, and the whole procession of boats went right round the city.[72]

Once free from war, the country began to recover. The population was about four million, and they were largely self-supporting agriculturalists, paying no direct taxes other than corvée work. The revenue was from indirect taxes such as those on alcoholic drinks, gambling dens, market garden rates, a percentage amount of the rice they produced, but these taxes alone would not be sufficient to run the State even in those more simple days. The bulk of the revenue came from the junk trade to China, and the royal ships were built both in Bangkok and other Thai seaports. Besides the king, many of the princes and nobles had sea-going junks, and together with Chinese junks coming

70 Dibakarawongse: *History of Rama I, op. cit.*, pages 264-276.

71 *Ibid.*, pages 276-277.

72 *Ibid.*, page 305.

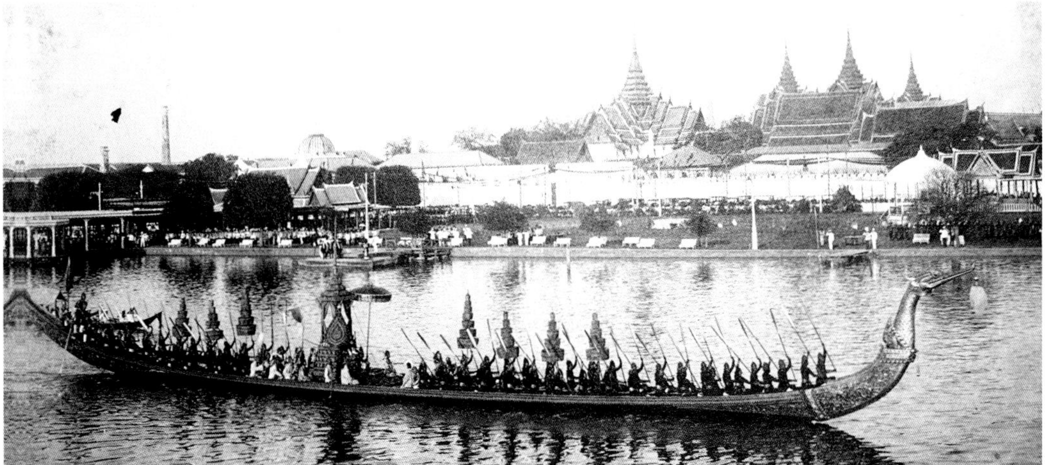

The royal barge, Suphanahong created during the reign of King Rama I. The current barge was built in the reign of King Rama V. (River Books)

in, all had to pay the king export and import duties. The Thai merchants, when they arrived in China, did not only sell their goods but sometimes the junk itself.[73]

Amongst Rama I's colleagues in his great task had been his brother, Boonma, later the Uparaja Sura Singhanat, but this great general did not shine in peace as he did in war. Then there was his nephew, the Deputy-Uparaja, a steady worker. Amongst the non-royal colleagues, his former secretary was appointed the Kalahom, another important minister was the author, Hon, who was Chao Phraya Phra Klang and Nai Bunnag, brother-in-law of Queen Amarindra, the ancestor of the Bunnag family, was Chao Phraya Akara Mahasena. Three of his progeny were to reach the extra high noble rank of *Somdet Chao Phraya*, and one would be Regent. However, most of Rama I's colleagues died before him and left him lonely in his last years.

His typical daily routine when in Bangkok has been described elsewhere.[74] He rose early and offered food and alms to the monks who were doing their early morning round with their food bowls.

At 10.30 a.m. a set of invited monks took regular turns to eat their main meal in the royal presence in the council chamber. After their departure at about 11.30 a.m., the king received verbal reports of the daily expenses of the Treasury. Then he mounted the throne to give his daily audience. First he received members of the royal family. After them came officers of the *Tamruat Luang* (the Royal Bodyguard of Gentlemen-at-Arms) with reports on particular crimes which had been referred to them for their opinion so they could assist the king in giving his judgment. Thereafter the audience was open to all who had the right to be received, and it continued until the king retired for his luncheon. This was taken in the Inside and he ate alone. This was a time when his daughters, other princesses, the *Chao Choms*, and other eligible ladies, could come and see him. After luncheon and the audience for the Inside, Rama I had his afternoon rest.

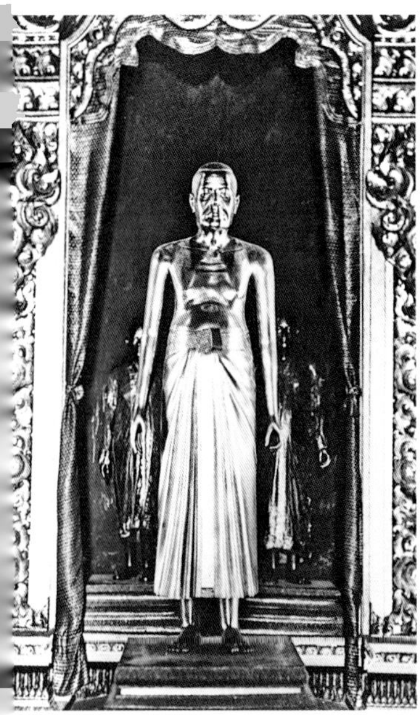

A statue of King Rama I within Prasat Phra Thep Bidorn. (River Books)

The king had his evening meal early – about 6 p.m. – again with the Inside, but with fewer people present. After that he went to the Audience Chamber and sat or lay on a low wide bench with many cushions, while the high officials, however important, crouched on the floor. The evening audience always opened with a daily sermon preached by an especially chosen and invited monk. This was followed by a verbal report from the Treasury of the Bedchamber (Privy Purse). Then came reports from the court chamberlains sent out during the day on different errands, such as enquiries regarding the illnesses of members of the Royal Family or important nobles, or some prominent Buddhist prelates. When these were completed the king once again mounted the throne for the open evening audience which consisted mostly of reports from the provinces requiring the royal decision. Generally the audience ended between 9 and 10 p.m., but in times of crisis it might continue far into the night. This regular routine was maintained year after year until, in the last two years of his life, Rama I became ill and infirm. Then he appeared at the window of the Paisal Taksin Hall of the Inside, which looked down into the Amarindra Hall of the Outside, so he granted audiences almost to the very end.

After a short, sharp illness, Rama I died on September 7th, 1809, at the age of 72 and in the 28th year of his reign. He was sound in mind to the end and was able to designate his eldest son, the Uparaja, Prince Isarasuntorn, as the heir of his choice.

What did Rama I look like? This is not known and all "portraits" are imaginary. The artists talked with contemporary eye-witnesses who tried to describe him and they also compared various features to certain living descendants. After that an accepted conventional portrait was evolved, and this was followed by the bronze statue at the eastern end of the Chakri Memorial Bridge in Bangkok. It seems he had a fine and healthy constitution, as no record exists of his ever being ill, and it is likely that he had a face with strong features to match his character.

In the wars against Burma under his leadership most of the troops were conscripts. The generals and other officers, however, were regular serving soldiers, and the corps d'elite were composed of men who were in the permanent employ of the king, the princes, and the nobles. Although the bulk were conscripts, such men can only fight successfully if inspired by great causes and by respected or beloved leaders. In many wars all over the world and at any period, conscripts have deserted in their thousands. In his ability to weld together the Thai people and inspire them to repulse the enemy again and again, Rama I gave birth to the modem Thai nation.

Although royal polygamy was practised in Ayutthaya, we have no definite record of the number of wives and children each king had. In contrast, we have clear and definite records for the Chakri Family.[75] We know that Rama I had 42 children, comprising 25 daughters and 17 sons. Of these 42 children, nine were the children of Queen Amarindra, leaving 33 from 28 mothers or an average of about one child per mother. It gives an insight into the polygamy of the Chakri kings. Seeing that he had so many wives and children, one might say that he was the first of a line of highly amorous monarchs. But if he was so amorous, and given the same number of wives, would he not have had many more children? It is quite beyond dispute that birth control of any kind would not have been practised in those days. Thai royal polygamy was a custom rather than a sensual licence. It was more secure for the king in his private residence to be surrounded by loving wives to serve as his trusted attendants. Many of them were daughters of vassal princes and great nobles, who had been presented to the "high and mighty prince", so that there would be blood relations between them and the Siamese royal family, and given those kinds of offers, it would have been poor statecraft to decline.

One of the legends which many people have believed over the years is that Rama I prophesied that his dynasty would only last 150 years.

73 *Ibid.*, pages 306-307.

74 *Ibid.*, pages 308-310.

75 *List of Names of Princes and Princesses of the Chakri House, op. cit.*

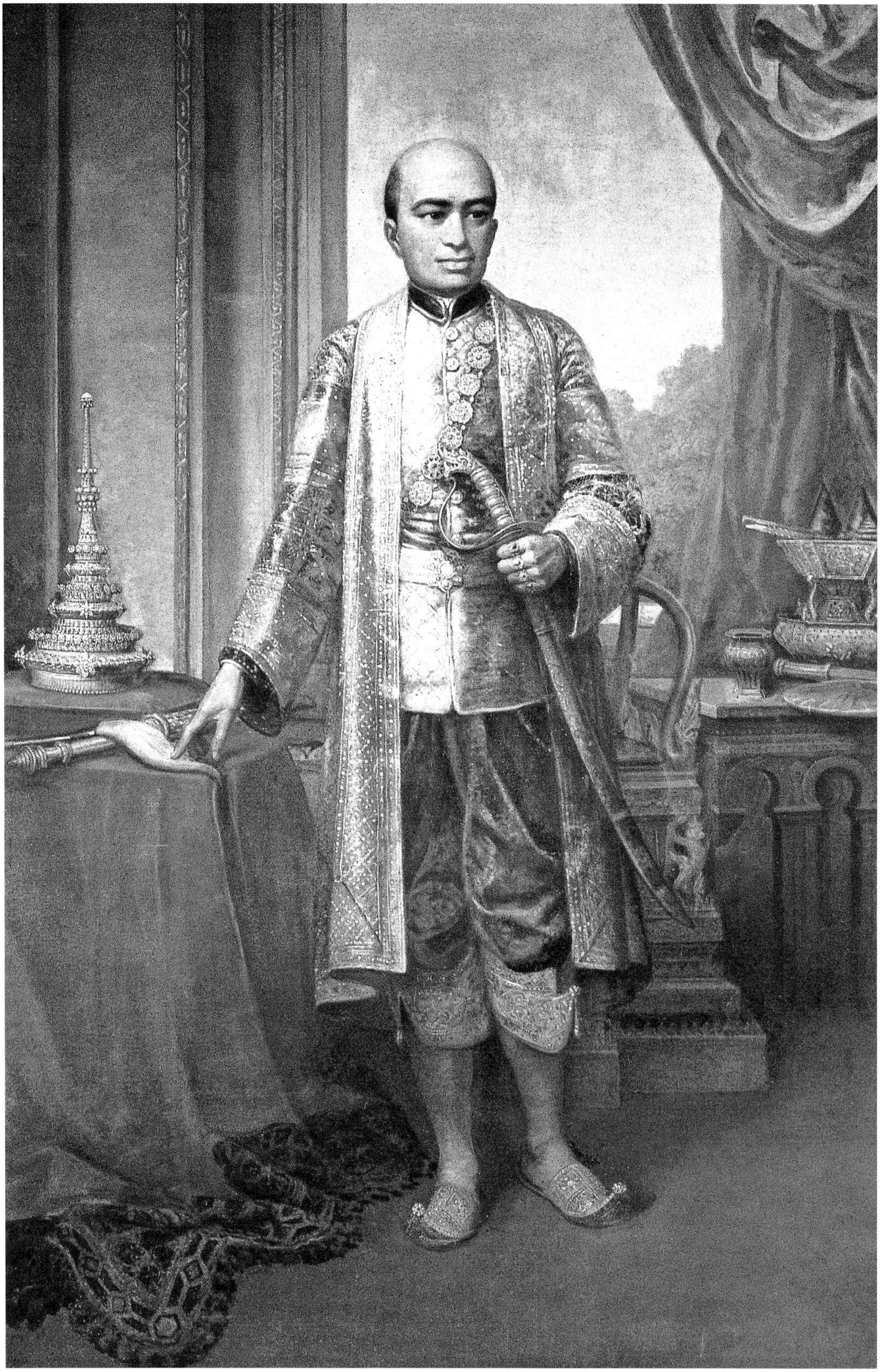

Chapter Two
THE ARTIST
(A.D. 1809 TO 1824)

A portrait of King Rama II within the Chakri Throne Hall.

For 76 years there had not been a peaceful succession to the throne of Siam. It was won after disputes or by conquest, thus the quiet and peaceful accession of Prince Isarasuntorn in 1809 was a happy contrast. He had three advantages. Of the late beloved Commander and Founder both of the new city and royal house he was the eldest son, amongst celestial princes and otherwise. He had been made *Uparaja* by his father in 1807, and was designated the heir of his choice by the late king on his death bed. Nevertheless the elective nature of the Thai monarchy was maintained by the Accession Council unanimously asking Prince Isarasuntorn to accept the throne, although they could hardly have another choice. This council, preside over by the Supreme Patriarch of the Thai Buddhist Church, was composed of princes, Buddhist prelates, and the high nobility. The water of fealty, after being cursed with menacing ferocity by the Brahmin priests according to their rites, was drunk in the capital and provinces, and disloyal subjects were expected to choke thereby revealing themselves.

The late king's body had been put into the silver Inner Urn, covered with the octagonal and ornate Golden Urn, both of which he had designed and loved, and was placed on the high golden catafalque in the Dusit Maha Prasat Throne Hall. The new king moved into the Grand Palace and set up temporary living quarters in the vast Amarindra Hall with its massive square pillars.[1] Until the coronation he was not yet a complete sovereign, his old style and titles were still in use, and he did not enjoy full ownership of the Inside of the Palace, and was, as it were, "camping" in the Outside.

The new "Lord of Life" was born on February 26th, 1768 when his father was a junior officer at Rajburi, but the family moved to Thonburi when he was two, and later he attended a temple school close by their home. He and his father were always very close, and General Chakri took his eldest son with him on his military journeys when the boy was only eight. They went together on most campaigns, and the son was with the father when he brought the sacred Emerald Buddha from Vientiane, and was with him again in Cambodia when General Chakri received the news of King Taksin's alleged insanity. He was sixteen when his father was offered and accepted the throne. After being created Prince Isarasuntorn in 1785 he was given the old palace of King Taksin as his residence and remained there for the rest of the first reign. He served directly under Rama I in four Burmese wars, and was once Quartermaster-General. In 1788 he spent the usual three months in a monastery as a monk, residing at Wat Samorai on the river, which

1 Prince Damrong: *History of the Reign of Rama II* (in Thai), page 5.

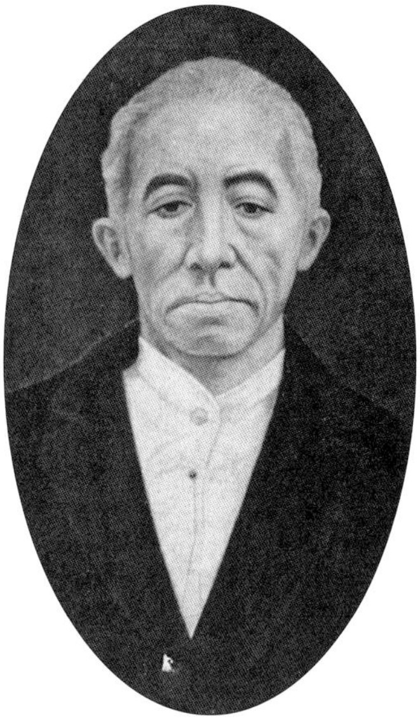

Prince Mongkut. (National Gallery Bangkok)

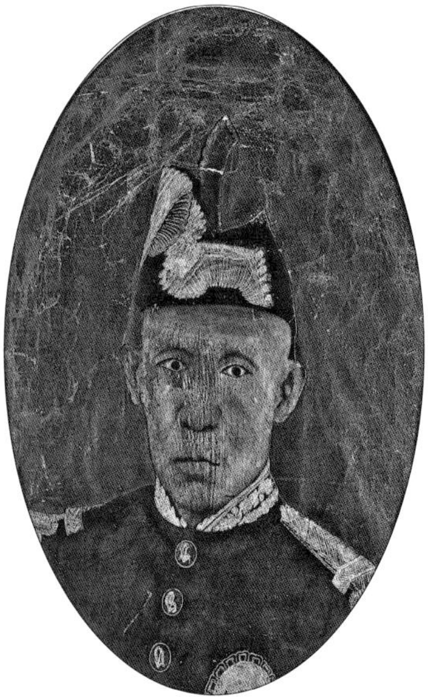

Prince Chudamani. (National Museum Bangkok)

was to become Wat Rajadhivas after it was made famous by its illustrious son. Besides having numerous minor wives, he married his first cousin, Celestial Princess Boonrod, a daughter of Rama I's second elder sister and her wealthy Chinese husband. Together they had three sons. The eldest died on the day he was born, and the remaining two, the first Chakri celestial princes at birth, were Prince Mongkut ("Crown" – born 1804), and Prince Chudamani (born 1808).

Although the succession went off smoothly, the situation both externally and internally caused anxiety. The Burmese were known to be waiting for an opportunity to attack. The elder and highly respected princes had passed away, and those remaining were not too well united. Within three days of the accession an anonymous letter was received by one of the senior ministers giving the warning that Celestial Prince Kasatra, together with some officials, was planning a revolt. This prince was the son of King Taksin and his mother was one of the daughters of Rama I, who had recognised him as a celestial prince, so in his veins flowed the blood of the two hero-kings. Soon the prince was arrested, and a commission of inquiry was set up with the king's eldest son, born of a minor wife, Prince Tup – later Prince Chesda Bodin, then only turned twenty-one, as President. Ten important officials were also arrested and all pleaded guilty to the charge. Prince Kasatra and his accomplices were in due course executed, and the last tie between King Taksin and the Chakri family was severed by this deplorable tragedy.[2]

The coronation was carried out with the full rituals of Ayutthaya as in the time of Rama I, but the important ceremony took place in the Paisal Taksin, or inner hall, of the Amarindra Group because the late king was lying-in-State in the Prasat building previously used. The new monarch's style and titles as inscribed on gold were the same as those of Rama I, and he is now generally known as Rama II. His son was to give him the posthumous title of Phra Buddha Loet La. After the coronation ceremony within the palace, there was a royal procession round the city in which 8,000 troops took part, including the artillery, probably for the first time. When the princes, prelates, and nobles were promoted in rank, Rama II followed his father in creating his only full brother, Celestial Prince Senanurak, *Uparaja*, who then went to live at the Palace of the Front. Part of the regalia which the king presented to him was a Japanese sword which became recognised as a special regalia for the Deputy King.[3]

It is curious that the ceremony for raising his mother to the exalted position of *Phra Pan Pee* (The royal lady of 1,000 years) or Queen-Mother was delayed by the king until 1810, when she was given the title and name of Somdech Krom Phra Amarindra, when both Buddhist and Brahmin priests took part. Despite the promotion of many princes and nobles, a contemporary English observer was right when he wrote, "In rank, there is no comparison between the sovereign and the most exalted of his officers or courtiers ".[4] In this the

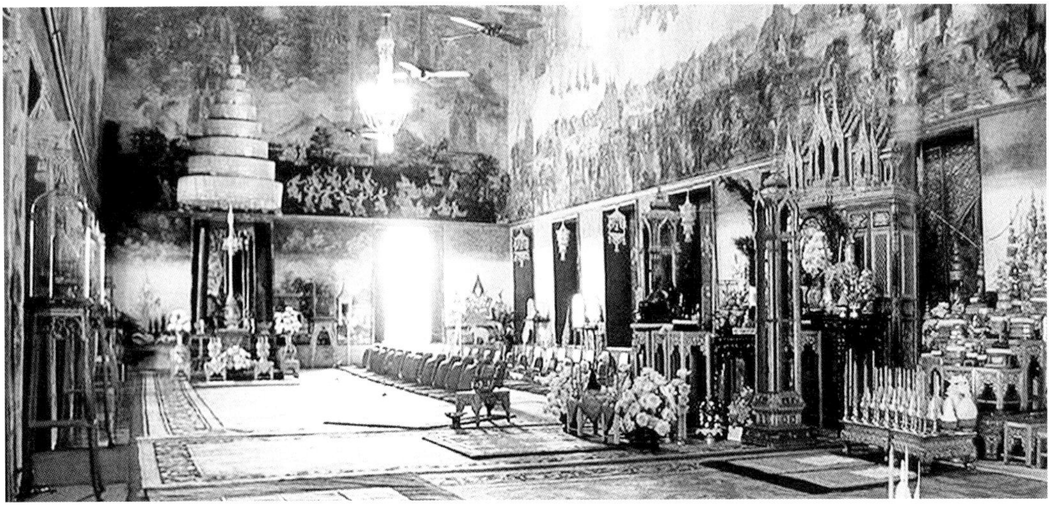

Within the Paisal Taksin throne hall. (River Books)

princes must also be included, and it is still the same in the present day. This utterly isolated glory of the king may be explained by the absence of any hereditary nobility, and the king therefore was not the *primus inter pares* as in European feudalism.

Owing to other pressing difficulties, such as threats of Burmese wars and Cambodian intrigues, the cremation of the late king did not take place until 1811, and it was the biggest affair of its kind since the fall of Ayutthaya. All details of the religious rites and the design of the huge crematorium – *Phra Meru,* or as pronounced by the Thais – *Phra Mane* – were carefully based on the examples of the old capital after meticulous research. The site of the *Phra Meru* was the south-western comer of the great lawn outside the Grand Palace, and it has ever since been the site for cremations of the king and queen as well as some of the highest royalty. With certain necessary modifications the procedure then adopted for the royal cremation has been maintained. The um left the palace in procession on a palanquin carried by sixty men shoulder high. After it had passed Wat Pho, it was transferred to the enormous golden funeral coach, called the Grand Chariot of Victory – 40 foot high and weighing over 20 tons – which required 160 men to pull with 135 men to hold it back, acting as brakes. Two such coaches, and many lesser vehicles, were constructed in the reign of Rama I, and they can be seen today in the National Museum. To take the heavy urn from the palanquin to the top of the lofty coach, an open lift, worked by a pulley, had been invented and it might well have been the first lift in the world. The coaches, the urn and the lift were all created in 1789. Many religious rites and alms-giving ceremonies preceded the actual cremation. Offerings were made to no less than 10,000 monks and coins enclosed in lime fruits were thrown to the masses from eight points around the *Phra Meru.* Clothing was distributed to the old and poor of over 70 years of age. There were ten open-air theatres, boxing matches, and colourful fireworks.

2 *Ibid.,* pages 12-14.

3 *Ibid.,* Note I, page 37.

4 John Crawfurd: *A Journal of an Embassy from the Governor-General of India to the Courts of Siam and Cochin-China,* page 373, London, 1828.

To the western mind it might seem strange to have such things at a funeral, but the king had been dead for some eighteen months, it was felt the people needed some entertainment. In addition, for the Thais it was only natural to celebrate the cremation of such an exalted personage and the end of mourning – for death itself was natural and inevitable. After the cremation the ashes were floated down the river, whilst the more solid bone relics were put into a miniature golden urn which was a replica of the *Thong Yai*. This was placed in the small mausoleum near the Amarindra Hall in company with the urn containing the relics of the Royal Premier and Supreme Ancestor.

The English envoy, John Crawfurd, whose mission to Rama II is described below, estimated that the population of Siam then was not less than five millions, and the area under cultivation was $4\frac{1}{2}$ million acres. The revenue was still from the same sources as those taxes collected under Rama I. Spirit taxes, of which the Chinese were the principal consumers, and many other taxes, were farmed out to professional tax-collectors, many of whom were Chinese. For their several privileges the Chinese had to pay a poll tax per capita. "The Siamese territory is so thinly populated, and there has been so little occasion to have recourse to land of an inferior description, that it is probable that very little of what is strictly rent exists . . . and as a natural counterbalance to the burthen of conscription, or public corvées, we find the land tax extremely light, in comparison with Hindustan, and other densely peopled countries of West Asia."[5] The minimum age for the corvée was 20, and one-tenth of the population had to give their service for three months in the year. Those exempted, other than the princes and nobles, were Buddhist monks, slaves, and the Chinese, of whom Crawfurd thought there were between 400,000 and 700,000, who had come to Siam without families, and inter-marriage with the Thais was flourishing. The rest of the free men could

BELOW RIGHT: The Ho Phra That Montien within the Grand Palace is where the ashes and relics of former kings of the Chakri dynasty are kept. (River Books)

The Maha Pichai royal carriage. (National Museum Bangkok)

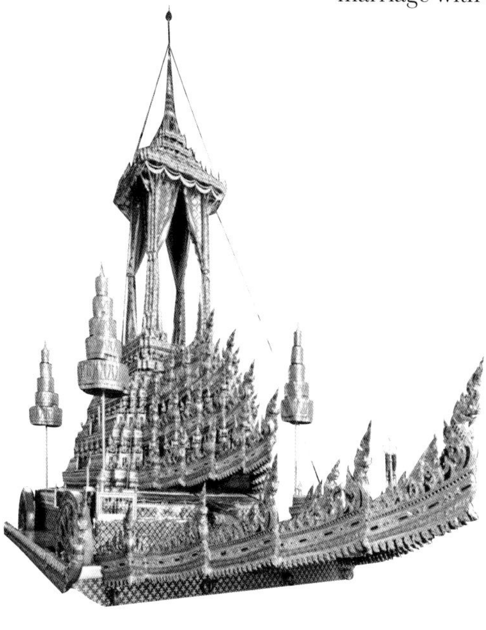

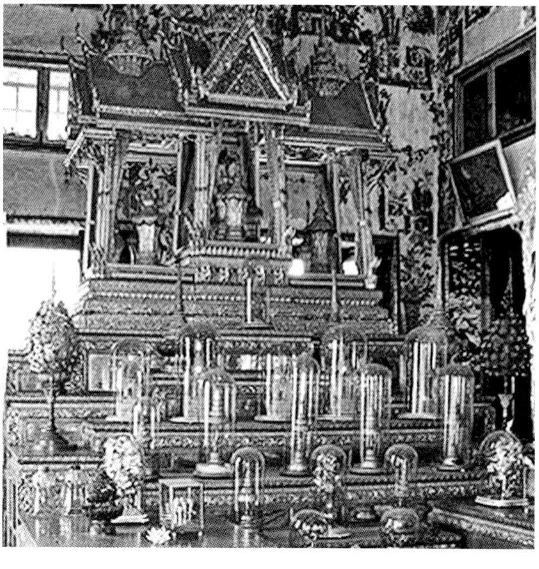

escape corvée service by payment in cash or kind, or they could provide their own slaves to do the work required.

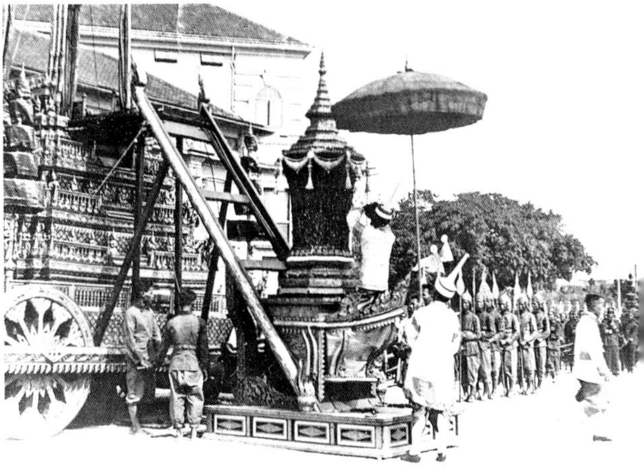

A simple lift was used to move the urn up onto the funeral carriage. (River Books)

Crawfurd[6] found that the great river Chao Phraya was fully navigable, and boats from Laos and other parts of the country would crowd the river, especially from August to December, bringing grain, salt, cotton, sapan wood, oil, and timber. On land, transport of goods was by elephants. The main foreign trade was still the junk trade with China, after which came the trade with Saigon and the Malay Archipelago. He estimated the size of the country as 190,000 square miles.[7] (198,247 square miles in 1959). Crawfurd found the climate most suitable for the production of rice, and he was enthusiastic about the fruits, finding them "excellent and various, surpassing, according to the experience of our party, those of all parts of India".[8] He went on, "The whole neighbourhood of Bangkok is one forest of fruit trees".[8] Happily for the Thais this is still the case, and most people would agree that "the most exquisite fruits of Siam are the mango, the mangustin, the orange, the durian (not eaten by royalty because of its unpleasant odour-Author), the li-chi, and the pineapple".[8]

In between family celebrations and funerals, over all of which the king of Siam had always been expected to preside, and his anxieties over Burma and the vassals, Rama II, who had come to the throne at the ideal age of 41, settled down quickly to governing his people. The registration of free men for conscription into the army or for corvée work had got into a terrible muddle during the long reign of his father, as registration was only done once in every reign. As a result it would be impossible to get the army ready in case of need. The king ordered a fresh registration, which was done by tattooing a small number on the forearm. They were registered as men of the Grand Palace, the Palace of the Front, of the princes who were *kroms*, or as men of the provincial governors. All men were permitted to change their overlords, and those who had disappeared into the jungle were given a grace period in which to return, register and receive pardon. Otherwise they would be rounded up and punished. The prescribed period of service was one month on and three months off to attend to their own livelihood, which meant corvée service for three months in the year.[9] Officials were sent out to examine the fruit orchards and rice fields for taxing. In the case of orchards only trees which were producing profits were taxed. For rice fields a proportion of the rice produced was required to be put into the royal silos. The fields were divided into two kinds. Those which had water from the river or a canal had to pay tax in relation to the size regardless of their results, whereas rice fields on high ground, depending solely on seasonal rainfall, paid taxes based only on the amount of

5 *Ibid.*, page 385.

6 *Ibid.*, pages 406-414.

7 *Ibid.*, page 452.

8 *Ibid.*, page 421.

9 Prince Damrong: *Rama II, op. cit.*, pages 48-52.

crops obtained. If it was seen that no serious effort to work the land had been made for three years, then the property reverted to the Crown.[10]

Fully aware of the evil consequences of opium smoking, which was a great source of crime, Rama I had enacted a law to forbid it. People would steal or rob to get enough money to buy opium, and the addicts fell seriously ill for lack of it. The Thai people had a belief that people who died from opium smoking became *prades,* a horrible type of malevolent spirit, as tall as the sugar palm trees, and having a long neck. It was always hungry because its mouth was so tiny that it could hardly eat anything, yet somehow it had a long tongue hanging out, and its body odour was so repellant that the *prade* itself suffered from it. On its head was a *chakra,* a sharp-edged discus which gradually cut the *prade's* long neck, causing a profusion of blood to flow; yet when the neck had been completely cut, the whole thing would grow again, thus giving the *prade* years of repeated torment. The *prade,* which could be male or female, heralded its approach with a blood-curdling shrill shriek, and its misery could only be ended by much merit being made on its behalf by close living relatives. Other evils, besides opium smoking, could also turn people into *prades,* such as being too miserly, and there are Thai people today who still believe in the phenomenon and say they have seen or heard one.

The sale of opium had also been prohibited, but neither law had proved effective. Rama II enacted a new law with more severe penalties. For smoking opium there was flogging, or being publicly exposed for three days on land and three days by boat. People who failed to inform government officials about opium offences were given sixty strokes of flogging. But anyone in possession of opium could sell it all off to the government within a prescribed period and escape any punishment.[11] It would then be exported for profit to the government. Rama II reformed the law in other ways, of which some of the more important changes can be mentioned. All contracts concerning matters of property had to be put in writing. A will had to be made in writing before four witnesses. A man could leave his property either to his wife or to his children, but he could not pass them over in favour of strangers and there was no preference for the eldest son. If a husband died intestate, the wife took the usufruct for her lifetime, and the capital was then divided equally between the children. The share for the child of a minor wife was half that for a child of the wedded wife.[12] Marriage then, as now, was purely a civil contract, with the monks only giving a blessing, and some payment had to be made by the groom on betrothal, which in theory was to compensate the bride's parents for the loss of their daughter's services. Divorce then, as at present, was possible by mutual consent; but if only one side desired it, then they had to go to

A painting by an English artist showing the Chao Phraya river and large junk. (From *The Kingdom and People of Siam,* Sir John Bowring 1857)

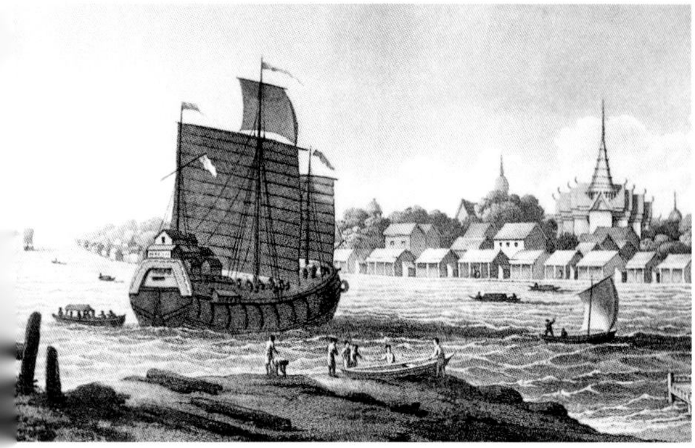

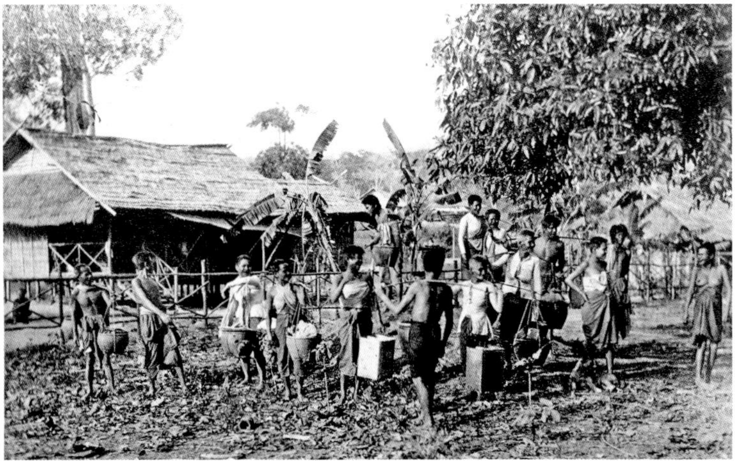

At the beginning of the Bangkok period, the majority of the population was engaged in agriculture. (River Books)

court. In any case, each side got back the capital which had been put jointly into the marriage coffer, except for the guilty party in adultery.[13]

There had already been a well-defined penal code as revised by Rama I. Punishment was mostly by flogging with a strong bamboo cane for different offences – between thirty and ninety strokes – and imprisonment was imposed only in serious cases of robbery with violence. For murder there was capital punishment, and the sentence was carried out by decapitation with a sword. For incendiary crime, the penalty was cutting off the offending hand. The old law had said that Buddhist monks found guilty of lack of chastity, after being expelled, could suffer death, but Rama II commuted it to life imprisonment with hard labour which consisted in cutting grass to feed the royal elephants. Sedition and treason were regarded as the most heinous crimes, and the punishment was death by decapitation, without any act of additional cruelty. One may find Rama II over severe in having Prince Kasatra and his followers put to death after they had all pleaded guilty. It must, however, be remembered that he had only been king for three days when the plot was discovered, and the dynasty, with which he identified the peace and well-being of the people, was only 28 years old and had to be protectol. Modem historians rightly stress that historical figures must be judged not by the moral standards of our own days, but by those of the times.[14] It is important to note that in the criminal law practices of both the first two Chakri kings, there was no class exemption.

The criminal law of any country at any time can only be judged by its results, namely, the peaceful security one can enjoy in the land. With this Crawfurd, in the reign of Rama II, was much impressed. "We walked for miles unarmed and unattended in the vicinity of Bangkok without receiving insult or offence from anyone, and never for a moment suspected danger to our person or property . . . I feel convinced that the property of a merchant or stranger visiting Siam is as secure from treachery or violence in Bangkok, either through the act of

10 *Ibid.*, pages 52-54.

11 *Ibid.*, pages 55-58.

12 Crawfurd, *op. cit.*, page 393.

13 *Ibid.*, page 394.

14 The Honourable Sir Steven Runciman: *The Writing of History*, a lecture in Kuching, March 20th, 1957.

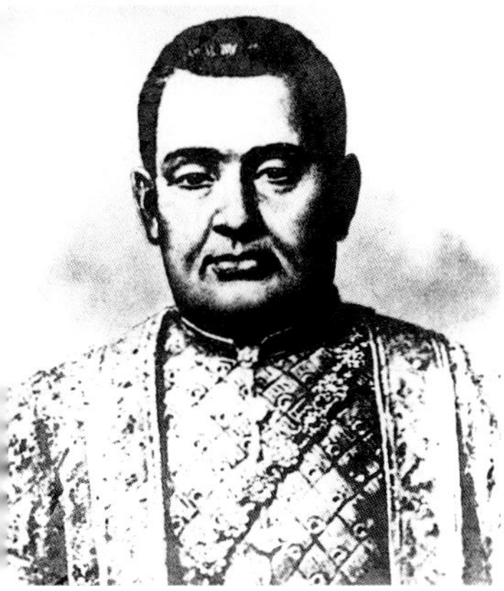

Krom Muen Chesda Bodin.
(River Books)

the government, or of private individuals, as it would be in the best regulated city in Europe."[15]

Overshadowed by his illustrious father, Rama II is more remembered today as a great artist than a good monarch. His own aims as a king were probably to consolidate the dynasty and to improve, where necessary, the reforms initiated by his predecessor. An impartial judge, such as Crawfurd, wrote that "the country prospered under his administration, that he was rarely guilty of acts of atrocity, and that upon the whole he was admitted to be one of the mildest sovereigns that had ruled Siam . . ."[16] There was one particular action of Rama II, however, which would have strong repercussions on the royal family, namely, he appointed senior princes to supervise the different departments of State even though there were noblemen as ministers. The princes acted as advisers but were senior to them. After this innovation, the princes would have more power and influence in the government until the change of regime in 1932. Gradually, but surely, the king's eldest son, Prince Tup, came more and more into prominence. He looked after the Treasury and the Port Authorities, and therefore had much to do with trade and foreign affairs. In 1813 he was created Krom Muen Chesda Bodin.[17] Some years later Crawfurd met him and was much impressed, writing that this prince was "the most intelligent of all the princes and chiefs of the Siamese court".[18] When Prince Chesda heard that Mr. Finlayson, who had accompanied Crawfurd, was a physician, he said that "he had heard that the English were acquainted with an antidote against the smallpox . . . His Highness wished to know whether the Governor-General of India would, if requested, send a skilful person to Siam to instruct the Siamese in the use of this antidote".[19]

Another prince who came much into the limelight was the king's half-brother, a non-celestial prince, Kraisorn, who was also in 1813 created Krom Muen Rakronnaret.[20] He was first in charge of the Royal Regiment of Elephants, but would later be given other important appointments. Although the princes were taking an active part in the administration, it may seem somewhat odd that they were not encouraged to travel about in the provinces, unless when in command of troops in wartime, or in the suite of His Majesty. It might have been due to a fear that the princes might intrigue with the local nobles and work up a rebellion. Even today in 1959, princes are in theory required to seek the king's permission before leaving the capital even to spend a few days at a seaside home, and it is willingly complied with as a traditional homage to the Head of the State and of the family.

Even though he was doing nothing to establish a more definite line of succession, Rama II let no suitable occasion pass when he could grant an extra mark of honour to his eldest celestial son, Prince Mongkut, born in 1804 and therefore five years old at the commencement of his father's reign. Having himself been the eldest celestial son of his own father, Rama II no doubt felt keenly conscious of the higher position of a *chao fa* or celestial prince. In 1812 Mongkut was given a grand ceremonial bath on a gorgeously decorated raft moored on the river near the Grand Palace, which was a revival of an ancient Brahmanic ritual from the Ayutthaya days. He was carried to the raft and back on a golden litter in a great procession. Although his mother, herself a celestial princess by birth, was now queen, there had been no special function to mark that fact. In 1816, when Mongkut underwent the Brahmanic tonsure ceremony – the cutting of the top knot of hair to symbolize puberty – Rama II again demonstrated, by the impressive grandeur of the occasion – greater than that enjoyed by his other and older sons – that a celestial child was truly superior to his other children.[21] It was repeated once more when in 1817 the young prince for a short while took the yellow robe as a *samnera,* or novice priest, and it is significant that his elder half-brother, Prince Chesda, was the most assiduous in rendering him the highest honours.

In the same year – 1817 – serious tragedy struck the royal family for the first time in the second reign, when the quiet, friendly, loyal, and unassuming Uparaja fell desperately ill.

The king was very upset, for he and his brother had been the best of friends, and not a cross word had ever passed between them. As his father had done for the Uparaja Sura Singhanat, Rama II went personally to nurse his younger brother, but it was of no avail, and aged only 37, the Uparaja succumbed to his disease. The inconsolable king did not appoint a successor for the rest of the reign, and the succession to the throne was left entirely vague.

Although there was a permanent Burmese threat, in reality it did not prove so serious. Rumours of a full-scale invasion in 1810 came to nothing as the Burmese lacked well organized forces in sufficient numbers. They did, however, attack in the south, and owing to the Thais' weakness on the naval front, they made some headway against Talang Island, Ranong, and Chumporn. But an army from Bangkok under the Uparaja, as well as Malay troops from Kedah, succeeded in expelling the traditional enemy. In 1819 Burma had a new monarch Bagyidaw and there were again reports of an impending Burmese invasion, but by that time the Thai army was well organised and ready for any eventuality. Crawfurd, writing only three years later,[22] said that the regular army did not fall short of 30,000 men armed with swords, spears, and European muskets. These were of British, Portuguese and American manufacture. In Siam there were between 20 to 30 walled towns which could be strongly defended. The king sent two armies to watch for the enemy. His eldest son, Prince Chesda, commanded the army placed between Rajburi and Kanchanaburi, whilst another senior prince commanded the army situated further south at Phetchaburi. It appeared that the southern army did not show such high standards of efficiency and good discipline as that under Prince Chesda.[23] This prince was then in command of an army in the field for the last time. Both forces remained on the watch until the rains came,

15 Crawfurd, *op. cit.*, page 347.

16 *Ibid.*, page 137.

17 Prince Damrong: *Rama II, op. cit.*, pages 96-99.

19 *Ibid.*, page 125.

20 Prince Damrong: *Rama II, op. cit.*, page 154.

21 *Ibid.*, pages 210-211.

22 Crawfurd: *op. cit.*, page 397.

23 Prince Damrong: *Rama II, op. cit.*, page 302.

but there was no sign of the Burmese. The bulk of the armies were then recalled to Bangkok, and only their remnants were left behind under the command of noblemen. Soon after that the Burmese ceased to cause the Thais any further anxieties, for they were to come into conflict with a far stronge opponent – Great Britain – who finally put an end to the Burmese monarchy in 1886.[24]

Cambodia presented the Chakri Dynasty with continual problems, which, in one way or another, were to persist for nearly one hundred years. At the beginning of Rama II's reign the Cambodian nobility was divided into two groups, one pro-Thai and the other pro-Vietnamese, and the king of Cambodia himself found it difficult to control either group, let alone his country. The new king, Ang Chan, claimed to have been offended by Rama I, who had not always complied with his requests. He failed to come to Bangkok for Rama I's cremation or to pay personal respects to Rama II, and instead sent his younger brother, Ang Imm. Cambodia in the past had had the positions of Deputy King and Assistant Deputy King. Rama II, exercising his rights as the overlord, appointed Ang Imm, and an even younger brother, to these two posts respectively, no doubt with a view to wooing them into greater loyalty.[25]

Emperor Gia Long of Vietnam, on the other hand, continued as always to be a good friend to the Chakri family, having sent an embassy to Bangkok to pay respects at the Lying-in-State of Rama I and congratulating the new King on his accession. Rama II naturally received the embassy as one from an equal sovereign, which indeed he was. Yet whenever any minor differences arose between Siam and Cambodia, it was always as a result of the influence of some Vietnamese officials in Phnom Penh. Rama II complained to Gia Long, who was always ready to render amicable mediation. Rama II took this somewhat placid line because he was more anxious about dangers from Burma, and it cannot be denied that in this way he showed weakness towards Cambodia. Once the Cambodians even went so far as to attack Battambang, but unsuccessfully, and on this occasion Gia Long declared that there had been faults on both sides. This was unacceptable to Rama II if he was to remain the overlord of Cambodia, so he ignored Gia Long's mediation, and the Cambodians did not try it again. All through his reign there were struggles between the pro-Thai and pro-Vietnam parties in the Cambodian capital, but because the great Emperor Gia Long was grateful to the memory of Rama I, things never quite came to a head. The only one serious anxiety came in 1819 when a canal was constructed from the Cambodian Great Lake to the Gulf of Siam by a joint Vietnamese-Cambodian effort as a short cut. Gia Long then informed Rama II that he had seized the Cambodian seaport at the canal's mouth, and the king of Siam accepted the *fait accompli,* being himself preoccupied with possible dangers from Burma. Nevertheless, he did retaliate by constructing the modern town of Paknam as the focal point for a

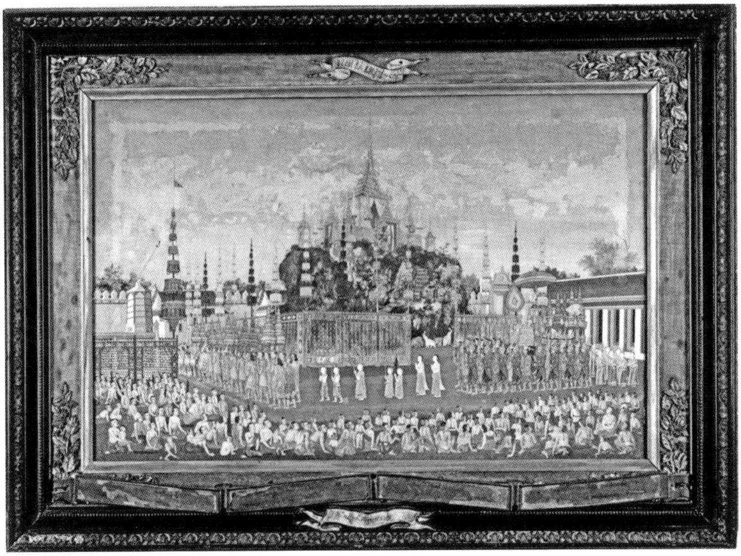

The tonsurate ceremony for Chao Fa Konton Thipayawadee.
(National Museum Bangkok)

system of forts to protect the mouth of the river, and it was to Prince Chesda that he confided the supervision of the work. Had Rama II then had the means to know that he had no need to be anxious over Burma, owing to the impending and disastrous war in which that country was about to be engaged with Britain, his entire foreign policy might well have been different.

Further Vietnamese expansion was temporarily halted when the great Gia Long died in 1820 at the age of 72. His son and successor, Emperor Minh-Mang, had different ideas from his father about dealing with Europeans, especially the French, and his new policy would alter the whole course of Vietnamese history, and indeed that of South-East Asia. There was a rumour that Gia Long had recommended Rama II to style himself Emperor as he had inherited so many vassal states from his father, but Rama II politely declined, saying that that was a Chinese custom, whereas the chief of the Thais had been known as king for centuries.[26] An important Thai embassy was sent to pay respects to the remains of Gia Long and to salute the new monarch.

In this second Chakri reign good relations continued with China. An embassy was sent in 1810, and the Chinese Imperial Court blithely went on regarding Siam as a vassal, yet as usual without the least attempt to assert any control. In June, 1821, the king heard of the demise of the Chinese Emperor and he sent a mission to express his regrets and to bring presents to the new sovereign. Both of her powerful neighbours, Burma and Vietnam, had fought with and been defeated by China, and had therefore sent tributes on that score, whereas Siam had never at any time been in conflict with that great country, yet China regarded her as a vassal just the same.

24 D. G. E. Hall, *op. cit.*, page 555.

25 Prince Damrong: *Rama II, op. cit.*, pages 88-91.

26 Prince Damrong: *Rama II, op. cit.*, Note 8, page 283.

Siam's position *vis-a-vis* her Malay dependencies became more complicated as British influence and power grew in that peninsula, especially after the cession of Penang Island by the Sultan of Kedah. Another state, Kelantan, had always been ruled by Bangkok through Terengganu, but these two states quarrelled in 1814, after which both came directly under Bangkok control, and sent their tributes through the Governor of Nakhon Si Thammarat, mistakenly called the Raja of Ligor by the British at that time. Although the Sultan of Kedah had ceded Penang Island to the British in 1786 when Siam was fighting Burma, after Siam had recovered her power having defeated the Burmese more than once, Kedah again declared her fealty. She was, however, allowed to carry on in her own way as a semi-independent state. Once he was comfortable in his mind that he had no danger of direct control from Siam, the Sultan regretted the loss of Penang Island, but the British refused to let him have it back.[27] Kedah took some warlike actions against the British, but was quickly and easily defeated. The British had paid a rent of 6,000 dollars a year for Penang, now they were given a strip of mainland opposite the island which became known as the Province of Wellesley, and the total rent was increased to 10,000 dollars a year. When the Sultan of Kedah died, he left ten sons, who were mostly from different mothers, and they squabbled over the succession until appeased by the Governor of Nakhon on behalf of Rama I. Yet soon after there were always quarrels in the Kedah family except when they were planning a revolt against Bangkok. Finally, when the new Sultan was asked to go to the Thai capital and render account of his actions, he flatly refused and would not send any more tributes. In 1821 Rama II decided on a firm action and sent forces to subdue Kedah. The sultan appealed in vain to the British for help, but they had already refused his predecessor an alliance in 1791 on the ground that Kedah was not independent of Siam. The Thai forces were successful and the sultan escaped to Penang Island as a refugee to begin his self-imposed exile. The king of Siam then abolished the sultanate and sent a son of the Governor of Nakhon to administer the state as a governor of a Thai province.[28]

Emperor Minh-Mang of Vietnam. (From *Journal of an Embassy to the Courts of Siam and Cochin-China, exhibiting a view of the actual State of these Kingdoms* by John Crawfurd (1783-1868), London, 1828).

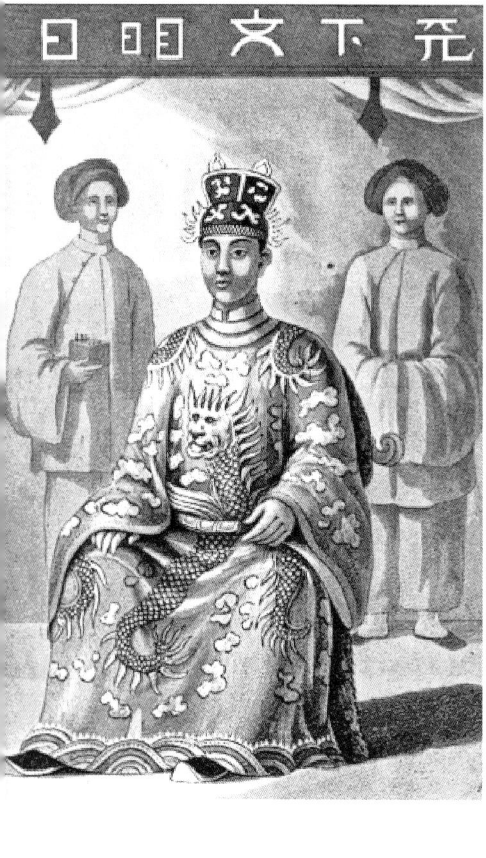

From the north-eastern frontier came tidings that the Governor of Bassac, a Laotian province under Thai rule in the north-east, had been defeated by a group of guerilla bandits. Prince Anu of Vientiane suggested to Bangkok that his own son should be sent to fight the bandits; and when he was successful, asked that he be rewarded with the governorship of the province. The matter was discussed by the king in open council, and it was strongly supported by Prince Chesda, but another, older prince opposed the idea with some heat, saying that it would make the Vientiane family far too important in that area. Prince Chesda eventually had his way, yet one day he would remember with bitterness how he had supported Prince Anu on that occasion.[29] Even in that second reign Anu took action against Siam. In 1819 he instigated his son, the Governor of Bassac, to fortify Ubol as a base for a future war against Bangkok, although he claimed at the time that it had been done for Siam's defence. He was also sending tributes to Emperor Gia Long of Vietnam which would cause trouble for the later Chakri kings, and Anu even offered to make a secret alliance with Luang Prabang against Siam.[30]

Although he was a great and successful monarch, Rama I did not have many " white " elephants. He was a connoisseur of elephants and had been presented by the different governors of provinces with six fine and powerful animals which were highly useful. In addition to these, only two white elephants were discovered and presented to him. Both were female and were by no means perfect according to the ancient treatises; with one having had its white tail cut off by its original owner in the hope of keeping the "white" elephant for his own use.[31] Rama II's reign was more auspicious in the matter of white elephants. His first, found at Battambang in 1812, was a perfect male specimen.[32] In June, 1816, the Prince of Chiang Mai discovered and gave to the king another perfect example of a male "white" elephant.[33] In the following year the Prince of Nan found yet a third male and most correctly presented it to Rama II. The king was more than delighted, for he now possessed three perfect first-class male "white" elephants which was more than any other Thai king had ever had before, as by no means all the seven "white" elephants of Maha Chakrapat of Ayutthaya were of that calibre. He had four stables built in the Grand Palace to house the four beasts, as one of the female "white" elephants of his father's was still alive.[34] Up till then the Thai national flag was plain red. Now, in order to celebrate his possession of three perfect specimens, Rama II put the symbol of a white elephant surrounded by a *chakra* in the middle of the red flag. In later reigns the *chakra* was removed, and the red flag, with the plain white elephant symbol, remained the national flag of Siam until 1917. Like his father, Rama II was deeply religious, and in 1817 he revived the big Wesak ceremonies, the occasion when the birth, enlightenment, and death of the Buddha, which had all occurred on the same day, were celebrated. He brought back the old Ayutthaya custom of a three-day great merit-making function. Animals awaiting slaughter were liberated and no killing of any kind was permitted during those days. Nor were any alcoholic drinks allowed. Instead there were continual services, sermons, and merit-making, and the whole city was tastefully decorated with bright lights and colourful flowers.[35]

Although in 1815 Ceylon already belonged to Great Britain, she remained a great Buddhist centre, and Rama II sent an ecclesiastic embassy with many presents for the monks of Ceylon. The Thai monks

27 *Ibid.*, pages 311-321.

28 *Ibid.*, pages 311-321. D. G. E. Hall, *op. cit.*, pages 434-435.

29 Prince Damrong: *Rama II*, *op. cit.*, page 272.

30 D. G. E. Hall, *op. cit.*, page 381.

31 Dibakarawongse: *Rama I*, *op. cit.*, page 215.

32 Prince Damrong: *Rama II*, *op. cit.*, pages 150-152.

33 *Ibid.*, page 207.

34 *Ibid.*, pages 213-214.

35 *Ibid.*, pages 215-220.

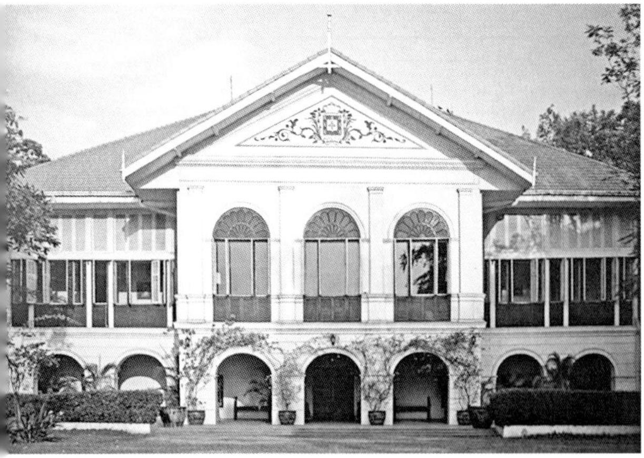

The Portuguese embassy on the banks of the Chao Phraya river. (River Books)

brought back seeds from the bhodi tree, derived from the original holy bhodi tree, under which the Lord Buddha had sat on the day of his enlightenment, which seeds had been sent to Ceylon by the great Emperor Asoka.[36] After a certain serious cholera scourge was over, Rama II, as a special merit-making gesture, caused the *mantras* or Buddhist hymns to be translated from Pali into Thai so that the congregations could follow and appreciate what the monks were chanting. Although he was a devout Buddhist, Rama II gave complete tolerance to all religions, and he protected the Christian priests and churches as much as he did those of Islam. By then the reforms of the Buddhist hierarchy by Rama had taken effect, and conversions to Christianity had begun to decline in number. Thai Christians were mostly descendants of the Portuguese, who, since Ayutthaya, had widely intermarried with the Thais. A contemporary English visitor thought that there were 800 Thai Christians in the whole of Bangkok.[37]

The first envoy to come to Bangkok in this second reign was once again a Portuguese, Carlos Manoel Silveira, sent by the Governor of the colony of Macao. As he had not been sent by the king of Portugal, Rama II received him not as a royal envoy, but a foreign merchant.[38] His mission was to investigate the possibilities of trade and, after the Portuguese vessel went back, Silveira remained behind. The Thais feared that there would be another war with Burma and they were eager to buy modern weapons for that purpose. The Portuguese were willing to sell muskets and other armaments which made Silveira popular. There was the usual exchange of presents, and according to Thai custom the king gave in return presents of the same value. Thus when one reads about the King of Siam receiving so many muskets as gifts, he had in reality bought them. The king made Silveira a junior nobleman with the rank of *Luang*, and also presented him with a house on the river which is today the site of the Portuguese Embassy. The Portuguese Government wanted Silveira accepted as their consul, but the Thais were not yet ready to sign a treaty, and the Portuguese were only given a trading permit,[39] which allowed them to put up a shipbuilding yard. Eventually, however, Silveira was accepted as Consul.

It was in 1822, under King George IV, that the British came fully into the Thai picture again with the mission of John Crawfurd, sent by the Marquess of Hastings, who was Governor-General of India. Crawfurd had been a physician in the Bengal Medical Service since 1803, had served under Stamford Raffles in Java, and had been British Resident at Singapore.[40] Besides his diplomatic mission, Crawfurd had been told to get as much information about Siam as possible, and so successful was he that his report became a large book. In the

Governor-General's letter introducing Crawfurd to Rama II, he wrote, "In token of the esteem and respect of the English nation for your Majesty, I send into your presence my Envoy, with an earnest desire to promote the friendship and intercourse which has of late so happily recommenced between the English and Siamese nations . . . The influence and authority of the British nation extends from Ceylon to the mountains which border upon China, and from the confines of Ava to those of Persia, over ninety millions of subjects, and we desire not to increase it . . . we are at peace and friendship with . . . the Kings of Eastern and Western Persia, with the Princes of Arabia, with the Turkish Sultan, and with the Emperor of China. The great King of England, separated from his Indian dominions by distance of half the globe, is too far away to govern them directly himself, and has delegated to me his authority. I anxiously desire the happiness and prosperity of the people thus entrusted to my care, and solicit for them the advantage of an intercourse and friendship with so great a monarch as your Majesty . . . I desire from your Majesty neither port, settlement, fort, nor factories; neither do I claim that our merchants resorting to your Majesty's country should be exempted from its laws. But if any regulations touching foreign commerce should be found to bear hard upon our merchants . . . I shall trust to your Majesty's wisdom and friendly disposition to have them modified or removed . . . Mr. Crawfurd . . . I have selected him . . . because he is well acquainted with the manners and customs of the nations to the Eastward, from his long intercourse with them . . . Mr. Crawfurd will offer your Majesty certain gifts in my name."[41] The presents were 300 muskets, much desired by Siam, a carriage complete with a horse to draw it, and many other objects.[42] The main aims of the Crawfurd mission were to get the duties reduced and to have the regulations against British ships modified, and to have the royal trading monopoly abolished. On the British side they were prepared to have the harbour dues raised.

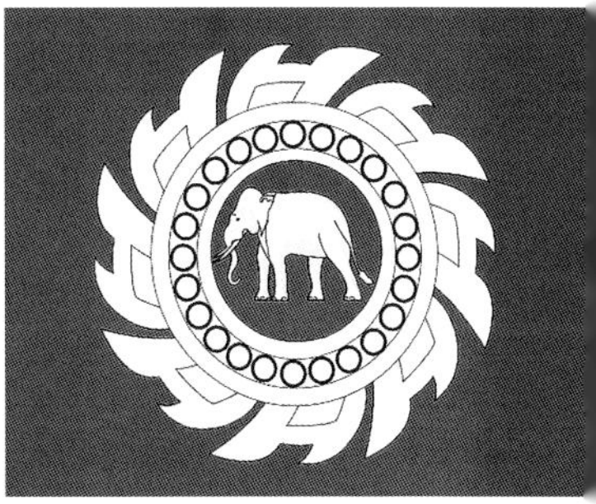

The Thai flag during the second reign. (River Books)

The mistake made by Lord Hastings was to imagine that because he had known other Asian peoples, Crawfurd would be in a position to understand the Thais. The Asian countries which Crawfurd knew were those already under British domination with their peoples docile and submissive. This was far from the case in Siam, and more than once in his book Crawfurd complained of the "vanity" of the Thais. "This people, of half-naked and enslaved barbarians, have the hardihood to consider themselves the first nation in the world, and to view the performance of any servile office to a stranger as an act of degradation."[43] Again he raged that " during our residence in Siam, we could obtain neither by intreaty nor promise of reward, the services of the lowest of the people for menial purposes."[44] "The lowest peasant considers himself superior to the proudest and most elevated subjects of any other country.[45] It is true that this proud people were, certainly to Crawfurd, indecently dressed, and even the Lord Treasurer chose to negotiate with him naked down to the waist.

36 *Prince Damrong: Tates of Ancient Times, op. cit.*, page 88.
37 Crawfurd: *op. cit.*, page 451.
38 *Collected History*, Part 62, page 12 (in Thai), *op. cit.*
39 *Ibid.*, pages 15-18.
40 D. G. E. Hal!, *op. cit.*, page 445.
41 Crawfurd, *op. cit.*, Appendix c, pages 595-596 and Prince Damrong's translation into Thai. *Collected History*, No. 62, pages 25-26.
42 *Collected History*, No. 62, *op. cit.* (in Thai), page 28.
43 Crawfurd, *op. cit.*, page 88.
44 *Ibid.*, page 345.
45 *Ibid.*, page 345.

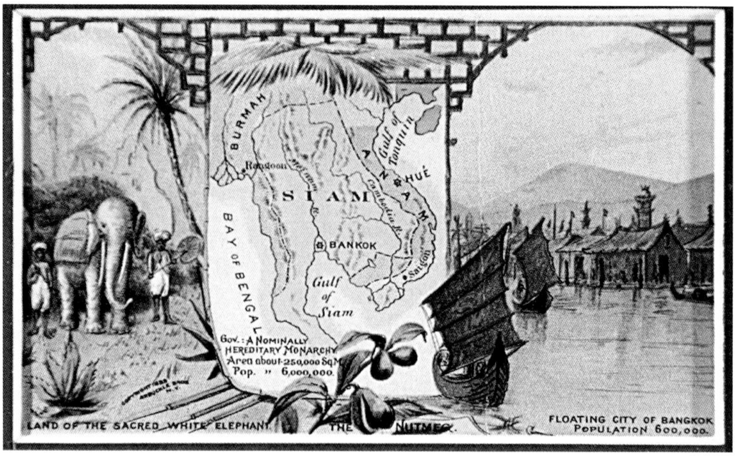

A postcard of the period which endeavours to capture the essence of Siam. (Paisarn Piemmettawat)

Thus there was a mutual antipathy from the very first. Yet Crawfurd felt that the Thais were "temperate and abstemious," and he noted the "absence of that implacable spirit of revenge".[46]

The British envoy was granted a royal audience in the Amarindra Hall, and of Rama II he wrote, "as he appeared seated on his throne, he had more the appearance of a statue in a niche, than of a living being. He wore a loose gown of gold tissue, with very wide sleeves. His head was bare, for he wore neither crown nor any orament on it . . . The words which His Siamese Majesty condescended to address to us, were delivered in a grand, and oracular manner."[47] There was the awkward question, "Have you been sent with the knowledge of the King of England?"[48] To which Crawfurd had to reply in the negative with the explanation that George IV was too far away. It was clear that Siam did not wish to deal with the Governor-General of India and would prefer direct intercourse with the King of England.[49]

The one great obstacle to both sides was that there were no Thais who could speak English any more than there were any English who could speak Thai. This resulted in much unfortunate misunderstanding. Interpreters on both sides were persons of very humble standing, hence the great reluctance to let Crawfurd take his own interpreters to the royal audience. They were Thais who had previously been domestic servants in Penang and could speak to Crawfurd in Malay.[50] Crawfurd had come to Bangkok imbued with all the prejudices of the British people in Penang, whereas the Thai high nobility were accustomed to deal with Chinese merchants who only thought in terms of huge profits and were willing to be humble and conform to Thai customs. Europeans, on the other hand, desired to preserve their dignity and prestige as well as deriving large profits in their trade.

The negotiation was slow and irksome to Crawfurd, being often interrupted by court mourning – a frequent occurrence in a large royal family – and there were other ceremonies as well. The State Monopoly and the prevailing customs of the time made it possible for the Thai government to buy the best foreign goods at the lowest price. They could also buy Thai goods at the lowest cost and then sell them to foreign merchants at the highest price. Despite the delays which upset Crawfurd, there were also some diverting entertainments. The Lord High Treasurer gave a dinner party for fourteen Europeans and Crawford said, "the table was abundantly furnished with viands, dressed in a cleanly way, not offensive to the European palate, as is most commonly the case with Indian cookery." The Phra Klang sat close to the table, but did not partake of the food.[51]

Another difficulty was that the Thais were clamouring for firearms, but the British were reluctant to sell as they knew that the weapons were needed for the possible war with Burma. Britain's own war with Burma was still two years off, so Crawfurd had to say that Britain could not sell arms which were intended to be used against her friend. The Thais wanted to sell large cargoes of sugar and other products, but the British would not commit themselves to any long-term promises. Crawfurd had been instructed to avoid discussing the cession of Penang to the British, the flight of a later sultan to that island, and his eventual restoration to Kedah, but the matter came up in the middle of a talk. The Thai position was that thc sultan was a vassal and he should have come to Bangkok and laid his complaints before the king in a proper manner, instead of running away and placing himself under foreign protection. If the sultan had done the right thing, they said, he would have obtained justice. Crawfurd had to admit that the British title to Penang was doubtful, and he praised the Thai prudence in not making claims which were impossible to enforce.[52] All was then at peace in Kedah, there was friendliness between the Thai and British-Indian Governments, and he later stressed that Kedah was indeed a vassal of Siam.[53] In the last talk with the Phra Klang, Crawfurd stated that British ships were well treated in the harbours and ports of Siam.

When he was shown a draft of a letter from the Phra Klang to the Governor-General, Crawfurd protested, but he was told that it was not etiquette for the king to write to anyone lower than another sovereign, so a compromise was reached whereby the letter would be from the Deputy of the Phra Klang to the Secretary of the Government of India. Crawfurd agreed that the Thai insistence on etiquette was mild for he remembered that the King of Burma had wished to address the king of England as one of his vassals.[54] Crawfurd did succeed in securing many modifications of the regulations hitherto imposed. The number of British ships admitted to Bangkok was to be unlimited, and if at least five British ships would come per year the duty would be reduced from eight per cent, to six per cent. But the ships would still have to be searched at Paknam and all canons and other firearms had to be put ashore before the vessels could proceed to Bangkok, where the Superintendent of Customs would assist the masters in the buying and selling of the goods, and the Thai government also promised that the harbour charges would not be raised.[55]

Crawfurd did not only have a farewell talk with the Phra Klang

46 *Ibid.*, page 346.

47 *Ibid.*, page 94.

48 *Ibid.*, page 95.

49 *Ibid.*, page 101.

50 *Collected History*, No. 62, pages 28-29.

51 Crawfurd, *op. cit.*, page 154.

52 Crawfurd, *op. cit.*, pages 159-160.

53 *Ibid.*, page 167.

54 *Ibid.*, page 169.

55 *Ibid.*, page 172.

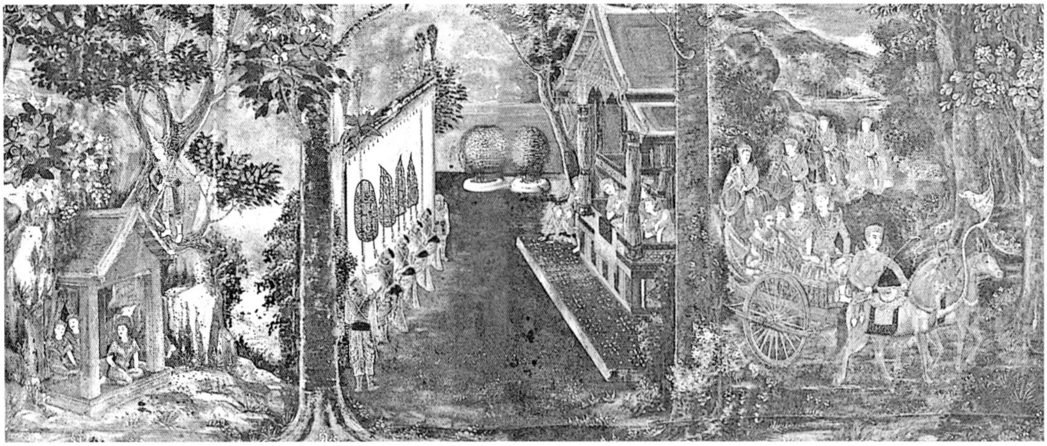

King Rama II was an artist who was also keen on poetry and drama. (National Museum Bangkok)

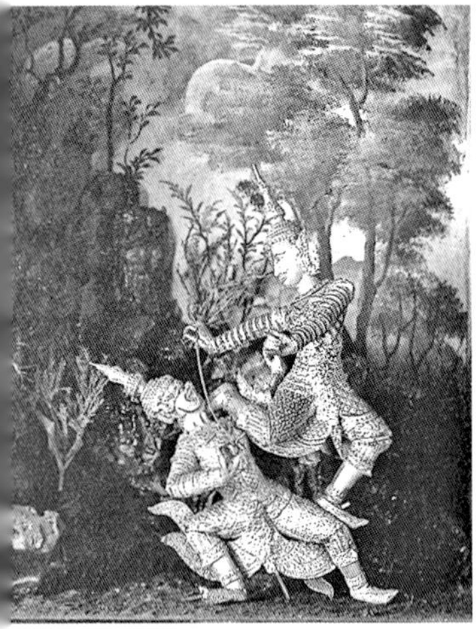

Dance drama derived from the writings of King Rama II. (National Museum Bangkok)

before he left Bangkok, but also another surprise audience with Prince Chesda who conveyed the king's regrets at not being able to grant him an audience for leave-taking owing to yet another Court mourning. The prince assured Crawfurd that the king was friendly and promised to protect all English merchants, adding that he himself was anxious to see plenty of trade between his country and British possessions. When Crawfurd's ship left there were no charges levied against it because it was carrying an embassy. Even though he did not obtain all that he had hoped for, Crawfurd wrote thus about the Thais : "The Siamese are one of the most considerable and civilized of the groups of nations inhabiting the tropical regions, lying between Hindustan and China."[56] He made good use of the time when he was waiting in between the talks – he spent four months in Bangkok – for he made soundings of the river, surveyed for map making, and obtained much information of all kinds. It was on July 16th, 1822 that Crawfurd left Bangkok.

Although his was a full and busy reign both in external and internal affairs, Rama II is best known today as a great artist. He had already been recognised as one of the greatest poets in his father's time and prominent in the group of friends who helped Rama I compose his immense and lengthy epic poems. Rama II was intensely interested in the Thai classical ballet, both the *khon* and the *lakorn*, and he personally supervised the revision and improvement of the dance steps and positions, thus it is to him that the Thais of today owe the high and pure standard of their classical dancing. He found that it was difficult to fit the steps and positions to the chanting of the poems from Rama I's period, and himself caused seven epic poems to be written or re-written. One of these – *Inao* – a romantic and amorous story with Javanese background – he wrote entirely himself and it covered forty-five volumes of the old type of Thai books. This poem was his best, and the poetry was not only exquisitely beautiful in the descriptive parts and the love scenes, but there was also a great deal of humour, and the story further served as an accurate account of the Thai habits, manners, and customs of his time, even though the story was meant to

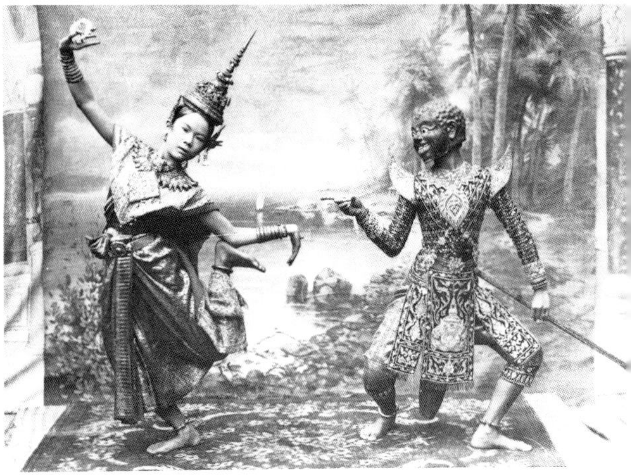

Dance drama from Sangh Thong, a story written by King Rama II. (River Books)

be set in Java in earlier times. For the six other poems – a new version of the *Ramakien* being the longest at thirty-three volumes – he recruited other poets as Rama I had done. However Rama II wrote most of it himself and the number of collaborators was smaller. He took pleasure in providing inspiration for other poets, and the best and his great rival at the time was a commoner by the name of Phu (1787-1855). The king enjoyed working and discussing poetry with Phu and he was never put out by the latter's sharper wit, and, to some critics, greater artistry. Phu was made a noble as Khun Suntonwohan (Beautiful Speech) and he wrote many long poems of his own. Amongst other collaborators of Rama II was his eldest son, Prince Chesda, and it has been said that he sometimes bitterly resented Phu's witty criticism of his work, when they all met to have the different parts read out aloud and discussed, making various alterations before the king accepted the final version of their joint work. Often they had the dancers brought in to try out the steps to fit the poetry which was altered whenever it did not match the ballet.[57] Thus in the reign of Rama II the Thai classical ballet was fully restored to its status before the collapse of Ayutthaya or it might even have been improved. While on the subject of Thai dancing, it may be as well to stress that the Thai ballet performances are not religious or temple dances, for there is no music or dancing connected with the Buddhist religion. Some misconceptions in the west may be due to the fact that they are sometimes performed at festival times, or at cremations, but these are not part of the religious observances.

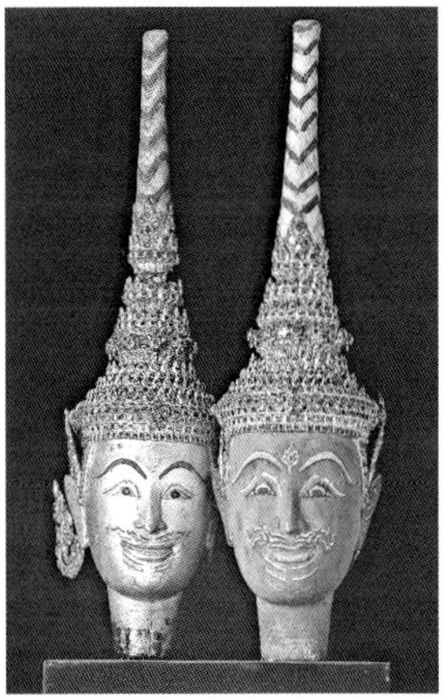

Two puppet heads created by King Rama II. (National Museum Bangkok)

Rama II was also responsible for commisioning architectural work and interior decoration. His father had concentrated on rebuilding Ayutthaya in Bangkok, so that everything was in Ayutthayan style. Rama II incorporated other styles such as Chinese and European, so that today, it is difficult to single out those parts which date solely to the reign of King Rama I. Rama II ordered the design and laying out of the "Garden on the Right" in the Grand Palace compound. It had a large lake, lined with bricks, which had several islands, large and small, all connected together by charming little bridges of diverse designs. On some of the islands there were Chinese pagodas, on others little European pavilions, and the king took his meals or listened to music in these delightful buildings. There was boating on the lake, and sometimes evening parties were held when the court wore fancy dress, and all the little canoes which were paddled round the islands had bright lamps of myriad hues. On such occasions there were competitions of poetry and song. In a small theatre on one island a ballet drama was staged. All round the lake there were many kinds of beautiful birds, some in large cages with others tethered to open perches, and their

56 *Ibid.*, page 310.

57 Prince Damrong: *Rama II, op. cit.*, pages 257-261.

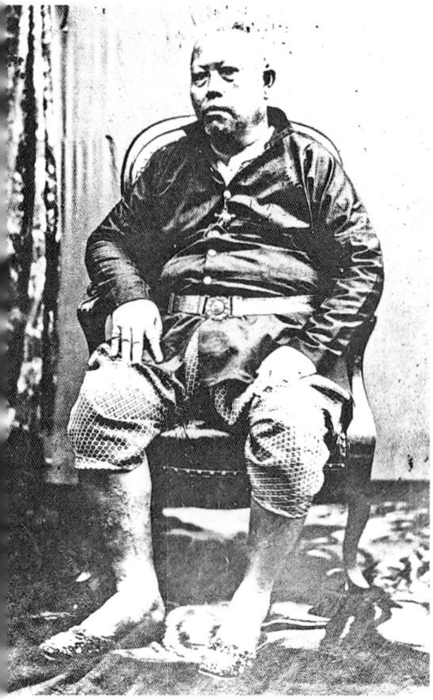

Prince Pramoj, 61st child of Rama II. (National Archives Bangkok)

The construction of the *prang* of Wat Arun was ordered by Rama II but it had not progressed very far by the end of his reign. (River Books)

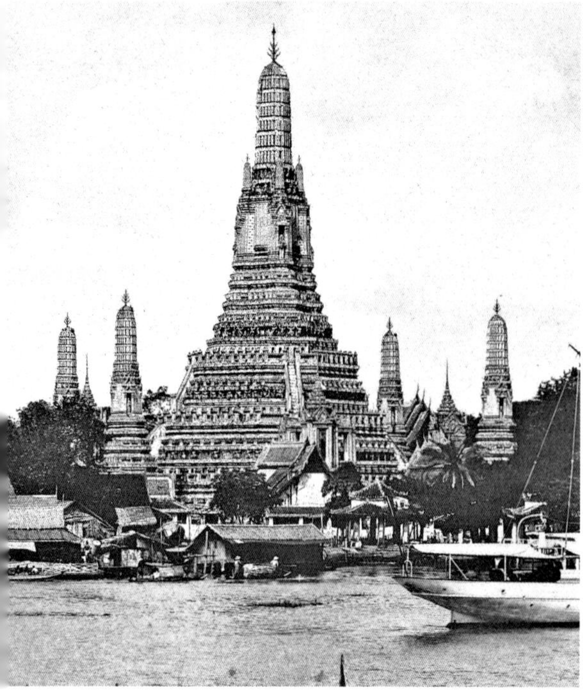

cries were sometimes deafening. But the "Garden on the Right" had not only been laid out for the royal pleasure. When the king was not using it, and particularly on special days during festivals, it was open to the public which included foreigners from the west and the vassal states. Sadly, the "Garden on the Right" no longer exists.[58]

Amongst the building work conceived by Rama II, the greatest was the tower of Wat Arun which dominates the Bangkok river on the west bank. It was not, however, completed until the following reign. It is a highly decorated building with thousands of cups and saucers broken up and then fixed on the walls to look like flowers. This has resulted in the erroneous but amusing story that the king had asked his devoted subjects to donate their crockery to decorate the temple.

In 1823 the king suffered a bereavement in the death of his full sister, his last surviving sibling. After her cremation there was a fight between the entourages of two important ministers as to who had seniority in passing through the main gate of the Grand Palace. Many wise old courtiers observed that this was an ill omen for the king, something further confirmed by the two deaths, in quick succession of two of the king's white elephants. Rama II was so distressed by all these events that when his eldest celestial son, Prince Mongkut took the yellow robe as a bikkhu, a fully-fledged monk, the king had the ceremony performed privately instead of making it an important function as on all previous occasions connected with that prince. The prince-priest went to reside at Wat Samorai on the river where Rama II himself had been a monk during the former reign.[59]

The routine of Rama II's daily life was largely similar to that of his father's, except that he undertook a good deal of artistic work himself. After luncheon he spent his time engaged in sculpture, both carving and modelling. Some of the exquisite carving on the doors of Wat Pho and other temples were the work of his own hand. According to Crawfurd, Rama II himself gilded a Buddha image every day.[60] He went out often to inspect the work being carried out on different buildings. In the evening he first listened to a sermon, then after the affairs of state were over, he discussed or composed poetry with his relatives and friends. His other favourite recreation the ballet, and he much enjoyed the amenities of the pleasant "Garden on the Right." Although he did not appear to neglect his duty of giving official audiences and carried them out as his father had done when affairs of State were over, he was able to relax more than his father could.[61] Rama II was a mild and gentle person and he was clearly as much loved as he was respected. No real first-hand portrait of him exists, but all accounts agree that he had a kind face, was almost bald, with a slight and graceful figure. Such features appear in the composite picture of him which hangs in the Hall of Kings in the Chakri Building of the Grand Palace.

Rama II, like most of the Chakri family, had many children. Altogether he had 73 – 38 boys and 35 girls from 38 different mothers, with 51 being born before his accession. Of these there were seven celestial children, six boys and one girl. The one Thai royal mother was Princess Boonrod, his first cousin, with three boys of whom Mongkut and Chudamani survived to maturity. The other four celestial children were those of a Laotian princess of Vientiane, and one, Prince Maha Mala would become prominent in later years and was the founder of the important family of Malakul, one of whom is Thai Ambassador in London at the time of writing, and another a highly efficient Minister of Education. Although most of the minor wives had only one child each, there were some who had five or six children.[62]

None of Rama II's daughters ever married. His 61st child, Prince Pramoj, was to have successful and important descendants in Seni Pramoj, leader in the U.S.A. of the Thai Resistance Movement in World War II and a very eminent lawyer, and Kukrit Pramoj, one of the foremost Thai journalists and intellectuals of today. The present Queen Sirikit, is descended through her mother from Rama II's 49th child, Prince Nuam, founder of the Snidwongse family.

Within a few days of Celestial Prince Mongkut's initiation into the Buddhist priesthood, the king fell seriously ill. The early symptoms were those of general giddiness and stiffness in the joints. He chose to act as his own doctor and prescribed for himself different traditional Thai medicines which had previously suited him well and effected a good cure. When he felt cold he asked for a warming medicine, and when this made him too hot he took a cooling draught. However, his self ministration was of no avail and he eventually went into a coma for eight days. When the court physicians were at last called in, they made up other prescriptions which the king was no longer able to swallow. He died on July 21st, 1824, aged 56 years and 5 months. (Most Thai books give his age as 58).

No fixed order of succession to the throne had by then been established, and since the death in 1817 of his younger full brother, no prince had been appointed *Uparaja* in his place. Although Prince Mongkut, as the eldest celestial son, had at different ages been given the most high honours, there was no clear cut declaration that he was the Heir Apparent. Having fallen ill so suddenly and being so long in a coma, Rama II had not been in a position to designate a successor as his father had done in 1809. Thus when he died he left a vacant throne.

The keynote of his reign was the consolidation of the power and prestige of the Chakri Dynasty, so that the good work of its founder could be carried on, and Rama II himself no doubt will be known to posterity as one of the greatest artists of the Bangkok period.

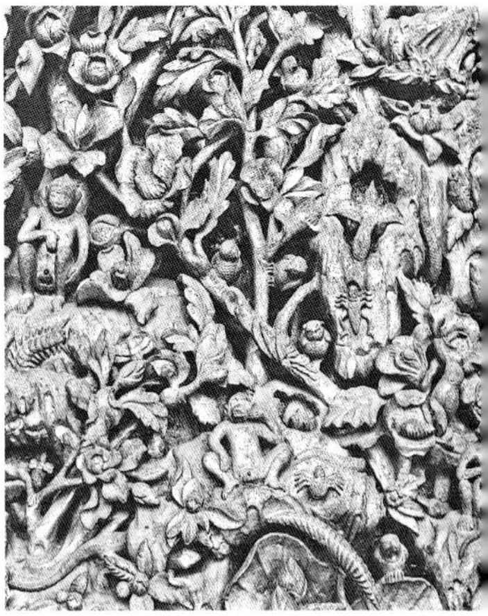

Carved doors from Wat Suthat. The portion personally carved by the king was damaged in a fire and is today conserved in the National Museum. (National Museum Bangkok)

59 *Ibid.*, pages 378-379.

60 Crawfurd, *op. cit.*, page 137.

61 Prince Damrong: *Rama II, op. cit.*, pages 393-394.

62 *List of Chakri Princes and Princesses, op. cit.*, pages 19-37.

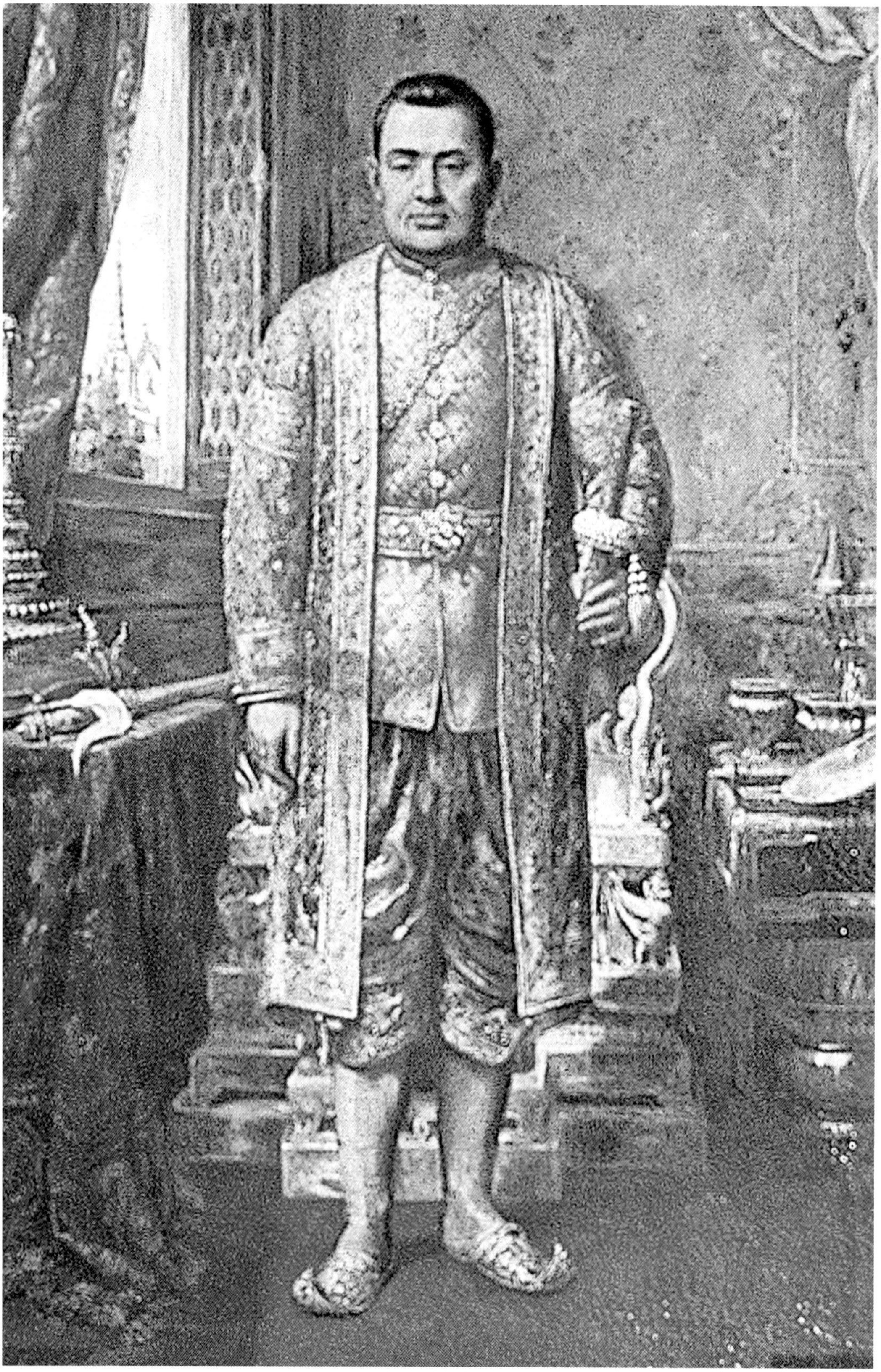

Chapter Three
THE RULER
(A.D. 1824 to 1851)

Imagined portrait of Rama III. (Chakri Throne Hall)

Prince Chesda, who then became king, was for a long time among the great majority of Thai monarchs who were almost completely unknown in the western world. But in 1957 there was published in the U.S.A. an excellent monograph on this king by an American scholar, Walter F. Vella.[1] The work is unique in being one of the few books on Thai history by a westerner wherein one finds Thai sources quoted and documentated as much as western ones. As Vella himself says: "The Third Reign of the Bangkok Dynasty is, in many respects, particularly rewarding for study. It is a period by and large typical of traditional Siam, unmarked by any drastic social, economic, or cultural changes. Yet, because it is relatively recent in time, a considerable quantity of Siamese documentation has been preserved for the period."[2] Taking full advantage of his considerable knowledge of Thai, he has made excellent use of the plentiful material.

One of his views, though very important, cannot, however, be sustained regarding the succession practices of those days. Vella says: "Rama II had one queen who had borne him two sons with the highest inherited title of *Chao Fa* – Prince Mongkut and Prince Chudamani. *The former prince had the clearest rights to the throne.*"[3] This is the view of many western writers and it dates from the reign of King Mongkut, owing largely to their mistaken belief that because he was the son of a minor wife, Prince Chesda was illegitimate. True enough in his father's reign his half-brother, Mongkut, had repeatedly been given the highest honours far above the rest, yet at no time did Rama II ever declare that the succession should go to the eldest celestial or *Chao Fa* son. The very position of the *Uparaja* in itself undermines this theory. The *Uparaja* of Rama II, like that of Rama I, was his full brother. Had either of these Uparajas survived his elder brother, he might well have succeeded to the throne. Rama II's own claims to the throne were based, not on his being a *Chao Fa*, but on his succeeding his uncle as *Uparaja*, and on the king's choice made on his deathbed, which was accepted by the Accession Council. Yet if an *Uparaja* was "an heir apparent"[4] why was the deathbed declaration made? In fact, it throws doubt on the automatic claims even of an *Uparaja*. The real claims of those days clearly rested on the choice of the dying sovereign and its acceptance by the Accession Council. No *Uparaja* had been appointed since 1817, and, being in a coma, Rama II could not declare his deathbed choice. Thus constitutionally the throne was vacant with no one having better rights than another, though different individuals

1 Walter F. Vella: *Siam under Rama III*. Published in New York for The Association For Asian Studies, 1957.

2 *Ibid.*, Preface.

3 *Ibid.*, page 4.

4 *Ibid.*, page 4.

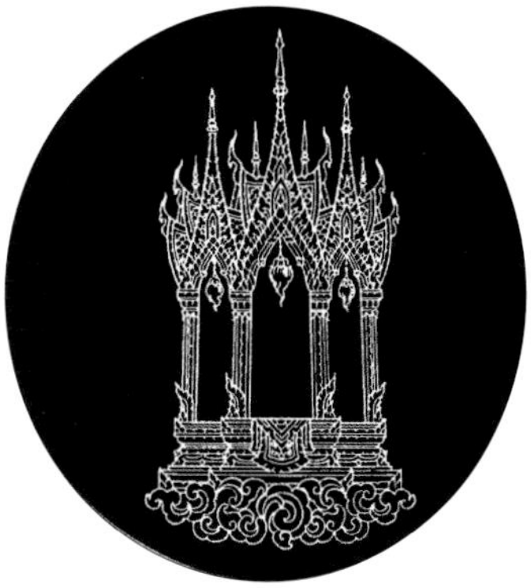

The symbol of King Rama III.

would naturally have their private preferences. The whole matter rested with the Council which proclaimed Prince Chesda as the new monarch with no dissenting voice, and any suggestion that he was a usurper is without constitutional basis.

Prince Mongkut had just entered the monastery as a monk, and he took no part in the proceedings. He would still be very young when he left the monastery after the customary period of three months, thus it was unlikely that he would be given any high or interesting post, seeing that the new king had many able men of his own age to assist him. The eldest *Chao Fa* therefore decided to remain in the Order and to make it his career.

Prince Chesda was his father's third child and eldest surviving son. His mother's name was Riem, and she was the only daughter of a nobleman created in the first reign – Phraya Nonthaburi and his wife, Peng. Phraya Nonthaburi had been in the service of Rama II since he was still Prince Isarasuntom, and it was while they were all living at the old palace of King Taksin that he took Riem as his third minor wife, and with her had three sons. Tup, later promoted to be Prince Chesda, was the eldest, and the other two died in infancy. When Prince Isarasuntom became King Rama II, the Lady Riem was recognized as a *Chao Chom* (Royal Lady Companion) First Class, and she was given charge of the royal kitchens.[5]

In his father's reign, at the early age of 21, the new Lord of Life had had the unpleasant task of investigating the alleged plot in favour of King Taksin's son and nephew of Rama I. By his ability and assiduity he progressively won his father's approbation and was given many highly important offices. Better perhaps, than anyone, he understood the necessity of foreign trade to supplement the national revenues. He himself owned many trading ships and was so successful that his father laughingly called him "The Merchant".[6] Despite his many offices he found time to visit the king every day at both his morning and evening audiences. Even a heavy tropical downpour of rain did not deter him, and when he got wet walking from his litter to the audience hall, he changed his clothes behind a screen in the ante-chamber. Popular with both princes and nobles, he kept an open house and entertained lavishly. He assisted his uncle, the *Uparaja*, as a supreme judge and was noted for his sense of justice and impartiality. He freely and constantly gave alms to the poor and aged, and on all festival days bought and set free all kinds of animals which would otherwise be slaughtered. After the death of the Uparaja in 1817 he was given command of the Royal Police, the forerunner of the Guards Division – the cream of the regular army.[7] Thus at the meeting of the Accession Council there was no question of their offering the crown to any other prince. The Council declared that the country was not yet in a settled state and there were many enemies abroad, thus a prince who was highly experienced in the affairs of State was needed as the new king.[8]

Following the demise of Rama II the now well-established

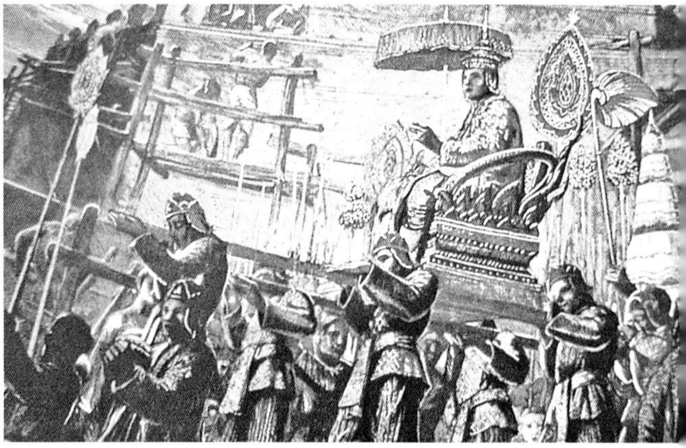

An imagined likeness of King Rama III in the Ananta Samakom throne hall. (River Books)

procedure was followed, and the golden urn containing the royal remains was placed in the Dusit Maha Prasat Hall, and all the rel igious rites followed at regular intervals. Then there was the drinking of the water of fealty throughout the kingdom. The full and elaborate ceremonies of the coronation took place on August 1st, 1824. However, Prince Damrong maintained that the third Chakri king did not once wear his crown during the whole reign.[9] The present author was told by his father that King Chulalongkorn told him that, when he was presented with the crown, the new king gave it to an official without first putting it on his head, saying, "I am only keeping it for him". In other words, he implied that he was keeping the crown for Prince Mongkut. The same style and title as those of his predecessors were used, which included Rama Tibodi, and he is now conveniently known as Rama III.

The coronation was followed by the customary promotions of the princes and nobles. If the Uparaja was intended to be the heir apparent, then Rama Ill's choice was indeed curious. He was without a younger full brother, and instead of a prince younger than himself, he appointed his uncle, the 17th child of Rama I, who was two years his senior. He was Prince Sakdibalasep who had been Commander-in-Chief, and nephew and uncle had always been great friends. He was the first non-*Chao Fa* to be *Uparaja*, a position he held for only eight years as he died in 1832, and no other prince would then be appointed to succeed him.

Another important appointment of Rama III was that of his mother, Chao Chom Riem, who was raised to royal rank as the Queen Mother Sri Sulalaya. Other promotions were fewer than at the beginning of most reigns because many of the ministers of the previous reign were still in their posts. It was the custom in those days for the new monarch to retain high officials in their posts unless there was some specific charge against any of them. Then after the many religious rites had been held, Rama III carried out with full pomp and ceremony, in accordance with the now defined order, the cremation of the remains of his father on April 29th, 1825.[10] This was attended by the governors of all the provinces and the vassal princes, including Prince Anu of Vientiane.

Like other Chakri princes of those days, Rama III had many children, namely 22 sons and 29 daughters by 35 wives. As he was 37 at his accession, 38 of his children were born before that event. He did not have a wife of royal birth so he had no queen and he raised none of his children to *Chao Fa*[11] or celestial rank, although as the all-powerful sovereign, he had every right to do so.

From the dynastic point of view one of Rama Ill's sons is highly

5 King Chulalongkorn: *Text for a sermon in honour of King Rama III,* (in Thai), page 16. Bangkok, 1939.

6 *Ibid.,* page 38.

7 *Ibid.,* pages 39-41.

8 *Ibid.,* page 44

9 Prince Damrong: *Rama II, op cit.,* page 29, note 18.

10 Dates and facts are taken from Chao Phraya Dibakarawongse: *Reign of Rama III* (in Thai), Bangkok, 1934.

11 *List of Chakri Princes and Princesses, op. cit.,* pages 38-50.

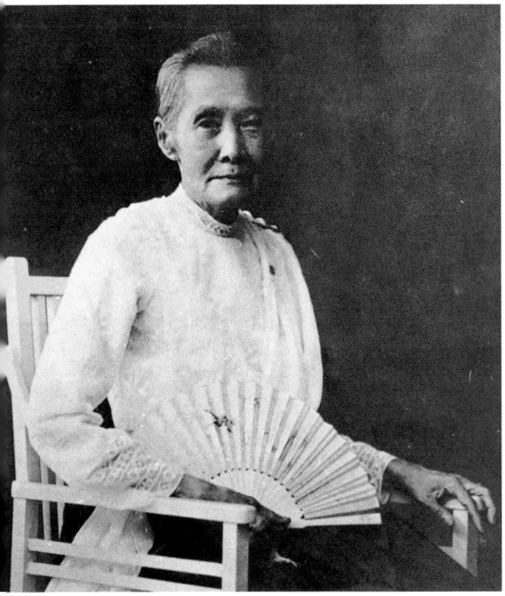

Princess Banarai.
(Paisarn Piemmettawat)

important. This was his sixth child, Prince Siriwongse (1812-1839), who was later promoted as Krom Muen Mataya. He was both a fine architect and artist, who was put in charge of the Mother-of-Pearl Department and the work of further embellishment at Wat Pho. The king was deeply grieved when Prince Mataya died at the early age of 27. He took Mataya's two daughters, Princess Rampoey and Princess Banarai, to live with him in the Grand Palace, and both girls became his favourite grandchildren.[12] As they grew up they were both to become royal wives of their great-uncle, King Mongkut. Princess Rampoey, as Queen Debsirindra, became the mother of King Chulalongkorn. Thus Prince Mataya is the great ancestor of all the descendants of King Chulalongkorn, including four kings, namely, King Rama VI, King Prajadhipok, King Ananda Mahidol, and the present reigning monarch – King Bhumibol.

The daily life of Rama III has been fully described by King Chulalongkorn,[13] who had no doubt heard about it from his nurse, Princess Sudaratana, the 26th child of Rama III. The king was such a heavy sleeper that he could not awake without being called which was usually at 7 a.m. The page, who carried out this duty, was forbidden to touch him. He could only tell him the time which often had to be repeated, and sometimes it was not until 8 a.m. that he was properly roused. After taking a bath and dressing himself, the king went out to the outer hall to present food to the monks, a number of whom were invited daily, before he had his own breakfast. But after the age of 50 he got so hungry early in the morning that he had to take his breakfast first. Next he made his quiet devotions in the private chapel with close members of the royal family, after which he fed his favourite pet – a tortoise. Then he appeared officially in the Amarindra Hall to receive the *Pancha Sila* (five precepts) from the leader of a chapter of monks, to listen to their chanting of prayers, and then present them with their lunch. The king sat near the senior monk and looked after him as he ate, while other princes attended to other monks in order of royal precedence – a practice which still continues today. After the departure of the monks, the king smoked a pipe as he discussed important business with some princes and high nobles. This was followed by a cup of tea which was the signal that he would now mount the throne for the general audience. This began with all the attending officials making a triple obeisance near the doors of the great hall, crawling towards the throne on their elbows, and near there reclining respectfully in their order of seniority. The morning audience lasted from one hour to one hour and a half, and, whenever pressure of business made it last longer the king complained that he was hungry. Usually he retired into the Inside by 12.30 at the latest to eat the big luncheon which he had been waiting to enjoy.

12 King Chulalongkorn: *Sermon, op. cit.*, page *at.*

13 *Royal Daily Life,* pages 7-14 (in Thai), Bangkok, 1946.

14 Luang Udom Sombat: *Journals* (in Thai), 2nd Edition. Bangkok, 1916.

After luncheon he received reports from the lady officials of the Inside before proceeding again to the Outside. It was then that artists were admitted to show their works, or the king would go out to the Royal Landing Stage to inspect new boats or ships, to the Emerald Buddha Temple to see some new building work, or else he went to watch the casting of some big artillery guns. From 2.30 p.m. Rama III relaxed and played with his children of whom he was extremely fond. He retired to bed at 4 p.m. and usually slept until 7 or 8 p.m., when he would take another bath before the evening meal. The full evening audience began at 9 p.m., and as in previous reigns, there was always a sermon before the business of hearing reports and the discussion which followed. It usually closed at midnight, but in a time of crisis it could continue until 2 a.m. or even later. Until his last and fatal illness, the king was robust enough to give these long, open audiences, and he never had to appear at a window of the Inside like Rama I in the last years of his life. A highly interesting book exists which records many of these evening audiences in detail, written by one Luang Udom Sombat.[14] It amply shows that Rama III was very much *The Ruler* of his country and kept in the closest possible touch with every aspect of national affairs. He was quick with his decisions, imposed strict but reasonable discipline, and his adverse comments and non-approbation were tinged with a strong sense of humour. He inherited his ministers from his father, and it was not until round about 1830 that most of them died, and he replaced them with men of his own choice. There was one outstanding exception, the Phra Klang – Lord High High Treasurer and Foreign Minister, who, despite having served Rama II in that capacity carried on for the rest of the third reign, and in 1830 received the additional post of Kralahom (Lord of the South). Even though he took such an excessive interest in State affairs, Rama III did

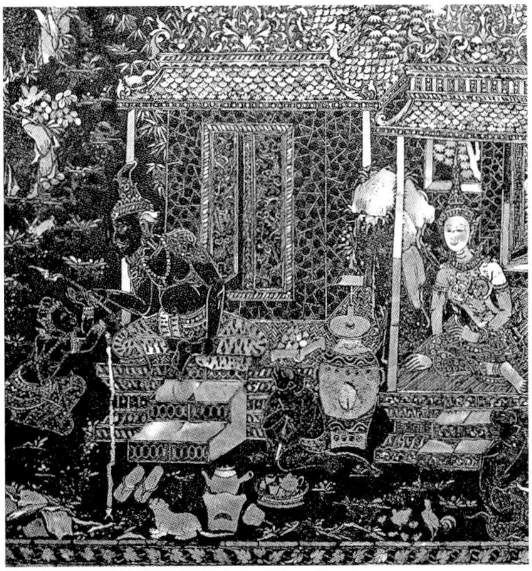

Detail of mother-of-pearl doors by Prince Mataya. (National Museum Bangkok)

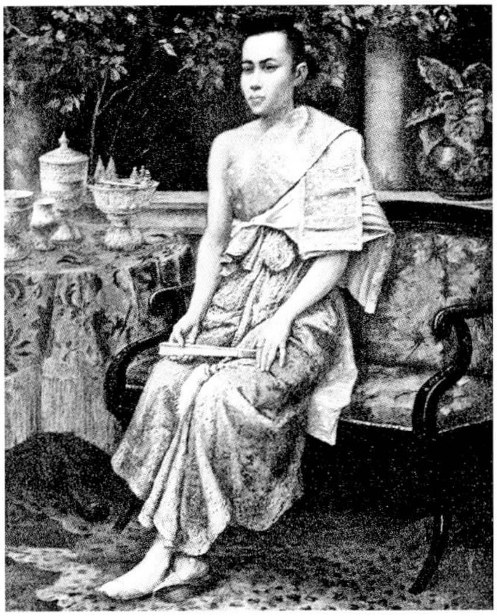

Queen Debsirindra. (Chakri Trone Hall)

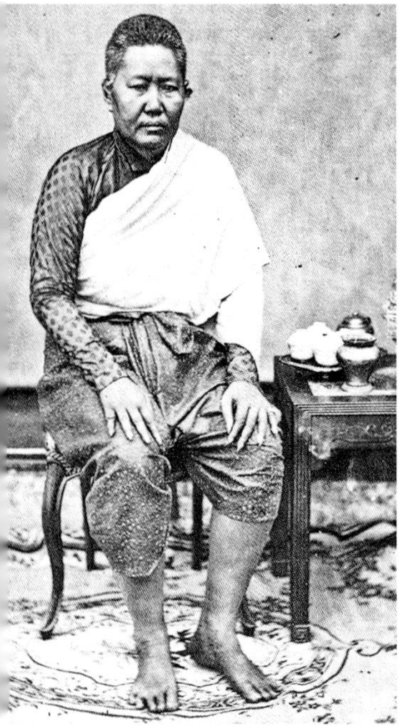

Princess Lamom, later Krom Somdet Phra Sudaratana Ratchaprayoon. (National Archives Bangkok)

not neglect those ceremonies over which he was expected to preside. Such court ceremonies were believed to be of benefit to the people as a whole, as well as increasing even further the glory and majesty of the king. Fortunately at Buddhist services one is expected to keep quiet only during the sermon, and the king could save time by sending for a prince or minister to have a quiet chat with him as the service continued.

The administration of the country followed the same pattern as under Rama I and Rama II, with the two heads of the North and South both having their headquarters in Bangkok. Of the provincial governors, those of Nakhon Sri Thammarat, Phitsanulok, and Khorat, all of these three being first-class provinces, enjoyed some independence in their actions. Corvée work continued as the heaviest form of direct taxation. Rama III was much concerned with the problems of serious crime, and he made many real attempts to suppress robbers and bandits. Sometimes relatives of criminals, or even whole villages, were held responsible for the misdeeds of their people.

Like his father, Rama III was determined to rid his country of the evils of opium, and in some cases an amnesty was promised if the drug was surrendered. The trade was largely in Chinese hands and it caused more crimes than before because it was being handled by Chinese secret societies which were established in Siam for the first time in this reign. The Chinese traders bought opium grown in India from British merchants and then sold it in Siam. The trade was so profitable that the Chinese secret societies had fierce feuds amongst themselves, resulting in violent fights which became a menace to public security. The government of Rama III took strong measures to break up these societies, and there was one large operation in the provinces when as many as 3,000 Chinese were killed.[15] All these warlike operations cost the government heavy expenses.

Over all, expenditure was rising as the government was now spending money in so many directions. With the king being a devout Buddhist, a great deal went in donations to religious bodies and for repairs to the great many temples as a result of constant new constructions. Then, there was the cost of armaments for internal security, which had become as important as external threats because of the Chinese secret societies. Although corvée service still continued, it was found that better work could be got out of paid Chinese labour. Building ships for seagoing trade, so necessary for the revenue, was costly; and more and more the government preferred taxes in money specie to goods or services rendered. As the balance of trade was favourable, with silver pouring into the country, and with Bangkok ever on the upgrade as a thriving port, things were going well for the government of Rama III. Ever since the time of Rama II the standard coin was the baht, which Crawfurd noted "Europeans, on grounds I do not know, have called a tical."[16]

Farming out taxes as an alternative to the royal monopoly on foreign trade had begun seriously under Rama II, and it resulted in

15 Prince Damrong: *Tales of Olden Times*, *op. cit.*, pages 238-241.

16 Crawfurd, *op. cit.*, page 331.

17 H. G. Quaritch Wales: *Ancient Siamese Government and Administration*, page 68, London, 1934.

18 Vella, *op. cit.*, page 31.

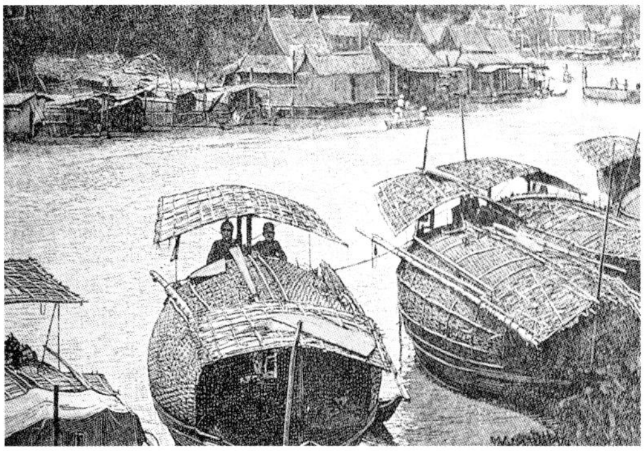

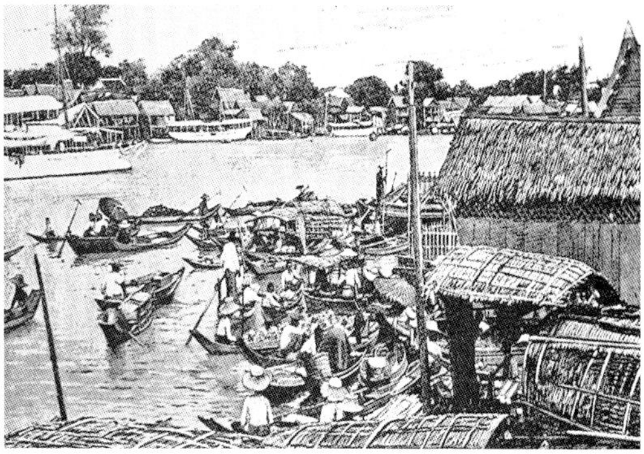

The Siamese economy and trade flourished during the reign of Rama III. Waterways provided the main transport network. (National Archives Bangkok)

rapid growth in the third reign when there were 38 different enterprises, most of which were taxed on production for export. Most of the tax farmers were Chinese and they had to bid against one another and pay for the privilege, an additional source of revenue for the State. Tax farming for gambling houses and the sale of alcohol had already existed since the time of Ayutthaya, and even then most of the tax farmers were Chinese. They had to guarantee the government a fixed amount, but they earned handsome profits in commissions.

Rama III was as fully alive to the importance of inland shipping as to the sea-going junk trade. He arranged for more canals to be dug, rivers to be dredged and widened, and of these there were four major projects, with one canal being 33 miles long and taking two years to construct.

The lives of the people had not changed much since the time of Rama I, except that corvée service was more carefully timed so as to interfere less with the people's livelihood. If the general run of Thai people did not have much cash, they were comparatively free and happy and had a higher standard of living than in most Asian countries. Slaves were mostly debtors who had the chance to redeem themselves. With inter-marriage flourishing or even on the increase, as hardly any Chinese women were coming to Siam, the Chinese majority remained small because the Chinese were quickly being absorbed into the Thai race in all classes. Their offspring were proud to be born Thai, although they always kept up their Chinese cultural background, such as ancestor worship, side by side with the newly acquired Thai form of Buddhism. That a Chinese minority continued to exist was because of continual immigration, the number being about 15,000 per year towards the close of this reign.[17]

Meanwhile the Thais practised their own mixed religion which was largely Buddhistic, with Brahmanic ceremonies being almost confined to the court. There a few Brahmin priests were retained, but, unlike in India or Cambodia, they had no political or restraining power.[18] The king himself was a most devout Buddhist. The daily sermon which he heard was not just an empty and sycophantic praise of him or his good works, but it had to be a

Ordinary people lived in wood and bamboo houses along waterways. (National Archives Bangkok)

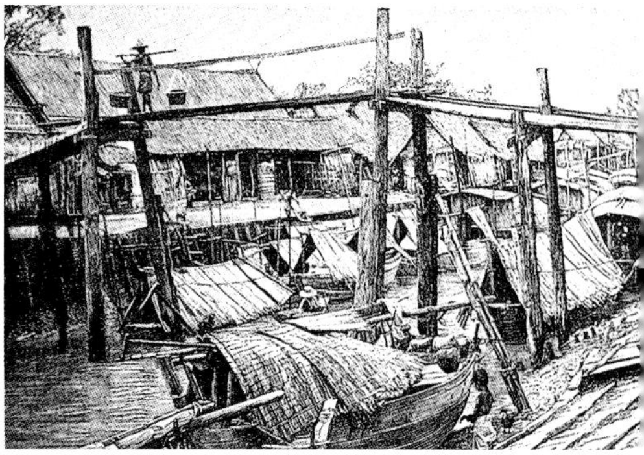

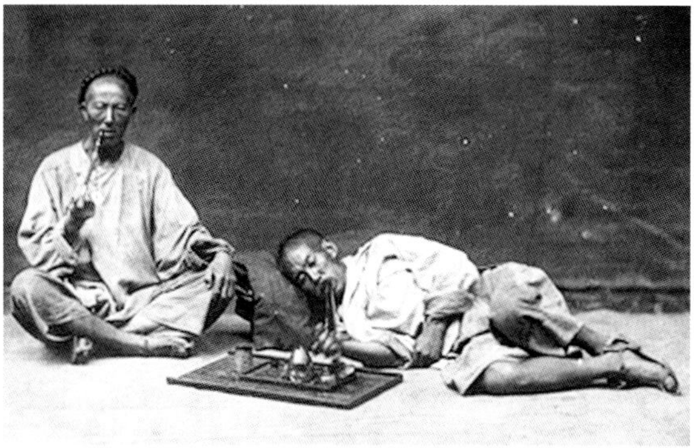

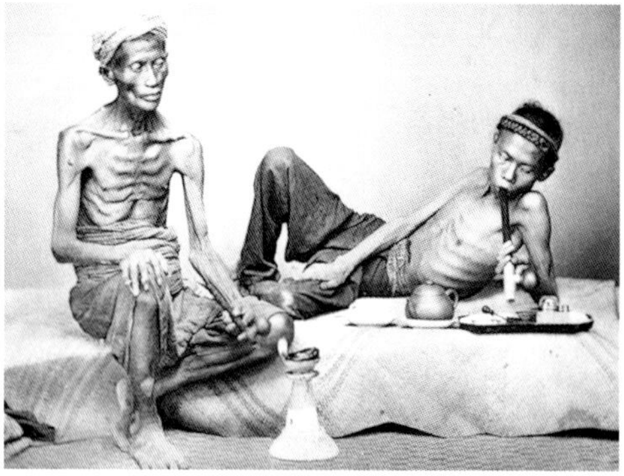

Opium smoking remained prevalent in the third reign. (National Archives Bangkok)

clear explanation and enlargement in Thai of different aspects of that vast compilation – the Buddhist canon. His former habit of giving alms grew greater after his accession, and he had several almshouses erected. The aged poor could buy state rice at very low token prices, and from time to time all the really poor had their taxes remitted. So great was his enthusiasm for the Buddhist order, that Rama III closely supervised the appointment of every prelate or abbott. He was deeply interested in the philosophical side of Buddhism, and he followed the results of the examination of brilliant young monks with special attention. His half-brother, Celestial Prince Mongkut, who had entered the priesthood shortly before their father's death, was a keenly studious monk and an eager Pali student. Through his good knowledge of the ancient language he was rapidly becoming deeply learned in the tenets of the religion. After three years, news of his brother's progress reached the king who asked Mongkut to sit for a high examination in Buddhism. This was held before a council of important prelates and in the royal presence in the Amarindra Hall. The prince-priest acquitted himself brilliantly and would have gone on much further in the examination, but for an unfortunate contretemps which will be related in another place. Up till then, no prince who had taken up the priesthood as a career, had ever gone in for a public examination, and, but for the invitation of Rama III, Prince Mongkut might not have broken that tradition. By passing the examination brilliantly he achieved much fame for himself and the Chakri family.[19]

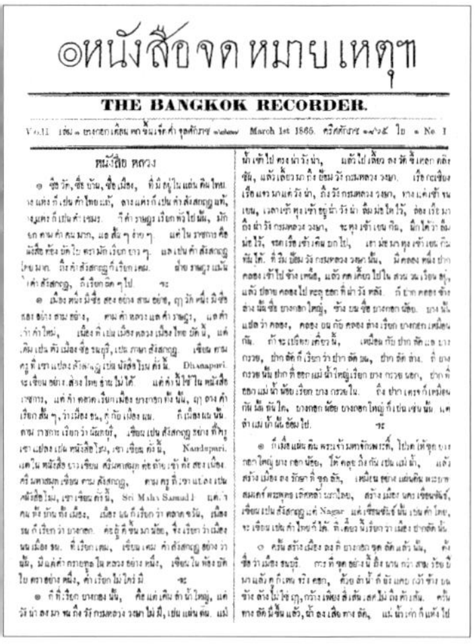

๏หนังสือจดหมายเหตุ

THE BANGKOK RECORDER.

Vol. II ... March 1st 1865. ... No 1

หนังสือ หลวง

The *Bangkok Recorder* was Thailand's first newspaper. It was published by Dr. Dan Beach Bradley with the first issue appearing on 4th July 1844.

Despite his devotion to Buddhism, Rama III followed the royal tradition of giving help to the Christian missionaries, although sometime he was much annoyed by them. Protestant missionaries came to Bangkok in 1828 but they stayed only a short time because of their lack of success. "Buddhism was deeply ingrained after hundreds of years and most of the natives found it impossible to accept a faith whose confession of sin and other doctrine appeared in no way different to their religion. The first missionaries went to Thailand in 1828. Many followed but after 18 years, 22 missionaries had failed to make one convert."[20] The continuous residence of American missionaries dates from 1833 onwards. Although their evangelical work was "almost or altogether fruitless",[21] – they baptized mostly their servants, many of whom were not Thai – their non-religious impact was profound. They practised western medicine which gradually gained acceptance, and they brought modem scientific knowledge to many Thais, such as Prince Mongkut and his friends, who were thirsting for it. In 1835 the American missionaries, led by Dr. Bradley, set up the first printing press in Bangkok, and they printed books and newspapers with type which they had prepared of the Thai alphabet. This was an event of incalculable importance to the Thai people as a whole. The Catholics returned to Siam in 1830 and had a community with a bishop, eight priests, and also some nuns.

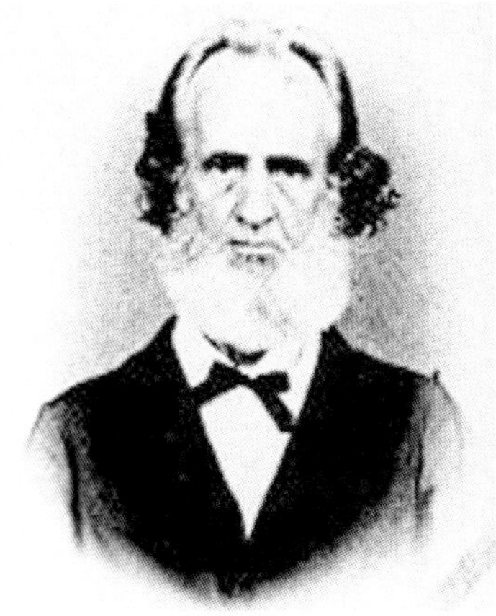

Doctor Dan Beach Bradley, an American missionary who devoted his life to Siam in the fields of medicine, writing and printing. (Wikimedia Commons)

Vella makes the interesting suggestion that the advent of the Christian missionaries provided the stimulus for religious reform in Buddhism led by Prince Mongkut at Wat Samorai. The prince-priest and his brethren found that a sizeable majority of the monks were content to lead a contemplative life. Not only did many of them neglect serious study of the Buddhist scriptures, but they did not keep strictly enough to the *vinaya* (rules). He found inspiration in this respect from the Mon priests resident in Siam, and he invited some of them to come and reside at Wat Samorai. It was in 1837, when he was 33, that Wat Bowonniwet – whose name was picturesquely translated into English by Alexander Griswold as the Monastery of the Excellent Abode[22] – had a vacancy in the office of abbot, and Rama III appointed his celestial brother to that office. As a result many young monks, who thought and felt like him, elected to join him there, and they formed a nucleous from which he founded a strict new sect – Thammayut Nikaya – which was to transform the lives of Buddhist monks in Siam. Mongkut sent for books from Ceylon to compare points in the doctrine, and in 1842 five Thammayut priests selected by him were sent to Ceylon by the king with Singhalese monks who had come to Bangkok earlier. The Thammayut sect into which five other monasteries joined, showed their modern views by preaching their sermons in Thai, and they even translated into Thai the Pali text with which every sermon had to begin. This new practice soon spread to other monasteries of the Maha Nikaya (The Big Sect). Although he quietly supported his brother's efforts behind the scene and the Thammayut sect was firmly established by the end of his reign, Rama III did not like the way they wore their yellow robe in the Mon style. Yet the formation of this new sect caused the king to make inquiries into the general conduct of all members of the Sangha in Siam, which resulted in some 500 monks being expelled in 1843. Despite this, more monks had become thoroughly learned in the true Buddhist doctrine in this reign than ever before.[23]

Most of the arts continued to prosper under Rama III as they had done in the time of his father. Bangkok was the centre, and the artists did not rely so much on their fees as on the patronage of the king, princes, and the nobility. Of all the patrons the king was by far the most important, and he continued the policy of beautifying the capital.

19 Prince Damrong: *Memoirs*, pages 51-55 (in Thai), Bangkok, 1946.

20 Mr. Eric Beresford to the Malvern Branch of the China Inland Mission *Malvern Gazetteer*, May 29th, 1959.

21 Sir John Bowring, *op. cit.*, Vol. I, page 336.

22 Alexander B. Griswold: *The Real King Mongkut of Siam*. Published in *Eastern World*. London, March, 1955.

23 King Chulalongkorn: *Sermon, op. cit.*, page 93.

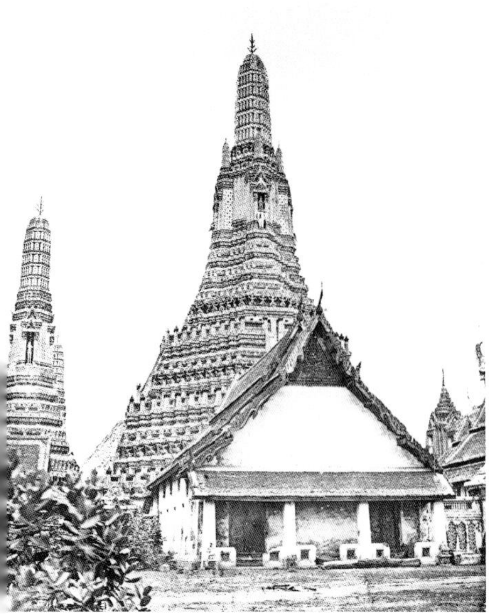

The central *prang* of Wat Arun which was completed by Rama III in honour of his father, Rama II. (River Books)

Within the Grand Palace, it was more a question of keeping abreast of continuous repairs rather than adding something new. Being deeply religious, Rama III was more interested in the temples and monasteries. He was active in expanding and repairing existing edifices, as well as having new ones constructed, and other rich patrons were inspired to follow his example. Altogether nine new temples were built and over 60 were repaired and added to.[24] It cannot be denied, however, that these artistic and architectural endeavours of the time have become a burden to the government of later days, for the number of temples and the separate buildings within each are now so great that it has become impossible today to produce the funds to keep them up to the desired standard. The towers in the temples are of two kinds, the bell-shape *chedi* with the spiral top such as the enormous one at Nakhon Pathom, and the more elaborate *prang* of Wat Arun which is 227 feet high, covered with china cups and saucers broken up to produce floral designs.

One of Rama Ill's important contributions to the arts was the huge 90-foot-long image of the reclining Buddha at Wat Pho, built of brick and mortar, covered with gold, and housed in a *vihara* a prayer house. The king also ordered for the Emerald Buddha Temple the casting of two large standing gilt images of the Buddha crowned and elaborately attired as Thai monarchs, which were placed in front of the Emerald Buddha itself. He named the images: Phra Buddha Yod Fa and Phra Buddha Loet La. The Thai people in general had been in the habit of referring to Rama I as the First Reign and to Rama II as the Middle Reign. Rama III suspected that they were now calling him the Last Reign, which would be an ill omen for the dynasty, so he gave orders that his two predecessors would henceforth be called by the names of these two new images respectively. Phra Buddha Yod Fa means the Buddha atop the Heavens, and Phra Buddha Loes La means the Buddha above the Skies.

The large reclining Buddha in the *vihara* of Wat Pho. (River Books)

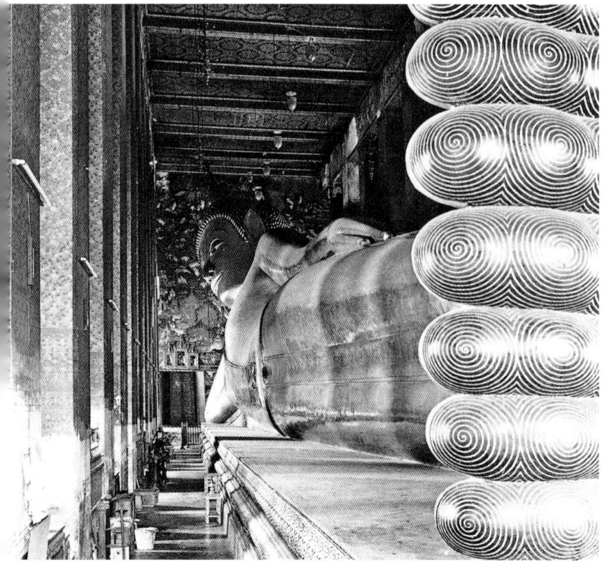

Like all the other arts in Siam, literature still relied on patronage, and printing, begun by the Americans in 1835, was still in its infancy even by the close of this reign. Rama III supported only religious literature and history, although he had himself tried his hand at poetry to please his father. Up until his time most of fine Thai writing had been in verse, and it was really only in his reign that good Thai prose began to develop. One of the king's uncles, the 28th child of Rama I, Prince Paramanujit Jinorot, although a monk in the Sangha, was one of the eminent poets and prose writers of the period. One of his

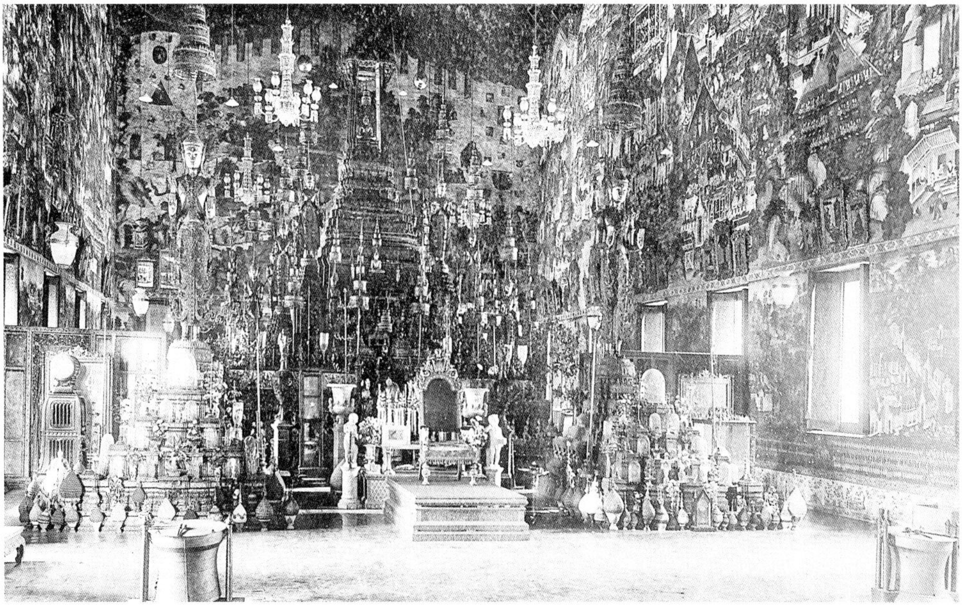

important epic poems was a description of the great deeds of King Naresuan of Ayutthaya, culminating in the single combat on elephants when he slew the Crown Prince of Burma. It is curious that besides serious works of religion and history, he translated an Indian poem about a girl called Kritsana, who taught a younger sister how to be a good wife, as she herself had seven husbands simultaneously. Rama III turned the main building of Wat Pho into a library, but a strange one as it had no books. On the walls were painted encyclopaedic murals depicting Religion, War, Medicine, Astrology, Poetry, Plants, Provinces, History Geography, Biographies, Fables, and Nursery Rhymes, and these narrative pictures even extended to the window shutters. There were also images of the different types of people of the world, and although they may not be accepted as great works of art, they are very interesting. He forsaw that one day the Chinese junk would no longer hold the important position it enjoyed in his time, so in order that the people of Bangkok would remember the principal way in which the city had become rich, he had the main building at Wat Yannawa designed in the shape of a Chinese junk.

Buddha images dedicated to Kings Rama I and II were installed on the right and left in front of the Emerald Buddha. (River Books)

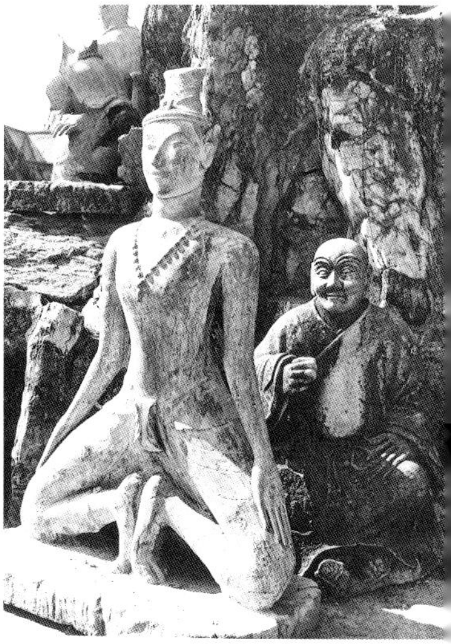

Statues of *rishii* in yoga postures within the grounds of Wat Pho. These were installed in the reign of Rama III together with instructive verses. (River Books)

Being so pious and something of a puritan, Rama III did not care for the ballet and he disbanded the royal troops of male dancers for the *khon* and the female dancers for the *lakhon*. Between arising and his bedtime the king would not listen to any singing or playing of any musical instruments, let alone wishing to watch the ballet.[25] Yet despite his disapproval and refusal to see the ballet, the art flourished in his reign, as princes and nobles vied with one another in having ballet troops of their own. These were female groups for the *lakhon*, and, strange as it may seem, the male costumes best showed off the female form, with many male dance poses being especially designed to suit the figuress of certain dancers.

24 Dibakarawongse: *Rama III, op. cit.*, pages 346-358.

25 King Chulalongkorn: *Sermon, op. cit.*, page 94.

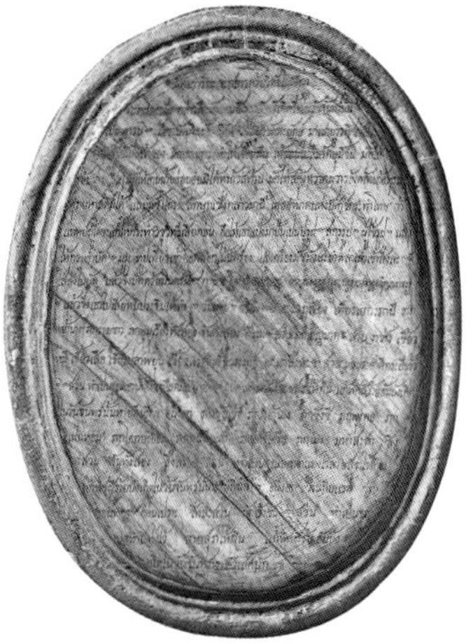

A marble plaque with recipes for herbal medicine were installed in Wat Pho at the order of Rama III. Somdet Phra Maha Sommana Chao was responsible for writing up the various recipes and organising their installation. (River Books)

It was with the practical matters of being the ruler that Rama III was by choice chiefly concerned, and he not only revised many of the laws, but often enjoyed judging cases in person. Finding that the population had much increased in 21 villages, he raised them to the rank of township. In the past, wars were mostly with Burma when boats were but little required, but in his reign campaigns would be fought in Cambodia, Vietnam, or in Malaya, which necessitated boats of all kinds. The king was active in overseeing their construction, and during his time a new style of seaworthy rowing boat, 9 foot wide and 33 foot long, with two lines of rowers, one on each side of the boat was invented with a large number of these boats being constructed.[26] In addition some 14 men-of-war with sails were also built in this reign. His knowledge of the multifarious affairs in every part of his domain was truly remarkable, considering that he himself never left the Grand Palace except to go to a few important temples and present the *Kathin* gifts at the end of the Buddhist Lent, or down to the landing stage to look at new boats or ships. Instead, he acquired all this information from the daily study of copious reports, followed by discussions during the evening audience when he often showed that he knew more about the country and terrain than the officials who had been on the spot.[27]

Rama III's reign coincided with the first British war with Burma, 1824-1826. At about the same time, the king had inherited a good deal of trouble in his Malay possessions. There was a difference of policy between the British Government of India, which preferred non-interference, and Governor Fullerton of Penang and the British merchants there, who desired to extend their influence and control over Northern Malaya. In 1825 Captain Henry Burney, an English official in Penang, was sent to Bangkok supposedly to ask for help in the war against Burma. Up till now Siam had done nothing about it beyond

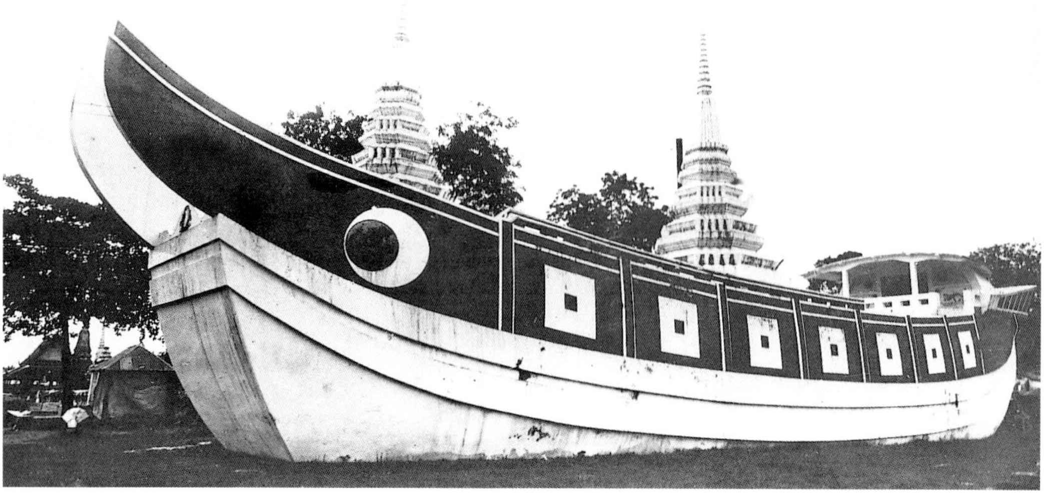

The large junk in Wat Yannawa was built by Rama III so that future generations could see what a junk looked like. (National Archives Bangkok)

sending an army to watch over events at the frontier. In actual fact Burney's real business was to negotiate about Malaya, and he consequently had to admit the correctness of most of the Thai claims to the northern part of the peninsula. The king himself did not wish to have any negotiation with Burney, but he was persuaded to do so by some of the important princes and nobles.

Troubles, however, persisted in the Thai controlled states of Malaya owing not only to political difficulties but also physical and economic causes such as the drought of 1829 and the floods of 1831. The British had the ex-Sultan of Kedah sent to Malacca from Penang as a favour to Siam, but his son revolted successfully for a time in 1831. In Siam proper there was jealousy between the Governors of Nakhon (Ligor) and Songkhla (Singora) which made suppression of the Kedah revolt difficult until strong forces arrived from Bangkok. The Malay states often quarrelled with one another and when one state revolted, the others often helped Thai troops in the task of repression. The real problem was how to prevent such occurences from breaking out, for a revolt in one state disturbed all the others. As Kedah was the state most often in revolt, it was felt that a satisfactory settlement with Kedah would bring peace to the whole region.

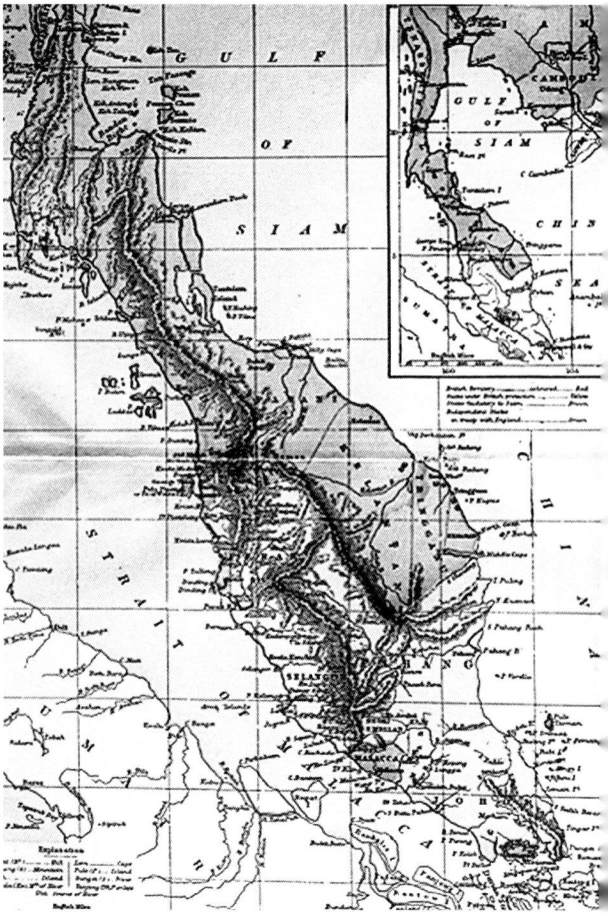

The Malay Peninsula and the southern Thai states.

The two great noblemen, Chao Phraya Yomaraj and Phraya Sripipat, who had been prominent in the work of repression, persuaded Rama III that it was essential to trust Malay relatives of the ex-Sultan and let them rule Kedah. In 1841, the ex-Sultan was allowed to return and be reinstated as sultan and the king's vassal after he had sent a son to Bangkok with a letter admitting his past misdeeds and asking the king's pardon. During the last ten years of the reign of Rama III, and with the helpful co-operation of the British authorities, the sultans of the different states under Thai suzerainty enjoyed almost autonomous rule and all was at peace. The many troubles between the Thais and the Malays probably would not have occurred, or not in that confused form, had the Malay people long ago been united as one nation as the Thais had been since the time of Ayutthya.

Although Britain had wanted Siam's help in her first war with Burma, it was in the manner of transports and animals, and not as an active military ally. The military defeats suffered by the Burmese worried the Thais, and, when Burney came in 1825 Bangkok was flooded with rumours that he was bringing an ultimatum and Siam was the next target for British attack. Burney was permitted to say that the

26 *Ibid.*, pages 90-91.

27 Luang Udom Sombat: *Journals, op cit.*

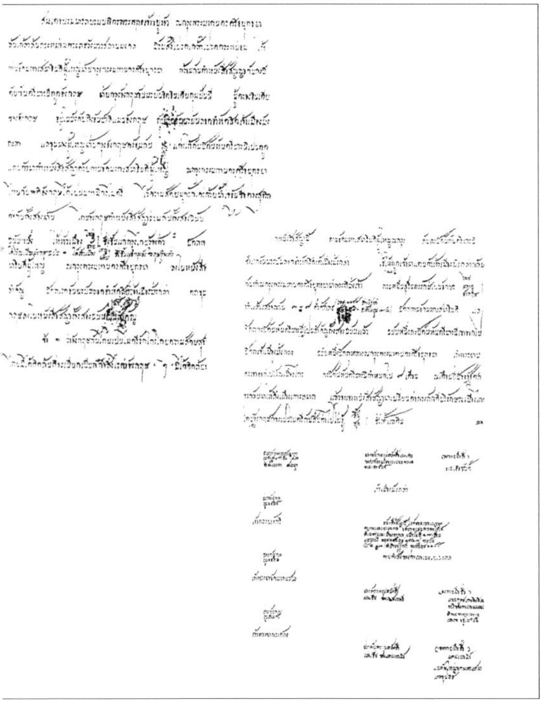

The first treaty between Siam and Britain. (The Secretariat of the Cabinet. (1995). *The Royal Emblems*. Bangkok: The Secretariat of the Cabinet Publishing House).

Thais could attack Burma in the north where British troops did not operate, but they should refrain from any intervention in the south. There was a germ of a British idea of setting up an independent Mon state between Burma and Siam which the Thais did not at all cherish, but this idea was quickly discarded.

Rama III had some knowledge of the British as he had met Crawfurd more than once, and the frontier of Siam now met that of the British for the first time in Burma. The king realized that, however undesirable it was to come out into the open, negotiations with Burney were inevitable, which was why he agreed to the advice of the princes and nobles. He ordered his ministers to be friendly and get on with the work, thus negotiations were rapid, and Burney having presented his first draft on March 29th, the first treaty between a king of the Chakri Dynasty and a western power was concluded on June 20th, 1826. Siam agreed not to interfere with British trade in the Malay states which the British admitted as belonging to Siam, and Siam also recognized Penang Island and the Province of Wellesley as British possessions. Britain accepted Kedah, Kelantan, and Terengganu as being under Thai suzerainty, whereas Siam recognized the independence of Perak and Selangor. The British admitted that the Sultan of Perak could send tributes to Bangkok if he wished, but Siam should not compel him to.

Article I opens in these terms: "The English and Siamese engage in friendship, love, and affection, with mutual trust, sincerity, and candour. The Siamese must not meditate or commit evil, so as to molest the English in any manner. The English must not meditate or commit any evil so as to molest the Siamese in any manner . . . the Siamese shall settle every matter within the Siamese boundaries, according to their own will and customs."[28]

There were 14 articles in the treaty, which was ratified by Lord Amherst, Governor-General of India, on January 17th, 1827. Perhaps he was accustomed to one-sided treaties between western powers and Asian peoples in that period, as Vella notes with apparent interest that: "One outstanding fact about the treaty was its absolute reciprocity on every point."[29] There were mutual pledges, equal responsibilities, with equal advantages. The two countries promised not to disturb the other's boundaries and territories, and to inform each other of troubles with vassals. Equality of extradition rights were confirmed. There was an explicit denial of any British claims to extra territorial rights in Article 5 thus: " The English subjects who visit the Siamese country must conduct themselves according to the established laws of the Siamese country in every particular."[30] There would be free trade according to the custom of the places, no rent of land for establishing a factory without permission, mutual aid for shipwrecked seamen, and an explicit English denial of the right to import opium into Siam.

In the Commercial Treaty of six articles, Siam agreed that 1,700 bahts' duty for each Thai fathom of a ship's beam should replace all other taxes on trade. The English agreed to the Thai ban on any export of rice, which was a staple food of the people, and not enough was then being grown for home consumption. It was largely Burney's own pleasant personality which made such a quick success of the treaty – he even tried to learn the Thai language. Vella writes with understanding: "He praised more, and criticized less, than any other Western diplomat who came to Siam during the reign. On July 17th, the day before he left Bangkok, Burney was accorded the honour that apparently had not been granted a foreign envoy since the seventeenth century,"[31] that of a farewell audience. Despite this honour, even in his own country Rama III had unwittingly acquired the reputation of being out-of-date and anti-Westerners.

The Burney mission caused one of Rama Ill's Laotian vassals, Prince Anu of Vientiane, to make one of the biggest and fatal mistake of his life, for believing the rumours that the English envoy had come to prepare the way for the British invasion of Bangkok, Anu decided to strike the first blow. The Laotian States had been vassals of Siam for a long time but not continuously, and they ringed Siam proper from the north-west down to the south-east. The Laos were generally easier for the Thais to get on with than the Malays owing to closer religious, linguistic, cultural, and racial ties. Some Laotian princes were linked to the Thai royal family by marriage, and several of their sons had been educated in Bangkok. Vella[32] quotes a French writer of 1901, who had found the Thai treatment of the Laos as "remarkable for the great liberty given the subjects of the Laotian tongue: the Court of Bangkok completely respected their customs, dress, and institution." The Laotian states can be conveniently divided into two groups. The western group consisted of Chiang Mai, Lamphun, Nan, and Phrae. The eastern group was formed by the two Mekong states of Luang Prabang and Vientiane, which in the eighteenth century had been united as one state. All through the reign of Rama III there was peace and harmony between Bangkok and the Laotian states with the exception of Vientiane.

At the accession of Rama III, Prince Anuwongse, more conveniently called Anu, had been the ruling prince of Vientiane for 17 years. With the support of the king when he was Prince Chesda, Anu's son was made Governor of Bassac, and this gave Anu's family power on both sides of the Mekong river. As stated in the last chapter, Siam had not presented a strong front to Vietnam in the second reign because she was concentrating on her defence against Burma, and Anu made the mistake of thinking it was because of Siam's general weakness. Anu himself was sending tributes to Vietnam after the accession of Rama III. In accordance with the correct etiquette he came to

28 *Siam's Case for Revision of Obsolete Treaty Obligations, etc.*, page I, 1919.

29 Vella: *Siam under Rama III, op. cit.*, page 120.

30 *Siam's Case*, etc., *op. cit.*, page 9.

31 Vella: *Siam under Rama III, op. cit.*, page 121.

32 *Ibid.*, page 79 quoting Eugène Picanon: *Le Laos français*, Paris, 1901.

Bangkok in 1825 for the cremation of Rama II, but during his stay he became offended because the new monarch had refused his two requests. One was for a troupe of ballet girls, and Rama III disapproved of the ballet. The other was for the return of descendants of families which had been taken to Siam in 1778. However, Rama III contended that their ancestors had been living on the west bank of the Mekong, and therefore were Thai proper who had been removed to the east bank. The rumours concerning Burney's mission spread to Vientiane in 1826 that the British had quarrelled with Siam and that the British navy would soon be attacking Bangkok. Thus Anu thought it was the right time to begin his grand revolt, and his ambitious aim went as far as to take Bangkok first and the whole of Siam later. If this task should prove too difficult, then he would endeavour to remove as much of the population and national wealth as possible and leave Siam too weak to retaliate. In his three-pronged plan, the force under his personal command aimed at Khorat, which he succeeded in taking partly by surprise and partly by pretending to be marching to help Bangkok against the British. His main army reached Khorat on February 17th, 1827, when his forward elements were already at Saraburi – three days' march from Bangkok.

It was only then that the Thai government became fully alerted, corvée conscripts were called up, and two large armies were formed with one independent brigade. Following news of this action, the Vientiane troops quickly retreated from Saraburi as the Thai armies approached that town. One army under the *Uparaja* was designated for the grand counter-attack, being despatched towards Vientiane itself. Another army under an able general, later to be promoted Chao Phraya Bodin, aimed to attack Anu's forces in the eastern provinces as far as Bassac, whilst the independent brigade was to operate west of Khorat. The Thai armies were successful in every direction with the troops advancing easily at first. Anu retreated from Khorat after first destroying the town and taking away thousands of prisoners, both men and women. They camped every night with the men in close captivity, but the women were ordered to serve the Laotian officers and men with food and drink. One night the wife of the murdered Governor of Khorat led other women to lure their Laotian captors into a drunken orgy, after which they were able to free their menfolk, who having killed some 2,000 Vientiane troops, were able to rejoin the Thais. After the revolt was over the governor's wife was elevated to Tao Suranaree and her statue now stands in the modern town of Khorat.

Anu then ordered his main army to make a stand and they came to grips with the army of Chao Phraya Bodin. A prolonged pitched battle – said to last a week – then took place; and, although Chao Phraya Bodin was wounded by a spear thrust, his army won a decisive battle which was fought near a large lake. Anu lost heart and, after deserting his army, he fled back to Vientiane, collected his valuables, and fled again with some relatives into Vietnamese territory. His forces were subsequently defeated everywhere, the city of Vientiane was occupied by the middle of May, 1827, and all the Thai forces converged there. Loyal Laotian states in the west sent troops to help Bangkok but they arrived too late to do any fighting.

The army of occupation then set to work in Vientiane. All the walls and forts were demolished, all movable weapons, elephants, and horses were despatched to Bangkok, and Anu's deputy, who had surrendered the city, received a full pardon. Rama III wanted to destroy Vientiane as a military base so as to prevent further revolts rising therefrom, as much as to warn other Laotian vassals what would be in store for them in case of treason. When the *Uparaja* and Chao Phraya Bodin returned to Bangkok, the latter was sent back north-east as the king feared that Vietnam might take over the weakened city of Vientiane. Meanwhile, helped by the Vietnamese, Anu returned to Vientiane with some remnants of his army which he had been able to gather together. Chao Phraya Bodin exercised caution and feigned a retreat, but when Anu unwisely sent his army after him, it was decisively defeated, and on October 19th, 1828, Chao Phraya Bodin re-entered Vientiane. Once again Anu was in flight, and it was some time before he was captured, betrayed by those he believed to be his friends. He and his immediate family were sent to Bangkok where they arrived on January 15th, 1829.

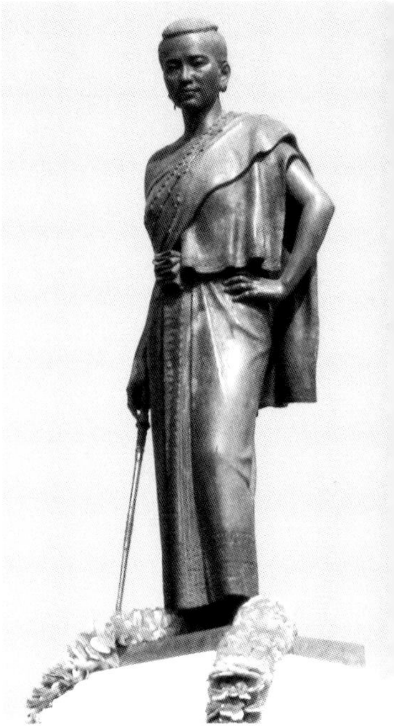

Statue commemorating Tao Suranaree. (River Books)

Rama III was bitterly angry with Anu. He had befriended him and supported him in the past against some weighty advice. There was no clear reason why Anu should revolt, given that he had been allowed freedom to run his state in his own way. The king ordered Anu to be placed in a very large iron cage and exposed by day to the public gaze. His wives were permitted to tend to his wants and give him food, and by night he was removed to sleep in reasonable conditions. An enormous crowd came every day, and the widows and children of Thai soldiers killed in the war lamented their loved ones and reviled Anu in front of his cage for hours on end. Within seven or eight days Anu was dead. He was 60 years old and died from a disease contracted earlier.[33] Standards of conduct and the treatment of opponents vary from age to age, and by some standards Rama III's treatment of Anu may be considered cruel. But it should be remembered that, apparently unprovoked, Anu had planned to destroy the Siam of Rama III when he thought that there was danger for her from the British. As a result of this prolonged insurgency, the principality of Vientiane was abolished, and her provinces came under the direct rule of Bangkok.

All through this revolt the state of Luang Prabang remained loyal to Bangkok and grew even closer in spirit. The provinces of Vientiane north of the Mekong had looked to Vietnam during the struggle, and despite the suppression of the rising, they still remained under the commercial influence of Vietnam. From 1833 onwards there was sporadic fighting between Thai and Vietnamese forces over these provinces, but without any lasting results. The Vientiane provinces close

33 Dibakarawongse: *Rama III, op. cit.*, pages 86-87.

to Luang Prabang, on the other hand, preferred at the time to be under Siamese control. As for the western Laotian states, all of them remained loyal to Rama III throughout his reign.

The British defeat of Burma in 1825-26 put an end to any danger from that country, and Siam's attitude naturally stiffened towards Vietnamese influence over Cambodia, which Siam still firmly regarded as her vassal. The complete suppression of the Vientiane rebellion gave encouragement to the pro-Thai elements in Cambodia. The Cambodian king, Ang Chan, usually in favour of Vietnam, was said to have sent a secret message to Rama III regretting his failure to take firmer action against the Vietnamese, giving as his excuse the fact that the Cambodian nobles were too divided.[34]

In July, 1833, the Vietnamese of Cochin China rebelled against their central government at Hue and sought to establish an autonomous state. The rebels asked for help from Bangkok which was granted. Two main Thai forces were quickly prepared, namely, an army of 40,000 men under Chao Phraya Bodin, the victor over Vientiane, and a naval force – using the new war boats – of 10,000 men under the Phra Klang. There was also a reserve force of Laotian conscripts. General Bodin was accompanied by two Cambodian princes who had been to Bangkok, Ang Imm and Ang Duang, and it was hoped that the Cambodian people would rally to them.

The Thais began with successes, and Bodin advanced through Cambodia as fast as his army could march. King Ang Chan now showed his true colours towards Siam by running away from Phnom Penh towards the Vietnamese generals who had come to repress the revolt. Thus when Bodin reached Phnom Penh easily, he decided to leave the two princes there to organize some sort of order and rally more Cambodian supporters. The Phra Klang's naval forces took the seaport of Hatien with no trouble; then having advanced through the canal to Chodoc, which he took after a brief battle, Bodin joined up with him and the two commanders held a conference. It was decided that the two forces should now combine, and, making use of the boats, they travelled down the Mekong towards Saigon as the water was deep enough at the time. All seemed set for a Thai victory, but they met with a check at Sadek, where the Vietnamese made a strong stand. The Thai assault on Sadek was to be simultaneously launched by Bodin and Phra Klang, but when the battle was joined on January 29th, 1834, the war boats did not make a determined attack and the whole operation was a failure. Bodin wanted to punish timid officers in Phra Klang's force, but Phra Klang staunchly defended them. As they were commanders of equal rank there was nothing Bodin could do, and they both decided on January 31st to withdraw. Phra Klang having declared that supplies were getting low and the water level of the river was falling, he and his boats returned to the port of Hatien, thence back by sea along the coast to Bangkok. Bodin marched back to Chodoc where he took up a defensive position which was twice counter-attacked by the Vietnamese, who were repulsed with some difficulty. Chao Phraya Bodin then went to Phnom Penh and followed the prevalent tactic of demolishing its walls and defences before taking his army back to Siam, bringing Prince Imm and Prince Duang with him. Rama III's idea of a double command was proved a total mistake, and the Thai failure brought Ang Chan back to his throne in Phnom Penh, backed by Vietnamese forces whose Commander-in-Chief, as the Resident, was the real ruler of all Cambodia.

In December, 1834, the adventurous and unfortunate career of Ang Chan came to an end with his death. As he left no sons, Vietnam took the unprecedented step of having one of his daughters, Princess Mey, elected Queen Regnant. It was bitterly opposed by the majority of Cambodian nobles. Furthermore, the fortunes of the Cambodian Royal Family were not helped by the intrigues between Prince Imm and Prince Duang, which ended in one being imprisoned in Hue and the other for a time being held under house arrest in Bangkok.

Vella[35] has well described the situation in Cambodia, deriving his information mainly from the French historian – Leclerc.[36] For seven years all power in Cambodia was in Vietnamese hands; the Cambodian Government, having become a legal fiction, only ruled through the strength of the occupying force of 12,000 first-class troops. Even the name of Phnom Penh was altered to the Vietnamese form of Nam Vieng, and the provinces were administered under the Vietnamese system of law. By 1840 the Vietnamese had even attacked that most revered institution – the Hinayana Buddhist Church. After the queen's sister had been accused of treason and duly executed, the royal family, with other Cambodian notables, was removed to Saigon. The limit came when a census of the population and a registration of all lands was carried out to facilitate more rigorous taxation. The ordinary Cambodian people then staged simultaneous revolts throughout the country. This resulted in the towns being still under Vietnamese control, but most of the countryside was under Cambodian patriots. As no leadership was forthcoming from their own royalty, the Cambodian people asked Rama III for help and this was speedily granted by sending an expeditionary force which was once again commanded by Chao Phraya Bodin. A slow ding-dong campaign followed in which either side supported one of the two rival princes, both of whom had been freed.

In May, 1841, successes crowned the Thai efforts and Prince Duang was accepted by the Cambodian partisans as their chief. After that Bodin marched with some ease into the heart of the country. The Vietnamese were facing troubles at home, what with a cholera epidemic and a revolt in the north – in Tongking. They withdrew their army, taking with them the rejected Prince Imm, who later died in 1843. By December, 1841, Duang was in control of Phnom Penh and all of Cambodia except in the south. The general situation of the country was bad as the farmers were thoroughly discouraged by the ravages inflicted on their lands by the continuous fighting, and they did so little

34 *Ibid.*, page 93.

35 Vella: *Siam under Rama III, op. cit.*, pages 100–108.

36 A. Leclère: *Histoire de Cambodge,* Paris, 1914.

work that they were near starvation. The Thai army itself was badly off with poor delivery of supplies from Bangkok, and it was not possble to live off the country in those conditions.

Late in 1844 the Vietnamese were able to return from Saigon to resume the war and they began with some successes. Then in one of his big counter-attacks from Udong in 1845, Bodin, who had gathered together a large number of combat elephants, used them like the tanks of modern times. These well-trained animals, closely followed by the infantry, attacked and chased the enemy with resounding success.[37] The Vietnamese began peace talks when the Cambodians promised to send tributes to their emperor at Hue, and a lengthy negotiation followed. It was a tripartite conference and Bodin, who felt that the Cambodians were utterly tired of the long war, persuaded Rama III to agree that the Cambodians should be permitted to send tributes to Hue as well as to Bangkok. The Emperor of Vietnam, who now recognized Duang as king of Cambodia, was to receive a tribute every three years. When a tribute was again sent to Bangkok in May, 1847, it was solemnly promised that the king of Siam would henceforth receive one every year. Chao Phraya Bodin was then able to return to Siam with his army. It should be noted that he was the distinguished forbear of the well-known family – Singhaseni. Rama III sent a crown, together with other objects forming the royal regalia, to Phnom Penh, and Prince Duang was duly crowned king in March, 1848 (or according to Leclerc late in 1847).

Thus Siam became the dominant foreign power in Cambodia, and it has been admitted, by such as Vella, that she exercised her control with moderation. She had no further territorial designs, and even in the provinces actually absorbed into Siam proper, Cambodian governors were appointed. Rama III won great esteem in preventing further Vietnamese encroachment against Hinayana Buddhism. He wrote to King Duang: "I do not seek any reward in Cambodia beside having the honour in time to come of having saved the country, and not allowing Buddhism to die out in Cambodia."[38] King Duang sent three sons, including his heir, to serve the king of Siam for a time in Bangkok, and in Cambodia he himself carried out legislative reforms on the Thai model.

Apart from her vassals, Siam only had direct contact with China, Vietnam, and Burma. Three ambassadors with three assistants were sent in a special mission to Peking to announce Rama Ill's accession in July, 1825, and in February, 1827, the Emperor sent gifts and acknowledged him as king of Siam.[39] Rama III sent tributary gifts to China every two years in order to maintain good trade relations which he considered more important than anything else. As always China made no attempt in this reign to exercise any control over Thai policy, external or internal.

Despite the struggles between the Siam of Rama III with Vietnam over the Laotian vassals in the north-east, and Cambodia, there was no real bitterness between the courts of Hue and Bangkok, and at no time did the army of one side penetrate the proper territory of the other, with full peace reigning between the two countries after 1847.

As for Burma, Britain's successes in the first war had finished her off as a threat since Burma had by then lost all her southern provinces bordering on Siam. All through the war, Siam was a cautious neutral, being content with guarding her frontiers. Britain had promised Siam the Mergui-Tenessarim region, lost to the Burmese sixty years before, if Siam would help with food and transport animals for the war, but Rama III had preferred friendly aloofness. By 1825 Britain was winning so easily that she ceased to press Siam for any help, and she did not make any further promises. After 1826 there were but few contacts between Burma and Siam, but Rama III was still keenly interested in that country and closely questioned anybody who came over the border.

The year 1833 saw an event of the utmost importance to Siam – the beginning of her friendship with the United States of America.

Before the arrival of Edmund Roberts, the U.S. envoy whom the Thais called "Emin Rabad – a nobleman from America", the U.S.A. had only been known through her merchant ships and her missionaries. Edmund Roberts, representing President Andrew Jackson, had first been to Vietnam and was then going on to Muscat, and he published his book about his mission in 1837.[40] He said that he was well received by everyone including the king himself . . . "His Siamese Majesty immediately ordered his best unoccupied building to be prepared for us, two of his war-boats to be sent to bring us to the city, and feast to be prepared by the Governor of Paknam, and on our arrival at the house, every comfort and every luxury were spread on the table; and cook, purveyor, servants, interpreters, and guards at our service. The Phra Klang was ordered to facilitate the speedy execution of the treaty . . ." Prior to the envoy's arrival the following royal proclamation was issued in Bangkok,[41] "Chao Phraya Phra Klang . . . received His Majesty's royal commands announcing that the Ruler of the American Country has entrusted Emin Rabad, a nobleman, with a letter to come over here with the purpose of promoting friendship and commerce. The said Emin Rabad came riding on a ship of so great a draught that it could not enter the mouth of the river. Arrangements, however, had already been made by sending boats to bring Emin Rabad himself and two noblemen of lower ranks, and the twelve servants who accompanied him . . . The Officers of the See Tamruat are to provide three bedsteads for the use of Emin Rabad and the two lesser noblemen. The Office of the Phra Klang Wiset is required to provide silken mosquito nets, whilst the Phra Klang Nai Office is entrusted with supplying three mattresses, three sheets, three pillows, and six bolsters for their use. The Royal Guards are expected to furnish three green Shanghai basins, whilst the Department of Defence has to provide the Metropolitan Department with four large water jars, and the Metropolitan Department is responsible for the carrying out of the order. The Department of Agriculture is required to supply the visitors with eight barrels of polished rice once every

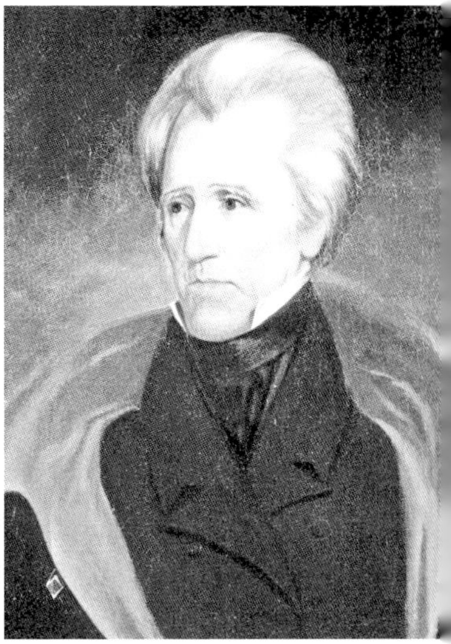

The US president, Andrew Jackson. Painted by Ralph Whiteside. (Wikimedia Commons)

37 Prince Damrong: *Tales of Olden Times, op. cit.*, pages 405-406.

38 *Collected Works of Rama III*, page 148, (in Thai), Bangkok, 1929.

39 Dibakarawongse: *Rama III, op. cit.*, pages 22-23 and 46-47.

40 Edmund Roberts: *Embassy to the Eastern Courts of Cochin-China, Siam, and Muscat*, New York, 1837.

41 *Collected History*, Part 62, *op. cit.*, pages 51-52. Translated by Nai Sukich Nimmanheminda for his lecture. Bangkok, 1958.

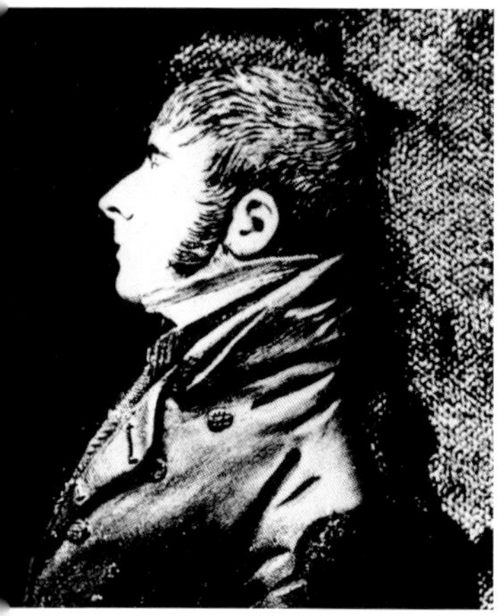

Edmund Roberts, the American envoy sent by President Andrew Jackson to develop diplomatic relations with Siam. (Library of Congress)

ten days throughout their stay, and the Phra Klang Rajakarn is required to see that sufficient firewood and coconut oil be amply provided . . . the four lesser pillars of State (ministers) are entrusted with the task of visiting the American visitors every third day with appropriate greetings and presents throughout the whole of their stay . . . As usual there was an exchange of presents of equal value, one of the American gifts being a watch studded with pearls.

Roberts' task was made easier than Burney's as the Thai themselves actively wanted to get on with him and his country, and there was no embarrassment such as the Malay question to stand in the way. The only difficulty was that Roberts tried to get more rights for his country than those granted to Britain through Burney, such as asking to establish a consulate, whereas the Thais were determined to go no further. But once Roberts realized what he was up against and accepted the situation, things moved at a rapid pace. The talks were concluded and the treaty initialled on March 20th, 1833, after only 22 days of negotiations. Apart from the king's enthusiasm for commerce. Roberts was assisted by the king's new fears of the British after their easy victory over Burma, and he wished to have the U.S.A. to balance Great Britain. The Thais' efforts to seek a balance of power has often been referred to in the west as "typically Siamese", and she has been accused of "playing one power against another." But what country has not tried to achieve the same aim at one time and another, and such a policy surely runs as a thread through the whole of history. In 1840 Thai officials told the French Consul in Singapore that they would like to see diplomatic and commercial relations established between Siam and France, but the French were not yet interested.[42]

Burney heralded satisfactory Thai relations with western powers and in the thirteen years between 1826 and 1830 Rama III gave six audiences to western diplomats, "a figure that probably cannot be matched by any other Asiastic country during that time."[43] Prosperity and trade were on the increase and there were usually over 50 large ships in Bangkok at a given time – mostly British. At that time sugar – not rice as yet was the principal export. An Englishman, Robert Hunter,[44] came to set himself up permanently in Bangkok and became a partner in trade of the government with influence at court. It was only when more and more Thai nobles began to enter business that Hunter lost his large profits as his position as a middleman was no longer necessary to the Thais. And at this point Hunter made a wrong move by resorting to the import of opium which was against the law. Further serious trouble arose in 1844 between Hunter and the government when Thai officials refused to pay for a steamer which Hunter had imported into Siam. It was not clear whether the boat had or had not been actually ordered, but the Thais said it was not good enough and the price was exorbitant. According to them Hunter then lost his temper and in his anger said many insulting things. Typical of many *farangs* then operating in Southeast Asia, Hunter threatened to ask the

42 Vella in page 124 quotes Capitaine Seauve: *Les Relations de la France et du Siam,* page 26, Paris, 1908.

43 Vella: *Siam under Rama III, op. cit.*, page 125.

44 Not a relative of the wife of the present author.

45 Vella: *Siam under Rama III, op. ci,* page 129.

46 *Ibid.*, page 130.

47 *Ibid.*, page 128.

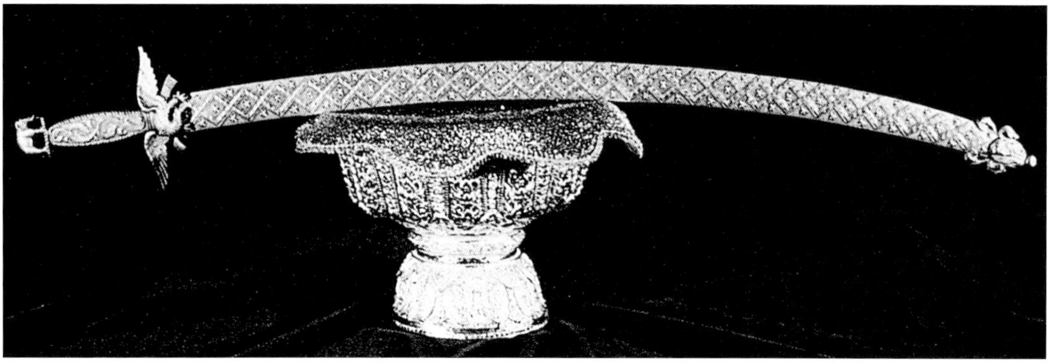

British Government in India to send warships to keep the Thai government in order, but in the end his request was refused by the British authorities on the grounds that the case was not clear. Surprisingly the usually scholarly and impartial Vella notes, "There is little doubt that the refusal of the British Government to support Hunter encouraged the Siamese in their restrictive trade policy."[45] One might well think that he was endorsing the general western feelings towards Asians in the nineteenth century if he had not added the words of Spencer St. John, the secretary of the next British envoy, Sir James Brooke: "As we only heard the English account of these quarrels, I have no hesitation in saying how ill they (the English) behaved. Had we heard the king's account we should have probably to speak even more strongly."[46] The government of Rama III had signed treaties with Britain and America in the hope of having diplomatic and commercial relations on equal terms, but veiled threats from the west did not seem to cease as was shown in the Hunter case, and the local western traders would probably have liked to see these threats implemented by acts of force. The idea that an Asian people had the justifiable right to enjoy and control their own trade might have been understood and supported by the liberal-minded Europeans in their own countries, but it was anathema to the local western people "out east". Vella quotes an American merchant in 1849: "The Siamese government and (tax) farmers have been going little by little, for the last ten years, to get the trade of *this place* (my italics) into their own hands, and which they have pretty well accomplished, from the fact that both the American and British governments have, for many years past neglected to visit this port and to see that their respective treaties have been abided by."[47]

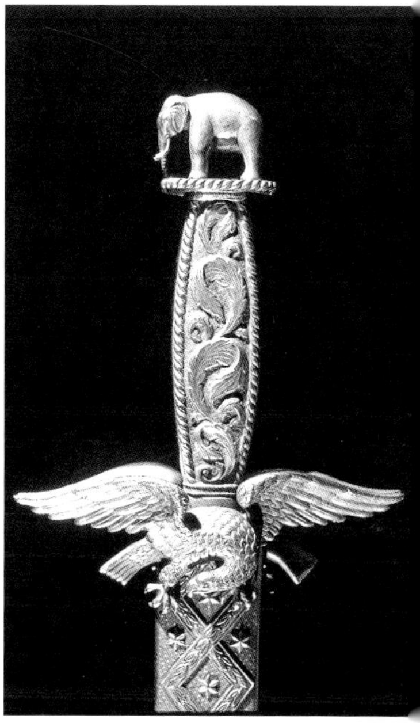

ABOVE AND TOP LEFT: A golden sword carved with an elephant and an eagle, symbols of the two countries, which was gifted to Rama III by Andrew Jackson in 1833. (US National Archives)

It was the usual cry that Rama III was not keeping to the terms of the treaties because he was trading with his own ships and had farmed out the collection of internal duties. But Rama III claimed that internal duties were not prohibited by the treaties, and that surely he could do what he liked with his own Thai subjects. He also insisted that his officials could operate their own European-type ships of which there were 17. That the British had their own conception of equal relations was demonstrated in 1840 when the Thai navy captured Chinese boats sailing into Bangkok with a cargo of opium which was strictly

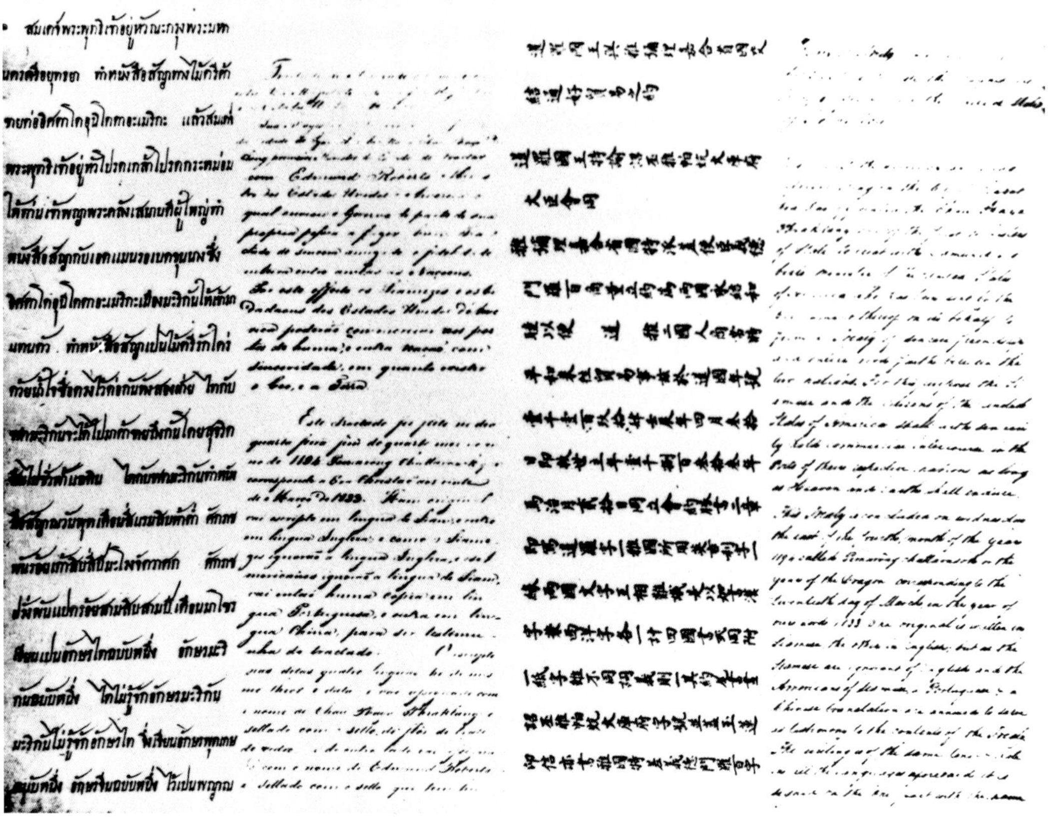

The first diplomatic and trade treaty between Siam and the United States. Within the treaty, four languages were used – Thai, Portuguese, Chinese and English. (US National Archives)

prohibited by Thai law. Because these Chinese ships were from Singapore and the owners and sailors were British subjects, the Singaporean authorities protested most vigorously against the capture, and the Chinese smugglers were released to avoid any rupture with the British. Between 1839 and 1842 Great Britain had won the first China War, had acquired Hong Kong, and China had been forced to open up a number of ports to trading vessels of all nations. It was only natural that in a far smaller country like Siam both the British and American merchants would want trading conditions similar to those in China, so both powers sent new diplomatic missions.

Joseph Balestier, an American merchant and U.S. Consul in Singapore, was commissioned by the President as a special envoy to Bangkok in 1849 with the aim of securing more favourable trading terms by a new treaty and also to establish a U.S. Consulate in in the capital. He arrived by a warship at the mouth of the Bangkok river on March 24th, 1850, but unlike Edmund Roberts, he was not accompanied by any "lesser noblemen" or U.S. naval officers coming ashore. Instead his suite consisted of local American missionaries, an interpreter, and a Chinese servant[48] The Phra Klang was away on official duties in the south of Siam and Balestier was received by his deputy, Phraya Sripipat. The very first interview proved disastrous as Balestier was very rude when Phraya Sripipat according to Thai

48 *American Envoys in the Third Reign – 1850*, pages 11-12 (in Thai), Bangkok, 1923.

49 *Ibid.*, page 15.

custom, asked after the health of the President Zachary Taylor and whether Balestier himself had had a pleasant voyage. Such questions were brusquely brushed aside as a waste of time and let's get on with business".[49] He had brought two letters, one with his own credentials and the other containing the objects of his mission, and he wanted to present these two letters to the king forthwith. The minister asked to see the letters first which greatly upset Balestier. It was explained to him that the Thais regarded a letter from a Head of State as an object of great importance. It had to be carried in State, translated and read to the king before the envoy was received, and Edmund Roberts had agreed to the entire procedure. Balestier then consented to let the minister take the letter, with the proviso that it be returned to him to deliver to the King in person. The minister insisted that it was not the custom, and after further altercations, Balestier walked out of the room in a towering rage. When he later met the minister again, besides complaining over trivial matters, Balestier declared that tax-farming by Siam was a violation of the treaty concluded with Roberts. Phraya Sripipat finally said that it was useless to discuss anything with such a difficult and intemperate man, but the Thai people desired to continue friendly relations with the American people. Although the Phra Klang returned on April 12th, the situation did not improve as he ignored Balestier's demands that Sripipat should be punished for insulting the U.S. envoy and the American people. Balestier had to leave without achieving his objective and the Thai ministers wrote to the captain of the U.S. warship who had brought him that they could not risk an audience with the king for such an ill-tempered man.

The British sent Sir James Brooke, who had distinguished himself in Borneo and become the first white Rajah of Sarawak, who arrived on

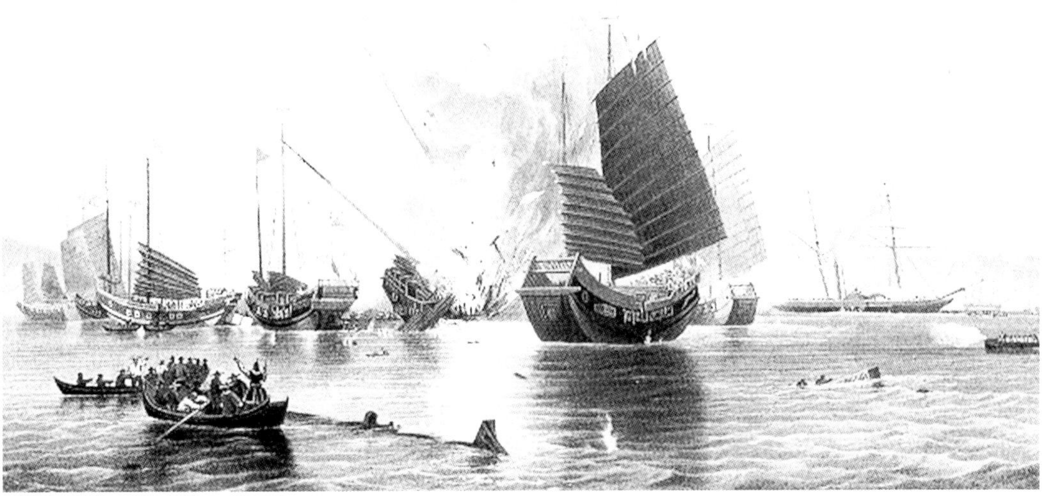

A painting showing a Chinese war junk being destroyed by the British during the First Opium War of 1839-1842. (http://ocw.mit.edu/ans7870/21f/21f.027/opium_wars_01/ow1_gallery/pages/1841_0792_nemesis_jm_nmm.htm)

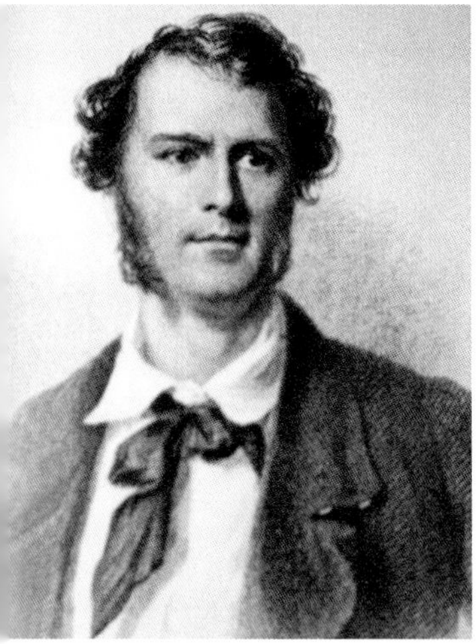

Sir James Brooke, the British envoy sent to Siam by Queen Victoria. (London, National Portrait Gallery)

August 10th, 1850, and stayed six weeks, having been accredited from Queen Victoria and not from the Governor-General of India. He came with a large suite, including three British officers, and travelled in three ships. The main English account of his stay in Bangkok comes from his secretary, Spencer St. John.[50] At first there was some doubt on the Thai side concerning his credentials, and Rama III thought that if the treaty of 1826 was to be revoked, it should be revoked by Burney coming back himself or by someone else sent from India, but Brooke explained that he was in a stronger position, having been seen by Queen Victoria herself.

Although he met the Phra Klang on August 25th, it was decided to negotiate by letters, and by September 10th Brooke had sent four letters,[51] and a draft of the revised treaty. He warned the Thais that treaty violations over trading matters had to cease, and darkly reminded them that Chinese obstructions of trade had led to the war and the defeat of China in 1840. Britain desired only to strengthen friendship and trade, but the 1826 treaty had to be drastically revised.

The Thai minister replied with three letters. The British request for the right of residence was rejected on the grounds that they did not want the possibility of having another quarrelsome person like Hunter in Siam. The Thais maintained that their only action which might be interpreted as treaty violation was when they caught the Chinese opium smugglers from Singapore. To the British demand for religious freedom, they said it was unnecessary as the Christians and missionaries were free already. No *farang* merchant had complained of any obstruction of trade. The British wished to have a resident consul in Bangkok, and for the first time the demand for extra-territorial rights was made. The Thais replied that since 1818 the presence of the Portuguese consul had not brought any increase in trade or benefits, that Thai officials could decide disputes with foreign merchant ships without a consul, and in any case it was not the Thai custom to send consuls abroad. As for extra-territorial rights, which Burney had not claimed, the Phra Klang said that Thai citizens in foreign countries would abide by the laws of those countries, so they expected foreigners to do the same in Siam.

Brooke's draft of the commercial agreement was not a revised version of that made in 1826, but a new one altogether. Most articles of imports were to be duty free, and a limited number of articles would pay moderate duties. Ship measurement duties were to be reduced to one-third of those then existing. The request that rice should be free for export the Thais could not agree to, saying that as it was the staple food of the people the government could not permit it to be exported in case of crop failure. It is clear that the king's ministers were suspicious of Brooke's draft and they sent him a joint letter of great length on September 27th, 1850, a part of which said, "Sir James Brooke is a very clever negotiator. From the time we became officials in the government of the king, in some cases 70 years, 60 years, 50 years, 40 years, 30 years and 20 years ago, we have not encountered anyone else who came to conduct diplomatic negotiations like a professor giving instructions –

instructions that pour forth like waters flooding forests and fields. Obsessed with arranging commercial matters, he thinks exclusively of getting results and advantages for merchants, he has no feelings for the interests of the population as a whole."[52]

Brooke had already announced his approaching departure before he received this long letter. He did not have an audience with the king because Rama III was very seriously ill at the time, and as a result there was no treaty. Together with the joint ministerial letter to Brooke, the Phra Klang sent him a letter for Lord Palmerston, then British Foreign Secretary, which stated that a new treaty was unnecessary as the Thai government was upholding the Burney treaty of 1826 in every way and the Thai desire for friendship was strongly stressed.[53] Brooke refused the usual offer of stipends for the stay of a diplomat, and Rama III spent the money so set aside to buy ornaments for a Buddhist temple. Sir James left Bangkok on September 28th, 1850.

Although any danger from Brooke's veiled threats was averted for the time being, the Thai ministers were fully aware of the growing British power in South-East Asia after Britain's defeats of Burma in 1826 and of China in 1840. As for Burma, Hall says, "Her military power, once the terror of all neighbours, was broken beyond recovery".[54] Regarding the British attitude, also according to Hall,[55] Lord Dalhousie, then Governor-General of India, said, "The government of India could never, consistently with its own safety, permit itself to stand for a single day in an attitude of inferiority towards a *native power* (my italics) . . ." He wrote to a friend,"We can't afford to be shown the door anywhere in the East." Some of the Thai intelligentsia, especially the few, who, like Prince Mongkut, had begun to learn English, knew what to expect from the West, for the Thais "had always been better able to accommodate to change than their neighbours." "They were better able than most East Asians to admit the superiority of the West in certain aspects."[56] But Rama III did insist on strengthening the forts at Paknam and an iron chain was made ready to be strung across the mouth of the river against hostile ships.

There was one major family tragedy in this reign. One of his uncles, Prince Rakronaret, had already been prominent in the second reign. When Rama III's *Uparaja* died on May 1st, 1832, Prince Rakronaret himself as well as many other people thought that he would be appointed to that high post, but instead the King merely promoted him from *Krom Muen* to *Krom Luang*. By 1838 he was the senior prince of the family, and he continued to be given more responsibilities and power. Then gradually the king began to receive complaints that the prince was abusing his power and privileges. In November, 1848, after complaints had become so frequent and persistent, Rama III decided to set up a special court of inquiry. Rakronaret was charged with taking bribes and of embezzlement, all of which the court decided were true. His private life was also in question and it was alleged that he preferred the company of his ballet dancers to his wives. When asked whether he thought this was

50 Spencer St. John: *The Life of Sir James Brooke, Rajah of Sarawak: From his Personal Papers and Correspondence*, London, 1879.

51 *Collected History*, No. 62, *op. cit.*, pages 118-219.

52 *Collected History*, No. 62, *op. cit.*, pages 200-217. Vella's English translation. pages 138-139.

53 *Ibid.*, pages 214-215.

54 D. G. E. Hall, *op. cit.*, page 519.

55 *Ibid.*, pages 526-527.

56 Vella, *op. cit.*, page 143.

improper, his brave reply was that his private life was no concern of the king. He was further accused of high treason in plotting to obtain support for himself to be King. This charge he most vehemently denied, admitting only that he had made up his mind not to serve another monarch if Rama III should pass away. He did not say how he proposed to avoid this, but it was known that he had shown antipathy towards Prince Mongkut even though the latter was a monk. One of the many departments he was in charge of was that of religion. Present in the Amarindra Hall when Prince Mongkut, as a priest, was sitting for his examination, and being so successful, Rakronaret exclaimed, "How much further is this going on?" Being deeply hurt, Mongkut begged leave to discontinue the examination. The court considered that the charges against him were proven and the hapless Prince Rakronaret was executed on December 13th, 1848.[57] He was, so far, the last person to be despatched in the manner reserved for princes by being beaten on the back of the neck with a sandalwood club.[58] Later kings did not hold this sad affair against his descendants, and they were to be prominent in the service of King Mongkut and King Rama VI.

During the reign of Rama III three senior ladies of the Royal Family passed away. His grandmother, Queen Amarindra, the wife of Rama I, died on May 25th, 1826. Ten years later Prince Mongkut's mother and celestial princess in her own right died on October 18th, 1836. Then the king's mother, Queen Sri Sulalaya, died on May 18th, 1837. A grandiose cremation was arranged for all three.[59] Rama III had no wife of royal rank and appointed no queen, thus he had no children of *Chao Fa* rank.

Although more than ten fine elephants of different unusual colours were presented to him, mostly by his Laotian vassals, no fully qualified "white" elephant was found for Rama III. Himself a pious and devout Buddhist, he was tolerant of other faiths except once in 1849 when he was extremely annoyed with eight Roman Catholic priests. That year saw the outbreak of a serious pestilence and the king ordered a period of deep devotion and piety to be observed. He himself spent enormous sums buying up large numbers of animals awaiting slaughter and then set them free, and he asked the public to do the same. Eight Roman Catholic priests declared that the idea was nothing but superstition and useless. They not only refused to comply, they told the Thai Christian converts under their care to refuse also. The king was furious, saying that he would expel all Christian priests and have all their churches pulled down. Fortunately Bishop Pallegoix declared that the eight priests had shown excessive zeal and there was nothing in the Christian religion against setting free animals which were to be slaughtered. The Bishop sent the king some chickens, ducks, and geese, so that he could set them free. Rama III was therefore pacified and all was forgiven.[60] Despite the popular belief that he was reactionary and ultra conservative, it was Rama III, who, impressed with the results of anti smallpox vaccination by Dr. Bradley, the American missionary, with dried scab from Boston in 1840, ordered more to be brought from India, had Thai doctors taught how to vaccinate and had over 10,000 people so treated.[61]

The king had been healthy most of his life and when he had his last illness he knew it was fatal. He sent for the princes and senior statesmen and asked them to remain united to serve the kingdom and the dynasty which had by then lasted 69 years. Although there were many princes, the king told the council not to ask him to name his successor, wanting them to take responsibility for choosing one of the princes themselves. Above all he begged them not to be ambitious, fight and kill one another for power. They should be like him in thinking only of the State, and he had no natural urge to choose one of his own sons as king. He asked them to be firm in loyalty to the kings of the first three reigns and their memory. He criticized several of the princes individually, declaring that Prince Mongkut was the only sound and good prince, but he was afraid he would make the entire priesthood wear the yellow robe in the Mon fashion. He asked the council to set aside 80,000 bahts and some gold from the Privy Purse to be spent on restoring and maintaining some temples in his memory. As his mother and her parents were commoners and thinking that they would not be regarded as the direct forbears of future monarchs, he asked that their relics be removed from the Grand Palace to avoid being an embarrassment to future sovereigns. He did not, of course, know that his successor, King Mongkut, would take two of his granddaughters to wife, and that King Chulalongkorn and all future monarchs would be his and their descendants. He even asked, when already desperately ill, to be moved from the Chakrapat Hall as the new king might not like his dying there.[62] His mind was clear and he was fully conscious until he passed away on April 2nd, 1851. He was 63 years old and had been king for 25 years, 7 months, and 23 days. He had continued the work of the dynasty in improving the strength and prosperity of Siam, and there can be no question that in his long reign it was he, and he alone, who was the Ruler.

57 Dibakarawongse: *Rama III, op. cit.*, page 317.

58 The Author asked King Prajadhipok in 1951 whether there was an executioner still capable of carrying out this method of execution and the reply was in the affirmative.

59 Dibakarawongse, *op. cit.*, pages 35, 167, 174.

60 *Ibid.*, page 351.

61 King Chulalongkorn: *Sermon, op. cit.*, pages 94-97.

62 *Ibid.*, page 97.

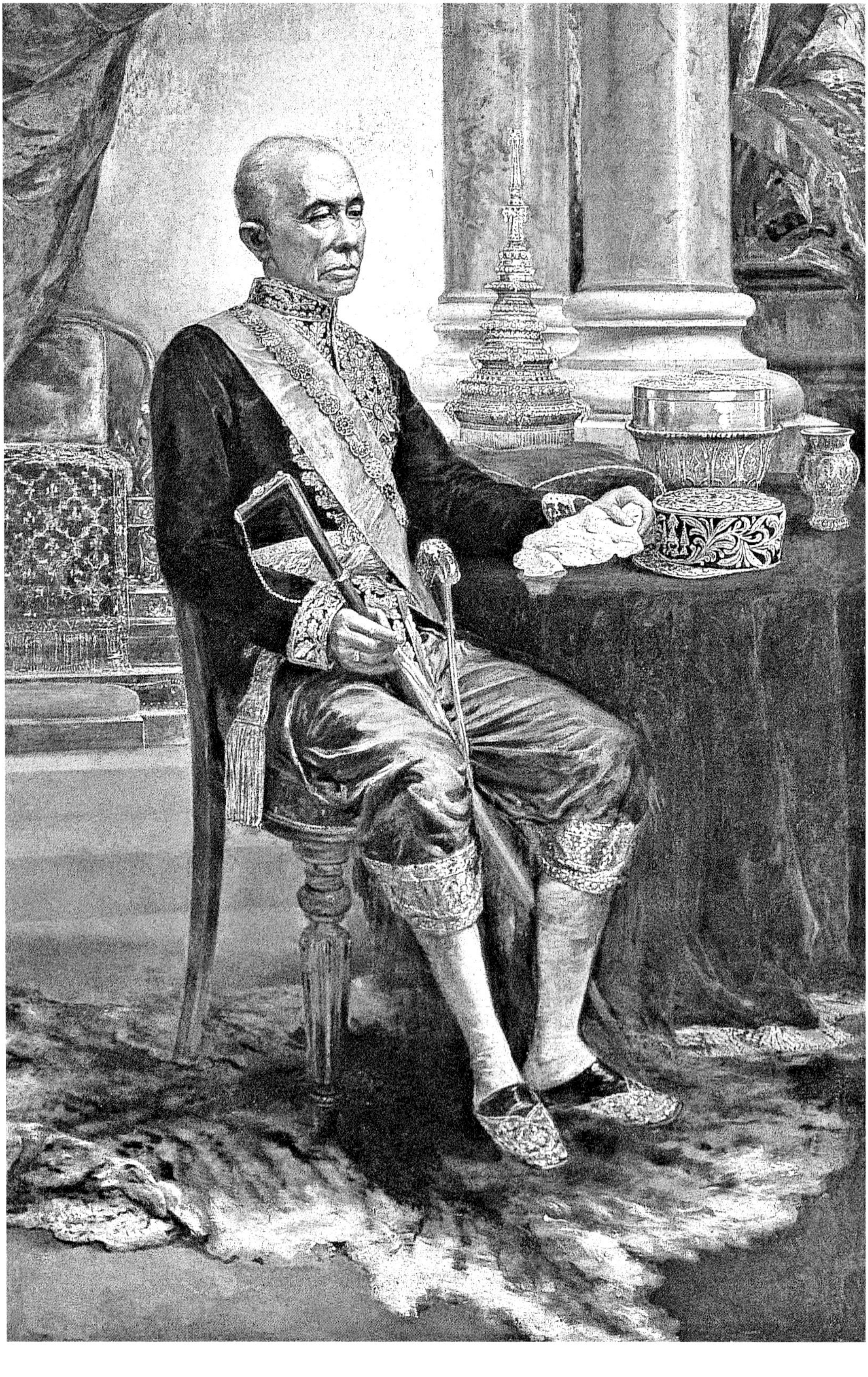

Chapter Four
THE ENLIGHTENED
(A.D. 1851 to 1868)

Portrait of King Mongkut, Rama IV, within the Chakri Maha Prasat Throne Hall.

It was an abbot of a monastery, a monk of 27 years' standing, who was invited to be king of Siam. Since the second world war, this fourth Chakri king, best known in the West as King Mongkut, has become the most renowned monarch inThai history. This is not due as much to his own great qualities and achievements, which in themselves entitle him to a full-length biography, but more to an American novel, a black and white film, and also to a musical play which was later made into a technicolour film.[1] All of this should perhaps be ignored by one who seeks here to be a serious historian, but the incidents and scenes from the above have become so familiar to so many people throughout the world as to be believed as real facts, and it is difficult not to refer to some of them. For this lapse, the author hopes for some sympathy, as much as for the difficulty of compressing King Mongkut's full life into one chapter.

Although Mongkut was the senior *Chao Fa* there was no rule in his time to make him more of a legal heir than the other princes, but the council was in one mind about the succession to Rama III, and even before the king's death the Phra Klang had been to see him at the monastery to warn him of this. Not wishing to risk the rivalry of others and an upheaval, the prince-priest promised to give up the yellow robe and accept the crown. News of the illness of Rama III was received in Singapore by the Editor of the *Singapore Free Press.* The letter, dated March 29th, 1851, was written by John Taylor Jones, an American missionary who had ccme to Siam in 1833.

He had become one of Mongkut's friends and, having been asked to call on him at the monastery, Mongkut told him that he would be elected as the next monarch. He had agreed to accept the offer, and Jones added: "So that no serious disturbances are apprehended".[2]

Rama III had breathed his last at 4 a.m. on April 2nd and later that forenoon prince-priest Mongkut was escorted from his monastery in a grand procession, watched by many of his future subjects, to reside at the Emerald Buddha Temple in the Grand Palace. A company of soldiers accompanied him while another was guarding his younger brother at the latter's own residence.[3]

That the enlightened Prince Mongkut would bring about many progressive reforms was anticipated in Singapore. "The new monarch is a man of liberal sentiments, and far in advance of the generality of his countrymen . . . we think the present sovereign will make great improvements in the country, will be very liberal to foreigners and their trade."[4] Mongkut, however, had first received the normal education of

1 Margaret Landon: *Anna and the King of Siam,* New York, 1944. The film *Anna and the King of Siam* with Rex Harrison as King. The musical play *The King and I,* and the musical film of the same name, both with Yul Brynner as the King.

2 *News of the beginning of the 4th Reign in a Singapore newspaper* (in Thai and English). Bangkok, 1932.

3 Dibakarawongse: *History of the 4th Reign,* pages 2-3, Bangkok, 1935.

4 *News . . . from Singapore, op. cit.,* pages 9-19.

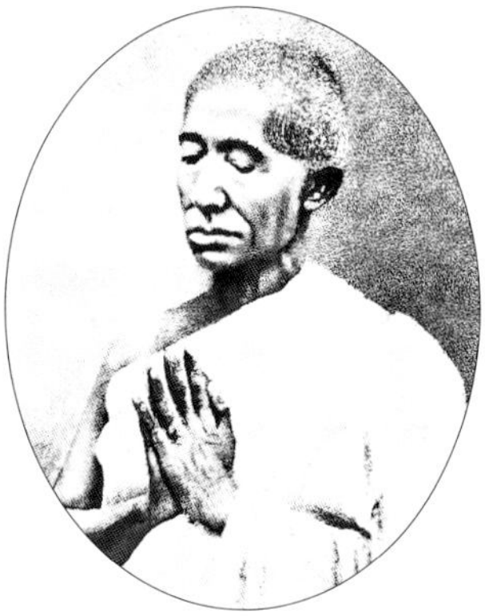
Prince Mongkut in his monk's robes. (Paisarn Piemmettawat)

a Thai prince of his time, being initially brought up in the Inside of the Palace amongst women, and had passed his earliest years in the feminine atmosphere of "domestic art of unheard of virtuosity".[5] The palace women cooked delicious dishes to be eaten with rice, and they delicately pealed luscious fruits into artistic patterns; they weaved as well as embroidered silken cloth, while with deft fingers they created exquisite garlands and bouquets out of fresh flowers. In addition, they could dance in the ballet and play musical instruments. As in the time of Ayutthaya, for the women to go and live in the palace was like attending a university of feminine accomplishments.

From this gentle background the prince was transferred to the care of men on the approach of puberty. He now learned to read and write more advanced Thai as well as elementary Pali, he was taught to ride and to shoot and to practise the ancient art of fencing, but no foreign language was included in the curriculum as no pureThai could then speak English or any European language. With such upbringing Mongkut might have grown up a normal and conventional Thai prince of the highest rank, but for the fact that after entering the Buddhist priesthood at 21, he did not come out after the usual three months but stayed on for 27 years. Why he stayed on, how he passed his time, and how he reformed theThai priesthood has been related in the previous chapter. His varied experiences as a monk were of incalculable advantage to him and to theThai nation when he came to ascend the throne. The life of a monk was strict, for unlike the layman with five precepts, the monk lives under 227 rules which includes among other restrictions abstention from all sex, the shaving of the hair on the head and eyebrows, a ban on touching gold, silver, or any money, or attending any place of amusement, or eating after midday, as well as leading a communal life in the monastery with few possessions apart from the yellow robes, the food bowl, and bare necessities. Thus the monastic life taught him strict discipline, as much as the Buddhist doctrine which was a fine philosophy combined with a profession of faith. As with all other monks, Mongkut was given a priestly name and his was Vajirayana.

A monastery was a democratic place, for the monks were drawn from all classes, and only their seniority in the order prevailed, so that the prince-priest mingled intimately with people he would otherwise not have seen, let alone spoken to, while the laity who came to worship were also from every walk of life. As the American admirer of King Mongkut, Alexander Griswold, explained, the experience made him think of himself more clearly as an ordinary human being and his subjects were almost his equals and not his chattels. Thus although he would expect complete obedience from them, his laws and his commands must be just and for the common good. As a monk he travelled widely throughout the country, an experience then denied to princes except when on war service. He had even gone into the jungle and up the mountains where he met the primitive hill tribes. From all of this, he developed his sense of duty to the whole people which was to be the guiding principle of his career.[6]

When he was a monk, Mongkut thought deeply about Buddhism. As the doctrine was first written down 400 years after the death of the Buddha, he felt that there must have been some mistaken beliefs in it. This testing of the doctrine was quite in order for a priest, for the Buddha himself had asked people not to believe or accept anything on blind faith – not even his own teaching. In testing the doctrine, he made judicious selections and rejections, and as Griswold observed, Mongkut created a new Buddhism while modestly thinking that he had merely revised the old doctrine. He claimed that Buddhism did not conflict with modem science, although the doctrine was based on the transmigration of souls, and Karma was the consequence of deeds in past, present, and future lives, an idea which had not yet been scientifically proven as a fact. Griswold suggested that Mongkut's mind might have run like this: "If you can't believe it, then follow the Buddha who said, 'If you are not sure, you had better be on the safe side. If you believe in it you will lead a good life, gain the respect of all, and lose nothing even if it turns out that you have guessed wrong. But if you reject it, you will very likely follow your own evil desires; and in this case, if it turns out you have guessed wrong, you will be like a traveller without provisions.' "[7]

Good Karma follows from the carrying out of acts of merit, and Mongkut made a clear distinction between good and foolish merit making. Some of the latter were considered harmless enough such as building sand pagodas in the monastic grounds at festival time or carrying images in a procession, as these could be regarded as simple reminders of the doctrine. Real merit, however, must be of social value. The rich could build monasteries (or today hospitals, dispensaries, schools, or libraries), but the poor could actively bridge a stream with a few bamboo poles or clear a path of sharp thorns; and all could give alms in proportion to their means.

Once he felt that he had absorbed enough of the Buddhist doctrine, Mongkut began to study other subjects. Although a Buddhist monk, he was friendly with the Roman Catholic bishop, Pallegoix, for the latter's Church of the Immaculate Conception was next door to Wat Samorai. From the bishop he learned Latin and in turn taught him Pali. He had English lessons from his American missionary friends, the Rev. Dr. D. B. Bradley and the Rev. J. Caswell. One of his English teachers is reported as saying: "He spoke it fluently but with a literary tinge, as if he had acquired it from books rather than conversation".[8] The prince-priest wanted to pay Mr. Caswell for the lessons, but the latter refused and asked instead to be allowed to preach the Christian doctrine to the Buddhist monks in their monastery, and to this request Mongkut agreed without hesitation.[9] He learned English with Mr. Caswell for nearly six years, and became proficient enough to understand all that he read, and he himself wrote English in his quaint

5 Alexander B. Griswold: *The Real King Mongkut of Siam. Eastern World,* London, March, 1955.

6 A. B. Griswold: *King Mongkut in Perspective. J.O.S.S.,* Vol. XLV, Part I, April, 1957.

7 *Ibid.*

8 Quoted by Dr. Malcolm Smith, *op. cit.*, page 24.

9 Prince Damrong: *Memoirs, op. cit.*, pages 68-71.

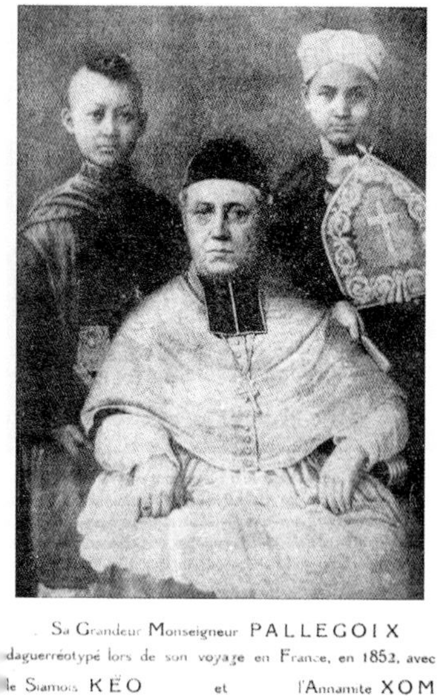

Bishop Jean-Baptiste Pallegoix was the first to introduce photography to Siam. (From *Description du Royaume Thai ou Siam*, Paris, 1854)

manner which was often forceful and apt in expression. Some other princes, including his full brother, Chao Fa Chudamani, and some of the young noblemen followed his example in learning English, but apparently none could match him in his knowledge, and he was the first Asian king to be able to understand, speak, and write English.

His knowledge of English was the key which unlocked the door to other studies, and he then began to read books on modern science, geography, history, mathematics, and astronomy – the last being his favourite subject. He was greatly interested in comparative religion and many a discussion took place with Bishop Pallegoix and the American missionaries. Griswold thought that his Christian friends once felt that they were on the point of converting him, but he could not accept Divine Revelation or the Redemption of Sin, only human reason; yet he admired Christian ethics. He is said to have told the missionaries : "What you teach them to *do* is admirable, but what you teach them to *believe* is foolish."[10] But if Christian faith helped other people he saw no harm in it, and, both as a monk and later as king, he helped the Catholic priests and missionaries in every possible way. He knew the Bible well and later surprised the English teacher of his children with : "Do you know the word 'Charity' or *Maitri* as your apostle St. Paul explains it in the thirteenth chapter of the First Epistle to the Corinthians?"[11]

At the Accession Council assembled in the Grand Palace, while Mongkut, still a priest, was waiting in the Emerald Buddha Temple, the noble ministers had more power and influence than ever before owing to the fact that by the end of Rama III's reign there were no prominent senior princes. The meeting was brief for all agreed on Prince Mongkut. When he was told of their decision he modestly said that he accepted in order to avoid any trouble, and he proceeded to take leave of the Order. However, once he was king he was quick to show them all that he was the master by the first edict which he issued about dress. Formerly those who attended the royal audience could do so naked to the waist when it was very warm. Part of the edict said "Those who do not wear jackets are as much as being naked altogether. Their torsoes might be blemished by skin troubles or they might be heavily perspiring, in both cases it was utterly disgusting. In all countries which are great powers men wear jackets and are properly dressed. People who do not dress properly are uncivilized or they are primitive savage tribes. Henceforth you will all wear jackets when attending my audiences."[12]

For the fourth time in Bangkok, a grandiose and traditional coronation ceremony was carried out. The Grand Palace alone was decorated for several days with 7,000 oil lamps of different hues arranged with artistry, and there were illuminations everywhere. The series of ceremonies began on May 15th, 1851, and finally when the crown was presented to him King Mongkut put it firmly on his head. The usual lengthy styles and titles were presented to him as for his three predecessors, but King Mongkut had three new and significant titles. One was that he was born "of royal parents on both sides". The next was that he was "admirably well versed in the *Tripitaka*"– the Buddhist canon. The third and also significant was "elected by all the people", for the Accession Council had always claimed to represent all Siam. Besides these and the old titles he added *Maha Mongkut* to preserve the name which he had made so famous already, especially with western people. It was the firstThai coronation ceremony watched by Europeans and Americans. The *Singapore Free Press* reported thus: "The Europeans were invited to witness the ceremony and met with a gracious reception. A dinner was provided for them in the European-style and presents were afterwards distributed to them consisting of gold and silver coins of the new issue."[13] On May 20th there was a procession by land round the city with 10,000 troops, both infantry and cavalry, together with troops in European dress drawing artillery pieces and carrying muskets. By then many beautiful royal barges had been constructed, and the king felt that the people would enjoy seeing them in a river procession. Thus one was held the next day when all the gorgeous long boats were brought out and the one carrying the king was propelled by one hundred men in scarlet using paddles with gold painted blades. The boat procession went right round the city by river and connecting canals, and the king alighted at Wat Bowonniwet to worship the presiding Buddha image of his old monastery.[14]

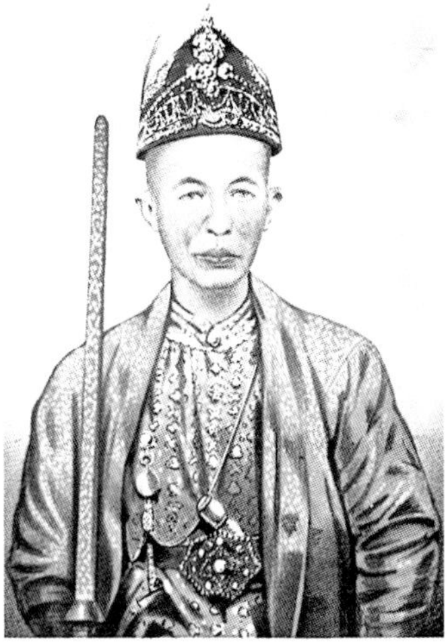

King Mongkut sketched by a foreigner. (From *King Mongkut of Siam*, A.B. Griswold, 1961)

Soon after the coronation it was the occasion for the king to appoint his deputy – the *Uparaja*, and his choice could hardly fall on anyone else but his full brother, Prince Chudamani. However, instead of merely appointing him Deputy-King, Mongkut returned 250 or so years to the reign of King Naresuan, and, like him, appointed his brother to be Second King with almost equal status and a coronation of nearly the same splendour, with the Second King then going to live at the Palace of the Front which had been empty for some years. The Thais did not like to call exalted princes by their proper names, and King Mongkut conceived the new idea of giving the monarch an additional and individual title after his coronation. Upon Rama III he bestowed the posthumous title of Phra Nangklao, for himself he chose Phra Chomklao, and for his brother Phra Pinklao, all of which were puns on their proper names. Rama III had originally been called Tup, which means being on top of something, and Nangklao means sitting on the heads (of the people over whom he ruled). Mongkut means a crown and Chomklao means an object crowning the head, while Chudamani means a hairpin for the children's top-knot, and *pin* is aThai word for a hairpin.

There is a substantiated story that King Mongkut had wanted the council to offer the throne jointly to his brother and himself, hence he went on to make him an almost equal Second King. This was also because Prince Chudamani's horoscope was so strong that he was likely to be a king one day, which made Mongkut feel that, if he were

10 Griswold: *The Real King Mongkut, op. cit.* Griswold: *King Mongkut in Perspective, op. cit.*

11 Anna Leonowens, *op. cit.*, page 165.

12 Dibakarawongse: *Rama IV, op. cit.*, page 6.

13 *News . . . from Singapore, op. cit.*, page 10.

14 Dibakarawongse: *Rama IV, op. cit.*, pages 7-38.

king alone, he would not live very long.[15] As he had been for 27 years a strict and progressive monk, the founder of the new Thammayut sect, it is difficult, even in the face of seemingly good evidence, to believe that he could have been influenced by such a superstitious idea. Perhaps it is more likely that he loved his brother as dearly as Naresuan had loved Ekatotsarot, yet felt in his brother a feeling of rivalry, and by making him the Second King he was able to demonstrate his great love yet put an end to any ambition which the younger prince might have entertained.

Just before he died one of the things which had disturbed Rama III was that, if Mongkut should succeed him, which was likely, he would abolish the Maha Nikaya sect and turn the entire priesthood into the Thammayut, and, as he put it, make them all wear the yellow robe in the Mon fashion. The king's feelings were conveyed to the prince-priest by one of the ministers. Mongkut immediately wrote to the king saying that in forming the Thammayut sect, he was thinking only in terms of religion and not of politics. He then ordered the Thammayut priests to return to wearing the robe in theThai way and they were to do so for the rest of his reign, only taking up the Mon fashion again after his death in 1868.[16] In fact, throughout his reign King Mongkut showed no special favours to the Thammayut over the Maha Nikaya and both sects prospered in harmony and improved themselves in every way.

King Pinklao, photographed in 1851. (National Archives Bangkok)

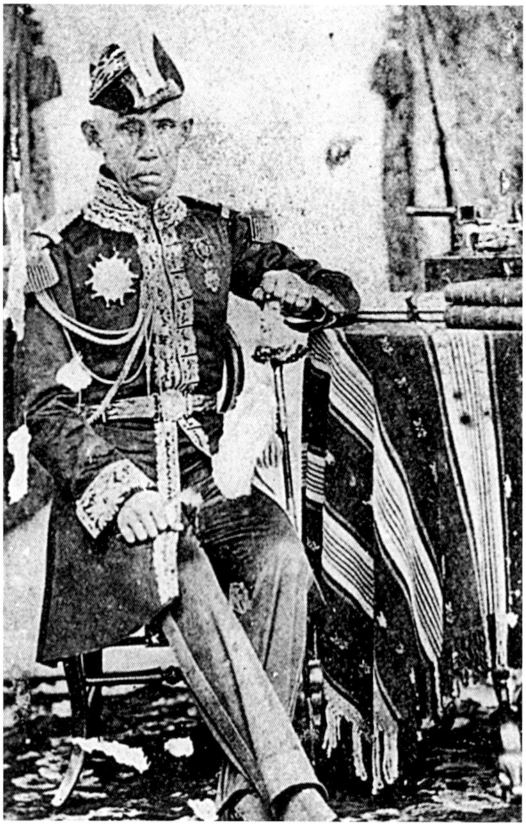

One of the princes promoted in rank, as was the custom after the coronation, was the prince-priest, a son of Rama I, who was also a great poet. He died on December 9th, 1852. King Mongkut's own two sons, born before he took up the yellow robe, were also promoted to *Krom Muen* rank. The elder of the two, Prince Nobawongse, became Krom Muen Mahesuan, and his grandson was to become the Supreme Patriarch in the reign of the present monarch, King Bhumibol, until his demise in 1958. Towards the close of Rama Ill's reign the highest position of Chief Minister fell vacant and it was offered to the Phra Klang, who declined the post saying that the holder of that high position did not live very long. He became the Kalahom as well, holding two seals, and was by far the most powerful man after the king. The new monarch promoted him to the specially exalted noble rank of *Somdech Chao Phraya* (a title King Taksin was alleged to have conferred on Rama I when he was General Chakri), and his younger brother, Phraya Sripipat, also received the same rank. They both had lengthy titles, Borommaha Payurawongse and Borommaha

Bijayayati respectively, and they were accorded almost the same honours as princes. But they were generally called *Ong Yai* (Senior Lord) and *Ong Noi* (Junior Lord). The elder was in charge of all the provinces, with the younger in control of the metropolis. This set the seal on the power and glory of the Bunnag family which was to endure until the close of the nineteenth century. With *Ong Yai* now showing signs of old age, his eldest and very brilliant son, Phraya Suriyawongse (Chuang Bunnag) was by then already the acting Kalahom. He was a close friend and contemporary of the king as well as his most trusted counsellor and minister.

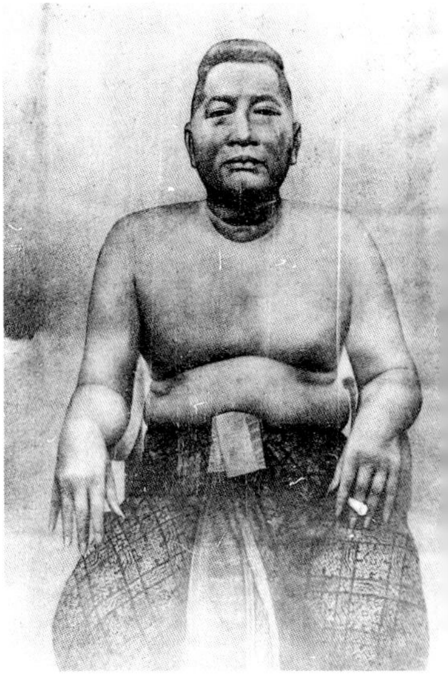

Somdet Chao Phraya Borommaha Bijayayati (Thad Bunnag), son of Chao Phraya Mahasena (Bunnag) and Chao Khun Nual, younger sister of Queen Amarintara. (National Archives Bangkok)

The cremation of Rama III took place with the usual great pomp and ceremonies on April 25th, 1852. Princes of the family, and especially the sons of Rama III who might have been in an anomalous position, were all treated with the highest honours in front of the vassal princes and western foreigners, presumably to show the unity and strength of the Chakri Family.[17] After the cremation ten monks were sent to Ceylon with rich offerings for the sacred temple of the Holy Tooth at Kandy.

Early in the reign the king had posthumously raised his mother, formerly known as Somdech Phra Panvasa, to be Queen Mother with the new name of Queen Sri Suriyendra. He had also taken to wife Princess Rampoey, the daughter of Prince Mataya and therefore a granddaughter of Rama III. She was the first wife of aThai king to be given the newly created title of Queen, namely, *Somdech Phra Nang*. On September 20th, 1853, she gave birth to a son who was given the name Chulalongkorn. With characteristic modesty King Mongkut did not designate the rank of the boy until the princes and noblemen begged him to confirm that he was Chao Fa, especially as no one of that rank had been born for a long time, and this the king was delighted to do. The queen gave him three more children, a daughter and two sons – Prince Chaturonrasmi (born in 1856), the ancestor of the Chakrabandhu branch, and Prince Bhanurangsi (born in 1860), the ancestor of the Bhanubandhu branch. It was one of the features ofThai polygamy that a man often chose, if he could, to have two or more women who were sisters as his wives, and King Mongkut proved no exception. He also took to wife the queen's younger sister, Princess Banarai, with whom he had two children. The Princess herself was not created another queen and the children were born *Phra Ong Chao*. One of them, born in 1863, inherited to the full his grandfather's artistic and architectural gifts. Among his superb creations is Wat Benjamabophit, known to countless foreign tourists as the Marble Temple. Later in the reign of his half-brother, King Chulalongkorn, he was created *Chao Fa* with the title of Prince Naris.

Like all Asian monarchs of his time King Mongkut naturally was a polygamist. He had already had two sons before he entered the monastery. During his 27 years in the priesthood all sources, Thai and western, confirm that he abstained completely. This has never at any

15 Prince Damrong: *Memoirs, op. cit.*, page 83.

16 *Ibid.*, pages 80-81.

17 Dibakarawongse: *Rama IV*, page 78.

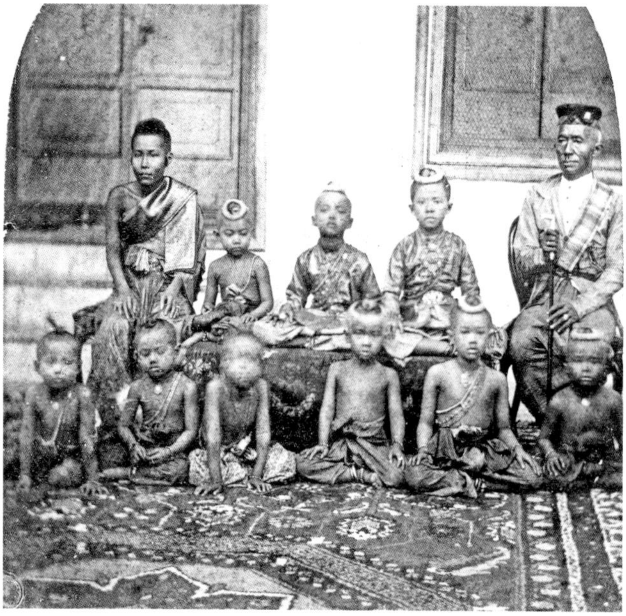

King Mongkut and Queen Debsirindra together with their children. (Jeffrey Spencer)

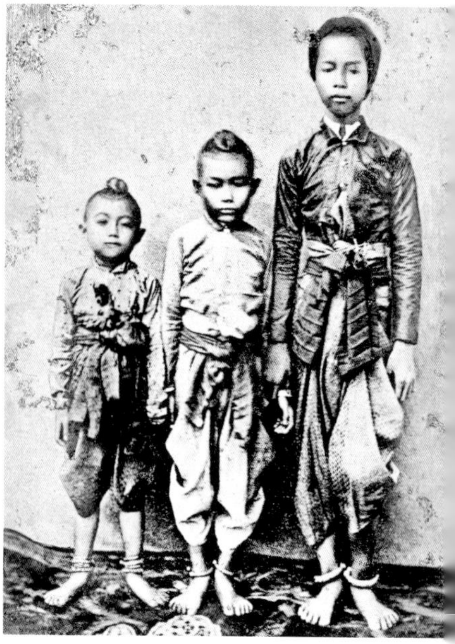

LEFT TO RIGHT: Prince Chulalongkorn, Prince Chaturonrasmi and Prince Bhanurangsi Sawangwongse. (National Archives Bangkok)

time been doubted, not even immediately after the end of the Absolute Monarchy in 1932 when there was a good deal of writing and talking in denigrating terms of the House of Chakri which had just lost power. Thus King Mongkut did not really begin his real polygamous life until after he was 47. His way of life with his wives resembled that of previous kings which has already been related. His polygamy was partly statecraft, and many of the wives were presented to him by their parents who were vassal princes or noblemen, in which case they were often accepted as a means of helping to cement the ties between them and the royal family. He had altogether 82 children – the largest number among Chakri kings – from 35 wives. There were 43 daughters and 39 sons, many of whom were to give splendid service to the country. The king was so busy that he was far from being absorbed in his harem, as the Inside has often been called by western writers, and especially Mrs. Anna Leonowens, the English schoolteacher whose books have become so famous through later works. She related that a wife of King Mongkut, who had run away with a renegade priest, was publicly burned at the stake with her lover, which Griswold has strongly maintained was impossible, for if it was done it would have been well known, yet it was never mentioned by any other writer of the period, be they Thai or Western. It is most unlikely that the Roman Catholic priests or American missionaries, the latter often sending news of the happenings in Bangkok to the Singapore newspapers, would have kept quiet. Griswold also contended that it was most unlikely that a man, who would sit up all night being so upset at having to sign the

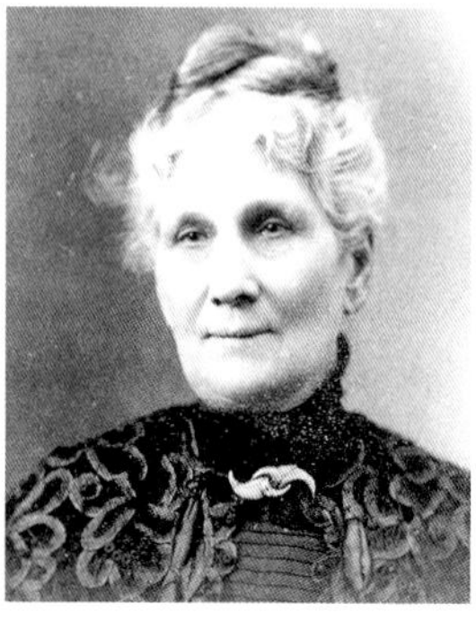

Anna Leonowens. (From New Mandala | Web Design: Code and Visual)

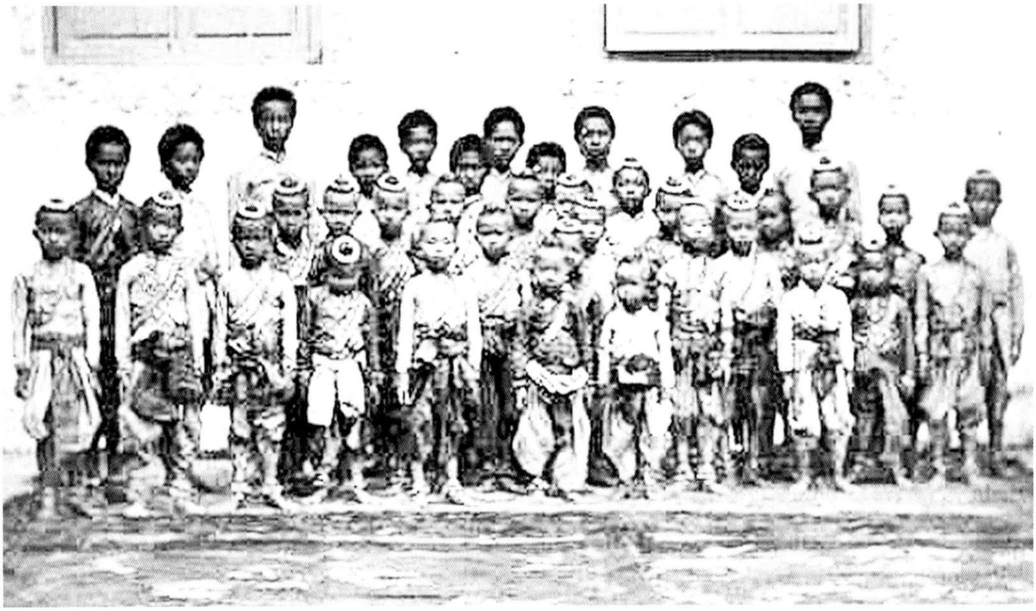

A group of sons and daughters of King Mongkut. (National Archives Bangkok)

death warrant of a convicted criminal, could order the public burning of a runaway wife. Seni Pramoj, the eminent lawyer, states that the couple were tried and that both the wife and the lover had to pay fines, and the priest was unfrocked. As an unfrocked priest he had to be punished for his immorality in breaking the rule of chastity, and for this he would be sentenced to cut grass for the royal elephants for a certain time. According to one of the edicts, the king's wives could resign at will unless they had already given birth to royal children.[18]

Reading and writing were the real relaxation of King Mongkut's life, and, with his knowledge of English he did not only have Western friends in Siam, but also many "pen friends" abroad. With many of these he continued corresponding after he had ascended the throne. Some of his letters – 125 of them – have been published in Thailand in six volumes. One in English was to Lieutenant-Colonel Butterworth, Governor of Prince of Wales Island (Penang) to whom he wrote on April 21st, 1851, and signed himself "newly elected President or Acting King of Siam"; it was not until after his coronation ceremonies were completed that he signed himself the "newly enthroned King of Siam".[19] One may well be surprised to read of an Asian sovereign signing himself as "newly elected President". Although once in power and conscientiously thinking that his rule was for the good of the whole, King Mongkut expected complete and immediate obedience, yet he was at heart a democrat. This can be seen in one dramatic and charming gesture. From time immemorial the princes, great officers, and officials had to drink the water of fealty to the sovereign at the beginning of every reign and again every year. One can imagine the surprise of the assembled company when the king himself took a cup of the water to his lips, thereby offering "voluntarily to pledge himself to the People as their sovereign by partaking in drinking of the Water

18 M. R. Seni: *King Mongkut as Legislator*, pages 28–33 (in Thai version), Bangkok, 1949.

19 Quoted by Dr. Smith, *op. cit.*, page 30.

to Truth, thus making it for the first time a bipartite instead of the former one-sided oath of allegiance".[20]

But the Siam ruled by King Mongkut was still far from being as democratic as he was himself at heart. All through his letters one can see again and again that he was highly conscious of the elective nature of his high position. Besides the number of people who were in voluntary and paid service of the Crown, the princes, and the nobles, the freemen still had to give corvée service. There were also serfs, usually called slaves by Western writers. But according to Sir John Bowring, the British envoy who will have his place later, "Bishop Pallegoix states that slaves are well treated in Siam – as well as servants are in France; and I, from what I have seen, would be inclined to go even further, and say, better than servants are treated in England . . . In small families the slaves are treated like the children of the masters; they are consulted in all matters, and each man feels that as his master is prosperous, so is he."[21] As in the time of Ayutthaya, rarely was a serf sold to another owner without his consent. The hierachy of ranks was so rigid amongst the free people that everyone had to pay respects to his superiors even to the point of prostration, the king being the apex of the pyramid so that reverence to him even extended to his palaces, and hats were removed when passing them.

What was King Mongkut really like? He was the first Chakri king of whom we have photographs. Admittedly he was irascible, but he usually got over his temper quickly. He was much closer to his subjects than his predecessors, except Rama I, who had been born a commoner, because Mongkut had lived and moved freely amongst them as a monk, both in town and country. As his reign progressed he became unique in being an Absolute Monarch who was the Leader of the Liberals at the same time, and in this aspect he had stout-hearted devotees such as *Phraya* (later *Chao Phraya*) Suriyawongse of the Bunnag family and many others. Yet the king realized that his progressive views did not find favour with everyone, and some of the opposition were not without influence. As he knew that Siam needed unity, he trod his way warily and made sure that the change from the old to the new was gradual.

The observatory and palace built on a small hill near Phetchaburi. (National Archives Bangkok)

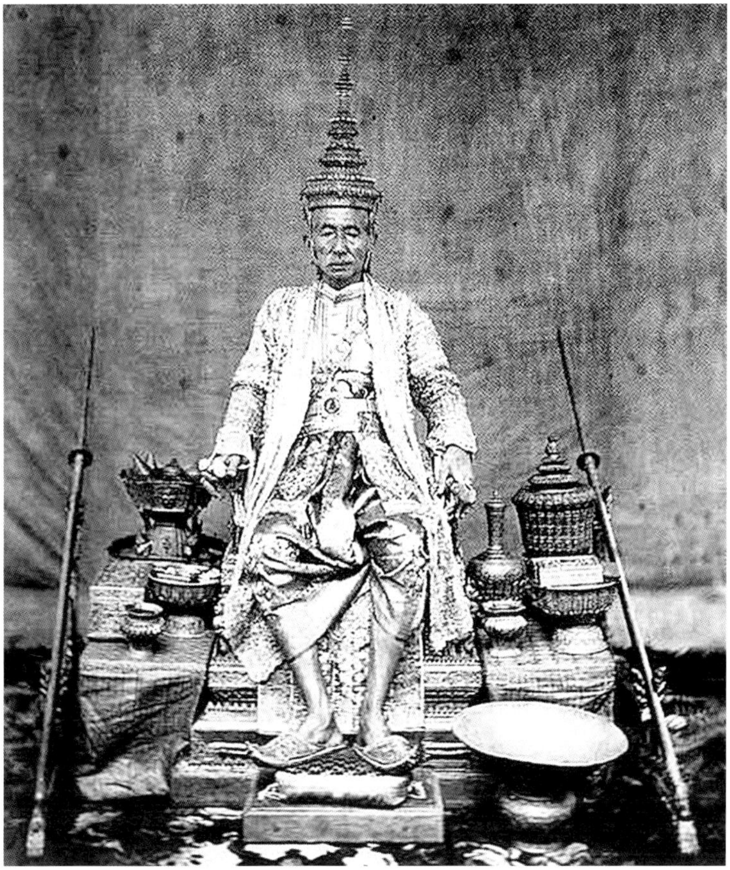

King Mongkut in traditional attire. He is wearing the Maha Pichai crown and has items of regalia on either side. (National Archives Bangkok)

There had been a tradition that a dissatisfied subject could go and hit a drum outside the palace and the king would appear to hear petitions, but the privilege was in disuse as no one hardly dared to hit the drum. Now King Mongkut decided to appear in public once a week to hear petitions in person. After his accession he travelled throughout the country even further and more widely than before. He made sea trips in the Gulf of Siam in his paddle steamer, in the west going down south as far as Songkhla (Singora), and he visited many places on the east coast. The island palace of Bang Pa-In, neglected since the time of Ayutthaya, was restored, and a delightful European-style palace was built on a hill near Phetchaburi within sight of the sea, which is described by Griswold as "a dream of beauty". Travelling by land he rode on horseback and could do so for hours on end.

He broke the back of old-world opposition with different royal edicts which began, as charmingly translated by Griswold, with the royal styles and titles and: "By royal command reverberating like the roar of a lion". Of course, Griswold presumably did not know that such titles and formula were traditional and did not originate from King Mongkut personally, but being an American, his further observations are interesting. He found that the grandiose formula was followed by an almost conversational preamble, outlining the circumstances and

20 Prince Dhani: Review of *Anna and the King of Siam* by Margaret Landon. *Standard,* Bangkok, 1946.

21 Sir John Bowring, *op. cit.,* Vol I, pages 193-194.

reasons that made him issue the edict, often adding gentle ironical comments before beginning the decree itself.

The edicts varied widely over countless subjects. TheThai lawyer and one-time Prime Minister and a descendant of Rama II through one of his younger sons, M. R. Seni Pramoj, in a lecture on King Mongkut,[22] informs us that the monarch was responsible for no less than 500 acts of law and decrees filling four large volumes, with much of it being personally drafted by the king, and a good deal of it light hearted and amusing in tone. Even though he was the all-powerful Lord of Life, Mongkut did not choose always to use his full power. For example, he decreed that senior judges were to be elected by the princes and officials on a classless basis, "nor should the electors hesitate, thinking that perhaps their choice would not meet with His Majesty's approval".

There is also his characteristic edict dealing with religion which states that: "No just ruler restricts the freedom of his people in the choice of their religious belief by which each man hopes to find strength and salvation in his last hour, as well as in the future beyond . . . there are many precepts common to all religions". But this was by no means new, for the idea of religious persecution had always been repugnant to Buddhism as practised in Siam. It will be remembered that already in Ayutthaya, King Narai had helped to build a Roman Catholic church, so in Bangkok King Mongkut gave money towards building Roman Catholic and Protestant churches as well as an Islamic mosque. There was no aspect ofThai life in which he did not show deep interest. One of his edicts was entitled: "Advice against the inelegant practice of throwing dead animals into the waterways."

In this all too brief summary of his life one case must be cited. A young woman of twenty, who was being coerced by her father to marry a man she did not love, appealed to the king because she was in love with another. The king decreed that she was to be allowed to marry the man she loved, but the man had to compensate her father for the loss of her services to him in the event of her marriage. He further decreed that henceforth women should only become wives through their own free will.

Two innovations among so many must also be mentioned in this limited space. He tried as quickly as possible to reduce corvée service, and he chose to pay for the labour required for construction work. As the Thais preferred to stay at home and tend their land or else enter the services, this paid labour became overwhelmingly Chinese. That corvée work which remained was run on lenient lines, and Bishop Pallegoix[23] was so impressed with the attitude adopted towards the Christian Thais that he wrote: "I have already said that the government allowed to the Christians (Thais) full liberty for the exercise of their religion. This liberty goes so far, that never are Christians employed in the king's service on Sundays or saints' days, at least unless there was some urgent and necessary work to be done."

22 M. R. Seni Pramoj: *King Mongkut as Legislator. J.O.S.S.* No. XXXVIII, and also unpublished English MS. with M. R. Kukrit Pramoj *The King of Siam Speaks*.

23 Mgr. Pallegoix, *op. cit.*, Vol. II, page 327.

Another innovation was that he wished to be seen by his people, whereas few people outside his entourage had ever saw Rama III. When King Mongkut went about, whether in Bangkok or in the provinces, his people were not to be shut away frorn him, but drunken men were to be chased away before his arrival, not by the royal guards who accompanied him, but by local authorities; and as for foreigners, they were permitted to pay respects to him according to their own custom. Up till then royal contacts with Westerners had been difficult as everyone had to crawl on the floor before the king with the exception of the envoys and their staff. The new king abolished crawling for all Westerners, who were to behave as they would in the presence of their own sovereigns.

King Mongkut recognized the value of history, and he said that "the ancient history of Siam is rather obscure and fabulous". As the bulk of historical records had perished in the flames which enveloped Ayutthaya in 1767, he now found that the new annals put together from scattered fragments, often wrongly or carelessly copied, showed little accuracy in dates and events. As Rama I had found it necessary to revise the Buddhist canon, so King Mongkkut felt it imperative to set up a committee of learned men to reviseThai history.

King Mongkut's daily life followed a fixed pattern. During the early part of the reign and until 1859 he lived in the Chakrapat building in the Amarindra group. He began the day with presenting food to a number of invited priests at 9 a.m. after which they departed with their well-filled bowls. The king then went to the Phaisan Hall to give an audience to royal and noble ladies. He entered the Amarindra Hall at 10 a.m. and presented food to more monks who this time ate it in the royal presence. After their departure he mounted the chair-throne from which he granted an official audience. At midday he retired to the Inside for luncheon which was followed by an afternoon rest. At 4 p.m. he appeared at a pavilion in front of a huge birdcage (the site now occupied by the great Chakri building) and received people informally, which was the time when *farang* friends usually called to see him. After that he went to the outer gate when the people would present petitions to him, or on some days he would go out in a horse-drawn carriage and tour the city inspecting some new works. Near dusk he usually sat at a window between the Amarindra and Phaisan Halls and here he received more petitions which had been brought by officials, being served his evening meal at about the same time. At 8 p.m. or later, depending on how busy he had been with reading and writing after his meal, he went down to the Amarindra Hall again for the evening audience which always began with a daily sermon by a priest. Then he listened to various and innumerable reports on affairs of State until it was time to retire to bed, which was often late. King Mongkut had more children than any of the Chakri kings, most of whom were born in the 17 years of his reign, and one cannot but wonder how he fitted in any time for his marital life. His children generally saw him at meal time but did not eat with him, and some of them were permitted to accompany him when he went out in Bangkok or on his travels in the country.

After 1859 King Mongkut moved to the new group of European-style buildings put up in the "Garden of the Right," as the puritan-minded Rama III had long ago removed all its charming features and presented them to the different temples. After this move King Mongkut altered his routine as there was now even more work which he had to attend to himself. There were many letters in English to write to Western heads of State and their envoys, which no one else could draft or write for him. No Thai record exists to show that the English teacher, Anna Leonowens, ever helped him. She was not there until 1862, and if help was asked, it would probably be the occasional choice of a word or some spelling doubts, as all the English letters had the stamp of his own quaint style. Even as a priest in the previous reign he had translated into English the letters which the ministers sent to Sir James Brooke. In theThai language he is recognized by many scholars as the founder of modernThai prose.

Besides this mass of correspondence in English, the king took most seriously the petitions of the people, and he had more reading and writing to do than any previous sovereign. He was inclined to be later and later for his evening audience, and even in those autocratic days, there were murmurs of complaint amongst the ministers and courtiers.[24]

Although the priests still came to receive food twice in the morning, the king did not now always appear personally but would delegate one of the senior princes to take his place, for he thought work was more important, and he also gave up more and more of his time to go out amongst the people. The evening sermon, however, was never missed, but sometimes it began rather late owing to pressure of work. Ruling Siam was a full-time job even if the population then was not more than five million.[25]

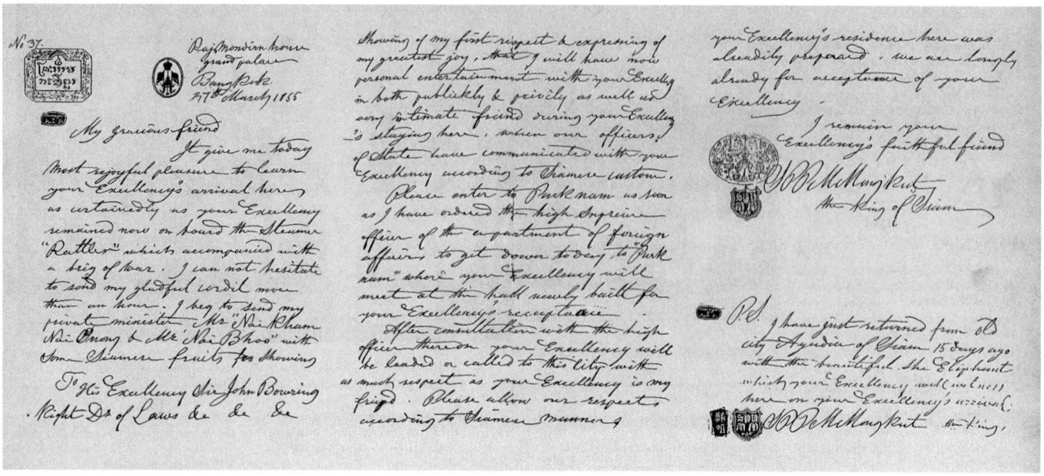
No 37.

Raj Mondirn house
grand palace
Bangkok.
27th March 1855

My gracious friend

It give me today most rejoyful pleasure to learn your Excellency's arrival here as certainedly as your Excellency remained now on board the Steamer "Rattler" which accompanied with a brig of war. I can not hesitate to send my gladful cordil more than an hour. I beg to send my private minister Mr "Nai Kham Nai Omong & Mr Nai Bhoo" with some Siamese fruits for showing of my first respect & expressing of my greatest joy, that I will have now personal entertainment with your Excellency in both publickly & privily as well as very intimate friend during your Excellency's staying here, when our officers of State have communicated with your Excellency according to Siamese custom.

Please enter to Paknam as soon as I have ordered the high Supreme officer of the department of foreign affairs to get down today to Paknam" where your Excellency will meet at the hall newly built for your Excellency's receptance.

After consultation with the high officer thereon your Excellency will be landed or called to this city with as much respect as your Excellency is my friend. Please allow our respects according to Siamese manners your Excellency's residence here was alreadily prepared. we are longly already for acceptance of your Excellency.

I remain your
Excellency's faithful friend
S.P.P.M. Mongkut
the King of Siam

To His Excellency Sir John Bowring
Right Do of Laws &c &c &c

P.S. I have just returned from old city Ayudia of Siam 15 days ago with the beautiful. The Elephant which your Excellency will see here on your Excellency's arrival.
S.P.P.M. Mongkut the King.

Letter from King Mongkut to Sir John Bowring. (From *The Kingdom and People of Siam - with a Narrative of the Mission to that Country in 1855 by Sir John Bowring*, 2 volumes, 1857)

24 Prince Damrong: *Memoirs, op. cit.*, pages 107-108.

25 *Royal Daily Life, op. cit.*, pages 15-18.

26 Prince Damrong: *Memoirs, op cit.*, pages 19-21.

27 Anna Leonowens: *The English Governors, etc., op. cit.*, page 208.

Although, according to one of his sons, Prince Damrong,[26] King Mongkut had a European two-wheel two-horse buggy which he drove himself, his reign was very much the bridge spanning the new and the old, and he was often carried on a flat-floor palanquin on which his favourite children were allowed to sit. Princess Saowabha, later to be the mother of two monarchs, was the daughter who most often sat on the king's lap. Her mother, Chao Chom Piam, was a much-loved wife, and was described by Anna Leonowens as "the only woman who ever managed him with acknowledged success ".[27] There was at that period a fifteen-day steamer service between Bangkok and Singapore, and when the steamer came in, the king was busy for three days with his foreign correspondence. Ice blocks from Singapore were brought into the palace and were much enjoyed by the children, but the older people complained that it gave them toothache.

Soon after his accession King Mongkut began to organize a modern army on European lines – albeit very small. There had already been a company of soldiers dressed in Western uniforms since Rama II had had some copied from the uniforms of the sepoys who came with Crawfurd. An English officer by the name of Captain Impey, who had heard of the King's enthusiasm for modern military training, resigned from his own service and volunteered to serve King Mongkut as the training officer of an infantry battalion. He gave his words of command in English, a practice that continued for the rest of the reign. When repeated many years later by old and retiredThai officers, they

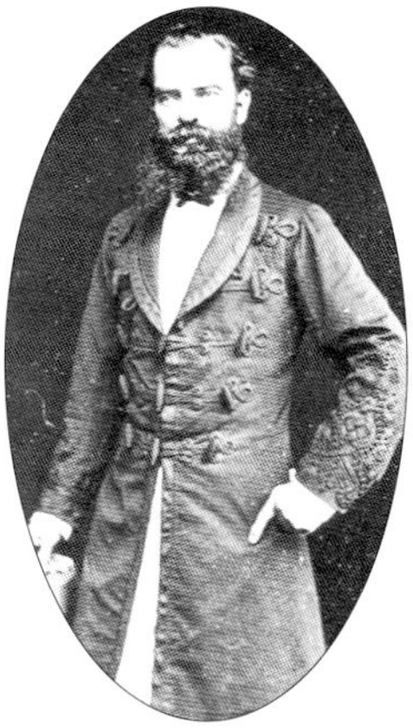

Captain Impey. (National Archives Bangkok)

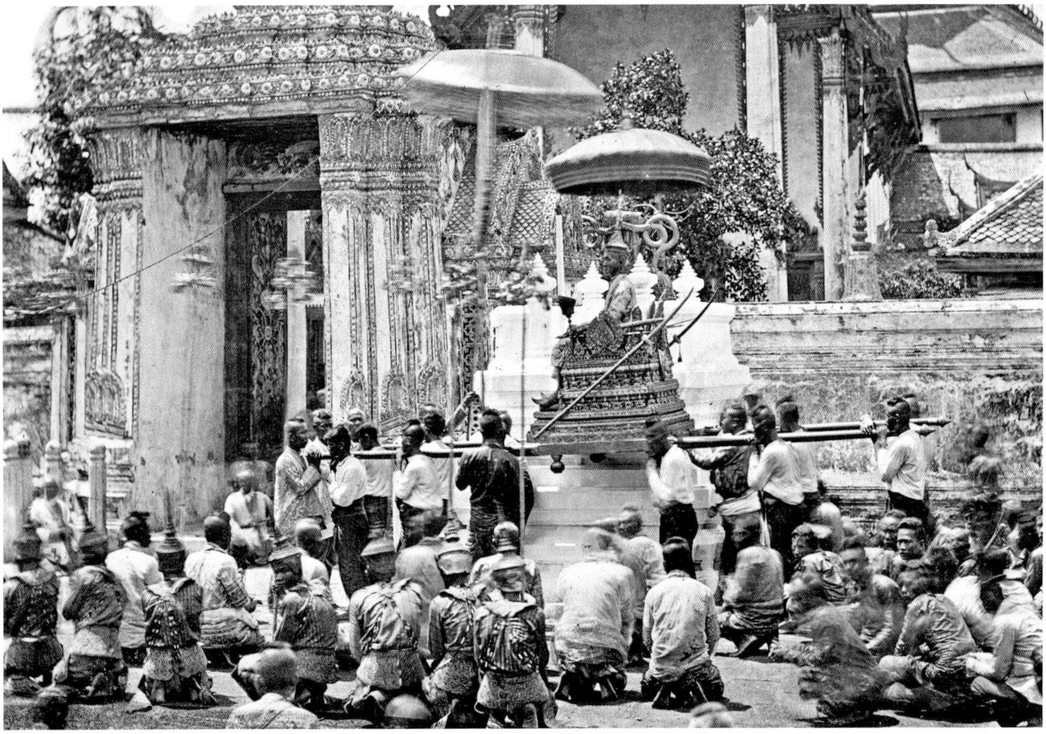

King Mongkut being borne on a palanquin to deliver *Kathin* robes at Wat Pho in 1866. (Wellcome Collection)

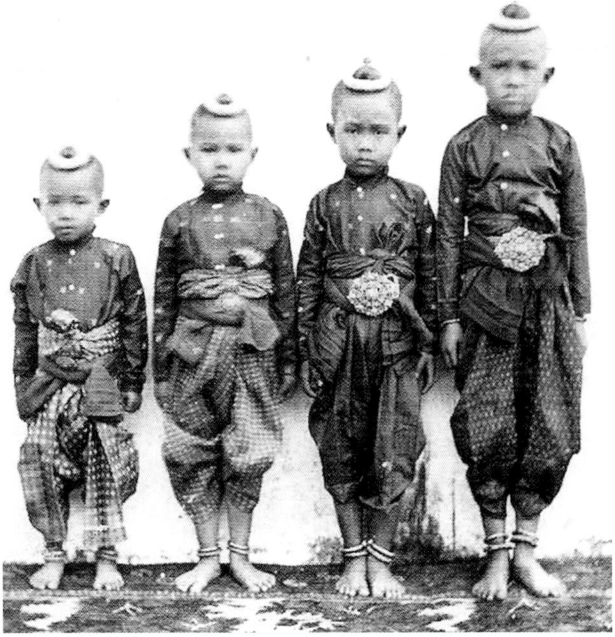

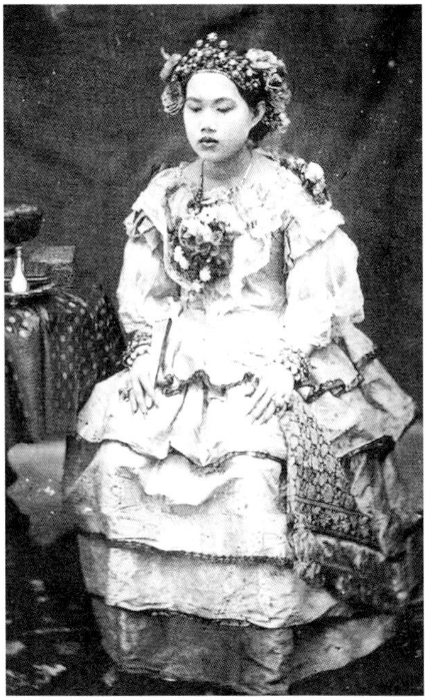

The children born to King Mongkut by Chao Chom Manda Piam. From left to right: Princess Sawang Vadhana, Princess Sunanta Kumarirat, Prince Thewan Uthaiwong, and Prince Unakun Anantanorachai. (National Archives Bangkok)

ABOVE RIGHT: Chao Chom Manda Piam. (National Archives Bangkok)

proved utterly incomprehensible. Later there were added a regiment each of Infantry, Artillery, and even Marines. The artillery was in the charge of the Second King, Phra Pinklao, assisted by another English officer, Captain Knox, who came to Siam shortly after Impey.[28] The Second King was so absorbed in the artillery that everyone in his service had to be gunners, even royal bath attendants and gardeners. When the English envoy, Sir John Bowring, went to call on him, he saw "a park of artillery, served by men dressed like English artillerymen, and obviously well disciplined".[29] The Second King had already been Chief of the Artillery in the third reign, and as he also knew English well, he translated intoThai in 1841 an English manual of artillery of 1823, but kept all the words of command in English.[30] Despite his fondness for the army, Mongkut was the first Chakri monarch to never command an army in the field, and the only warlike operation carried out in his reign was an unsuccessful expedition to Kengtung in the Shan States.

Rama III had had several men-of-war with sails. The acting Kalahom, Chao Phraya Sri Suriyawongse, had already been an adept shipbuilder then, and under King Mongkut he supervised the building of steamers with engines and fittings imported from England. He designed both warships and transports, and he organized the nucleus of aThai navy. Bowring said that "to him Siam owed her fleet of merchant ships".[31] The Second King was also highly interested and had a naval squadron of the Palace of the Front. It is fitting there that in 1959 a destroyer which the Royal Thai Navy received from the United States has been named *Pinklao.* In those days, all the steamers were commanded by English captains, the sailors were Asians of various nationalities, and all the engineers were Thais.[32]

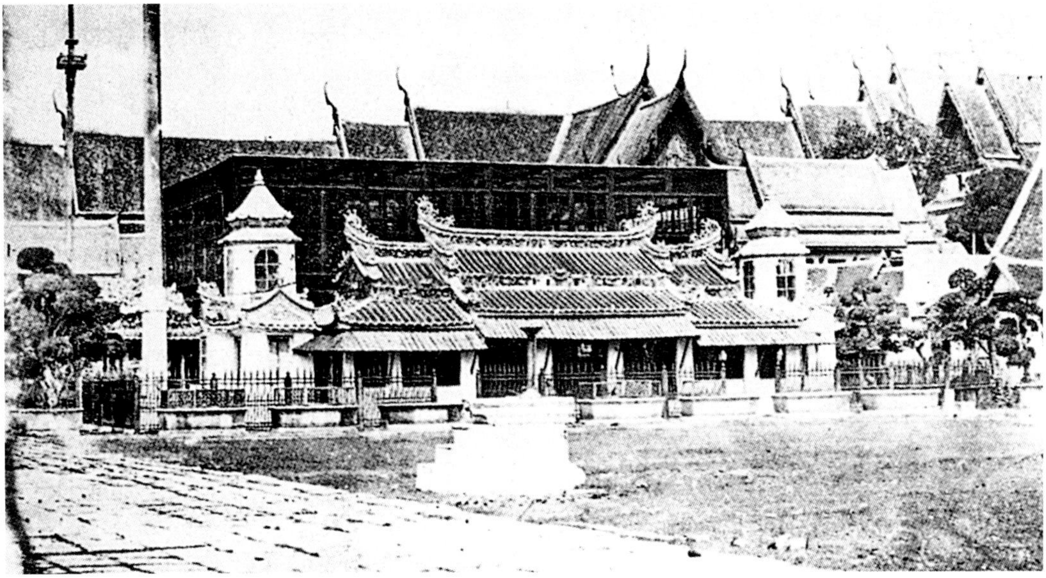

The area where King Mongkut received petitioners and visitors – the so-called large birdcage within the Grand Palace. (National Archives Bangkok)

Although progressive and Westernized in his thinking, Mongkut was enough of a traditionalist to enjoy all the age-old traditions of his country, and he was well satisfied with the appendages of majesty vouchsafed to him, namely, the four white elephants found in Siam and presented to him in his reign. He himself wrote a book on the qualities to be looked for in a white elephant. Having described many points such as yellow eyes, white hair, white nails, pink skin, a beautiful snore, and other qualities, he added that similarly it was not possible to lay down the law on the points of a woman's beauty, as each man had his own individual taste.

Although he attended to many matters of home affairs, such as the digging of canals, the construction of roads, the introduction of modern currency, the overhauling of the governmental and palace services with a whole lot of new titles for the officials, the most important feature of King Mongkut's reign was his relations with Western powers. As Griswold aptly said: "he mounted the throne . . . when European imperialism was tearing Asia to pieces ".[33] From Hall we hear that "it is perhaps not too much to say that Siam owed to Mongkut more than anyone else that she preserved her independence when by the end of the nineteenth century all the other states of South-East Asia had come under European control".[34] King Mongkut had already known when he was in the monastery that Siam had to get on with the West or perish. Robert-Martignan[35] declared that King Mongkut realized that the British defeat of China in 1840-42 was but the beginning of European influence in Asia, and collaboration by Siam with European states was necessary, if Siam were to preserve her independence. That nearly the whole of the Chakri family understood this was emphasized by Sir Josiah Crosby, who, off and on for 40 years, lived and worked in Siam in the British Foreign Service: "To the

28 Prince Damrong: *Memoirs, op cit.*, pages 116-118.

29 Sir John Bowring: *op. cit.*, Vol. II, page 315.

30 Phra Pinklao: *Manual of the Artillery* (in Thai), Bangkok, 1924.

31 Sir John Bowring: *op. cit.*, Vol. II, page 304.

32 Prince Damrong: *Memoirs, op. cit.*, page 118.

33 A. B. Griswold: *King Mongkut in Perspective, op. cit.*

34 D. G. E. Hall: *op. cit.*, page 579.

35 Robert-Martignan: *op. cit.*, page 201.

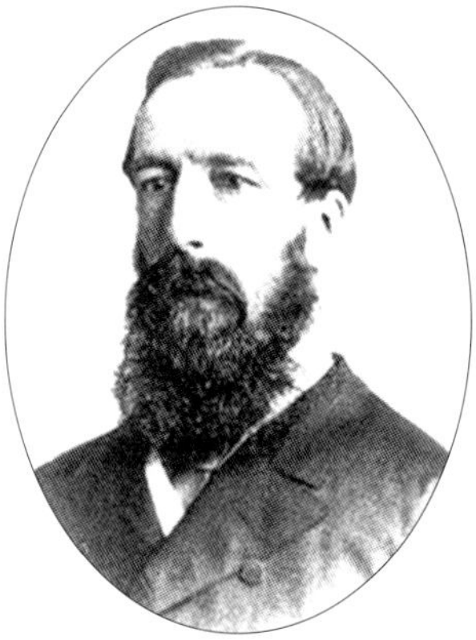

Captain Thomas George Knox. (National Archives Bangkok)

sagacity of the members of the Royal House of Chakri, indeed, the Siamese nation owes an incalculable debt, both for the preservation of its sovereign status through the wise policy of compounding with the advance of Western civilization, instead of resisting it, initiated by King Mongkut and continued by King Chulalongkorn, and for their services as its most enlightened, most capable and most progressive leaders".[36] But to state, as has been done by several western writers, that that was why Mongkut decided to learn English seems exaggerated. He had learned it in the monastery when there seemed but little, if any, chance of his ever becoming the ruler of Siam and the director of its foreign policy. The Thais, especially members of the Chakri family, are highly curious by nature, and it is more likely that Mongkut was spurred on by a simple desire to learn – a genuine craving for knowledge. Once he had learned English, he was naturally influenced by what he read, and he knew that Siam had to try to acquire in a decade what had taken the West hundreds of years to achieve.

The sudden departure of Sir James Brooke in 1851, after his failure to conclude a new treaty, caused the belief in Bangkok that he would soon return with warships from Hong Kong to force the issue, but Rama III died before it could come to that.[37] King Mongkut's fame had spread to Singapore where it was known that he spoke English and was liberal minded. As a result, it appeared that the British had given up the idea of using force in the new reign. Accordingly Sir John Bowring was sent to Bangkok in 1855, and again like Brooke, was the direct envoy of Queen Victoria. Bowring's first impressions were that surprisingly many Thais spoke English – even an unimportant official who brought him a letter.[38] He had also heard that the Second King had read a book by Sir Walter Scott and had called one of his ships by its name,[39] and that one Thai young man had already been to England to study navigation.[40]

Bowring came in the *Rattler* from which he transferred at Paknam to a State barge to proceed to Bangkok, the *Rattler* following the next day. At Paknam the British ship had fired a salute of twenty-one guns to theThai flag, and a Thai " park of artillery, exceedingly well served, returned the salute . . ."[41] At first Bowring was informed that the king did not want any salutes in Bangkok for fear that the people might be alarmed after rumours of a possible British invasion. But Bowring was so adamant about the salutes that King Mongkut wrote to him,"I beg, therefore, to permit or agree that twenty-one guns on board the steamer *Rattler* shall be fired in salute on her arrival at directed place of anchor, rear of new fort".[42] The king then issued a proclamation to his people warning them of the firing of salutes and its friendly nature. Another thing which worried Bowring was that he might not receive the high honours appropriate to the envoy of a great queen. Fortunately both he and King Mongkut had read the French account of how King Narai had received the envoys of Louis XIV, and they agreed on the same formula.

36 Sir Josiah Crosby: *op. cit.*, pages 48-49.

37 *Collected History*, No. 62, *op. cit.*, page 225.

38 Sir John Bowring: *op. cit.*, Vol. II, page 251.

39 *Ibid.*, page 254.

40 *Ibid.*, page 257.

41 *Ibid.*, pages 262-263.

42 Sir John Bowring: *op. cit.*, Vol. II, Appendix g., page 427.

43 *Ibid.*, pages 270-271.

44 *Ibid.*, Vol. I, pages 410-411.

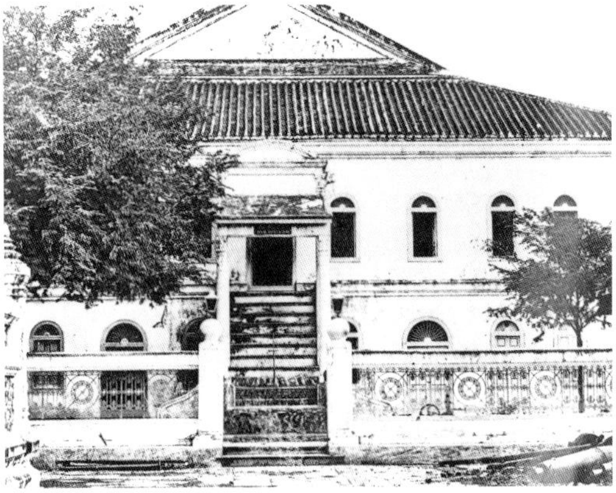

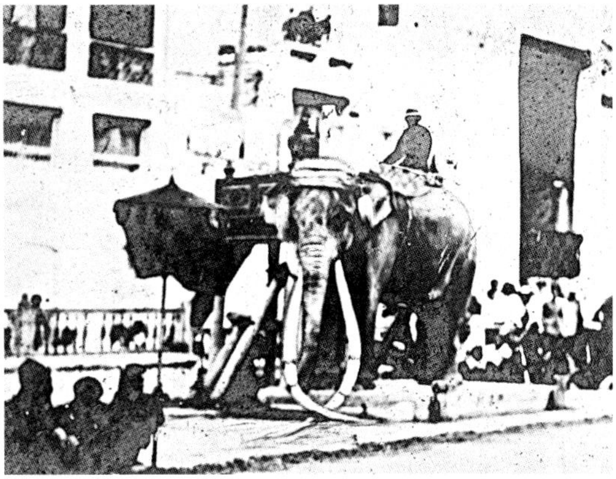

TheThai problem was how to act towards the British. Defiance as practised by the Chinese and Burmese would bring war and defeat, yet if there was to be any cringing fear then any advantage to be gained from the treaty would be lost. TheThais had to negotiate in a friendly way to obtain the most equal terms possible. The king first received Bowring privately and according to the envoy: "It was a beautiful moonlight, and in an open space, on a highly ornamented throne, sat His Majesty clad in a crimson dress, and wearing a head-dress resplendent with diamonds and other precious stones, a gold girdle . . . His Majesty offered me cigars with his own hand, and liqueurs, tea and sweetmeats were brought in".[43] The rest of the British diplomatic mission were then brought in to the royal presence.

Bowring went to see the king again more than once, and much more privately. He thus described King Mongkut's private apartments: "They were filled with various instruments, philosophical and mathematical, a great variety of Parisian clocks and pendules, thermometers, barometers, in a word all the instruments and appliances which might be found in the study or library of any opulent philosopher in Europe".[44] Appropriately Queen Victoria's presents to him were a watch set with diamonds and a travelling writing case with many useful gadgets. When the present writer went for the first time to lunch with King George V and Queen Mary at Windsor Castle in 1932, he saw King Mongkut's presents to Queen Victoria which consisted of a gold and enamel crown and several other objects of royal regalia. Bowring had his official audience with the king on April 16th, 1855, when he was received most graciously and with much pomp. He had been fussily anxious that he and his officers would not be allowed to wear their swords, as the French envoys had worn theirs before King Narai in the seventeenth century, but all was agreed to, and he was dressed in exactly the same way as he would appear before his own sovereign. The best times he and King Mongkut had together were during the informal visits. The king showed Bowring the Crown Jewels, and the latter was especially impressed with the Sword of State with the gold scabbard richly embossed and covered with diamonds and other

One of the white elephants discovered in the reign of King Mongkut, Plai Hom, in front of the Sutthai Sawan throne hall. (National Archives Bangkok)

ABOVE LEFT: The Royal Mint within the Grand Palace. (National Archives Bangkok)

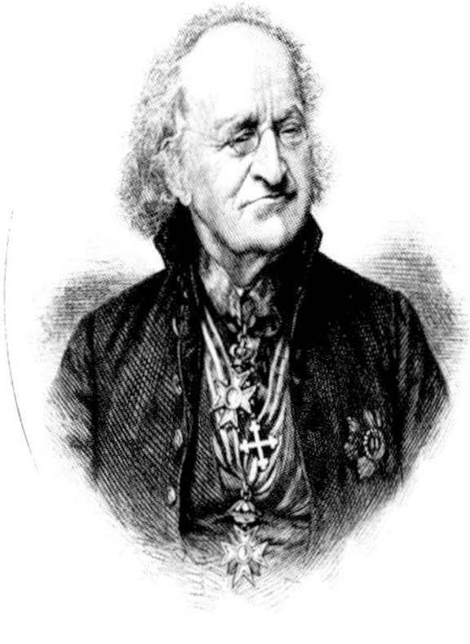

Sir John Bowring, the British envoy from Queen Victoria. He brought a letter from Her Majesty and negotiated a treaty with the Siamese which was signed in 1855.

jewels; and when he unsheathed it there were two swords, one within the other – the inner of steel, the outer of heavier metal.[45] Of the political conversations with the king, Bowring observed: "In all my relations with him when I had occasion to convey to him the motives of my conduct, he was invariably willing to accept those explanations and to assure me that he should attribute my proceedings not to any want of respect for himself, but to my sense of the duties I owed to my sovereign and my country".[46] Bowring must sometimes have been taken aback by some of the things which Mongkut said to him, such as when he enquired about the recent discovery of the planet Neptune and went on to say: "You have two terms, one the vulgar – leap year, and the other the classical – bissextile – when February has twenty-nine days."[47] Although he had never visited England, he said to Bowring: "Your country is a garden".[48]

The main task of getting the treaty completed was left to the new Kalahom, Chao Phraya Sri Suriyawongse, who had succeeded his father, the Phra Klang in his old age and Bowring wrote: "Such promptitude was, I believe, never before exhibited in an Asian Court. It is mainly due to the Phra Kalahom's energetic influence: he has a great deal of work to accomplish, and he is working while it is day – ay, and by night as well ".[49] Yet revealing some mistrust of the Asian by the European, Bowring had to follow such praises with: "If the Kalahom be sincere, matters will end promisingly; if not, he is the most supereminent of hypocrites".[50] Bowring's suspicions were ill founded. The new treaty was signed on April 18th, 1855.[51] Practically all the concessions asked for by the British were given.

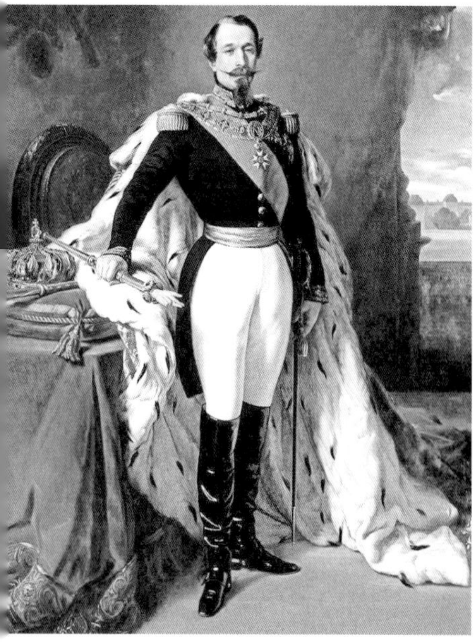

Emperor Napoleon III by Franz Xaver Winterhalter. (Napoleonic Museum)

A permanent British Consul would be nominated to Bangkok who would supervise British commerce which was granted far greater freedom. The king was anxious that the Consul might not be his friend, but Bowring assured him that only a person fully acceptable to him would be chosen to fill the post. The British Consul would hold jurisdiction over all British subjects resident in Siam, both Europeans and Asians, as Siam had by this treaty accepted British extra-territorial rights in her own sovereign territory. Siam agreed not to impose duties on any British goods at more than three per cent, *ad valorem*. Perhaps the most important concession was that the evil drug most hated by the Chakri kings – opium – could now be imported by the British from India *duty free*. The British were furthermore permitted to purchase land within four miles of the city walls. This second Anglo-Thai treaty was to act as a charter for the rights of all other Europeans and of Americans in Siam for some fifty years to come, because treaties with other nations would follow the same pattern.

Sir John Bowring had a private audience with the Second King, Phra Pinklao, whom he found "a sensible, quiet, and amiable person, who from prudence and policy, takes little part in public affairs", and in his private apartments Bowring found that the "furniture and ornaments would lead you to believe you were in the house of an Englishman", and that he "conversed in excellent English".[52] Bowring had a farewell dinner with the Commissioners for the Treaty, a senior prince – Prince Wongsasdhirajsanid, a younger half-brother of the monarch, the two great Elder Statesmen, and the Kalahom. Bowring was amused that when they drank the health of the two sovereigns there was general cheering. When a British commissioner later returned with the ratification of the treaty, further presents were brought from Queen Victoria which included a model railway (now in the Bangkok National Museum) and a model ship.

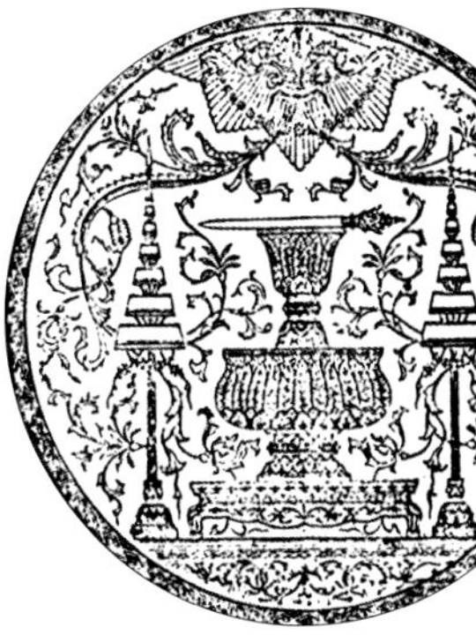

The emblem of the Second King Pinklao.

The First King showed many concessions and great restraint towards the Second King, he would never even depart from Bangkok on a journey without first writing to ask leave of his younger brother. Mongkut's modesty showed right through his correspondence, and again and again in hisThai letters he referred to his royal position as an elective one. His politeness to other princes, especially those senior to him in age, makes one feel that he did not consider himself the great autocrat over and above his relatives, but rather a *primus inter pares*. It is thus sad to relate that the two brothers did not get on, and there were both suspicion and jealousy on the part of the younger. On many important family occasions, the Second King pleaded illness and would not attend, while the real reason was that he feared that he and his family would not be given high enough places, and on such occasions Mongkut, as one can see from his letters, was deeply hurt. The Second King had many domestic troubles, and he once even accused a senior wife, who had borne him twelve children, of nearly poisoning him by giving him love potions. He was incapacitated by illness during the last five years of his life, and retired from all public affairs. In his last illness King Mongkut gave him the most devoted care until Phra Pinklao died on January 7th, 1866, at the age of 58. It was by now clear that under modem conditions the position of a Second King or Deputy King had become an anomaly. Although King Mongkut survived his younger brother by two years, no new *Uparaja* was appointed. Despite his western ideas, however, King Mongkut did not feel that the Thais had moved on far enough for him to appoint his eldest son as Crown Prince, although he must have had some hopes. Like his father had done for him, he gave special honours whenever there was a suitable occasion to his eldest and celestial son, Prince Chulalongkorn. The situation was better than when Mongkut was young, for towards the end of the fourth reign both princes born before he entered the priesthood had died, and Chulalongkorn was in every sense the eldest son.

Once the treaty with Britain was signed in 1855, much diplomatic activity followed. On April 15th, 1856, a treaty was signed with France, then under Napoleon III, whose envoy, M. de Montigny, brought as imperial gifts bronze busts of the Emperor and Empress and a carriage complete with horses. Later still the French Emperor added a

45 *Ibid.*, Vol.II, page 318.

46 *Ibid.*, Vol. I, page 409.

47 *Ibid.*, Vol. II, page 280.

48 *Ibid.*, Vol. II, page 310.

49 *Ibid.*, Vol. II, page 304.

50 *Ibid.*, Vol. II, page 287.

51 *Siam's Case, etc., op. cit.*, page 22.

52 Sir John Bowring: *op. cit.*, Vol. II, page 324.

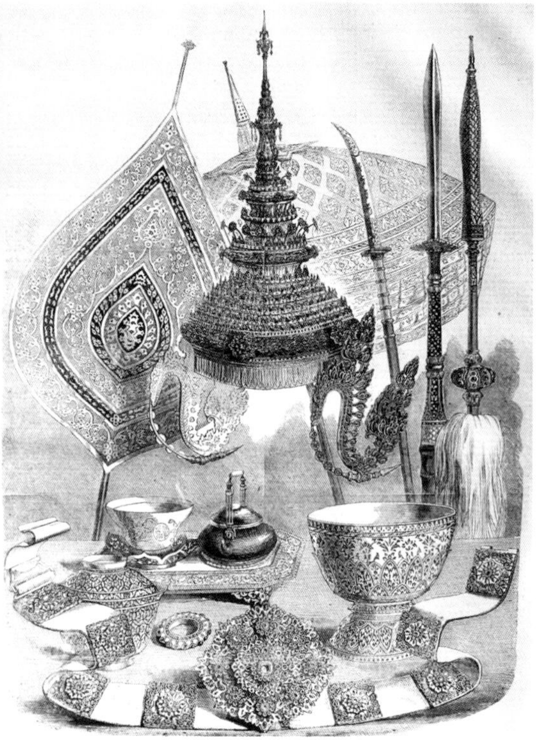

Gifts of King Mongkut to Queen Victoria. (National Archives Bangkok)

steamboat. The same year President Franklin Pierce of the United States of America sent Harry Parkes as his envoy and a new treaty was negotiated and signed. Other treaties quickly followed with these countries : The Hanseatic League in 1858, Denmark the same year, Portugal 1859, Holland 1860, Prussia 1862, Sweden and Norway 1868.[53] Prince Damrong suggested that King Mongkut wanted to have treaty relations with as many nations as possible so as to avoid having one paramount power. In return for the embassy of Sir John Bowring, King Mongkut sent an embassy to Queen Victoria which was conveyed to England in a British ship, taking the presents which have been described already. Queen Victoria received them with the Prince Consort standing by her side, and they had an interesting and happy time in London which the Ambassador described later in a lengthy poem.

Hall has made some interesting comparisons between King Mindon of Burma (1853-1878) and King Mongkut such as: "like his contemporary, Mongkut of Siam, he felt the challenge of the West, but in his land-locked kingdom, now more than ever isolated from the outside world, his handicap in the effort to meet it was the immeasurably greater . . . But unlike his contemporary, Mongkut of Siam, whose country had not been defeated and carved up by a European power . . . Mindon was himself too ignorant of other systems of administration to carry out any far-reaching reforms . . . and unlike Mongkut of Siam, he knew no European language and did not employ English tutors for his children".[54] The treaties with Western powers had enormous economic consequences for Siam because they allowed rice, hitherto forbidden, to be exported by foreigners, which in turn forced the Thais to grow more rice which soon became their principal export. Nature had provided the Thais with a soil and climate suitable for growing the best quality rice. To improve rice growing, King Mongkut had many new canals cut to improve irrigation. Already a thriving port in any case, Singapore greatly benefited from the almost free trade with Bangkok, and the rice was distributed to the rest of the world through Singapore.

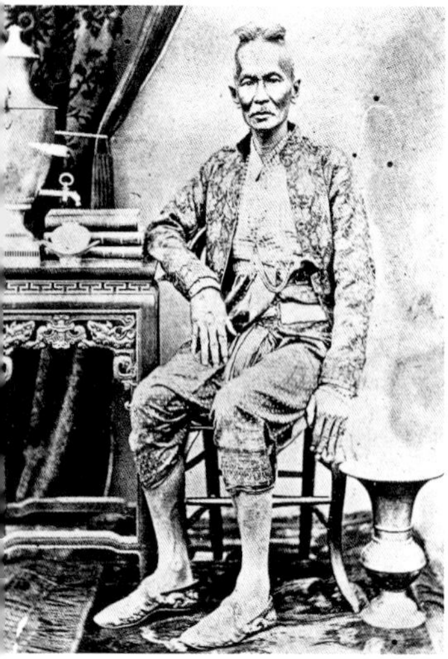

Mom Rajawongse Kratai Issarangkul was sent as an interpreter on the mission to Queen Victoria. (National Archives Bangkok)

Official relations with China continued for a while on the old lines. After the cremation of Rama III, an embassy went to Peking with the usual presents for the Emperor. Later a mission from China marked the passing of one emperor and the accession of another. The Chinese mission consisted of Chinese merchants with a letter from a commercial agent. As a result, the ministers did not show the letter to the king, and the ministers replied that the last time they sent an embassy to Peking it was attacked by Chinese bandits on the way. In July, 1863, the Governor of Canton sent on three letters which had been delayed at

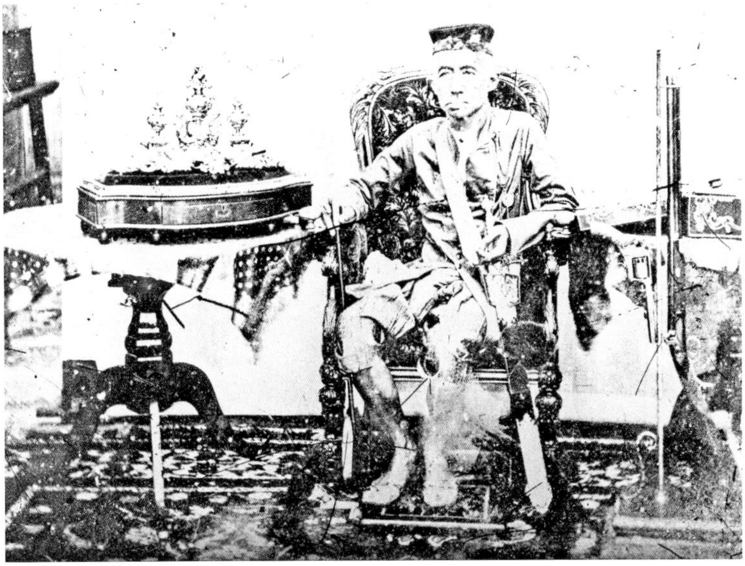

Photograph of King Mongkut sent by him to Queen Victoria. (National Archives Bangkok)

Canton, and in these King Mongkut was reminded that he owed the Emperor of China five tributes. It was decided to ignore the rebuke and thereafter no letters or tributes were sent to China again.

After the Bowring treaty relations between Siam and the British were better than ever. Hall showed some surprise when he wrote: "Mongkut and his successor, Chulalongkorn carried out the treaty faithfully".[55] There were three Anglo-Thai commissions to decide on the frontier between Siam and Burma. TheThais agreed with everything the British decided on and the work was a resounding success. Between 1858 and 1863 there was trouble in Malaya owing to a family feud in British controlled Pahang in which dispute Thai-controlled Trengganu intervened. The British carried out a moral and physical intervention, namely, protests and the shelling of the forts of Trengganu by British warships, under pressure of British merchants in Singapore, but Siam stood aside and everything was settled. Hall has shown that this was yet another instance when the liberal-minded House of Commons in England objected to the use of force by the Colonial authorities.[56] The Colonial authorities deserve our sympathies for thinking that force was the easiest and most swift policy. They could not have known that the Japanese would catch up with the west technically and would in 1942 send the towers of western domination in South-East Asia crashing to the ground, towers which were not to be re-built until after the crushing defeat of Japan herself.

The real border problems in King Mongkut's reign were with the French, and these he inherited from his father, Rama II, who had let the north-eastern Laotian states and Cambodia pay tribute to Vietnam as well as to himself. The problems would get even worse when inherited by his son, Chulalongkorn. After the death of the great friend of Rama I, the Emperor Gia-Long, his successors returned to the persecution of Christians and the closed-door policy against the West,

53 *Siam's Case, etc., op. cit.*

54 D. G. E. Hall: *op. cit.*, pages 532-547.

55 D. G. E. Hall: *op. cit.*, page 581.

56 *Ibid.*, page 452.

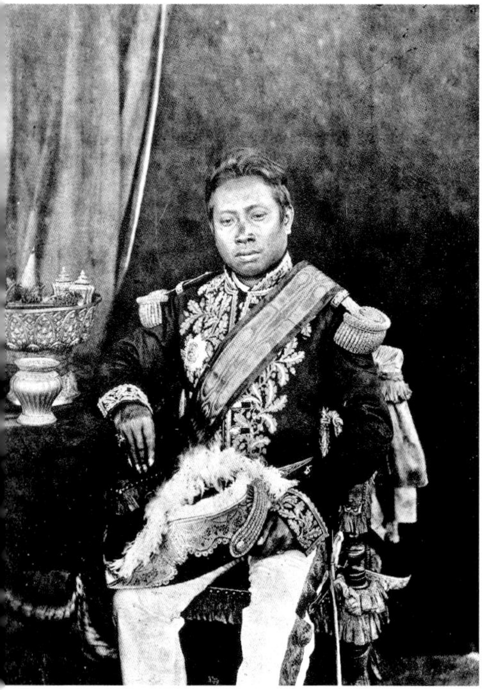

King Norodom of Cambodia. (Wellcome Collection)

for they had not correctly read the meaning of the British victory over China and Burma. The Emperor Tu-Duc (1848-1883), according to Hall[57], in 1852 had two French priests put to death. M. de Montigny, the French consul in Bangkok, was sent to Hue to make a strong protest but he could obtain no results. When the French wanted to send an embassy to negotiate a treaty, it was refused entry. Gun-boat policy was considered the only method and French warships shelled a Vietnamese fort, signalling the beginning of the struggle which would lead to the end of Vietnamese independence. By March, 1861, France had firmly occupied the six southern Vietnamese provinces of Cochin China. The French therefore claimed that they were entitled to the tribute which neighbouring Cambodia had been sending to Hue. Now that they were in control of the Mekong Delta, the French became anxious to maintain Cambodian freedom and independence. It happened that in 1860 King Norodom of Cambodia was driven out of his capital by a rebellious brother and he sought refuge in Bangkok. The Cambodian king was supported by a French priest, Mgr. Miche, the Vicar Apostolic of Cambodia, who asked the French consul in Bangkok to obtain help from King Mongkut. This was granted and Norodom was conveyed back to Kampot in a steamer, and he eventually re-entered his capital in March, 1862. Thai moral backing appeared to be suffcient as no armed forces accompanied him.

France now wished to be the sole protector of Cambodia, but Norodom said he owed the existence of his country to Rama III who had freed it from Vietnamese domination, yet at the same time declared that he was completely free *vis a-vis* Siam. The French admiral, Bonard, conqueror of Cochin China, visited Norodom in September, 1862 and pressed for the tribute owing to Hue. Hall wrote that "France, *it seemed* (my italics), was much more concerned with pressing her claims than with safeguarding the independence of Cambodia".[58] The newly established French Resident in Cambodia reported to the French authorities at Saigon that in Cambodia the King of Siam was more powerful than her own king.

Pierre-Paul de La Grandière, who succeeded Bonard, went to see Norodom also and urged him to sign a treaty accepting sole French protection, to which Norodom agreed. Meanwhile, in Paris the French Foreign Minister hesitated to advise Napoleon III to ratify the treaty as King Mongkut had protested that Norodom was his vassal and could not act without his consent. In this contention Mongkut was supported by Great Britain, then the active rival of the French for power and influence in South-East Asia. A compromise was reached whereby the French, as *de facto* protectors of Cambodia, recognized ancient Thai suzerainty over her. The Thai Resident at Oudong, then the capital,

57 *Ibid.*, chapter 34.
58 *Ibid.*, page 562.
59 Dibakarawongse: *Rama IV, op. cit.*, pages 326-327.

succeeded in persuading Norodom to style himself "Thai Viceroy of Cambodia".

Norodom had not yet been crowned as the crown and other regalia had been left in Bangkok for safe keeping. King Mongkut was prepared to go to Oudong to crown him, but when La Grandière objected he suggested a compromise whereby Norodom could go to Bangkok for his coronation, and the latter agreed to leave on March 3rd, 1864. The French had to decide on swift action – the race was on between them and the British for power and prestige in South-East Asia. The French Resident threatened to seize the palace in the event of Norodom leaving for Siam, and asked for military reinforcements from Saigon. When Norodom departed, French marines entered the palace and hoisted the tricolour. Norodom, thoroughly alarmed at the news, returned to find waiting for him the treaty of protection now duly signed by Napoleon III. He accepted the inevitable and the treaty was ratified on April 17th. The French organized his coronation on June 3rd, and the French Resident refused to let the Thai Representative of King Mongkut place the crown on Norodom's head. The French did, however, agree in April, that Norodom should go to meet Mongkut at a border town but the Thai king did not come.

All of the above were the results of *de facto* arrangements which did not appeal to the tidy mind of King Mongkut, and something of a *de jure* nature had to be devised. In consequence there were fresh negotiations in Bangkok with a new French envoy, M. Aubaret. This arranged for King Mongkut to accept the Emperor Napoleon III as sole protector of Cambodia, but King Norodom was to do homage both to him and to the King of Siam, and the treaty was signed in Bangkok on April 14th, 1865. King Mongkut then sent an embassy to France in 1867 which went first by a Thai steamer as far as Singapore where they arrived on January 20th. The Thai embassy to London had travelled by a British ship, so the embassy to Paris transferred to a French vessel.[59] The embassy was well received by Napoleon III with as high honours as

The Thai embassy being received at Fontainebleau by Napoleon III. (Musée national du Château de Versailles)

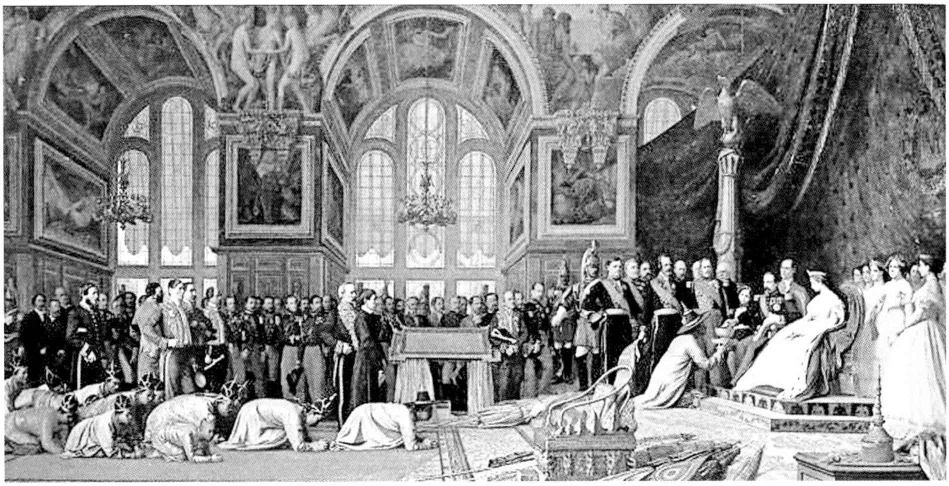

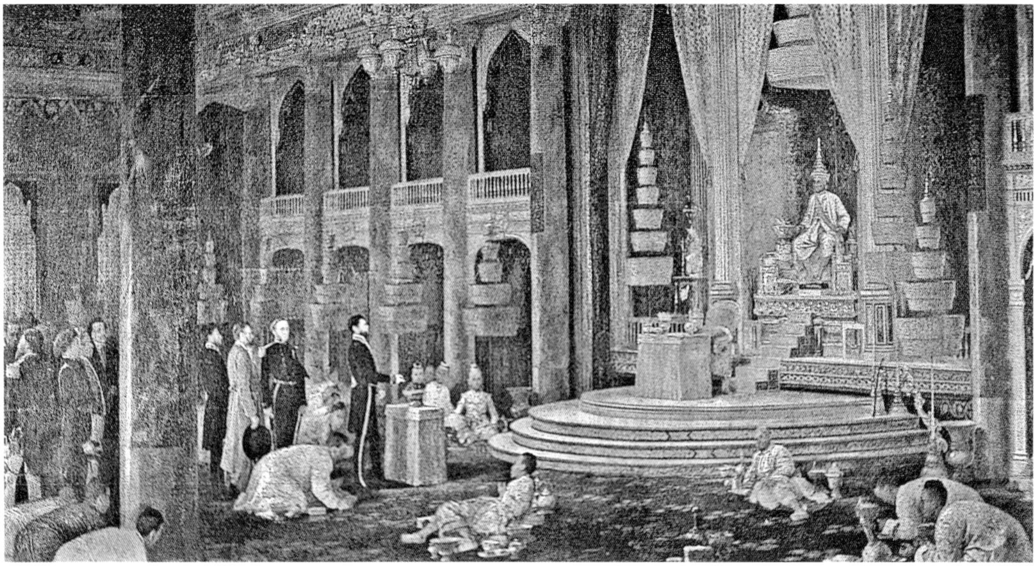

King Mongkut receiving the French embassy sent by Napoleon III. (National Archives Bangkok)

Louis XIV had granted to the embassy of King Narai from Ayutthaya. When Aubaret himself returned from his leave in Paris he brought back many more presents including a dress sword for Prince Chulalongkorn. He came in a new type of steamer with a single screw astern which caused much interest. He had with him the ratification of the treaty and the king gave him both an official and a private audience. In June, 1863, Admiral Bonard had sent on the Emperor's behalf the stars of the Legion of Honour especially studded with diamonds for both the First King and the Second King. Siam had no order of chivalry of the European type, honours had been bestowed by means of objects of utility such as gold tea pots, gold trays, swords with gold scabbards and so on. King Mongkut felt that the time had come when a European type of order should be instituted. The highest honour so far bestowed had been a gold chain decorated with the nine gems, which heralded propitious good fortune. On this basis King Mongkut created the Most Ancient Order of the Nine Gems which he bestowed on the French Emperor. This order has since been made available to Buddhists only and is now most rarely given. King Mongkut had it in mind to create two more orders, one to be called the White Elephant after the national emblem, and the other the Crown after his own name, but he did not live to put the scheme into practice.

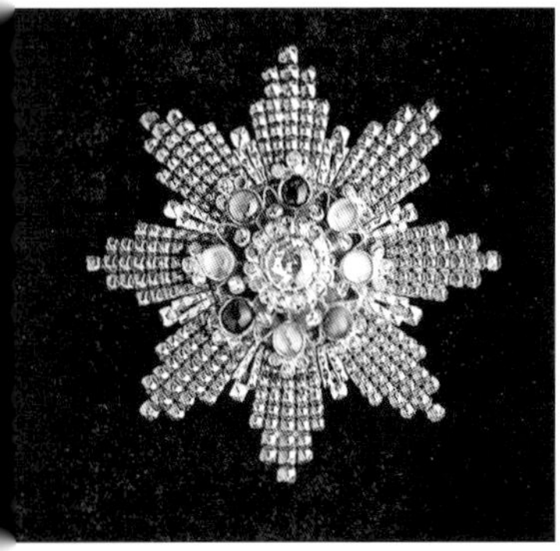

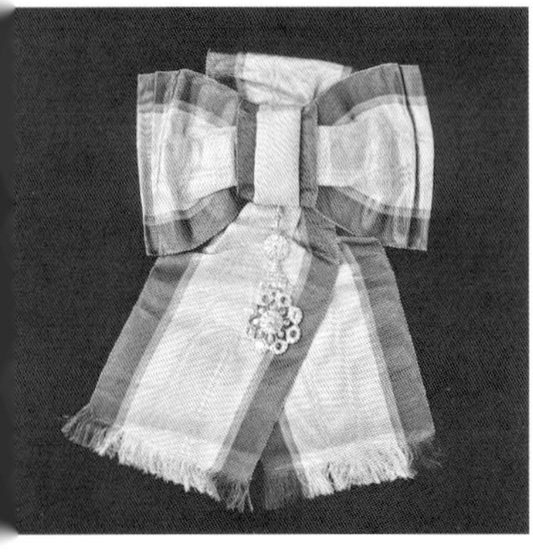

The Order of the Nine Gems created by King Mongkut. (River Books)

Of King Mongkut's achievements in internal affairs, Hall[60] put it briefly and succinctly thus: "He had European advisers and teachers who, in the absence ofThais with technical skill, became heads of departments. He had promoted the digging of canals, the construction of roads, shipbuilding, and especially the teaching of foreign languages. He had established a mint in the palace and from 1861 minted flat coins in substitution for round lumps of gold or silver previously in circulation". It was in 1862 that he laid down Charoen Krung Road in

Bangkok, still known to English speaking people to this day (1959) as New Road, and he built on either side of the road commercial premises which were to be let – a complete innovation. He had already built three other modern roads as the result of complaints by foreign consuls. They had said that western people had been accustomed for their health to take the air of an evening, riding in horse-drawn carriages, and owing to lack of suitable roads in Bangkok, they were suffering from bad health and illnesses. The king said he was grateful for their complaints, and added that he felt ashamed of the dirt and filth of the narrow lanes of Bangkok, and he began a road and bridge building programme. The foremen in charge of those operations were Thais, but the paid labourers were Chinese.[61] Another important means of transport – the waterways – were not forgotten and four major canals were dug in the provinces connecting important towns.

King Mongkut's building scheme was immense and some of it has already been related in passing. Prosperous Bangkok then had up to 300-400 foreign ships in port a year, and, with rice being exported, the income of the ordinary people had much increased. The king bought and had built several steamers and his own new paddle-steamer was capable of 11 knots. He loved cruising in the Gulf of Siam, and if other

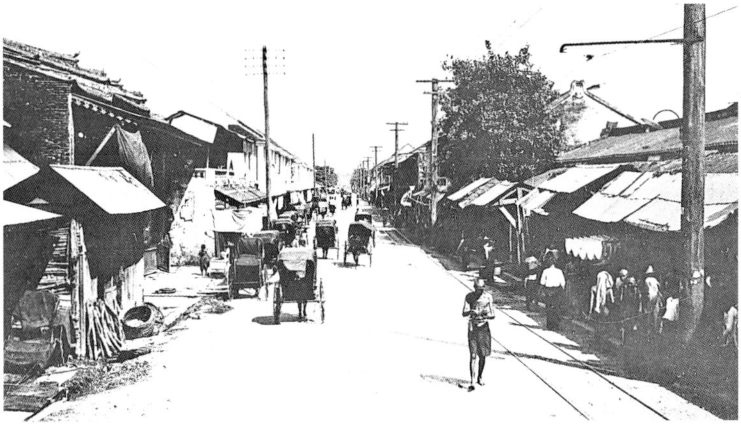

Charoen Krung Road. (National Archives Bangkok)

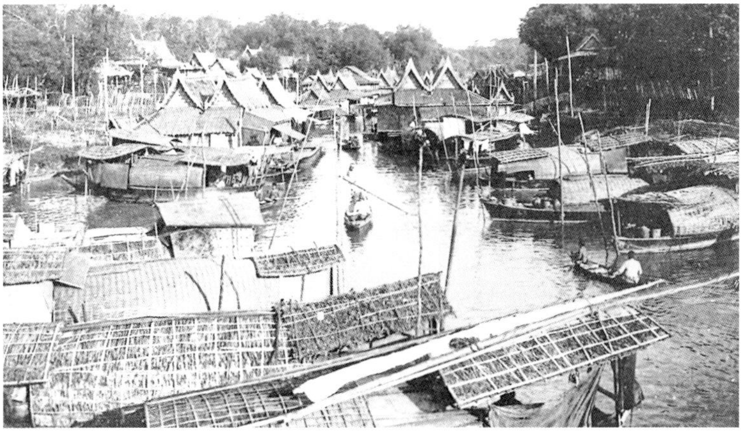

The junction of Mahanak and Padung Krung Kasem canals. (National Archives Bangkok)

60 D. G. E. Hall: *op. cit.*, chapter 36.

61 Dibakarawongse: *Rama IV*, pages 235-243, 278-279.

steamers were too slow to keep up, he went in the paddle-steamer alone without any escort. Although he had inherited many gorgeous State barges, he himself added perhaps the most exquisite of them all – the one with the Seven-headed *Naga* (The King Great Snake).

The Grand Palace was further enriched with new buildings in both Thai and European styles. He founded five new wats in the capital and restored twenty. He built new wats in the country such as Wat Kema, charmingly situated by the river near the present Rama VI railway bridge, and the *wat* on Sichang Island in the Bight of Bangkok. Then there was the *wat* on the Palace Hill near Phetchaburi which formed a counterpoint to his scientific observatory of the stars. He also had built in Bangkok, not far from the Grand Palace, the European-style Saranrom Palace now housing the Ministry for Foreign Affairs. It was said at the time that he intended to retire to Saranrom Palace in his old age. This could mean that he had intended to abdicate at 70 or 75, for a man with Mongkut's temperament would not like to be a king who was too old to rule his country actively, and his son might by then have shown his mettle, and be accepted by everyone if nominated as his heir.

As a monk he had roamed the country widely and on foot. Once in the jungle he came across the enormous ruins of an ancient shrine –Phra Pathom Chedi – then lost in the tangled wilds of a tropical jungle. He recognized it as the oldest and largest Buddhist shrine in the kingdom and told Rama III about it. The latter said that it was not worth restoring as it was too remote from anywhere. However, once he became king, Mongkut set his heart on its restoration, and it was raised and finally covered with orange-coloured tiles as seen by the hundreds of thousands of visitors today as it stands close to the southern railway main line and also the motor highway, and a new town – Nakhon Pathom – has grown up around the great *chedi*. King Mongkut carried out some of the bricklaying himself and worked from some very high scaffolding.[62] The work was unfinished in his lifetime and was completed by King Chulalongkurn. One of Mongkut's generous gestures was to return the revered image – Phra Bang – back to Luang Phra Bang in 1866.

The Ananta Nagaraj state barge constructed in the reign of King Mongkut. (Wellcome Collection)

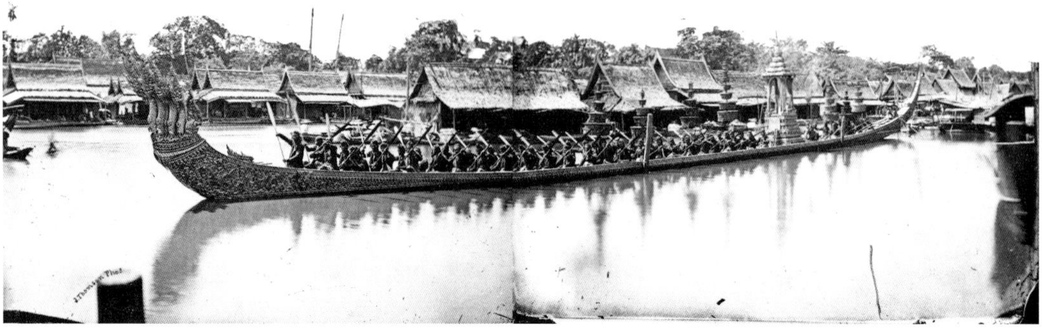

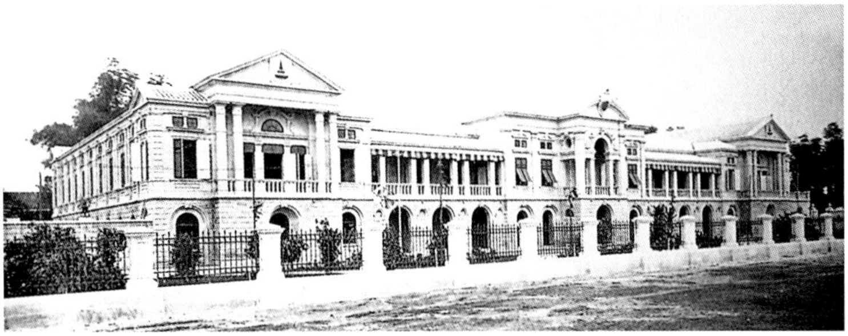

Saranrom Palace where the king intended to retire. (River Books)

Being in treaty relations with so many foreign countries and with their consuls being in Bangkok, King Mongkut also had his consuls in some of those countries. Sir John Bowring, now retired, was appointed Thai Consul in London with the Thai title of nobility in the rank of Phra. There was a consul in Paris, a vice-consul at Marseilles, a consul in Berlin and another at Lisbon – all of them Europeans. At Penang, Singapore, Hong Kong, Macao, and Batavia, his consuls were Chinese merchants.

Knowing that knowledge of English, which he had learned with great perseverance, was of incalculable benefit to him, Mongkut was determined that his children, especially his eldest son, Chulalongkorn, should be properly taught that language. The prince had more than one teacher. At first there were the wives of the American missionaries, then the English widow – Mrs. Anna Leonowens, and finally the Englishman – Francis George Patterson. The present writer has had the good fortune in the last ten years to have travelled widely and been round the world, and has found that the majority of English-speaking people now think that every enlightened action or progressive thought displayed by the two monarchs – father and son – were the results of Mrs. Leonowens' influence and teaching. As these beliefs are so general, it is necessary here to make some observations. First of all it must be remembered that King Mongkut had learned English and admired Western views – or some of them-when he was still a monk. Mrs. Leonowens did not come to Bangkok until 1862 – after he had been on the throne for *eleven years,* when most of his reforms had been decided upon and his important treaties with Western powers already concluded, so she could hardly claim any influence on his internal or external policies. In fact to engage her as a teacher of English was part of a progressive policy which had been settled in his mind long before her arrival. The general misconception about her position and influence did not arise from her own book, published in 1870, which had lain forgotten for over 70 years. Nor did it owe its rise so much to Margaret Landon's best-selling American novel, but rather, and absurdly so, to the widely popular musical film, *The King and I.* Since then it has become most difficult to get even reasonable western people to believe that the film was almost entirely fictional except for the use of real names. In fact,

62 Dibakarawongse: *Rama IV, op. cit.,* page 441.

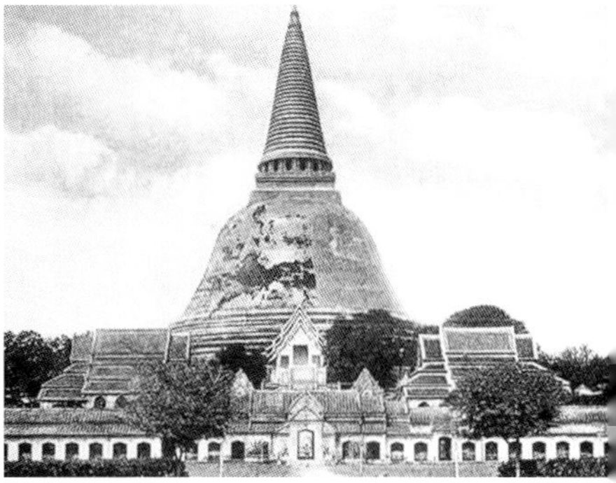

Phra Pathom chedi in Nakhon Pathom. (National Archives Bangkok)

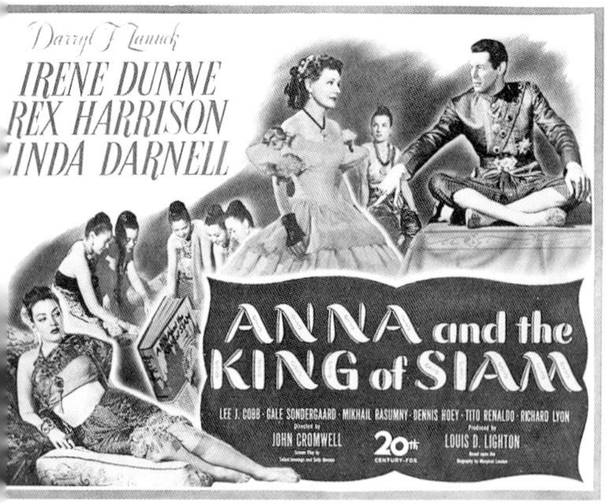

Poster for the film Anna and the King of Siam. (EuroGraphics)

it is almost as fictional as *The Mikado* of Gilbert and Sullivan, but in its case it was advertised as a documentary.

Of the original book of Mrs. Leonowens : *The English Governess at the Siamese Court,* some of Griswold's shrewd observations are worth repeating for those who did not read his articles.[63] Mrs. Leonowens claimed that she understood Thai (or Siamese). Griswold says: "But Siamese is a tricky language, and it is clear she never understood it. He asked, how much did she understand what she was told? His answer was: "less from Thai women, but she relied more on European gossip and her own imagination." *Romance of a Harem* was written in 1873 – six years after her departure from Siam. It was reprinted in London in 1952 as *Siamese Harem Life*, presumably because of the success of the film.

Mrs. Margaret Landon's novel, published in 1944, was based on *both* books by Mrs. Leonowens. Mrs. Landon herself admitted that her novel was 75 per cent fact and 25 per cent fiction, which caused Prince Dhani to observe "this would imply that Mrs. Landon believed in most of the statements in the original books of Mrs. Leonowens".[64] Griswold said that Mrs. Landon did not correct Mrs. Leonowens' faults, and I myself asked in a previous book whether by *fact* Mrs. Landon meant everything that Mrs. Leonowens had written?[65] *Siamese Harem Life* in its 1952 edition had an introduction by Miss Freya Stark, saying, "harassed and indomitable, she loved the women in this royal slavery and trained a new and happier generation of children to carry light into the future and few people can have wielded a stronger influence in that corner of Asia". Even much more recently, in 1959, an Englishman who had taught in Siam, wrote, "Anna Leonowens, King Chulalongkorn's professor, achieved so much single handed !"[66] If the parts played in his upbringing by his father and Thai teachers are to be ignored, what about the missionaries' wives and Mr. Patterson? To all such queries Griswold has the answer: "It has become almost an article of faith among westerners that every virtue the (Thai) Royal Family has displayed since Anna's time stems from her tactful inculcation of the Christian ideals In the musical play King Mongkut is required to sing a song: "It's a puzzlement." It seems that it is westerners who have been puzzled that an Asian king could be enlightened and progressive on his own, so Anna has been used as a romantic explanation.

Concerning Mrs. Leonowens' knowledge of the Thai language, Prince Dhani wrote: "unacquainted with the Siamese . . . most of her translations of Siamese passages, accepted without question by Mrs. Landon, are either unrecognizable or quite wrong". An Englishman who spent many years in Siam and was a physician to the Queen, Dr. Smith, wrote of her: "Her books, particularly her second one, show that she was gifted with vivid imagination which at times took charge of her pen".[67] Hall also wrote of the different Western portrayals of King Mongkut: "Mrs. Leonowens . . . the lady was gifted with more

63 Alexander B. Griswold: *op. cit.*

64 Prince Dhani's Review of Margaret Landon's novel, *op. cit.*

65 Prince Chula: *The Twain Have Met, op. cit.*, page 32.

66 D. J. Enright: Review of *The Mask of Siam* by David Barnett. *The Spectator,* August 14th, 1959.

67 Dr. Malcolm Smith: *op. cit.*, page 42.

68 D. G. E. Hall: *op. cit.*, page 579.

69 Anna Leonowens: *The English Governors, etc., op. cit.*, page 238.

imagination than insight. Margaret Landon's (book) is even more unfair to Mongkut. The fairest estimate of him is in Malcolm Smith's (book)".[68]

Anna Leonowens, who sailed from Bangkok on July 5th, 1867,[69] left Siam a year before Mongkut's death, and, even if she could have possibly been allowed to be there, could not have been present at the king's death bed and make the promises about helping King Chulalongkorn to rule Siam as portrayed in the musical play and film. If the above discussion is considered to be unnecessary "white-washing" of King Mongkut, may I say that I am fully aware that his memory has no need of it. But a situation has developed which is somewhat alarming, especially so to historians, namely, that a musical film based on a novel, which was made for commercial purposes, should have been able to alter history in the minds of hundreds of millions of people.

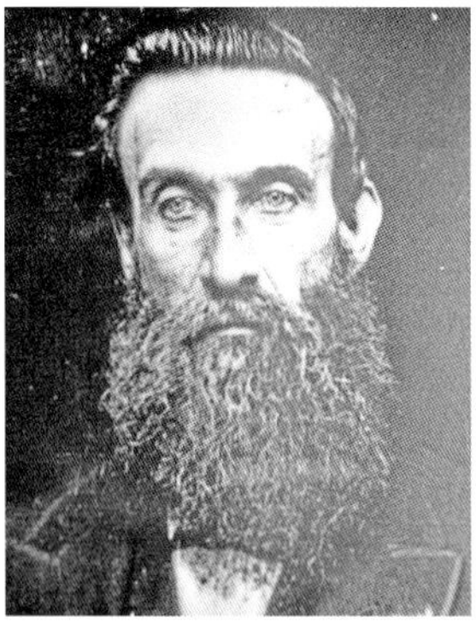

Francis George Patterson, one of the English teachers to the royal children. (National Archives Bangkok)

Among the many subjects studied by King Mongkut, astronomy was his favourite, and today the glass dome of his observatory on the Palace Hill near Phetchaburi can still be seen glinting in the sun. The chronicles of the time frequently record his taking the positions of the stars by night and the sun by day. On his travels he would often stop, get off his horse, and take a reading of the sun so as to know his exact position in relation to the longitude and latitude. Accordingly, he was highly elated to learn from his and other scientists' calculations that there would be a total eclipse of the sun in the southern part of Siam in 1868. The Thai belief regarding eclipses was that a colossal giant swallowed the sun or the moon for a while, and the people would beat gongs or anything that would make a loud noise in the belief that this would frighten the monster and make it disgorge the sun or the moon. According to ancientThai astrology, a total eclipse of the moon was known, but a total eclipse of the sun was thought to be impossible. Most important of all they did not know that the occurrence of an eclipse could be calculated in advance. When King Mongkut announced that he had calculated exactly when and where the eclipse would take place, even the most intelligent among his entourage were incredulous.

The best account of the eclipse comes from Prince Damrong, who was present by his father's side as a boy of rising seven.[70] The king found that the eclipse would be visible at Sam Roi Yod, a remote village near a group of mountains called "Three Hundred Peaks" on the west coast of the Gulf of Siam not far from the modern resort of Hua Hin. When the king ordered preparations to be made for the Court to move there to view the eclipse, most people thought the entire enterprise a waste of time. Even the clever Prince Maha Mala told Prince Damrong afterwards that he did not believe the king. A part of the jungle was cleared near the beach and a camp was set up which was a veritable wooden palace with many guest houses and pavilions.

King Mongkut invited Sir Henry Orde, then Governor of Singapore, to come as his most honoured guest, and the French government was sending a large party of scientists, who arrived on July 25th. In his letter to Sir Henry Orde, who was coming by sea, King

70 Prince Damrong: *Memoirs*, *op. cit.*, pages 26-30. Rendered into English by Dr. Smith, *op. cit.*, page 45.

Mongkut told him to come to the place at "East Greenwich longitude 99 degs. 42' and latitude North 11 degs. 39'." He had taken more trouble than usual with his calculations because he knew that if where they were the eclipse was not total, the sceptics would laugh at him, if only behind his back. The king himself left Bangkok by steamer on August 8th, and Sir Henry Orde arrived on August 16th. Being a devout Christian he asked to be excused from landing on a Sunday, and Mongkut naturally understood. All the Europeans in Bangkok were invited – there were 84 of them in his service alone, as well as others in business. The large Thai party included the ladies of the palace and several children. Many famous Thai astrologers had been summoned and they came full of disbelief. The sea was rough and many were seasick, a fact of which King Mongkut complained in his letter to Bangkok. Prince Maha Mala was so fearful of being seasick that he endured the exhaustion of riding an elephant all the way from Phetchaburi. The hospitality was lavish, and the Europeans were served with European meals prepared under the expert eye of a French chef, with large blocks of ice were very much in evidence to cool the drinks.

The eclipse was expected on August 18th, and when the day opened with clouds and rain, one can imagine the agony of King Mongkut's mind. Everyone else was also depressed, especially the French scientists who wondered if they had travelled thousands of miles in vain. Then what seemed like a miracle occurred – the sky suddenly cleared and the most wonderful sight was soon seen – a total eclipse of the sun exactly as the king had predicted. As the last bright part disappeared, one of the astrologers gave a shout despite standing next to His Majesty. The totality lasted 6 minutes and 46 seconds and Prince Damrong remembered that it was dark enough to see many stars. The king was overjoyed. The Europeans admitted that he was a brilliant mathematician and a real astronomer, while the old Thai sages were proved quite wrong. What a tremendous moment it must have been for him, and how he must have enjoyed the party which he gave that night.

It is poignantly sad to relate, however, that the great party was followed by tragedy. The king's pavilion was built on the exact line of totality according to his calculations. It was on low ground and at a fever-infested spot, whereas if the king had not been such a purist and had it built a little way off, all might have been well. Prince Damrong in later years found a brick platform which was probably where his father had placed his telescope. In 1929 there was another total eclipse of the sun in Siam, this time at Pattani, and King Mongkut's grandson, King Prajadhipok, used the same telescope to view it.

Soon after returning to Bangkok the king fell seriously ill from malaria caught in the fever spot. The fever, which would not leave him, took a serious turn because he was so exhausted. Dr. Bradley and other American physicians asked to attend him, but, despite his otherwise progressive mind, he now clung rigidly to Thai medicine, and it was soon obvious to him and everyone else that he was dying. It was even

71 Dibakarawongse: *Rama IV, op. cit.,* pages 478-481.

more critical because the king's eldest son, Chulalongkorn, who had also watched the eclipse, was equally stricken. He was then living in his own establishment known as the Rose Garden Palace. With the situation becoming so serious, Chao Phraya Sri Suriyawongse had the guards augmented at the palace of the prince.

When he realised that his malady was fatal,[71] King Mongkut sent for Prince Wongsa and his senior ministers, led by Sri Suriyawongse. Both the Ong Yai and the Ong Noi had already passed away. Through the ministers the king returned several personal gifts, received over the course of many years, back to their donors. He worried about the illness of Prince Chulalongkorn and was asking after him the whole time, but they would not tell him that he too was very ill. He sent for his secretary and dictated a farewell letter to the prelates of the Buddhist Church, which was in Pali, after which he spoke to his secretaries in English. It was his wish to live to the last in the hallowed example set by the Lord Buddha, especially in dying with a completely conscious mind. He was proving that his mind was unimpaired by speaking and dictating in two languages. He was even glad that it was his birthday, for the Lord Buddha had died on his own birthday. He asked that none of his small children were to be allowed to approach him as he did not wish to be distracted from his quiescent readiness to leave the world. He asked to see the senior princes, ministers, and some of the noblemen and officials of higher ranks. In taking leave of them, he begged for their forgiveness if he had been impatient, wounding, or offensive to them in any way. They were moved to terrible sobs and tears and utterly unable to reply. He calmly and gently admonished them, reminding them of the words of the Lord Buddha: "All which are born must die."

Like his father and half-brother, Rama II and Rama III, King Mongkut designated no heir. He declared that his eldest son, Prince Chulalongkorn – then aged 15 – was too young to rule. He said how deeply he regretted having to leave them because he would no longer be able to *serve* the State with them. They were to choose a prince whom they thought best fitted to *serve* the State in his place. To them he commended his children's welfare; and if they had loved him, he asked that, should any of his children offend in any way, their lives might be spared for his sake and exile should be their only lot. Finally he asked to be turned on to his right side in the way the Lord Buddha had died, and his last words clearly spoken were: "This is the correct way to die." He was fully conscious and clear of mind when he breathed his last on October 18th, 1868.

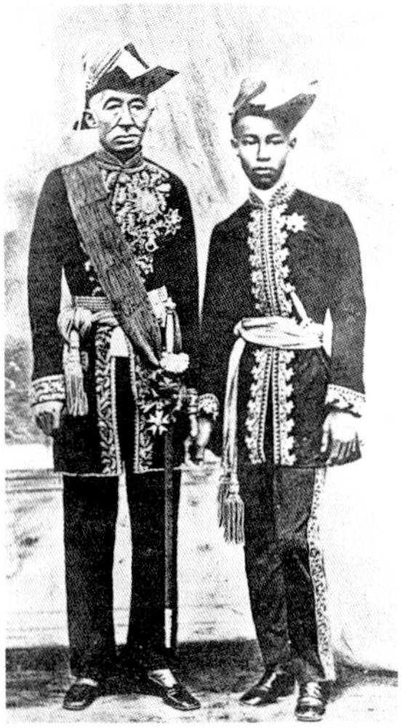

One of the last photographs of King Mongkut and Prince Chulalongkorn. (National Archives Bangkok)

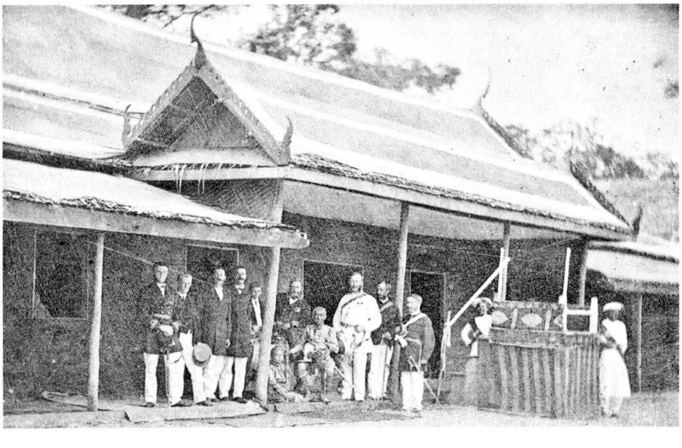

King Mongkut and Sir Henry Orde in the pavilion built to observe the total eclipse in Prachuab Khiri Kahn. (Tringanu Historical & Pictorial Archivist)

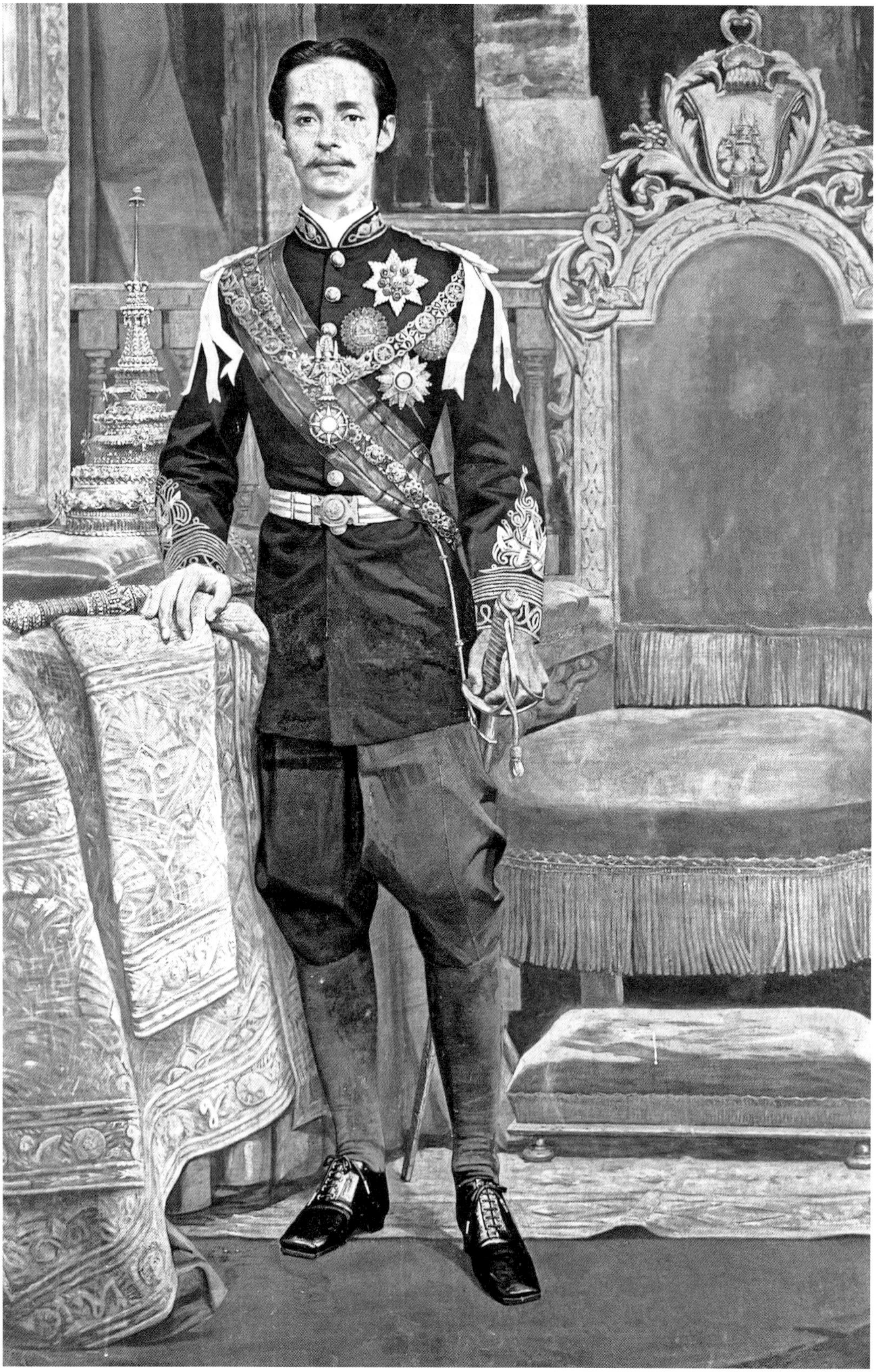

Chapter Five
The Revolutionary
(A.D. 1868 To 1910)

King Chulalongkorn's reforms were of such magnitude that his son, King Prajadhipok, once said that it was *revolutionary*, but unlike other revolutions it was carried out from the throne. His reign of 42 years took up almost one-third of the period of the absolute, or rather paternal monarchy of Bangkok. If King Mongkut deserves a full-length biography, King Chulalongkorn needs one of two or three volumes. Pending that event only a brief summary of his life and reign will now be attempted.

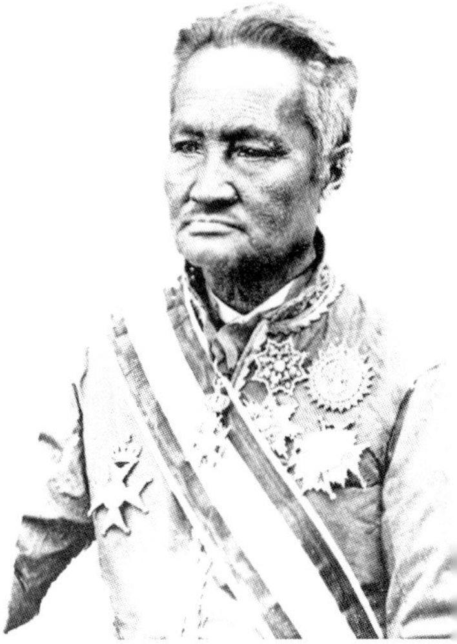

Somdet Chao Phraya Sri Suriyawongse (Chuang Bunnag), who was Regent at the beginning of the Fifth reign from 1868-1873. (River Books)

OPPOSITE: A painting of King Chulalongkorn by Carlo Rigoli. (River Books)

It was at nine p.m.[1] that King Mongkut had died, but it was round about midnight when the Accession Council, having been summoned by the Chief Minister, met in the Grand Palace. There was no clear right to membership of this council and it usually consisted of the Patriarch, prelates, senior princes, and ministers, with membership determined by the most powerful minister at the end of each reign. In this case it was Chao Phraya Sri Suriyawongse who invited the Patriarch, Prince Pavaret (a son of the *Uparaja* of the 2nd Reign), and 24 prelates. Of the 16 princes present there were seven half-brothers of Mongkut, six sons of Rama III, and three sons of former *Uparajas*. None of Mongkut's own sons were old enough, but seven who were in the junior priesthood as *samnera* were invited to watch the proceedings. Twenty noblemen were admitted to the council, led by the Chief Minister himself, with other ministers, lesser officials, and guards officers girded with swords. These latter were only watching or providing security. They were all sitting on the floor and the Chief Minister then assumed the kneeling position, and with hands joined in the attitude of prayer, declared that the late king had designated no heir. Instead he had left it to the council to choose a prince who was considered suitable, and he now asked them to make a suggestion without any qualms. Prince Deves, the eldest half-brother of the late monarch, said that as a sign of love and loyalty to his late majesty, they should offer the throne to his eldest son. The Chief Minister thereupon asked them one by one to give their vote, except for the prelates, of whom he only asked the Patriarch, and one by one they all assented. The Chief Minister then said that the late monarch had been anxious because his son was too young, to be an effective ruler. Prince Deves suggested and the council concurred that Chao Phra Sri Suriyawongse should be Regent until the young King was old enough to enter the priesthood, namely had reached the age of twenty. The Chief Minister accepted the position and said he would do his best, but because he knew so little of royal ceremonies and court affairs, he asked Prince Maha Mala to take charge of the Royal Palace.

1 *Collected History*, No. 52, *Death of King Mongkut* (in Thai), Bangkok, 1929.

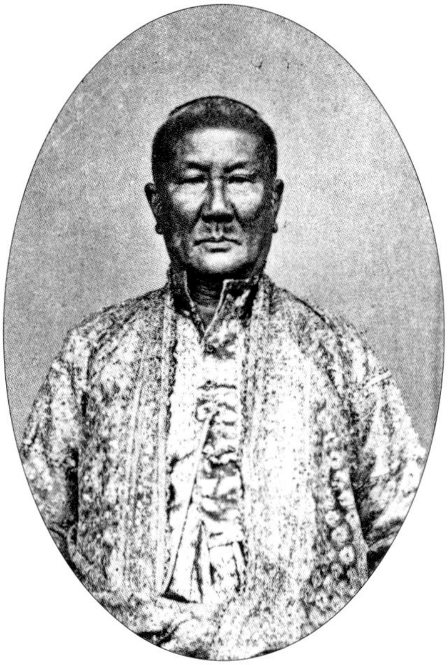

Prince Deves, a half-brother to King Rama IV. (National Archives Bangkok)

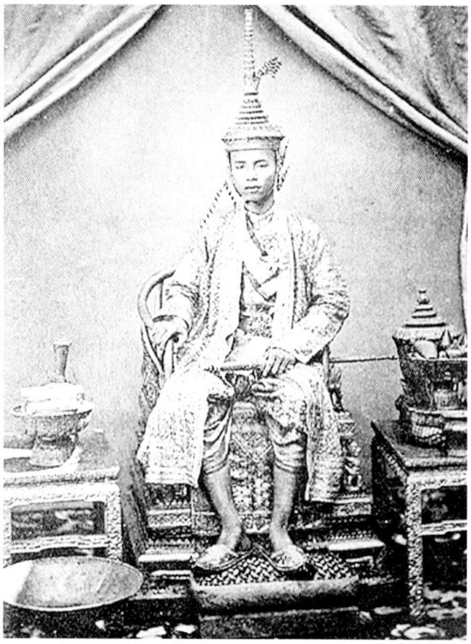

King Rama V on the occasion of his first coronation. (National Archives Bangkok)

Prince Chulalongkorn, photographed by John Thomson in 1865. (Wellcome Collection)

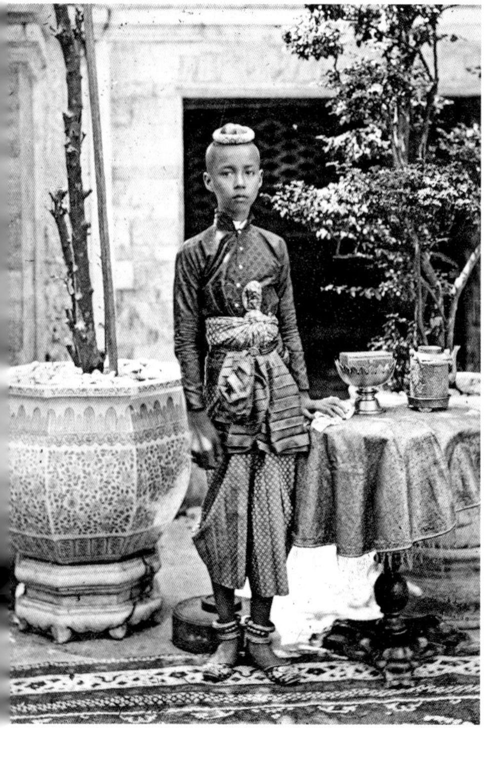

Prince Deves further declared that they also owed a debt of gratitude to the late Second King, Phra Pinklao, so they should elect his eldest son, Prince Bavorn Vichaiyan, as the new *Uparaja*. On this question the Chief Minister also asked the opinion of each member of the council. All agreed or abstained except for another half-brother of King Mongkut, Prince Varachakra, who said that in former times it was the king himself who chose the *Uparaja* and in the Chakri Dynasty it had either been the brother of the king or an uncle in the 3rd Reign, but never the son of the late *Uparaja*. Accordingly, he suggested that they should wait until the king was grown up and could choose his Deputy for himself. Sri Suriyawongse was extremely angry, and after severely rebuking Prince Varachakra, asked him outright: "You don't agree. Is it because you want to be *(Uparaja)* yourself?" Prince Varachakra realized that it was time to give in and replied: "If you want me to agree, then I agree." There has been much speculation amongst Thai historians as to why the Chief Minister was so insistent on the appointment. One of the reasons given was that he wanted to have a grateful ally – the prince was fifteen years older than the king – should King Chulalongkorn turn against the Regent after reaching his majority. The new *Uparaja*, the last to be appointed in the Chakri Dynasty, had originally been named George Washington by his democratic father, and he would have very little to do in the 17 years that he held his high position.

As a result, when he died in 1885 at the age of 48, the position was abolished. It was in this manner that King Chulalongkorn, who was born on September 20th, 1853, became the fifth king of the Chakri Dynasty at the age of just 15 years.

The young sovereign had been devoted to his father and was nursing him in his last illness until one day King Mongkut felt his son's forehead and found that it was very hot. The prince, having a high fever, was sent back to his own palace and told not to return until he should recover. Sadly, he never saw his father alive again. At his accession King Chulalongkorn had been ill for over a month and he was in a very weak state. Unable to walk, he was carried to the Grand Palace, and when he saw the body of the late king he could hardly raise his arms in the attitude of salutation and just fainted away. When he was revived by the doctors, the senior princes decided that he was too ill to remain there, and it was Prince Maha Mala who presided at the official bathing ceremony, and it was he who placed the crown for the last time on the late king's head before the body was lowered into the inner silver urn and covered with the great golden urn – the Thong Yai. This was placed on the gold catafalque in the Dusit Maha Prasat Hall with full ceremony, followed by the age-old rites until the cremation took place in due course.

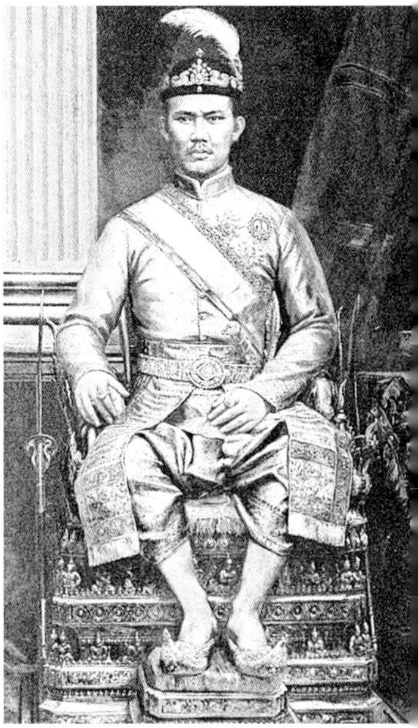

Krom Phra Bavorn Vichaiyan who was the Deputy King *(Uparaja)* during the fifth reign. After his death, this office was abolished. (River Books)

The Regent had worked closely with King Mongkut and he was equally progressive and open-minded, thus the young king was being trained to follow in the footsteps of his father, under whose direction his early education had been conducted. His mother had died when he was only nine but fortunately he had been under the constant care of his great-aunt, Princess Lamom, the full sister of Prince Mataya, whom he loved as much as his own mother. Chulalongkorn first learned to read and write Thai from the ladies of the Inside, who also taught him the complicated royal traditions and court etiquette. Later he learned advanced Thai and elementary Pali with male teachers as his father had done. Other subjects taught by men were boxing, wrestling, and Thai fencing. Horsemanship had been taught by King Mongkut himself, who was a skilful horseman and capable of driving as well as riding, despite his 27 years as a monk. Once, however, his buggy cart did turn over when one of the reins broke and the king had injuries to his side and legs, while the young Prince suffered three lacerations to his head. Government and statecraft he also learned from his father, chiefly by being in attendance when he was engaged in State affairs at night, during which in between reading State papers the old monarch would talk to him and explain important matters. He also learned a great deal by being the bearer of verbal messages to the Chief Minister the following morning. For the Buddhist doctrine, Chulalongkorn had expert teachers and he went into the monastery as a *samnera* in 1866. Thus despite his youth King Chulalongkorn had been well versed in the different branches of Thai culture of his time. As well as that he learned English from the wives of American missionaries and

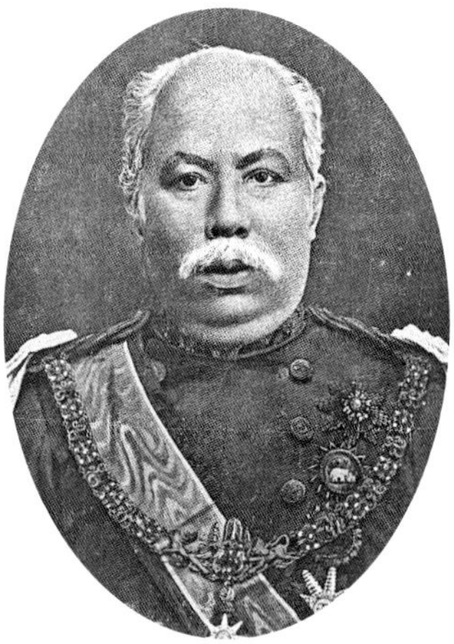

Prince Maha Mala, founder of the Malakul family. (Paisarn Piemmettawat)

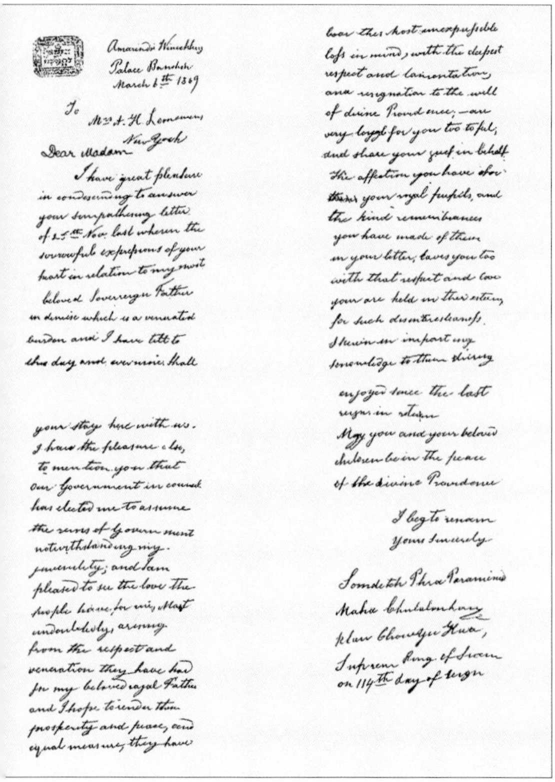

Amarindr Winichhay
Palace Bangkok
March 6th 1869

To
Mrs. A. H. Leonowens
New York

Dear Madam

I have great pleasure in condescending to answer your sympathizing letter of 25th Nov. last wherein the sorrowful expressions of your heart in relation to my most beloved Sovereign Father in demise which is a venerated burden and I have little to this day and evermore shall bear this most inexpressible loss in mind, with the deepest respect and lamentation, and resignation to the will of divine Providence; — are very loyal for you too to feel, and share your grief in behalf the affection you have shown to your royal pupils, and the kind remembrances you have made of them in your letter, leaves you too with that respect and love you are held in their esteem for such disinterestedness. I having imparted my knowledge to them during your stay here with us. I have the pleasure also, to mention you that our Government in council has elected me to assume the reins of Government notwithstanding my juvenility; and I am pleased to see the love the people have for me, most undoubtedly, arising from the respect and veneration they have had for my beloved royal Father and I hope to render them prosperity and peace, in equal measure, they have enjoyed since the last reign in Siam.

May you and your beloved children be in the peace of the divine Providence

I beg to remain
Yours Sincerely

Somdetch Phra Paramindr
Maha Chulalonkorn
Klau Chowyu Hua,
Supreme King of Siam
on 114th day of reign

Letter from King Chulalongkorn to Anna Leonowens after she had left. (PBA Galleries)

Mrs. Leonowens, who, according to Prince Damrong, ceased teaching him in 1866 – one year before she left Siam.[2]

After his accession he continued his English lessons in the evening with Francis George Patterson, but here again he was soon too busy and the lessons had to stop. However, being so fond of the English language – many words of which he mixed with Thai all his life – he went on studying on his own in his spare time, and he could read, write, speak, and understand English quite well – certainly as well as any educated Thais of his time. Despite his minority, the king gave audiences, the Regent being always present, took part in religious ceremonies, attended Cabinet meetings over which the Regent presided, and was informed of everything that went on in the country.

At the commencement of the Regency there were many in Bangkok who gravely feared its consequences, for it was remembered that five monarchs of Ayudhya had been assassinated during their minority, one of them by a Regent with the title of Chao Phra Kalahom Suriyawongse. The parallel in the title with the present Regent must have been in the people's minds, including that of the Regent himself. But the Kalahom Sri Suriyawongse of the Fifth Reign of Bangkok was a statesman of great integrity, as Sir John Bowring wrote of him in his diary: "He is a most sagacious man, towering above every person whom we have met – of graceful, gentlemanly maners and appropriate language . . . in a word, his language is of the most high-minded patriotism."[3] Although some clashes of temperament naturally occurred now and again between the young monarch and his mentor, the Regency passed off peacefully and safely for the king. Nevertheless, eighteen years later King Chulalongkorn was to admit that there were times when he found the relationship irksome.

Judged by any standards – and there are many photographs, paintings and sculpture from life of him at different ages – King Chulalongkorn was good looking, and Mrs. Leonowens conceded that "for a Siamese he was a handsome lad".[4] Like his forbears, and all the Thais of his time in a position to be so, he was a polygamist. Before his accession he already had two non-royal wives, one of whom was of the Bunnag family, and he had had two daughters. Although Prince Maha Mala had been asked by the Regent to run the palace, he did so on the official and ceremonial side. The young king appeared to have had unbridled control of the Inside despite the presence of his great-aunt and former nurse, Princess Lamom. Many more noble young ladies were again and again presented to him as minor wives whom he accepted in accordance

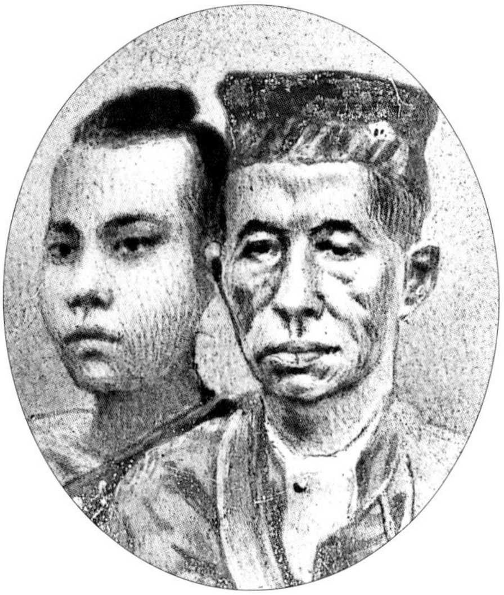

King Mongkut and Queen Debsirindra. (River Books)

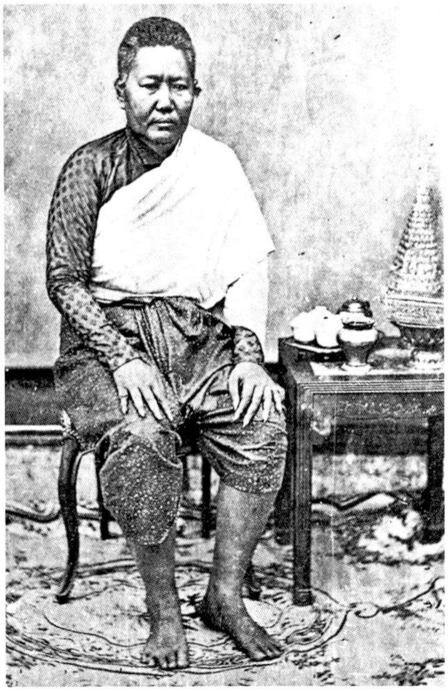

Somdet Krom Phra Sudaratana Rajaprayoon, King Chulalongkorn's nursemaid. (National Archives Bangkok)

with old custom. It must surely have beensomething of a novelty to have the presence in the Inside of many attractive, intelligent, and highly-educated young half-sisters who were under his sole guardianship. His own full sister had died in the reign of King Mongkut and was not there to help him look after them, while their mothers, being *Chao Choms*, were not in the position to treat the king as a stepson. A few of these half- sisters the king took to wife and raised them to the rank of queen, placing them high above former wives of noble birth. While this practice is admittedly shocking to the Western mind, it was based on the old Hindu system of keeping royal blood pure for the succession. It was difficult for the Chakris to inter-marry with foreign royalty, surrounded as Siam was by former enemies or vassals. Dr. Smith[5] has stated that such marriages were plentiful in the history of mankind, were mentioned in ancient Egyptian history, known amongst the ancient Hawaiians, the Incas of Peru, and the Kings of Ceylon and Persia, but in later years it was practised only by the Indo-Chinese races, namely the Thais, the Laos, the Cambodians, and the Burmese. Three of King Chulalongkorn's half-sisters who became his wives were daughters of the Lady Piam, already mentioned as the favourite wife of King Mongkut. They were Princesses Sunanta, Sawang, and Saowabha. The other half-sister who was also his wife was Princess Sukumala, whose mother was from the *Ong Noi* branch of the great Bunnag family. All these princesses were made *Phra Nang* – Queen, but some of them would be promoted higher still on different occasions.

Princess Sunanta, created *Somdech Phra Nang* (Her Majesty the Queen), died tragically in 1881 when she and her daughter were travelling up the river to the island palace of Bang Pa-In and the boat

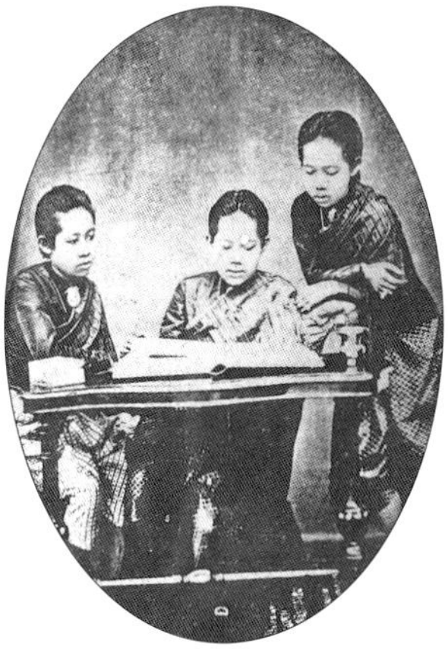

FROM LEFT TO RIGHT: Queen Sawang Vadhana, Queen Sunanta and Queen Saowabha. (National Archives Bangkok)

2 Prince Damrong: *King Chulalongkorn before his accession*, pages 4, 7, 8, 16 (in Thai), Bangkok, 1929.

3 Sir John Bowring: Vol. II, *op. cit*, page 282.

4 Anna Leonowens: *The English Governess, etc.*, *op. cit.*, page 218.

5 Dr. Smith: *op. cit.*, page 135.

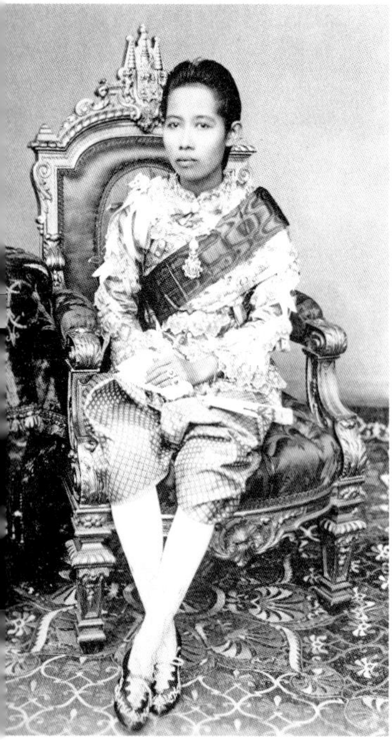

Queen Sawang Vadhana.
(River Books)

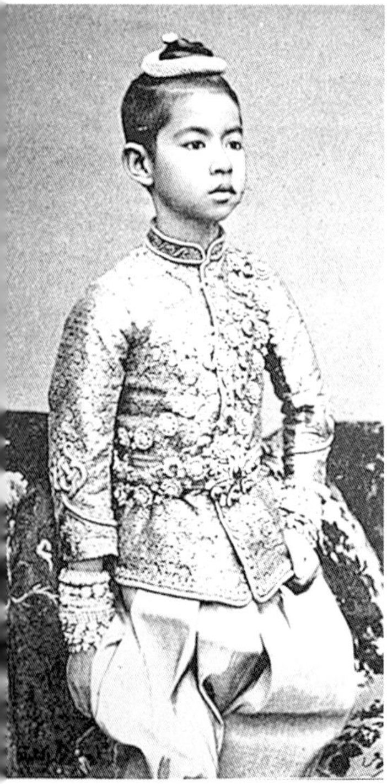

Crown Prince Maha Vajirunhis.
(National Archives Bangkok)

containing them capsized and they were all drowned. She was barely 21 and was pregnant at the time, and King Chulalongkorn mourned her most deeply as can be seen from the memorial he had put up in the garden of Bang Pa-In with inscriptions in Thai and English. The latter read: "To the beloved memory of her late and lamented Majesty, Sunanta-Kumariratana, Queen Consort, who was wont to spend her most pleasant and happiest hours in this garden amidst those loving ones and dearest to her. This memorial is erected by Chulalongkorn Rex, her bereaved husband, whose suffering from so cruel an endurance through those trying hours made death seemed so near yet preferable. 1881."

Her next sister, Princess Sawang (born 1862), also created *Phra Nang*, had eight children, while her younger sister still, Princess Saowabha (born 1864), also created *Somdech Phra Nang*, had nine children. Princess Sukumala (born 1861) who remained only *Phra Nang* for reasons unknown to the present writer, had two children. This failure to elevate her is all the more surprising because King Chulalongkorn had great affection and respect for her, and her two children were on completely equal terms with the children of the two *Somdechs*, namely, being first class *Chao Fa*, and entitled on informal occasions to be called *Toonkramom* (carried on the head), sometimes shortened to *Toonmom*, except the current heir to the throne, who was always called *Toonkramom* in full.

Of the male children of these three queens, the senior in age was the eldest son of Queen Sawang, Prince Vajirunhis (born 1878), who was created Crown Prince by his father, an entirely new position and an unprecedented step seeing that the *Uparaja* was still alive, thus putting an end to the old theory that an *Uparaja* might succeed to the throne instead of a son of the monarch. Nevertheless, the succession was not yet by law according to primogeniture, and the king still reserved to himself the right to appoint his heir. Crown Prince Vajirunhis died at the early age of 17 in 1895 whereupon King Chulalongkorn appointed Queen Saowabha's eldest son, Vajiravudh, as Crown Prince, and not the next son of Queen Sawang. At about the same time he raised Queen Saowabha to be what may conveniently be termed the Supreme Queen as such a title had not existed in Siam before, and this was *Somdech Phra Boromma Rajinee*.[6] For the rest of the reign she alone was called in European languages "Her Majesty the Queen of Siam," was entitled to the Queen's Royal Standard and was received, when alone, with the National Anthem. The same titles and honours have since been accorded to the sole consorts of King Prajadhipok, and the reigning sovereign, His Majesty King Bhumibol.

Queen Saowabha had five sons who grew to maturity: Vajiravudh (born January 1st, 1881), Chakrabongse (born March 3rd, 1883), Asdang (born 1889), Chudadhuj (1892), and Prajadhipok (November 8th, 1893). Queen Sukumala had only one son (and a daughter), Paribatra (born June 29th, 1881 and only six months younger than Vajiravudh).

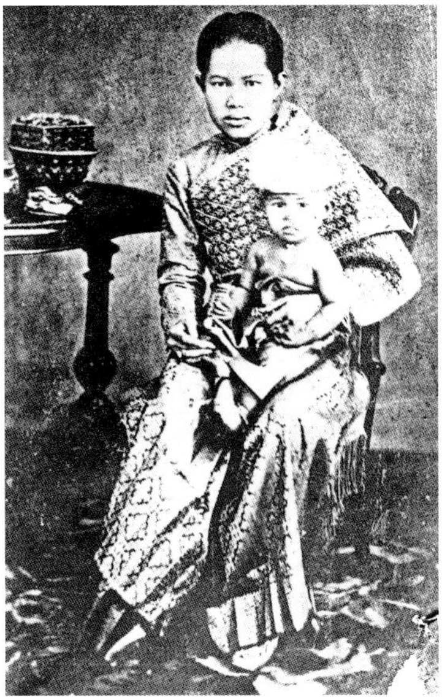

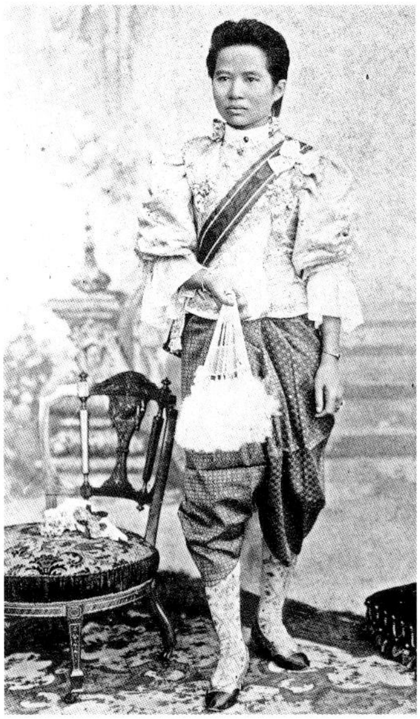

Far left: Queen Sunanta with her daughter Princess Kannabhorn on her lap. (River Books)

Left: Queen Sukumala Marsi, the mother of Prince Paribatra. (Paisarn Piemmettawat)

Of Queen Sawang's eight children, only two survived to maturity, namely, Princess Valaya (born 1884), and Prince Mahidol Adulyadej (born January 1st, 1892).

The well-known cartoonist, Ripley, once stated in his "*Believe it or not*" series that King Chulalongkorn had 3,000 wives and 370 children,[7] and more recent writers have either repeated this or had other erroneous figures of their own. It had been difficult to say exactly how many wives King Chulalongkorn did have, as the official records only gave the names of those who bore him children. Recently the present writer has with some difficulty succeeded in obtaining the reluctant help of his four surviving wives, and it is now possible to say that King Chulalongkorn had 92 wives. He had 77 children, 32 sons and 44 daughters, and one unborn when Queen Sunanta was drowned. These children were from 36 mothers.[8] Dr. Smith has pointed out an interesting feature. Of these wives only two had more

6 One lady was created *Boromma Rajini* by King Rama VI, but was demoted soon afterwards.

7 Ripley: *Believe It or Not,* page 78, London, 6th Impression.

8 *List of Chakri Princes and Princesses, op. cit.,* pages 81-107.

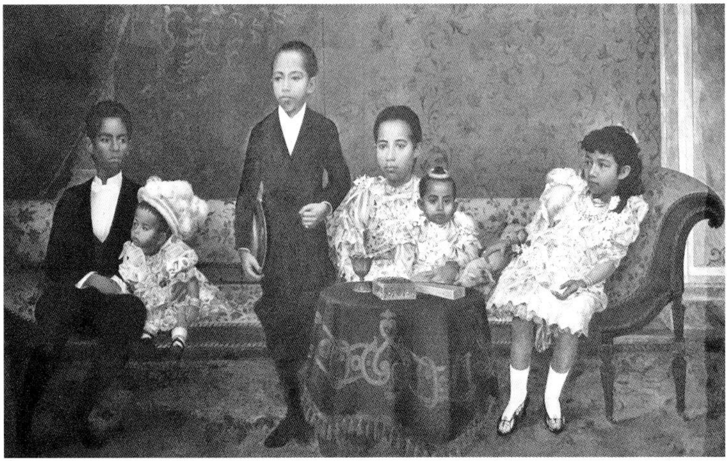

Queen Sawang Vadhana with her sons and daughters. From left: Crown Prince Maha Vajirunhis, Prince Mahidol, Prince Sommotiwong, Princess Siriporn, and Princess Valayalongkorn. (National Gallery Bangkok)

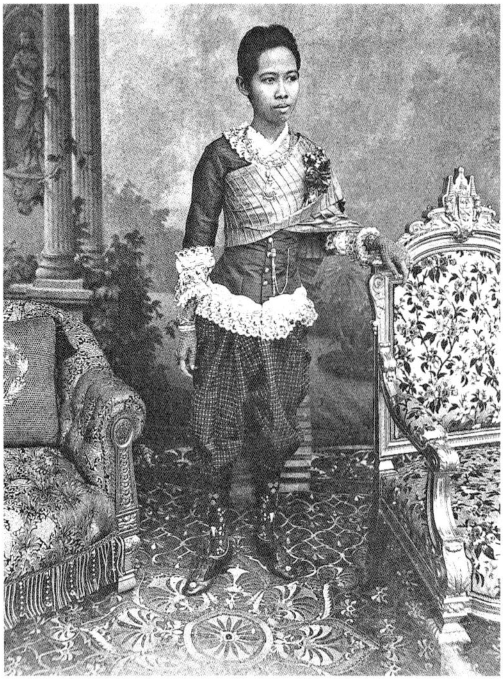

Queen Sawang Vadhana. (Paisarn Piemmettawat)

than four children, namely, Queen Sawang (8) and Queen Saowabha (9); three of the other wives had four, four had three, nine had two, and eighteen, or half their total number, only had one child each. As it is inconceivable that birth control was practised, many of the wives could have but little or no marital relations. As in previous reigns, many of them were accepted for reasons of statecraft or politeness. They were given honours, were well looked after and all the wives could come to the audience for the Inside in the yellow room. Hence the term grew up for the wives who did not see the king otherwise, to be called "The *Chao Choms* of the Yellow Room".[9]

Meanwhile we must return to the beginning of the reign and the Regency. King Mongkut had hoped to go to Singapore sometime after the eclipse and make a return visit to Sir Henry Orde. Now King Chulalongkorn was pressing to be allowed to carry out his father's thwarted plan. The Regent, who had been to Singapore himself, was sympathetic, and so the king went to Singapore in 1871 – the third year of his reign – when he was 18. From Singapore he went on to Java, and both the British and Dutch authorities were highly pleased and most hospitable. When he left Bangkok by ship he was the first Thai sovereign to journey out from his kingdom since King Naresuan went to war in Burma in the seventeenth century. Altogether he was away 37 days and received gratifying public receptions in both Singapore and Batavia (Jakarta). All the while he was observing everything and learning a great deal. He was deeply impressed with what the Europeans had done in the countries they had colonized. When he returned to Bangkok his vision had widened, his ideas profoundly changed, and he was more than ever convinced that the way towards progress lay in education with an emphasis on the knowledge of English.

With the Regent's support he decreed changes in court etiquette in the Outside amongst the men, while the ladies of the Inside could carry on with their age-old customs. The men now wore European-style uniforms or civilian clothes with close-neck jackets, but retaining the traditional *panung* (which the Thais originally took from the Khmers) – derived from the Indian *dhoti*, but worn more tightly and looking like modem plus-fours. They were made of silk and in different colours, with royal blue for official wear, with which they wore European silk stockings and shoes. They sat on chairs instead of reclining against cushions on the floor. King Chulalongkorn was determined that in the future the princes and nobles of Siam would be better educated than his own generation. He founded a model school for the sons of princes and high nobles which was in the Grand Palace and was called

9 Dr. Smith: *op. cit.*, page 140.

Rajkumar College. His younger brothers and half brothers were made to attend, followed later by his own sons, and English was widely taught by newly imported English masters. One of these was Robert Morant, who also gave private lessons to Princes Vajirunhis and Vajiravudh, but never taught King Chulalongkorn himself. After the success of this experimental school, he founded another modern school – the Suankularb or Rose Garden School – attended by sons of even junior officials and merchants, which became the forerunner of many government secondary schools. When he opened it he said: "All children from my own to the poorest should have an equal chance of education." That was his dream, and all through his reign he tried to widen the scope of education, although it was not possible to put all his dreams into practice owing to financial limitations. Like his father before him, Chulalongkorn was determined that Siam was not to be a Western colony, and one of the ways to avoid it was to pay for their own path towards progress.

Throughout his reign King Chulalongkorn continued the work of enlarging and improving the army, which was necessary for internal security, as it was to be called upon more than once to put down riots by Chinese secret societies and revolts by Chinese Boxer troops who had escaped into North-eastern Siam. It was also required to defend the dynasty and, if need be, to enable the country to become an ally of one *farang* power against another. His own special creation was the *Mahadlek* (Royal Pages) Guards Regiment. At the age of fifteen the young sovereign was intensely interested in everything military, and he went to watch the training of different Bangkok regiments every afternoon. In the palace he formed his young royal pages – boys of noble birth who were his playmates – into a tiny regiment of 24 boy-soldiers, affectionately known as the "two-dozen" regiment. The number soon increased, and as the boys grew up with the king they were employed as his closest bodyguards. On ceremonial occasions they marched in single file on either side of the king – a privilege enjoyed to this day only by their successors. In 1870 their number rose to be 72. By 1873 the king and most of them had reached the age of 20, and serious recruiting began for young men outside the palace, but only men of good birth and education were admitted. Other officers, besides the king, were appointed, and ranks were for some time designated in English, the king being colonel. Two companies were formed which soon increased to six, and a lieutenant colonel was appointed to be in real command who was some times, but not always, a prince. The king took the closest interest and visited the regiment in his spare time, but this became more rare after the end of the Regency when the king became his own Prime Minister. Eventually this special regiment was integrated with the

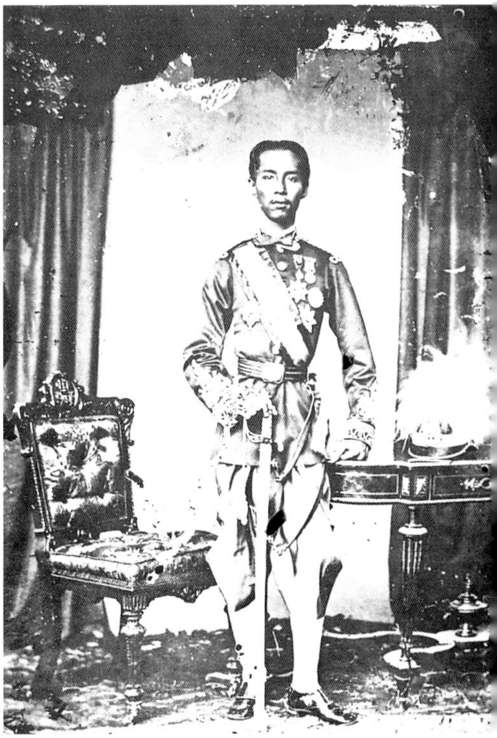

King Chulalongkorn in royal guards uniform. (National Archives Bangkok)

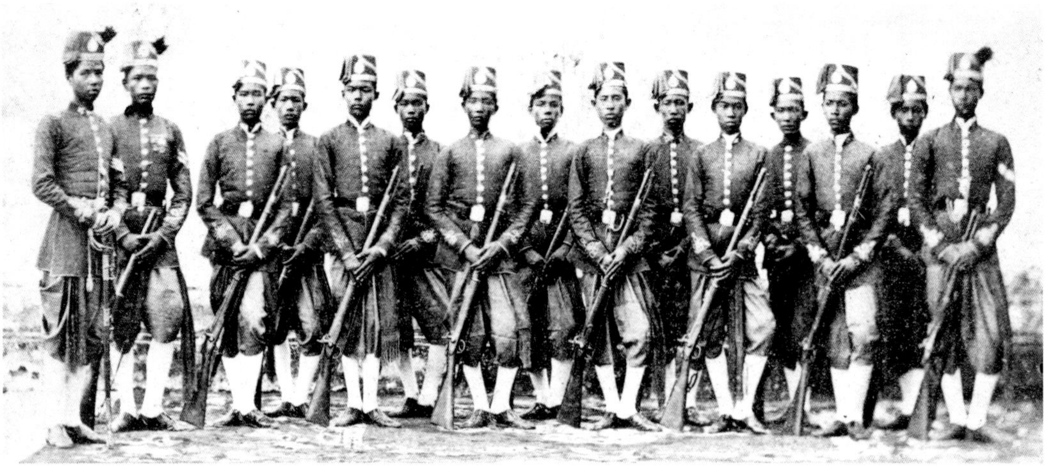

The first company of King Chulalongkorn's own body guards. (National Archives Bangkok)

regular army as the 1st Infantry Regiment of Guards, and was and continues to be the only regiment to wear scarlet for full-dress. When King Chulalongkorn died in 1910, his son and successor added to the name, "King Chulalongkorn's Own Bodyguard". The regiment wear that great king's cypher in his perpetual memory.

After his visits to Malaya and Java, King Chulalongkorn told the Regent that, having seen European colonies, he would now like to tour Europe itself. The Regent felt that Europe was still too far at that early part of the reign and India was agreed upon as a compromise. The king left by ship on December 18th, 1871, and he was away for four months with no ladies accompanying him. He was well received by the British Viceroy at Calcutta and thoroughly enjoyed his stay in the sub-continent, which included a visit to Bodh Gaya and other places of interest in the Buddhist Holy Land close to Benares, being the first, and so far the only, king of Siam to have done so.

In 1873 he was 20, considered to have reached his majority, and was given a full coronation ceremony. After he had placed the crown

10 Prince Damrong: *The Introduction of Western Culture in Siam, J.O.S.S.*, Vol. XX, Part 2, page 100.

11 It is from this "Chula" that the present writer's name is derived.

12 For a full description of the Grand Palace, see Prince Chula *The Twain Have Met, op. cit.*, pages 88-89.

King Chulalongkorn's trip to Malaya in 1871-72. (British Library)

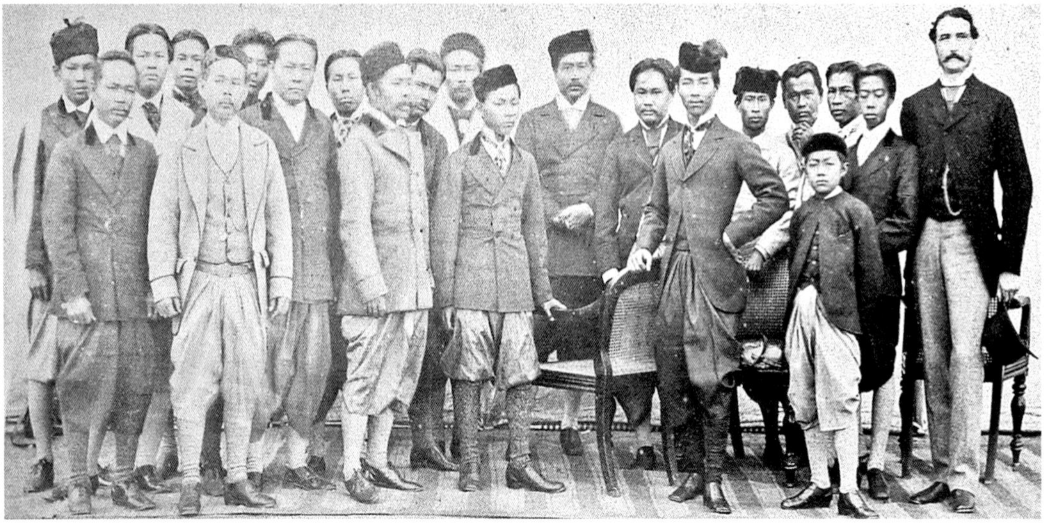

on his own head he proclaimed that from then on all ceremonial prostration to the king was abolished, and he asked the whole assembled company to stand up. Prince Damrong,[10] an eye-witness, later wrote: "I can assure you that it was a most impressive and memorable sight." The monarch received the same style and titles as his predecessors with emphasis on "born of royal parents on both sides" and the somewhat contrasting one of elected by all the people." His own personal title was Chula Chom Klao,[11] based on his father's title of Chom Klao, Chula being the Sanskrit term for small or junior. The king on that occasion gave his mother the posthumous title of Queen Mother with the name of Debsirindra. The Regent was given the highest rank of nobility with the style and title of Somdech Chao Phraya Boromma Maha Sri Suriyawongse.

At 21 the king became a monk for a short while, and as he had to surrender the crown on taking up the yellow robe, he had to have a second coronation, but it was a far less grandiose one.

For the greater part of the reign King Chulalongkorn lived in the Grand Palace.[12] He had to pull down a group of European-style buildings of King Mongkut because the wooden framework had begun to rot. He replaced them with new buildings, the most important edifice being the Chakri Building of three tapering spires which was begun in 1876 and completed in 1880, two years before the centenary of the Dynasty. It is a unique building, having a Thai roof with spires and ornate gables, yet the body is of Italian style. The outer part of this huge building consists of a throne hall (where the present king receives ambassadors when they present their credentials) and ante-rooms; with the inner part having King Chulalongkorn's private apartments and the living quarters of Queen Saowabha and her children. Her bedroom was so large that it was divided by wooden screens with photographs so that it was like living within a family album. There was the charming blue room with screens depicting scenes out of the *Inao* of Rama II

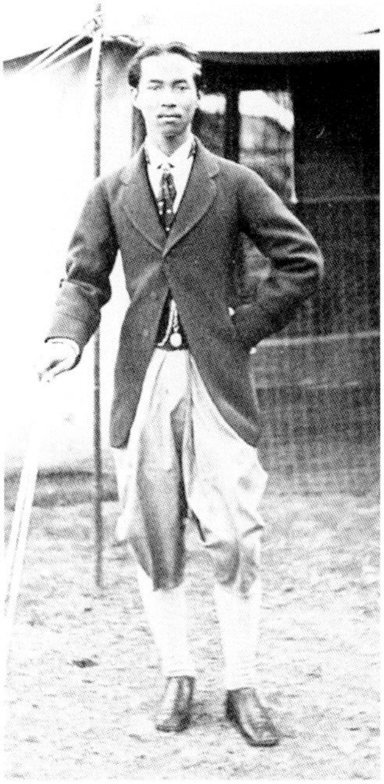

King Chulalongkorn's trip to India in 1871-72. (British Library)

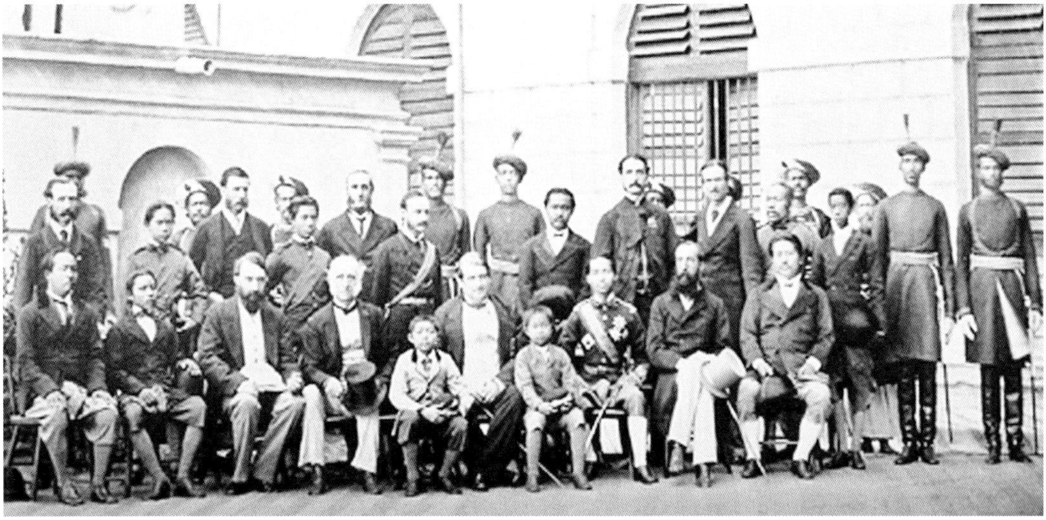

King Chulalongkorn, his entourage and Lord Mayo on his trip to India in 1871-72. (British Library)

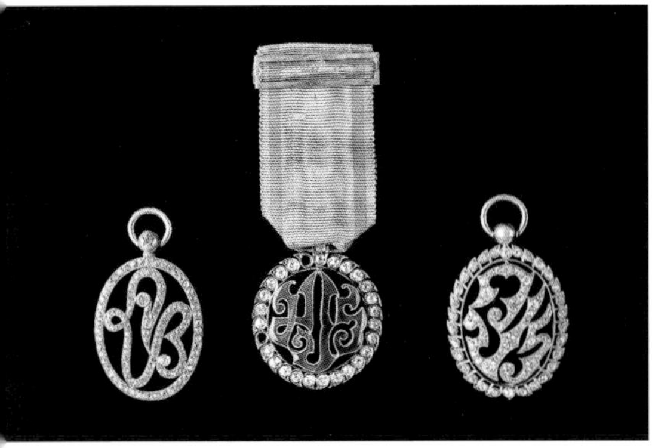

The Rattanabhorn medals from the Fourth, Fifth and Sixth reigns. (River Books)

where the present writer spent many happy days of his early youth having his meals and early lessons. The other queens and lesser wives had their own houses within the Inside, and Queen Saowabha alone was without a house and shared with the king the private portion of the great Chakri Building.

In 1882, when the dynasty was one hundred years old, King Chulalongkorn established the Most Noble Order of the Royal House of Chakri, which had a riband of bright saffron yellow of the robes of the Thai Buddhist monks, with an exquisite star, collar, and badge. This order was reserved for worthy and senior princes and princesses of the Chakri Family and for friendly foreign royalty. He then founded the Order of Chula Chom Klao, awarded to princes and officials and their ladies, which was partly hereditary, and which had a pink riband and the badge had his portrait in miniature. He furthermore carried out his father's wishes in creating the Order of the White Elephant and the Order of the Crown of Siam for services to the State. Then besides the usual bravery, campaign, commemorative, and long service medals, Siam has one unusual order which King Chulalongkorn first instituted posthumously for King Mongkut and which has since continued with every monarch. It is the Royal Cypher Medal for personal services to the sovereign which has five classes. There is a new order for each reign, and the distinctive feature of the order is that the first class medal is entirely covered with diamonds – so far unique of any order in the world.

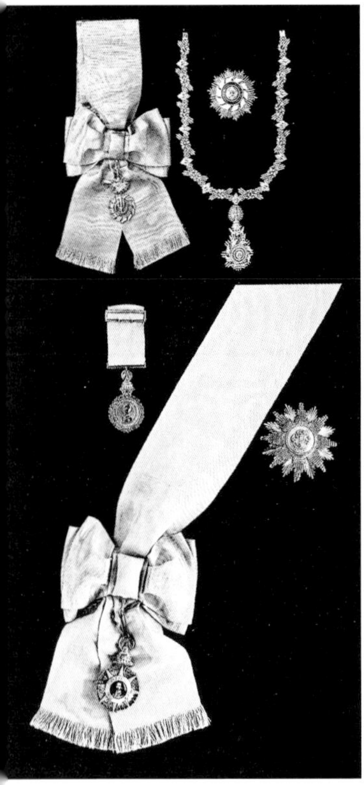

The Chakri order and the Chula Chom Klao decoration. (River Books)

King Chulalongkorn enjoyed his life, for he worked very hard and also played hard. He had simple health aims: to eat well and to sleep soundly. Himself an excellent cook, he enjoyed every kind of succulent food, Thai, Chinese, Malayan or European. He wrote a book of recipes of European food which included the following recipes: 46 kinds of soup, 36 for meat, 15 for pork, 49 for fowl, seven for lobster, 31 for fish, crab, and other shellfish, 14 for sandwiches, and 12 for salads. Best of all he loved to cook and eat at a picnic. As he became older he kept later and later hours – undeniably a family trait inherited by most of his descendants – and he seldom got up before noon (unless there were some important morning functions). Luncheon taken alone, but watched by some of his wives and children, was at three p.m., and it was during this meal that he read through most of his state papers. His evening meal was taken soon after dusk under the same conditions. He only ate with other people at state banquets which had the direct supervision before and during its courses by Queen Saowabha behind the scenes if she was not present, as it was more often for men only. After cabinet meetings in the early evening and after his meal he worked far into the night and hardly ever retired to bed before three a.m. Round about 1895, or just after, Queen Saowabha was often alone with him, when they discussed State affairs,

13 The author was told this by Queen Saowabha herself, and by her lady attendants.

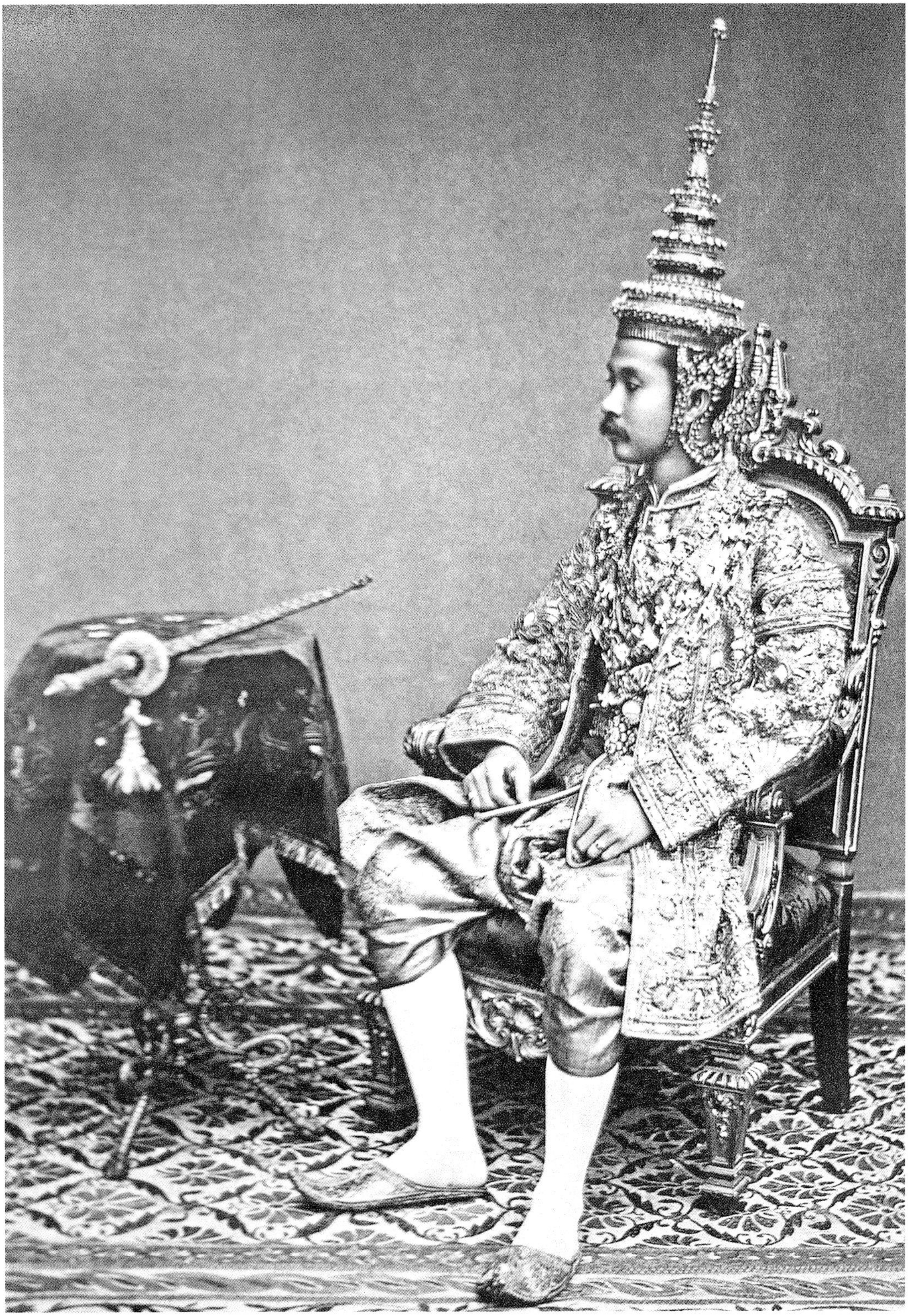

King Chulalongkorn during his coronation ceremony. (River Books)

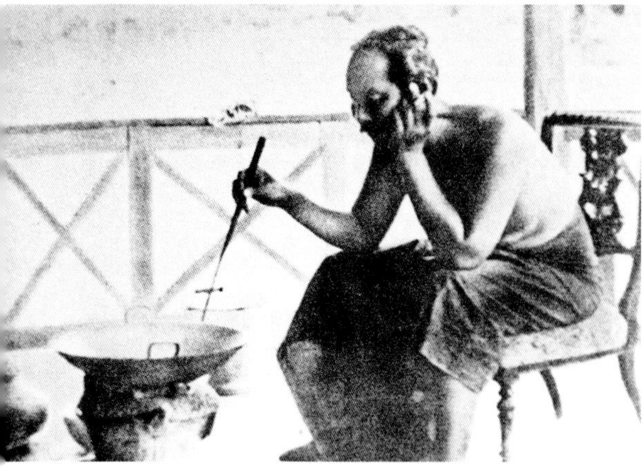

King Chulalongkorn cooking at Ruen Ton, the Thai-style house in the grounds of Dusit Park. (National Archives Bangkok)

and she sometimes made a joke to relieve any tension which was inevitable now and again.[13]

Later in the reign King Chulalongkorn built Dusit Palace which was well outside the city walls and to the north-east of the original city of Bangkok, and he connected it with a magnificent boulevard – the long Ratchadamnoen Avenue – based partly on the Mall in London and partly on the Champs Élysées in Paris, and it had three beautiful marble bridges of Parisian style to cross canals. Dusit Palace had dwelling houses for the king and his family – Amporn Sathan Villa being his own house – and he added the great high domed marble throne hall in Italian style which was not completed until his son's reign and was called the Ananta Samakhom Throne Hall. Around Dusit Palace he designed a modern garden city wherein he laid plans for every street and even chose the tree species that would to line them. Personally he supervised the building of the palace and the laying out of the garden city, where he would drive round between 4 and 6 p.m., at first in a horse and carriage and later in a motor-car, for he was one of the first owners of these new machines round about 1902 and 1904. Best of all probably he liked to drive himself in his yellow, open-topped, electric car with one or two of his older grandchildren.

In 1892 he ordered a steam yacht from England at the time that he was enlarging his tiny navy. For the sake of national economy he had the yacht built as a gun-boat. She was of 3,000 tons, painted white with two graceful yellow funnels, and armed with four 4.7 inch guns, ten six-pounders. Later, probably after his time, six machine guns were added, Her deck had 2-inch steel armour plating and she could reach a speed of 14 knots. After her arrival a few more gun-boats were bought from Britain. It was in 1892 that King Chulalongkorn came face to face with gun-boat diplomacy, and he probably felt that if he had a few efficient gun-boats of his own, gun-boat threats would cease and the Western powers might find peaceful negotiation more profitable than sending larger forces. That has always been the strategy of the Thai armed forces to have enough to make threats more expensive to implement than they would otherwise have been. At no time since the reign of King Mongkut has a Thai government thought itself strong enough to withstand an invasion by a major power. The gun-boat yacht, which was named the *Maha Chakri*, was at the same time well furnished and equipped, and had a round smoking room at the stern with a circular bench seat under the stern portholes. The king liked to tour the coastal districts of the Gulf of Siam with the yacht, and later he made many informal visits to Malaya and Java in the yacht which was commanded by a Dane by the name of Richelieu, with Thai officers and ratings.

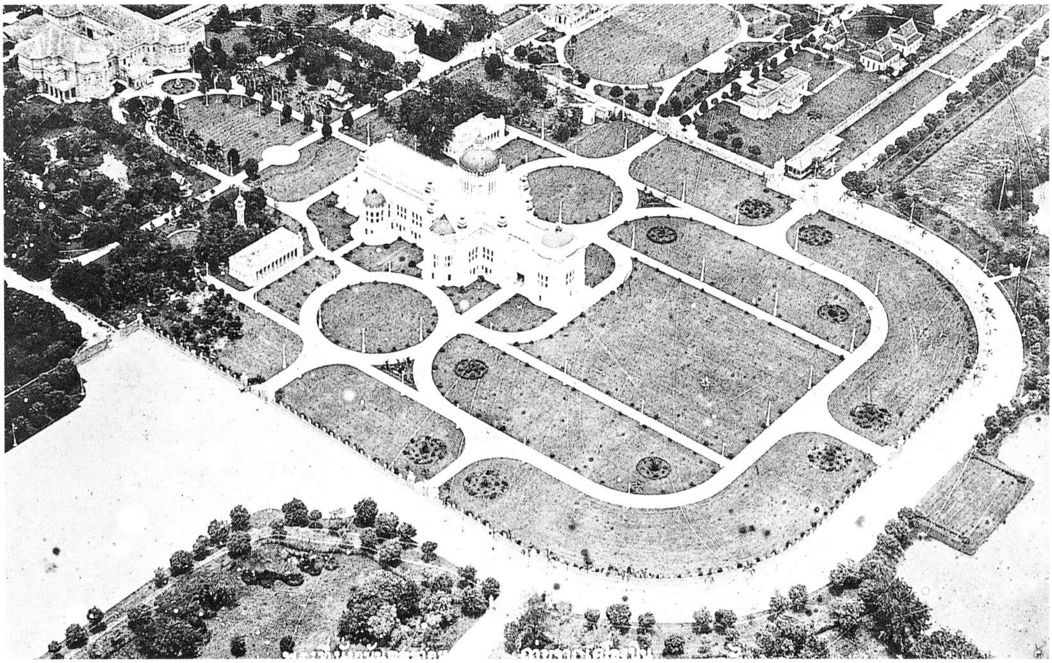

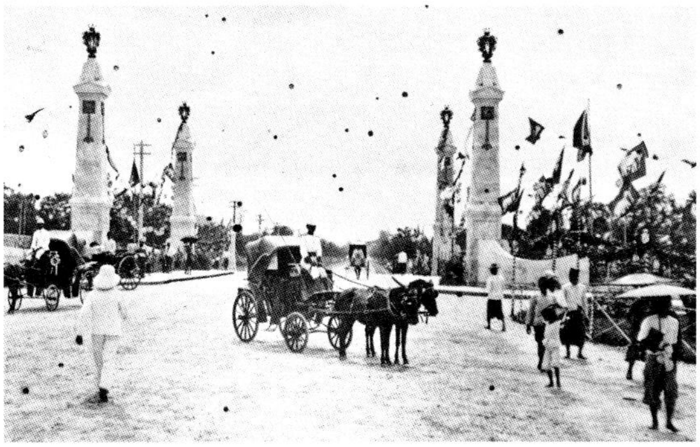

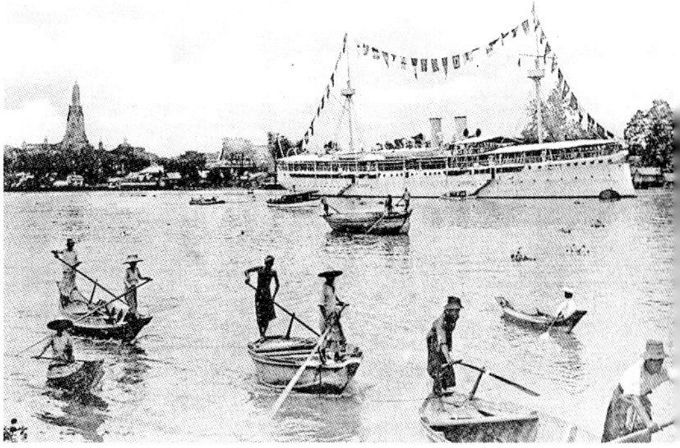

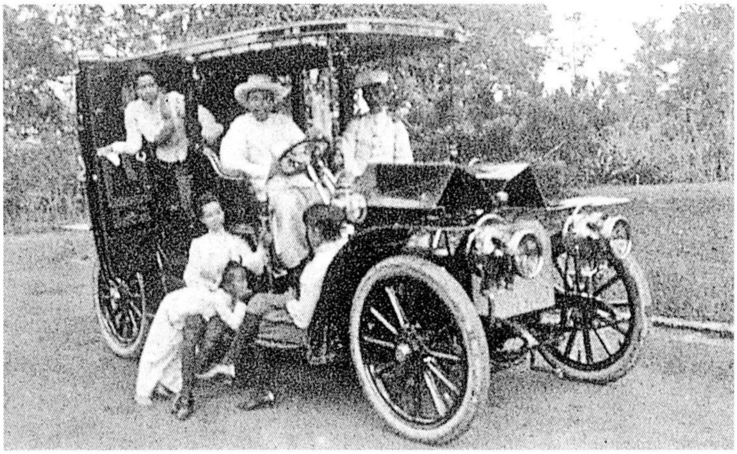

Top: Aerial view of Dusit Park. (River Books)

Above left: Makkhawan bridge. (River Books)

Above: The royal yacht Maha Chakri. (River Books)

King Chulalongkorn in his car with Queen Sukumala Marsi. (National Archives Bangkok)

King Chulalongkorn travelled a great deal and almost all over his kingdom except for his Laotian provinces. He travelled both in the grand ceremonial manner of the *Lord of Life* and also as a private individual in disguise in the *Arabian Nights* style. He was extremely fond of the *Arabian Nights* and rendered one story into an exquisite Thai poem. On such occasions he was accompanied by some of his brothers, his children, and close friends, for it was not unusual for well- to-do Thai families to journey together in a group. They would visit remote up-river or canal-side villages in a little fleet of small paddle boats. With the scarcity of photographs and newspapers, he usually remained unrecognized for a long time. On these occasions he accepted simple hospitality, sometimes himself helping to cook a meal, or attending a village wedding. Of even greater importance was that he heard and saw at close quarters the results of his benevolent rule and increasing reforms. At one house the son of the host kept staring at the king during the meal and muttered to himself: " So very like him, very like!" His father had to ask him what he meant and he pointed to one of the guests from Bangkok and said that he resembled the *Lord of Life* whose photograph he had once seen in a town hall. The game was up but the king put the peasants completely at ease. There was one villager whom the king had visited regularly for some time whose name was On. One day he was astounded to receive a present with the crown over the royal cypher and the inscription: "From your friend, C.P.R." (Chulalongkorn Boromma Rajadhiraja). King Mongkut had come to know his people through his travels as a monk for 27 years, his son met and got to know the ordinary people when he was already king through these unconventional and amusing trips in disguise.[14]

Apart from the unfortunate Queen Sunanta, both queens of King Chulalongkorn, who were the daughters of the Lady Piam, survived him. With all the honours, titles, jewellery, and properties bestowed upon her, as well as apparently the greater part of his company, it would be difficult even for the prejudiced to deny that Queen Saowabha was King Chulalongkorn's most beloved wife and helpmate. Countless joint portraits and entwined names on all kinds of ornaments (many in the possession of the present writer) and even on a set of coffee cups, together with the official medal awarded to commemorate her regency in 1897, fully testify to this fact. Queen Saowabha was born on January 1st, 1864 (in her eldest son's reign it was celebrated on December 31st so as not to clash with his, which was also January 1st). She was therefore ten years younger than the king. Having many children of her own – nine were born to her – she was intensely interested in the improving science of midwifery, and in 1883 she sent four young girls to study midwifery in England. After that many other Thai girls qualified, so the queen founded in Bangkok a modern school for midwives in 1897. All through her husband's reign, indeed throughout her life, she continued her good works, such as founding the Thai Red Cross Society, of which she was an active president for 26 years,

14 Prince Damrong: *Tales of Olden Times*, pages 32-33.

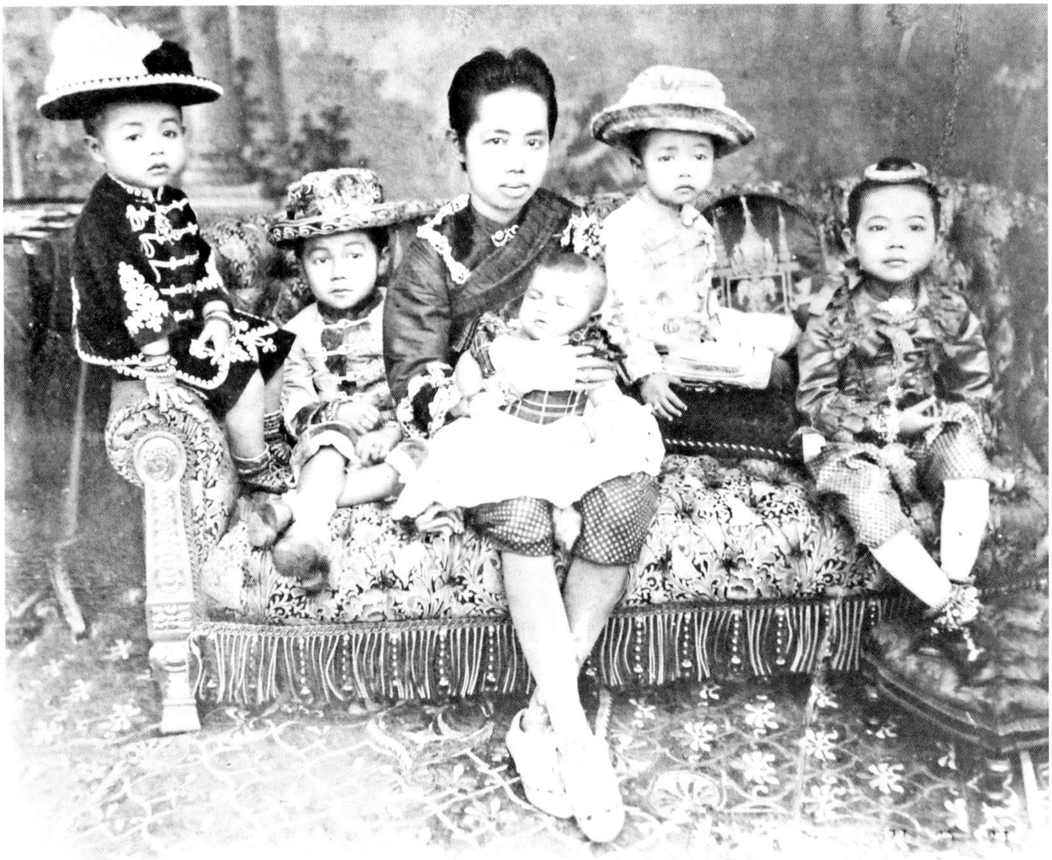

Queen Saowabha with five of her children. Left to right: Prince Chakrabongse, Crown Prince Vajiravudh, Prince Siriraj, on her lap Prince Tripetch and Princess Pahurat. The latter three all died at a young age. (River Books)

and was succeeded at her death by her sister, Queen Sawang, who has since been succeeded by her beautiful and gracious granddaughter-in-law, Her Majesty Queen Sirikit. Queen Saowabha built and endowed two girls' schools in Bangkok and four in the provinces. She sent to Europe at her own expense many students, both male and female, to study all manner of subjects. Her court was the centre of feminine arts and grace, and indeed for a young girl to be attached to her was like being sent to a university, as had been the old custom.

Except for the new title of *Somdech Phra Borommа Rajini*, which was given to Queen Saowabha, Queen Sawang had rank, honours, and riches almost parallel. Such riches she dispensed for good works with equal generosity. One very pretty and charming girl called Sangwalya, whom she sent to study in the U.S.A., was one day to play a surprisingly important part in the history of the House of Chakri. The two sister-Queens were the best of friends. Queen Sawang gave to her younger sister the deference due to her rank, both in life and in death, without sacrificing any touch of intimacy. The present writer was present on many an occasion between 1912 and 1919 when Queen Sawang visited her sister and all the lady attendants were ordered to leave the room, the nieces of both and the only grandson of one being permitted to

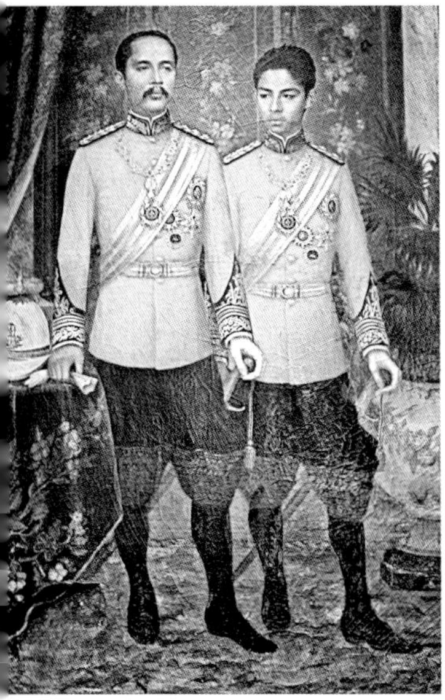

King Chulalongkorn and Crown Prince Vajirunhis. (National Gallery Bangkok)

remain to serve them so that the two sisters could converse in intimate privacy. The children of both queens behaved towards one another as if they were full brothers and sisters from the same mother, which indeed they almost were.

King Chulalongkorn took the greatest interest in his children. All his sons, *Chao Fas* or *Phra Ong Chaos*, unless unfit in health, were in due course sent to be educated in Europe. This was one step further than King Mongkut, who had had English teachers brought to Siam. The only one of the older boys not sent was the Crown Prince Vajirunhis, who was being groomed as the future King and was to go later just for a big sightseeing grand tour which he never lived to do. Most of the others went to England, but some went to Germany, Denmark, and one to Russia. France was omitted as being a republic, but they were allowed to go there on holiday. The amazing thing was that with all the burden of work he had to do, all King Chulalongkorn's sons in Europe had letters from him almost regularly. The important letter he wrote to the first four elder sons – all sons of *Chao Choms* and therefore not celestial princes – who had gone to England in 1885, has often been published and once with an English translation.[15] They were Prince Kittiyakorn (grandfather of the present Queen Sirikit), Prince Rabi, Prince Pravitra, and Prince Chira. "There is no need," the king told them, "for you to style yourselves princes ... It is my desire that you should regard yourselves merely as Siamese boys of good birth . . . The decision is not the result of a lack of paternal affection . . . Your father openly owns you as his sons . . . In Europe princes are few; in our country they are many. Because their princes are not numerous, it is practical for them to maintain their dignity at a higher standard than is possible in our country . . . Princes who give out their rank without being able to afford the upkeep of their dignity will only bring contempt upon the royalty of their country . . . Again a prince in a foreign country has no privilege above a commoner, his only advantage is perhaps that he can enter good society, which any other person of good birth can also do . . . The notion that you have been born princes and can be comfortable through life without doing useful work is one which does not place you above the lower animals, which just come into life, eat and die. But even such animals are useful, for they leave their hides, skins and bones . . . Wealthy people in Europe, from generation to generation, derived their income from rents and interests. You receive your allowances through me from the people, and such grants are only sufficient for your support and the upkeep of your dignity . . . If after acquiring proficiency in foreign languages you cannot turn them into Siamese, little advantage will have been gained, *for we can employ as many foreigners as we need* (my italics). What will be required of you IS an ability to turn a European

The first four sons of King Chulalongkorn sent to study in England: Prince Rabi, Prince Pravitra, Prince Kittiyakorn and Prince Chirapravati. (National Archives Bangkok)

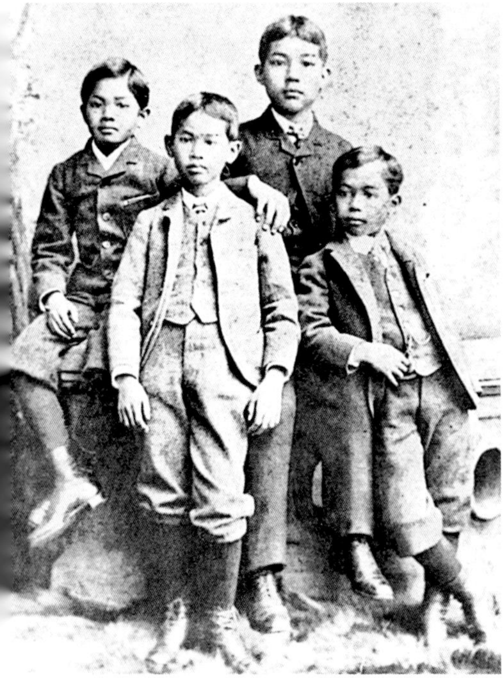

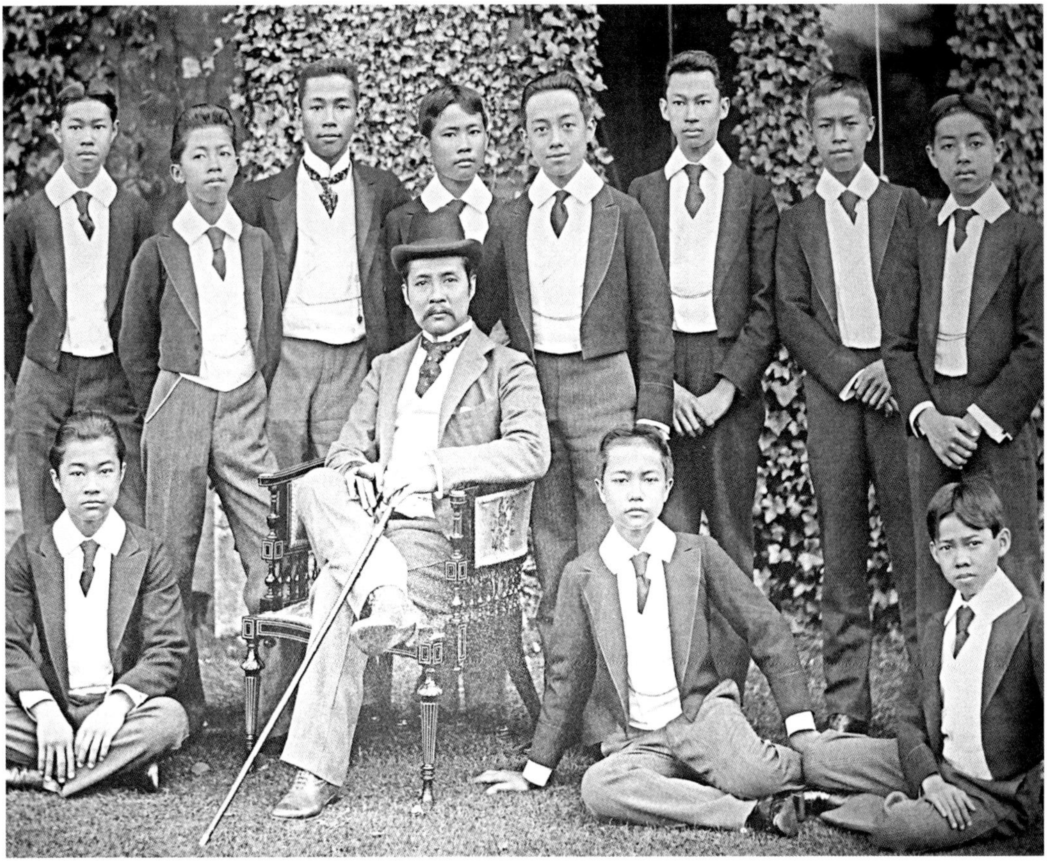

King Chulalongkorn photographed at Taplow Court during his first European tour in 1897, with those sons who were sent to study in England. (River Books)

language into Siamese, and Siamese into a European language. You would be useful then."

Although King Chulalongkorn was obviously sincere in trying to give all his children equal love and attention, he was but human and must have had his favourites. It was also essential to give closer attention to the upbringing and education of the celestial princes as he had made it clear, in appointing their senior to be the first crown prince, that the succession would first go through the line of the *Chao Fas*. As there were many of them, the chance of a son of a *Chao Chom* ever succeeding to the throne was very remote. Furthermore, the young *Chao Fas* lived nearer his own quarters – especially the children of Queen Saowabha – and he could see them more easily and more often. Queen Sukumala's residence was only a stone's throw away from the Chakri Building, and although Queen Sawang's house was further, it was connected with the Chakri edifice by an overhead bridge. Queen Saowabha's first child was a daughter, her third and fifth were sons; these three were unfit and died young. The two elder sons who survived were great friends, and they were Vajiravudh (nicknamed Toe – Large) and Chakrabongse (nicknamed Lek – Small). All the children, regardless of mothers, mostly played together and the leader of them all was Crown Prince Vajirunhis (Yai – Big). Photographs tend to show that he was very

15 *Collected Royal Writings*, pages 41-50 (partly in Thai), Bangkok, 1951. English translation by Prince Bidya.

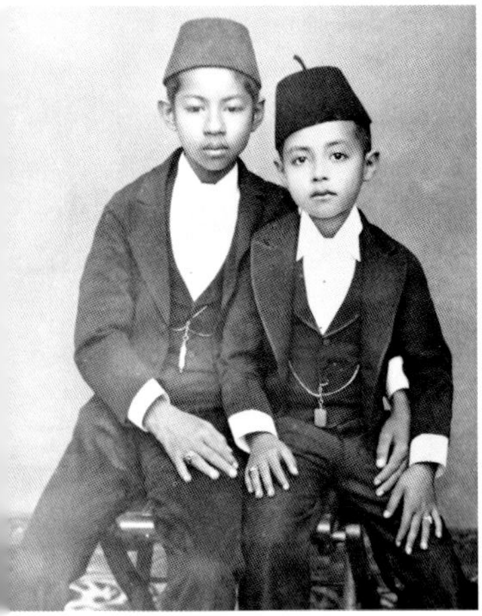

Crown Prince Vajirunhis with Prince Chakrabongse. (River Books)

fond of Lek, who was most often close to him. When any of them were old enough they attended the Rajkumar College, where, besides the usual studies, they were taught to ride and shoot as well as different forms of the old Thai fencing art. Other students included their cousins, the sons of the other sons of King Mongkut, such as the great scholar, Prince Dhani. These grandsons of King Mongkut, like all grandchildren of a sovereign who are not also grandchildren of a queen, had the junior princely title of *Mom Chao*.

At that period children still wore the top knot until the age of puberty when they would go through the Brahmanic tonsure ceremony which brothers, half-brothers, and cousins, both boys and girls, of the same age shared together – 13 for boys and 11 for girls. Children of both sexes were clad in gorgeous costumes, were bedecked with necklaces of diamonds and other gems, and wore a jewel-studded crown according to their rank. At an early age the *Chao Fas* were created *Krom Khun* and instead of just having another title, King Chulalongkorn began the new practice of giving his children the names of cities and towns, whereas his brothers and half-brothers continued with the old system, as for example Prince Dis became Prince Damrong. Amongst the *Chao Fas*, Vajiravudh became Prince of Dvaravati (Ayutthaya), Chakrabongse at the age of nine, Prince of Phitsanulok, and Paribatra Prince of Nakhon Sawan. Even if the children were playing, they were kept under strict etiquette and discipline, but the punishment was always given by their mothers, and never by the king. Queen Saowabha did not spare the cane. Girls had their fingers or their arms bent back at the joints, which helped to achieve the supple shape considered graceful by the Thais.

In due course the sons were sent to Europe except Crown Prince Vajirunhis, and the departures were terrible times for their mothers and loving nurses. Vajiravudh had his entire education in England, first with a private tutor, then at Christ Church, Oxford, where he studied history. He entered happily into the life of the university, rode to hounds, and belonged to clubs, making many friends. He then entered the Royal Military Academy at Sandhurst, and after being commissioned was attached to the Durham Light Infantry. In 1948 the writer met an old D.L.I. soldier who was a car park attendant in Durham who remembered him as his platoon commander. He also attended the famous School of Musketry at Hythe. He loved the British Army, its drills, training, uniforms, and mess life. He talked about it all with nostalgia, and would demonstrate his love when he became king. It was his deep regret that he had not been sent to a public school, like his brothers, but King Chulalongkorn felt that he was too close to the throne. Although he travelled widely in Europe, even to Russia, it was to England that he lost his heart. It was at the Thai Legation in London in 1895 that he received his appointment as Crown Prince. For some strange reason many Western people often assumed that various Thais were the Crown Prince or Heir Apparent.

16 *Queen Sukumala to Her Son.* (in Thai), Bangkok, 1950.

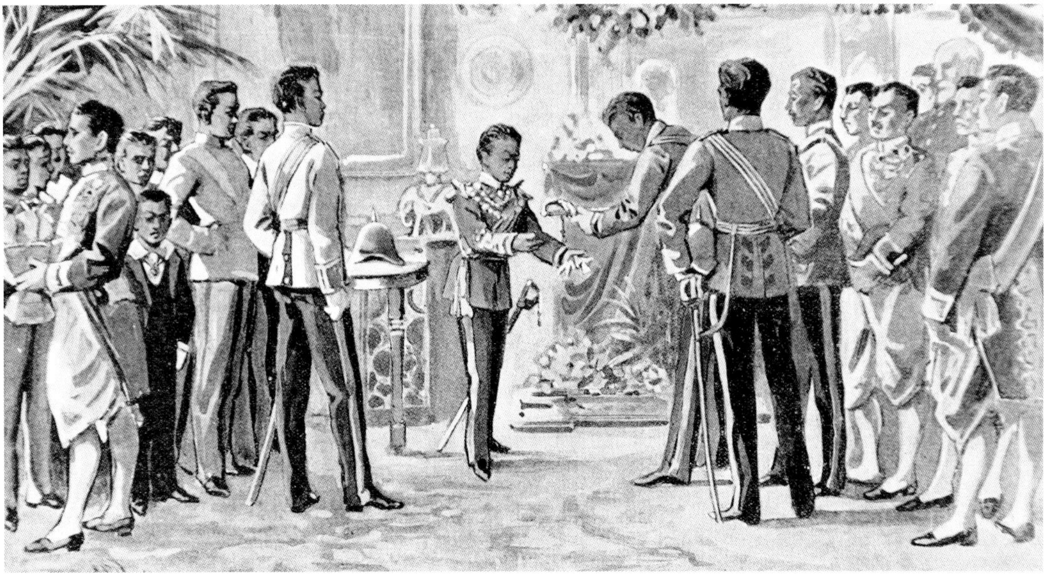

The elevation of Prince Vajiravudh to Crown Prince was noted in *The Illustrated London News*.

Let it therefore be stated here without equivocation that Prince Vajiravudh (later Rama VI) was the only Crown Prince of Siam or Heir Apparent so far to have ever set foot in Britain, Europe or America (written in 1959). It was in England that he became one of the first patients to be operated upon for appendicitis. While there he was received by Queen Victoria, attended certain functions at Court, and was the first Chakri prince to be made an honorary Knight Grand Cross of the Royal Victorian Order. Before the close of his stay in England he founded the Thai Students' Society – Samaggi Samagom – which meets for ten days every year, and despite two World Wars has survived to this day.

Prince Paribatra was educated in Germany under the guiding eye of the Emperor, William II, and he distinguished himself in the German Army. He was also a keen musician and able to play most Western musical instruments as well as finding time to study the art of composition. King Chulalongkorn was fond of and had great trust in this son, with whom he corresponded regularly, while the son's love for his father was both deep and selfless. He was barely six months younger than Vajiravudh, and might well have thought with regret that in 1895 he missed being Crown Prince by such a narrow margin. But there was nothing in his conduct then or subsequently to show that he ever felt that way. He had a wise mother, a princess with a perfect understanding of royal Thai polygamy. In one of her frequent letters to him in Europe, she wrote: " You know about Tounkramom Toe (Vajiravudh) and what he is going to be. Apply yourself to love him and be loyal to him. You are both far away from home, so if you can be intimate and affectionate to him now, it will smooth the way for both of you in the future. As for the rest of your half-brothers in Europe, remember that they are all your father's sons, be correct, affectionate, and united with them all."[16] It should be added that even though the brothers studied

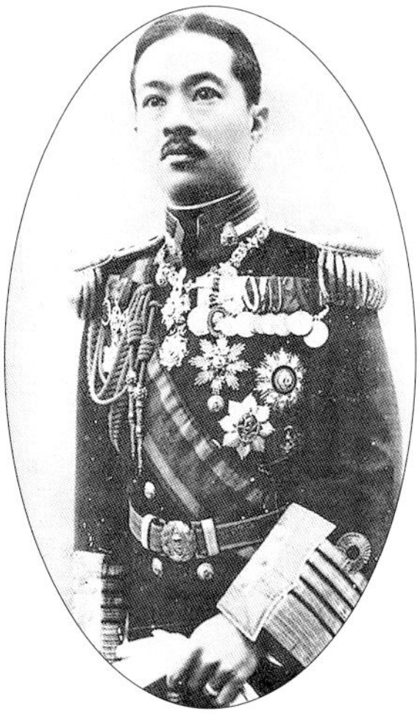

Prince Paribatra. (National Archives Bangkok)

in different countries they met frequently during their vacations. Repeatedly Prince Paribatra was told to be affectionate to his stepmothers (who were also his aunts), even with such details as to what size of photographs of himself he should send them. Queen Sukumala's love and loyalty for her husband, who was her king, and her attachment to the Chakri Dynasty as a whole should prove an inspiration to others. Later on, when her son had been commissioned in the German Army after passing out of the Military Academy, and there was a question as to whether he should return forthwith to serve in Siam and be near her, or proceed first to the German Staff College, she advised him to remain in Germany so as not to be less qualified than Lek, who was entering the Russian Staff College.

This Lek was Chakrabongse, Prince of Phitsanulok, the second adult son of Queen Saowabha whose education was more unusual than any of his brothers. There had been much trade between Denmark and Siam and the Danish firm, East Asiatic Company, had teak concessions in the northern Thai forests as well as engaging in other trades. In democratic Denmark junior princes went into business even in those days, and one of these, Prince Waldemar, the youngest son of King Christian IX and brother to Queen Alexandra of England and the Empress Marie of Russia, had for business reasons often visited Siam and had become a close personal friend of King Chulalongkorn. He spread the news all over the courts of Europe of the high qualities of his Thai royal friend, and soon European royalty began to visit Bangkok. In 1893 an important visitor came in the person of Prince Waldemar's nephew – Nicholas II of Russia – then Tsarevitch or Heir Apparent – who had just been to India. He and King Chulalongkorn at once became friends.

King Chulalongkorn and Prince Chakrabongse, photographed in England in 1897. (River Books)

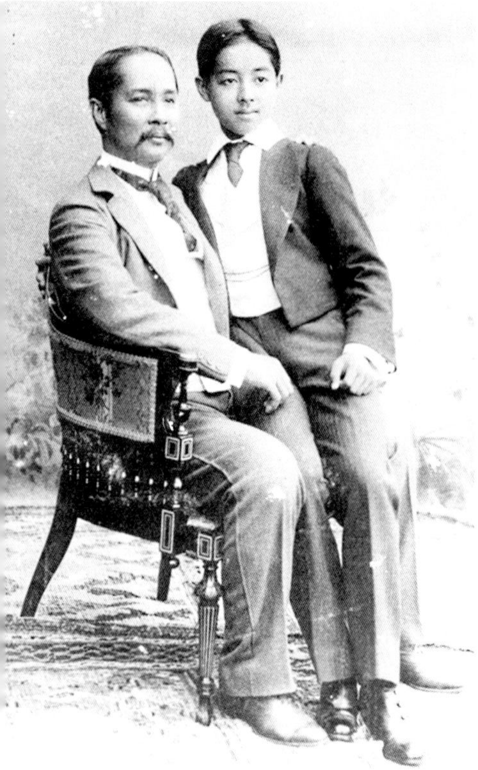

Prince Vajiravudh had already gone to England, and in 1896 it was the turn of Chakrabongse. From all accounts it appears that he was the favourite son of both his parents. Many of King Chulalongkorn's letters to his sons have been published and invariably – even in those addressed to the two successive Crown Princes, Vajirunhis and Vajiravudh – the king employed what may be termed the condescending use of the second personal pronoun of *chao*. In his letters to Chakrabongse, however, the second personal pronoun was dispensed with, and whenever he had to say "you", he wrote Lek, a usage considered by the Thais to be most intimate and affectionate, which from published letters King Chulalongkorn appears to reserve for him alone. The considerable correspondence between father and son, hitherto unpublished, is in the possession of the writer pending the possible appearance of a full length biography of King Chulalongkorn. Again and again in his letters to Chakrabongse, even shortly before his death, the king stressed the tremendous sympathy and understanding between them, and it would be all the more tragic when Chakrabongse would for once disappoint his father so gravely.

After Chakrabongse had been in England for barely a year and came to know English really well, judging by his letters, his father made his first European tour which will be described later. When he went to St. Petersburg, his friend Nicholas was Emperor of all the Russias. Nicholas II asked him to send one of his sons to Russia to be brought up by him. He was not only going to guide his education as William II had done for Paribatra, but he would pay for his entire stay, and have the boy live permanently in an apartment in the Winter Palace. King Chulalongkorn accepted the offer and chose Chakrabongse who then began to learn Russian as well as English. The king felt that his son would work even harder if he had competition from another Thai boy. Education in Europe was not only provided for Thai boys who were royal or noble, as there was also the king's scholarship for which everyone could compete. It was one of the scholarship boys by the name of Poum, who was jointly chosen by father and son to accompany Chakrabongse to Russia.

They arrived at St. Petersburg in 1898, and, after being received by the Emperor, both boys lived together in the Winter Palace and shared the same privileges, so much so that some of the Russian aristocrats thought that Poum was an illegitimate son of the King. After some intensive coaching they entered the *Corps des Pages*, the Eton of Imperial Russia except that it was a military secondary school and military academy combined founded by Alexander I in 1802. Besides military training and a first-class secondary education with a heavy syllabus of languages and sciences, the cadets, who wore magnificent uniforms, were required to attend all the important court functions as Imperial pages. The two Thai were day-boys, travelling to the school from the Winter Palace in one of the Imperial carriages. Despite their luxurious and princely life, no privileges existed at the school where they worked hard and drilled hard, rode a great deal, did not play much, and they made many friends.

In the annual examination of 1900 Chakrabongse was placed second and Poum fourth which made them personal pages for the Empress Mother and the Empress Consort. The pages had to serve at State banquets and the present writer was told by Poum that a page once dropped some soup on the Empress Mother, and after a rebuke by the Emperor, the boy proceeded to rub her corsage with a napkin and with much vigour. In the final examination of 1902, out of the total marking of 12, Chakrabongse obtained 11.75 and Poum 11.50, thus passing out first and second into the Russian Army with record marks, and the Prince's name was chiselled on the marble wall of the main hall of the school. As successful studies were highly prized in the family, it can be imagined how he became more than ever the apple of his parents' eyes. On being commissioned the two Thai young men chose the cavalry and served in the Emperor's Own Hussar Guards in which

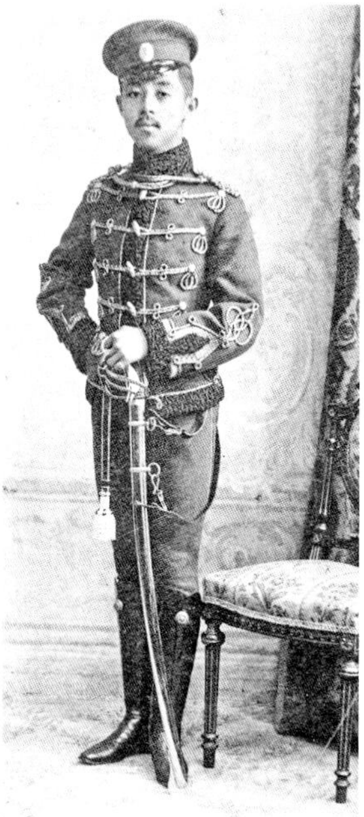

Prince Chakrabongse in Hussar Uniform, 1902. (River Books)

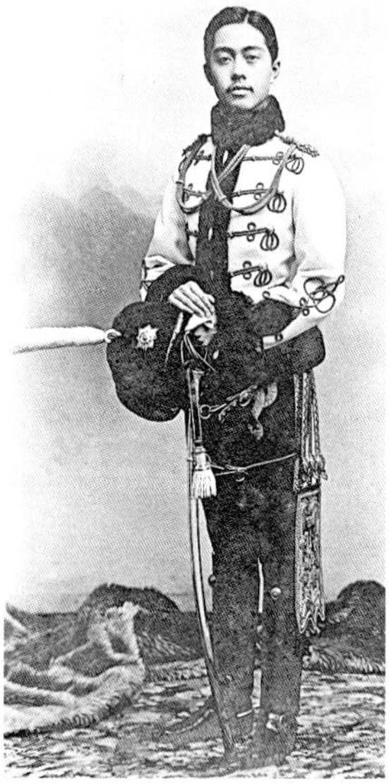

Poum was sent as the companion to Prince Chakrabongse. (River Books)

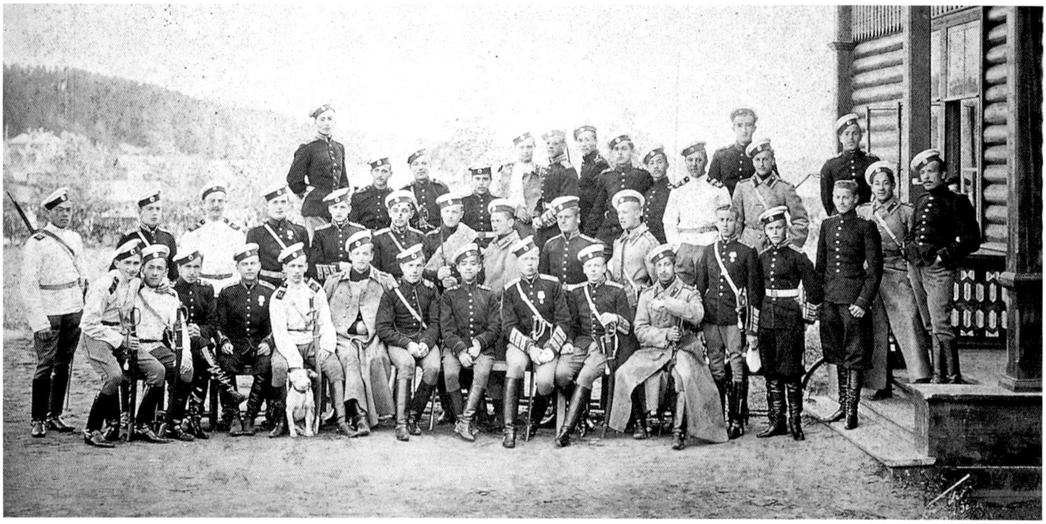

Prince Chakrabongse and the Corps des Pages class of 1902. (River Books)

regiment Nicholas II had himself served when Heir-Apparent. Later both Chakrabongse and Poum attended the Russian Staff College, and together with Paribatra in Germany, they were the first three Thai officers to have passed Staff colleges.[17]

Few of King Chulalongkorn's sons who studied in Europe failed to reach the required standards. One, Prince Asdang, was so homesick that he was allowed to return, and Prince Urubongse (born 1893) was too frail to leave Siam. Two of the princes did very well in England, both going to Harrow and Trinity College, Cambridge. Prince Purachatra (born 1882) went on to Chatham and joined the Royal Engineers. Prince Yugala (born 1883) distinguished himself as a cox and might have got his "blue" for Cambridge if he did not have to give up coxing in his last year to concentrate on passing his final examination. Of the king's younger sons, although they departed for Europe in his lifetime their education belongs to the next reign.

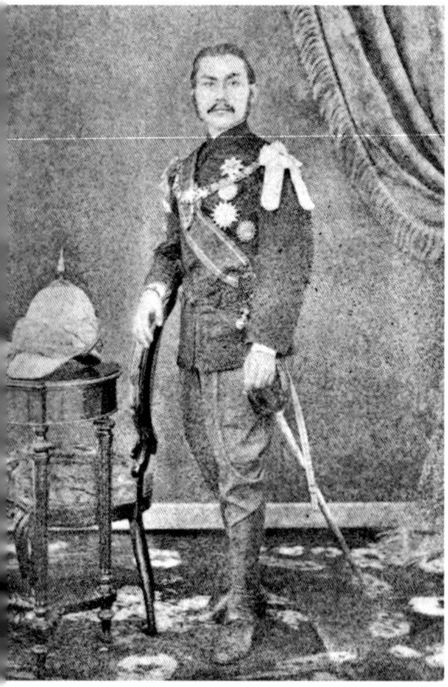

Prince Chaturonrasmi. (Paisarn Piemmettawat)

It seems clear now that, brought up by his enlightened father and by the Regent, King Chulalongkorn was intent from the beginning on reforms of every kind, and if he did not carry them all out it was because 42 years was not long enough. Robert-Martignan wrote: "One stands confounded before the grandeur of such work accomplished".[18] As his son, King Prajadhipok said, "it was *a revolution from the throne*." The administrative reforms which were undertaken gradually were more or less completed by 1892. Besides the experienced noblemen and their descendants, the king was much helped by his brothers and half-brothers. His next full brother, Prince Chaturonrasmi, was for a time in charge of Finance, but he was in poor health and died in 1900. The next brother, Prince Bhanurangsi, was in charge of the Armed Forces, and throughout the country he was most popular and highly respected. Amongst the many able half-brothers, two must be deemed the most useful, namely, Prince Damrong (born 1862) who, with immense energy and enterprise, took

17 Full details can be found in Prince Chula: *The Twain Have Met,* etc., *op. cit.,* pages 58-61.

18 Robert-Martignan: *op. cit.,* page 235.

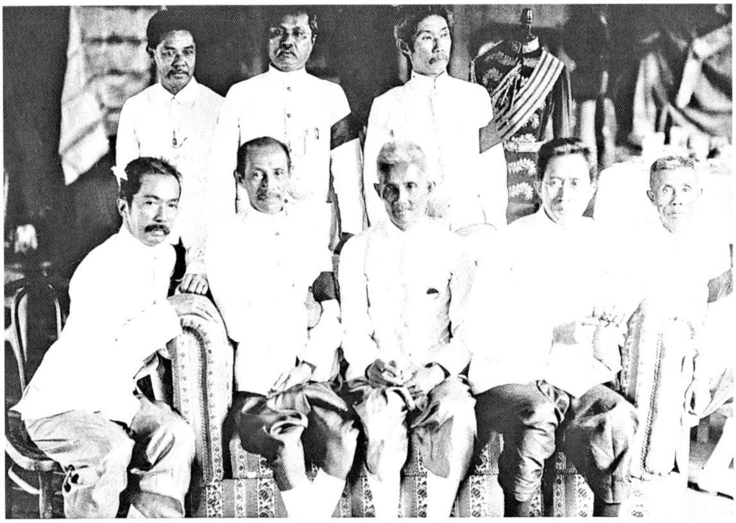

Some of the sons of King Mongkut. Front row, from left: Prince Damrong, Prince Adisorn, Prince Sampasit Prasong, Prince Naris, Prince Rajasak Samosorn. Back from left: Prince Prachak, Prince Sampasat and Prince Pitiyalab. (National Archives Bangkok)

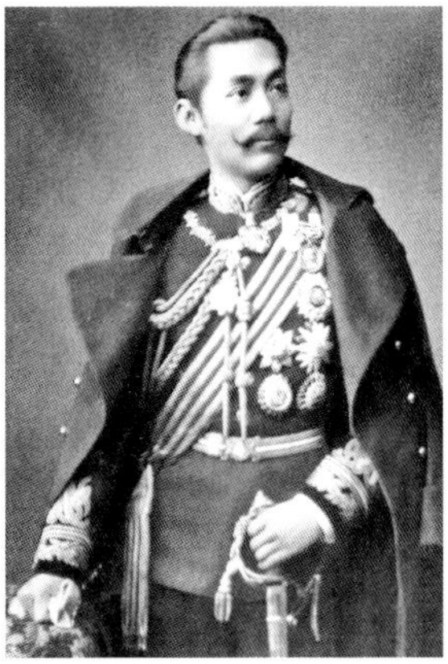

Prince Bhanurangsi. (National Archives Bangkok)

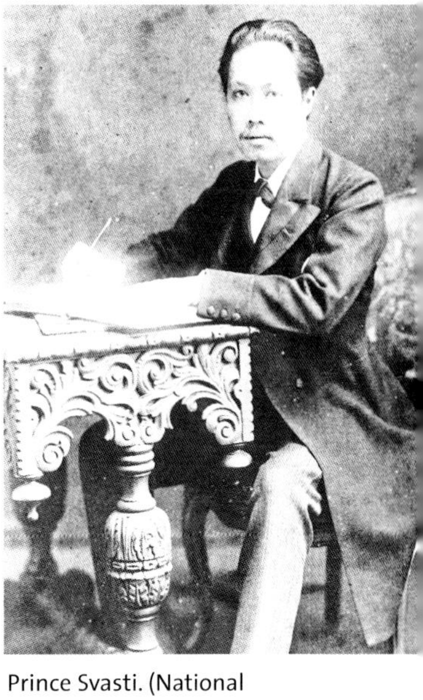

Prince Svasti. (National Archives Bangkok)

charge in turn of Education and the Interior. In his spare time he was interested in history and archeology and can be regarded as the Father of Modern Thai History. The other was Prince Devawongse (born 1858), a son of the Lady Piam and therefore a full-brother of Queen Sawang and Queen Saowabha, who was for over 40 years Minister of Foreign Affairs in two reigns. He understood to perfection King Mongkut's policy of accommodating the threatening attitude of the West in the nineteenth century with gentleness and dignity. There were also many who made themselves useful to the king in diverse ways. Prince Naris (born 1864) was the greatest artist and architect of his time; Prince Vajirayana (born 1859) followed his father's footsteps in becoming a monk and eventually became the Supreme Patriach, exercising strong moral influence on the monks and laity alike for many years; Prince Sommot (born in 1860) was in charge of the King's Private Secretariat and Prince Mahisara (born 1866) was Minister of Finance. Unless they were in bad health, all the princes worked in some capacity, with some sent to rule in the provinces such as Prince Prachak (born 1856) who was Viceroy of the North-East and was responsible for suppressing the revolt of the Chinese Boxers whio had crossed into Siam. Another, Prince Nares (born 1855) was an envoy to both Britain and the United States. Although too old to have been educated in Europe, most of King Chulalongkorn's brothers had learned English in Bangkok and had a chance of touring Europe. The only brother young enough to have been sent to England as a student was Prince Svasti (born 1865), the youngest son of the Lady Piam, who was the first Thai to study at Oxford. One son of King Mongkut, Prince Naradhip (born 1861), strangely combined the abilities of a great poet and dramatist with being a daring and enterprising businessman, and was incidentally the first Thai to insure his life with a European firm.

In the choice of foreign advisers King Chulalongkorn went further than his father in the diverse nationalities employed. At first they were

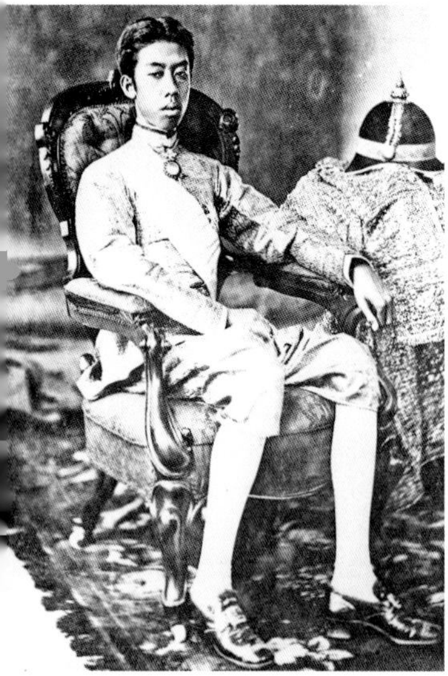

Prince Nares. (National Archives Bangkok)

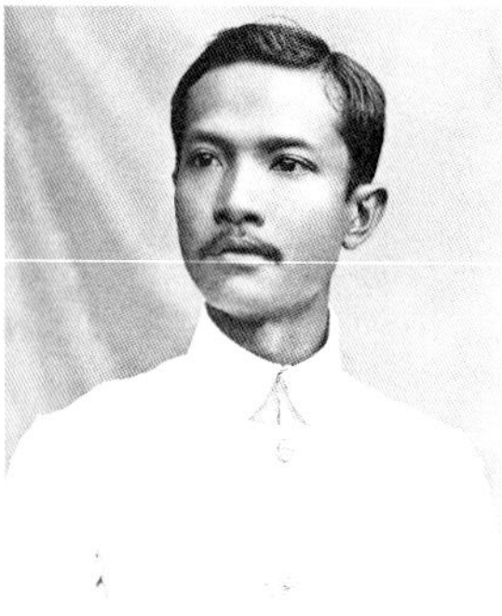

Prince Rabibhadana. (National Archives Bangkok)

mostly British who had had experience in Burma, but they were soon joined by Belgians, Danes, French, Germans, and Americans. Many of them were not advisers but teachers and technicians, and most had far greater influence than merely giving advice, yet they were not given any portfolios and were not entrusted with any ministerial responsibilities. One of the most successful of the advisers was Rolin-Jacquemyns, a Belgian international lawyer of great repute. There was a vacancy for the post of Adviser in International Laws and Foreign Affairs in 1892. Although the pay was good and the job interesting, Siam was considered very far from Europe in those days and suitable men were difficult to find. It was on his way home from England that Prince Damrong encountered Rolin-Jacquemyns in Cairo. The Belgian had had a distinguished career at home and having been Minister of the Interior was now retired at the age of 60. However he was in financial difficulties after helping a brother in an unsuccessful business. He was in Egypt negotiating for a post with the Egyptian Government, but a suitable one had not be offered. He was quickly chosen for the post by King Chulalongkorn on the advice of Prince Damrong, and with the full support of Prince Devawongse. Owing to his past record and his high international reputation, a higher post, namely, that of General-Adviser was created for him. He proved a great success in his work, and the neutrality of his own country was an asset. In 1896 he was made Chao Phraya Abhai, thus being the second *farang* to reach that high noble rank since Phaulkon in the reign of King Narai, though without the same dire consequences to himself. Owing to ill health he retired in 1899 with a good pension and loaded with honours.[19]

At the turn of the century the first four princes, who had gone to England, had now returned. One of them, Prince Rabi, created Prince of Rajburi, became a highly efficient Minister of Justice and put into practice the law reforms of Rolin-Jacquemyns. He was also responsible for the founding and running of the Law School, the proper examination of law students, and of the institution of the Bar Society. Hall quotes J. G. D. Campbell as saying that in Siam there was "a universal horror of anything in the nature of a permanent European Civil Service"[20] and that it arose from the fear of losing independence. It is surely natural for an independent country to wish to preserve that independence and to build up her own Civil Service. Yet in reading what Europeans living in South-East Asia thought or said at that time; one must sympathize with them in thinking that the *natives* were on the whole incapable of doing things for themselves.

The educational scheme, initiated by Prince Damrong after his visits to Britain and the continent of Europe, was to adapt the old monastic school buildings to modem educational needs, and the use of monastic grounds as schools was to perpetuate the old tradition where education had been in priestly hands. The first fundamental aim was primary education, but at first progress was slow because funds were being urgently needed elsewhere, and also because of the lack of

19 Prince Damrong: *Tales of Olden Times, op. cit.*, pages 96-101.

20 J. G. D. Campbell: *Siam in the Twentieth Century*, page 172, London, 1902. D. G. E. Hall: *op. cit.*, page 590.

trained teachers. It is here that criticism might be directed at the Buddhist Church for not making learned monks more available for secular schools. A teachers' college was set up but naturally it was some time before its graduates could be sufficient. It was in 1899 that the government asked for and obtained the loan from Britain of J. G. D. Campbell to assist Prince Damrong for two years. Side by side with the newly-founded State schools, Christian missionary schools continued to flourish, and private Thai schools were encouraged.

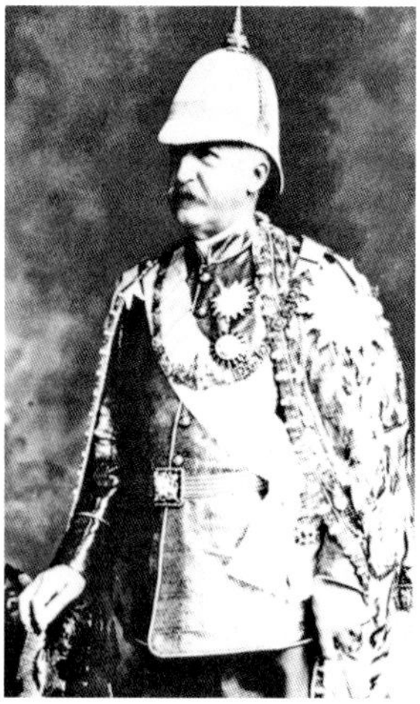

Rolin-Jacquemyns,
Chao Phraya Abhai Raja.
(National Archives Bangkok)

Following the formation of the Ministry of Justice in 1892, a new system of criminal and civil courts were set up, those for Bangkok in 1894, and for the provinces in 1896-7. There was no jury system but there were three judges, the accused was considered innocent until proved guilty, and there was the Court of Appeal. The king no longer judged any cases himself, but in theory the decisions of the highest court, the Supreme Court of Appeal, were in his name. The procedure in court was similar to English practices and most of the earlier modern barristers had been called to the English Bar. Thus English judicial traditions once begun have persisted with success to this day.

The Ministry of Finance was also founded in 1892 when, among other changes, the system of farming out the rights to sell opium was stopped, and a limited amount of opium was dispensed through Treasury agents. The king knew well that it was immoral for the State to obtain revenue from opium, but it was necessary to find money to pay for all the reforms. Although because of increased trade and prosperity, imports were simply pouring in, Siam could not raise legitimate revenue by increasing import duties as she was bound by her treaty obligations with Western powers to keep them at *three per cent.* The official in charge of agriculture had held but sixth place in the old hierachy, now a ministry was established for that essential industry.

For administrative purposes the kingdom was divided into *monthon* (circle), *changwad* (province), and *amphoe* (district), all governed by officials from Bangkok. The people of the villages and hamlets, however, could elect their own headmen. The Laotian vassal princes, so long as their conduct was lawful and loyal, were left as titular heads of their provinces and received subsidies additional to their private income, but they could not touch public funds and their provinces were administered by Bangkok officials. The four Malay Sultans, before cession to Britain, had almost autonomous rule. In order to find the right men to administer these circles, provinces, and districts. King Chulalongkorn founded the Civil Service College as well as the Military and, later still, Naval Colleges. A police force on western lines was organized, first under British senior officers, and there was a gendarmerie for the provinces. The postal and telegraphic systems were set in motion. It is difficult to recount briefly in these few pages the stupendous task accomplished under his leadership.

When British engineers first surveyed the route for possible railway construction between Burma and China, the King's thoughts turned to

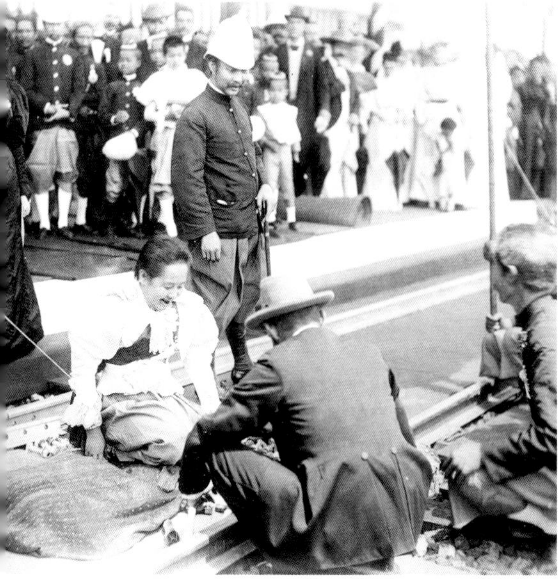

the possibility of Siam having railways, and he was determined that she should build her own railways, being convinced that otherwise the British or French, who had become his neighbours in Burma and French Indo-China respectively, would ask to extend their own systems into his country. The first railway in Siam was a private enterprise, built by a Belgian-Danish company and it was sixteen miles long connecting Bangkok with Paknam – the town at the mouth of the river. The king even bought shares for himself and his sons. The first State railway line conceived was to be from Bangkok to Khorat. A Royal State Railway Department was formed, and the king cut the first sod in 1892, the spade and wheelbarrow used by him being now in the National Museum. In order to present an attitude of neutrality the State lines were built by German engineers. The first to be completed was from Bangkok to Ayutthaya in 1897, but progress was slow owing to disagreements between the German engineers and British contractors. In later years Thai railways would be constructed by Thai engineers who had studied abroad with a sprinkling of British engineers to help them for many years to come. The line to Khorat was completed in 1900, that to Lopburi in 1901. The remarkable thing, as W. A. Graham has pointed out,[21] was that the railways were built out of ordinary revenue. It was not until 1903 that King Chulalongkorn's Government floated in London the first ever foreign loan of £1 million, which was immediately oversubscribed, to pay for further railway construction. The southern line went as far as Phetchaburi by 1903, and by arrangement with British Malaya in 1909 this line was

Queen Saowabha participating in hitting in the divets for the new railway. (River Books)

The opening of the Bangkok-Ayutthaya in 1896. (River Books)

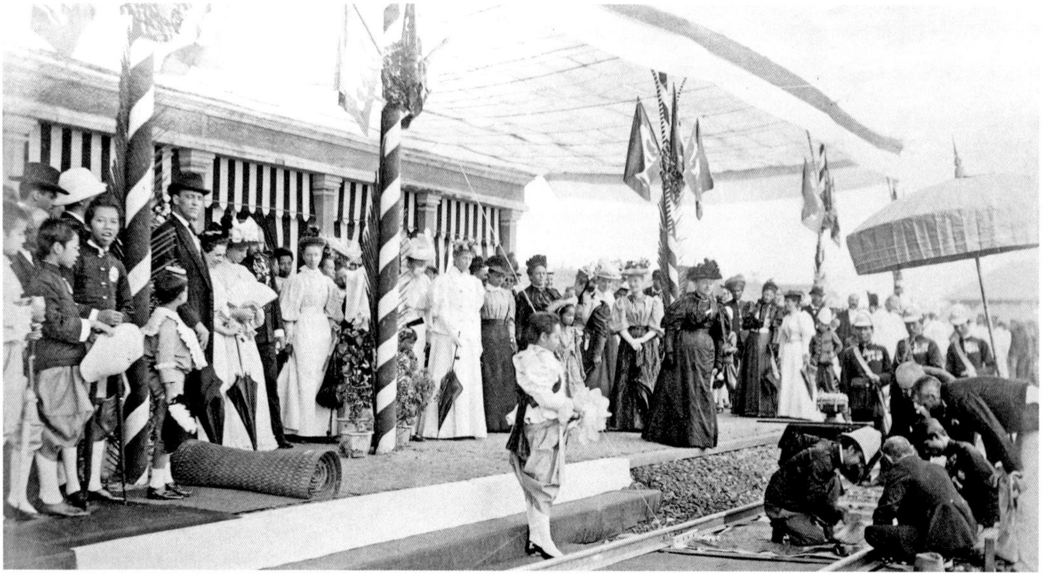

extended to the frontier.[22] In order to run the country with the minimum amount of direct taxation, the Chakri Monarchy concentrated on railway construction and only built roads in areas not already served by railways, and all these roads led to different rail-heads, such that at the close of the fifth reign the total length of railways was 520 miles.

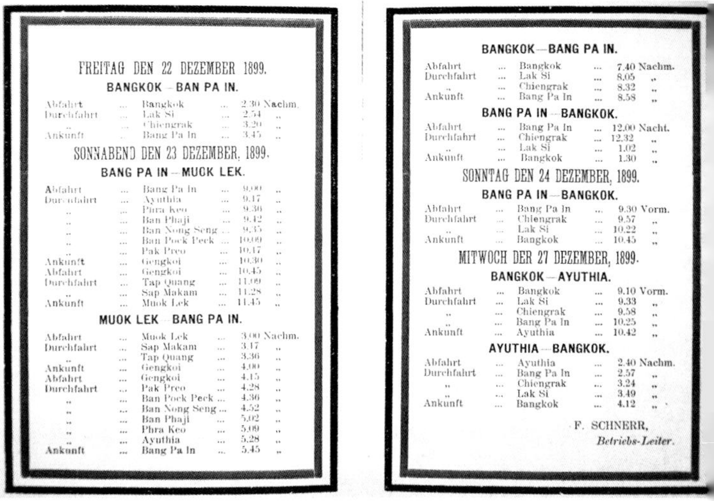

FREITAG DEN 22 DEZEMBER 1899.

BANGKOK – BAN PA IN.

Abfahrt	Bangkok	2.30	Nachm.
Durchfahrt	Lak Si	2.54	„
„	Chiengrak	3.20	„
Ankunft	Bang Pa In	3.45	„

SONNABEND DEN 23 DEZEMBER, 1899.

BANG PA IN – MUOK LEK.

Abfahrt	Bang Pa In	9.00	„
Durchfahrt	Ayuthia	9.17	„
„	Phra Keo	9.30	„
„	Ban Phaji	9.42	„
„	Ban Nong Seng	9.35	„
„	Ban Pock Peck	10.09	„
„	Pak Preo	10.17	„
Ankunft	Gengkoi	10.30	„
Abfahrt	Gengkoi	10.45	„
Durchfahrt	Tap Quang	11.09	„
„	Sap Makam	11.28	„
Ankunft	Muok Lek	11.45	„

MUOK LEK – BANG PA IN.

Abfahrt	Muok Lek	3.00	Nachm.
Durchfahrt	Sap Makam	3.17	„
„	Tap Quang	3.36	„
Ankunft	Gengkoi	4.00	„
Abfahrt	Gengkoi	4.15	„
Durchfahrt	Pak Preo	4.28	„
„	Ban Pock Peck	4.36	„
„	Ban Nong Seng	4.52	„
„	Ban Phaji	5.02	„
„	Phra Keo	5.09	„
„	Ayuthia	5.28	„
Ankunft	Bang Pa In	5.45	„

BANGKOK – BANG PA IN.

Abfahrt	Bangkok	7.40	Nachm.
Durchfahrt	Lak Si	8.05	„
„	Chiengrak	8.32	„
Ankunft	Bang Pa In	8.58	„

BANG PA IN – BANGKOK.

Abfahrt	Bang Pa In	12.00	Nacht.
Durchfahrt	Chiengrak	12.32	„
„	Lak Si	1.02	„
Ankunft	Bangkok	1.30	„

SONNTAG DEN 24 DEZEMBER, 1899.

BANG PA IN – BANGKOK.

Abfahrt	Bang Pa In	9.30	Vorm.
Durchfahrt	Chiengrak	9.57	„
„	Lak Si	10.22	„
Ankunft	Bangkok	10.45	„

MITWOCH DER 27 DEZEMBER, 1899.

BANGKOK – AYUTHIA.

Abfahrt	Bangkok	9.10	Vorm.
Durchfahrt	Lak Si	9.33	„
„	Chiengrak	9.58	„
„	Bang Pa In	10.25	„
Ankunft	Ayuthia	10.42	„

AYUTHIA – BANGKOK.

Abfahrt	Ayuthia	2.40	Nachm.
Durchfahrt	Bang Pa In	2.57	„
„	Chiengrak	3.24	„
„	Lak Si	3.49	„
Ankunft	Bangkok	4.12	„

F. SCHNERR,
Betriebs-Leiter.

A train timetable in German from 1899. (River Books)

In his great zeal to promote the welfare of his people the king did not neglect public health and hospitals, and in 1886 set up a committee of nine consisting of princes, officials, and the king's *farang* personal physician, Dr. Peter Cowan. The task of organizing the first hospital was entrusted to Prince Damrong and Prince Sri (born 1862), another son of King Mongkut.[23] It was felt that as the idea of a hospital was an innovation, there should at first only be one experimental hospital, and it was built in Thonburi out of rather modest funds. The first difficulty was to find doctors, as all of them were still practising the traditional Thai medicine using herbs and tree bark – often with most successful results.[24] However, because of jealousy, none of the royal Thai doctors would work together or divulge any of their knowledge until finally Prince Sri found a royal doctor of good repute who had retired, and let him appoint two of his own pupils as his assistants. Dr. Cowan also went to the hospital and there dispensed western medicine in which science the king now believed, despite in some special cases still clinging to Thai practices.

The next obstacle was to find patients, for at first only those who were so ill that they could not be cured by their own doctors, ever went to the hospital, where they then almost invariably died. As a result, the general public were apprehensive that to go to the hospital was to die. Dr. Cowan suggested collecting some of the beggars with skin troubles and sores whom he guaranteed to cure rapidly, but the beggars were indignant, saying that to cure them would be to deprive them of their legitimate means of livelihood. Finally the committee found it necessary to force their servants and dependants to go to the hospital, and when they came out fully restored to good health, the hospital became so popular that in no time at all there were not enough beds for the would-be patients. It was then the custom that the king would dispense some form of charity at the time of an important royal cremation. In 1887 there took place the cremation of Prince Siriraj, the fourth son of Queen Saowabha who died at the tender age of three. The king and Queen Saowabha decided that the charity connected with it should take the form of adding more to the funds of the hospital which they called Siriraj Hospital. In addition, Prince Sri

21 W. A. Graham: *Siam*, 3rd Edition, 1924, Vol. II, page 145.

22 D. G. E. Hall: *op. cit.*, page 588.

23 Prince Damrong: *Tales of Olden Times*, pages 124-205.

24 The author, the son of a Thai educated in Europe and a European mother, was, when a boy, treated by both western doctors and Thai doctors of the old school.

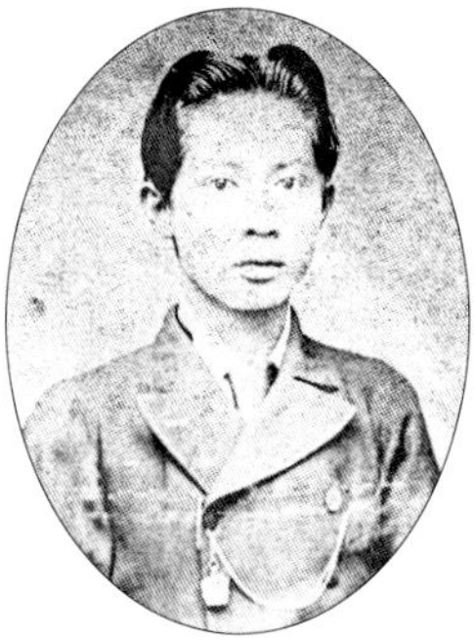

Prince Sri who was in charge of the Department of Health and established Siriraj Hospital. (National Archives Bangkok)

enlarged the scope of his work for public health by organizing large-scale vaccination against smallpox and founding a hospital for mental diseases. In time more hospitals were built in Bangkok and the provinces, and everywhere they received the full confidence of the public. A medical school was instituted at Siriraj Hospital which in due course began to produce Thai doctors of western medicine in addition to those who returned from their studies in Europe and America. This medical school was to grow from strength to strength, and in the next reign would have much support from the Rockerfeller Foundation and from Prince Mahidol, a son of King Chulalongkorn and Queen Sawang, and father of the present reigning sovereign – His Majesty King Bhumibol. Nevertheless, the number of fully qualified Thai doctors was far from adequate, and European doctors of different nationalities would reap a rich harvest for years to come. Some years later there were at least enough Thai doctors to be appointed as government doctors in the various provinces.

In order to persuade the general public to take to western prescriptions, which were not only more efficacious but also did not need to be taken in such large liquid quantity as Thai medicine, a ruse had to be resorted to. It was not stated on the bottles or boxes that the medicine was of western origins, and the labels merely said "For Fever", "For Dysentery , or "For Indigestion", and so on. After the people had taken the remedies and found them curative, western medicines soon became popular. Once this was so, surgery followed in good time. There was unfortunately a sad side to this successful picture in that Prince Sri had so overtaxed his strength with his great efforts that he died of consumption at the age of 27.

The achievement of King Chulalongkorn which most caught the western imagination is the abolition of slavery. The system itself was described by Hall as "Not as harsh as the plantation system of America . . ."[25] Already in King Mongkut's reign, edicts had been issued to ameliorate the lot of the serfs. Slavery of some kind has been known in the world since the dawn of history, with some Thai Buddhists claiming that the Buddha was the first person to condemn the practice.[26] Originally the Thai were one of the few races which did not know serfdom, hence the name of Thai – Free, and the system was adopted from the Khmers when the Thais migrated into the Indo-China peninsula.

There were seven types of serfs in 1868: 1. Serfs purchased from a previous owner. 2. Children born from serf parents. 3. Serfs given as presents. 4. People who had been helped with payment of fines after criminal conviction. 5. People who were helped in times of high prices for rice. 6. Prisoners of war. 7. Children given to gambling houses as payment for gambling losses. This latter type deeply distressed the young king who found it a wicked practice.

However, the abolition of slavery in various parts of the world had not gone smoothly. In the U.S.A. it caused a cruel and prolonged war, while in Japan there was a revolution. Similarly, two liberators of

25 D. G. E. Hall: *op. cit.*, page 584.

26 *The Abolition of Serfdom in the 5th Reign* (in Thai), Bangkok, 1956.

slaves, Abraham Lincoln and Alexander II of Russia, were both assassinated. With the support of the Regent, King Chulalongkorn at his coronation issued the *revolutionary* decree that all the people born in his reign would eventually be free. Thus the year 2411 of the Buddhist Era (April, 1868 to March, 1869), became known as the year of freedom from slavery, but although it was easy to decide to abolish serfdom, how was it to be carried out? When the king, after reaching his majority, first informed the ministers and other noblemen of his idea, most of them were in disagreement. When news reached the serfs themselves, not a few of them showed clearly that they would prefer to remain as they were because their situation was not as bad as might be imagined; they were secure in their board and lodging, paid no taxes, and had no responsibilities. As they were bond slaves, if they were displeased with their owner they could try to get a kinder one to buy them at a good price, thereby ensuring that most of the owners had to be benevolent to their slaves. To protect them from forced sales, King Mongkut had already decreed that serfs over 15 years old could not be resold without their consent. When the news of the coming abolition reached the owners, they were also against the idea as they needed the service of serfs which was cheaper than hired labour. Thus, all in all, the king's initial project clashed with public opinion, and the titular *Lord of Life* had to find a suitable stratagem. First he carefully examined the existing law dealing with slavery and found that the value of slaves was set based on their age, beginning cheaply at one to three months old – 6 baht for a boy and 4 baht for a girl – before gradually rising to peak prices for men aged between 26 and 40, and for women between 21 and 30. After this the value declined until really old people of 91 were

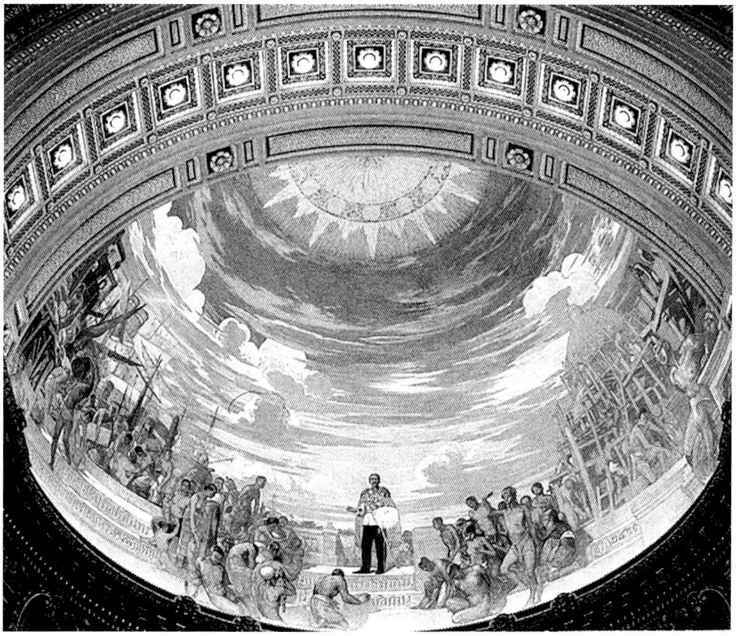

A painting in the dome of the Ananta Samakhom Throne Hall showing King Chulalongkorn abolishing slavery. It was painted by Galileo Chini. (River Books)

only worth 4 baht for men and 3 baht for women. In order to let them buy their freedom or have their freedom bought for them cheaply, the king's new plan was to link the peak price to the age of 7 to 8 years after which the value dropped sharply at once, and at the ages of 18 to 21 their set value by law would only be 3 baht. Children of slaves were automatically to cease being slaves at the age of 21, and no one over 21 could be sold into serfdom. In fact, the king had wanted to abolish the value of all the children of slaves immediately and set them free, but he realized that unkind owners of parent-slaves might jeopardize their upbringing by withholding essential facilities from the parents, and he had to be content with the practical plan outlined above.

King Chulalongkorn set up a committee to draft the new law and it met for the first time on July 12th, 1874. No princes were members of this committee which consisted entirely of commoners. The king, himself not quite 21 years old, was present at this first meeting. In his address he emphasized that progress had to be gradual and cause no undue hardship to owners or slaves. He added: "I do not want anyone to be serfs, but there are people who still want to remain serfs, as they pay no taxes and need not follow any profession, and sometimes when there is. no work for them to do they still have plenty of food to eat. This will not be so when they are free, thus full freedom can only come when there is lucrative work available for everyone. This task of freeing slaves is too big for one man to decide upon. Please give me your advice, each one of you". After their deliberations the committee fell into line with the king's plan, and the law was drafted and enacted on October 18th, 1874. To enable slaves to get better work when they were freed, some alms houses were turned into schools for slaves. As it was voluntary insufficient numbers of slaves attended, so the king bought many slaves from their owners on the condition that these slaves attended the schools. Following these measures the number of slaves gradually dropped, and by 1905 the great task of abolition was completed. The Malayan states of Kedah, Terengganu, and Kelantan were still under Thai rule, but the abolition of slavery did not extend to them, and they were permitted to follow their own Muslim customs.

King Chulalongkorn's foreign policy was concerned largely with difficult relations with the French who had now secured the position of being the Protectors of all Vietnam, then called Annam. As Hall[27] says, France's prestige had become dangerously low in Asia after her overwhelming defeat in the Franco-Prussian War of 1870-1 and the fall of Napoleon III. It was felt in France that the best way to revive her prestige was to recommence the policy of expansion in Indo-China which had been interrupted. Meanwhile, Burma had ceased to exist as an independent state following the disastrous conduct of King Thibaw who succeeded his father in 1878. He was finally removed from the throne, the Burmese monarchy abolished, and Burma annexed to the British Empire as a province of India from 1886. This event naturally made King Chulalongkorn and his ministers view their difficult relations with the French with some alarm and trepidation. At the same time the French were suspicious of the British and they thought that they were encouraging Siam to expand towards Annam.

Thus troubles with the French stemmed from the French protection of Annam in 1883 because the boundaries between Siam and Annam were not precise, and the French claimed that the River Mekong should have been the natural frontier. Although admitting the vassalage of the Laotian King of Luang Prabang (now the kingdom of Laos) to Siam for many years, the French insisted that he was a vassal of Annam as well because he had also sent tributes to Hue in 1831 and 1832. Hall[28] thus sums up the situation: " the fundamental fallacy in such an argument lay in reading European ideas into the relationship between the states of the Indo-Chinese peninsula. But the French did it consciously and deliberately, and with the single-minded aim of exploiting to the full any situation which could be used to their advantage."

The Chinese warlike refugees, known to the Thais as "Ho" or "Haw", had poured into Tongking and the Laotian states in 1864 and remained in the district. In 1872 they threatened Luang Prabang and Nong Khai. Following the requests for help from the 75-year-old King of Luang Prabang and the Thai Governor of Nong Khai, troops were sent from Bangkok who dealt successfully with the Haws. But despite these men confining themselves to fortified areas, they were still a menace, so Thai troops were maintained there in order to protect Luang Prabang. By 1883 when the French had completed their annexation of north Annam, they complained that Thai troops had frequently penetrated into Annamese territory. Franco-Thai negotiations were concluded by the treaty of May 27th, 1886, when Siam ceded to the French all territories on the eastern bank of the Mekong, while retaining Luang Prabang. Nevertheless sporadic frontier raids continued on both sides.

Great Britain, now in full control of Burma, wished to see a reasonably strong Siam as a buffer state between the French and themselves, as she was anxious about France's growing power and influence in Indo-China. It is curious to observe that ever since France became a republic it was less easy for Siam to obtain a sympathetic understanding than in the time of Napoleon III, but whether this was because things had been easier between two monarchies cannot, of course, be determined with certainty. As the Haws were still active, the French forces under Auguste Pavie and the Thai forces under Chao Muen Wai Woranart (later Chao Phraya Surasak) who were there to keep the Haws in order, sometimes clashed between themselves in minor actions said to be due to the vagueness of the boundary lines. By the end of 1889 Pavie had become French consul in Bangkok during which time there were constant consultations between the British and French Governments regarding the boundaries of Siam, and both countries were anxious that the power and influence of the other should not be increased. Frontier incidents between Siam and the French persisted with both sides blaming the other, while in Bangkok

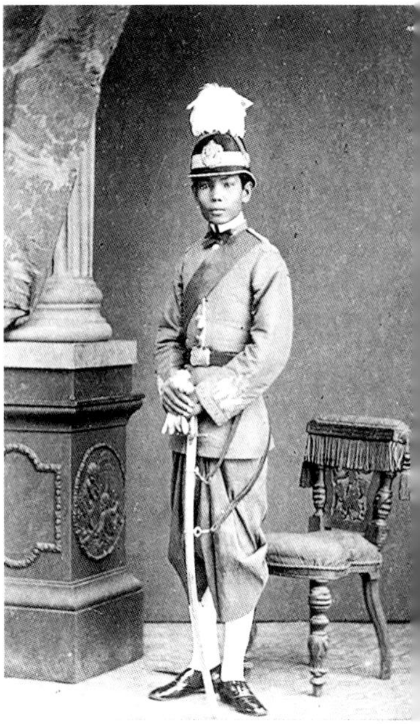

Chao Muen Wat Woranart later Chao Phraya Surasak. (National Archives Bangkok)

27 D. G. E. Hall: *op. cit.*, page 569.

28 E. V. G. Kierman: *British Diplomacy in China, 1880-1885*, page 591, Cambridge, 1939, quoted by D. G. E. Hall.

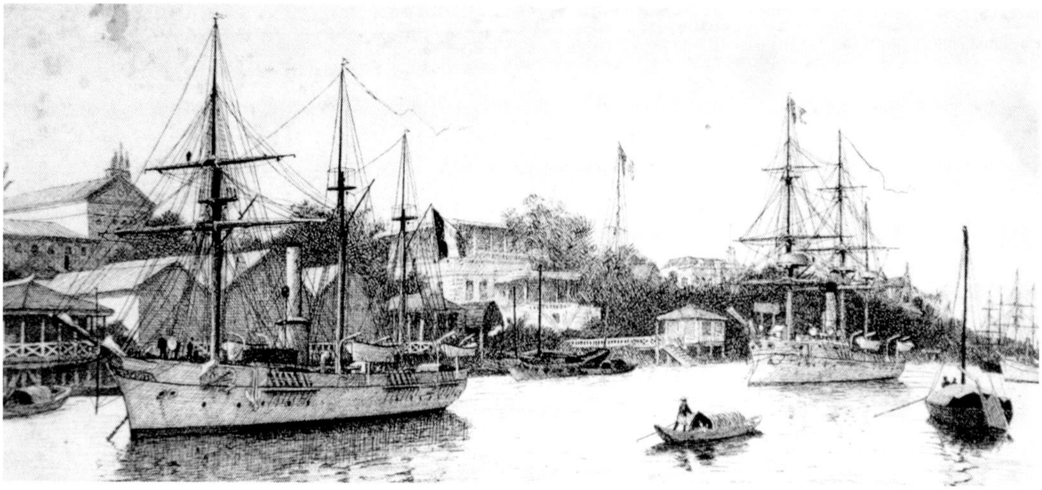

Drawing of the French ships *Lutin* and *Comete* which were moored in the Chao Phraya river in front of the French Embassy. (Dawlish Chronicles)

King Chulalongkorn was preoccupied with his administrative reforms, which were largely accomplished by 1892 when the different ministries had been formed. Meanwhile, the French consulate in Bangkok was raised to be a legation and Auguste Pavie became the first resident Minister Plenipotentiary. It was then that the Belgian General-Adviser, Rolin-Jacquemyns, was being heavily attacked by the French who alleged that he was secretly a British agent.

In 1893 frontier troubles became extremely grave and there were allegations on both sides of frontier violations, of murders and of kidnapping, until finally the French charged that the Thai had launched a strong attack across the Mekong on April 6th, 1893. The French now asked for more territory and for the Thai officers alleged to have led the attack to be punished. On July 13th, two French gunboats were at the mouth of the Chao Phraya river waiting to go up to Bangkok to show the flag on the French National Day, July 14th, opposite the French Legation on the river where it still stands today. Virginia Thomson[29] states that the French Government in Paris had decided at the last moment to hold the two warships outside the bar of the river, but the order was not received in time. When the two vessels began to cross the bar they were fired upon by the Thai forts, the French returned fire and there were casualties on both sides, but the ships got through and finally anchored opposite the Legation. Because of the prolonged political tension between France and Siam, two British warships, H.M.S. *Swift* and H.M.S. *Pallas* had been sent to hold a watching brief outside the river. The British told the French that they had urged caution on the Thai government and the French promised to inform the British of their every move. A great deal of what followed is still a matter of conjecture, for, as Hall[30] relates, the French archives concerning this question has not (1955-1959) been thrown open to the public. It is, however, known that Britain had suggested moderation from both sides, but when the Thai Foreign Minister, Prince Devawongse, asked for British help in arbitration over

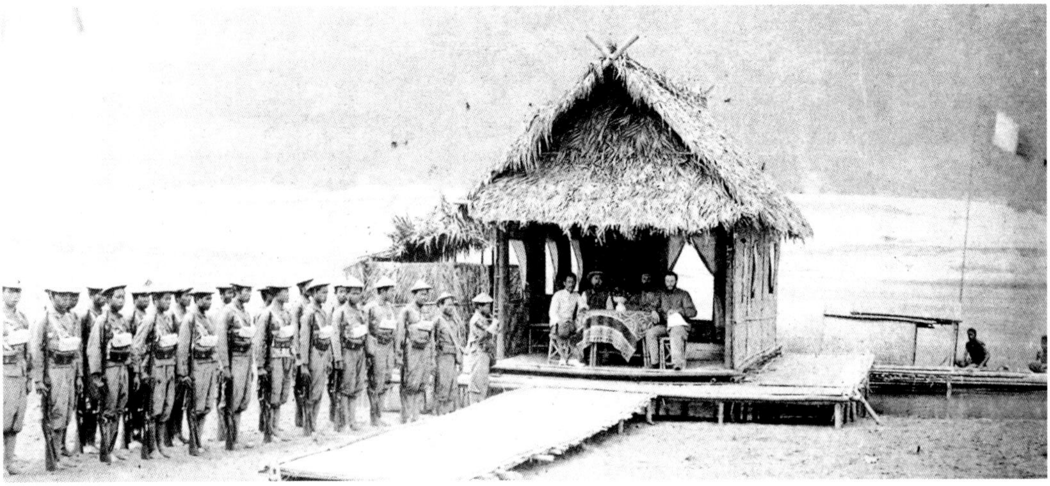

Auguste Pavie in negotiations with the Lao leader. (Wikiwand)

the frontier incidents, his British counterpart, Lord Rosebery, advised the Thais to act with even greater caution, and he sent a copy of his communication to the French Ambassador in London.

Following the shooting at Paknam, Auguste Pavie received an order to deliver the following ultimatum to Prince Devawongse: 1. That France as the Protector of Annam and Cambodia should have all the territory on the eastern bank of the Mekong even if any part of it was inhabited by Laotians who were then under Siam. 2. Punishment of all Thai officers responsible for frontier incidents. 3. Siam to pay France an indemnity of three million gold francs (25 francs to the £). The French Foreign Minister told the Chamber of Deputies in Paris that the French Government wished to avoid war as Bangkok was a city of 350,000 inhabitants and would require a large army of occupation. Also they knew that Britain did not want France to upset the balance of power in that region, especially when there were other difficulties between Britain and France in Africa and elsewhere.

With the Thai Government being slow to reply, Pavie left with the warships for Koh Sichang, a Thai island near the mouth of the river, and the French gunboats now proceeded to blockade Bangkok. There was a small group amongst the Thai statesmen who thought that French demands should be resisted, as they did not know that Lord Rosebery had telegraphed Prince Devawongse advising that the Thai government should accept the French terms and thereby making it clear that there was no likelihood of British help in the event of war. Prince Dhani has said that the Emperor Nicholas II of Russia, by then an important ally of France, strongly urged France to be moderate out of his friendship for King Chulalongkorn."[31]

That monarch, who had believed the troubles with France settled in 1886, was so upset by the Paknam incident that he fell ill. He refused to take any medicine, and from his sick bed wrote a poem of heartbreaking misery to some of his brothers. However, he was soon cheered by the protestation of loyalty and confidence in him shown by

29 Virginia Thomson: *Thailand, the New Siam*, page 188, New York, 1941.

30 D. G. E. Hall: *op. cit.*, page 605.

31 In his notes to the author in 1958.

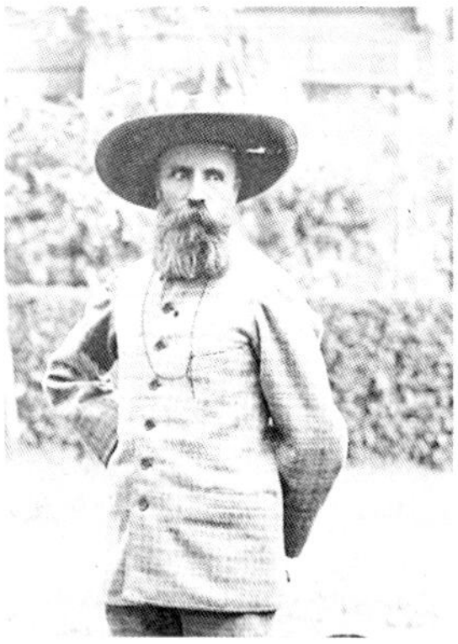

August Pavie in 1893. (Wikiwand)

Prince Damrong.[32] The moderates led by Prince Devawongse and fully supported by the king, won the day and all the French demands were agreed to by the draft treaty of October 3rd, 1893. The Thais were to demilitarize the territory immediately to the west bank of the Mekong, and the province of Chantaburi in the south-east near the coast was occupied by French troops to guarantee all the promises in the treaty being carried out. Only then did Pavie return to Bangkok. It was in August, 1893, that J. G. Scott was appointed British Minister in Bangkok and through him and Pavie there were continual negotiations concerning the respective spheres of influence in Indo-China.

Fortunately the situation calmed down, and in 1896 Britain and France agreed to accept the existing boundaries of Siam and jointly guaranteed her integrity against any third power. Now fully aware of her weakness in the absence of possible British support, Siam agreed to the French extension of extraterritorial rights in Siam not only to French subjects, European *and* Asian, but also to any refugees from French territories and their descendants living in Siam. The French Legation registered almost anyone who presented themselves with such claims, and even a French writer[33] admitted that no proof of any kind was required by the French authorities. Sir Josiah Crosby[34] wrote that, although the inhabitants of Luang Prabang and Vientiane were clearly of Thai race, Thai control over those cities and their provinces had not always been effective. In 1904, in return for the earlier ending of the occupation and the evacuation of French troops from Chantaburi, Siam finally ceded both Vientiane and Luang Prabang to the French. The Anglo-French *Entente Cordiale* was now in place, so the new cession received British approbation.

Thai map with shaded area showing territory lost to France in 1893.

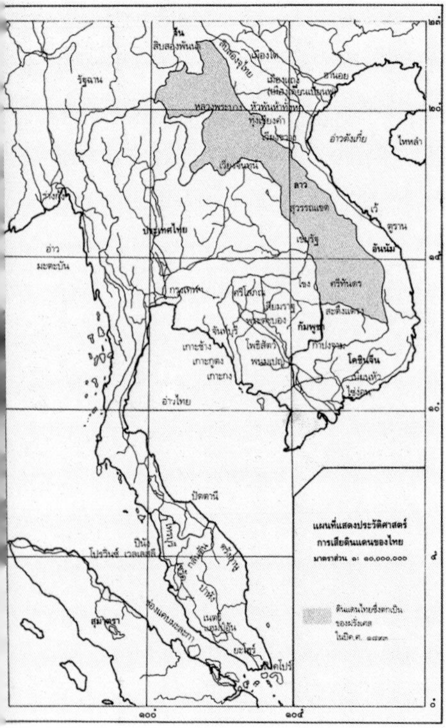

By 1907, the administrative reforms of King Chulalongkorn were fully completed, and a new adviser-general was appointed – again a neutral – Mr. Strobel, of U.S. nationality. Another treaty was concluded with France when Siam gave up her last three remaining Cambodian provinces, Battambang, Siem Reap, and Sisophon, whose population were of a mixed Thai-Cambodian stock. By this cession Siam lost the renowned Khmer ruins of Angkor which was probably a good thing for the world in general, as the French were more capable of restoring them both in terms of finance and the intense interest and deep learning of their scholars in oriental studies. In return France surrendered her extra-territorial rights over her *Asian subjects only.* This was an important gain for Siam as her police had found it difficult to differentiate between Thai subjects and French Asian subjects, and there had been frequent complaints that the latter had been arrested by mistake. Relations with France improved further when a number of French jurists were appointed to the committee to codify Thai laws. Thai students went to France and many more Thai people could speak French as well as English.

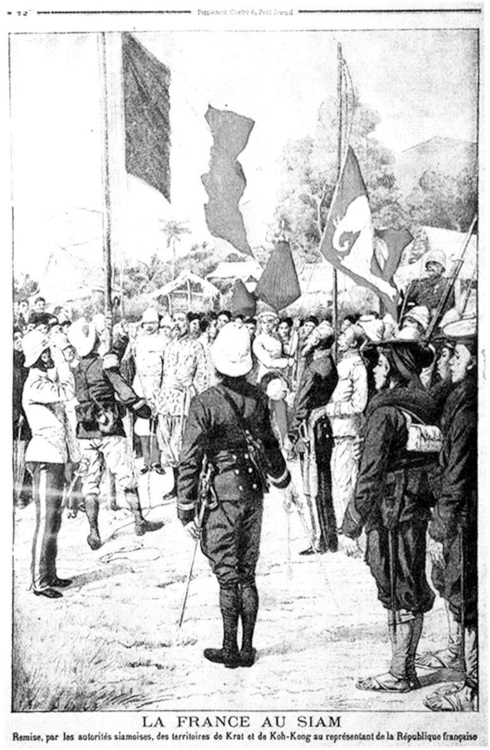

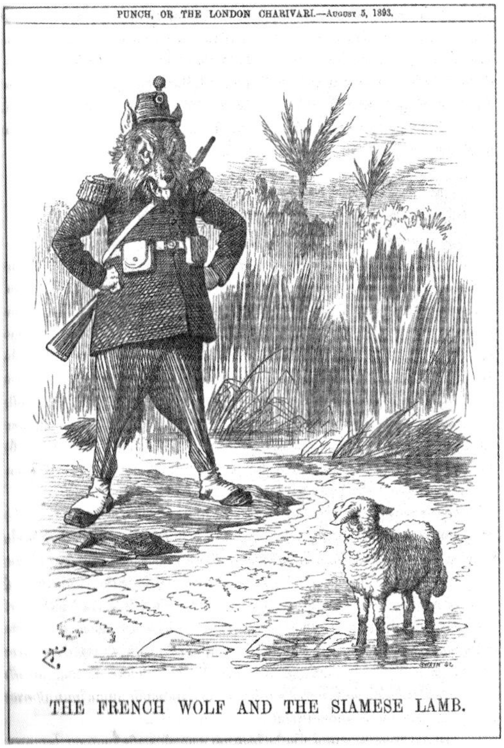

A cartoon from *Punch* in 1893.

ABOVE LEFT: Lowering the Siamese flag and raising the French one on Koh Kong during the Paknam crisis. (*Le Petit Journal*, 1905)

Soon after the troubles with France, in 1898, a treaty was concluded with Japan, who would herself reach a position of eminence after her victory over a European power – Russia – in 1904. In 1909, a most important new treaty was signed with Britain, and was ratified on July 15th, being the last treaty of King Chulalongkorn's reign. Siam gave up her sovereignty over the four Malayan sultanates of Kedah, Kelantan, Terengganu, and Perlis, which in practice meant their cession to Britain – a territory of 15,000 square miles and one million inhabitants. Britain in return surrendered extra-territorial rights not only for British Asian subjects, but Europeans as well, thereby becoming the first European power to do so. Thus although he had lost 90,000 square miles of territory to the French and British, King Chulalongkorn's foreign policy ended on a happier note, and it has been said by Virginia Thomson that Siam "gained morally by this physical loss",[35] in that she became a more compact and homogenous country. Her independence remained intact, if incomplete, and she would avoid the growing pains suffered by ex-colonial Asian countries. Yet these necessary losses of territory to two overwhelmingly stronger western powers would later be used as pretexts for attacks on the king by Thai anti-Chakri politicians after 1932.

Owing to the international troubles the much desired European tour had to be postponed until 1897. It was during this and the subsequent tour of 1907 that King Chulalongkorn had the gratification of seeing how high his prestige was in the world. Queen Saowabha was

32 Princess Poon Diskul in *Collected Royal Writings*, *op. cit.*, page 71.

33 Col. F. Bernard in Robert-Martignan, *op. cit.*, pages 135-136.

34 Sir Josiah Crosby: *op. cit.*, page 61.

35 Virginia Thomson: *op. cit.*, page 163.

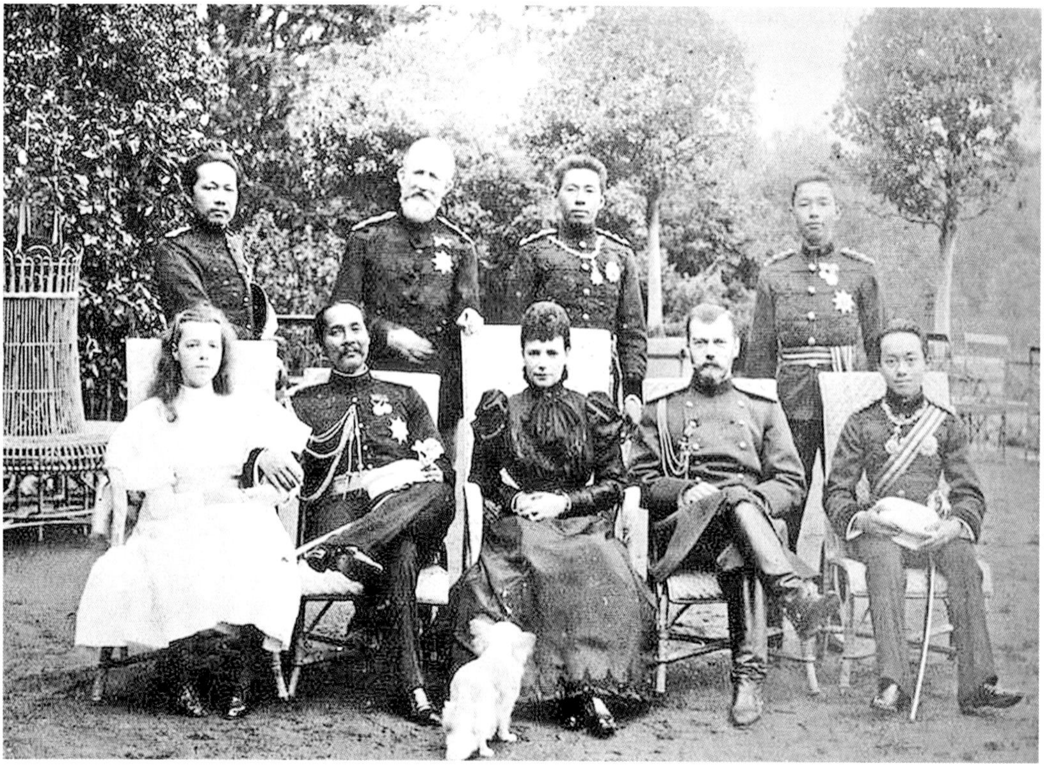

King Chulalongkorn and Tsar Nicholas II, together with the Empress and members of the Siamese and Russian royal families. (River Books)

appointed Regent during his absence and was the first Thai Queen ever to be jointly called with the king as the *Two Sovereigns.* Queen Sukumala wrote to her son in Germany that from then on, apart from minor details, Queen Saowabha was to be treated in the same way as the king himself.[36] Excitedly King Chulalongkorn wrote to his son, Chakrabongse (Lek), then a boy of 14 and in England : "Mother will be proclaimed Regent on the 21st of this month, the ceremony will be similar to the appointment of a crown prince, except that Mother will have to take the oath in front of the council. I have personally drafted the order of the ceremony, and it is really going to look important. Her title of *Parama Rajinee* will have the addition of *Nart* (Ruling). She will henceforth be addressed as to the Sovereign (in Thai he wrote *Chao Pandin)* . . . I am so excited that we shall meet soon, but feel so sorry for Mother in her upset at my departure and her anxieties over her heavy task".[37] To commemorate the first regency of a queen a medal was issued attached to a plain blue ribbon.

For the first tour of 1897 he travelled the whole way to Europe and back in his yacht *Maha Chakri.* Among the many countries he visited was France where he was agreeably surprised to find that he was well received both officially and spontaneously by the French people who gave him a hearty cheer when he appeared with the President of the Republic in a horse-drawn carriage after being met at the railway station. In Russia he cemented his friendship with Nicholas II, in

Germany he got on splendidly with William II, in London he stayed at Buckingham Palace and was received by the Prince of Wales (later Edward VII), the Duke of Connaught, and the Duke of York (later George V), as Queen Victoria was resting quietly at Windsor in preparation for the fatigues of her forthcoming Diamond Jubilee. He did, however, get a sightseeing tour of Windsor Castle and would remember every detail ten years afterwards. In Austria he stayed with the Emperor, Franz Joseph at both the Hofburg and Schoenbriinn. He visited Italy, Sweden, Belgium, and other countries, and was particularly friendly with the royal families of Denmark and Mecklenburg. The tour was a real success because he could converse easily and intimately with European royalty, being the first Asian monarch to talk with them directly in English instead of through interpreters. His delightful letters to Queen Saowabha, giving his well informed, lively and humorous impressions of the first tour have been published in book form.[38]

Ten years later he made his second visit to Europe, travelling this time by a German liner of which he took the entire first-class accommodation. He was not in good health and it was more of a private trip, but he saw several old friends. He spent a week-end at Windsor Castle with King Edward VII and Queen Alexandra. A charming description of that stay was given in his letters to his favourite daughter, Princess Nibha (born 1886), dated June 22nd, 23rd, and 24th, 1907, which have also been published in book form and the book has proved extremely popular.[39] Apart from a garden party for 8,500 people, and a formal dinner party, it was a friendly family week-end. Amongst European royalty present, most of whom he had already known, King Chulalongkorn met Prince and Princess Andrew of Greece, the parents of Prince Philip, Duke of Edinburgh. He spoke to the Prime Minister, Sir Henry Campbell-Bannerman[40] whom he

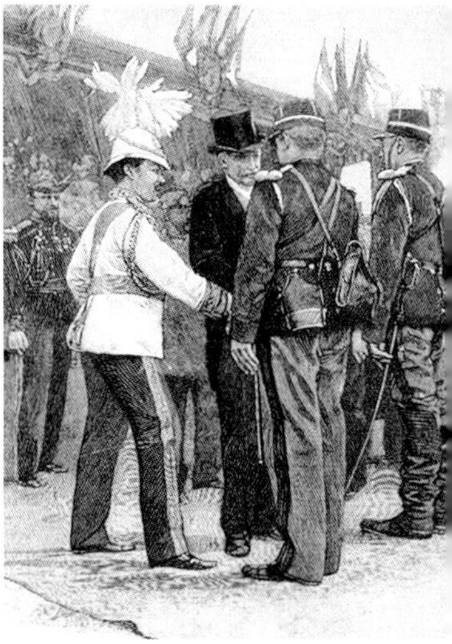

King Chulalongkorn was well received by President Félix Faure. (National Archives Bangkok)

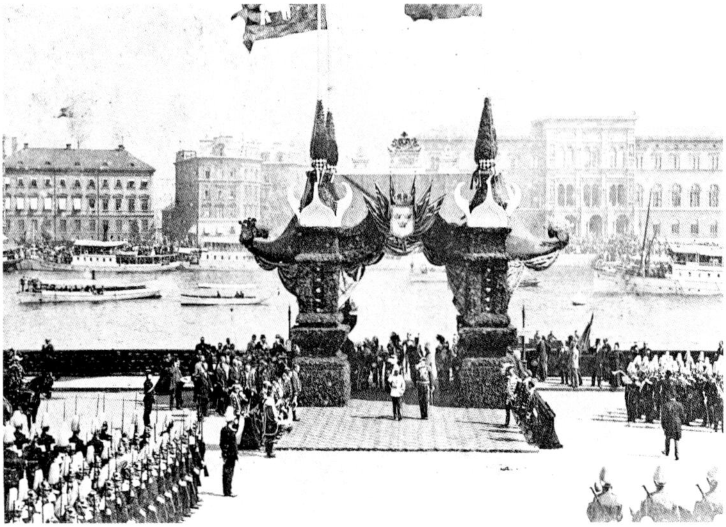

The reception of King Chulalongkorn in Stockholm on 13th July 1897. (National Archives Bangkok)

36 *Queen Sukumela to Her Son, op. cit.*, page 108.

37 The original in Thai, dated March 3rd, 1897, is in the possession of the author.

38 *King Chulalongkorn's Letters to Queen Saowabha during his European tour of 1897* (in Thai), Bangkok, 1919.

39 *Klai Ban (Far From Home)*, in Thai, Bangkok, 1924.

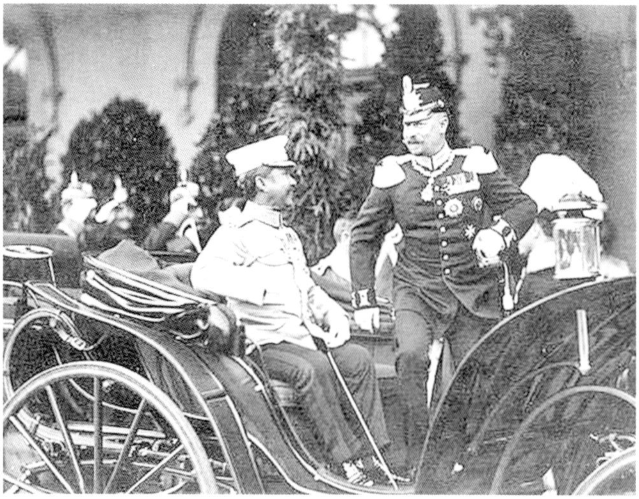

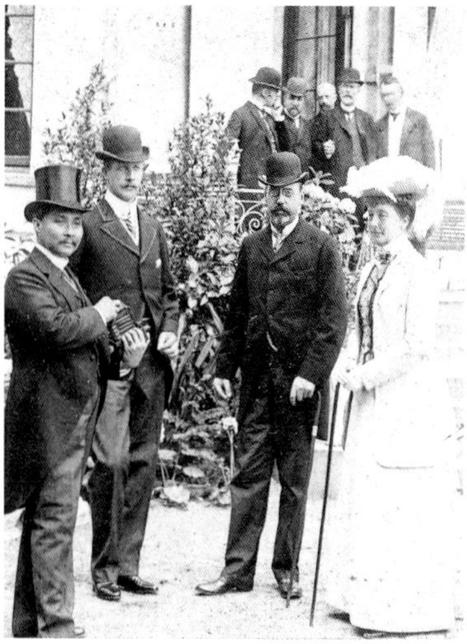

King Chulalongkorn on his second trip to Europe with the Duke of Mecklenburg Schwerin about to get into the carriage in Brunswick. (National Archives Bangkok)

King Chulalongkorn with Prince George of Greece and Prince and Princess Waldemar of Denmark, 1907. (River Books)

On his second trip, the king visited the Riviera together with Prince Urubongse, Prince Prajadhipok and Prince Mahidol. (National Archives Bangkok)

found " quiet and retiring, not at all like Lord Salisbury",[41] whom he had met ten years previously. He remembered most of the changes which had been made at Windsor since 1897, even the absence of one of a pair of huge Chinese jars. "Atmosphere at the English Court is very much like in an ordinary home, not so royal and formal as on the continent". At breakfast "the king read the newspapers and we exchanged news." He told his daughter that before dinner on the Sunday King Edward VII "handed me a gold cigarette case with his initials set in diamonds beneath an enamel crown . . . He would not wait for any thanks, but hurried me off to dinner". Light descriptive touches in the same vein pervade the letters about every European court he visited. His conclusions regarding the Windsor stay were: "It must be pleasant to be a British King, so long as one does not want to have too much of one's own way. One must let others do the work. They usually come and tell you about it before, and if you have any ideas of your own you can always state them. But if they persist in having their own way you must let it go, otherwise it might lead to a disastrous quarrel. This system works well in England, and this king knows very well how to make it work. He knows when to give way, yet he is clever enough to win respect. He has carried out some ideas of his own. He is large-hearted, a sportsman, and so very gay. I am most impressed with him, and no wonder he is so popular ".

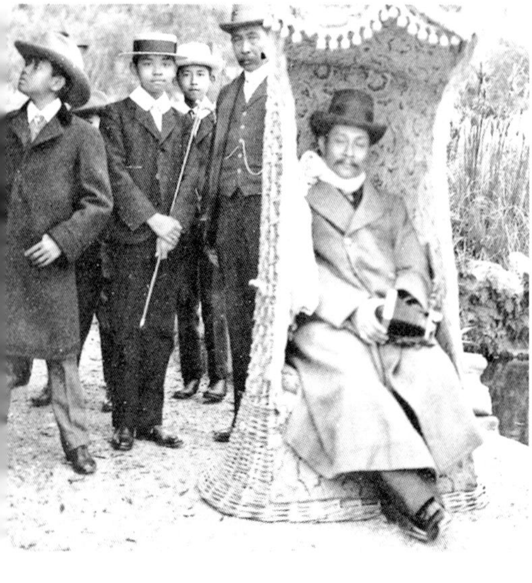

Apart from the royal visits, during both tours he enjoyed seeing his sons and for a brief while watched their education closely and discussed problems with their preceptors. He loved European food, enjoyed eating in restaurants especially in Paris, but he would not sit down in one without first visiting the kitchen and meeting the chef. Both books of correspondence, already referred to,

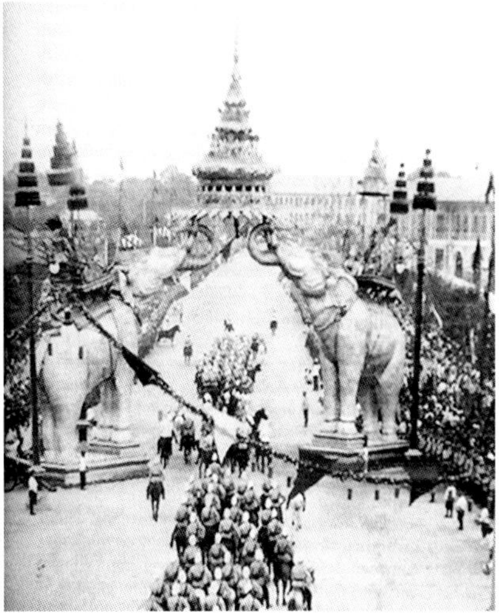

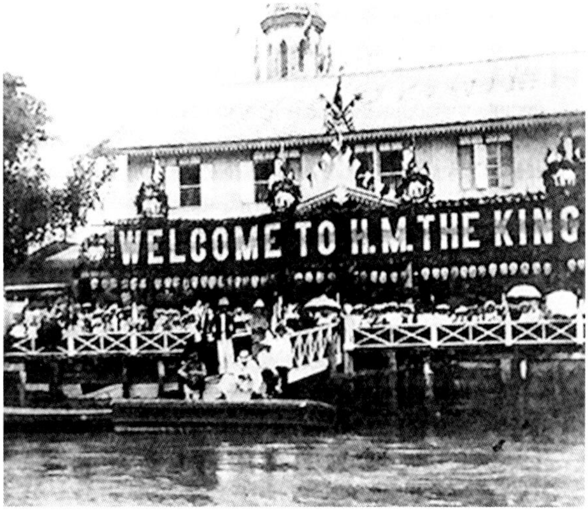

Lavish decorations were arranged to welcome the king home, 1907. (National Archives Bangkok)

show the wide knowledge which he had acquired of the world, not only geographically, but historically and constitutionally. Unfortunately in 1907 it was also a health-seeking trip for he had become quite ill with a serious kidney complaint. Although he saw many European doctors who thought it could be cured, so ardent was his wish to return to his work that he would not consent to remain away long enough. The European tours were of benefit to the country as a whole. He took people with him who held important posts in the government service, he took young students, and he brought back many new ideas. Bangkok, in particular, was further beautified, and nearly every year he had a bridge built across the canals to open on his birthday. The Chakri family have sometimes been blamed for focusing too much on Bangkok, but as it was the city which they had built, it was perhaps understandable.

On his return home in 1907 King Chulalongkorn had as tumultuous a welcome as in 1897, but suddenly his health sharply declined. He had worked hard all his life, and besides affairs of State and innumerable hobbies, among which keeping Leghorn chicken and photography were the favourites in his last years, there was also the prodigious amount of his writing work. He wrote diaries, travel books, history books, and also some of the best of Thai poetry, and his grandchildren have often wondered in awe how he found time for it all.

Although as sovereign and *Lord of Life*, he had owned all the land in Siam, King Chulalongkorn had voluntarily surrendered such legal rights – another revolutionary step – without any outside pressure. He set up his Privy Purse which was kept apart from the National Treasury. He also instituted the holding of land in Siam by title deeds. It was with Privy Purse income that he sent his sons to be educated in Europe. With his savings he bought land in Bangkok and elsewhere which he gave to his children, and as they had title deeds they were private owners and could bequeath the properties to their descendants or anyone they chose. Thus the grandchildren of King Chulalongkorn have not had to depend on any Civil

40 Liberal Prime Minister, 1905-1908.

41 Conservative Prime Minister, 1885-1886, 1886-1892, 1895-1902.

List, but on their own lands or their work. Admittedly the celestial princes had greater shares, and most of their children have been better off than the children of the *Phra Ong Chaos*.

Round about the turn of the century most of the older sons had returned from their studies. Crown Prince Vajiravudh was carrying out the general duties of the Heir Apparent as well as serving in the army, and during the king's second tour of Europe in 1907, it was he who was appointed Regent. He had returned home via the U.S.A. and Japan. Chakrabongse accompanied him as far as America where they visited President Theodore Roosevelt at the White House, and among other sightseeing opportunities, they were both impressed with the outstanding discipline and drill at the U.S. Military Academy of West Point. In Bangkok the Crown Prince first stayed at Saranrom Palace before moving to Chitralada, then the name of one of the two houses forming the Paruskavan compound near Dusit Palace.

Prince Chira, created Prince of Nakhon Chaisri, one of the first four sons of the king to go to Europe, had studied in England and Denmark and returned to be Minister of Defence. In May, 1903, Celestial Prince Patibatra, Prince of Nakom Sawan,[42] returned to join him and served as Chief of the Army General Staff, being the first fully qualified Thai staff officer, but strangely enough he held this high office at the lowly rank of a second-lieutenant. In February, 1904, he was suddenly recalled from a military exercise near Rajburi and told by King Chulalongkorn that he had to go into the Navy as the Commander-in-Chief because there had been some irregularities with naval finances and senior officers were divided into cliques. Although disappointed at not being able to follow his real profession, Prince Paribatra obeyed his father without demur. Assisted by Prince Abhakorn (born 1880), who had been in the British Navy, he reorganized every branch of the naval service, and was the founder of the Naval College in 1906 with the sailor, Prince Abhakorn, in close professional charge. He was the first of the *Chao Fas* to marry, and he had the good fortune to make a love match as well as a suitable one for he married his cousin, Princess Prasongsom, a daughter of Prince Mahisara, the Minister of Finance. On December 5th, 1904, their first child, Prince Chumbhot was born. Later five daughters were born to them, and Prince Paribatra also had a son and a daughter from another wife.

The sons of King Chulalongkorn who were involved in reforms of the armed forces.
From left to right: Crown Prince Vajiravudh, Prince Chakrabongse, Prince Purachatra and Prince Chirapravati. (National Archives Bangkok)

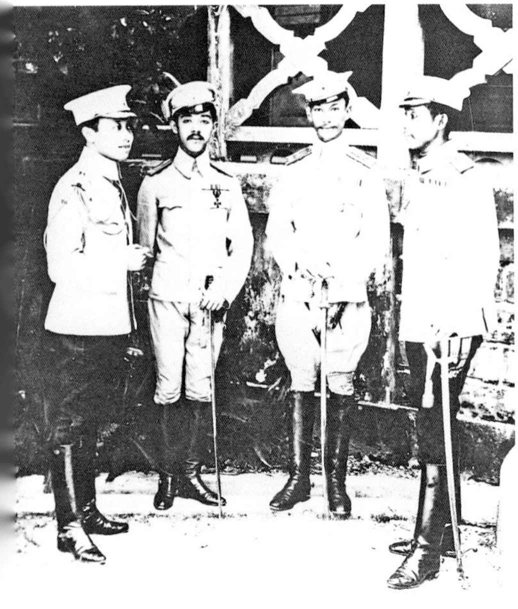

Before the birth of Prince Chumbhot several grandchildren had already been born to King Chulalongkorn. The rule in the Royal Family was that grandchildren of a sovereign had the princely rank of *Mom Chao*, the equivalent of His (or Her) Serene Highness, and if these princes did well in the royal service they could be raised to *Phra Ong Chao* with the prefix of His Highness. Only children of the king by minor wives or children of an *Uparaja* were

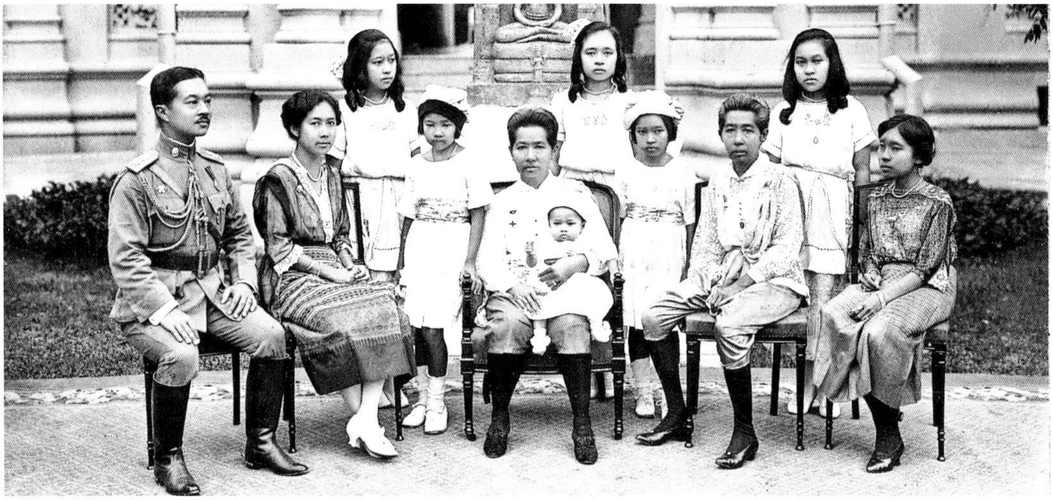

Prince Paribatra, Queen Sukumala and other members of the Paribatra family. (National Archives Bangkok)

born *Phra Ong Chao*. As the position of *Uparaja* had been abolished, the king's nephews and nieces who were children of his full and celestial brothers were only *Mom Chaos* like children of the king's half-brothers. King Chulalongkorn decided that henceforth his full nephews and nieces, born from the chief wife, should be *Phra Ong Chao* with the prefix of Royal Highness. In a similar way Prince Chumbhot became a Royal Highness together with the five sisters born of the same mother. *Mom Chao* is the last of the princely ranks, their children having the noble rank of *Mom Rajawongse* (M.R.), and their grandchildren *Mom Luang* (M.L.) For all subsequent generations there were no titles, they have the surnames surviving from their ancestors having been the son of a king – with *na Ayudhya* added.

It was in 1906 that Chakrabongse, Prince of Phitsanulok, returned to Siam and it was then that he caused his father great disappointment and anguish. When he was home on leave in 1903-4 he had fallen in love with one of his half sisters, but the king disapproved, saying that marriages of that kind were out of date. When the prince returned to Russia he met a young and attractive Russian girl, Catherine Desnitsky, who was born in 1888. Her father was Ivan Stepanovitch Desnitsky, Chief Judge of the Lutz Province, and her mother was from a family of landed gentry in Ukraine with the name of Khijniakoff. By 1904 both her parents were dead, and she was in St. Petersburg studying to be a volunteer nurse for service in the Russo-Japanese War. Her brother was also in the capital, being a brilliant student at the university, who later joined the Diplomatic Service.

Chakrabongse met Catherine at the home of a mutual friend and he fell in love with her almost immediately. She insisted on going to the war at the age of 17 and she had a distinguished record, gaining three decorations, including the Order of St. George. On her return to St Petersburg in 1905, Chakrabongse proposed, but she did not accept until he had seen her brother and received his consent. To his own

42 Princess Prasongsom Paribatra: *Memoirs* (in Thai), Bangkok, 1956.

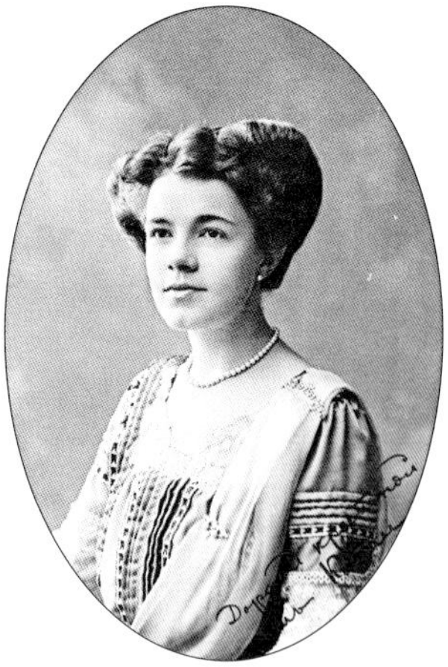

Catherine (Katya) after her marriage to Prince Chakrabongse. (River Books)

father and mother the young prince sent no word, his reason being that if they were to refuse their consent, he would not be able to marry her; but as they had said nothing, he could do so. Nor did he tell his guardian, the Emperor, who must have been deeply hurt when he heard the news. Forgiveness, however, followed in full measure; for when Chakrabongse returned to Russia in 1911 the Emperor made him an honorary colonel in the Hussar Guards and bestowed upon him the highest Russian honour, the Order of St. Andrew, the equivalent of the Garter in England. It was in 1906 that Chakrabongse and Catherine were married in Constantinople, and after a honeymoon in Egypt, returned to Siam. As he had not told his parents about his marriage, Chakrabongse played for time by leaving his wife behind in Singapore, while returning himself to Bangkok to live at the main building of Paruskavan Palace next door to his brother – the Crown Prince, and took up his post in the Army as Commandant of the Military Academy.

Bangkok gossip soon reached the king's ear that there was a Madame de Phitsanulok staying in Singapore, and the King asked him jokingly at a public audience whether he was married to a Russian woman when he was quietly told that it was true. The king's grief was acute, and Queen Saowabha was both furious and sad. Once the news was out, Catherine was sent for and she came to live at Paruskavan. At first she led a secluded life which became a blessing in disguise as she learned Thai and English – having already spoken French as a child – as well as the manners and customs of the country, and wearing Thai dress. Chakrabongse went about his business as usual and was assiduous in his regular visits to his parents. They had overcome their anger and disappointment and now chose to ignore the whole thing. Queen Saowabha, having been more violent in her disapproval, was the more ready to forgive; also her feminine curiosity could not be indefinitely curbed, and when she finally received her daughter-in-law, the young Russian wife could already speak Thai and was well versed in the intricacies of court etiquette, such that mother-in-law and daughter-in-law liked one another immediately.[43] The king, although still not receiving her, began to ask his son about his wife and expressed his pleasure that she shared some of his hobbies such as keeping Leghorn chickens. He was also delighted that Chakrabongse and his wife enjoyed going for a walk along his new tree-lined avenues.

Paruskavan Palace. (River Books)

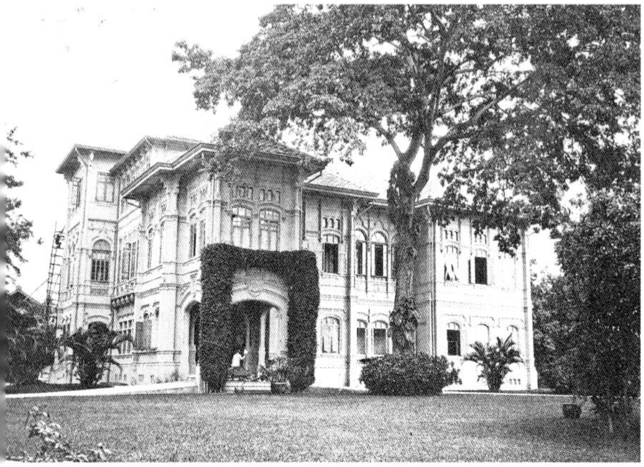

On March 28th, 1908, a son was born to Chakrabongse and Catherine, and his birth gave his grandmother great happiness and he was the only grandchild she ever lived to see. Her English physician, Dr. Smith, wrote, "The Queen's first and only grandchild. She was overjoyed. The boy became her greatest favourite".[44] The Queen called him *Nou* which means mouse a nickname most commonly given to children. When asked before his birth what rank he thought the boy should be, Chakrabongse replied to the King : "Oh, he can be just a plain Mister". The king therefore ignored his grandchild, much to the grief of the Queen. After the child was two, the king agreed to see him both at his grandmother's new home at Phaya Thai and at Dusit Palace as eye-witnesses, older grandchildren or youngest wives of the king, have testified. The king is reported by them to have told Queen Saowabha: "I have seen your grandson today, and he looked sweet and resembled his father. As soon as I saw him I loved him, for after all he is of my own flesh and blood, and there were no European looks about him".[45]

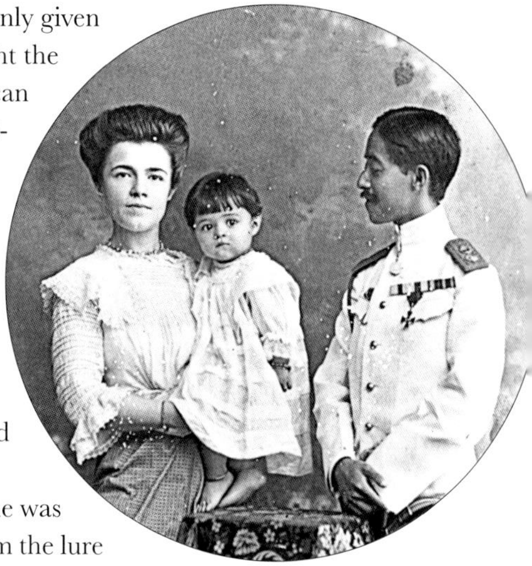

Katya, the author and Prince Chakrabongse. (River Books)

Phra Sarasas wrote thus of King Chulalongkorn:[46] "But he was not unlike other despots, who cannot extricate themselves from the lure of despotic power. While attaching the utmost importance to fortifying his country with Western techniques, he was all the time haunted with the problem of how to perpetuate his despotic rule. This nightmare made him advance the civilization of his country only when such advancement would help and not hinder absolute kingship".

There is, however, reliable evidence that after his second European tour, King Chulalongkorn was thinking of abdicating at 60. He might have known that in building Saranrom Palace, his father, too, had thought of abdicating when not fit enough in health to rule. That King Chulalongkorn well understood the principles of Constitutional Monarchy has been shown by his remarks about King Edward VII of Britain. He bought for Queen Saowabha some farmland a little way north of Bangkok and there he built a conglomeration of comfortable wooden buildings which he called Phaya Thai (Lord Thai) Palace, where he intended to retire with Queen Saowabha as a farmer after his abdication. He pondered thus: "I will not for all my life remain king, but instead I want to be the king's father". After his tour of 1907 he must have realized that the days of the absolute monarchy even one as benevolent as his own were numbered. But it would be better for his son to be the one to grant the constitution because he had been educated in England and, being an ardent Anglophile, would know all the better how to make the system work. Meanwhile, Queen Saowabha had already gone to live at Phaya Thai in the hot months, and the king drove himself there nearly every day in his yellow electric car from Dusit Palace two miles away to visit her round about tea time.

A document has recently been published in a Thai journal[47] which shows what the king had already thought about this problem earlier in his reign. Although the king had assumed full powers and the Regency ended in 1873, the Regent, Sri Suriyawongse, continued as Chief Minister and greatly assisted the king in running the country. As Minister of Interior he was highly successful in suppressing bandits in

43 If requiring details see Prince Chula: *The Twain Have Met,* etc., *op. cit.,* Chapter V.

44 Dr. Smith: *op. cit.,* page 116.

45 Signed statements are in the author's possession.

46 Phra Sarasas: *op. cit.,* page 128.

47 *Siam Samai* (Weekly Thai journal), Vol. 9, No. 444, November 15th, 1955.

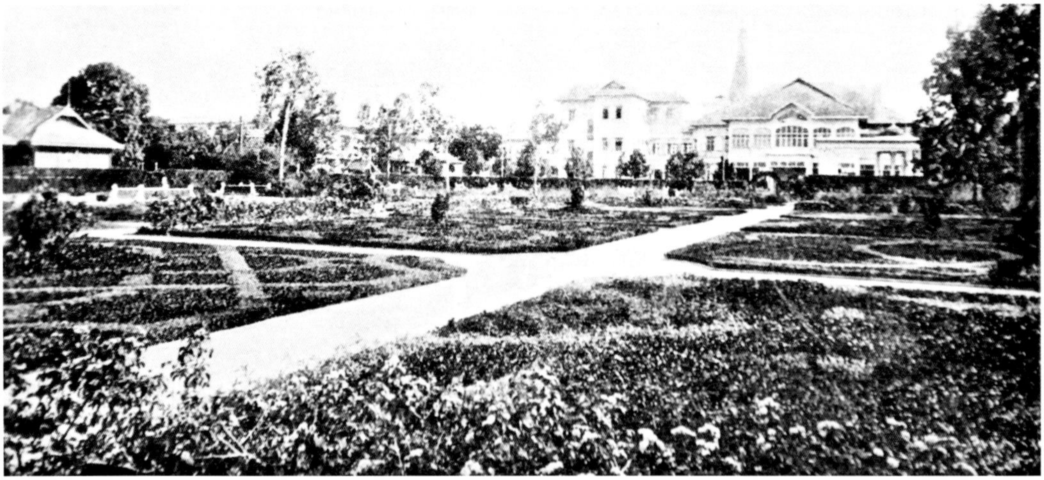

A view of Phaya Thai palace. (National Archives Bangkok)

the provinces and Chinese secret societies in Bangkok. It was on January 19th, 1882, that the Regent died and after that date King Chulalongkorn, then 29 years old, was alone and ruled with unfettered power. It was in 1886 when he was 33 and had been king for 18 years, that a petition of 60 pages was presented to him signed by eleven persons who had all been to Europe to study or on visits, with four of them being princes. The petition was couched in language which can only be described as plain speaking. It pointed out that with all power being concentrated in the king, his authority was hanging only on a thread. A constitutional parliamentary system was essential if independence was to be preserved from the colonizing powers (Europeans), especially as the king had been too lenient with ministers who were lazy, and bad choices of ministers had been made. Accordingly, it was desirable that there should be collective responsibility vested in a cabinet headed by a prime minister. The petitioners admitted that the time was not ripe for a fully-elected assembly before going on to say much about the right of free speech and equal justice for all classes.

By law all were guilty of *lese-majeste*, and the king could have been angry and had them severely punished, the law even permitting the death penalty; or he could have refused to be bothered with reading the document at all. King Chulalongkorn studied the petition carefully and gave the following reply "Having examined all that you said, I thank you for your patriotic interest. I would never stand in the way of progress, for I suffered much when I was a powerless figurehead during the Regency, just as I now find full powers heavy with responsibility. I would be glad of the compromise of constitutional government, thus there would never be any need to compel me to accept such a situation as European kings have been compelled to accept. I have now been king for eighteen years and I well understand our situation. The weakness of the king to which you refer has not been my fault or the fault of my predecessors, and if the ministers have always been so powerful, it is because they as a class have made so many kings in our history. I was a boy when I became king, and any senior people will tell you of my difficulties. Do not imagine that I have been sitting stupidly on the throne for eighteen years without giving thought to this problem.

"You should first study how this country has been governed before you find yourself sufficiently equipped to give me advice. Both the *executive* and *legislative* [he used English words here in his Thai text, C. C.] powers were vested in the king, or rather the Regent at the beginning of the reign. I found the Regent and ministers absorbed in the executive but uninterested in the legislative. When I reached my majority I founded the Legislative Council *(Rata Montri)* wherein I became myself the Leader of the Opposition against my own ministers which was why the Council was at first so strong. As the work became more difficult to cope with, the old ministers began to fail; I had to take over more and more responsibility in the executive until now I alone am the government, and without my active support the Council was losing its influence and prestige, thus it is true that I have neglected the Council because I have been too busy with increased executive business.

"I am now my own Prime Minister almost exactly like the British Prime Minister, but the British Prime Minister only has to concern himself with principal matters, while I have to know every minor detail. On the other hand, the British Premier has to sit and answer questions in the House of Commons which I do not have to do, but I have had so much to occupy my mind that I have failed to further develop the Legislative Council as I should have done.

"That we need in this country a reform of the whole system of government I entirely agree, but then members of an effective legislative council must be independent men. Where are we to find such men? Most of the present members all have administrative or executive posts of some kind, and I cannot abandon my personal responsibility to the present ministers as they are not fully capable. The older ones, who know their limitations, now hardly ever dare to speak. What should they do? Should they resign *en bloc*? Such a thing has never occurred here and it would likely cause panic amongst the people. I, too, want political reforms, but at present there are other matters more pressing". What these matters were has already been related. King Chulalongkorn added: "We must first of all see that we can get the right kind of people to be our future legislators, or we are better off without them." It should be noted that King Chulalongkorn wrote this reply to the petition *eleven years* before he went to England and Europe for the first time.

Among King Chulalongkorn's countless useful measures, the creation of the National Library must be included. It was his wish to commemorate his father in that way, and in 1904 the long planned project came to fruition. A National Library Committee was set up

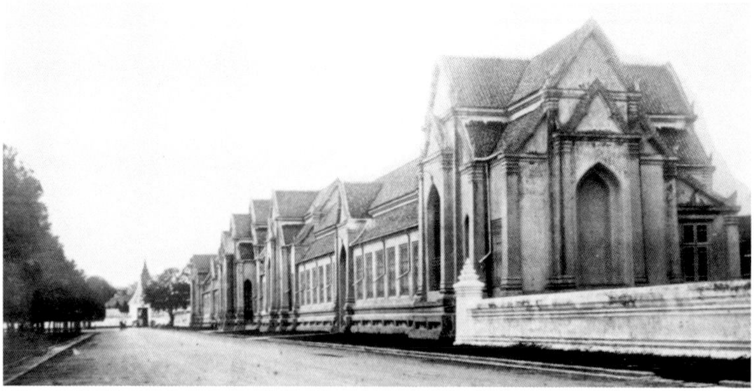

Tuk Thavorn Watthu, when it used to be the Vajirayan Library. (National Archives Bangkok)

headed by the Crown Prince Vajiravudh, assisted by Prince Damrong, Prince Sommot, Phra Prajakij, and Phra Borarn. Books and manuscripts were collected from three old libraries, and the Vajirayana (King Mongkut's priestly name) Library for the City was founded. From that early institution finally sprang the National Library of today which owes a tremendous debt to the ceaseless efforts of Prince Damrong and his team of officials in searching the country for manuscripts. The most notable find was that by Luang Prasert, whose discovery of some historical manuscripts has altered many accepted facts regarding the history of Ayutthya.

Formerly it had been the custom to give beautiful, expensive and often useless objects as tokens of thanks to guests attending cremations. With so many manuscripts gathered together or freshly found, the heavy expense of printing them for publication became a problem. Families of the dead had begun to distribute books at cremations, but they were always books relating to Buddhism. It was in 1904 that King Chulalongkorn issued public advice that the best way to give away presents at cremations was to pay for the printing of manuscripts in the National Library for distribution, and most families accepted the suggested choices of the Library committee. The practice continues, but today many other unpublished works and even entirely new ones are also distributed at cremations.

Hall[48] found that the long term results of King Chulalongkorn's measures of reforms were most striking, especially by contrast with Siam's two neighbours – French Indo-China and Burma – and he agreed with W. A. Graham that the Thai peasantry, the backbone of the country, had become "a sturdy and independent class free from the ancient thraldom, owning its own land, depositing money in the savings bank, in fact, acquiring a stake in the country."

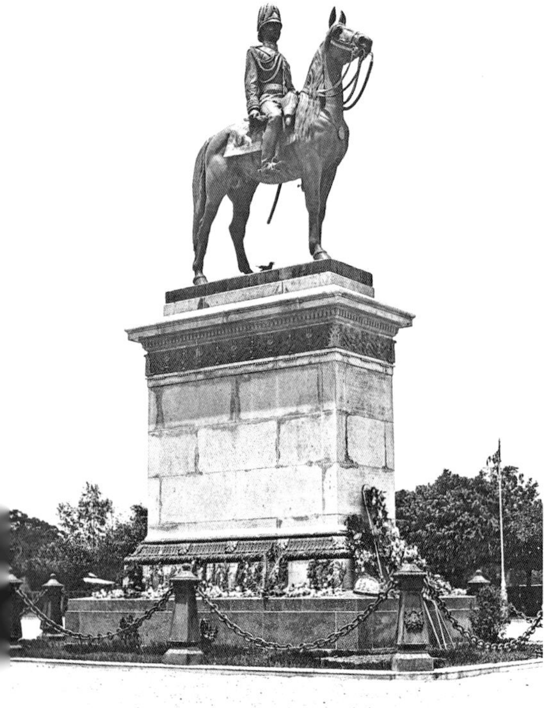

The equestrian statue of King Chulalongkorn was created following public subscriptions. (National Archives Bangkok)

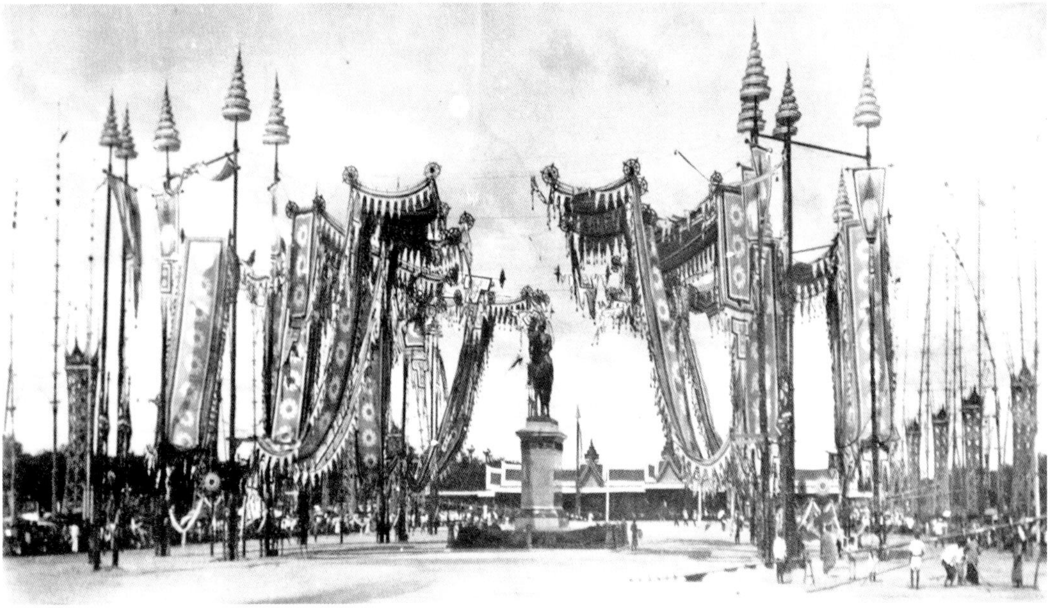

Opening ceremony for the equestrian statue of King Chulalongkorn. (National Archives Bangkok)

The reports of the Financial Adviser, who was always British while the Foreign Affairs Adviser was American and the Legal Adviser French, was first published for the financial year of 1901-02 by C. Rivett-Carnac to the Minister, Prince Mahisara. It shows that the year 1899-1900 had closed with a surplus of nearly 3 million baht (at 13 baht to £). The profitable gambling tax-farms were being reduced for moral purposes, for gambling often resulted in the wicked sales of children into slavery, but there were still spirit sales and opium farms in full swing. There was no national debt, and the prosperity of the country over the past years made possible the formation of good reserve funds for lean years. The allowance for Education of 2 million bahts against 6 million for the King's Civil List can be explained by the fact that the Court was still the cultural and artistic centre, and a great deal of the Civil List was spent on adult education in the forms of museums, libraries, art schools, ballet, repairs of royal buildings and monasteries and royal barges, all of which were important parts of the national heritage, and only a small portion of the money went to the king and his family.

The budget of 1900-01 had expected a surplus of 330,034 bahts, but the real surplus amounted to 3,770,940 bahts. There were satisfactory revenues from paddy field taxes, fisheries, forests, tin, Judicial Stamps, Capitation Tax at 2 baht per head, and from savings. C. Rivett-Carnac said the increased revenue was due to improved methods of administration which enhanced the prosperity of the people, a direct result of better government. The increase in the Land Tax was due to a greater area under cultivation. It made possible the abolition of 12 gambling farms in keeping with the avowed policy to abolish such farms altogether. Among the many items of public

48 D. G. E. Hall: *op. cit.*, page 585.

expenditure was electric lighting for Bangkok. The most essential telegraphic lines had by then been established throughout the kingdom and the service was being run at a loss, whereas the State Railway in that year earned a net profit of 400,000 baht.

The report of the new Acting-Adviser, W. J. F. Williamson, for 1904-1905, shows that in 1902-1903 the volume of Thai exports had reached a record level, and despite heavy expenditure for the public benefit, the real budget deficit was only 96,420 baht. The expenses included public buildings, roads, irrigation, locks, dredging, military barracks, and police stations. The Acting-Adviser made the following comments: "State regulated gambling is, doubtless, indefensible on moral and other grounds, but the practical administrator has to take facts as he finds them, and on a balance of the advantages incidental to this form of revenue, it is probable that, in this country at least, the evils are outweighed by the benefits which the government is enabled to confer on the community at large by reason of its freer expenditure on objects of public utility. The question in Siam is entirely one of ways and means, and the government, having once put the hand to the plough in the matter of progress on modern lines, cannot afford, for merely sentimental considerations, to cripple the administration by surrendering so large a portion of its annual income as the abolition of the Gambling Farms would entail. At the same time His Majesty's Ministers are fully alive to the evils inherent in this method of raising revenue, and any well thought out scheme which provided for a sufficient sum from other sources, would receive their most careful consideration". The greater volume of exports naturally meant a larger volume of imports, and higher duties on these to a reasonable degree would make it possible to abolish evil methods of raising revenue such as through gambling and opium. But such a course of action was not open to King Chulalongkorn as all his treaties with Western powers still retained the restrictive clause first agreed to by his father in 1855 which forbade the Thai government from imposing duties on Western imports at higher than three per cent, *ad valorem*.

An author writing a full length biography of King Chulalongkorn will be able to make fuller use of these highly interesting reports of the Financial Advisers, but here the last report of the reign must suffice. It was presented by W. J. F. Williamson to Prince Kittiyakorn, Prince of Chantaburi, the eldest son of the king, who had become Minister of Finance in 1908. The actual revenue for 1909-10 was over 60 million baht as against 30 million in 1900, and the surplus was 3,834,782 baht. The foreign exchange situation was so satisfactory that the Adviser congratulated the government. Exports exceeded imports by as much as 40,702,493 baht, which showed that the country was in a healthy state in trade and finance, with the population now reaching the 9 million mark. The Chinese minority were mostly happy and content to get on with their work. Immigration continued but Chinese wives began to come with their husbands after the turn of the century, and

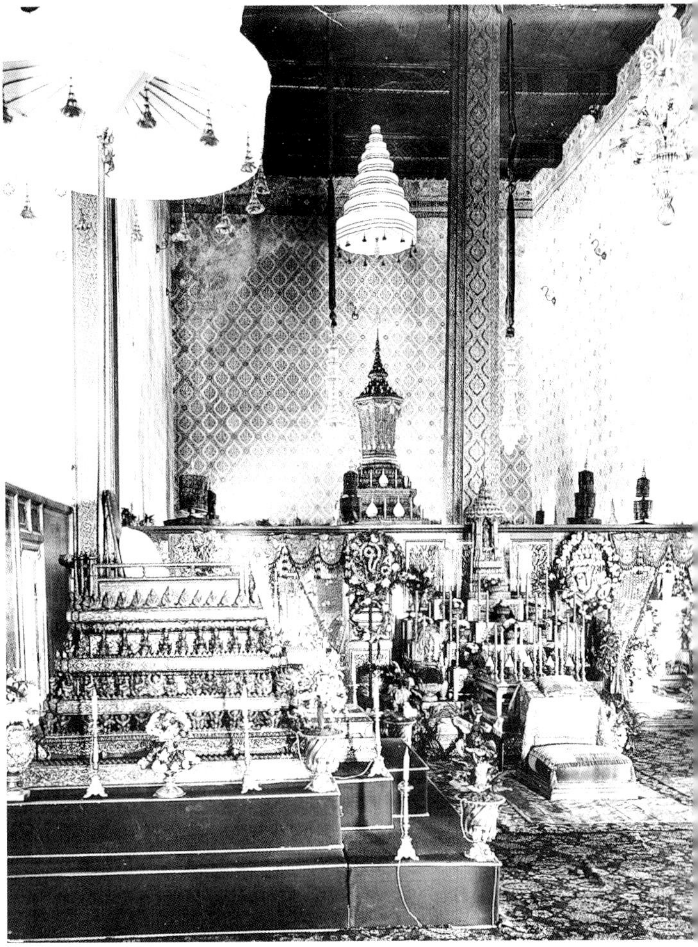

The urn containing the body of King Chulalonkorn installed within the Dusit Maha Prasat Throne Hall. (River Books)

inter-marriage declined, but by that time Thais with Chinese connections were already in large numbers throughout Bangkok and other towns. There were clashes and riots between Chinese secret societies which were suppressed at times by force and at other times by clever efforts at reconciliation by government authorities. It is interesting to observe that the Suez Canal, which brought the lands of South-East Asia into closer trade relations with Europe, was opened for traffic in 1869 after King Chulalongkorn had been on the throne for one year.

In 1908 King Chulalongkorn celebrated the forty years of his reign amidst unparalleled public jubilation and displays of loyalty. The people subscribed a large sum of money to erect a visible memorial to him, an undertaking never before attempted for a Thai individual alive or dead. It is said that they wanted a grandiose marble memorial like the one in Rome for King Victor Emmanuel II. King Chulalongkorn accepted a modest equestrian statue outside his own Dusit Palace, desiring that the rest of the money should be spent on improving and increasing the scope of the Civil Service College which has since become Chulalongkorn University. With more subscriptions pouring in after his death, the new king and other family members would found Chulalongkorn Hospital for the Thai Red Cross Society.

The king had suffered from a chronic kidney disease for some years, and becoming critically ill on October 16th, 1910, he died in a coma at 45 minutes past midnight on the 23rd. The intense grief of his family and all the people in general cannot be adequately described. As for Queen Saowabha, she was for the rest of her life inconsolable and always wore black. Since then, on October 23rd of every year, thousands upon thousands of men, women, and children have gone with floral tributes to pay homage at the foot of his statue. Thus his real memorial is in the hearts of the people of Siam.

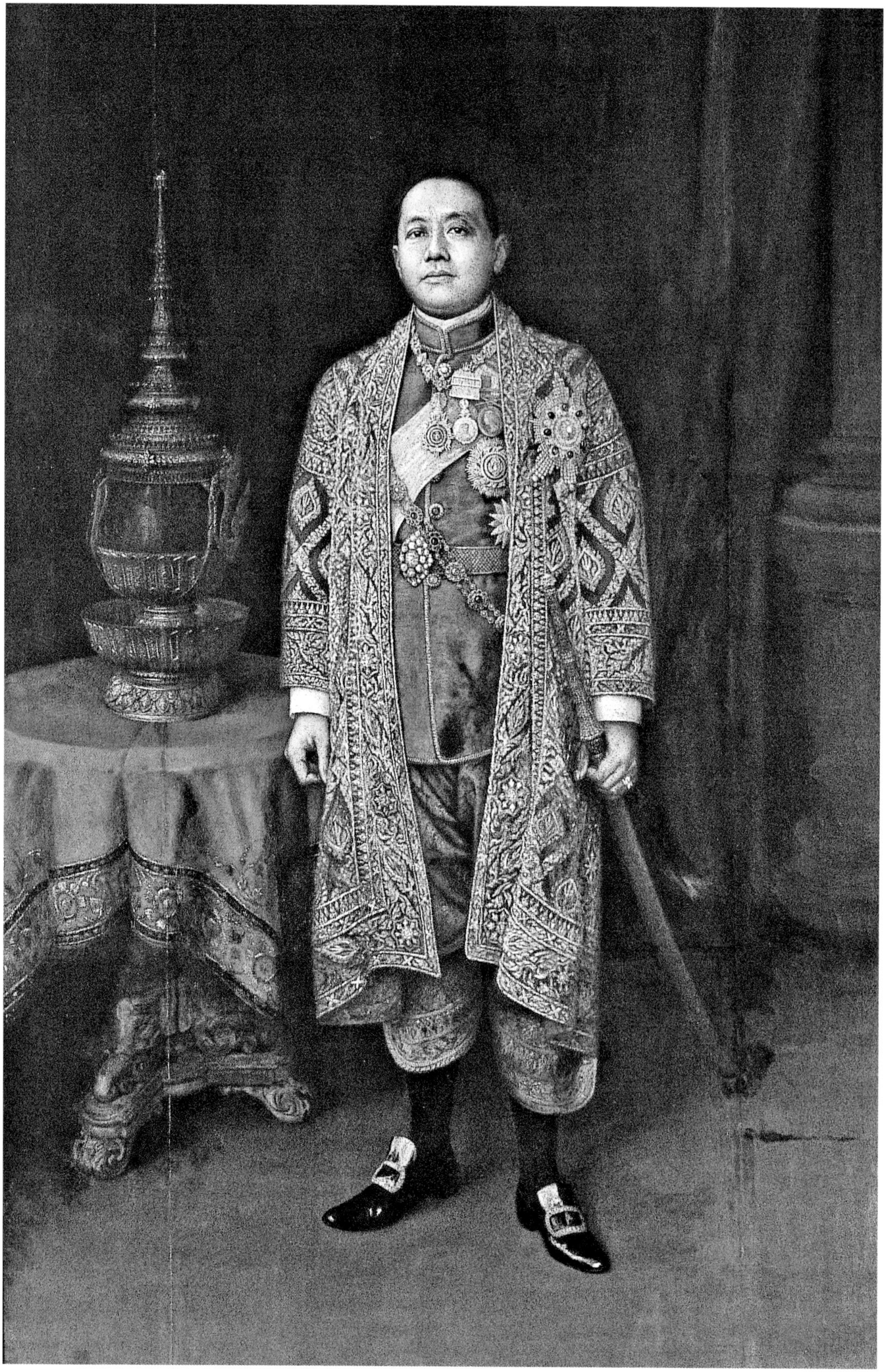

Chapter Six
The Liberal
(1910-1925)

OPPOSITE: King Vajiravudh, Rama VI.

The reign of King Vajiravudh, or Rama VI as he later preferred to be called, is still so close to us (1959), and so many of the personnages who occupied the stage or their children are still alive, that the events of that epoch can only be lightly touched upon and reviewed in outline. For the first time in the history of the House of Chakri an Heir Apparent had been legally and officially proclaimed fifteen years earlier, and there was no question of election by an Accession Council. Accordingly, the new monarch ascended the throne with the full loyal support of the Royal Family, the great ministers, the senior officials, and the Thai people at large. Rama VI was just under thirty – a splendid age to ascend to a throne, and no monarch of Siam had ever succeeded to such a noble or well secured heritage. He had charming looks and natural dignity, despite being of short stature and somewhat plump, and he was endowed with the gift for public speaking with a soft and melodious voice.

Queen Saowabha became Queen Mother with the title of Queen Sri Patcharindra, but colloquially she was called the Queen of One Thousand Years – the old title for the Queen Mother. She continued to occupy her old quarters in the private side of the Chakri Building, but preferred more and more to reside at Phaya Thai Palace, which, with the continuing growth of the capital, was now in one of the new suburbs.

One of the early acts of the new sovereign was to recognize the

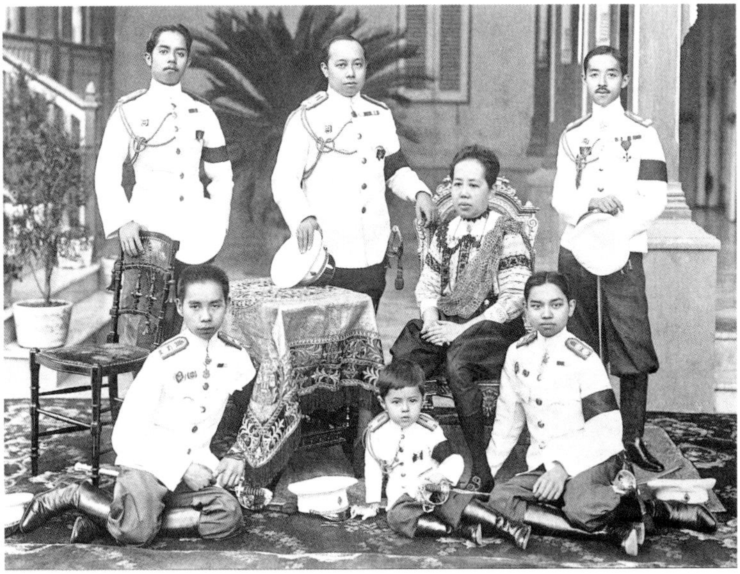

The Queen Mother with her five sons and grandson. Standing from left: Prince Asdang, King Rama VI and Prince Chakrabongse; seated: Prince Chudhadhuj, Prince Chula and Prince Prajadhipok (later King Rama VII). (River Books)

marriage of his brother – Chakrabongse. Although she had already been thus called for four years, his Russian-born sister in-law officially became *Mom* – a title given to a commoner who marries a prince. It is like being called "princess" without the prefix of Royal Highness, and it does not confer any attributes of royalty. It is a title held by Thai women as well. Catherine now received the Chula Chom Klao Order, and her son was recognised as a prince – a *Mom Chao* – namely, of Serene Highness rank. In due course the king gave him the name Chula Chakrabongse, inspired, so he said, by King Chulalongkorn's reigning style of Chula Chom Klao.

As the king was a bachelor, Prince Chakrabongse, who was the next full brother, became Heir Presumptive to the Throne, and the ladies of the Court called him *Toonkramom* only instead of Toonmom Lek as before. As the king naturally hoped to marry and one day have a son and heir of his own, no proclamation was made. He was following the Western system of regarding the next brother of a childless king as automatically the heir. Similarly no proclamation was felt necessary in the reign of King Edward VIII of Britain to the effect that Albert, Duke of York, was his heir. This system was new to Siam, and it gave rise in later years to the idea that Chakrabongse was never at any time heir to the throne. The people, who thought thus, confused his position with that of the *Uparaja* who had to be appointed and proclaimed, but that title had already been long abolished. It appears that Rama VI held a meeting of senior princes[1] at which he produced various items of evidence to show that it had been the intention of King Chulalongkorn that the line of succession should first pass through the descendants of Queen Saowabha. As an absolute Thai monarch this meeting was unnecessary and he could designate his heir or the line of succession as he pleased. But Prince Paribatra was older than Prince Chakrabongse, and Rama VI undoubtedly wanted to rely on the immense moral prestige of his father to keep the Royal Family united on the succession question. One feature of the reign which shows that Prince Chakrabongse was the heir was the fact that, although he never held a ministerial portfolio, he was required to attend cabinet meetings – one of the duties of the Heir.

The Chakri Family have one peculiarity not seen in western royal families, namely that the seniority of princes did not rest on their proximity to the throne in the line of succession, but on their rank, generation, and respective individual age. The equal celestial princes or *Chao Fas* came first, so the senior prince now was Prince Bhanurangsi, the only surviving full paternal uncle of the king. Prince Paribatra (born 1881) came next, followed by Prince Chakrabongse (born 1883) and the other *Chao Fas*. Then came the king's non-celestial uncles and half-brothers, and because they were one generation older, the king's first cousins were senior to his nephews. All but one of the latter were sons of half-brothers, and until 1922 Rama VI had only one full nephew – Chula Chakrabongse.

1 A copy of the report of the meeting, inherited from his father, is in the author's possession.

It was as Heir to the Throne that Chakrabongse was sent to London in 1911 to represent his brother at the coronation of King George V of Britain, which was when he was made a Knight Grand Cross of the Royal Victorian Order.[2] Both in his father's and brother's reigns, Chakrabongse represented the Sovereign at many royal functions, and he received altogether sixteen grand crosses of European countries. While he was away Paruskavan Palace was redecorated, and he now had the whole compound with the two houses as his residence.

During his stay in Europe it was part of Chakrabongse's mission to invite European royalty to Bangkok for the full coronation of King Rama VI in December, 1911. (A quiet religious ceremony had taken place on November 11th, 1910). He discussed the matter with King George V of Great Britain who expressed his regret that his sons were too young to go, the eldest, the Prince of Wales (later Edward VIII) being then only seventeen. Finally George V chose his brother-in-law, Prince Alexander of Teck (later Earl of Athlone), who was accompanied by his beautiful wife, Princess Alice of Albany, a granddaughter of Queen Victoria. Chakrabongse was otherwise also successful. The Emperor of Russia was sending the Grand Duke Boris, the King of Sweden was represented by his younger son, Prince William, whose Russian wife – the Grand Duchess Marie – was a friend of Chakrabongse's from St. Petersburg. Prince Waldemar came on behalf of his brother, the King of Denmark, and he brought two sons with him, one of whom Prince Axel has ever since been a good friend of the Chakri family and of Siam. It was the biggest gathering of European royalty in Asia, and it was further enhanced by the presence of Prince Fushimi of Japan – the most powerful Asian nation.

The ancient rituals of the coronation as revived by Rama I were faithfully carried out as they had been by each Chakri king, and the new reigning title chosen by King Vajiravudh was Phra Mongkut Klao. Prince Chakrabongse told the present author that, being so fond of many European ways, King Mongkut had asked King Chulalongkorn to call his future heir Mongkut so that there would one day be

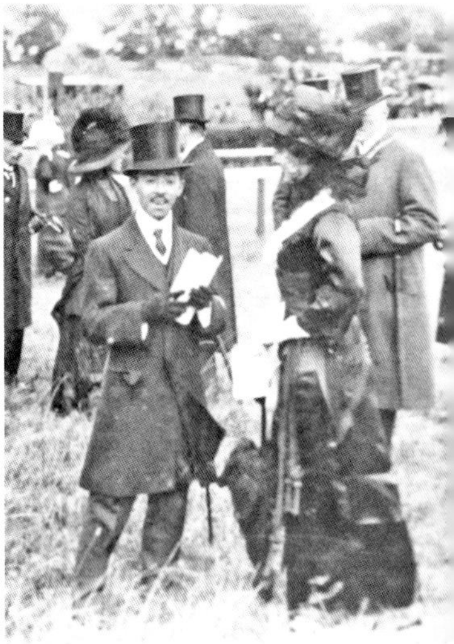

Prince Chakrabongse at one of the events which formed part of the coronation ceremonies for King George V. (River Books)

2 *In The Ceremonies to be observed at the Royal Coronation of Their Majesties King George V and Queen Mary*, 1911. Procession of Royal Representatives, Royal Guests, and their Suites, page 8: "His Royal Highness Prince Chakrabongse of Pitsanulok, Heir Presumptive of Siam."

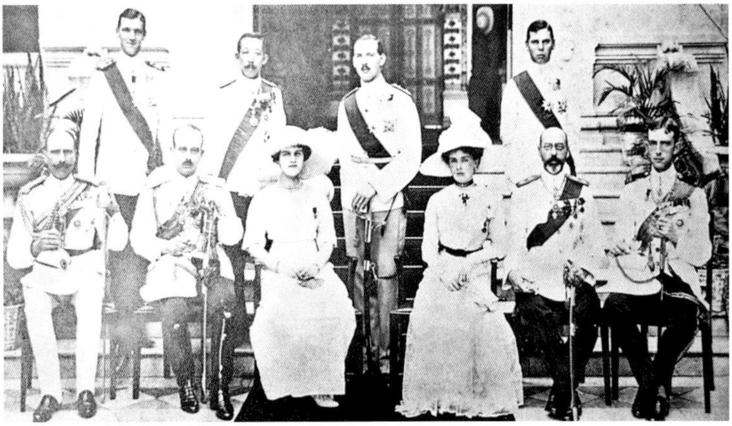

Representatives of foreign heads of state attending the coronation of King Rama VI. Front row, l to r: Prince Alexander of Teck, Grand Duke Boris Vladimirovich of Russia, Princess William of Sweden, Princess Alexander of Teck, Prince Waldemar of Denmark and Prince William of Sweden.
Back row, l to r: Prince Axel of Denmark, Prince Fushimi of Japan, Prince Oke of Denmark and Prince Erik of Denmark. (River Books)

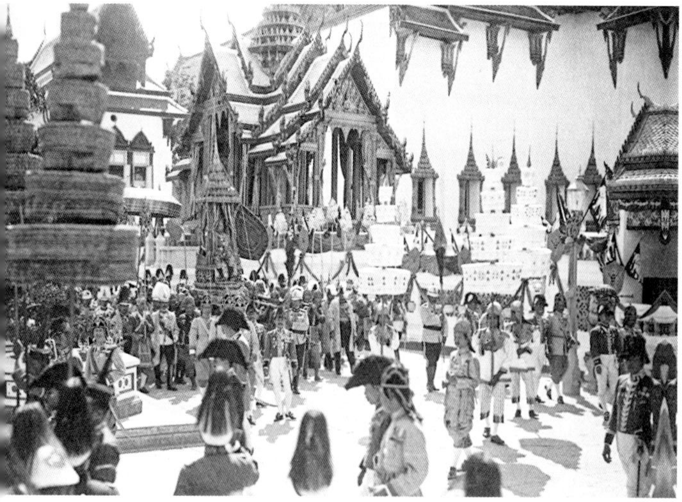

King Rama VI being borne on a palanquin around the Grand Palace to celebrate his cornonation. (River Books)

King Mongkut II as in the European custom. As King Chulalongkorn had failed to carry out this wish, he asked Crown Prince Vajiravudh to use the name Mongkut as his reigning title. Although the new king kept his promise, some years later he preferred to call himself Rama VI, and also changed the names of his five predecessors to Rama. This practice has not been followed in this book for the fourth and fifth kings as they had become so well-known under their old names. Both the father and grandfather of the newly crowned monarch had had as parts of their royal styles "born of royal parents on both sides" and "elected by all the people". For Rama VI the first of these two was retained, but the latter one was altered to "appointed by his royal father". The coronation ceremonies went off to perfection and the only difference from the past was that, besides the king himself and his immediate attendants who were in full royal regalia and ancient dress, everyone else was in the European-style uniforms.

In a polygamous society half-brothers can love each other deeply, but there is naturally a stronger feeling between brothers born of the same mother, and Chakrabongse, in his exultation at seeing his full brother crowned king, wrote to him the same night in English as follows:[3]

"My dear Brother,

Though you have received plenty of congratulations and good wishes today, I think you will not mind receiving a simple but nonetheless hearty expression of congratulations from your loving brother, who has been near you from childhood and has passed through stress and storm with you in Europe and elsewhere.

Though I have had the bitter experience of losing dear Father, but I am extremely satisfied that I saw my beloved brother crowned king today and no other person. May Heaven grant you, my king, long years of peaceful and useful life, a long and prosperous reign, may Heaven grant you the possibilities of fulfilling all your good and *liberal* [my italics] intentions to lead the State towards real progress and that these intentions may not be stifled by anyone, so that our dear country may reach the level of the most forward State and command the respect of the whole world during the reign of King Vajiravudh.

Your affectionate brother and Your Majesty's most obedient and loving servant.

Lek."

3 Members of the Chakri Family have often written to one another in English to avoid the elaborate language required for the different ranks even amongst relatives.

King Vajiravudh promptly replied on the same day and also in English:

"My dear Lek,

I am deeply touched by your personal letter of congratulations on this the greatest day of my life. When the water of consecration fell first upon my head this morning, my tears fell with it. They were tears of mingled joy and sorrow. There is no need to explain further to you, who know my thoughts as I know them myself.

You have always been more than a brother to me, you have been my friend. With you by my side, I feel sure I shall be able to bear the heavy burden of the crown more easily and with greater credit to myself and our family. Just at first things are bound to move rather slowly, because of the many obstacles I have to surmount. We are living in a difficult time, a time when antiquated traditions are struggling against change. But I do not despair. I still hope to live long enough to see the time when Siam shall have truly entered and be honoured in the Family of Nations as an equal in every sense of the word.

Be my friend as you have always been, and we will face the future together.

Your loving brother,
Vajiravudh R."[4]

4 Both original letters in English are in the possession of the author.

The coronation was covered in the press of the day such as *The Illustrated London News.*

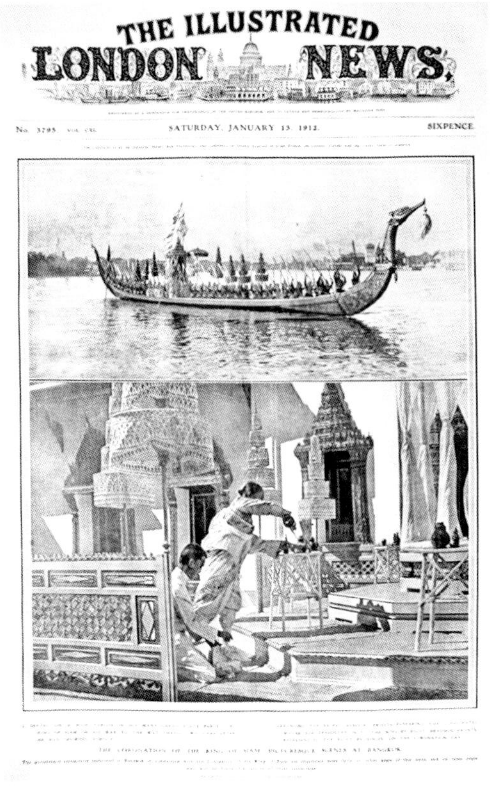
THE ILLUSTRATED LONDON NEWS

No. 3795 VOL. CXL SATURDAY, JANUARY 13, 1912. SIXPENCE

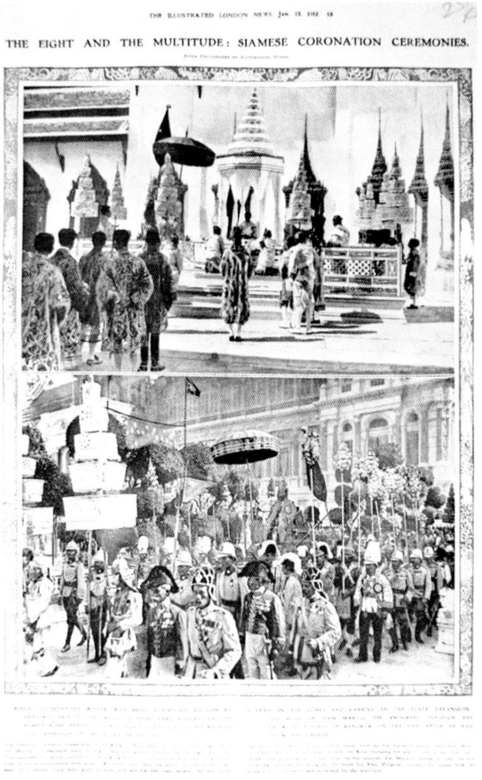
THE EIGHT AND THE MULTITUDE: SIAMESE CORONATION CEREMONIES.

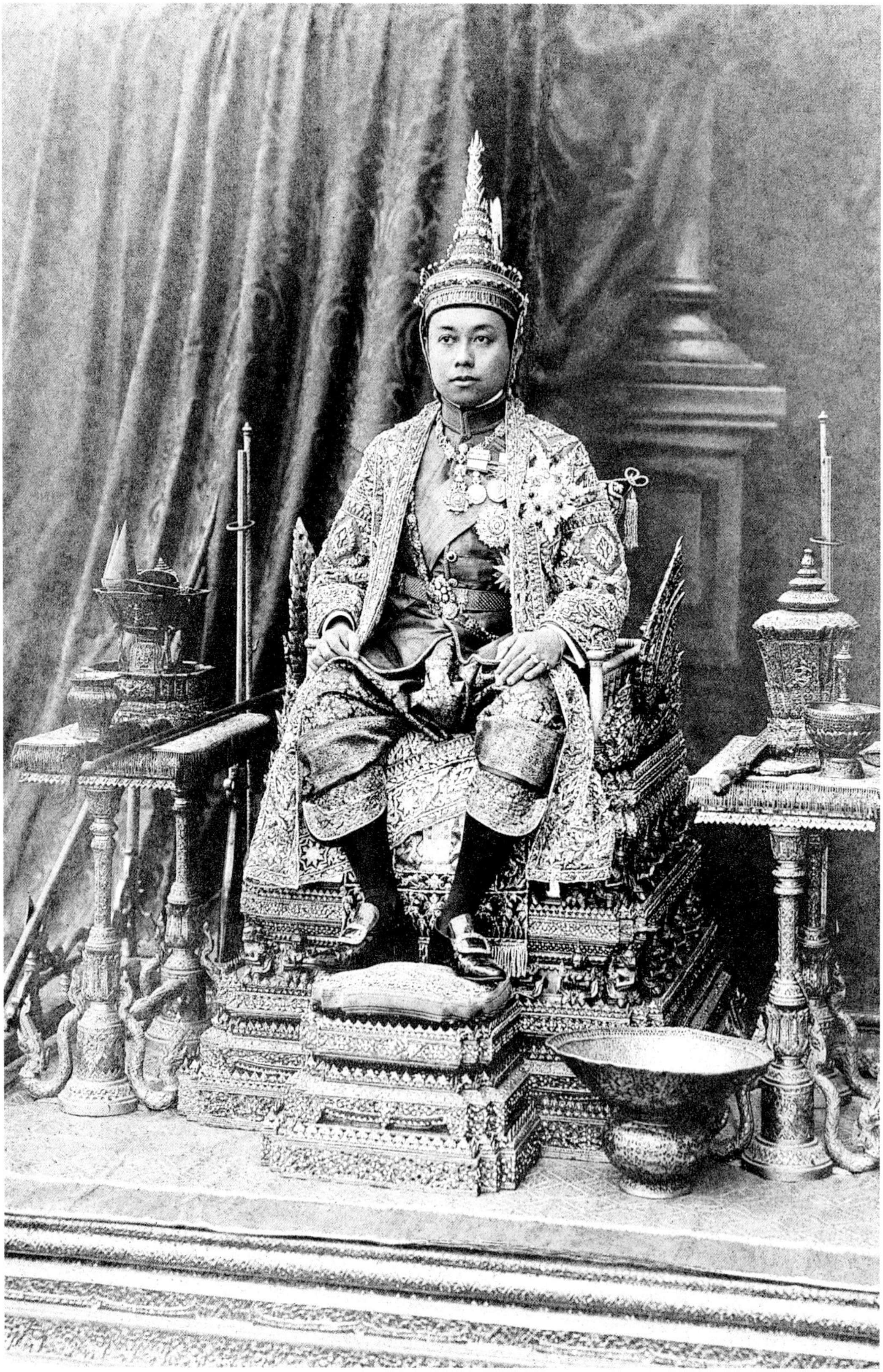

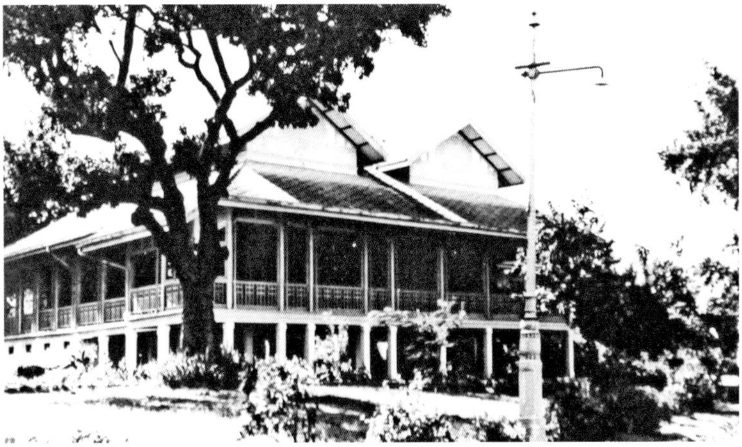

Chakrabongse House, Hua Hin. (River Books)

OPPOSITE: King Rama V in his coronation robes. (Paisarn Piemmettawat)

In the light of subsequent knowledge it is melancholy to reflect that only nine years after this exchange of enthusiastic and hopeful letters, Chakrabongse would be dead, and King Vajiravudh would follow him within five years. It is indeed difficult to write of this sixth Chakri reign without risking rebuke for mentioning Chakrabongse too often. When he wrote the preface to a book distributed at Chakrabongse's cremation in 1920, Rama VI said that it was customary to include a brief biography of the deceased, but this he could not do as he would be writing his own biography as much as part of Thai history.[5]

At the close of the brilliant coronation festivities, the foreign royalty were taken on expeditions into the country with Prince Chakrabongse and his Russian wife as their guides. This resulted in the birth of the now popular seaside resort of Hua Hin near an old fishing village on the west coast of the Gulf of Siam. There Chakrabongse and Catherine found an ideal spot for a camp from which the European princes went forth into the jungle to shoot game of different kinds, from tigers to wild pheasants. The sand on the beach was as white as snow, and Chakrabongse and his wife liked the place so much that they built a house there. Together with Prince Nares, who had also built his place, they began the growth of the seaside resort which has since grown to a large size, with a railway hotel and golf course.

Although the greatest enthusiasm was shown by all classes during the coronation, when he seemed to be riding on the crest of popularity, Rama VI did not enjoy such a happy position for long. Now he is seen as a progressive king, who was a nationalist, a democrat, and a man-of-letters, yet in his own time popularity quickly escaped him, owing partly to his secluded life, as for most of his reign he was unmarried and passed his time amongst courtiers. He showed himself to the people only on important ceremonial occasions, and his private life was shut off from his family and subjects, so much so that between 1910 and 1920 he and a brother as close as Chakrabongse hardly ever had a quiet chat together, let alone a private meal. They met at cabinet meetings, which the king presided over less and less, preferring to work

5 King Rama VI: Preface to *History of Warfare* (in Thai), by Prince Chakrabongse. 2nd Edition. Bangkok, 1920.

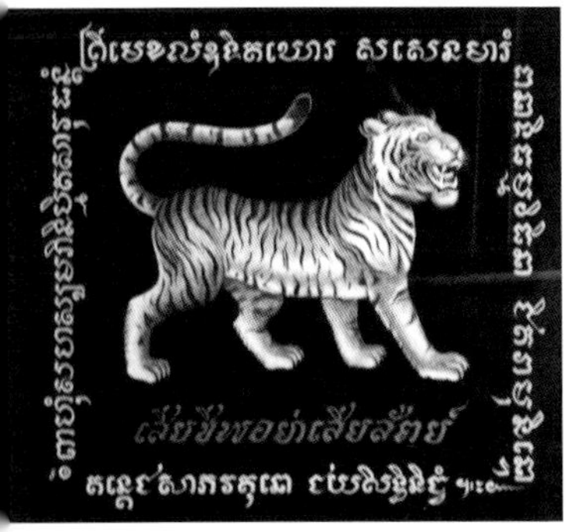

The Wild Tiger Corps flag. (Paisarn Piemmettawat)

directly with individual ministers, or else they met at large family dinners, ceremonies, or receptions when naturally they could never be alone. Instead the brothers wrote to each other intimately and frankly, and Chakrabongse often put forward ideas, some of which were adopted, while others were rejected after clear and patient explanations.[6] In fact, once his inner all-male court was established, Rama VI became increasingly shy of anyone outside his immediate circle, and it seemed that he could only be natural when he put pen to paper.

His contemporary lack of popularity was also due to his being ahead of his time, which caused his people to misunderstand him. By the people – in Siam of those days – one means the officers of the armed forces, the civil servants, some retired members of both, and the small and slowly growing group of professional men – mostly lawyers, and a few Thai merchants. Most of the trade and business were in the hands of Westerners, Chinese, and Indians, who had little or no influence in Thai politics. It was estimated in the Budget Reports of 1925-26 that in 1914 the Chinese sent 126 million baht (then at 13 baht to the £) of their profits to China.

One of the first and major ideas of the king which misfired was the creation of the Wild Tiger Corps. He knew that Siam had escaped European domination by her good fortune in being placed between the rival British and French colonial powers, and through the brilliant, if inglorious, diplomacy of his father and grandfather. Rama VI felt that in his reign liberal thoughts had made such progress in Europe that colonial conquests by force of arms would no longer meet with the support of the European peoples at home. On the other hand, a move to restore order and protect "their interests" in a chaotic country would be well supported by the same people. Thus the continued policy of neutrality must be backed by sufficient force to maintain internal order and spare no excuse for a European power to obtain cheap conquests by means of easy "police actions." In this idea he had the full support of Chakrabongse, who had become Chief of the Army Staff and a general. In the absence in Europe of Prince Chira for health reasons, he was Acting-Minister of Defence. After Prince Chira's death in 1913, an old soldier with a long career, Chao Phraya Bodin, was made Minister of Defence as Rama VI held that it was not suitable for the heir presumptive to have a ministerial portfolio. For the navy, a new Ministry of Marine was created and Prince Paribatra became the Minister. He continued to work hard and was responsible for the construction of the naval dockyard in Bangkok and other useful measures.

Despite a century of almost complete peace which the Thais had enjoyed, they were still a military race at heart, and Rama VI considered the armed forces to be the best rallying point of Thai nationalism which to him spelled unity. As the Chakri paternal monarchy had tried to run the country with the minimum of taxes, the king knew that, although the army was improving all the time, cash was lacking to make it sufficiently strong. He was an admirer of the British Territorial Army, so he decided to supplement the regular army, which consisted of professional officers and N.C.O.s and national service troops, with a volunteer Territorial Army which he maintained out of his Privy Purse.

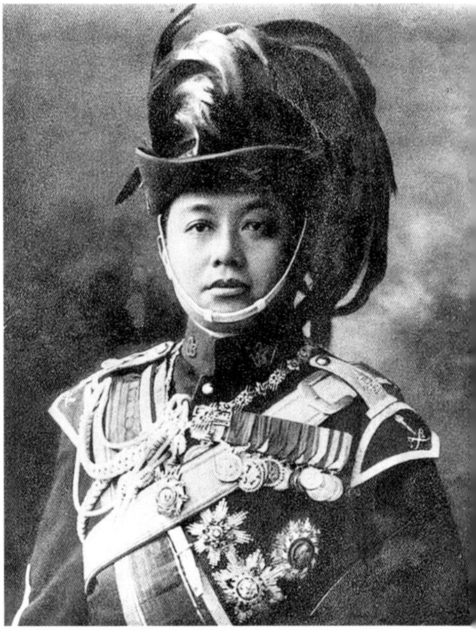

King Rama VI in the uniform of the Wild Tiger Corps. (Paisarn Piemmettawat)

Unlike in Britain his Territorial Army was not placed under the War Office, and its regiments did not form parts of regular regiments as additional 4th or 5th Battalions. Instead Rama VI organized a new force under his own direct command independent of the army and the Ministry of Defence, which he called the Wild Tiger Corps after King Naresuan's guerillas, the Wild Tigers and Peeping Cats. In addition to the provincial regiments, he made the mistake, albeit with a good intentions, in forming a Wild Tiger Brigade of Guards, raised among his courtiers, in which the king took the closest interest. The Bangkok Command of the Wild Tigers had a comfortable and well-equipped clubhouse where the king went most days between 5 and 7 p.m., and it was open to all ranks. There he gave inspiring patriotic lectures and mingled with one and all, such that civil servants and business men hurried to join the Wild Tigers so as to be well within the royal aura. Members of the regular armed forces were excluded, which caused some bitterness until the rules were relaxed and they could join the Wild Tiger Corps itself and not the club only. Furthermore, commissions in the regular forces did not necessarily entail getting one in the Wild Tigers, and there was the odd spectacle of senior military and naval officers appearing on certain evenings dressed as privates in the Wild Tiger Corps. The princes showed their loyalty by accepting honorary colonelship of provincial regiments, and Chakrabongse had the Phitsanulok Regiment.

Some of the dissatisfied elements, mostly military and three naval officers, together with some civilians, had felt confident that King Rama VI would grant a constitution, yet by 1912 there was still no sign of it. They then became restive, with bitterness about the Wild Tigers adding fuel to the fire. In consequence, a plot was prepared to arrest and depose the king. A recently published book by one of the military leaders said that the military conspirators wanted to set up another prince in a limited monarchy, but some of the civilians envisaged a republic.[7]

Prince Chakrabongse had been suspicious for some time and was watching the army closely. Then one of the military leaders became stricken with conscience, confessed, and told him about the whole plot, whereupon its suppression was planned with great care and secrecy. The plot, as Hall[8] says, was "nipped in the bud" by his (the king's) able brother, the Prince of Phitsanulok". The move by the prince on February 27th, 1912, was so rapid that the conspirators were arrested before they even knew that they had been betrayed. When he went to

6 A large collection of the letters of the two brothers, written in their own hand, is in the author's possession.

7 Captain Leng Srichandra: *The Revolution of 1912* (R.S. 130), (in Thai), Bangkok, 2nd Edition, 1946.

8 D. G. E. Hall: *op. cit.,* page 673.

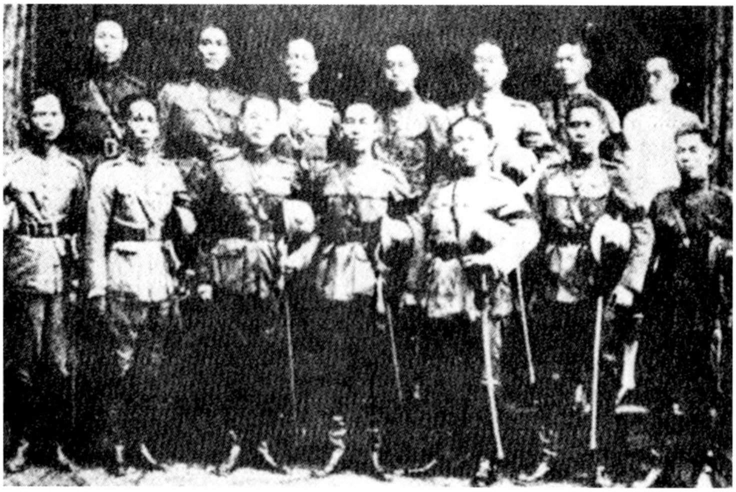

The army officers involved in the coup plot. (National Archives Bangkok)

see the king at a manoeuvre of the Wild Tigers near Nakhon Pathom, he was able to inform his brother that the plot had been suppressed. At the trial which followed some of the rebels were condemned to death according to the law, others to life and other terms of imprisonment, but the king commuted the death sentences. Hall[9] has suggested that there was another military plot in 1917, but neither Prince Dhani[10] nor the present writer can find any trace of it. Hall[11] says that in his lectures Rama VI declared that only Buddhists could be patriots, but Prince Dhani is strongly of the opinion that the king said only that to be without a religion was like being naked, but not that the religion had to be Buddhist.[12] If he had said that, he would have been going back on the attitude of his predecessors.

The Wild Tigers flourished until the end of the reign, but it was never popular, and it was wound up by Rama VI's successor, King Prajadhipok. The real success of the movement was its junior branch – the Tiger Cubs – which was recognized by the World Organization as true Boy Scouts, and today they are one of the best monuments to his memory.

With his English outlook Rama VI wanted the Thais to play football and he chose soccer, believing that it was more suitable to the

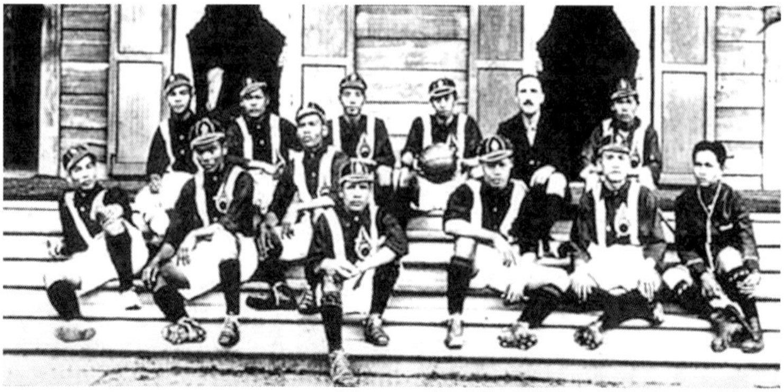

The Wild Tigers football team. (National Archives Bangkok)

climate. Soon clubs and leagues were formed, at first with English schoolmasters and residents as coaches, and in due time matches were played before excited crowds of thousands. Unfortunately the king's enthusiasm for the Wild Tigers intervened, and he wanted the teams of their Guards Regiments to win always. This meant that good players in rival clubs were lured away and given minor posts at Court so that they could join those regiments. The fact that cups were constantly won by the king's Wild Tigers caused discontent. However, in time feelings mellowed and soccer became popular, with rugby football now a close rival.

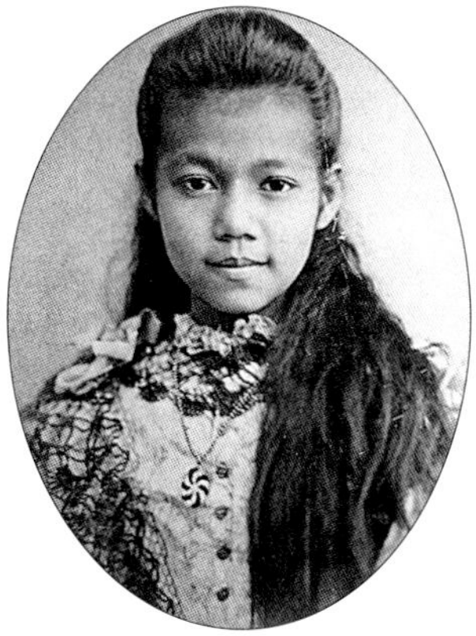

Princess Valayalongkorn with her long hair. (National Archives Bangkok)

Like the army, the navy was a conscript force, the men mostly coming from seaside towns and villages, and they were considered tough in mind and body, while the officers, mostly products of the Bangkok Naval College, with a few who had been in the British and Danish Navies, were also looked upon as being tough, having modelled themselves on their professional chief, Prince Abhakorn, and they were often suspected of being ready to join any unruly elements. In fact, Prince Abhakorn himself was unjustly suspected of plotting against the king in 1912, and troubles came to a head when one of the king's pistols was lost when he was cruising in the Gulf of Siam in the royal yacht. Prince Abhakorn was retired from the navy which caused Prince Paribatra much grief, but the Navy Minister was persuaded by naval friends not to resign.[13] It has been stated that only three naval officers were really involved in the plot, and they were handed over by Prince Paribatra to Prince Chakrabongse to be tried with the military.

One of the instantly popular and lasting reforms of Rama VI concerned women. Thai women of the central region – forming the majority – had for some time worn their hair almost as short as men and were dressed in the "plus-fours" – like *panung*. The king persuaded them via his writings to wear their hair long and to dress in skirts like the Laotian women of the north, but soon the fashion changed to Western styles. One of the first women to have long hair was Princess Valaya (born 1884), the only surviving daughter of Queen Sawang.

Literature was one of Rama VI's greatest loves, and he is recognized as one of the major Thai poets of his day, yet it must be confessed that his style was academic, and, apart from patriotic songs, his poetry lacked deep feeling. His knowledge of English was perfect and he was especially impressed with the works of Shakespeare, and his translation of three of the master's plays were not only close in idiom and accurate even to punctuation, but were also poetic. While a student in England he had loved the theatre, and back in Siam he wrote or translated from English and French, of which he also had good knowledge, nearly one hundred plays. His attempt to create a Thai theatre on Western lines did not succeed, although he acted in many of his plays himself with his company of amateurs, giving the proceeds to charities, which caused much adverse criticism as people were distressed to see their revered monarch perform on the stage. Despite

9 D. G. E. Hall: *op. cit.*, page 673.

10 Prince Dhani: Notes to the author in 1958.

11 D. G. E. Hall: *op. cit.*, page 673.

12 Prince Dhani: same notes.

13 Princess Prasong Paripatra: *Memoirs, op. cit.*, page 17.

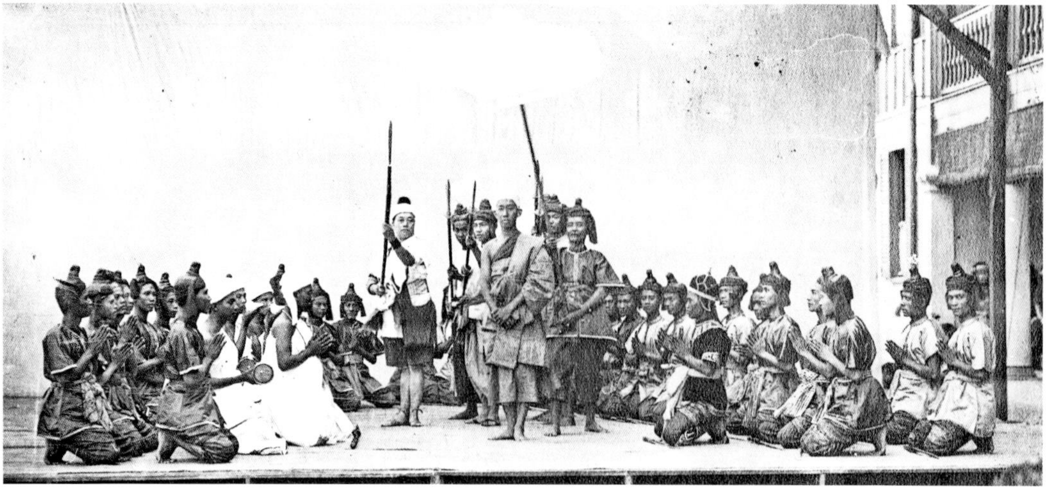

The king acting in a play about King Ramkhamhaeng in his seaside palace, Maruekhathaiyawan. (National Archives Bangkok)

his encouragement, the theatre in Western style has not made any progress beyond amateur clubs, and the bulk of Thais prefer their traditional ballet in different forms with intervals of buffoonery by clowns and comics.

One of the major events in the reign of Rama VI took place in 1916 with the enactment of a law requiring all families to have surnames – another successful and lasting reform. The king himself, the princes, and the high officials were besieged with requests to invent surnames for countless families. The king had a department to help him think up names, but others had to do it themselves – an arduous task.

It was early in this reign – in 1911 to be precise – that a French pilot first brought an aeroplane to Bangkok for demonstrations, and Prince Chakrabongse and Prince Purachatra, in uniform with riding boots and spurs, went up with him one at a time, but no record exists to show who went up first, and it will never be known who was the first Thai to leave the ground in an aeroplane. Prince Chakrabongse had no doubts about the future of aviation for military and civil purposes, and, as Chief of the Army Staff, he was instrumental in sending four young officers to France to leam to fly. Upon their return a flying section was formed under the auspices of the Engineers under the command of Prince Purachatra. When the section was enlarged into the Flying Corps, it was transferred to the command of the Chief of Staff – Prince Chakrabongse. It was he who chose Don Muang as the first airfield, later to be the airport of Bangkok, and his statue now stands in front of the civil side of the combined airfield. After his death, Prince Paribatra, who took his place, was equally enthusiastic and did much for the advancement of Thai aviation.

The Queen Saowabha Memorial Institute. (River Books)

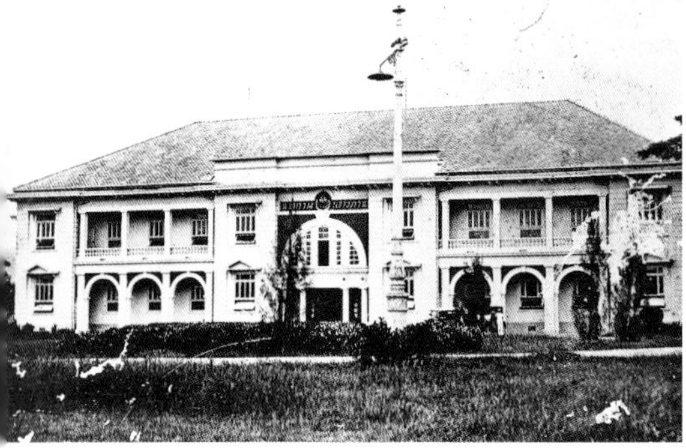

The year 1912 saw a severe outbreak of smallpox which greatly distressed the king, and he ordered the Ministries of Interior and Local Government (Bangkok)

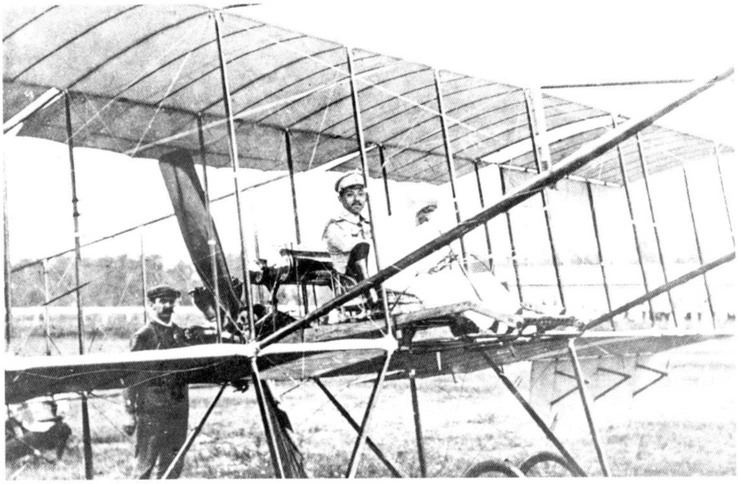

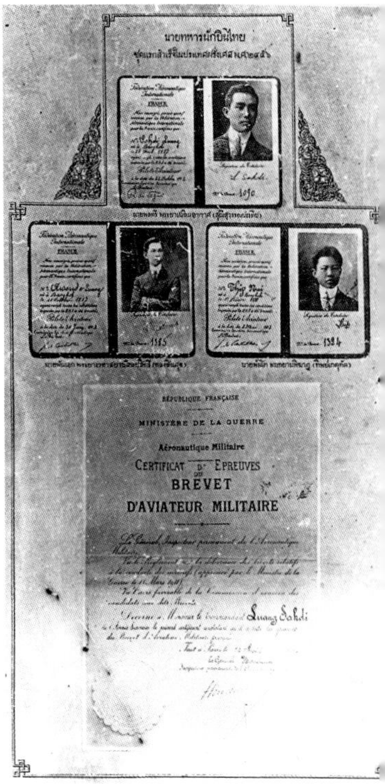

ABOVE: Passports of the three army officers sent to train as aviators in France. (National Museum Bangkok)

ABOVE LEFT: Prince Chakrabongse in the biplane. (River Books)

to consult one another on immediate measures to suppress the disease. It was decided not to use compulsion, but rather persuasion, to get people to come forward to be vaccinated, and the king contributed a large sum from the Privy Purse towards the heavy expenses. The campaign was a success and thenceforth vaccination became universally popular, and in time smallpox was almost entirely eliminated. Rama VI was also much concerned with the incidence of rabies in Siam, and he was active with the help of Prince Damrong, one of whose daughters died of the dread disease, in founding the Pasteur Institute in Bangkok. At first staffed with French doctors, it is now in Thai hands, where there is also a snake farm for preparing serums against poisonous snake bites. The Institute also served as a memorial to the king's mother, Queen Saowabha.[14]

It was on the initiative of Rama VI that the huge surplus of money subscribed for King Chulalongkorn's equestrian statue was spent to found Chulalongkorn University, and he donated a large plot of highly valuable Privy Purse land for the purpose. He also founded the Royal Pages School on English public school lines, which, after his demise, became known as Vajiravudh College – a worthy memorial.

It has been said earlier in this chapter that Rama VI had succeeded to a noble and well secured heritage, and this is particularly true with regards to finance. The actual figures for the first year of the reign showed the revenue at 63.5 million baht (a 3 million baht increase) against an expenditure of 59 million, giving a surplus of 4.5 million baht. The Prince of Chantaburi was still Minister of Finance, and the Englishman, W. J. F. Williamson, remained the Financial Adviser. There were the first signs of the king's increasing requirements for the expenses of the Royal Household, and the Civil List was now

14 Prince Damrong: *Tales of Olden Times, op. cit.*, pages 206-213.

Vajiravudh College. (National Archives Bangkok)

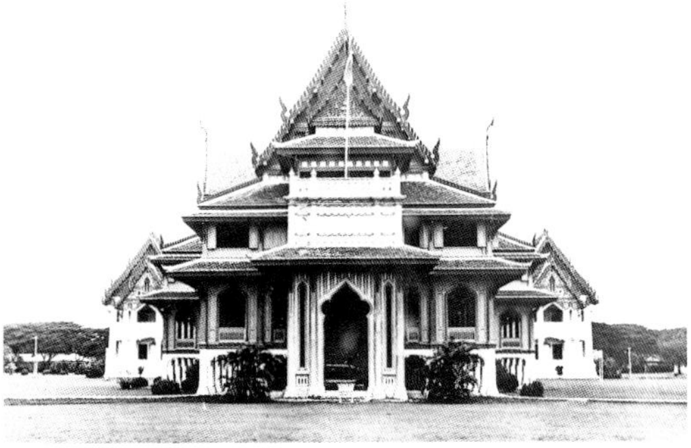

7 million. But the king would claim that the Court was still the centre of the arts and culture of the country, and the training ground for future administrators who were seeing the king daily at close quarters, and therefore would better understood his progressive and liberal policies for the betterment of the people.

In the second year – 1911-12 – the national account showed a deficit of 2.5 million owing to the king's coronation, which cost over 3 million, and unfortunately it had taken place in a year of poor rice crops following a partial drought. But the enormous reserves built up in his father's reign could easily take care of that, and there was in this year an important financial event, namely the founding of a Treasury Savings Bank, which owed its inception to Rama VI's personal initiative.[15] The bank was to continue to grow larger in the number of deposits from year to year. By the following year the situation was back to normal when the actual revenue exceeded estimates by 5.5 million and there was a comfortable surplus of nearly 3.5 million baht. The country's trade was highly satisfactory, with exports exceeding imports by some 25 million, and the purchasing power of the baht had improved after a good harvest. The exchange rate was strong because of large gold standard reserves in London of over one million pounds sterling.

Rama VI was himself a *liberal* idealist, but to carry on without heavy direct taxes, the government had derived a good income from duties paid by Chinese gambling houses and from the sale of government owned opium purchased from abroad. The king was convinced of the evils of these two sources of State income and he sought to abolish them forthwith. As the *Lord of Life* he should have been able to do so, but the Minister of Finance and his English adviser stated that it was not yet possible because other sources of revenue could not be found to replace them. King Chulalongkorn had already abolished gambling houses in the provinces, now Rama VI wanted the Bangkok ones closed, but he was told quite plainly that it could not be done until the great Western powers would lift the limit of import duties set at three per cent *ad valorem* by the treaties signed over fifty years ago in the reign of his grandfather, King Mongkut. Negotiations with the great powers over this matter had failed, but the king nevertheless insisted on closing down six of the Bangkok gambling houses, thus leaving only five. In 1914-15 these provided only 6.7 million baht out of the total revenue of 73.9 millions. By April 1st, 1917, Rama VI had his way and all gambling houses were finally closed down.

Siam already had a much enlarged State railway system which was a paying concern, as noted by the Financial Adviser: "In its railway property, the government possesses an asset of considerable value which brings in an appreciable and steadily increasing revenue."[16] By then, and at Prince Chakrabongse's suggestion, the army had lent Prince Purachatra to run the railways, which he did with great enthusiasm and ability.

15 *Report of the Financial Adviser, 1913-1914*, W. J. F. Williamson.

16 *Report of the Financial Adviser, 1917-1918*, W. J. F. Williamson.

Although he was surrounded by many princes and princesses of an age senior to him, including his full paternal uncle – Prince Bhanurangsi – there is no doubt that amongst the elders Rama VI loved and respected most were his mother, Queen Saowabha, and his half-uncle, the Prince Patriarch Vajirayana, who had initiated him into temporary priesthood when he was Crown Prince. The Prince Patriarch resided at Wat Bowonniwet, the monastery of the Excellent Abode, where his father – King Mongkut – had once been the abbot as he now was. Regardless of his higher rank in the Buddhist Church, an abbot always remained the abbot of his own monastery.

In the absence of a queen consort, during the coronation festivities the Queen Mother was one of the central figures next only to the king himself. Beside other occasions the public saw her during the review of the troops when the king and the princes, Thai and foreign, were all mounted. Queen Saowabha sat in an open carriage drawn by four horses, and on her lap was her only grandchild – Chula Chakrabongse.[17] She had taken the death of her husband very badly, and after the cremation she was persuaded to go on a cruise in the yacht *Maha Chakri*, accompanied by her grandson, but the ceremonies for the coronation of her eldest son did much to occupy and console her.

Residing usually at Phaya Thai Palace, she maintained a large establishment and most of her entourage were women, all her ladies-in-waiting being of noble birth, but unlike those at European courts, they did not only attend the Queen on official occasions, but actually lived in and looked after her, while they themselves were attended to by ordinary domestics. Over the entire establishment presided Lady Pam Malakul, whose brother, Chao Phraya Dharma, was the King's Minister of the Royal Household. King Chulalongkorn had hardly ever gone to bed before 3 a.m., so Queen Saowabha was firmly entrenched in that habit; and now that she was a widow, she completely turned night into day, and except on special occasions when she felt she should attend some important functions, she slept all day and quiet descended on Phaya Thai like the palace of the Sleeping Beauty. Her grandson did not go there until the evening, and after two hours of fun with his playmates, he would have time for a chat with her before going to sleep on a mattress on the floor behind her bed.

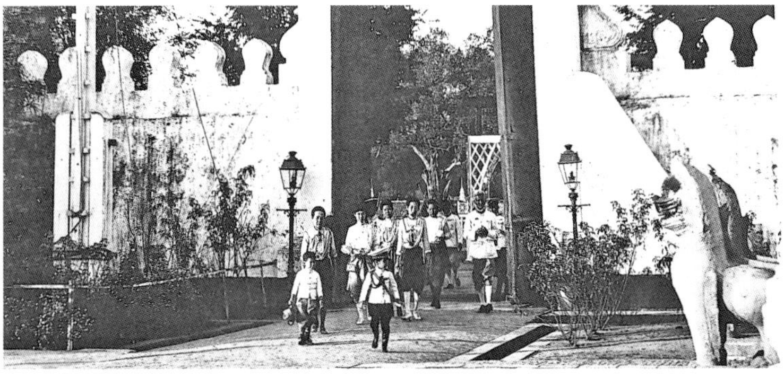

Queen Saowabha walking in the Old Palace at Ayutthaya with Princess Valaya and the author. (River Books)

17 From a personal letter to the author from H.R.H. Princess Alice of Albany, Countess of Athlone, October 23rd, 1959.

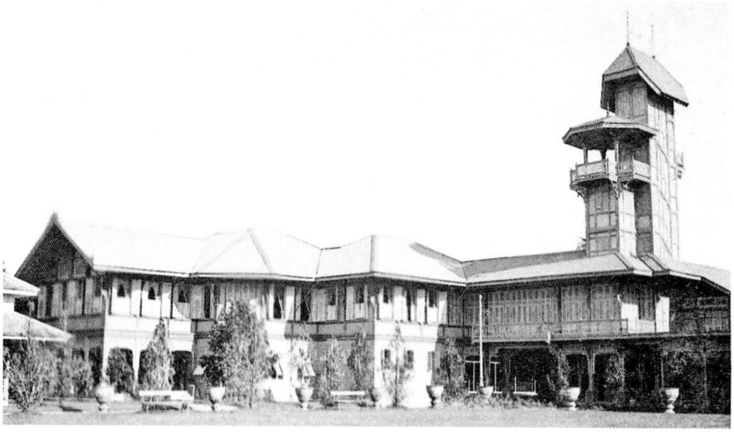

Phaya Thai Palace, where Queen Saowabha spent the last years of her life. (National Archives Bangkok)

As time went on the queen became more and more bedridden, taking her meals on the bed, with breakfast at about 10.30 p.m. Visitors began to arrive after 11 p.m., and animated conversation went on all night, for she was keenly interested in every topic and her mind was fully active. Some of the time she would be working on her Red Cross affairs, the governing of the Grand Palace which the king placed in her care, the distribution of Orders for ladies, or her household business. She had her lunch or dinner at 2.30 a.m., and the last visitors left at 5 a.m. shortly after the queen herself went to sleep. Her sons went to see her often except the king, who only did so about every four months. When he did, it was an occasion when many of the young princesses and ladies of high-birth hoped to catch his eye for marriage, but it was of no avail. Queen Saowabha's niece, Princess Valaya, lived with her at Phaya Thai, and somewhat confusingly called her "Mother", and called her own mother, Queen Sawang, "Aunt".

By 1918 the Queen Mother's health took a sharp decline; she hardly ever got out of bed and spent more and more time sleeping. Even her favourite son, Chakrabongse, often had to wait for hours before seeing her. "Why don't you complain?" asked Dr. Smith, who was her English physician. "After all, she's your mother." "Yes, but she IS also the Queen Mother," replied the Prince, "and that makes it quite different."[18] Queen Saowabha had an unexpected passion for cars of different makes, sizes, and prices. She kept a few cheaper ones for her household use, while remaining faithful herself to a huge red Napier of a type which was a forerunner of the present-day station wagon or shooting brake. Round about the London Motor Show time she read the English magazines, *The Motor* and *The Autocar,* assiduously, and she ordered several cars each year, mostly from England. Once arrived in Bangkok they were paraded before her, then she would give most of them away to her sons, brothers, and friends. She prided herself on her ability to choose the right type of car for each person's needs and means to maintain it. She was not only generous with cars, she was generous with everything, giving away houses, plots of land, furniture

18 Dr. Smith: *op. cit.*, page 116.

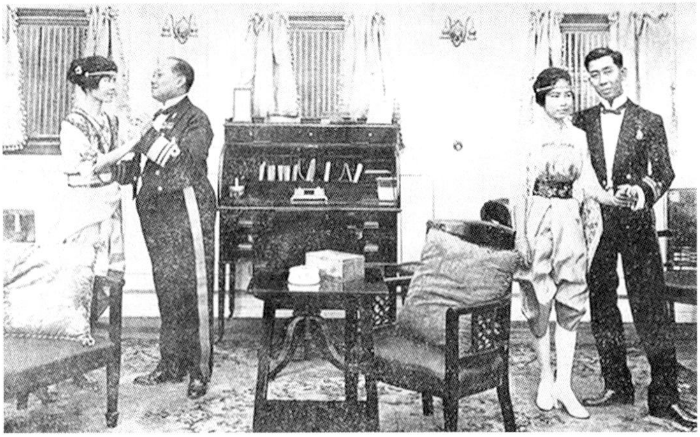

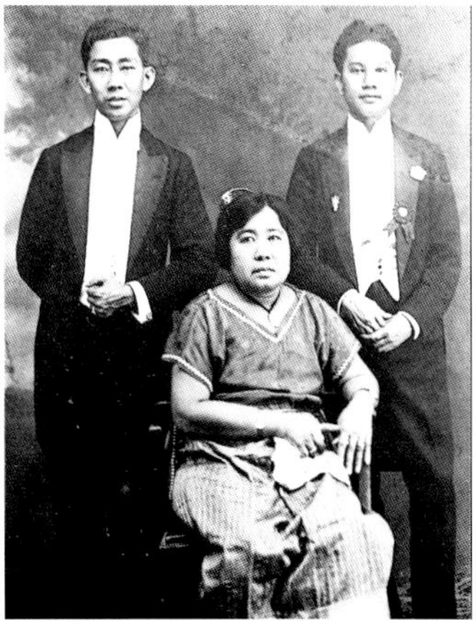

and jewellery. When she died, apart from the fabulous amount of jewellery which she had received from King Chulalongkorn, she left comparatively little capital. Her public charities have already been recounted in the previous chapter.

For those who had to work by day, going often to see the Queen Mother was hardship. This was especially so for Prince Chakrabongse, who often left his mother at 5 a.m. and went straight to watch troops training at 6 a.m. After a bath and change at home, he would be in his office by 10 a.m. The person who should have minded her odd hours the least was the king, who himself turned night into day. Although there were many brilliant personalities at his Court, two brothers especially shone far above others. They were from a collateral branch of the Royal Family, being of *Mom Luang* rank, and descendants of Rama I's 34th son. They were called Feua and Fuen Puengbun and were completely devoted to the sovereign, looking after his every mood, wish, or whim, and almost knowing what he wanted before he asked for it. Not surprisingly they gained his complete confidence, love, and friendship. They were his closest companions in all his interests and enterprises, especially the Wild Tiger Corps and play-act ing. In return for their selfless service, honours and riches were

ABOVE, FROM LEFT: Chao Phraya Ram Rakop (M.L Feua Puengbun), Tao Indra Suriya (M. L. Cheua Puengbun) and Phraya Anirudh Deva (M. L. Fuen Puengbun). (National Archives Bangkok)

ABOVE LEFT: King Rama VI acting in the play *Pongpang* with Chao Phraya Ram Rakop. The king was acting with his fiancé Princess Vallabha Devi. The other female part was played by Princess Lakshami Lawan. (National Archives Bangkok)

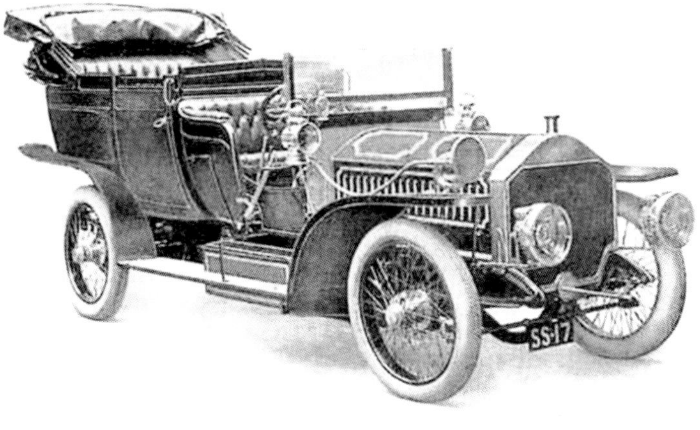

A Napier car of the type owned by Queen Saowabha. *(Autocar)*

showered on them, for Rama VI inherited to the full his mother's generosity. The elder brother became a general in the army and Chief A.D.C. to the king, yet keeping full control of the Inner Court (Department of *Mahadlek),* assisted by his younger brother as his deputy. For most of the reign it was difficult, if not impossible, for anyone to approach the king except with their help. M.L. Feua finally achieved the highest title of nobility as Chao Phraya Ram Rakop, while Fuen became Phraya Anirudh Deva. It was truly remarkable that these two men still found time to lead their own lives, meet young women and marry and have families.

When World War I broke out in August, 1914, Rama VI's government declared itself neutral, which was only natural as far as the Thai people were concerned. But there were a few Thais who were positively pro-Allies, and the most ardent of these was Rama VI himself. He sent a large donation to the welfare fund of his old English regiment, the Durham Light Infantry, and he subscribed to many Allies' charities. He wrote pro-Allies articles in the newspapers under different assumed names, as well as translating both general and technical war articles from English magazines, all of which were favourable to the British cause. Although all of these were printed under many different assumed names, everyone knew from the style that they were written by the king. Of course, he continued to receive the German and Austrian Ministers at Court, yet he was reluctant to attend any functions organized by them for their charities, while treating the British Minister as a personal friend. Even the French felt themselves rather left out in the cold, and to redress the balance Prince Chakrabongse made it his business to be extra friendly to them. With his close Russian connections he was pro-Allies himself, while Prince Paribatra, despite his German education, remained quiet and tactful. If he could have had his way, Rama VI would probably have joined the Allies from the beginning, but even the *Lord of Life* had to heed public opinion. The Thai people still felt resentment against the French for having taken a large part of Thai territory, and although there was less ill feeling against the British, there was a suspicion that the only reason they had not harmed Siam was because of some bargaining and understanding between them and the French. The Germans, on the other hand, had never done Siam any wrong, and they were known to the Thais only as friendly traders selling the kind of goods which most appealed to them. British goods were considered to be of the highest class, but they were too expensive for the majority, while German goods were cheaper and almost as durable.

The war brought some of the king's younger celestial brothers who were being educated in Europe back to Siam a few years earlier than otherwise would have been the case. The first to arrive was Prince Prajadhipok (born 1893), the youngest son of Queen Saowabha, who was then twenty-two. In England he had been at Eton and the Royal Military Academy, Woolwich, where he was happy and successful.

He was commissioned in the Royal Horse Artillery, and when war came he was enthusiastic to go to France with his battery. Years later King George V told the present writer that Prince Prajadhipok tried in every way to get to the war. Lunching one day with the king at the Aldershot Royal Pavilion, he begged for royal help. "I told him I was sorry," the king went on, "you're not a subject, you can't go." As there was nothing for him to do in England, he returned home to join the Thai Army and served as a subaltern in the 1st Regiment of Artillery. Until he was married and had a home of his own, Prince Prajadhipok lived with his mother at Phaya Thai.

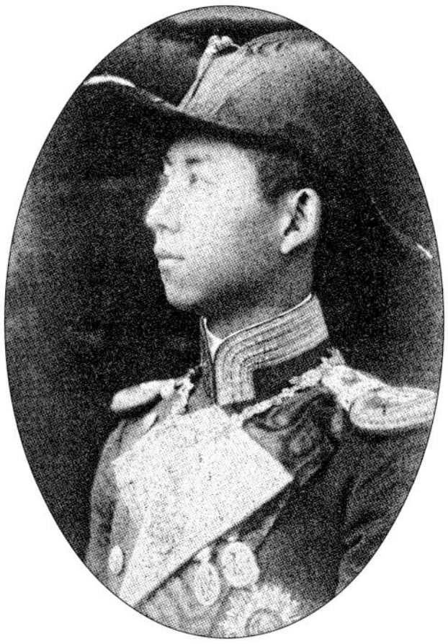

Prince Mahidol.
(Paisarn Piemmettawat)

Prince Mahidol (born 1892), the only surviving son of Queen Sawang, returned shortly after him. Although he was a half-brother of Chakrabongse, their relationship was close because they were also cousins, their mothers being sisters. He and Chakrabongse were the best of friends, and he was extremely fond of Catherine, who once nursed him through a dangerous illness. Prince Mahidol was extremely handsome with seemingly a fine physique, though actually his health was poor. He had first been to Harrow School in England before he was transferred to the German navy. He had just been commissioned when the war caused him to leave, and he returned home to join the Thai navy and lived with his mother at Sapatoom Palace. Queen Saowabha's third son, Asdang (born 1889), did not like England and returned very early to undergo a Thai military education. When the war came he was a battalion commander in the 1st Regiment of Foot Guards. It was not until 1918 that the Queen Mother's fourth son, Chudadhuj (born 1892), came back from England. He had been at Magdalene College, Cambridge, and being musical and artistic, he was the only one of her sons who was not a soldier. He took the liveliest interest in the School of Arts and Crafts, and in the Thai classical ballet and traditional music.

Despite being a soldier Rama VI was proud of his navy, and he liked to go to sea and watch naval exercises as much as he enjoyed army manoeuvres directed by Chakrabongse, and those of the Wild Tigers directed by himself. The army manoeuvres were family affairs, for Queen Saowabha also went to watch as four of her sons took part. Besides the king and Chief of Staff, who was Director, Asdang was a battalion commander and Prajadhipok an artillery subaltern or captain. The Queen Mother followed the army exercises by boat along the river and was carried to different prepared covered stands where she watched with a large party. The navy then consisted of coastal gunboats and small torpedo boats, all of which were remarkably well handled. In the war the king was impressed by the exploits of the German light cruiser *Emden,* which went so far east as to bombard Penang. As he had it in mind to join the Allies one day, if there was a Thai light cruiser which could attempt such deeds on its own, it would bring lustre to the country's name. As there was no money to buy such a vessel without extra taxes, Rama VI formed a Navy League to collect

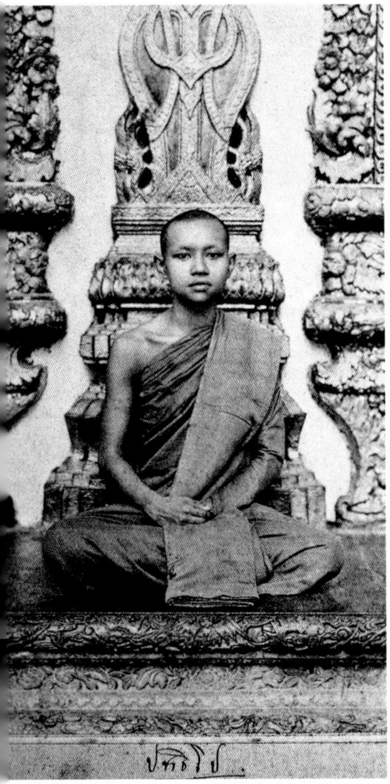

Prince Prajadhipok while in the monkhood. (National Archives Bangkok)

money by public subscription. The heads of different departments of the government service and governors of provinces, in order to please the king, semi coerced the people to subscribe, which made the whole idea unpopular, and Rama VI's attempt had misfired again. Finally only enough money was collected by the end of the war to purchase an old British destroyer which was named *Phra Ruang* after the early Thai hero-king of the Sukhothai period. In war-time Prince Abhakorn, who had led an eventful retired life as a quack doctor and a patron of pugilists, was recalled to the navy, and it was he who went to England to bring the *Phra Ruang* back to Bangkok.

In August, 1917, the king's youngest full-brother, Prajadhipok, became a monk for three months and resided at the monastery of the Excellent Abode under the supervision of the Prince Patriarch Vajirayana. The Patriarch knew English well, although he spoke it with a completely Thai accent, and like his father, King Mongkut, he enjoyed religious discussions with visiting Christian priests and clergy and usually surprised them with his knowledge of comparative religion. Towards the end of Prajadhipok's sojourn in the monastery, the Patriarch sent for him and pointed out that the young Prinee Priest was the *fourth* full-brother of the monarch, thus he was not likely to attain a high position in the Army or Civil Service, for good positions would be taken by his elder brothers and half-brothers. Would it not be wise, he asked, to stay on in the priesthood permanently, and perhaps one day himself become the Prince-Patriarch for the good of Siam and the Chakri Family? The bhikkhu Prajadhipok agreed in principle, but regretted that it was impossible in practice as he was already in love with a girl before taking the yellow robe.[19] Strangely enough within eight years all his brothers would be dead and he would himself become king. Although the young prince's term in the yellow robe gave great happiness to his mother, it completely ruined his health, as, having already had weak digestion, not eating between midday and early the next morning made it worse, and he was never properly fit again.

In 1918 Prince Prajadhipok's great love for his beautiful first cousin, Princess Rambai Barni, a daughter of Prince Svasti and therefore a niece of Queen Saowabha, reached its happy culmination in their marriage. The Queen Mother was so delighted that all the women guests at the wedding were given diamond rings. Prince Prajadhipok, already

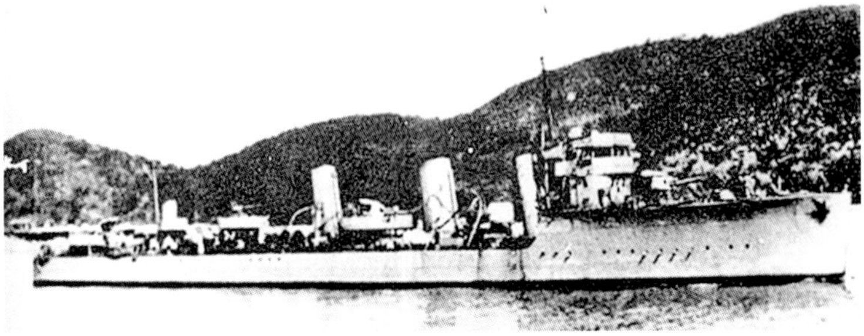

The destroyer *Phra Ruang* bought from the British navy. (National Archives Bangkok)

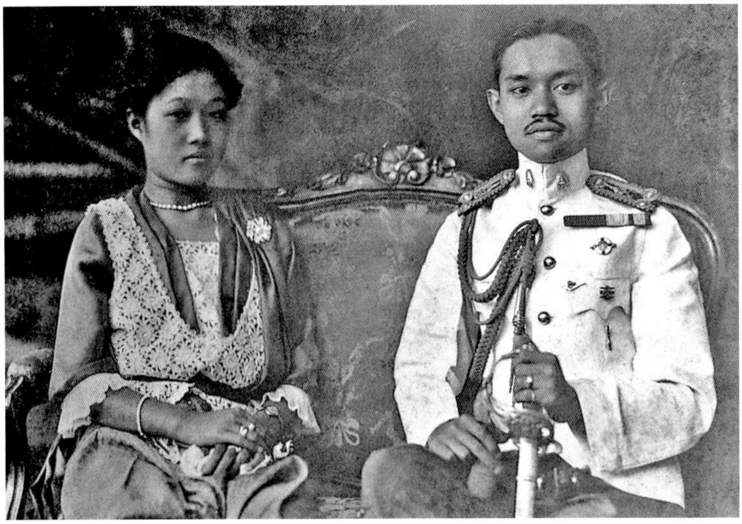

Prince Prajadhipok and Princess Rambai Barni after their wedding. (Paisarn Piemmettawat)

a captain for some time, was then promoted major, and he was transferred from the artillery to command the Junior Military School.

Harking back to 1917, Prince Chakrabongse and his wife nearly went to Russia in that year as the Emperor Nicholas II had invited the prince to visit him at the front, and King Rama VI had given permission. All was ready for the trip when news came of the Russian Revolution and the Emperor's abdication. How Catherine felt about the whole thing can be easily imagined, for apart from being worried about her former country, she was also anxious about her relatives.

By 1917 the king had received full support from all sides in his determination to join the Allies; and the United States of America, when declaring war on the Central Powers, sent a circular appeal to all neutral countries to join in the struggle to support Right against Might. Chakrabongse was enthusiastic, and Robert-Martignan[20] went so far as to say of him: "The Prince of Phitsanulok, the principal and prime mover of the alliance, showed his most clairvoyant sense." Under his direction all Germans and Austrians were quickly arrested and interned, while the Thai navy rapidly seized and took over some forty German merchant ships which had taken refuge in the neutrality of the Bangkok river. The German crews tried to blow the ships up, but in nearly all cases their attempts were foiled, and the ships were taken intact to form the nucleus of the future merchant fleet. Although well looked after and satisfied, the European internees were then sent to India to be interned by the British at their persistent request. It was believed that the British did not relish the idea of white men – albeit enemy subjects – being kept under the direct supervision of Asians.

Prince Chakrabongse put his heart and soul into the war effort, and if possible he would have liked to see at least a Thai mixed brigade in France, commanded probably by himself. In this hope he was fully supported by the king, for they had plenty of men who were intensely

19 This was told to the author by King Prajadhipok himself.

20 Robert-Martignan: *op. cit.*, page 294.

keen to go, and they only lacked modern equipment. If they had gone they would have been the only Asian troops of an independent Asian nation fighting in Europe. The Japanese, although allies, sent no troops to Europe, the Chinese were only there as a labour corps, and all fighting Asian troops came from colonies of the Western Powers. There seemed to be a complicated kind of colour bar, and the Allies were not prepared to equip a full fighting force from Siam. Instead they said they would accept a motor transport corps, and were finally persuaded to have air pilots also. At this point, the king decided that the entire expeditionary force was to be composed of volunteers, and the regular forces volunteered to a man, with thousands of civilians also pouring into the recruiting offices. The king thanked everyone by a circular letter, and eventually about 1,200 men were accepted. Prince Chakrabongse took the closest interest in their training, clothing, and equipment, then went to see them off in their ship at Paknam. He reminded them that they were going to Europe as representatives of the Thai people as a whole. The men acquitted themselves well; but those aspiring to be pilots were still being trained and acclimatized in the south of France when the Armistice came in November, 1918, and they never saw any action. They returned home to serve in the gradually enlarged Air Force. The Motor Transport Corps operated with the French Army under heavy shell-fire before crossing the Rhine into Germany after the Armistice with other allied forces. It was during their stay in France that the Thai men became friendly with U.S. troops, a friendship which has endured to this day. There were Thai contingents in the victory marches in Paris, London, and Brussels. When they got back to Bangkok big parades and receptions were organized for them, and the king was magnificent on these occasions with his patriotic speeches. He had been made an honorary general in the British Army, which pleased him. He made his brother a Field Marshal, which did not please Prince Chakrabongse, who felt that no one should receive a baton without having been in action.

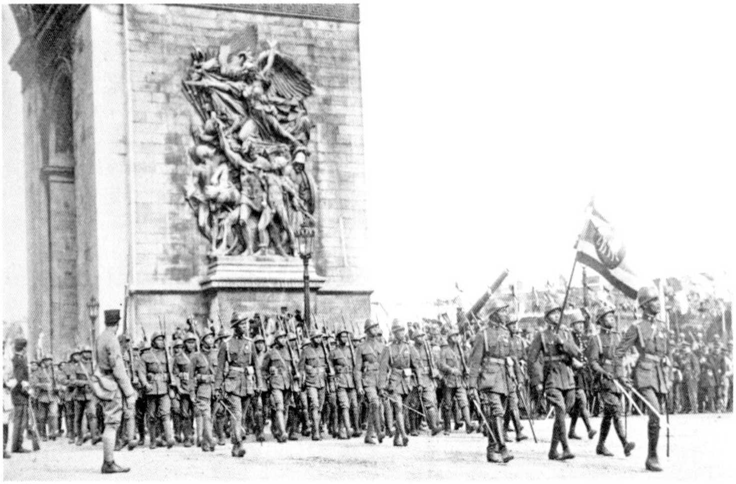

The Thai Expeditionary Force participating in the Victory Parade on the Champs Élysées on 14th July 1919. (River Books)

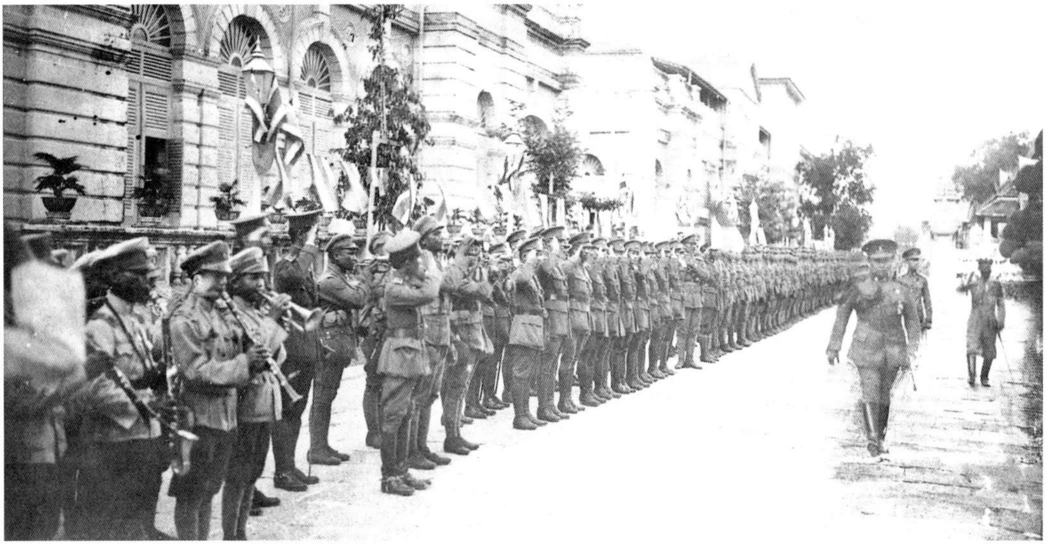

King Rama VI inspecting the Thai Expeditionary Force upon their return to Bangkok. (River Books)

After Siam had joined the Allies, the Thai flag was often flown in Europe and the U.S.A. at Allied functions. If the white elephant on the red ground was not always well made, the king felt that it more often resembled a pig. He was fond of change anyhow, so the national flag was altered. It became a flag of five horizontal stripes of, from the top, red, white, double dark blue, white, and red. It has remained the Thai flag ever since – another lasting memorial to King Rama VI.

It was in 1917 that criticism of the king and attacks against the Court again became widespread and were largely centred in a newspaper called *The Daily Mail* which was published in two versions, English and Thai. However, it was in the Thai versions that the strong attacks appeared. Prince Chakrabongse was distressed about all this, feeling that in a paternal or absolute monarchy the king had to bear too much responsibility and was the sole target for all recriminations. Nevertheless drastic suppression or prosecutions seemed no longer possible. He put pen to paper and submitted a lengthy memorandum to the king on April 21st, 1917, in which he suggested that the Legislative Council of King Chulalongkorn should be revived. As before, its President and members should be appointed by the Sovereign, and the Council would review each draft of an act of law before its promulgation, the members would have the right to question ministers, and the proceedings of the Council should be held in public and be fully reported in the newspapers. In this way he thought the ministers would be less certain in their power and less arrogant, and the king's heavy burden of sole responsibility would be alleviated.

The king replied in a personal letter of April 30th addressed to "My dear Lek." He thanked him for the memorandum and then declared that, with his English upbringing, he did not cherish power for its own sake, and he was a constitutionalist at heart. If he had proceeded only by theory, and had not looked at the practical side, he would have granted a constitution already in 1912. But he was advised by eminent Thai, British, and American advisers alike that the bulk of the Thai people were not well educated enough to know how to elect their representatives to a legislative assembly. The half-way measure suggested by Lek would not solve the problem, for a legislative council with members nominated by the king would only be considered a group of his "yes men," and he would continue to be personally criticized. Rama VI thought that if Siam was not yet ready to have a real parliament, it was better to do without an imitation. The matter was dropped, and, as far as is known to the present writer, it was not raised again for the rest of the reign.[21]

Siam is a country prone to flooding, and the high water season of 1917 brought disaster, with most of Bangkok being under two or three feet of water for some weeks. Some people, especially the young, thought it highly diverting to paddle their boats along the avenues and across the square where the statue of King Chulalongkorn stood, but the losses to the country were enormous, especially to the rice crop. Amongst individual sufferers was Catherine, whose ten-year work in her garden was washed away in a few hours. She had already suffered mental anguish over the Russian Revolution, and being in poor health on top of it all, it was obvious she was close to a breakdown. Normally she and Chakrabongse would be due for a holiday in Europe, but unable to leave his war work, he sent his wife off on a prolonged holiday in Japan and Canada. Their son was now at the Junior Military School, which would later prove of great benefit to him, for apart from a thorough early military training, he met and got to know well boys who would be leaders of the country in years to come.

Prince Mahidol's active service with the Thai navy was short-lived. He was considered too important a prince to go to sea constantly in command of a small torpedo boat, which was what he wanted to do. He was disappointed and annoyed at being made an instructor ashore,

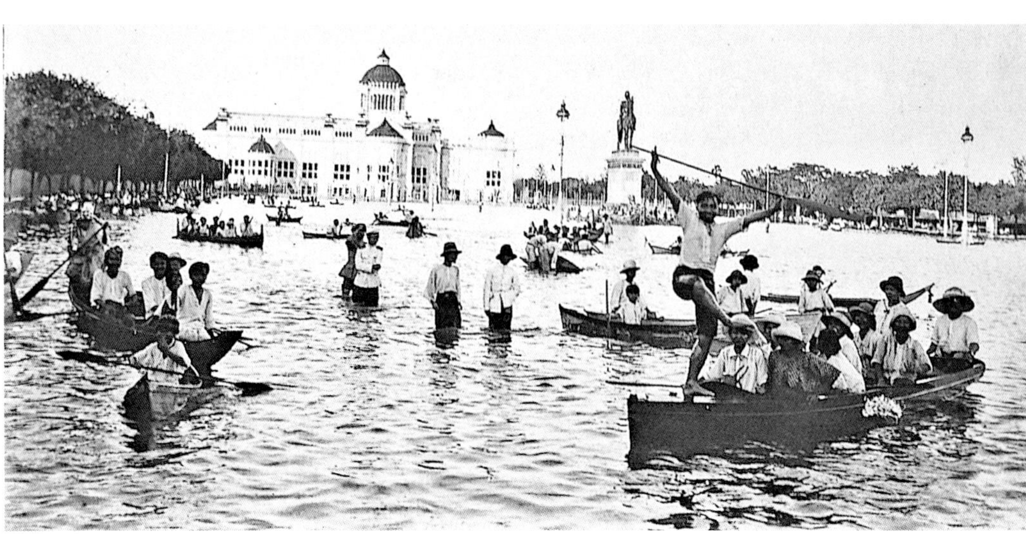

During the floods of 1917 the area around the equestrian statue of King Chulalongkorn was completely inundated. (River Books)

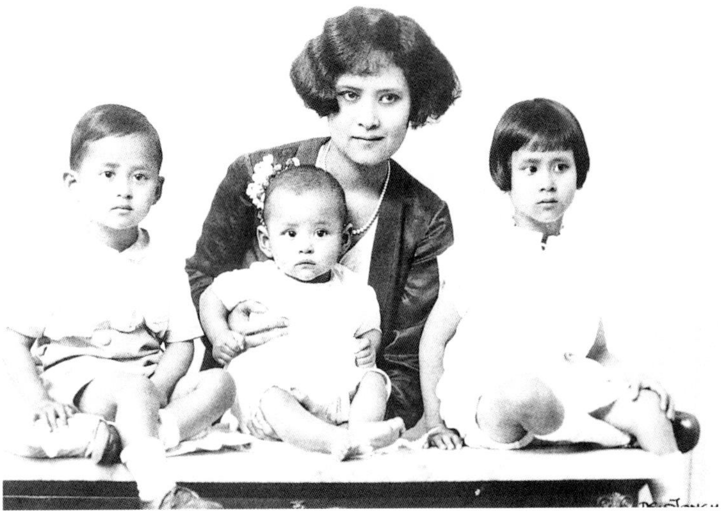

Mom Sangwalya with her three children: Prince Ananda, Prince Bhumibol and Princess Galyani. (River Books)

but after a while he was permitted to leave the navy. He went to the United States to study public health at first, then he took up medicine and finally obtained his M.D. at Harvard University. While living in Boston, Mass., he met and fell in love with a Thai girl who was a nursing student. Called Sangwalya Chukramol, she was pretty, charming, and intelligent. After obtaining permission from the king and his mother, he married her in Bangkok in 1920. He returned to the United States for further studies and at intervals worked in Britain and Germany. Three children were born to the couple and they had the junior princely rank of *Mom Chao* or Serene Highness. They were Princess Galyani (born in London on May 6th, 1923), Prince Ananda Mahidol (born in Heidelberg, Germany, on September 20th, 1925), and Prince Bhumibol Adulyadej (born in Boston, Mass., on December 5th, 1927). Both of the boys succeeded to the throne as the 8th and 9th monarchs of the Chakri Dynasty.

The great friendship between Prince Mahidol and the Chakrabongse family grew ever stronger over the years. Extracts from a letter which he wrote in English and sent from Boston to Catherine in Canada on September 24th, 1918,[22] when she was on the eve of her return to Bangkok, shed some interesting light on the character, feelings, and thoughts of the father of two future sovereigns :

> " The (your) letter having been addressed to a Prince Mahidol of Siam, of course, cannot reach me so soon, because I am known around here only as Mr. M. Songkla. (He was the Prince of Songkla). Nevertheless they seem to have discovered that I am somebody else too . . .
>
> . . . In my early days (as a student) in Europe I never did realize what my country, my home, was to me. Not until I have learnt to love my people through contact with them, have I known their valuable and lovable qualities. I am not exactly homesick, but I

21 A copy of each of these unpublished documents were found among Prince Chakrabongse's papers in the author's possession. Knowing the styles of both brothers, there can be no question of their not being genuine.

22 The original letter was given to the author by his mother.

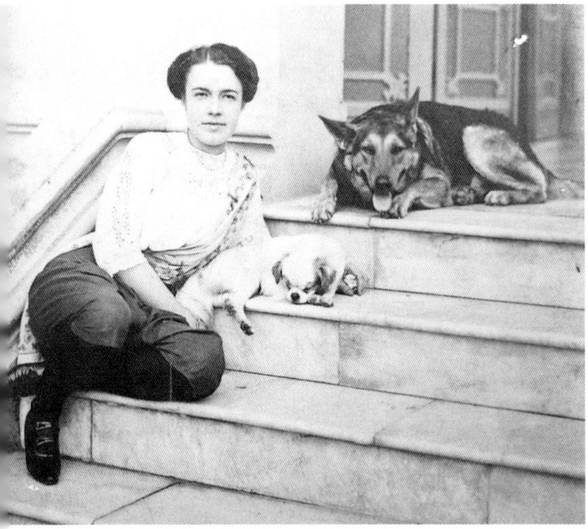

Mom Catherine with her dog L'Or at Paruskavan Palace. (River Books)

have learnt through my work here that my place in the world is among my people, the Siamese.

Do you remember our trip to Chiang Mai? [This was a big trip to the North which he made with the Chakrabongses between November 12th and December 27th, 1916[23]]. What a pleasant time! I now feel that it was more than pleasant, it was a revelation to me. I shall never forget to thank you and Lek for having invited me on that trip. And I shall try to make it worth your while to have asked me to accompany you, for I have learnt how to help those people whom I have seen and thus help Lek in his work to make Siam a good country to live in.

I cannot express to you my feelings of satisfaction that you are given the opportunity and you yourself are wise enough to take care of your health.

Your life, dear Catherine, and your health means so much happiness to Lek and our dear little Nou . . .

. . . You see, Siam has joined the Allies in the war. Although having been educated in Germany and still being thankful and true to those friends of mine in that country, I nevertheless rejoice at the king's decisive policy. My country and my people first, then afterwards my own feelings. I therefore think it right for the king to do so. We are sending troops to France. We send the sons of our peasants to fight and be killed by the Germans, but we have not sent the sons of our rulers to share their hardship. [One prince of Serene Highness rank did go to France as a captain – Author]. I am therefore resolved to go to France and to share the fate of those peasant boys in whatever capacity I will be most useful . . . The Royal (Thai) Navy is not so active so that joining it again would only mean a stay in Bangkok doing office work . . . As I have studied medicine now for two years, I would be somewhat useful in this line. [The war ended before he had time to carry out any of his plans – Author].

. . . You asked me whether I wish you to take anything to Bangkok. Yes, take the enthusiasm, the love for my country and people, the devotion to the king, that I have only faintly expressed to you in this letter. Also the devotion to those whom I love and respect, my mother above all, and Lek, and every loved one.

May the feeling that your life is precious to so many of us give you the health and happiness you need to cheer up those who are far away waiting for your return.

A happy voyage and au revoir from your very faithful,

Mahidol."

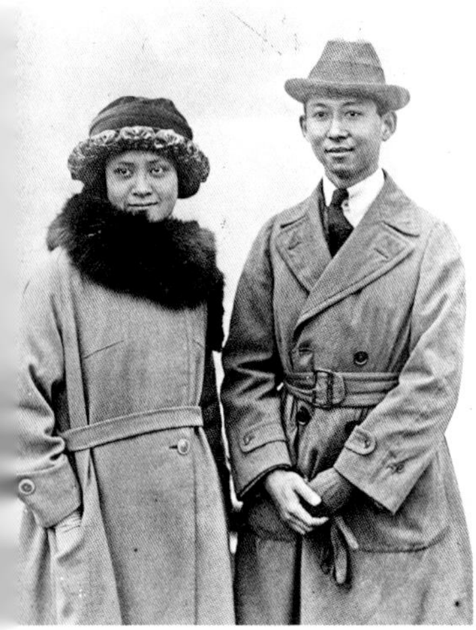

Prince Mahidol with Mom Sangwalya in U.S.A. (Paisarn Piemmettawat)

Prince Mahidol's loving wishes and hopes did not come true. During Catherine's prolonged absence Chakrabongse was working harder than ever, and his only relaxation was when he went to his seaside home at Hua Hin where he had a large house parties which included young relatives of both sexes. He fell in love with a very pretty girl, Chavalit, the daughter of Prince Rabi. Someone wrote and told Catherine, but instead of hurrying back she stayed away longer. When she came back she asked him to give the girl up or grant her a divorce. Chakrabongse pleaded for time to think, but what his real plans were will never be known.[24] This was not only the calamity of a small family, as it also upset King Rama VI, the Queen Mother, members of the Royal Family, who loved both husband and wife, and it gravely disturbed the army. Most people had not liked the Prince marrying a European, but they had become reconciled to it, and the happy and virtuous family life of Prince Chakrabongse had become an example. Everyone tried to arrange a reconciliation, but finally a divorce was decided upon and carried out. Feeling that she had nothing to offer him, a Thai prince, Catherine left her son behind with his father and grandmother, and she herself went off to join her brother in China. She accepted only a small allowance from her husband, intending at first to join the Russian White Forces as a nurse in their struggles against the Bolsheviks. The fight ended before she could get there, and she settled down in Shanghai to take up full-time work helping Russian refugees who were pouring into that large port. Thus did she made her dignified exit from the stage of Thai history. (She died in Paris in January, 1960).

The divorce cast a gloom over the family of Queen Saowabha. The king had been entirely against it, and later when his brother asked for permission to marry Chavalit, Rama VI flatly refused. The Queen Mother, who loved Catherine, was also against the idea of divorce, but when it was persisted in she became angry and hurt. Once it had gone through, she thought her son had better marry Chavalit; the king's refusal of permission annoyed her, and she smothered her grief in declining to take her medicine or any remedies for her health. When Rama VI went to see her, she turned her back on him and would not speak to him. He remained sitting in silence for nearly an hour before he left, never again to return to Phaya Thai in her lifetime; thus was how mother and son met for the last time. When her grandson visited her for the weekend, now that he went to school, in October, 1919, he found her asleep all the time, and he left for school on the Monday morning without her once waking up to speak to him. On that very morning-Monday, October 20th – Queen Saowabha passed away. She was 55 years and 9 months old when she died. She was deeply mourned by her sons, grandson, and her other close relatives, as much as by all who had known her personally and benefited from her boundless generosity. But on the public her death probably did not make a great impact, as she had been out of the limelight for some years. Nevertheless there was a general feeling that with her passing the curtain had finally descended on the golden epoch of King Chulalongkorn.

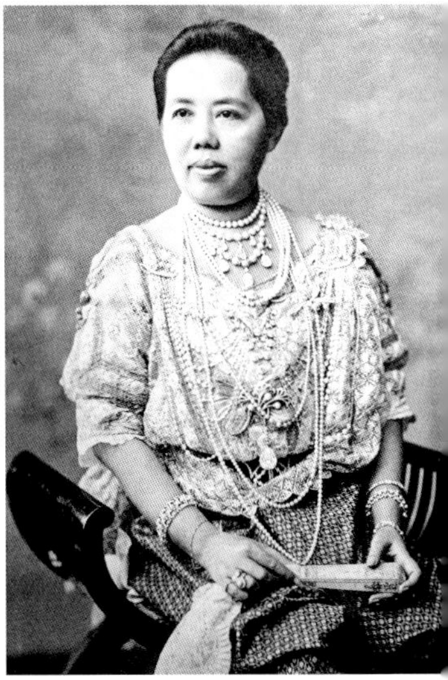

Queen Saowabha.
(Paisarn Piemmettawat)

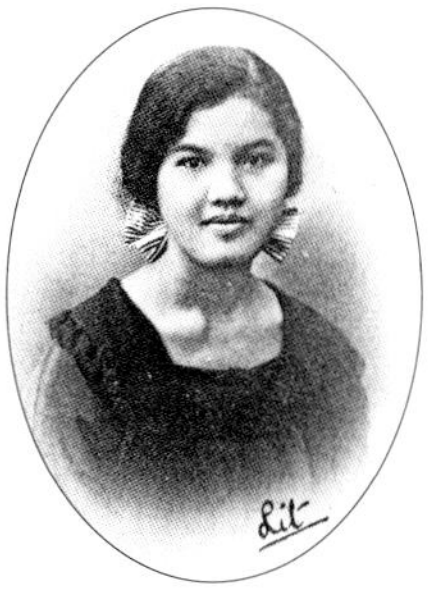

Princess Chavalit Obhas.
(River Books)

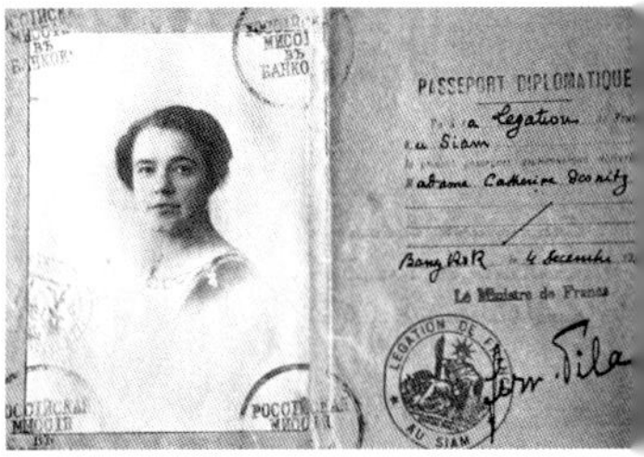

The passport used by Catherine after her divorce.
(River Books)

23 Details in Prince Chula's *The Twain Have Met*, etc., *op. cit.*, pages 94–96.

24 In 1921, a year after Prince Chakrabongse's death – she married Harry Clinton Stone, a U.S. citizen who was then working in China.

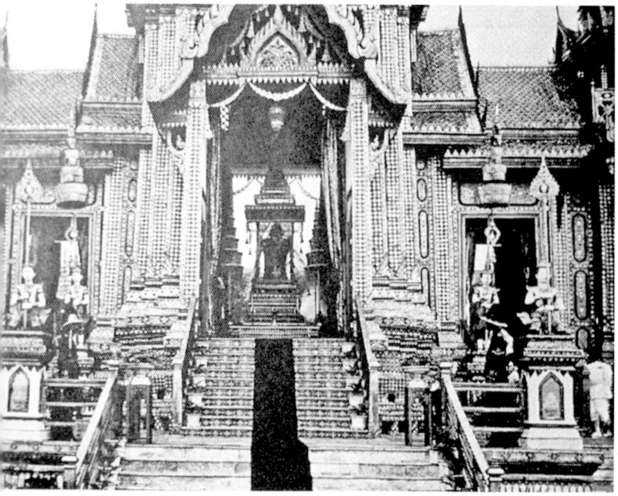

The urn of Queen Saowabha within the *Meru* on Sanam Luang. (River Books)

In accordance with tradition her body was placed in the Thong Yai urn and set up on the high catafalque in the Prasat Hall of the Grand Palace, with religious ceremonies going on for seven months before the cremation took place with full pomp in June, 1920. All honours were rendered to the Queen Mother, yet throughout the ceremonies the atmosphere was uncomfortable and even more depressing than funeral rites need be, for everyone knew that relations between the king and his closest brother had become severely strained. Also there were wild rumours of plots against the king, and Chakrabongse himself received an anonymous letter stating that his own death by poisoning had been planned. Even the name of the officer who was going to carry out the deed was given, but with his characteristic boldness the prince sent a copy of the letter to the officer, much to the latter's consternation and embarrassment. During the months preceding the cremation he had been working especially hard on a scheme to retire some inefficient senior officers. By the time the strenuous cremation ceremonies were over, he was utterly exhausted.

The king gave him leave to have a long holiday, and taking Chavalit and his only son along with him, he left Bangkok for Singapore by boat, intending later to travel north slowly up the Malay Peninsula by rail, and complete his leave with a stay at Hua Hin. Already on the boat Prince Chakrabongse became ill, and when they arrived in Singapore and went to stay with a Chinese rice merchant who was a friend, he was found to be suffering from a severe bout of Spanish 'flu complicated by double pneumonia. Three English doctors were called but he became rapidly worse, and he died in the morning of June 13th, at the age of 37 years, 3 months, and 10 days. Prince Prajadhipok had rushed down from Bangkok by train only to arrive too late and merely in time to take the body home. The remains of Prince Chakrabongse were borne on a British gun-carriage escorted by British troops and followed by the Governor of the Straits Settlement, his brother and son, to the railway station. When the body arrived in Bangkok, the young officer commanding the Guard of Honour was so choked with grief that he found it difficult to give words of command. The king met the body at the station, and as he bent down to kiss his nephew on the cheek, he made it wet with his tears, all the estrangement with his late brother forgotten. In July, Chula Chakrabongse was created a prince of Royal Highness rank in an official proclamation. Owing to rumours, the known existence of the anonymous letter, the illness and death of other General officers who had collaborated with him in the army retrenchment scheme and had had similar symptoms, many people thought that Prince Chakrabongse and they had been poisoned by some germ at a dinner held shortly before he left for Singapore. No investigation was ever held.

The effect of Prince Chakrabongse's death, cannot be better demonstrated than by quoting three western writers. The French, Robert-Martignan[25] stated: "His death deprived Siam of one of her best sons. His intelligence, his military worth, the loyalty of his character, and the clarity of his spirit, the Sovereign and the nation would lack at a time when they were most needed". From Sir Josiah Crosby:[26] "The demise of the Prince of Phitsanulok, was a national misfortune, for he possessed strong character and acknowledged ability". It was a coincidence that when the Queen Mother and the Prince died, their physician and friend, Dr. Malcolm Smith, was on leave in England. He wrote later: "The death of Prince Chakrabongse was a calamity for the country. Had he lived to become king as he undoubtedly would, the whole course of history might have been changed for he was popular with a large class of people ".[27] The king wrote that he felt as if one of his arms had been amputated. The Thai writer, Phra Sarasas, wrote in his English book: "It was a misfortune for the country that Prince Chakrabongse who was the king's next brother and heir to the throne, should have died before he was crowned. He epitomized in his personality all the desirable characteristics in a king. His character was a compound of earnestness, deference, pleading, irresistibility, impertinence, and dignity with a profound sense of patriotism and democracy".[28] After his death all proclamations mentioning his name had the new royal prefix of *Somdech Phra Anujar Dhiraj* previously used only for brothers of the king who had been *Uparaja*.

25 Robert-Martignan: *op. cit.*, page 283.

26 Sir Josiah Crosby: *op. cit.*, page 46.

27 Dr. Smith: *op. cit.*, page 117.

28 Phra Sarasas: *op. cit.*, pages 139-140.

The urn of Prince Chakrabongse was placed in the Chitralada building of his palace. (River Books)

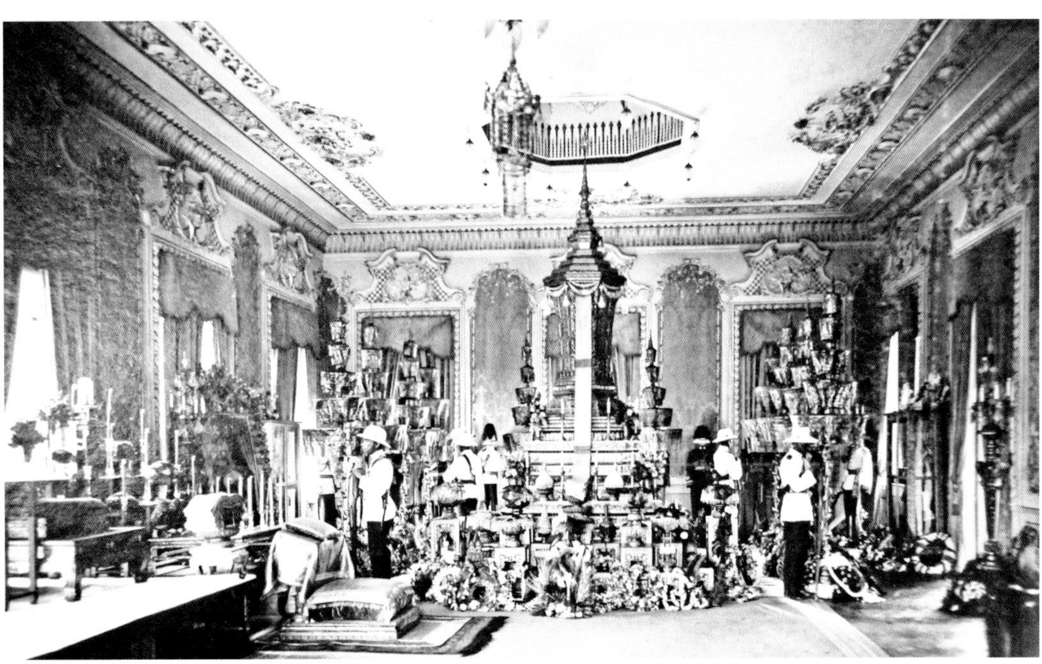

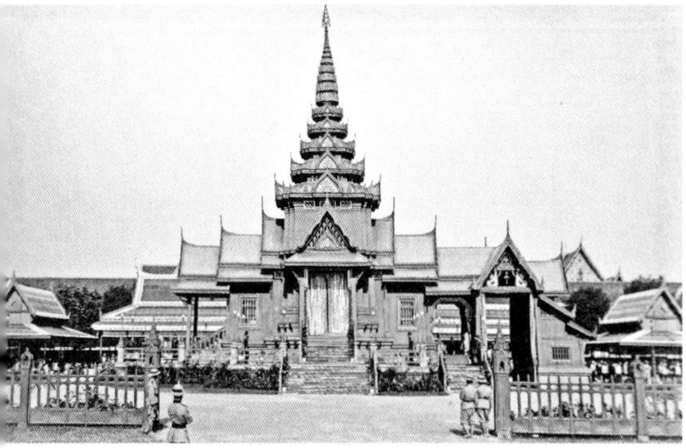

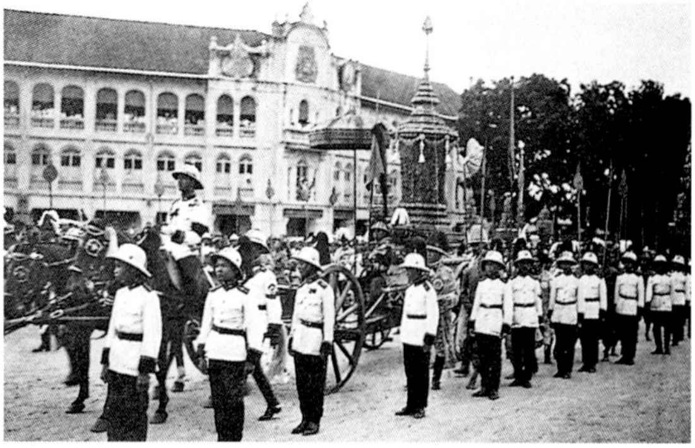

The *Meru* for Prince Chakrabongse. (River Books)

ABOVE RIGHT: The urn of Prince Chakrabongse is taken in procession from Paruskavan Palace to Sanam Luang. (River Books)

The passing of his mother and closest brother saw a profound change in the king's way of life, although it cannot be known whether it was by coincidence or deliberate design. He had previously been completely happy as a bachelor living amongst men, but soon after the cremation of Chakrabongse in October, 1920, Rama VI began to invite young women into the Court, mostly his cousins who were daughters of Prince Naradhip and their friends. In a short time plays were written for them to act in with the king and the male courtiers.

After a meeting of the Privy Council, which had rarely been called, the king on November 9th announced his engagement to Princess Vallabha Devi (born 1892), a daughter of Prince Naradhip, who like the king was a grandchild of King Mongkut. She was 28 and thus of a suitable age to be the bride of a man of 39. The news was received with great joy by the Royal Family, and the senior celestial princes vied with one another in providing entertainments for the king and his fiancee. A close family atmosphere was stressed, and certain well-known personages of the Court felt that they were left out in the cold. The public at large were pleased at the king's approaching marriage and the prospects of there being an Heir Apparent, a true male heir. After Prince Chakrabongse's death it had been assumed that Prince Asdang was the heir presumptive. However, although he had been married for some years, he was still childless. Because he did not like Europe and associated little with Europeans, he was believed by them to be unintelligent. Actually he had had a good education in Siam, understood English quite well, was an able army officer, and had a profound knowledge of Thai affairs, but his childlessness was a handicap. At a large party given by the former Thai students in Britain, the king said he intended to set an example of monogamy. Throughout the innumerable festivities in their honour, Princess Vallabha Devi conducted herself with great dignity and charm.

During the engagement period the king put at her disposal the new palace, Chitralada. (It is now the favourite private residence of the present monarch, King Bhumibol). There she had a minor court of her own, and she was surrounded by young ladies which included many pretty younger sisters, the most prominent of them being Princess Lakshami (born 1899). The king himself had moved to Phaya Thai

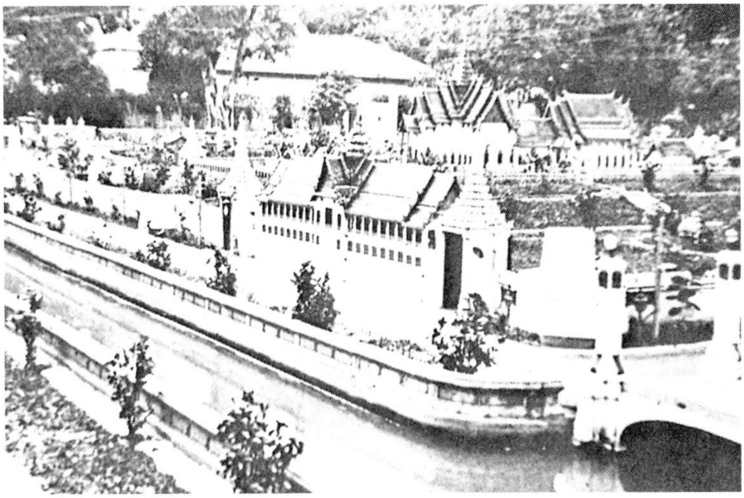

'Dusit Thani', King Rama VI's model town in the grounds of Phaya Thai. (National Archives Bangkok)

which he was going to alter vastly. (It is now the Phra Mongkut Klao Military Hospital). Although he visited his fiancée every day at tea time, and they frequently attended parties together, the king also telephoned her daily from his study. This was personally seen and heard by the present writer, who, being without parents, spent a certain amount of time each day with his uncle. In the large garden of Phaya Thai, Rama VI had a vast miniature city built, which was complete with a perfect copy of the main buildings of the Grand Palace, some temples, shops and stores, theatres, hotels and private houses with gardens, some having miniature trees sent from Japan. There was a winding river flowing through the city which was fed by a water tank hidden behind a "mountain ", and the river debouched into a large lake. When it was all lit up at night the miniature city was like fairyland. His courtiers rented houses and elected a Mayor and Councillors to run the city, and they held meetings which the king attended. He said that in this way he was teaching them to understand municipal politics which he intended to introduce in Bangkok in the future.

Soon after the passing of his mother and brother, Prince Prajadhipok became seriously unwell. When he was better, it was decided that he should go to Europe for recuperation, and he left Siam on February 2nd, 1921, with a large party which included his wife, Rambai Barni – they were also childless – his father and mother-in-law, his nephew, Chula Chakrabongse, and other students. The Prajadhipoks stayed for a while in Egypt, but the students proceeded direct to England for their education. Prince Prajadhipok arrived in Europe in the summer for further medical treatment, and made such good progress that he chose to make up for his lost education due to the

Prince Prajadhipok and Princess Rambai Barni, together with various nephews, from left, Prince Chula, Prince Aditya, Prince Subha Svasti. (River Books)

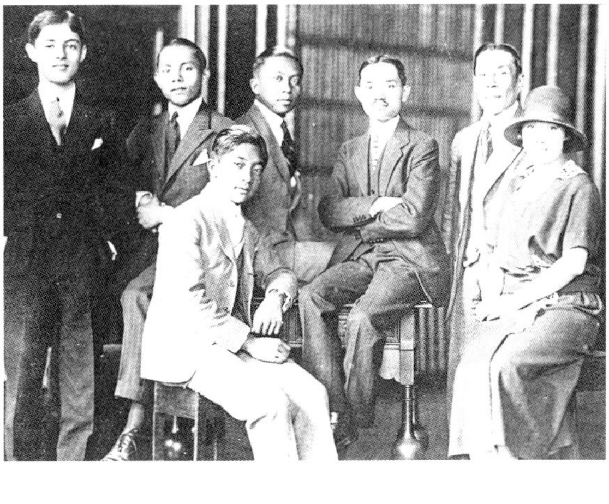

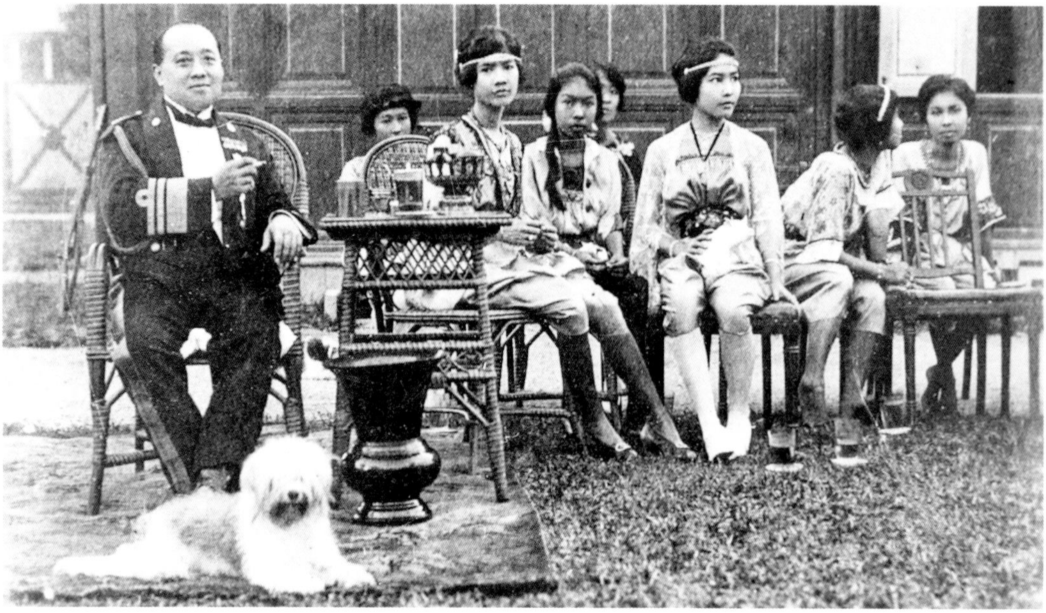

King Rama VI together with Princess Vallabha, Princess Lakshami and other more junior princesses. (National Archives Bangkok)

war. With the king's agreement he took a house at St. Cloud, near Paris and entered the French Staff College. He did not return to Siam until 1924 when he was promoted to Major-General in command of a division in the provinces.

Meanwhile Rama VI's matrimonial aspirations did not turn out as he had hoped. By March, 1921, there was an announcement that, through incompatibility of temperament, the engagement with Princess Vallabha Devi was broken off. In September, 1921, the king announced his engagement to her younger sister, Princess Lakshami, whom he married and raised to the rank of *Phra Nang* (Junior Queen) in August, 1922. The union was not blessed with issue, and after a time the couple lived apart, but they were on amicable terms and Queen Lakshami's loyalty to the king never diminished. It seems that at this point Rama VI's enthusiasm for monogamy had definitely waned. In October, 1921, and January, 1922, he had taken to wife as per former custom two sisters of good birth, Prueng and Prabai Sucharitakul, and they became *Chao Choms* with new and poetic titles. The younger, who suffered more than one miscarriage, was in the same year created the Supreme Queen with the identical title first granted to Rama VI's mother by King Chulalongkorn, namely, *Phra Boromma Rajinee*. Then on September 15th, 1925, there came the dramatic proclamation that she lacked the capacity for the rank of Supreme Queen, and her title was altered to be that of an ordinary queen. In the following October, it was announced that another lady was soon expected to give birth to His Majesty's child, and she was created a junior queen as Phra Nang Suvadhana. The abandonment of the new idea of monogamy by one so enlightened and westernized as Rama VI, and his frequent matrimonial changes have proved puzzling to students

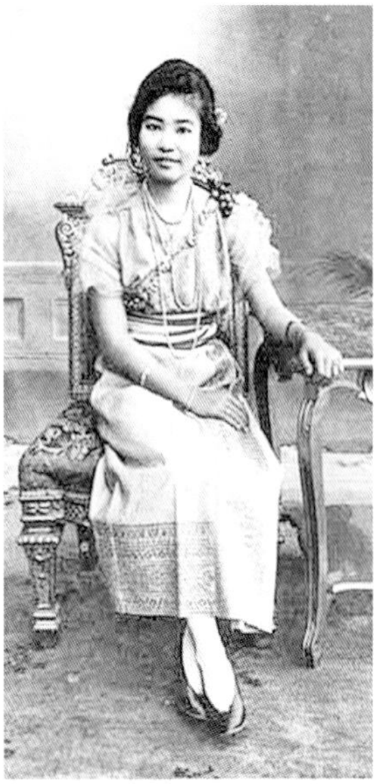

Princess Lakshami Lawan. (National Archives Bangkok)

of the history of the Chakri House. The monarch's copious journals, now in the Royal Archives, have not been published, and one can but wait for his own account. One can, however, be certain that he was an unhappy man in the last five years of his life, and that above all he was frantic in his eagerness to provide a male heir. In view of the fact that his successors, King Prajadhipok and King Bhumibol have been strict monogamists and there has been only one queen in each reign, the title of *Phra Nang* for Lakshami and Suvadhana has been rendered in English by the authorities more often as Princess.

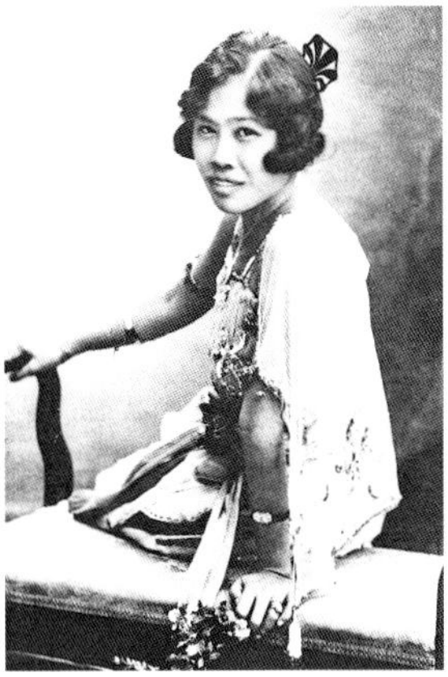

Phra Sucharitasuda, who was briefly one of the queens of King Rama VI. (National Archives Bangkok)

What was worse still for Rama VI was that during those five years his immediate family was being decimated by death. His third full brother Chudadhuj, died in 1923, and his second full-brother, Asdang, died in 1925, so there now remained only the king and Prajadhipok. In 1924 the king enacted as a Palace Law the first Law of Succession in Siam which followed the system of primogeniture, in which it was laid down that the son of a deceased heir would succeed before his uncle. The law also decreed that the line of succession should first pass through the sons of Queen Saowabha in the order of their ages, then through the line of Queen Sawang, namely Prince Mahidol, and then that of Queen Sukumala whose only son was Prince Paribatra. After that all princes were eligible for the throne in the order of seniority, but it was expressly stated that a princess could not become sovereign. Thus at first sight it would appear that if Prince Chakrabongse had been alive, he would have been the heir, and presumably his son after him. But later in the same law Prince Chakrabongse was posthumously disqualified for marrying a foreign lady, Catherine, and his son was automatically disqualified. The third brother, Prince Chudadhuj, had left a son by a Thai wife – Varanand – born in 1922, who might well have been the king's heir by law. Some people have said that he could not be as his mother was not royal, but there was nothing in the act to say that the mother of the heir had to be of royal birth and this would be confirmed some years later. In the beginning of the act, however, the king reserved the age-old right of nominating any prince as his successor. Thus when Prince Prajadhipok returned to Bangkok in 1924 via the U.S.A. and Japan, it was generally assumed that unless a son was born to the sovereign, he would be the heir to the throne of Siam.

At that time three grandsons of King Chulalongkorn of Royal Highness rank were being educated in England, namely Chumbhot, Chula Chakrabongse, and Bhanu, a son of Prince Yugala. Two of his grandsons of Highness rank who were also in England, namely Aditya, a son of Prince Abhakorn, and Prem Purachatra, a son of Prince Purachatra. Although the fathers of these two were not celestial princes, the boys had been created *Phra* Ong *Chao* because their mothers were of royal birth.

Siam saw much progress during the fifteen-year reign of Rama VI, and many facts pointing to this have already been related in the foregoing pages. At the close of World War I, Siam, as one of the Allies,

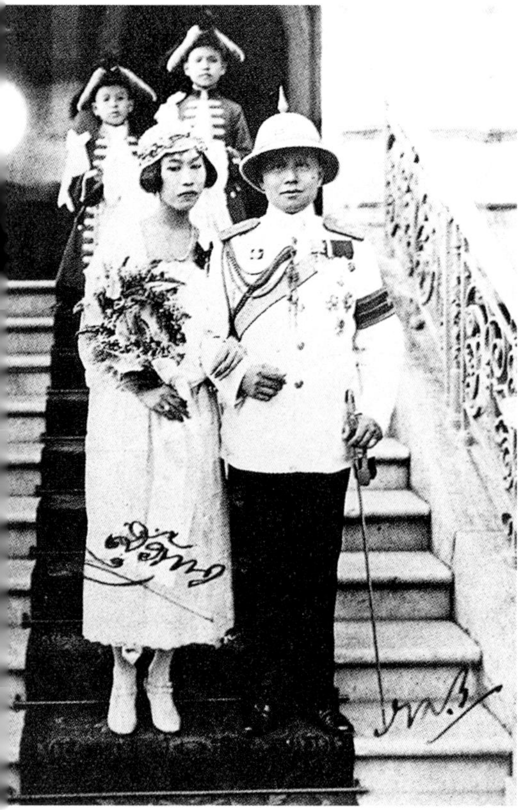

was represented at the Peace Conference of Versailles and became a founder member of the League of Nations, and in this reign most of the new and more just treaties with the great powers were concluded, giving Siam almost equal status. Thus many of the hopes expressed in his letter to Chakrabongse during his coronation had been achieved. He had also enacted a law requiring compulsory and free primary education. In addition, a big railway bridge spanning the Chao Phraya River near Bangkok had been constructed, thus linking the Northern and Southern lines.

Yet the king was not happy. He was in poor health, as the problems resulting from his appendicitis and peritonitis while at Oxford had worsened. His matrimonial difficulties and his lack of a male heir made him sad, and the frequent deaths of his close family appalled him. His household expenditure had got out of hand and risen in an alarming manner. Despite calling for a Civil List of 11.5 million baht in 1923-24, and more the following year, the king was encumbered with debts. The State finances also showed deficits year after year.[29] But the king's personal generosity could not be curbed, and people who had asked for monetary gifts, received royal bounty in instalments.

The wedding photograph of King Rama VI and Queen Suvadhana on their wedding day, 10th August 1924. (National Archives Bangkok)

In November, 1925, Rama VI became critically ill, and just as the malady took a more serious turn, Queen Suvadhana gave birth to a girl. When the baby was taken to the king on his sick-bed, he gently patted her head. Knowing that a daughter could not succeed, he murmured: "It's just as well." Realizing that the illness was fatal, he asked to be moved into the Grand Palace and he rested in a room within the Chakrapat Group where he had slept a few nights after his accession.

In the words of his successor, Prince Prajadhipok: "It was a nerve-racking day. I was called to the bedside five or six times, but each time the expected death did not take place. The king finally died after one o'clock on 26th November, after having been ill for fifteen days. I slept in the Amarindra Hall most of the time. I could hardly eat or sleep. Rumours were rampant and intrigues galore. The situation was most uncertain, my own comfort was that all the princes were highly patriotic and thought of nothing but the good of the country. No personal ambition ever came across their minds at any time, and their kindness to me was overwhelming. I feel that with such sentiments in the Royal Family, Siam and the Chakri Dynasty will live yet in spite of *everything*".[30]

Thus ended the reign of King Vajiravudh, or Rama VI the *Liberal*. He was 43 years, 9 months, and 25 days old, and he had had a reign of just over 15 years.

29 *Financial Adviser's Report (1925-26)* presented by Sir Edward M. Cook.

30 Personal letter in English from King Prajadhipok to his nephew, Chula Chakrabongse, dated May 7th, 1926.

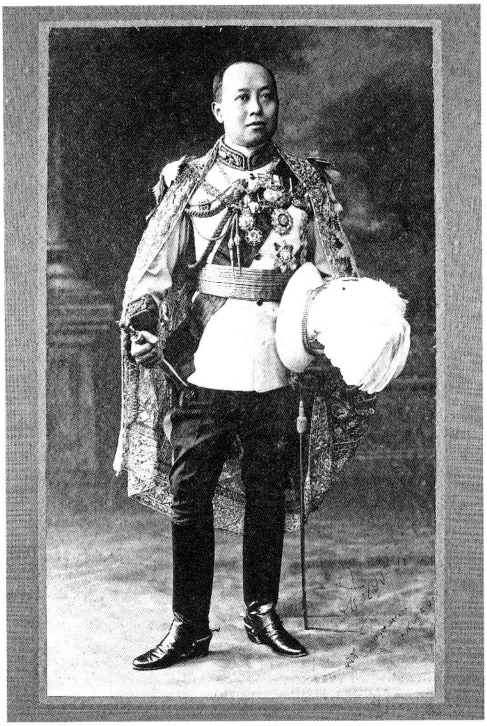

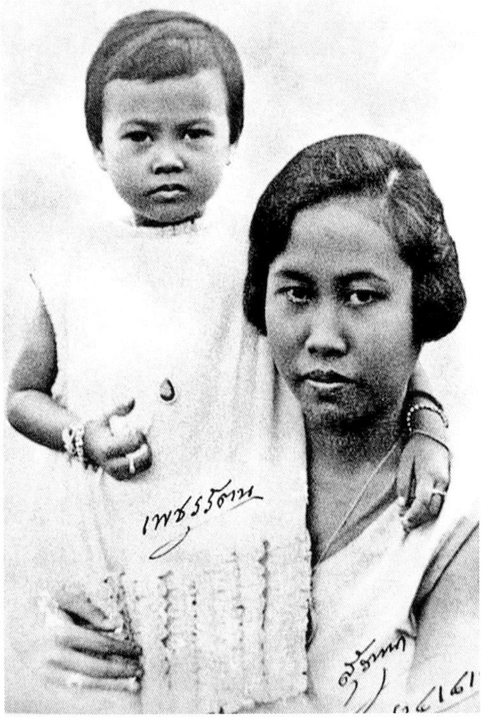

Princess Bejaratana together with her mother Queen Suvadhana. (National Archives Bangkok)

ABOVE LEFT: King Rama VI in the full dress uniform of a Field Marshal. (River Books)

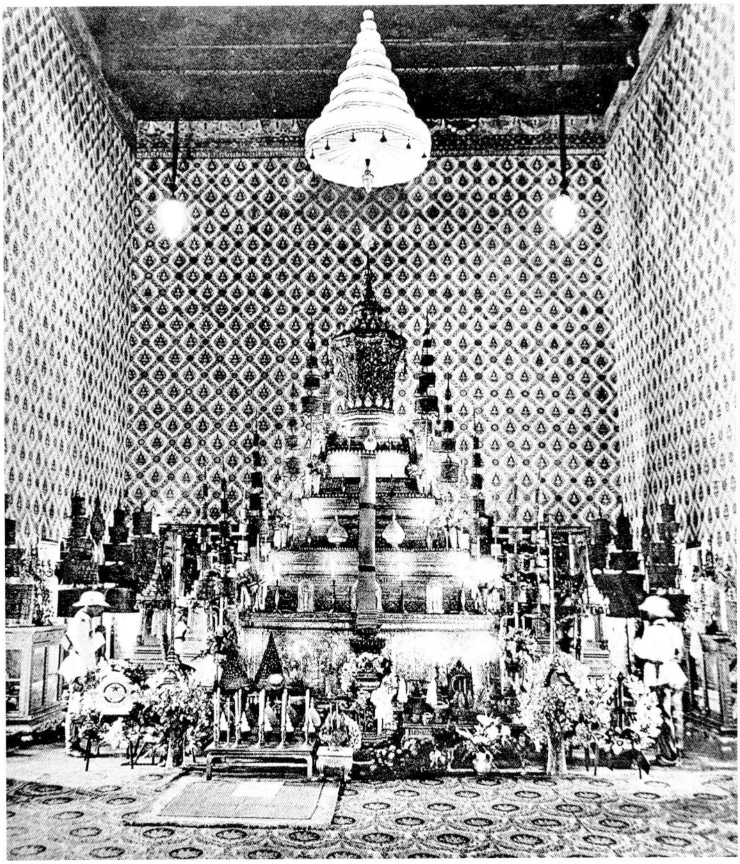

The lying-in-state of King Rama VI within the Dusit Maha Prasat Throne Hall. (Paisarn Piemmettawat)

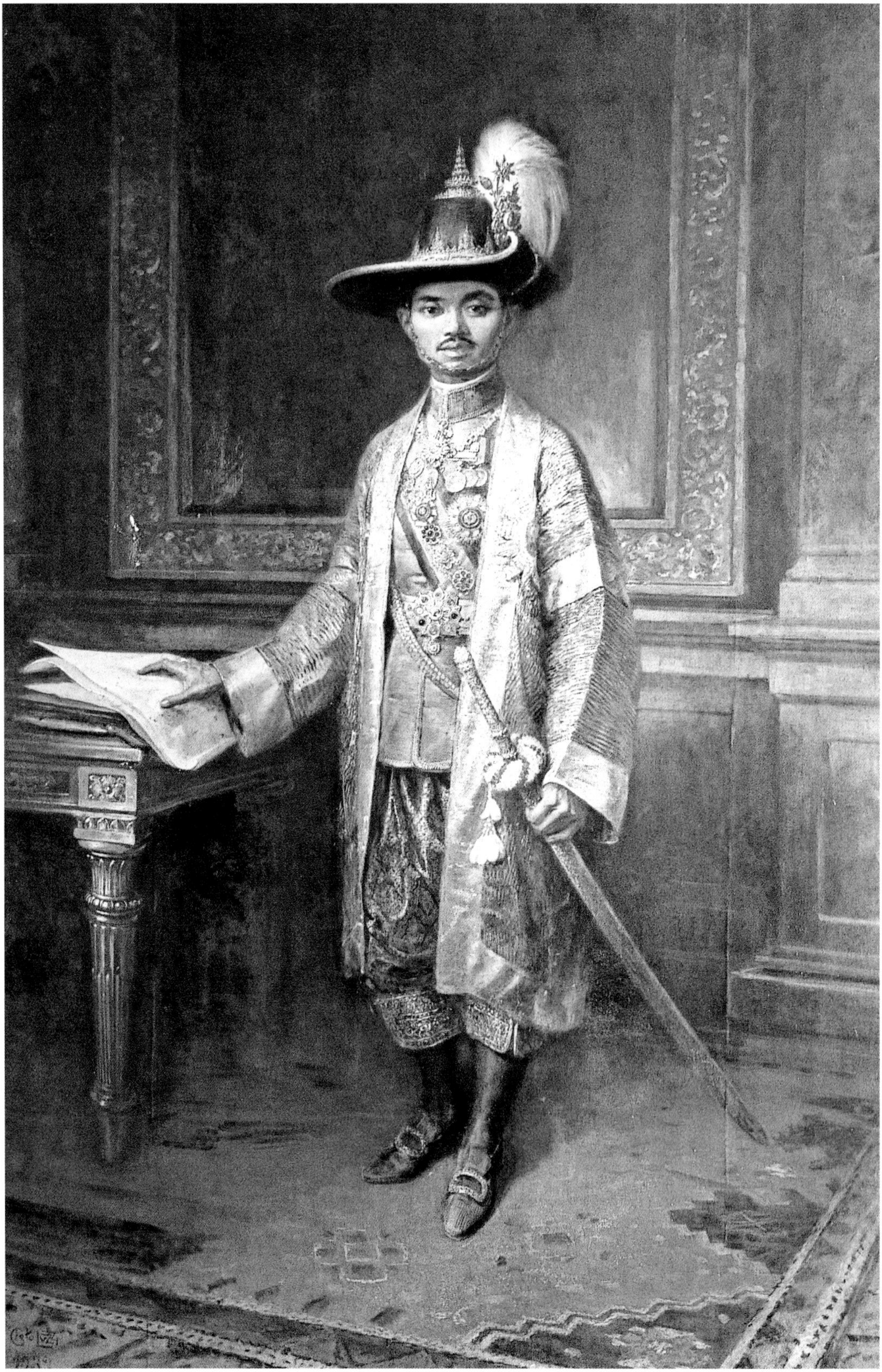

Chapter Seven
THE PHILOSOPHER
(1925-1932)

The law of Succession of 1924 had clearly stipulated that the time was not yet ripe for Siam to have a queen regnant, so there was never any question of Rama VI's baby daughter succeeding him on the throne. The late king had left a letter, which, when opened, contained what everyone had expected, his appointment of Prince Prajadhipok as the next heir, thus passing over his nephew, Varanand, the only son of Prince Chudadhuj, then only three years old. The royal decision was loyally accepted by the princes, the high officials, and therefore by the nation as a whole. Although he was by upbringing a soldier, it is felt that the following pages will show that the seventh king of the Chakri Dynasty was more of a *Philosopher,* and he would be able to appreciate and understand every side of every question. One of King Prajadhipok's first acts was to create his niece a *chao fa* or celestial princess, and she was given the name Bejaratana. He then made it clear that he wished to be known as King Prajadhipok, and not Rama VII. From then on the name of Rama was never used for him or his successors. For English readers it may be a matter of interest that he was the first monarch of any country to have been a boy at Eton.

Painting of King Prajadhipok in the Chakri Maha Prasat Throne Hall.

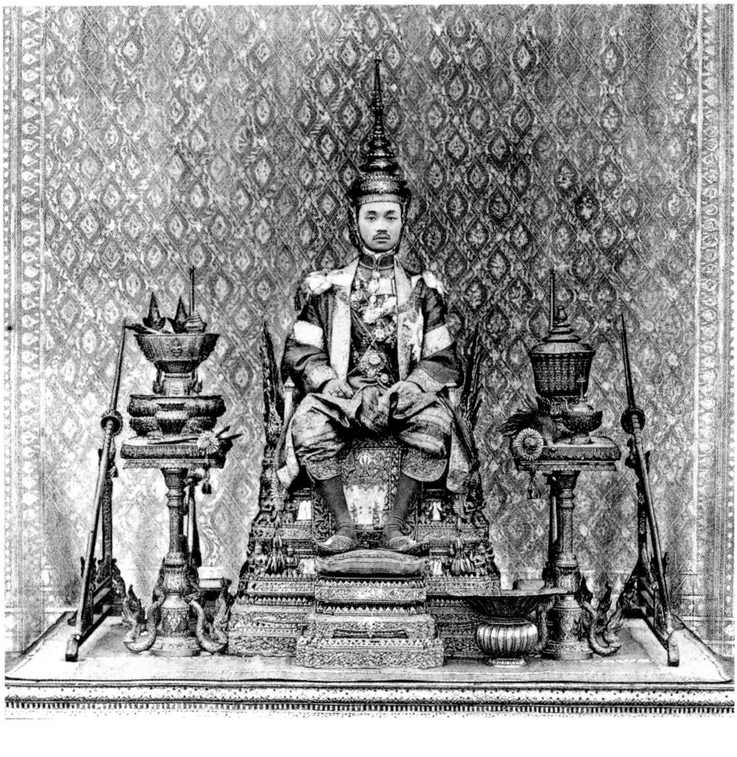

King Prajadhipok during his coronation ceremony, 1925. (National Archives Bangkok)

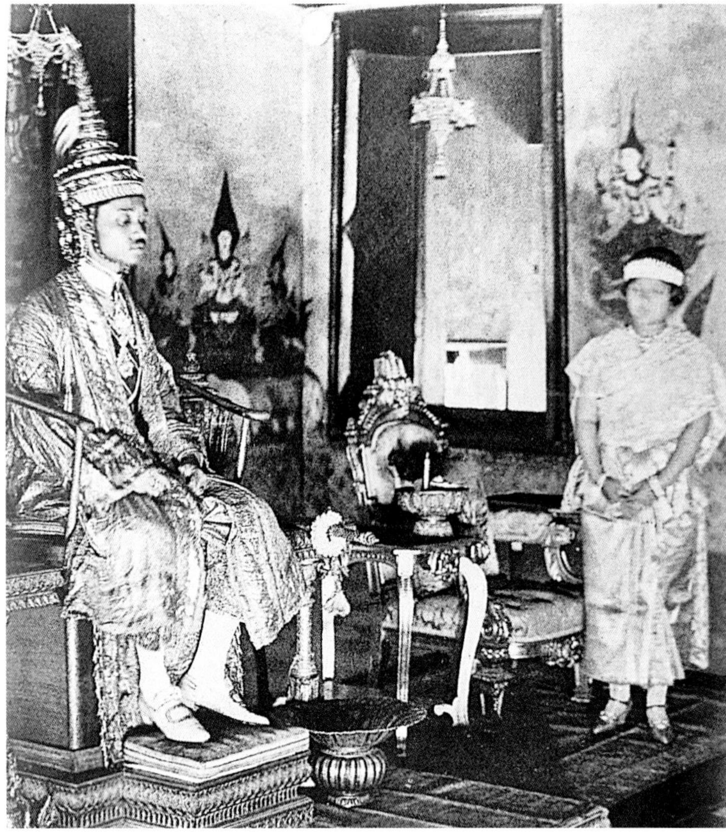

King Prajadhipok and Queen Rambai Barni during the coronation ceremony in the Paisal Thaksin Throne Hall. (National Archives Bangkok)

When he ascended the throne in November, 1925, King Prajadhipok had just turned thirty-two, and he made a decision which had some unexpected repercussions on the Chakri family. He announced that being the youngest child of his father, and having served the State only as a soldier, he lacked knowledge and experience in the art of government, and felt himself too young for his heavy task. Thus he decided to create a Supreme Council (Abirata Sabha), consisting of his uncles and elder half-brothers. The first President was the elderly and highly respected Prince Bhanurangsi, the king's paternal full-uncle. After his death, he was succeeded by Prince Paribatra, the eldest celestial half-brother of the monarch. The Council met every week, usually attended by the king, and it advised him on all matters of public and family affairs. As the king verbally confirmed with the present writer in 1931, even when he accepted their advice, as the Absolute Monarch he was solely responsible for all decisions made.

The Supreme Council was an excellent idea to start with, yet as its royal members died, they should perhaps not have been replaced so rapidly thereby creating the impression that the Supreme Council might continue for the rest of the reign, and leading some to say that the king was reluctant to rule personally. Furthermore, a vacancy was always filled by a senior prince; no commoner regardless of his ability or experience, was ever appointed. Originally the Council was designed to assist the king in supervising his cabinet of ministers; but gradually some of the new councillors were themselves holding ministerial portfolios and sat in the cabinet as well as in the Council. It made the Council seem like an inner cabinet in which non-councillors could not participate. The conscientious king attended the meetings of both the council and the cabinet if he was not away from Bangkok.

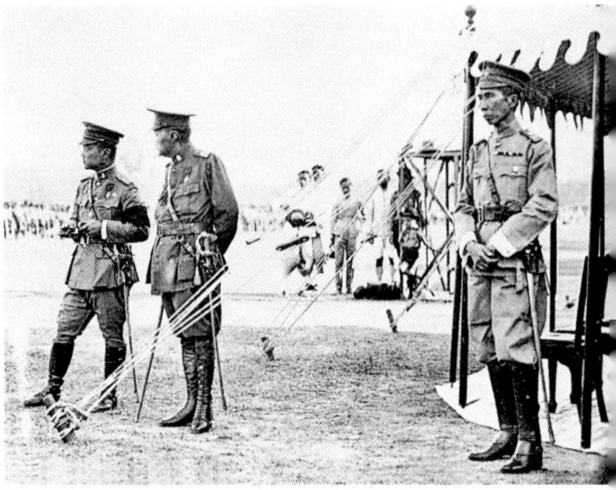

Senior members of the royal family who were made members of the Supreme Council created by the king at the beginning of his reign. From left: Prince Paribatra, Prince Bhanurangsi and Prince Naris. (National Archives Bangkok)

King Rama VI had been lavish with his personal expenditure, and towards the close of the reign had had to call on the Treasury to defray his deficits. King Prajadhipok right from the beginning had the worthy aim of practising strict economy both in the State and the palace. That he was uneasy about the whole state of affairs can be seen in his letter to the present author who was then in England: "The most important thing was the carrying out of the Retrenchment scheme. Few people in Europe (I mean the Siamese) knew that Siam was in a very precarious financial position. It was therefore quite necessary to cut down the expenses of the government. We decided on decreasing the staff of the various ministries, which meant turning out large numbers of officials, especially in the Royal Household, as I consented to reduce the Civil List by about 4 million baht. This action, of course, has raised a storm of criticism against the government, and has caused a certain amount of suffering among those who are turned out. But the results justify the action. Besides being able to balance the budget, which has been showing large deficits for several years, it has shown the people that other careers should be sought for besides government service. It is time for us to develop our commerce and industries."[1]

In 1929 another severe blow befell the Chakri family. Prince Mahidol had returned to Siam from the U.S.A. and served in the Department of Public Health, but soon became discontented, as he felt frustrated by the fact that he was not permitted to do all that he felt he could. He thought the other officials were inhibited by his rank of a celestial prince, so he returned to Boston for further studies and research which were continued in Britain and Germany. When Rama VI died and Prajadhipok succeeded him, Prince Mahidol should have been his heir according to the Law of Succession of 1924. But as King Prajadhipok was only 32 and married to a healthy young woman, Queen Rambai Barni, he still hoped to have sons of his own. No proclamation was made about Prince Mahidol, and there was no need for one. In any case, Prince Paribatra was by then so eminent and powerful, not unlike Rama III in his own father's reign, that most people thought that he would be designated heir in the event of the king dying childless. Many people had been surprised when Prince Paribatra had stood by and let his very much younger half-brother ascend the throne, for they did not know that he was far too high minded to challenge the legally-designated successor.

1 *Ibid.*

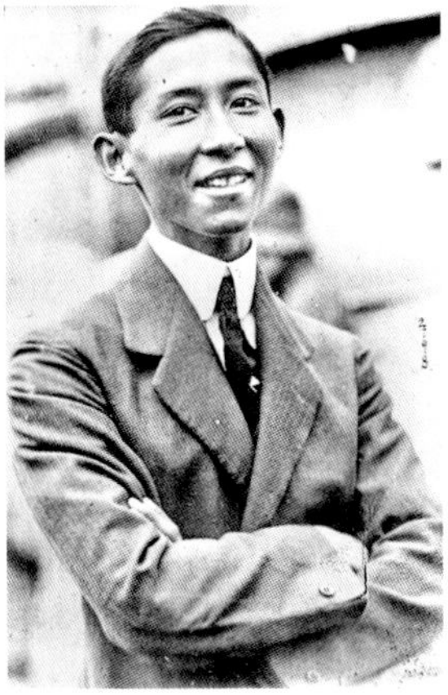

Prince Mahidol.
(Paisarn Piemmettawat)

After leaving the Department of Public Health, Prince Mahidol declined all offers of other government posts, preferring to go to Chiang Mai and work as a doctor in an American hospital which had been established in the northern city for some years. Leaving his wife and children in Bangkok with his mother, he led a most simple and austere life, throwing himself heart and soul into hard work. One of his extra interests was the Leper Colony nearby. Although giving the impression of being in fine physical condition, he had never been a fit man, and many illnesses of an internal and organic nature had left him weak. In 1929 he was taken ill, and although he was brought down to Bangkok, nothing could be done for him, and he died when he was only 37. In him, Siam lost another of her worthy sons at the same early age. He had given vast sums to the cause of medicine, he had been a great inspiration to the medical profession, and he was largely responsible for getting the Rockefeller Foundation interested in the Thai Medical College to its enormous benefit. Extremely handsome, he was amusing, witty, and a brilliant *raconteur,* with an immense fund of knowledge on all sorts of subjects. He was most courteous, but he could, when provoked, be very quick and hot tempered. His thoughts and ideas were far too democratic and ahead of his time, and his high rank and poor health came between him and the work he had set his heart on. His young family of three children were brought up with the utmost care and devotion by their mother. The elder boy, Ananda Mahidol, then four years old, was according to law now heir presumptive to the throne, but few people then thought that he would ever reign. Together with other children of celestial princes who were still *Mom Chaos,* the three were raised by King Prajadhipok to the rank of *Phra Ong Chao* or the rank of Highness. Amongst the others also raised, there was Prince Birabongse (born 1914), a son of Prince Bhanurangsi, who was later to be the first Thai sportsman of international fame.

The lying-in-state of Prince Mahidol in the throne hall of Suan Kularb Palace.
(National Archives Bangkok)

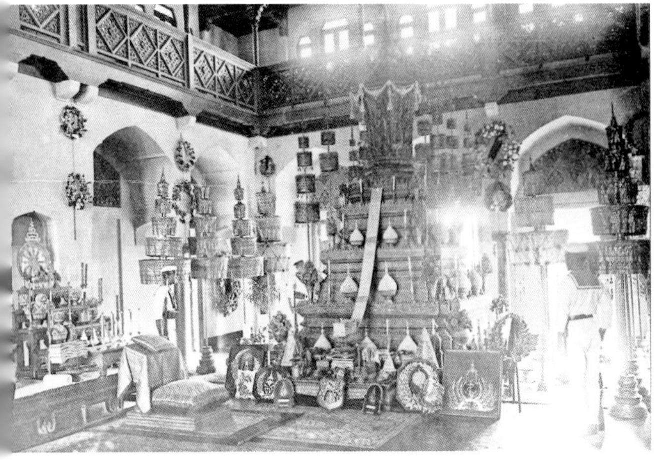

Another tragedy to strike at the House of Chakri was that King Prajadhipok, by then fitter than he had ever been through playing golf, lawn tennis, and squash, found himself going blind. He was suffering from cataracts in both eyes, with one worse than the other and ripe for an operation. In 1931 he decided to visit Japan, Canada and the United States, and to undergo an operation at the end of the tour. These State Visits – and he was the first Thai Monarch to make them to those countries – went off splendidly, and in America the king hinted to the press that he had in mind soon to grant a constitution.The successful operation took place at the home loaned to him by the wealthy Mrs. Whitelaw Reid in New York State.

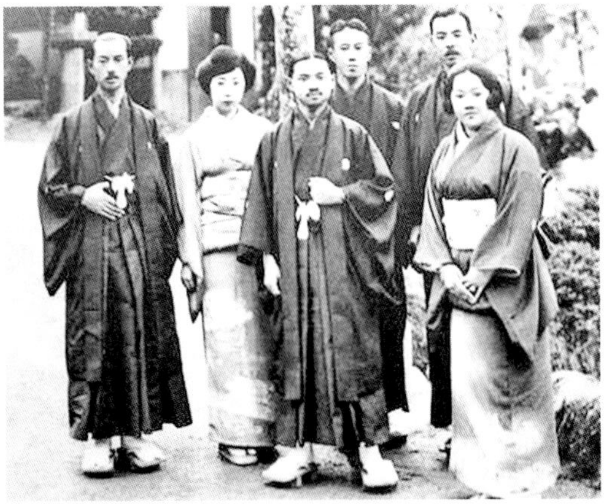

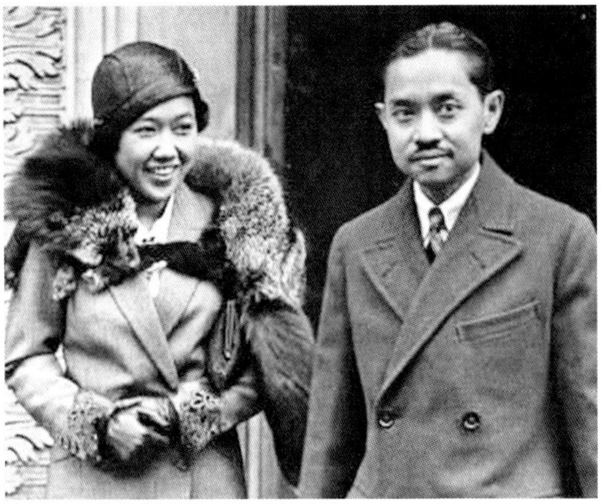

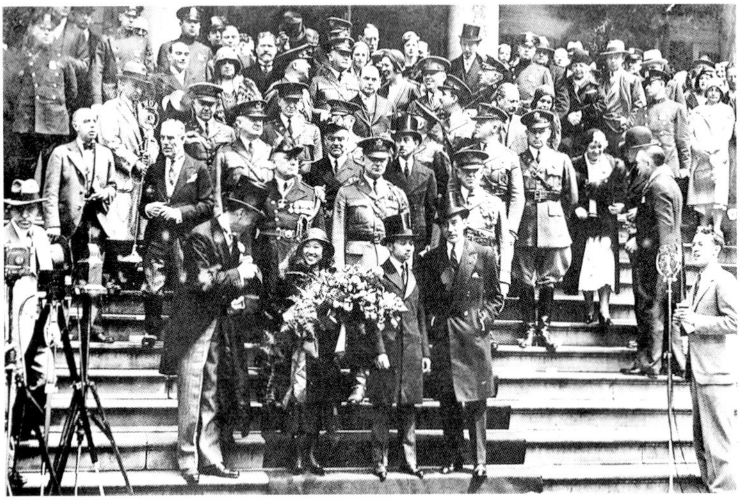

ABOVE LEFT: King Prajadhipok and Queen Rambai in Japan. (National Archives Bangkok)

ABOVE: The king leaving hospital after his eye operation. (National Archives Bangkok)

LEFT: Reception on the steps of the New York Town Hall for the king and queen. (National Archives Bangkok)

By now, Prince Bhanurangsi had been dead for three years, so while the king was away Prince Paribatra was made Regent. It was just at that time that the country was hard hit by the universal slump, and, as part of further economies, there was more retrenchment in the armed services – mostly in the army which was the largest of the three – all carried out by Prince Paribatra in the king's name. Prince Bavoradej, the Minister of Defence, who was *not* also in the Supreme Council, resigned in protest and instantly became a hero in the eyes of most serving officers. His position in the royal family was that of a minor prince, but he was senior in age (born 1877), and was a highly respected friend of the king's. He had been educated in England at Harrow and the Military Academy, Woolwich.

Prince Paribatra's son, Chumbhot, had gone to Harrow in 1921. After he left in 1925 he had a long holiday in Siam where he met and fell in love with an attractive and brilliant girl, Pantip Devakul, daughter of Prince Traidos Devakul, and therefore granddaughter of Prince Devawongse, Foreign Minister for over forty years, who had died in 1923. Prince Traidos had taken his father's place as Foreign Minister

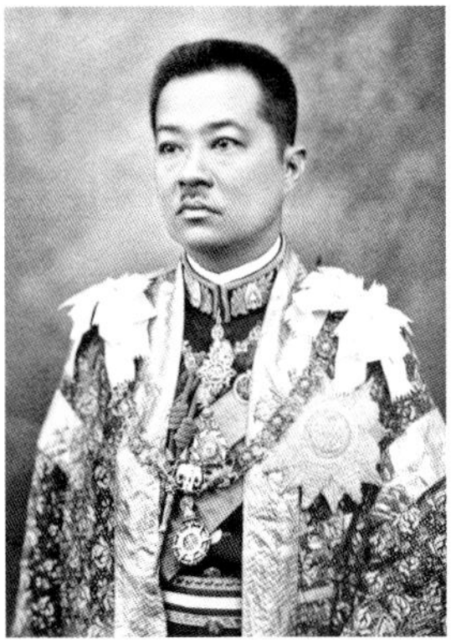

Prince Paribatra. (Paisarn Piemmettawat)

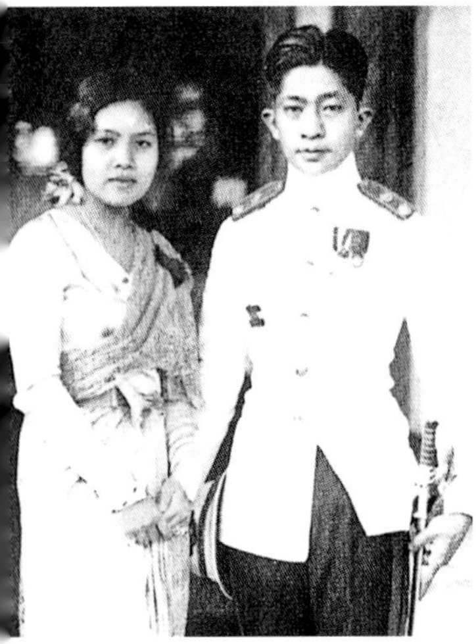

Prince Chumbhot and Mom Rajawongse Pantip Paribatra on their wedding day in 1930. (River Books)

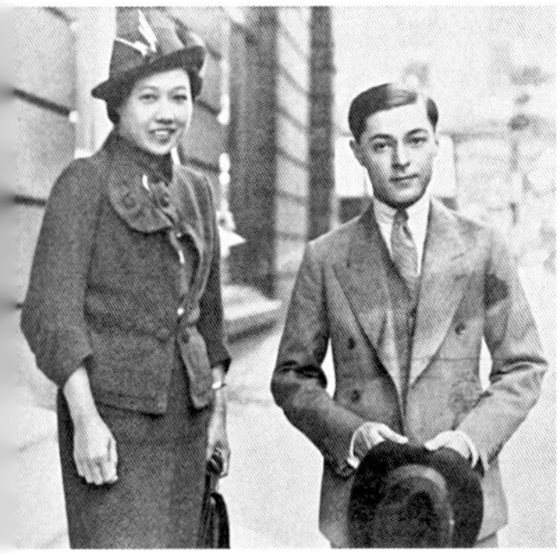

Prince Chula with Queen Rambai Barni. (River Books)

and had been created Prince Devawongse II. After Prince Chumbhot took his degree at Oxford in 1930, he returned to Siam and married Pantip, and they had a baby daughter. Prince Chumbhot was undergoing his apprenticeship in a junior post in the Ministry of Finance. The king's full nephew, Chula Chakrabongse, had also gone to Harrow in 1923, and from there had gone straight to Trinity, Cambridge, taking his degree in history in 1930. In September, 1931, the king allowed him to return to Bangkok for a few months' leave before continuing his historical research at Cambridge, and while he was in Siam he was in the position to observe at close quarters the twilight of the Absolute and Paternal Monarchy.

He went out by ship to Penang and thence by rail to Bangkok. The king met him at the private royal station which was a rare and high honour, as neither King Rama VI nor King Prajadhipok had ever gone to the station to meet anyone except the deceased senior members of the royal family. During his stay the king gave him the Ratanaporn or Royal Cypher Medal First Class, and when he later left by rail for Penang on his way to England, the king again went to the station to see him off. This led to a good deal of speculation about the young man's future which suggested that people did not expect the king to live for long, and many people were wondering who would ultimately be the heir, as the king had the right to nominate any prince.

The king was living mostly at Dusit Palace in the Amporn Villa where King Chulalongkorn had died in 1910. The third floor where he had lived and died was preserved as it was in his time and never again occupied. As King Prajadhipok was childless, he took much interest in his nephews and nieces, and his only other full-nephew, Varanand, was living with him. Chumbhot had been lent Suan Kularb Palace near by, and his lively wife, Pantip, was one of the king's favourite companions, and she and her husband visited him frequently. Prince Aditya had entered the Civil Service and was a successful provincial governor, having married Kobkaow Viseshkul, one of the most charming and possibly the best dressed women in Siam. Had it not been for circumstances beyond his control, Chula Chakrabongse would have returned in 1933 to serve in the Ministry of Education, and would very likely have married a cousin.

In November, 1931, Britain had just had the full taste of the world slump and had gone off the Gold Standard when the MacDonald-Baldwin National Government had been returned to power with a bumper majority. Siam had always traded largely with the sterling area, but following the advice of the Financial Adviser, E. L. Hall-Patch, as was generally believed, Siam decided to stay on the Gold Standard. Hall-Patch resigned shortly afterwards and as he never submitted a Financial Adviser's report no details are exactly known. Economic difficulties soon arose through Thai rice being too dear in the sterling market. This made the king anxious and unhappy, with Supreme Council and Cabinet meetings going on for hours, and the king often

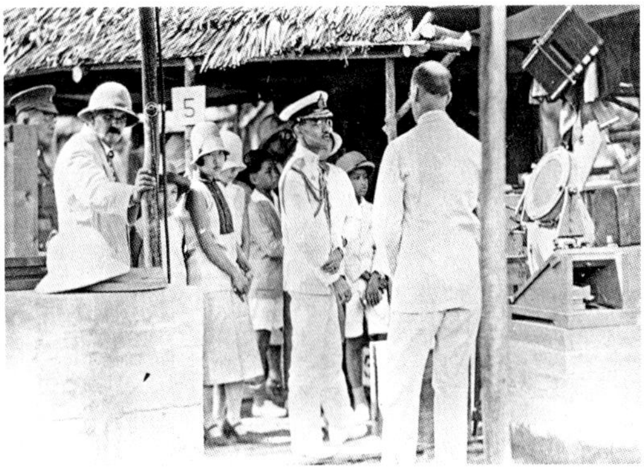

King Prajadhipok and Queen Rambai on a visit to Pattani. (National Archives Bangkok)

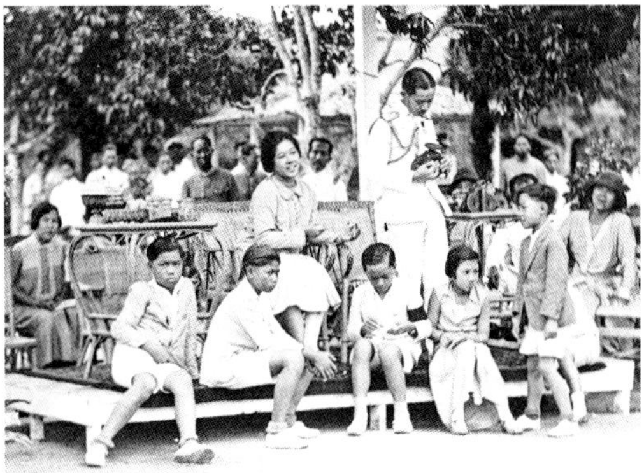

King Prajadhipok and Queen Rambai with various relatives and their entourage. (National Archives Bangkok)

did not sit down to lunch until 3 o'clock. However much advice he might get from other people, responsibility ultimately rested with the king alone. One day at a family dinner party he exclaimed: "I'm only a soldier, how can I understand such things as the Gold Standard?"

It soon transpired that amongst the intelligentsia, whether educated abroad or at home, there were many who, although loyal to the throne and the dynasty, felt that the situation had got beyond the king. Nor did they appear to have confidence in the Supreme Council. Prince Paribatra in particular was unpopular, which was unjust as he could in no way be blamed for the world slump which had hit the country. By and large the more highly educated people were convinced that they should be allowed a share in governing the country. The king decided in November, 1931, to talk to a large meeting of army officers and explain the current economic difficulties, as from one soldier to other soldiers, hoping that they would understand and sympathize. One of those officers told the present writer in 1937 that he left the meeting in tears, feeling that his king had become powerless. He was a young captain who for a while had been attached to the French army in the artillery, and his name was Luang Pibulsongkram (Plaek Kittasangha).

Owing to the continued and indeterminate existence of the Supreme Council composed solely of princes, there arose a strong feeling against princes in general, with Prince Paribatra the main and undeserved target of attack. The princes were believed to be enormously rich, so they were the butt of resentment following the slump. To Prince Paribatra were attributed, in imagination and talk, millions of baht which we now know for certain he could not possibly have had. The intrepid and enterprising Prince Purachatra was also criticised for being extravagant, but in reality his journeys to Europe, his cameras, his experimental radio sets, and other latest acquisitions, were part of the trials and tests for new equipment for the Ministry of Commerce and Communications, of which he was the Minister.

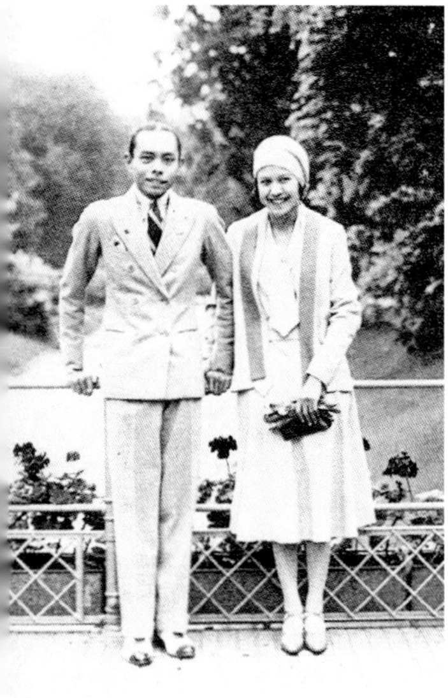

Prince Aditya and his wife, Mom Kobkaew. (National Archives Bangkok)

As he had given up an army career to go to Cambridge, Chula Chakrabongse received the king's consent to go back to Cambridge for two years' more research in history before finally returning to serve in the Ministry of Education. During his stay in Siam that autumn he had the opportunity to visit a large number of schools, both for boys and girls, run by the State, Thai private, Chinese, and Christian missionaries, as well as the University and Technical Colleges. Everywhere he found that the thirst for study and knowledge amongst the youth of Siam was keen and insatiable.

Chula Chakrabongse also had the chance to attend many religious and traditional ceremonies, some of which were being held for the last time in the twilight of the old regime. The most beautiful of these was the *Kathin* festival in which the king went to the great temples in full pomp. *Kathins* take place at the end of the Buddhist "Lent" or Wet Season, when people from all over the country make up parties to go to the temples to present useful gifts to the monks, followed by all kinds of harmless fun and games. It was after the *Kathin* that those men who had entered the monastery for the three months took leave of the hallowed Yellow Robe. The king went to the important Bangkok monasteries in full dress, accompanied by the royal family. By land he went in procession preceded by the Guards Division in full dress, as well as a Guard dressed in ancient style, with the sovereign himself borne on a golden palanquin held aloft by sixty mm, and surrounded by his entourage. For the river *Kathin* procession, the gorgeous and over 100-foot long gilded royal barges were used, and they were paddled along by men dressed in scarlet with the paddle blades painted in gold.

As he left Dusit Palace with the king to go to the private railway station on his return to Cambridge, Chula Chakrabongse did not know that he was seeing for the last time the Royal Standard – the red Garuda on the saffron yellow background – flying above the large marble throne hall of King Chulalongkorn. As the king bade him an affectionate farewell, it was the last time that he saw his uncle as the Absolute and Paternal Monarch of Siam.

King Prajadhipok is taken on a palanquin from the Borom Phiman Throne Hall to the Grand Palace during a royal ceremony. (National Archives Bangkok)

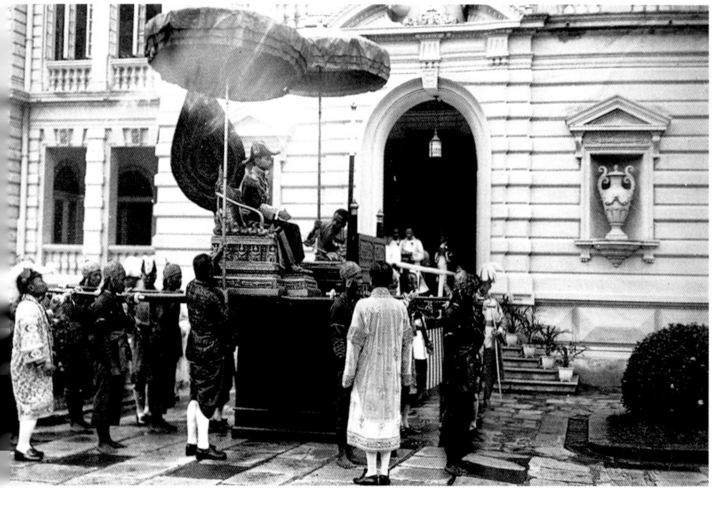

In Bangkok as April 6th, 1932, was approaching, preparations were in hand to celebrate the anniversary of one hundred and fifty years of Chakri rule, but all the while rumours were rampant. Superstitious pessimists were reminding one another of the alleged prophecy of Rama I that his line would only last for 150 years. Others were talking of an impending revolution or at least of assassinations of important personnages. But the ceremonies all

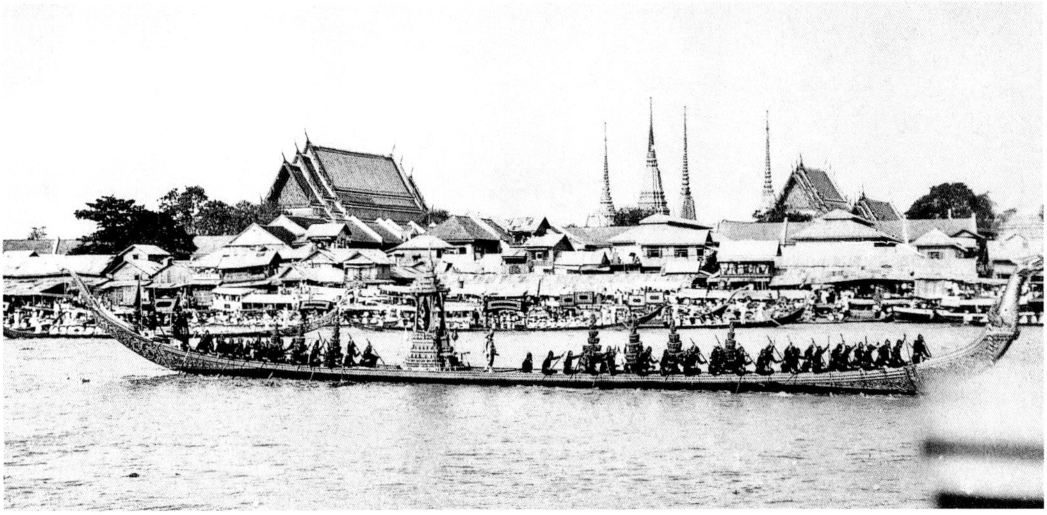

The Suphanahong royal barge on the Chao Phraya river at Ta Tien as part of the water procession in 1925.
(National Archives Bangkok)

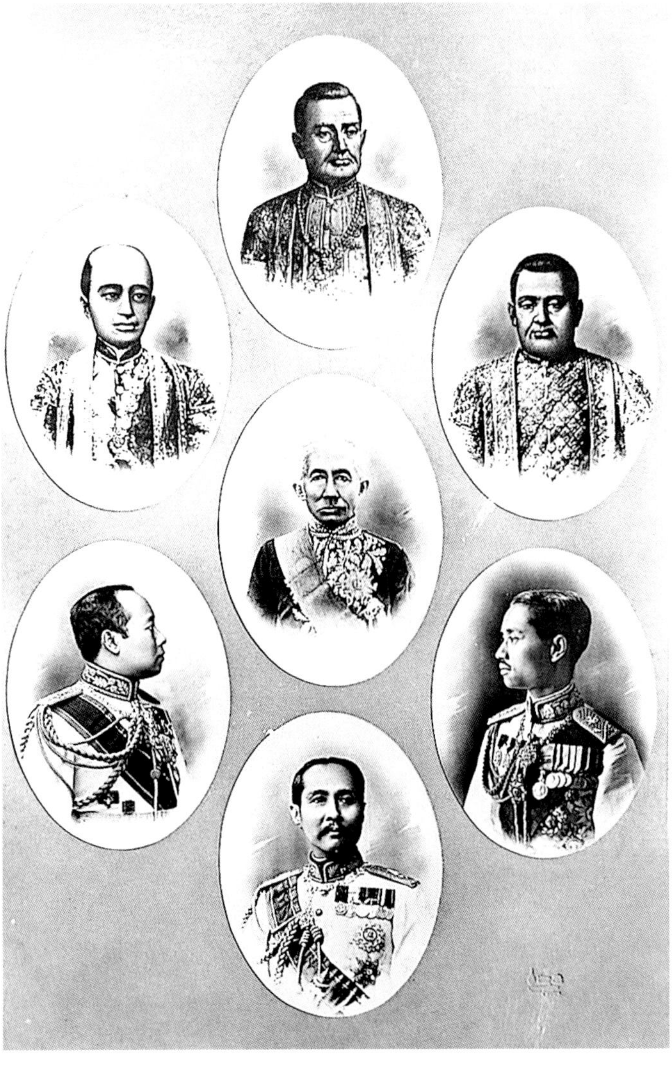

The seven monarchs of the first 150 years of the Chakri dynasty.
(National Archives Bangkok)

News reports of the celebrations for 150 years of the Chakri dynasty in *L'Illustration*.

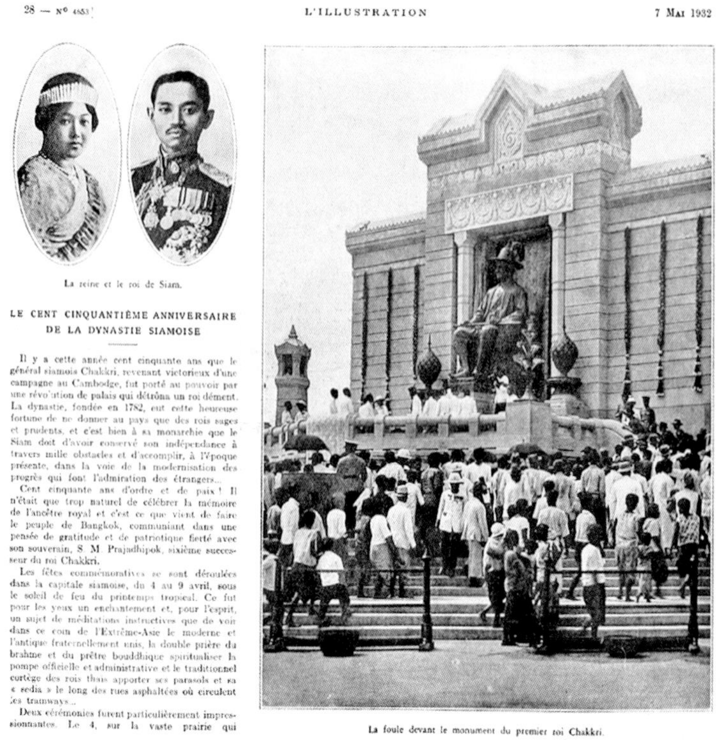

28 — N° 4653 L'ILLUSTRATION 7 Mai 1932

La reine et le roi de Siam.

LE CENT CINQUANTIÈME ANNIVERSAIRE DE LA DYNASTIE SIAMOISE

Il y a cette année cent cinquante ans que le général siamois Chakkri, revenant victorieux d'une campagne au Cambodge, fut porté au pouvoir par une révolution de palais qui détrôna un roi dément. La dynastie, fondée en 1782, eut cette heureuse fortune de ne donner au pays que des rois sages et prudents, et c'est bien à sa monarchie que le Siam doit d'avoir conservé son indépendance à travers mille obstacles et d'accomplir, à l'époque présente, dans la voie de la modernisation des progrès qui font l'admiration des étrangers...

Cent cinquante ans d'ordre et de paix ! Il n'était que trop naturel de célébrer la mémoire de l'ancêtre royal et c'est ce que vient de faire le peuple de Bangkok, communiant dans une pensée de gratitude et de patriotique fierté avec son souverain, S. M. Prajadhipok, sixième successeur du roi Chakkri.

Les fêtes commémoratives se sont déroulées dans la capitale siamoise, du 4 au 9 avril, sous le soleil de feu du printemps tropical. Ce fut pour les yeux un enchantement et, pour l'esprit, un sujet de méditations instructives que de voir dans ce coin de l'Extrême-Asie le moderne et l'antique fraternellement unis, la double prière du brahme et du prêtre bouddhique spiritualiser la pompe officielle et administrative et le traditionnel cortège des rois thaïs apporter ses parasols et sa « sedia » le long des rues asphaltées où circulent les tramways...

Deux cérémonies furent particulièrement impressionnantes. Le 4, sur la vaste prairie qui

La foule devant le monument du premier roi Chakkri.

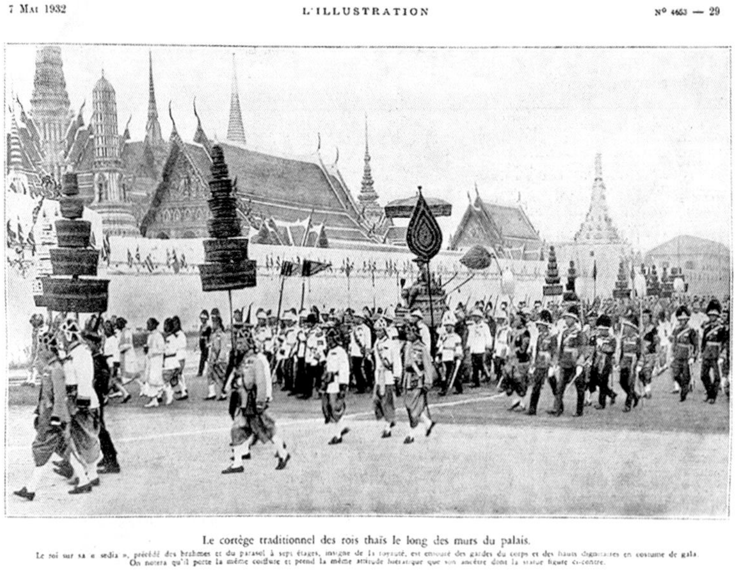

7 Mai 1932 L'ILLUSTRATION N° 4653 — 29

Le cortège traditionnel des rois thaïs le long des murs du palais.

Le roi sur sa « sedia », précédé des brahmes et du parasol à sept étages, insigne de la royauté, est entouré des gardes du corps et des hauts dignitaires en costume de gala. On notera qu'il porte la même coiffure et prend la même attitude hiératique que son ancêtre dont la statue figure ci-contre.

went off smoothly, and after the opening of the Rama I road bridge across the river linking Bangkok with Thonburi, the atmosphere was more calm and settled. There was one tragedy following these celebrations, the death of Prince Yugala on April 8th due to fatigue, as he was not really well enough to attend them. Then on May 11th, Siam suspended the Gold Standard, linking the baht to the £ at 11 baht, but it was too late.

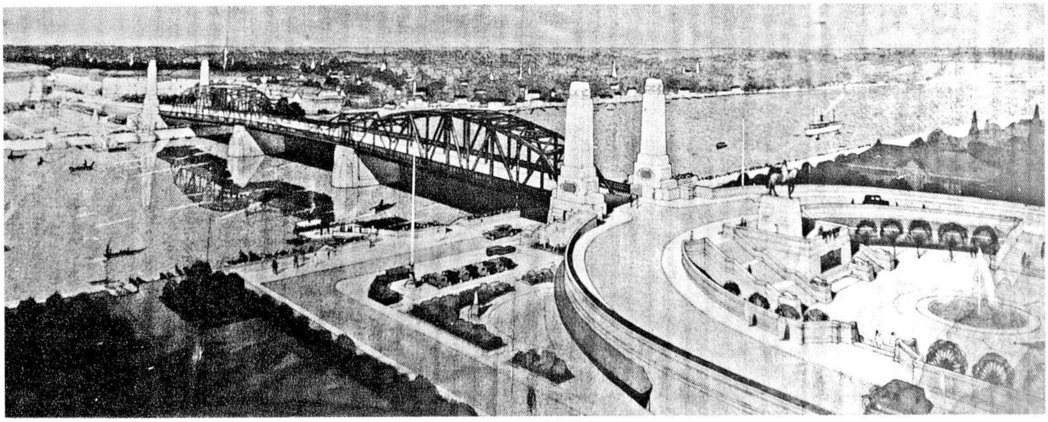

Memorial Bridge built to celebrate 150 years of the Chakri dynasty. (Paisarn Piemmettawat)

It all happened at dawn on June 24th, 1932, when a few tanks rumbled into the grounds of his palace and Prince Paribatra was taken away still in his pyjamas, his destination the marble throne hall of Dusit Palace over which the Royal Standard had flown until the day when the king had left for his annual summer holiday by the seaside. There the senior prince was joined by other princes and some ministers, who by chance were then in the capital. They had all been sent for and brought there at the same hour – reminiscent of Prince Chakrabongse's simultaneous arrests of the revolutionary leaders in 1912. They became hostages awaiting their fate while a letter was despatched to the king, then staying at his new palace at Hua Hin, ironically enough named Klai Kangwol, which meant "far from worries".

From all seemingly reliable accounts, mostly told to the author in 1937 by the persons directly concerned, this revolution had been prepared seven years earlier in Paris by some of the Thai students in France, the leaders being Pridi Banomyong, later appointed a junior judge with the title of Luang Pradit, and the soldier, Captain Luang Pibulsongkram, already mentioned. Upon their return to Siam these two began to work through secret channels, and it was reliably believed that amongst the military there were only 27 plotters, or *promoters* as they preferred to call themselves, while Pridi worked successfully amongst civilians, especially young lawyers. They based their reason for a change of regime on the world slump and the retrenchment scheme far more than the theory or the desirability of a democratic and parliamentary form of government. It was important that the military *promoters* persuaded Colonel Phraya Phahon of the Artillery, and Colonel Phraya Song of the Engineers, to join them, which was especially important because Phraya Song had the added advantage of being Commandant of the Staff College, with influence over the Weapons Training School, the Military Cadets Academy, and the Armoured Regiment. Luang Pibul, being junior in rank, was acting behind the scenes. Amongst the civilians, if Pridi was the most important person to deal with political propaganda and drafting a constitution, the most active was probably Kuang Abhaiwongse, also a former

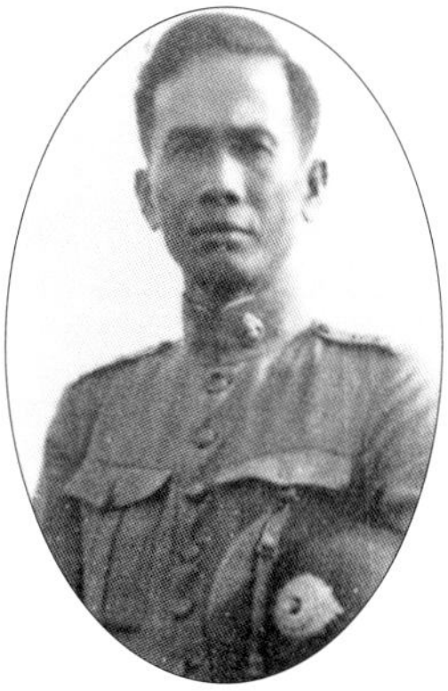

Luang Pibulsongkram. (National Archives Bangkok)

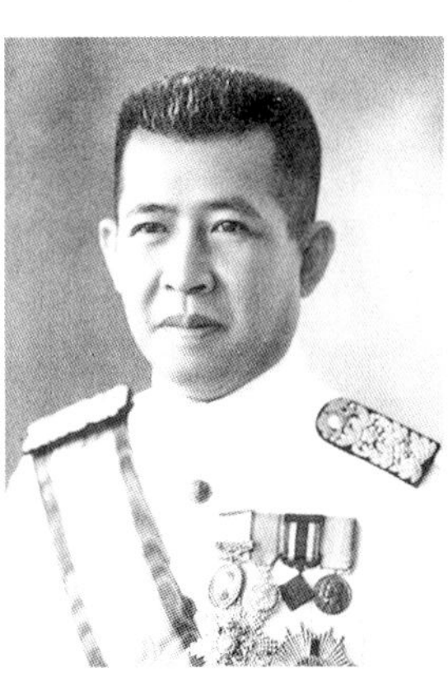

Pridi Banomyong (Luang Pradit Manutham), the civilian leader of the 1932 coup. (Paisarn Piemmettawat)

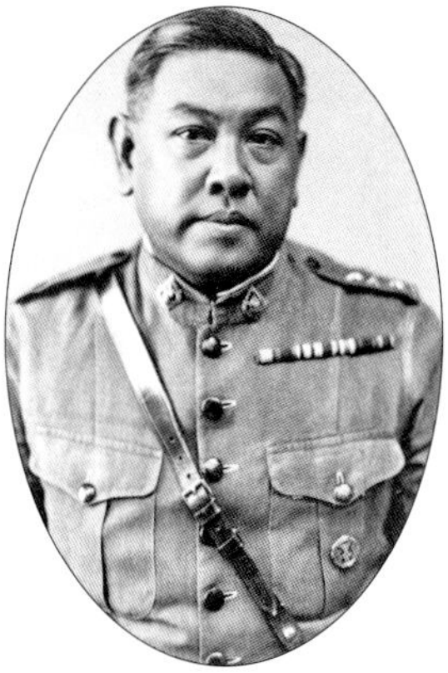

Phraya Phahon, the military leader of the coup on 24th June 1932. (Paisarn Piemmettawat)

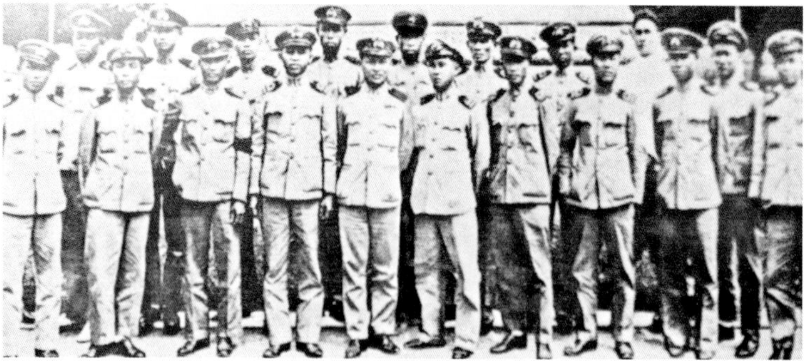

ABOVE RIGHT: The naval officers involved in the coup. (National Archives Bangkok)

student in France, who was in the postal services. It was he who saw to it that vital telephone and telegraph wires were cut if need be, and he directed the military to occupy important posts of communications such as radio stations and general post offices.

Ships and shore units of the Royal Thai Navy, in the absence of senior officers away on their annual holiday, were taken over by naval officers in on the plot, as with other vital services. The Royal Thai Air Force stayed aloof from the whole business. The remarkable feature was that not more than seventy men in all were in the plot, yet it was so daringly conceived and so perfectly carried out, that a one hundred and fifty-year-old monarchy could face a spectacular fall within a few hours. One of the reasons was that the upholders of the monarchy were so conscientious, that even though the Chief of Police had known of the plot for some time, the government had refused to permit early arrests because of insufficient evidence for legal warrants. Another interesting feature was that only a small portion of the army was in the know, while the majority, especially the infantry, knew nothing about it, and the provincial divisions had no share at all in the affair. The leaders arranged for the officer cadets, with some artillery and tanks, to assemble in the large square outside Dusit Palace where other units were ordered to converge for an exercise of internal security. Colonel Phahon then mounted a tank to declare that a revolution had taken place, its purpose being to ask the king for a constitution. Thus menaced by the guns of the artillery and tanks, the other units had no option but to give a cheer and join in. It was ironical that all of this took place within sight of the equestrian statue of King Chulalongkorn – the founder of the modern Thai Army.

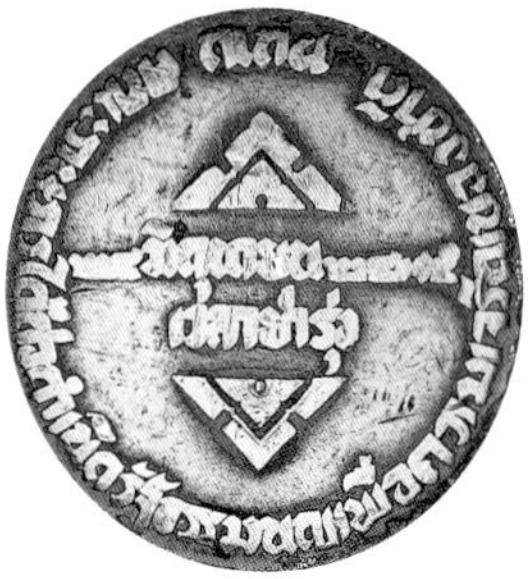

The brass plaque which until recently was set into the spot on the royal plaza where the revolution was announced. (River Books)

Many of the infantry units, who had not known of the plot, chose the passive role of shutting themselves up in their barracks. One of these was the 1st Infantry Regiment, King Chulalongkorn's Own Bodyguard, whose 2nd Battalion had barracks quite close to the square. A company commander later told the present writer that his battalion was all ready for action, but orders to move never came for the simple reason that the Guards Divisional Commander had been arrested. Later in the morning Prince Paribatra, from his captivity, issued a broadcast appeal that there should be no bloodshed between Thai people, and the affair was over as far as Bangkok was concerned. As Hall[2] says, "The public took no part

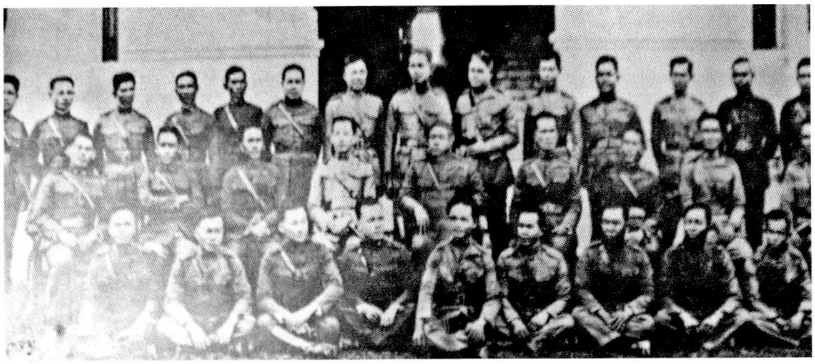

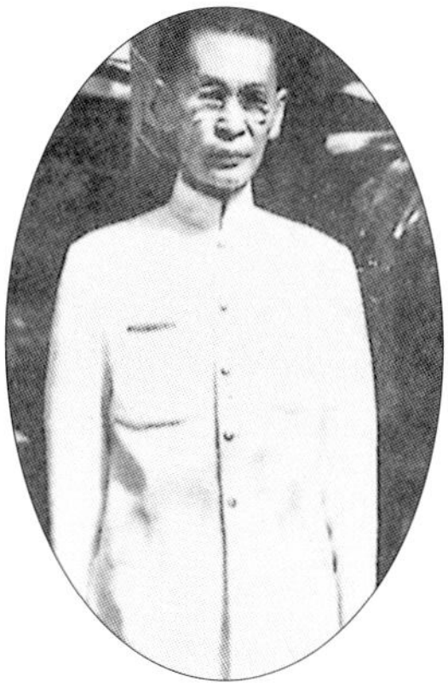

Luang Kowit Abhaiwongse, part of the People's Party. (National Archives Bangkok)

ABOVE LEFT: Army officers involved in the revolution. (National Archives Bangkok)

in the coup save as spectators." The scene now shifted to the king's summer palace at Hua Hin where, by coincidence, the princely heads of the army and navy were also on holiday, and they hurried to join the monarch, while Prince Purachatra, alone among the senior princes in Bangkok, escaped arrest by rushing down to Hua Hin in a detached railway engine. When unofficial news reached them, a debate began as to the line of action the king should take but as yet news from Bangkok was conflicting. The present narrative is largely based on the account given by the king himself. It had been stated in Bangkok that the aim of the movement was only to change the regime to that of constitutional monarchy with King Prajadhipok continuing to reign, if he accepted. But an anonymous pamphlet was widely distributed in which there was a vitriolic attack on the entire Chakri family, going right back to the founder, who for the first time was publicly branded as usurper to King Taksin. This pamphlet purported to have been composed by the People's Party, the name by which the promoters of the coup d' état called themselves.

Three courses were open to the king. One was to escape abroad, another was to return to Bangkok and accept to be a constitutional monarch, but the blood-curdling pamphlet which he had read was something of a deterrent. Thirdly he could attempt to rally the provincial divisions to fight the plotters, and some of the waverers in Bangkok might then join him. The king's father-in-law, Prince Svasti, constantly urged the king to return to the capital and see it through, for to fight would not only mean bloodshed between Thai people, but the senior princes in captivity might be massacred. The king wrote: "I felt I could not sit on a throne besmirched by blood."[3] King Prajadhipok was in favour of returning but the fierce manifesto made him hesitate. "I thought I would let the ladies act as a sort of penny that I toss up. Both the Queen and her mother firmly decided that we should all go back and I must say they deserve all honour and credit for making that brave decision because we were all quite aware that we were probably going to our death. The ladies preferred death to dishonour and that was enough for me."[4] They had been told by telegraph that a warship was being sent with an ultimatum, and according to the King, "I could hardly sleep at all and I suppose that my feelings were rather like the soldiers who will have to go over the top on the next day."[5]

2 D. G. E. Hall: *op. cit.*, page 677.

3 Letter in English: King Prajadhipok to Prince Chula, August, 1932. Original in author's possession.

4 *Ibid.*

5 *Ibid.*

The ultimatum which came the next day with the warship read as follows: "The People's Party consisting of civil and military officials have now taken over the administration of the country and have taken members of the Royal Family such as H.R.H. Prince Paribatra as hostages. If members of the People's Party receive any injuries the princes held in pawn will suffer in consequence. The People's Party have no desire to make a seizure of the Royal possessions in any way. Their principal aim is to have a constitutional monarchy. We therefore enjoin Your Majesty to return to the capital to reign again as king under the constitutional monarchy as established by the People's Party. If Your Majesty refuses to accept the offer, or refrain from replying within one hour after the receipt of this message, the People's Party will proclaim the constitutional monarchical government by appointing another prince whom they consider to be efficient as king."[6] It was signed by Phraya Phahon, Phraya Song, and Phraya Riddhi, all army colonels. It has often been a matter of speculation who this prince might be, and it is certain that by accepting to return to Bangkok, King Prajadhipok helped to preserve the succession in the lines indicated in the Law of Succession of 1924.

The king's reply was:

"To the Military in Defence of Bangkok:

I have received the letter in which you invite me to return to Bangkok as a constitutional monarch. For the sake of peace, and in order to save a useless bloodshed, to avoid confusion and loss to the country, and more, because I have already considered making this change myself, I am willing to co-operate in the establishment of a constitution under which I am willing to serve.

Furthermore, there is a possibility that, if I decline to continue in my office as king, the foreign powers will not recognize the new government (sic). This might entail considerable difficulty for the government.

Physically I am not strong. I have no children to succeed me. My life expectancy is not long, at least if I continue in this office. I have no desire for position or for personal aggrandisement. My ability to advance the progress of the (Thai) race alone constrains me.

Accept this sincere expression of my feelings.

Prajadhipok."[7]

The king returned to Bangkok by a special train after refusing to go by the warship which might make him seem like a prisoner. On his arrival at the private royal station he was silently met by seemingly sympathetic crowds, some of whom lined the roads from the station to Sukhothai Palace, his home before his accession. Once the king had returned to his capital, all thoughts of resistance ceased everywhere. Negotiations immediately began between the monarch and the promoters, who

6 English translation by *Bangkok Times*, June 24th, 1932.

7 English translation reproduced by K. P. Landon: *Siam in Transition*, page 10, London, 1939.

never admitted that they were rebels and he secured the release of the hostage princes, but they had to quit their official posts, and the Supreme Council was automatically dissolved.

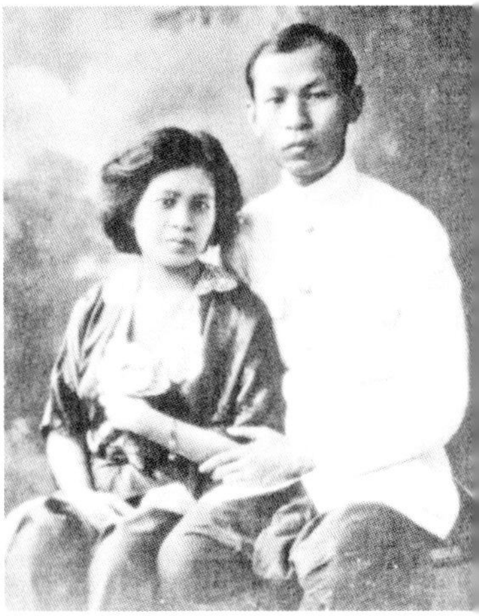

Phraya Manopakorn Nithithada and his wife Khunying Nid. (National Archives Bangkok)

The most important amongst the royal personages, Prince Paribatra, was requested to leave the country, and he departed for Java with his family never to return. Thus passed from Thai history this intelligent and sympathetic figure whose home was one of the centres of the arts of Siam and the Western world.

The Provisional Constitution which the king signed forthwith provided for one House of Parliament, which was called the People's Assembly, with the government being called the People's Committee, and the Prime Minister was to be known as Chairman of the People's Committee. Before a General Election could be held, deputies were nominated by the government in the king's name, and from then on legislation was in the hands of this Assembly. One of its first tasks was to pass the Act of Amnesty which absolved everyone in the coup from any guilt in an unlawful act. Within a short time the new government, which promised to adhere strictly to all treaty obligations, was recognized by the Powers. Having seen the actions of the Powers after the recent revolution in Iraq (1958), it is my belief that the new government of Siam would have been recognized whether King Prajadhipok remained on the throne or not.

When the list of nominated deputies was published, it was seen that they were composed largely of the promoters themselves or retired officials who had been out of favour in King Prajadhipok's reign. It was promised that a General Election, with universal suffrage for both sexes at or over 21 years of age, would be held as soon as possible, but it was laid down in the Constitution that the first ten years would be regarded as a trial period when for every elected deputy there would be one nominated, for the Thai people were considered to be insufficiently educated to rule themselves. The promoters thus showed themselves partly in agreement with King Rama VI. The Law of Succession of 1924 was accepted in this and the following Permanent Constitution, but with the proviso that the legal heir could only ascend the throne if approved by the Assembly, thus making a legal declaration that the kingship of Siam was partly hereditary and partly elective.

The big surprise was that the first Prime Minister was not chosen from one of the promoters themselves, which was probably to demonstrate their genuine good faith. Instead, he was Phraya Mano, President of the Supreme Appeal Court in the previous royal regime, and many of the newly-appointed ministers were senior men who had served royal masters before King Prajadhipok's reign. There were, however, many ministers without portfolios who were the young promoters, most prominent being Luang Pibulsongkram and Luang Pradit (Pridi Banomyong).

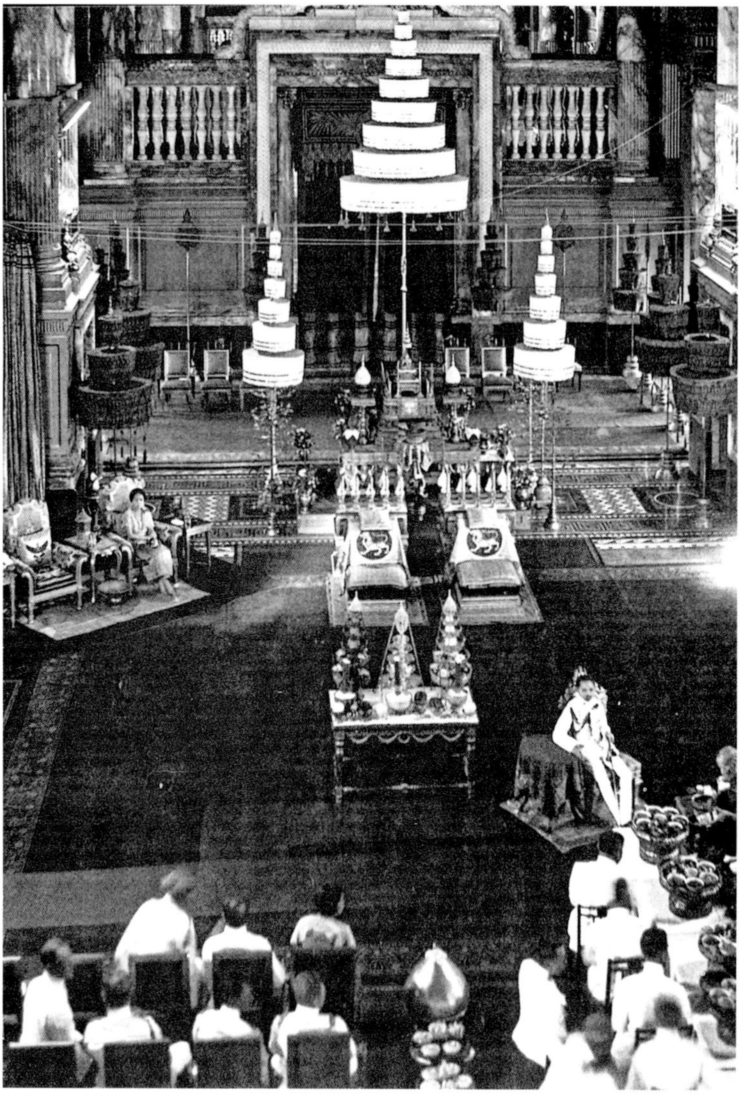

King Prajadhipok and Queen Rambai presiding over the constitution granting ceremony in the Ananta Samakhom Throne Hall on 9th December 1932. (National Archives Bangkok)

King Prajadhipok made a stupendous personal effort to negotiate for a sensible and durable "permanent" constitution, and the difficult task took over five months to accomplish. Although basically it had many points in common with the June constitution, the new one was much more to the king's liking. He obtained the right to dissolve the Assembly, and words which were distasteful to him were dropped. The Chairman of the People's Committee now became President of the State Council, the government was designated His Majesty's government, with Parliament known as the Assembly of the People's Representatives. Before signing the new constitution, the king requested that all the promoters should go as a body and pay homage and offer apologies not only to him, but to the royal family as a whole, for the bitter words of abuse of Rama I in the manifesto. This they agreed to do. When the time came there were a few absentees, but in any case all appeared to have been forgiven. Although the mutual suspicion was not really allayed, with the negotiation being concluded on a happier note, King Prajadhipok signed the "permanent" constitution on December 10th, 1932. For this the king devised a solemn ceremony and wore the crown for the first time since his coronation. He wrote thus about it all: "I had thought out the details of such a ceremony for years, knowing that it will have to come in my life time . . . Even the proclamation that was read had been drafted in my mind for a long time . . . I naturally regret a little that it could not come off as I had planned for such a long time, but really I suppose that it is best as it is. If I had granted a constitution myself those people who want power, and have now got it, would have been still left in the cold, and there might have been a severe agitation for a republic and a much worse form of rising . . . I feel that my life work is done and that I have nothing more to do except to live on peaceably if possible . . . I don't know whether you realize it or not, as you are far from Siam, but the actual fact is that this movement for a constitution is not as popular in Siam as one might expect."[8]

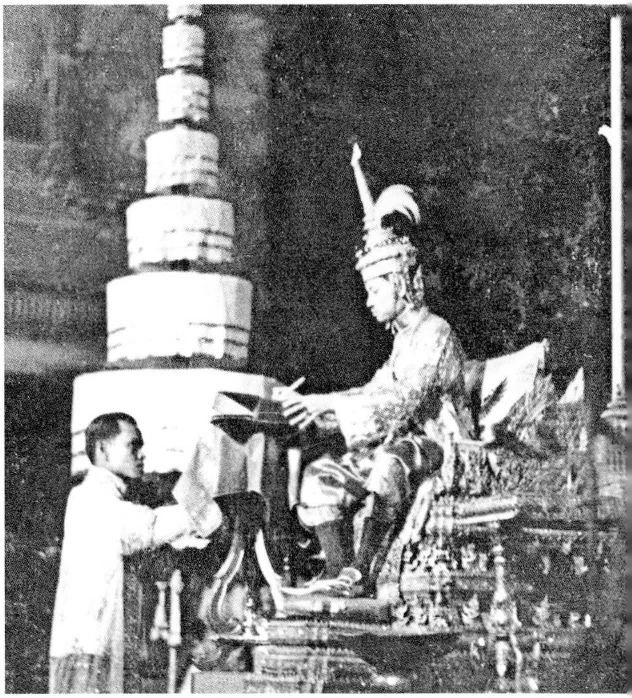

King Prajadhipok granting the constitution and wearing the crown for the last time. (National Archives Bangkok)

That was how the paternal or absolute monarchy of the Chakri Dynasty came to an end after just over 150 years. Many people remarked that Rama I's prophesy had been proved true. We have in the foregoing pages followed the last absolute monarch from his early youth, his education in England, and his mature life. Although not as handsome as some of his brothers, and extremely short, King Prajadhipok possessed great natural dignity always, and charm when his intense shyness allowed it to come forth. Although a soldier by upbringing and profession, he was marvellously well read in English and French in most subjects, and his fund of knowledge was astounding. A brilliant and indefatigable talker, he had a keen sense of humour, did not mind being argued with or contradicted, and could see every side of every question. As Hall[9] rightly said: "Prajadhipok had never expected or desired to become king." But if someone else had been king when the regime had to be changed, things might have turned out differently. In years to come King Prajadhipok might well be regarded as the true *philosopher*, who was the saviour of the Thai monarchy, and in that case possibly also of Siam's age-old traditions and ancient heritage.

On Decemher 10th, 1932, the seventh king of the Chakri Dynasty ceased to rule. The question was: Would he continue to reign?

8 Letter in English: King Prajadhipok to Prince Chula written during December, 1932, and January, 1933. Original in the author's possession.

9 D. G. E. Hall: *op. cit.*, page 675.

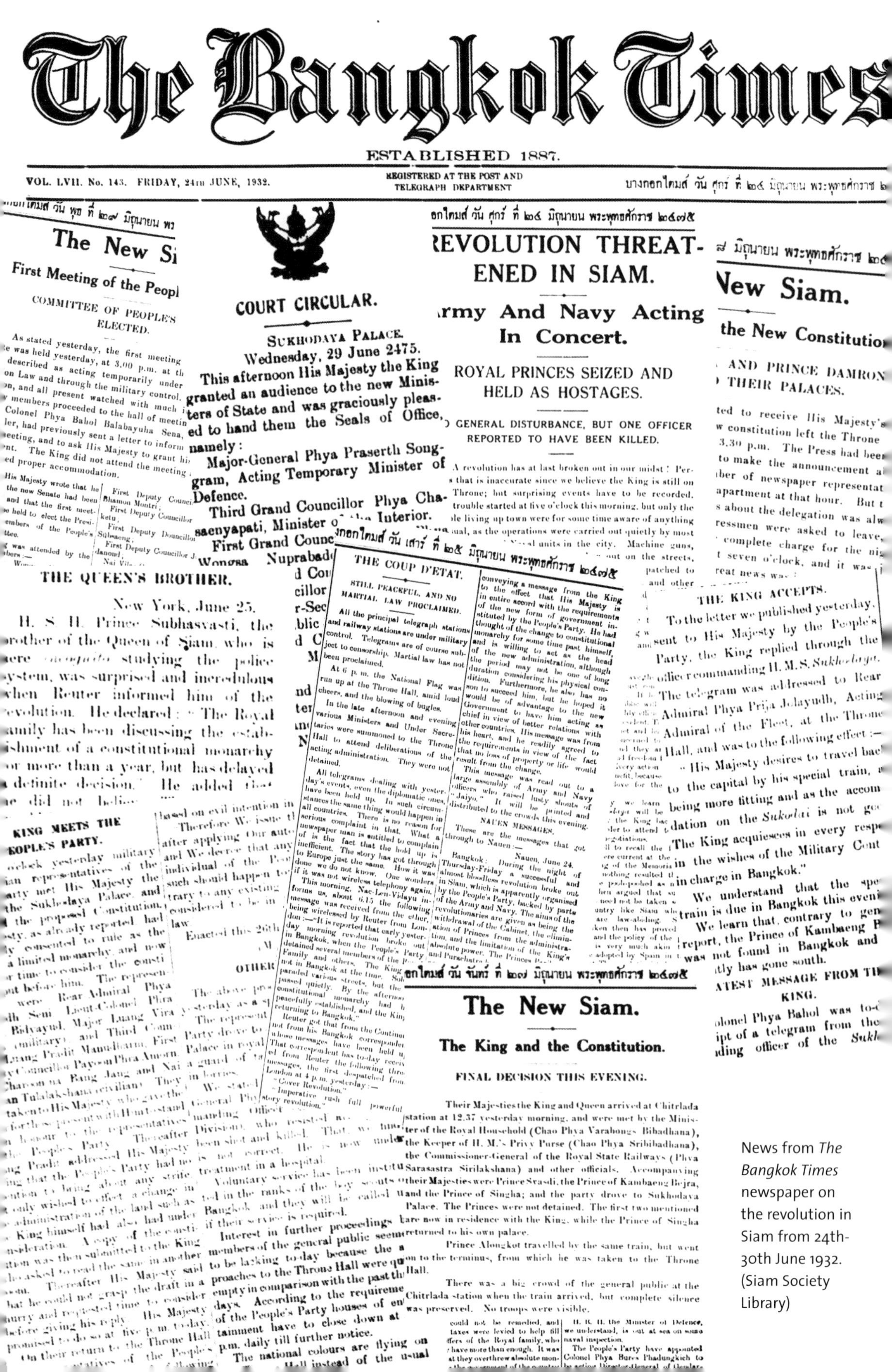

The Bangkok Times

ESTABLISHED 1887.

VOL. LVII. No. 143. FRIDAY, 24TH JUNE, 1932. REGISTERED AT THE POST AND TELEGRAPH DEPARTMENT บางกอกไทมส์ วัน ศุกร์ ที่ ๒๔ มิถุนายน พระพุทธศักราช ๒

The New Si...

First Meeting of the Peopl...

COMMITTEE OF PEOPLE'S ... ELECTED.

As stated yesterday, the first meeting ... was held yesterday, at 3.00 p.m. at th... described as acting temporarily under ... on Law and through the military control. ... and all present watched with much i... members proceeded to the hall of meetin... Colonel Phya Bahol Balabayuha Sena, ... ler, had previously sent a letter to inform ... meeting, and to ask His Majesty to grant hi... The King did not attend the meeting ... ed proper accommodation.

COURT CIRCULAR.

SUKHODAYA PALACE. Wednesday, 29 June 2475.

This afternoon His Majesty the King granted an audience to the new Ministers of State and was graciously pleased to hand them the Seals of Office, namely:

Major-General Phya Praserth Songgram, Acting Temporary Minister of Defence.

Third Grand Councillor Phya Chasaenyapati, Minister of the Interior.

First Grand Counc... Wongsa Nuprabad...

...REVOLUTION THREATENED IN SIAM.

...rmy And Navy Acting In Concert.

ROYAL PRINCES SEIZED AND HELD AS HOSTAGES.

...O GENERAL DISTURBANCE, BUT ONE OFFICER REPORTED TO HAVE BEEN KILLED.

A revolution has at last broken out in our midst! Per... s that is inaccurate since we believe the King is still on ... Throne; but surprising events have to be recorded. ... trouble started at five o'clock this morning, but only the ... le living up town were for some time aware of anything ... ual, as the operations were carried out quietly by most ...

...New Siam.

...the New Constitution

... AND PRINCE DAMRON... ... THEIR PALACES.

...ted to receive His Majesty's ... w constitution left the Throne ... 3.30 p.m. The Press had bee... to make the announcement a... ber of newspaper representat... apartment at that hour. But ... s about the delegation was alw... ressmen were asked to leave, ... complete charge for the ni... t seven o'clock, and it was ... reat news was:

THE QUEEN'S BROTHER.

New York, June 25.

H. S. H. Prince Subhasvasti, the brother of the Queen of Siam, who is here *incognito* studying the police system, was surprised and incredulous when Reuter informed him of the revolution. He declared: "The Royal family has been discussing the establishment of a constitutional monarchy for more than a year, but has delayed a definite decision." He added that he did not beli...

THE COUP D'ETAT.

STILL PEACEFUL, AND NO MARTIAL LAW PROCLAIMED.

All the principal telegraph stations and railway stations are under military control. Telegrams are of course subject to censorship. Martial law has not been proclaimed.

At 6 p.m. the National Flag was run up at the Throne Hall, amid loud cheers, and the blowing of bugles.

In the late afternoon and evening various Ministers and Under Secretaries were summoned to the Throne Hall to attend deliberations of the acting administration. They were not detained.

...conveying a message from the King to the effect that His Majesty is in entire accord with the requirements of the new form of government instituted by the People's Party. He had thought of the change to constitutional monarchy for some time past himself, and is willing to act as the head of the new administration, although the period may not be one of long duration considering his physical condition. ... This message was read out to a large assembly of Army and Navy officers who raised lusty shouts of "Jaiyo." It will be printed and distributed to the crowds this evening.

NAUEN MESSAGES.

These are the messages that got through to Nauen:—

Nauen, June 24. Bangkok: During the night of Thursday-Friday a successful and almost bloodless revolution broke out in Siam, which is apparently organised by the People's Party, backed by parts of the Army and Navy. ...

THE KING ACCEPTS.

To the letter we published yesterday, sent to His Majesty by the People's Party, the King replied through the officer commanding H. M. S. *Sukhodaya*. The telegram was addressed to Rear Admiral Phya Prija Jolayudh, Acting Admiral of the Fleet, at the Throne Hall, and was to the following effect:—

"His Majesty desires to travel back to the capital by his special train, as being more fitting and as the accommodation on the *Sukodai* is not go... The King acquiesces in every respe... in the wishes of the Military Com... in charge in Bangkok."

We understand that the spe... train is due in Bangkok this eveni...

We learn that, contrary to gen... report, the Prince of Kambaeng P... was not found in Bangkok and ... tly has gone south.

...ATEST MESSAGE FROM THE KING.

...olonel Phya Bahol was to-... ipt of a telegram from the ... nding officer of the *Sukh*...

KING MEETS THE ...EOPLE'S PARTY.

...o'clock yesterday military ... ian representatives of the ... arty met His Majesty the ... the Sukhodaya Palace, and ... the proposed Constitution. ...

The New Siam.

The King and the Constitution.

FINAL DECISION THIS EVENING.

Their Majesties the King and Queen arrived at Chitrlada station at 12.37 yesterday morning, and were met by the Minister of the Royal Household (Chao Phya Varabongs Bibadhana), the Keeper of H. M.'s Privy Purse (Chao Phya Sribibadhana), the Commissioner-General of the Royal State Railways (Phya Sarasastra Sirilakshana) and other officials. Accompanying their Majesties were Prince Svasdi, the Prince of Kambaeng Bejra, and the Prince of Singha; and the party drove to Sukhodaya Palace. The Princes were not detained. The first two mentioned are now in residence with the King, while the Prince of Singha returned to his own palace.

Prince Alongkot travelled by the same train, but went on to the terminus, from which he was taken to the Throne Hall.

There was a big crowd of the general public at the Chitrlada station when the train arrived, but complete silence was preserved. No troops were visible.

Interest in further proceedings ... members of the general public seem... to be lacking to-day because the a... proaches to the Throne Hall were qu... empty in comparison with the past th... days. According to the requireme... of the People's Party houses of en... tainment have to close down at ... p.m. daily till further notice.

The national colours are flying on ...

News from *The Bangkok Times* newspaper on the revolution in Siam from 24th-30th June 1932. (Siam Society Library)

After
(A.D. 1932 To 1959)

Although he no longer ruled after December 10th, 1932, King Prajadhipok still reigned. After the signing of the "permanent" constitution the political weather was calm for a while until a storm began brewing early in 1933. The People's Party had earlier declared its aims in six points, the third of which was "A national economic policy must be drawn up to provide remunerative work for everyone." This difficult task had been entrusted to Pridi, a lawyer by training, who in due time produced his plan. The gist of it was the nationalization of all agricultural land which would be purchased by the issue of bonds and not by cash, and all the farmers would then become government officials with a fixed salary. The salary to be paid to these farm workers was also in the form of cheques which could only be spent in government stores, thus reducing the price of consumer goods and destroying the profit system. The sales of rice at home and abroad would be undertaken by the government; so the middlemen – mainly the Chinese – would be eliminated.

The presentation of the Pridi plan split the People's Party, as some of its members, particularly the military, considered it Communistic, with a strong minority vehement in its defence. A serious rift in the Cabinet followed, the majority, led by Premier Phraya Mano, emphasizing its Communistic aspects, but Pridi nevertheless had some of the young civilians as his supporters. Mano submitted the Pridi plan to the king, who also declared that it was Communistic, giving many

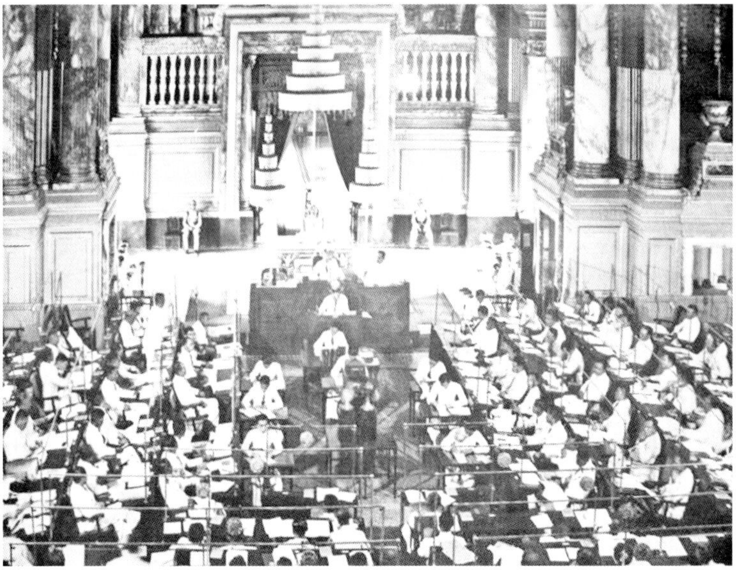

Early meeting of the People's Council. (National Archives Bangkok)

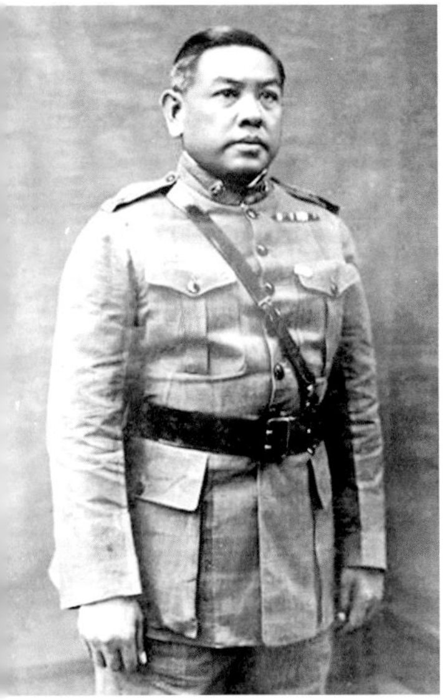

Phraya Phahon was Prime Minister five times between June 1932 and December 1938. (Paisarn Piemmettawat)

reasons to support his arguments. He further suggested that the plan would never be tolerated by the Thai farmers, who would sooner disappear to lead a rigorous and spartan life in the jungle than submit to such regimentation. Mano then published the king's review of Pridi's plan in pamphlet form, probably with the king's consent. He did not seem to think, although he was at the English Bar as a student and qualified, that this was contrary to the generally accepted principle that the sovereign's warning or advice to his ministers should not be made known to the people.

Feelings became so embittered in the Assembly that violence appeared imminent with some deputies brandishing loaded revolvers in the chamber. Things escalated to such an extent that Colonel Song felt it necessary to bring troops to guard the doors and search members for firearms. Owing to Colonel Phahon's personal regard for him, Pridi was enabled quietly to resign from the cabinet and permitted to leave the country for an indefinite period. Now, giving danger of violence as the reason, Mano obtained the king's consent to prorogue the Assembly on April 1st, 1933 – then still the Thai New Year Day for B.E. 2476 – after which he proceeded to rule by decree. Having thus far supported Mano, the two important colonels, Phahon and Song, then ominously resigned not only from the government but from their active posts in the army as well. Assured otherwise of the army's loyalty to his regime, Mano blithely accepted their resignations and was so bold as to appoint as the army C-in-C a retired general who had not been one of the promoters of the 1932 coup. During Mano's rule by royal decree, the "diehard" royalists rejoiced in their belief that the days of the absolute monarchy were returning.

On June 20th, 1933, a fresh blow was struck when, with less than four days to a year, history was repeated with the king again being at his seaside home at Hua Hin. The new coup was again made by Phahon, and for its complete success he was supported by the younger Pibulsongkram. This coup resulted in the exit from Thai politics of Mano and Song, although the latter continued to hover in the background until his death, while Mano went to Penang in exile and was not really heard of again. The aim of the new coup was to recall the Assembly, and at the same time send expressions of loyalty to the king, who accepted the *fait accompli* and asked Phahon to form a new government, which, after some show of reluctance, he agreed to do. As he was a soldier, he said, he needed expert civilian advice, and Prince Wan Waitayakorn (born 1891), a son of Prince Naradhip (born 1861 and a son of King Mongkut), formerly in the Foreign Office and then living in retirement, was given the post of general adviser to the Premier. He continued to occupy this post in nearly all subsequent governments, became Foreign Secretary and Deputy-Premier, and in time would play a prominent role at the United Nations, which included being President of the United Nations Assembly. Pridi soon returned at Phahon's invitation after a tribunal had cleansed him of the taints of being a Communist. The king agreed to his rejoining the government, and this time with a portfolio, namely, as Minister of the Interior.

The return of the promoters (nicknamed *Dee Nueng* as in Thai *Dee* means Good and *Nueng* means One or First Class) to full power in June, 1933, made the more active royalists, who were now largely constitutionalists too, feel that the *Dee Nuengs* could not be removed except by force. These men were mostly retired Army generals, led by Phraya Sri Sitthi Songkhram. Contrary to general belief, the former Defence Minister, Prince Bavoradej, joined in the plot later, and his princely rank made it a full-fledged royalist plot which was not to its advantage. Once again the king was at Hua Hin, where he tended to pass more and more time, when civil war broke out in October, 1933. Provincial troops led by Prince Bavoradej and General Sri Sitthi Songkhram converged on the capital with the declared aim of freeing the king from the People's Party and setting up a more genuinely democratic constitutional monarchy. Their hopes that some units in Bangkok would rise to give them support did not materialize and it was Pibul who conducted the successful defence which greatly increased his prestige in the People's Party. Phahon emphasized in his radio talks that he was the head of the king's legal government, designating the other side as rebels, and invited the king to return to Bangkok. Instead, the king decided to go further south, and after a perilous sea trip in a small motor-boat, reached Songkhla with the queen just before the "rebel" forces were defeated within the vicinity of the Don Muang Airport. Phraya Sri Sitthi Songkhram fell in action, while Prince Bavoradej and some other leaders made good their escape into French Indo-China, where they spent many years in exile. The others, who were captured or surrendered, were put on trial by a special court set up under a new law to protect the constitution, and were given various terms of imprisonment. Luang Prakob Nitisarn, a prominent Thai lawyer, who was put in prison to await trial as a suspect and was later acquitted and exonerated, has stated categorically to the present author that while in prison he talked freely with the "rebel" leaders. From these talks he formed the definite opinion that there was no

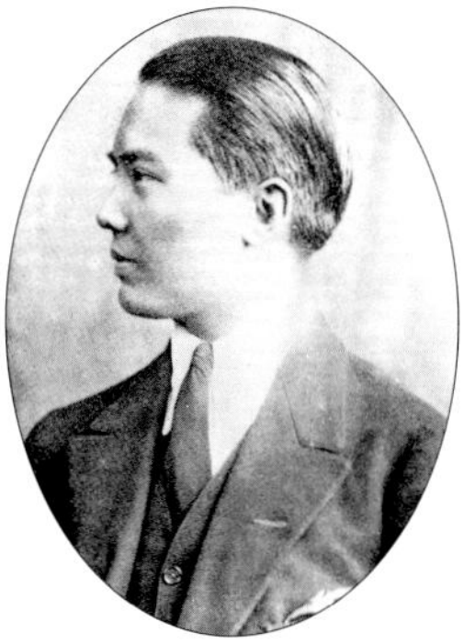

Prince Naradhip Pongprapan who was foreign minister and later deputy prime minister. (Paisarn Piemmettawat)

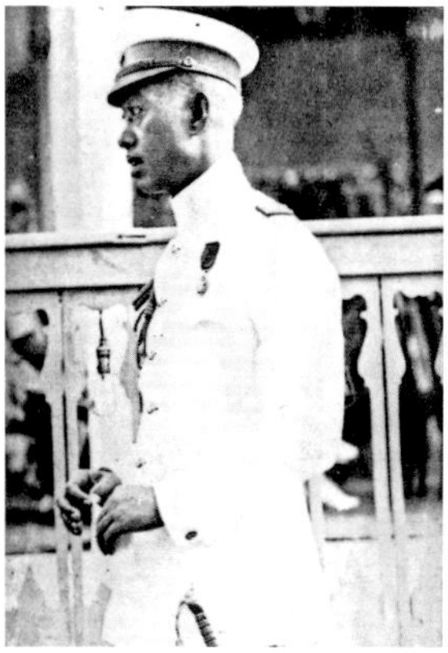

Prince Bavoradej while Minister of Defence in 1928. Later he led the failed coup of 1933. (National Archives Bangkok)

BELOW LEFT: Lak Si railway station was the rallying point for the plotters. (National Archives Bangkok)

BELOW: Government tank. (National Archives Bangkok)

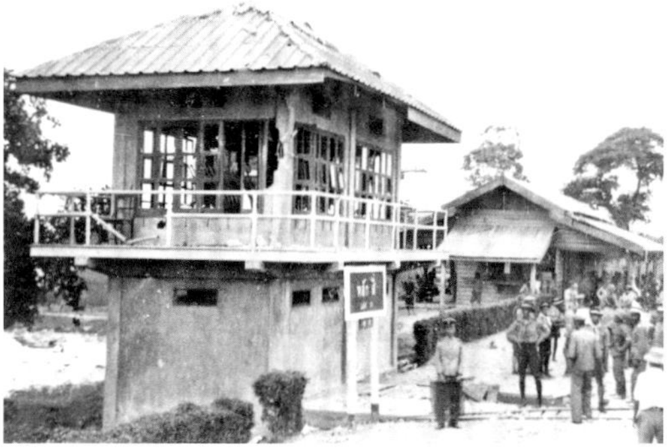

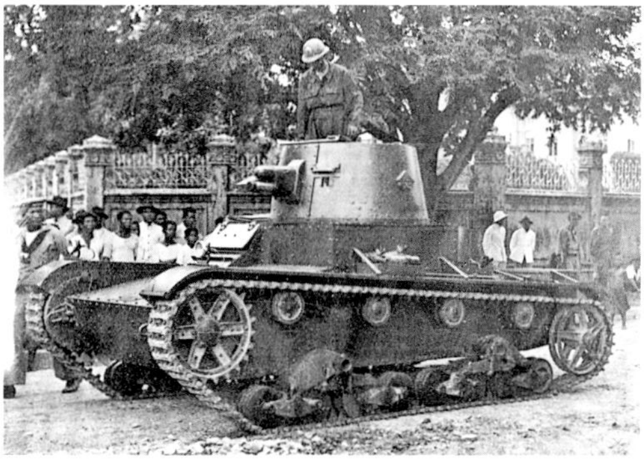

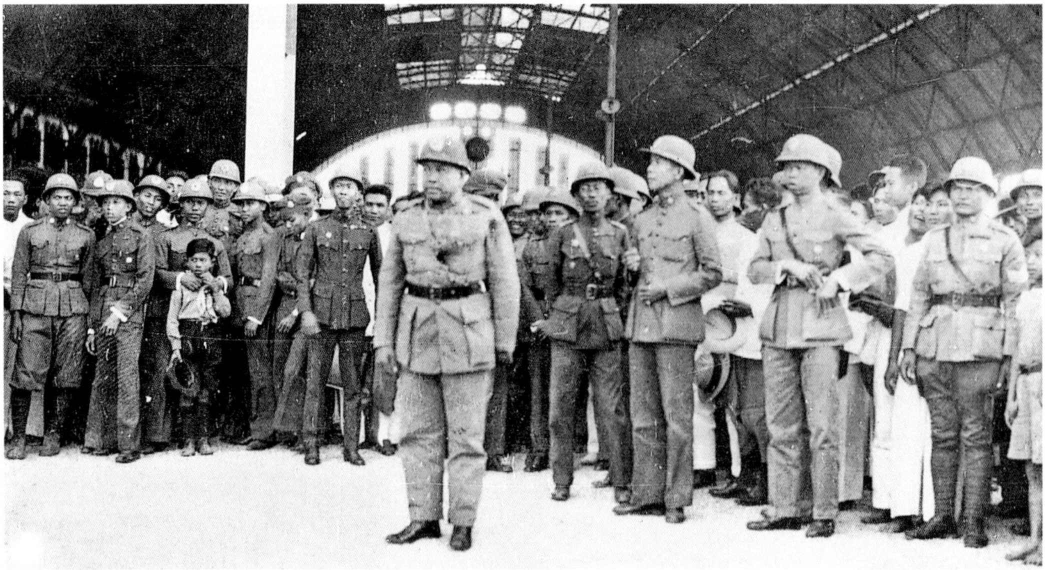

Phraya Phahon and other army officers waiting to greet those soldiers involved in supressing the Bavoradej Coup.
(Paisarn Piemmettawat)

substantial foundation for the suggestion that "most of the royal princes had given moral and financial support to the rebels."[1] In any case, none of the princes by then had much money.

On November 1st, 1933, the first General Election was held, which was not a direct election, for it was arranged that village representatives were elected first, and they in their turn became the electors of the deputies, with 78 deputies altogether. Hall[2] states that "less than a tenth of the electorate voted and comparatively few candidates offered themselves for election". According to many Thai persons consulted by the present writer, and from their memory, there were far too many candidates which created confusion. Official numbers of voters given by the Ministry of the Interior were as follows: Total electorate was 4,278,231. Those who actually voted were 1,773,532. Thus the percentage of voters was 41.45.[3] The people in the provinces voted more than those in Bangkok, who showed apathy. Colonel Phraya Phahon remained Premier, while Colonel Pibul became more important than ever and was the virtual Commander-in-Chief of the army except in name, and he now had only one serious rival, namely, Pridi.

The king's eyes had deteriorated further and he clamoured to go abroad for another operation. The government wanted him at home to add to the stability and prestige of themselves as the king's government, and they offered to send and pay for the very best of surgeons to come to Siam regardless of cost, but finally the king won the argument. With the queen and a small entourage, he left Bangkok by a Danish ship on January 12th, 1934. He arrived in France in February and had a restful stay at Beaulieu. His nephew's visit to him was cut short by the sudden death of King Albert of the Belgians, and King Prajadhipok sent him to the funeral as his representative. Before he left Beaulieu on his first mission, Prince Chula Chakrabongse was invested by the king

1 D. G. E. Hall: *op. cit.*, page 679.

2 *Ibid.*, pages 679-680.

3 Official letter to author, January 20th, 1959.

4 Exceptions have been six Presidents of the French Republic who were considered Heads of a neighbouring State, French Indo-China.

5 K. P. Landon: *op. cit.*, Appendix II, pages 257-259.

with the Order of Chakri, the highest Thai order reserved for the king and queen, senior princes and princesses, and some foreign royalty.[4] Thus he was the first of his generation to obtain this high honour and the last Thai to receive it from the last absolute monarch. King Prajadhipok and Queen Rambai arrived in London in April, 1934, on a private visit but they were nevertheless met at Victoria Station by the Duke and Duchess of York (King George VI and Queen Elizabeth), and were soon invited to lunch at Windsor by King George and Queen Mary. Later they met the British sovereigns again at Ascot. As the first constitutional monarch of Siam, King Prajadhipok made an extensive tour of European countries.

Since his departure from Siam, however, the king had been in disagreement with the government over constitutional differences, the king's main thesis being that he had given up his absolute power to the whole of the Thai people and not to any one group. He objected particularly to the law to preserve the constitution and the special court, while the government said that everything they did was necessary owing to conditions of emergency. A deadlock arose. The government sent a mission to England to see the king, led by an elder statesman, Chao Phraya Sri Dharma Dibes, who was then President of the Assembly, in an attempt to patch up differences and beg the king to return home. In February, 1935, the elder statesman saw the present author at the latter's flat in London and said that the talks had completely broken down, and the king had decided to abdicate. The abdication finally took place on March 2nd, 1935, at a house the king had taken at Cranleigh, Surrey. Among other things in the announcement, the king said "I am happy to turn over my power of rule to the people as a whole. I am not willing to give it over to any person or to any group to use in an absolute manner without heeding the voice of the people . . . I wish to give over all of my kingly privileges but I desire to retain all of those privileges which were mine before becoming king. I do not care to name my successor although it is my privilege according to law. Furthermore, I do not care to have anyone rise up in rebellion in Siam against the government on my behalf. If anyone names me as their instigator in rebellion kindly understand that I have no share in it and am not pleased. I am exceedingly sorry that I am unable to serve my people and country according to my plans and hopes which I received from my royal ancestors. There remains only a sincere prayer that Siam will prosper and that the people will have peace and happiness."[5] As no successor was designated by the king, Section 9 of the Constitution invoked the Law of Succession of 1924, and the legal heir, Prince Ananda Mahidol, then a boy of ten and living with his mother, brother, and sister at Lausanne, was proclaimed king. The aged Prince Naris, who had been sole Regent for King Prajadhipok, resigned, and the government set up a Council of Regency, consisting of His Royal Highness Prince Oscar, Krom Muen Anuvatana, His Highness Prince Aditya, and a commoner-nobleman,

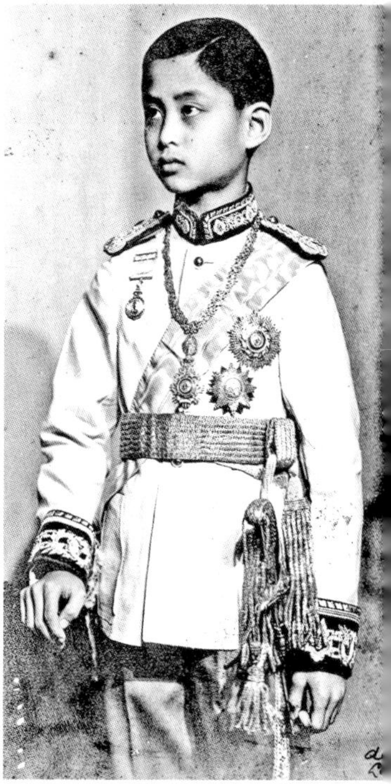

King Ananda Mahidol. (Paisarn Piemmettawat)

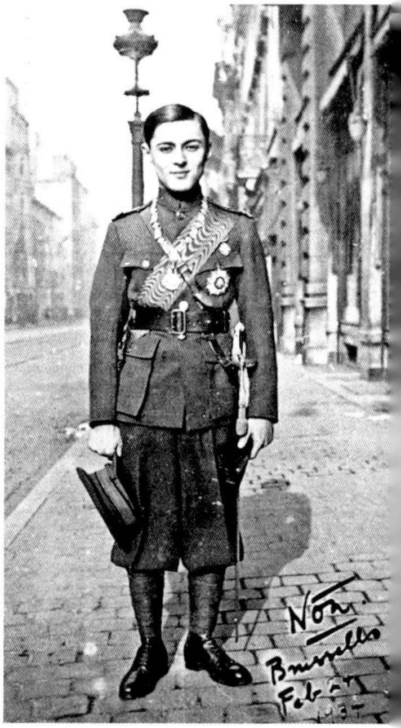

Prince Chula in army uniform and wearing the Most Noble Chakri Order bestowed on him by King Prajadhipok. (River Books)

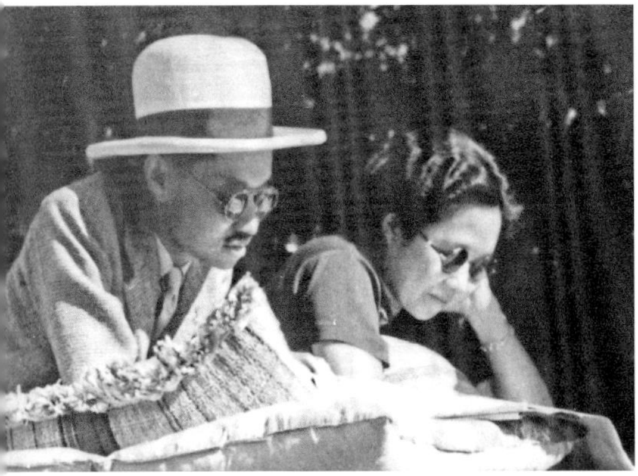

King Prajadhipok and Queen Rambai relaxing in England after the abdication. (National Archives Bangkok)

Chao Phraya Yomaraja. The last had served both King Chulalongkorn and King Rama VI as a cabinet minister, either of the Interior or of Bangkok Government. Thus began the 8th reign of the Chakri dynasty and the boy king continued to live in Switzerland for the sake of his health, for he was not robust, and all three children being educated there.

In January, 1936, the new sovereign was for the first time represented at an important foreign royal function by his cousin, Prince Chula Chakrabongse, namely, at the funeral of King George V, who had died on January 20th. Prince Chula had decided after the change of regime to live in London and devote himself to writing history books in Thai for publication in Siam. He was first presented to George V early in 1932 when he was invited to lunch privately at Buckingham Palace. Their Majesties continued to be most graciously kind to him, and he lunched privately with them regularly and was also invited to attend several royal functions, being placed amongst members of the British royal family. Prince Chula represented the king of Siam again at the coronation of King George VI and Queen Elizabeth in May, 1937. In January, 1938, he had the honour to present to King George VI the Order of Chakri on behalf of King Ananda Mahidol.

It was in March, 1935, that, under Prince Chula's financial backing and personal management, Prince Birabongse began motor-racing under the pseudonym of "B. Bira." He soon achieved many successes in Britain, Ireland, and the continent of Europe, and thus it was a Chakri prince who was the first Thai to become a successful and popular sportsman of international renown. His fame gave pleasure to Thai people of all sections, and his efforts were applauded by the

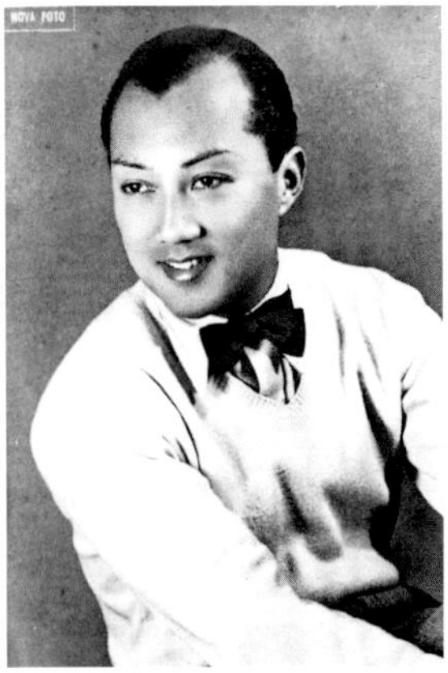

Prince Biraabongse became a famous racing driver under the pseudonym B. Bira. (River Books)

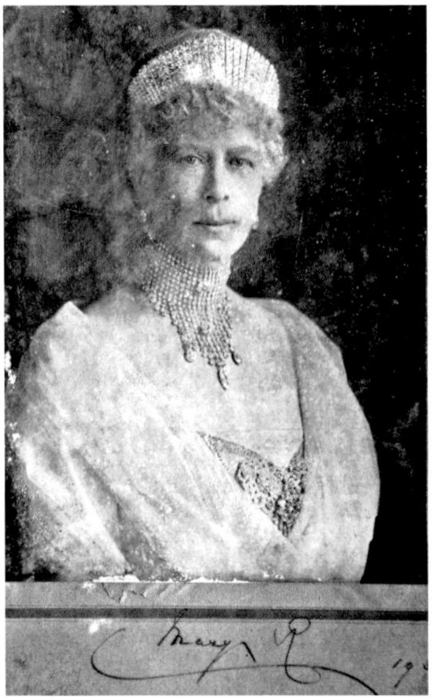

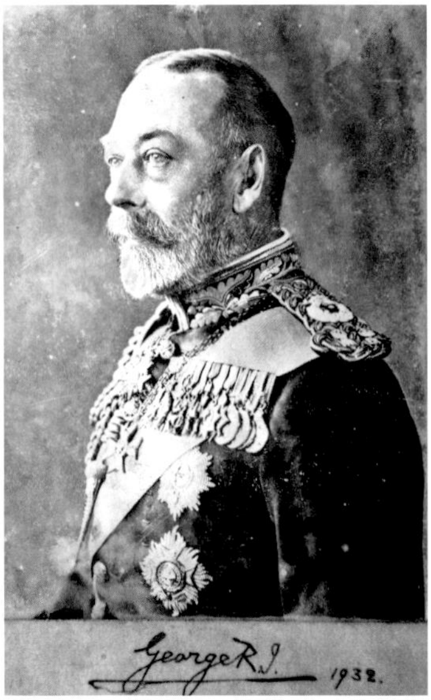

RIGHT: Queen Mary and King George V, with whom Prince Chula became quite close. (River Books)

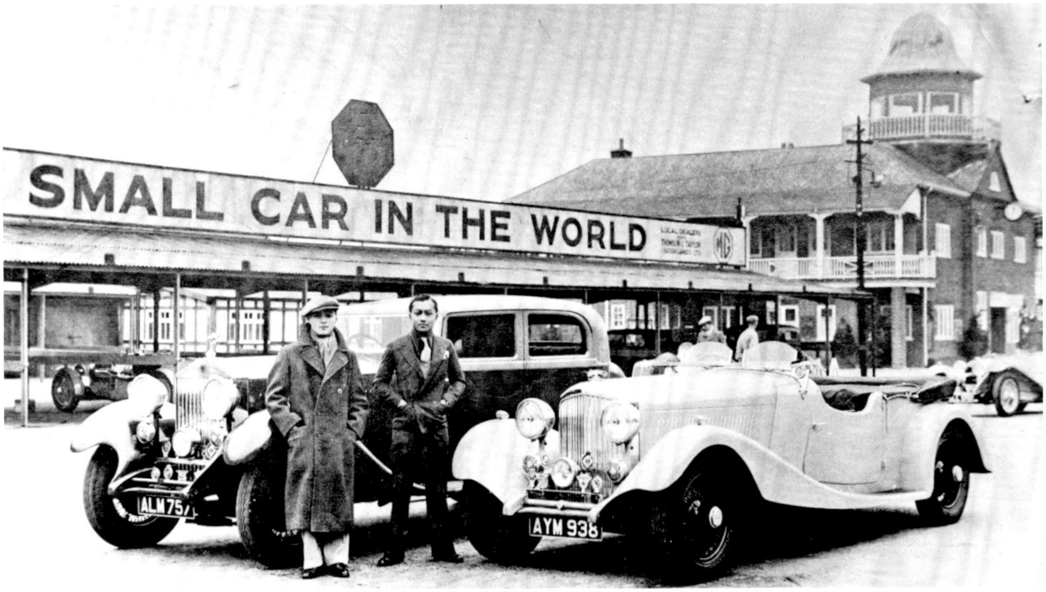

Prince Chula and Prince Bira with Bira's first car, an MG outside Brooklands. (River Books)

government. Together Prince Chula and Prince Birabongse went to Siam for a few months in the autumn of 1937 and they received a joyful welcome from the Regents, the government, the Press, and the people at large, for Prince Birabongse's many international victories well matched the upsurge of Thai nationalism.

Prince Oscar Anuvatana found the task of being President of the Regency Council too strenuous and upsetting for his frail health, and on August 12th, 1935, the royal family heard with deep shock that this gentle and kindly man had taken his life. Prince Aditya succeeded him as President of the Regency Council with Chao Phraya Yomaraja remaining, and Chao Phraya Bijaiyendra, an elderly retired general, appointed to support him as two other members. In 1937 Phraya Phahon was still Premier, with Pibul as Minister of Defence and virtually in charge of the army, and Pridi, then still Luang Pradit, was Minister for Foreign Affairs.

In the summer of 1937 there was a serious crisis known as the Land Scandal in which the Council of Regency was unfortunately involved. The king of Siam had owned a good deal of land in Bangkok which was now considered Crown property, detached from any particular sovereign, and being under the administration of the Regents. It transpired that they had allowed some 34 of the 1932 promoters to buy some of this land at a very low price and with unusually easy payment intalments, such that the purchases amounted to gifts. When it became known, it resulted in great and general public indignation. Pridi was innocent of all the charges as he had not purchased any land, but there was a *rumour* that Pibul had bought some but had quickly returned it when he saw the trend of public opinion.

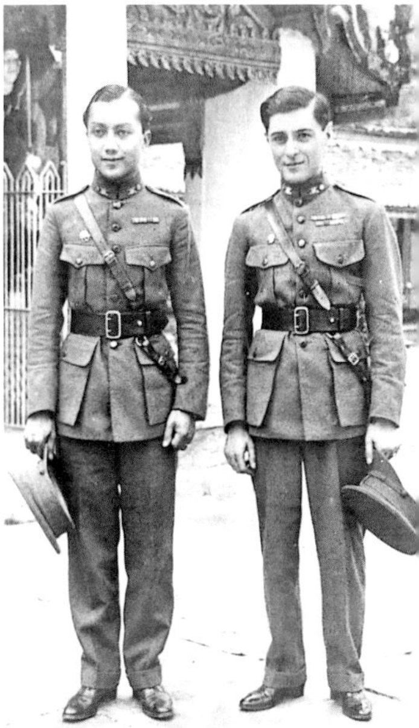

Prince Bira and Prince Chula on their trip back to Thailand in 1937. (River Books)

Taking the public anger as their cue, the elected deputies attacked the Regents and the government severely in the Assembly, using words and terms so strong that both the Regents and the Premier felt compelled to resign. As both the Regents and Premier held their positions by military support, the civilians in the government thought that their time of triumph had come. They clamoured for the resignations to be accepted, hoping to nominate new Regents and a new Premier, but Pibul successfully rallied the military to give yet stronger support to the Regents and Premier Phahon, who then withdrew their resignations as "the defence forces wished the present Regency Council to remain in office", and thus all was back to normal by August 11th. Pridi had kept well out of the entire affair, and, as Foreign Minister, he was usefully employed with Prince Wan in negotiations over the revision of the treaties, so that Siam should attain full freedom and equality in her relations with the Western powers, a delicate task in which they succeeded admirably. The treaties of 1925, the last year of Rama VI, had permitted the Thai government to raise import duties above 3%, but most of them were only at 5%, apart from some exceptions such as tobacco at 25% and beer and wine at 12%. Now Siam had full jurisdiction over all foreigners in her law courts as well as full fiscal liberty. Of these new treaties the last British-born Financial Adviser, W. A. M. Doll,[6] had this to say in his report: " Siam had just reaffirmed her political sovereignty by a series of brilliant treaties. The essential handmaiden of that political sovereignty is solvency, which is financial sovereignty, and without the latter, the former loses its substance and becomes a shadow." It should be noted that Siam had obtained the revision of these treaties by negotiation when the Powers had not been harassed or weakened by a World War, and it was therefore a purely moral achievement on both sides.

The new regime had certainly produced budgets with more than one surplus, and it had also brought in estate duties and income tax, both entirely unknown under the Chakri absolute and paternal monarchy. Of estate duties the estimate for 1935-36 was only 100,000 baht, yet it did not produce more than 43,955 baht and was given up as not worth collecting.[7] The income tax picture was not much brighter. The lowest exemption limit for income tax was 2,400 baht per annum, yet less than 3,000 Thais out of 12 million had incomes of more than £220 a year. Of these 94 had between 10,000 to 20,000 baht per annum, 35 had between 20,000 to 30,000 baht, and only 29 had over 39,000 baht (at 11 baht to £1). "In terms of monetary capital, Siam is a remarkably poor country."[8] The riches of the country lay in the soil and the work of the peasant cultivators of rice. As Doll so rightly said: "The debt owed by the country to its peasants is incalculable."[9]

In September, 1938, Prince Chula Chakrabongse was, with royal permission given by the Council of Regency, married to Miss Elisabeth Hunter, third daughter of Mr. and Mrs. Edward Hunter, of London. When the couple went back to Siam in October, 1938, they received a blessing with the pouring of the lustral water on their heads by the king's grandmother, Queen Sawang, who was Prince Chula's great

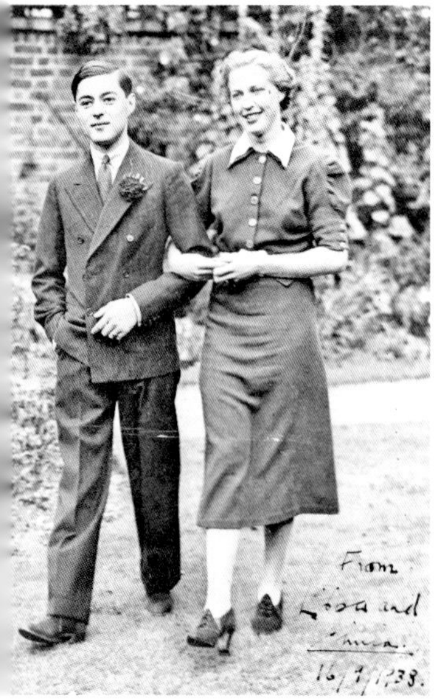
Prince Chula and his wife, Elisabeth. (River Books)

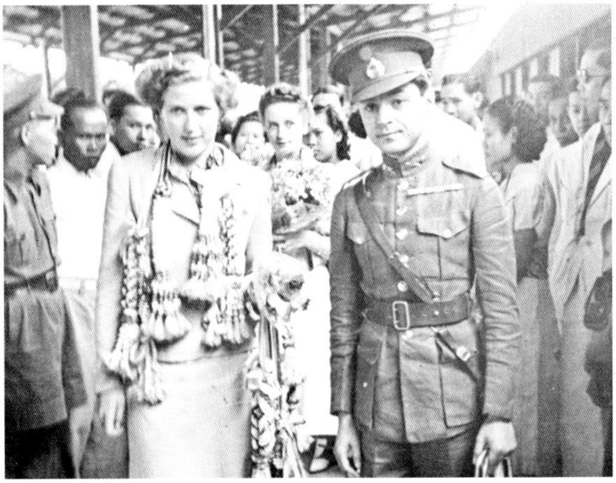

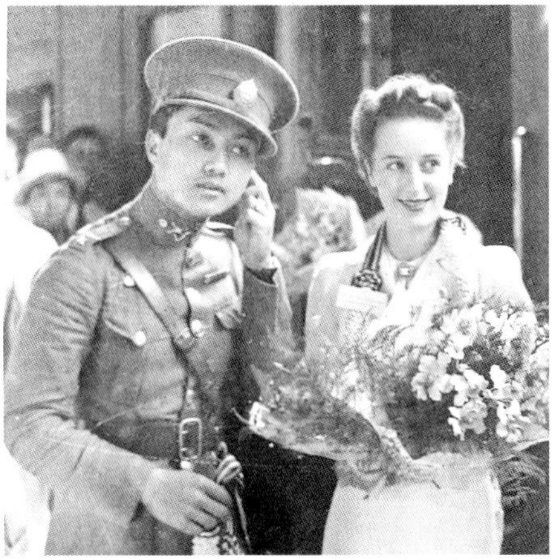

ABOVE LEFT: Prince Chula and his new wife, Elisabeth, arriving for their first trip in Thailand in October 1938. (River Books)

ABOVE: Prince Bira and his new wife, Ceril, during their trip to Thailand. (River Books)

aunt. Prince Birabongse had, with a similar permission, been married in January to Miss Ceril Heycock, the only daughter of Lt.-Colonel P. R. Heycock (Royal Marines, retired) and Mrs. Heycock.

Before the arrival of the four of them to stay in Siam for several months, a second attempt was made to assassinate Pibul. He had previously been shot at while getting out of his car at a football match. This time while dressing to go out to an evening party, he found his valet beginning to shoot at him. It was awkward for Pibul, who had his half-Wellington boots on already, yet had not done up his trousers, but he managed to evade the bullets, and the man was arrested and charged. It was alleged that he was in the pay of some mysterious group. Pibul was the only Thai politician of the period to be paid the unwelcome compliment of attempted assassination. Shortly after the event the young monarch, Ananda Mahidol, aged 13, arrived in Bangkok with his mother, brother and sister. The sight of the Royal Standard, not seen since King Prajadhipok's departure in 1934, moved many people to joyful tears.

The king and his family lived at Chitralada Palace. He was thought by many to be young for his age, yet he could sit patiently through long religious ceremonies in which he played his leading part well. Despite the king's presence, Bangkok remained seething with rumours of impending assassinations and coups d'état. News came of another attempt on Pibul's life, this time by poisoning. His wife was also stricken, and when seen by the present author at the Military Hospital, which Phaya Thai Palace had become, they both looked seriously ill. It was not surprising that after their recovery they would not eat or drink anything outside their home for some time. By the end of 1938 it was announced that Phraya Phahon had resigned the premiership, and Pibul was appointed to succeed him, with Pridi now Minister of Finance. After a successful stay of some months, the king left with his family on January 1st, 1939, to return to Switzerland for his further education.

6 *Financial Adviser's Report*, 1938-1939.

7 *Ibid.*, 1936-1937.

8 *Ibid.*, 1937-1938.

9 *Ibid.*

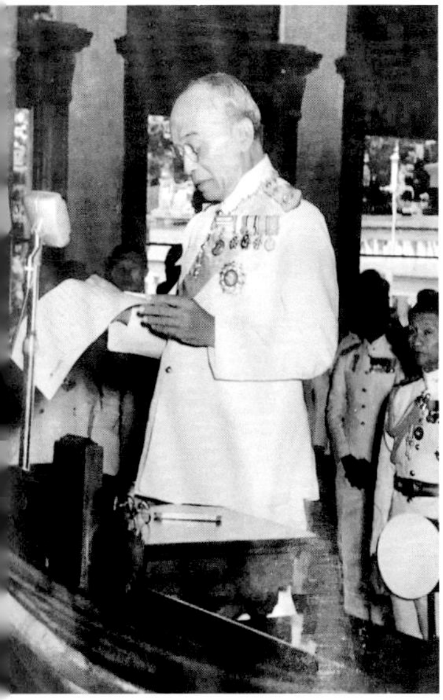

Prince Rangsit.
(Paisarn Piemmettawat)

One of the two surviving sons of King Chulalongkorn at that time was Prince Rangsit, a non-celestial prince who was therefore a half-brother of the king's father – Prince Mahidol. As Prince Rangsit's mother had died when he was very young, he was brought up by Queen Sawang, and was very close to Prince Mahidol in brotherly friendship. He had married a German lady – Elisabeth – when he was a student at Heidelberg, and they had two sons and a daughter. The Mahidol children loved him dearly and Prince Rangsit was prominent during the king's stay. He was clever, artistic, amusing, and well informed, never giving the least sign that he was interested in politics. There was complete consternation all round when the public was officially informed that, together with many other people, Prince Rangsit had been arrested and accused of complicity in a large-scale anti-government plot. He was thrown into an ordinary prison, and after a lengthy trial by the special court, he was condemned to death with some others. For the first time since 1932, a number of the accused were actually executed by shooting, but the sentence on Prince Rangsit and others was commuted to life imprisonment. As her daughter, Princess Valaya, died just about the same time, the news began the breaking up of the Queen Grandmother's health. The affair caused a thorough shock in the country, and the Chief Regent, Prince Aditya, was much blamed by many people for not preventing the incarceration of Prince Rangsit in a common gaol, but no one explained how he could have prevented it.

A big change occurred in 1939 when the Pibul government decided to drop the name Siam both in Thai and in European languages. In Thai *Prades Sayam* was altered to *Prades Thai,* and in English the name was Thailand with the equivalent form in other languages. In 1940 there was another important announcement that the year would no longer end on March 31st as before, but, to conform with universal practice, it would end on December 31st. Thus the Buddhist era year of 2483 had only nine months, and A.D. 1940 and B.E. 2484 began simultaneously on January 1st

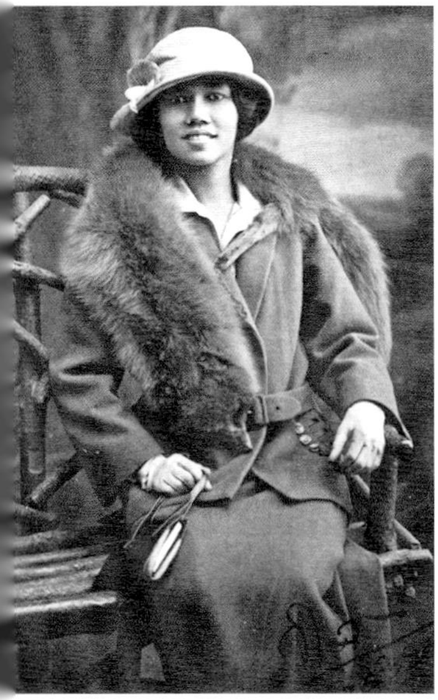

Princess Valaya Alongkorn died in February 1938 at the age of 54. (Paisarn Piemmettawat)

War had broken out in Europe on September 3rd, 1939, and as expected, Thailand declared her neutrality. There was great anxiety in the country as it was expected that sooner or later Japan would come in on the side of the Axis. Non-aggression pacts were negotiated between Thailand and Britain and France and were duly signed.

Prince Chula was in England when war broke out, having just completed helping Prince Birabongse in his fifth and highly successful motor-racing season. Although he made great efforts to get home, all kinds of unfavourable circumstances stood in the way. On April 4th, 1940, he was appointed by the Thai Government as Chief Thai delegate to the League of Nations. This put an end to his attempts to return home and when they were resumed it was too late.

On May 1st, 1941, King Prajadhipok died at his home at Virginia Water where he had lived for six years since his abdication. He was

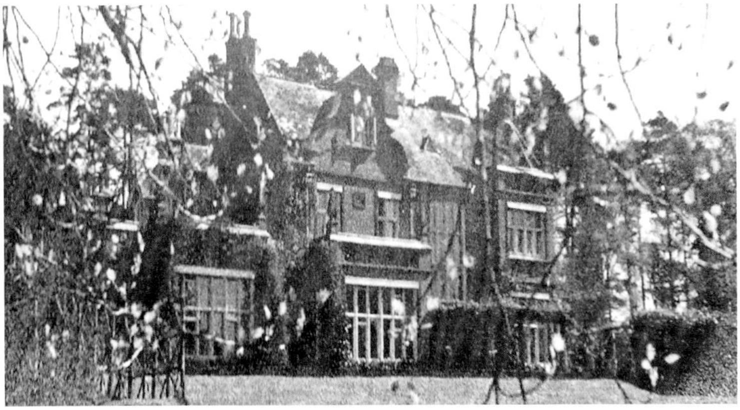

Glen Pamnet, the house in Virginia Water, where King Prajadhipok died in 1941. (National Archives Bangkok)

cremated at Golders Green after a simple but moving Buddhist ceremony. He was in his 48th year and thus lived longer than any of the children of King Chulalongkorn and Queen Saowabha. His widow, Queen Rambai, remained in England until after the war.

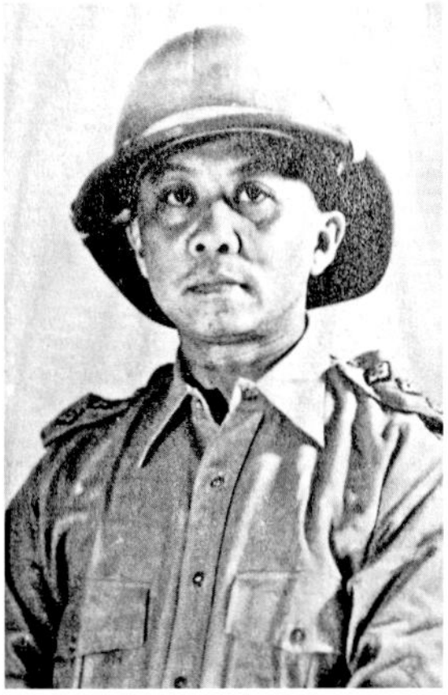

Prince Subha Svasti, the leader of the British side of the Free Thai movement. (River Books)

The year 1941 saw in Thailand a more aggressive form of nationalism directed against the French in Indo-China, which led to a war between the French and Thailand. This abortive war ended with Japanese mediation which was soon followed by Japanese occupation of French Indo-China with the agreement of the Vichy French Government. This, as Field-Marshal Smuts later said, turned the whole Western defensive system of Singapore and South-East Asia into an impracticable plan. By the end of November the Japanese began their threats against Thailand, and the events which took place everywhere on December 7th-8th have passed into world history. On December 9th it became known that the Thai Government had ordered all resistance against the Japanese to cease, and it is still little known throughout the world that heroic and costly fighting continued in the south for some time. By December 16th M.R. Seni Pramoj, Thai Minister at Washington, had announced that he refused to obey orders from Bangkok and was forming a Free Thai Movement in the U.S.A. which was supported in England under the leadership of Prince Subha Svasti. Towards the end of January, 1942, Bangkok was bombed for the first time and the bombing continued for most of the war. On February 4th the B.B.C. announced that Thailand had joined Japan and declared war on Britain and the United States.

Although everyone has ever since admired the fine spirit which animated the Free Thai Movement and their work of resistance both in Thailand and abroad, later opinion in Britain and the U.S.A. has been to the effect that, apart from avoiding complete ruin to the country,

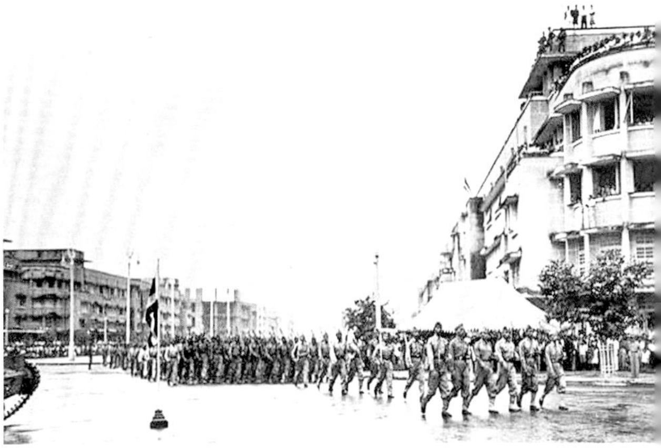

Members of the Free Thai marching down Ratchadamnoen Avenue at the end of the war. (National Archives Bangkok)

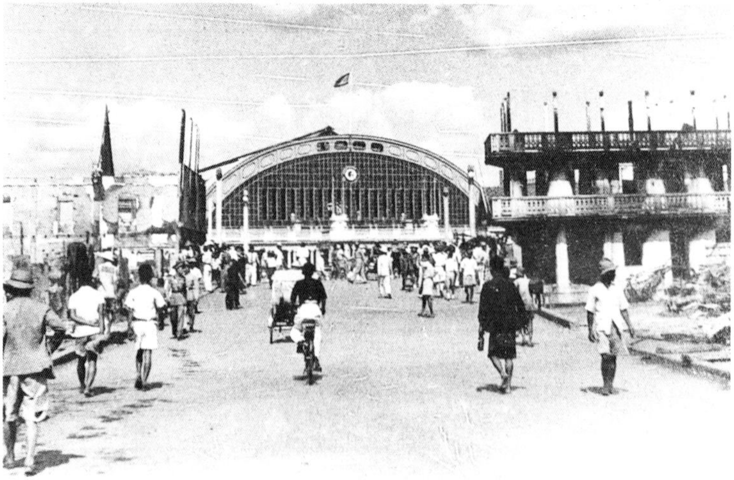

The area around Hua Lampong Railway Station was bombed in 1944. (National Archives Bangkok)

had Premier Pibul not joined the Japanese, British, American, and other allied prisoners-of-war of the Japanese incarcerated in Thailand might not have survived. The Japanese did not control their Thai "allies" very closely, and the Thai people were secretly able to give extra food and provide drugs and medicine, and generally assisted the prisoners in many ways. Pridi, who was sole Regent after the resignation of Prince Aditya, was the resistance leader in Thailand, while Pibul always maintained that he and his friends were also secretly working against the Japanese. Later in the war the nominated deputies got rid of Pibul as Premier, and Kuang Abhaiwongse was appointed Premier in his place.

Sir Geoffrey Thompson, the first British Ambassador to Bangkok since the war, has written, "although it was not realized at the time or for long afterwards, Siamese policy . . . turned out to our ultimate advantage, for it was the Siamese, and not the murderous and brutal Japs, who interned British subjects and seized British properties . . . Our internees, in strikingly favourable contrast to the British prisoners who worked and died in slave conditions on the Burma railway and elsewhere under Japanese custody, were well treated, well fed, and well housed by the Siamese. After the Japanese defeat and surrender, not only were our troops well received when they in turn occupied Bangkok and other areas in Siam, but it was a matter of comparative ease to negotiate the Anglo-Siamese agreement of January 1st, 1946, which terminated the state of war between the two countries on our terms, which were generous.[10] The Thai government had to pay compensation for damages to British property, which was paid without complaint. The U.S.A., however, had regarded the Thai declaration of war as null and void, so there was no peace treaty, and no compensation, and these were regarded by the Thais as more generous terms. It must in fairness be stated that U.S. properties in Thailand had been far less extensive. Although compensation was paid without rancour, it was more difficult for the Thai government to provide the agreed

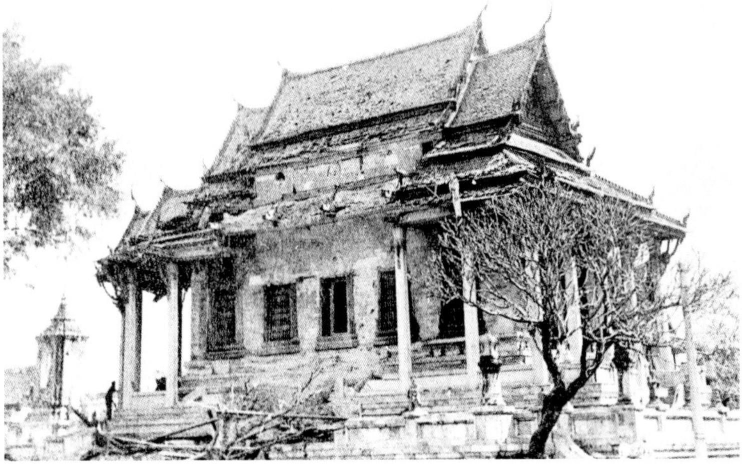

The Phra Buddha Rattanasathan building within the Grand Palace was bombed between 19th-20th February 1944. (National Archives Bangkok)

quotas of rice required by the British to feed other parts of South-East Asia and India, and much negotiation for various schemes had to be gone through before arriving at a successful conclusion.[11]

Many British ex-prisoners-of-war gave similar accounts to the present author: "From the small town of Kanchanaburi came our supply of drugs to combat the serious diseases, which were smuggled to us by the Thais such as Mr. Boon Pong. Many of us owed our lives to the resourcefulness of this Thai gentleman, who, if found out by the Japanese would surely have lost his head".[12] It was the same story in the U.S.A., and once an American naval officer brought his young wife to see the present writer at Memphis, Tennesee, saying that, but for the help he received from the Thais, he would never have returned alive to marry her.

Pridi was still Regent at the close of the war and, after his return from Washington, M.R. Seni Pramoj became Prime Minister. A new constitution was being drafted envisaging a two-chamber Assembly, with the lower house entirely elective. Seni was quickly followed by other premiers, none of whom stayed long in power. King Ananda Mahidol, who had spent the war years with his family in Switzerland, returned to Thailand at the age of twenty and immediately won the hearts of the people of all classes.[13] To celebrate his return the political exiles, including Prince Bavoradej, were permitted to come back from Saigon and elsewhere, the only gap in the general harmony being the arrest and trial of ex-Premier Pibul, who had become a Field-Marshal during the war, and some of his friends, all of whom were charged as war criminals for having drawn Thailand into the war on the side of Japan. The charges, however, were dropped, and after his release Pibul went into retirement. Prince Aditya, the former Regent, had been very ill for some time and died on May 19th, 1946. As things seemed calm and quiet, Pridi left for a triumphal world tour as the Elder Statesman and was particularly welcomed in the United States and Britain as the famous hero of the Resistance.

10 Sir Geoffrey Thomson: *Front Line Diplomat*, pages 188-189, London, 1959.

11 *Ibid.* for details. Chapter 16. pages 188-216.

12 Notes from Captain R. R. Fewell, late The Suffolk Regiment.

13 Pridi's tenure of the Regency naturally lapsed with the king's assumption of his full constitutional powers.

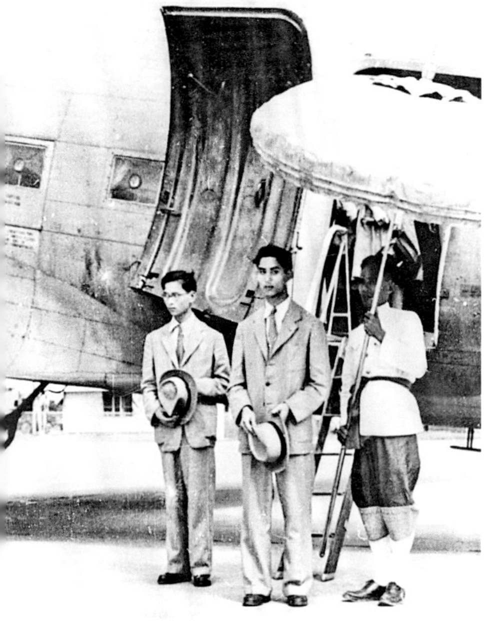

King Ananda and his younger brother, Prince Bhumibol, arriving in Thailand on 5th December. (National Archives Bangkok)

After his successful global tour and on his return, Pridi became Prime Minister, and it was said that the favourable results which he obtained in the general election were due to the cells which he had created during the war for the Resistance Movement. King Ananda, who had become so popular, was preparing to leave for Switzerland to complete his studies. Staying with his mother and brother in the Grand Palace, he was in the morning of Sunday, June 9th, found shot dead in bed. His own pistol, with which he had practised shooting, lay on the floor. Death had been caused by a shot through the forehead with a .11mm. bullet apparently from the same type of gun as his own. The profound grief of his mother, brother, and sister (married, with a young baby and living in Switzerland) was fully shared by all sections of the people, and deputies in the Assembly openly wept as they clamoured for a full investigation. His only brother, succeeding him as King Bhumibol (pronounced in Thai as *Poomipon),* was recognized as sovereign by the Assembly with general acclamation. In August the new king left for Switzerland for further studies, and Prince Rangsit, now fully restored to all his royal ranks, was appointed Regent, to the delight of the king and the people.

Premier Pridi ordered a public investigation of the late king's demise which went on for a long time. The proceedings did not satisfy the public, and indignation against Pridi grew so great that he resigned and was succeeded by Luang Dhamrong. (Some years later and after a long trial, two men, who were royal pages, were executed for the crime in connection with the king's death, and it was declared that other suspects had escaped). No one could hold any authority for long, as the uncertainties about the king's death underlined everything. On November 8th, 1947, Dhamrong was ousted by a bloodless coup d'état. Leaders of the coup were General Pin Chunhawan, his son-in-law Police General Pao Sriyanonda, Air Marshal Karch, and

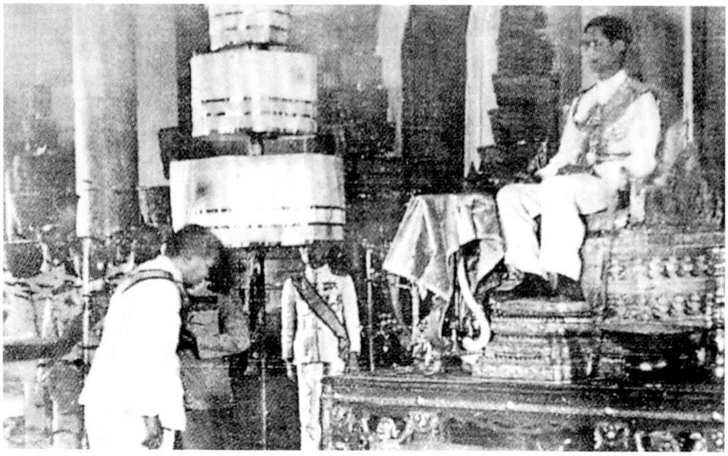

King Ananda granting the revised constitution on 9th May 1946, within the Ananta Samakhom Throne Hall to the Prime Minister, Pridi Banomyong. (National Archives Bangkok)

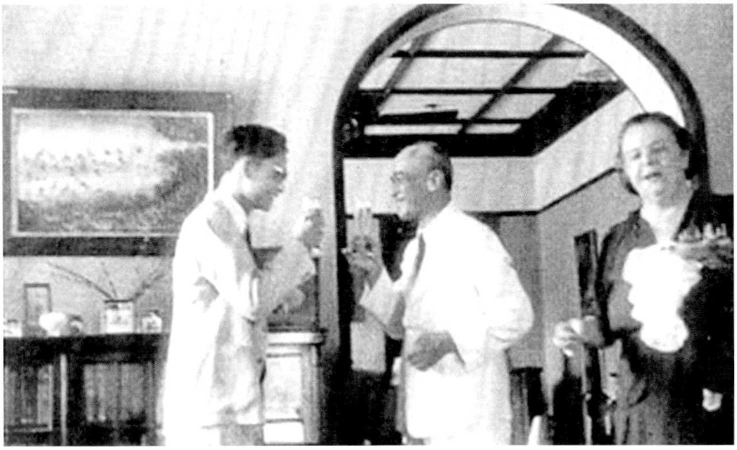

King Bhumibol, Prince Rangsit and Mom Elizabeth Rangsit in Witthayu Palace. (National Archives Bangkok)

General Sarit Thanarat (also spelt Dhanarajata), then Commander of the Bangkok Area. None of these had been in the original 1932 coup, and they invited Kuang Abhaiwongse to be premier for a short time before they asked Field-Marshal Pibul to return to politics and re-assume the premiership. Pridi had already left the country, it was said by the help of the British and via Singapore, and no one knew where he was. Thailand had by then become a member of the United Nations and the new regime was duly recognized by all the powers. All this while Prince Rangsit remained regent.

There were serious troubles in February, 1949, when Pridi was alleged to have returned to make his first attempt to seize power by force with the support of parts of the navy and marines. A fight broke out on February 26th, when the army and police remained loyal to Pibul and the elements of the navy and marines involved were defeated.

Different drafts for a new constitution had been made, and in all of them a nominated senate was included composed of men of recognized ability and experience, with the final form being promulgated on March 23rd, 1949.

In 1950 the king was again back in Thailand. He had become engaged to Mom Rajawongse (Lady of the Royal Line) Sirikit, a daughter of H.S.H. Prince Nakkhat, a son of the Prince of Chantaburi (eldest son of King Chulalongkorn) whose mother was the daughter of the old Prince Devawongse. M.R. Sirikit was in her late teens and most lovely, and the king married her in Bangkok before his coronation, when she became queen with the supreme title of *Somdech Phra Borommа Rajinee*. The king confirmed the new constitution of March 23rd, 1949, before departing for more studies in Switzerland.

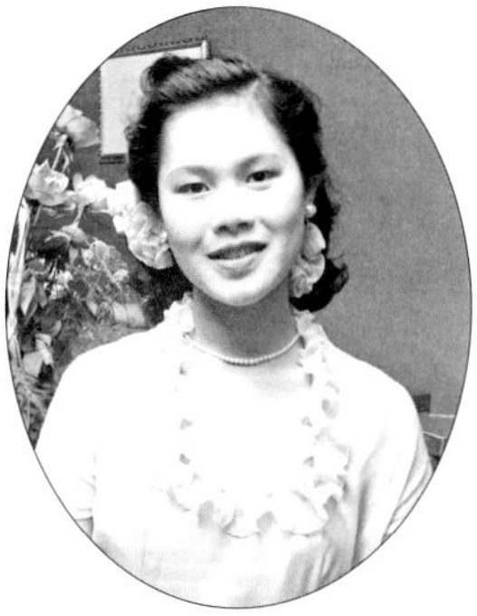

Mom Rajawongse Sirikit at the time of her engagement to King Bhumibol. (Paisarn Piemmettawat)

Their Majesties have three daughters and one son, Celestial Prince Vajiralongkorn who was bom in 1952. Prince Rangsit, who was the senior prince at all these proceedings and the cremation of King Ananda, died on March 7th, 1951. He was succeeded as Regent by Prince Dhani, who later became President of the Privy Council. On Prince Rangsit's death, the position of Senior Prince passed to

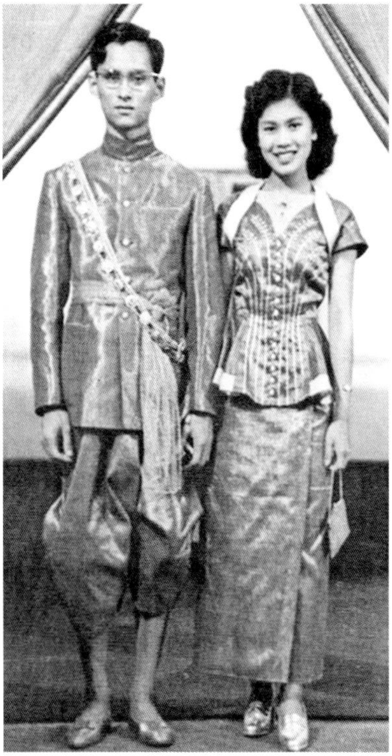

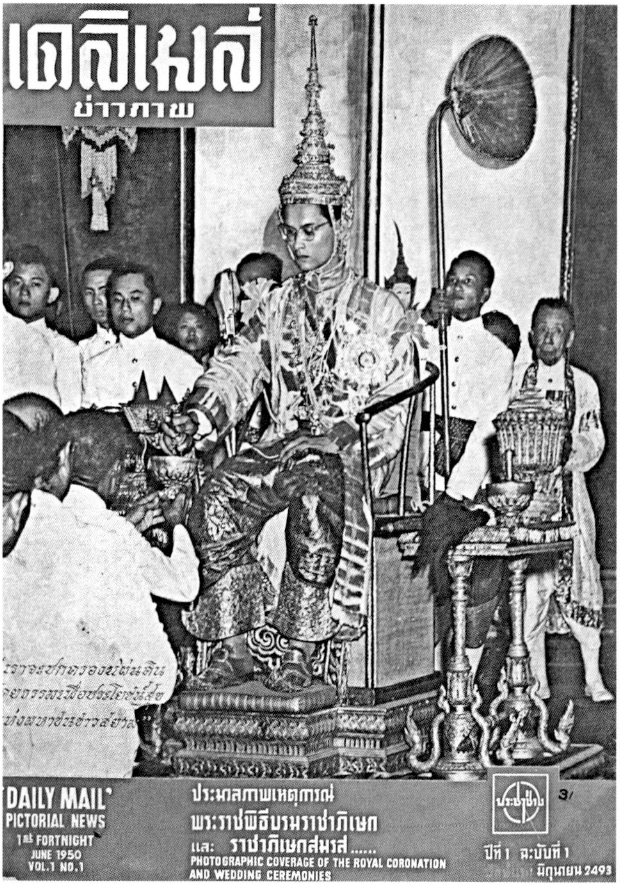

King Bhumibol and Queen Sirikit at their wedding before the coronation. (Paisarn Piemmettawat)

The coronation of King Bhumibol. (Paisarn Piemmettawat)

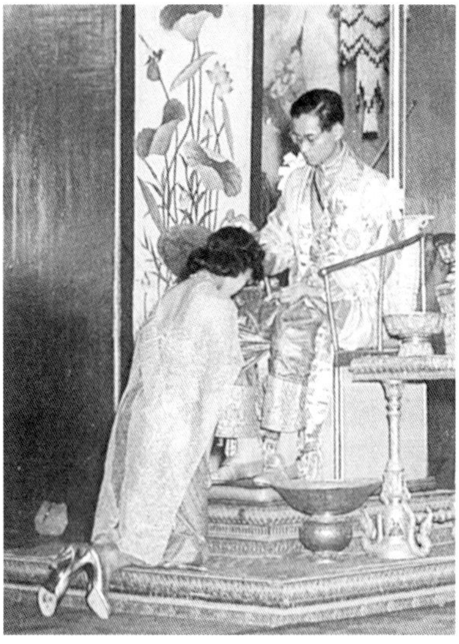

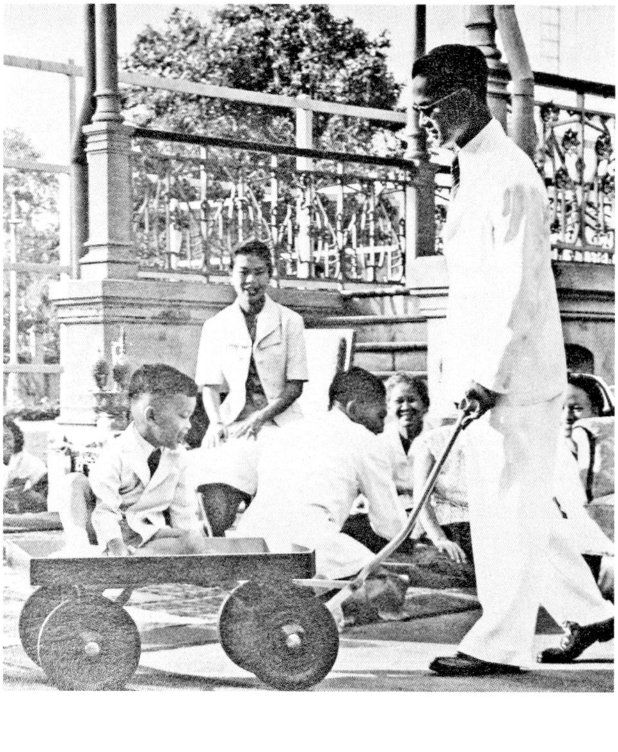

King Bhumibol bestowing her titles on Queen Sirikit. (Paisarn Piemmettawat)

King Bhumibol playing with Crown Prince Maha Vajiralongkorn. (Paisarn Piemmettawat)

His Royal Highness Prince Chumbhot, who was later promoted *Krom Muen* with his father's title of Nakhon Sawan.

On June 29th, 1951, parts of the navy struck again, and again it was said that Pridi was behind it. Field-Marshal Pibul was kidnapped while naming a new dredger presented by the U.S.A. He was kept prisoner on a warship as the pro-Pridi elements in the navy hoped that, with him as a hostage, they and the government forces could have a parley, for the Thais did not want to fight one another and most coups were really two sides playing for favourable positions. But this time there was even more severe fighting when the Thai Air Force joined the government side. The warships were bombed, but Pibul escaped by diving into the river and swimming ashore. The rebels were defeated and when order was restored Pibul was still using the Constitution of March 23rd, 1949.[14]

As the king and his family were returning to settle down in Thailand on the completion of his European education, there was a coup on November 29th, 1951, by the group forming the government, and as no forces were involved it became known as the silent coup. The Constitution of 1949 providing for a senate of men of ability was annulled and the original Constitution of December 10th, 1932, with a one-chamber Assembly of nominated and elected deputies in two equal halves was brought back, and another trial period of ten years was proclaimed. The king accepted this arrangement on his arrival, and Pibul remained Prime Minister, with General Sarit and Police-General Pao having gained much influence and power and were said to be rivals. Kuang was the natural Leader of the Opposition, but he and his Democratic Party boycotted the elections which followed. Although the elected deputies of the Opposition were few, they were very loud in their criticisms. Prince Wan Waitayakorn was Foreign Minister and later became President of the Assembly of the United Nations.

In June, 1953, Prince Chula Chakrabongse, accompanied by his wife, Elisabeth, represented the King of Thailand at the ceremonies and festivities for the Coronation of Queen Elizabeth II of Britain.

In the spring and summer of 1955 Field-Marshal Pibul made his world tour. When he returned he initiated the policy of allowing free public speaking "like in Hyde Park in London", and the park where the speeches were made became known as Hyde Park. With loudspeakers permitted, a crowd of 10,000 came to listen which led to abusive speech and rowdy behaviour. As a result the experiment was stopped, but not before the prestige of Pibul and Pao had been undermined by insulting remarks publicly made against them. Pibul now officially permitted political parties, and himself led his Seri Manangsila Party, while Kuang's Democrats officially re-entered the political arena. There were many splinter parties some of which showed obviously leftist tendencies and fiercely opposed the South-East Asia Treaty Organization (S.E.A.T.O.) formed in 1954 with Thailand as one of the

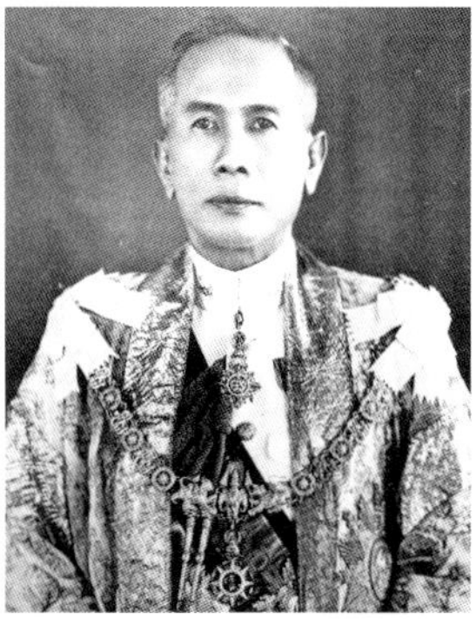

Field Marshal Pibul. (National Archives Bangkok)

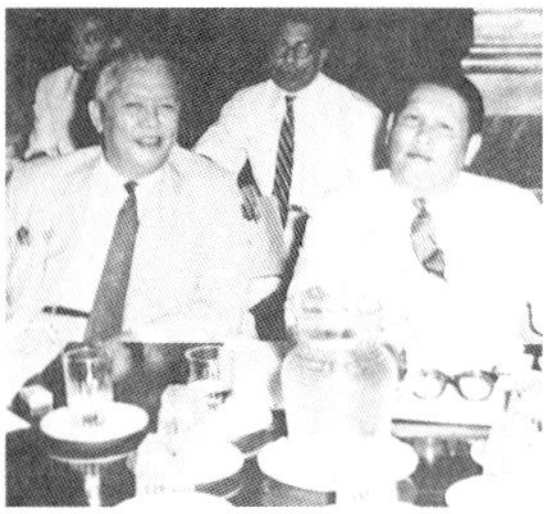

General Sarit and Pol. General Pao Sriyanonda. (National Archives Bangkok)

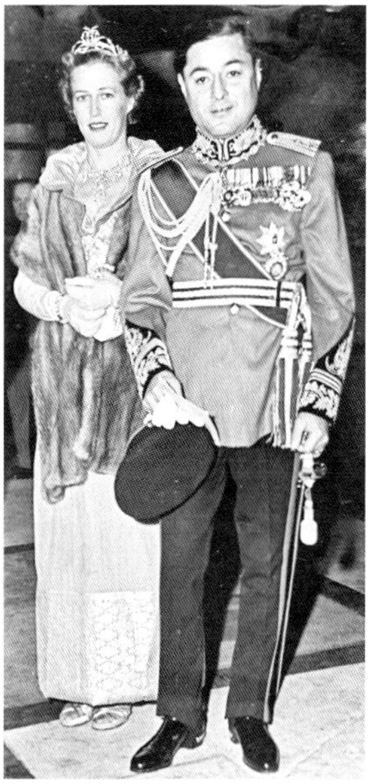

Prince and Princess Chula representing Thailand at the coronation of Queen Elizabeth II. (River Books)

14 For full details see Prince Chula: *The Twain Have Met*, etc., *op. cit.*, pages 272-274.

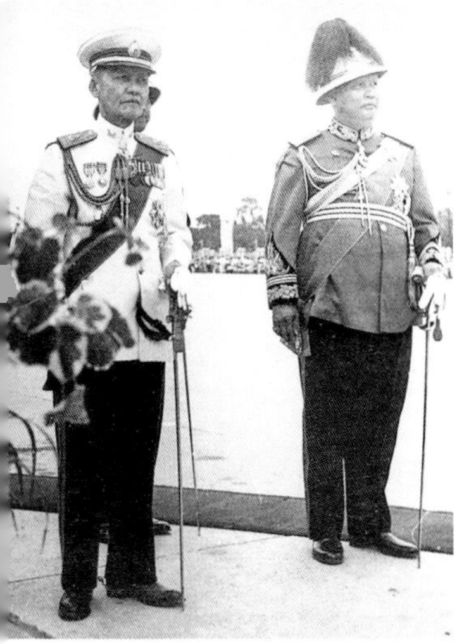

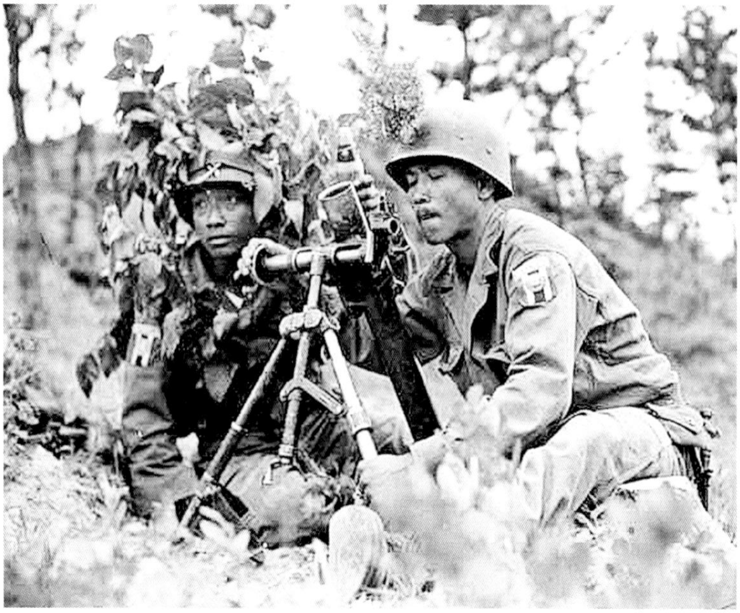

Field-Marshal Pin Chunhawan (left) and Field-Marshal Sarit, leaders of the 1957 coup. (Paisarn Piemmettawat)

Thai soldiers in the Korean War. (National Archives Bangkok)

members, and later with its headquarters established in Bangkok. In Korea, Thai soldiers had fought bravely for the cause of the United Nations, and there were two frigates from the Thai Navy and a squadron of transport planes from the Thai Air Force. All the Thai personnel received high praise from their allies.

The Pibul Government decided to hold a general election in February, 1957. Although nominated members would remain until 1962, intensive electioneering began in the autumn of 1956 for the coming election was looked upon as a rehearsal and a trial of strength between the Pibul and Kuang parties for 1962 when there would be no more nominated members according to Pibul's promise. The general election was held on February 26th, 1957, and resulted in a narrow overall victory for Pibul's party, with Kuang's Democrats obtaining the next largest number of seats, and the rest divided among the splinter parties. Pibul and Kuang headed the Bangkok poll in first and second places respectively. Before long accusations were made on all sides that the government had rigged the elections. Tempers became very frayed indeed despite the government's denials, and in the end Pibul admitted that there had been some irregularities. The situation became worse until it developed into students' demonstrations and marches of protest.

On September 16th, 1957, a coup d'état was staged by Sarit, now promoted Field-Marshal, which was entirely successful and met with more obvious public support than any coup since the first one in 1932 in which the public had shown apathy. Pibul and Pao went into voluntary exile, and Field Marshal Sarit assumed control. On his advice the king appointed *Nai* (Mr.) Pote Sarasin as Premier of a caretaker government for ninety days to keep order and supervize another general election. Pote Sarasin, a lawyer with private means, had been considered a sincere politician for some time and was once Foreign Secretary, and he had lately been Ambassador in Washington before becoming Secretary-General of S.E.A.T.O. from which post he obtained leave.

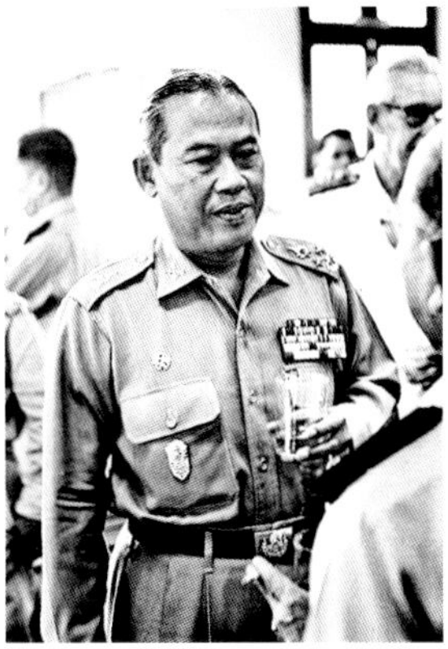

General Thanom Kittikachorn. (National Archives Bangkok)

All, includingly foreign observers, agreed that the general election of December 15th, 1957, was completely honest, and credit was given to General Praphas Charusathien, the Minister of Interior. There were 813 candidates representing 19 parties, and 403 independents, for the 160 seats. The party of Field-Marshal Sarit, the Unionists, obtained 45 seats, Kuang's Democrats 39, and Independents 58. The remainder were won by splinter parties, some of which formed a Left Block. The national turnout was 44.06%, the highest being the province of Ranong with 72.83/05, while only 33.96% of Bangkok electors voted.[15] General Thanom Kittikachorn, Deputy C.-in-C. was appointed Premier and had a comfortable majority based on the nominated members. Field-Marshal Sarit, the great influence behind the scenes, was at the height of his popularity when he became seriously ill and had to go to the US.A. for a major internal operation.

The Assembly proved unmanageable, every section, including the nominated members, pressing for what they themselves wanted before giving support to the government. The lack of unity between the Right and the Centre encouraged the Left to go all out to disrupt the country both in parliament and in the press, as well, it was alleged, as by subversive preparation for a Communist uprising. Bad news was continually being conveyed to Field-Marshal Sarit during his convalescence in the U.S.A. On March 30th, 1958, by-elections were held in five provinces whose electors had over 50% of passes in the primary grade of education and could elect new deputies to replace nominated deputies, even before the ten year trial period had run out. No substantial changes occurred in party strength, for the Democrats won 13 seats, the government 9, and Independents 4.

While Field-Marshal Sarit was enjoying a prolonged convalescence near London in England, worse news reached him of impending trouble. He envisaged the danger of further unrest and disorder, the overthrow of the monarchy, the subversion of Buddhism, and the destruction of all the institutions cherished and upheld at great cost by the Thai nation.[16] Secretly, Field-Marshal Sarit flew back to Bangkok in a chartered plane. On October 20th his friend, General Thanom Kittikachorn, resigned his post as Premier, and at 11.13 p.m. Field-Marshal Sarit proclaimed the Revolution with the support of the army, navy, air force, and some civilians, who now became known as the Revolutionary Party.

In its declaration No. 4 the Revolutionary Party stated that it would: "1. Respect human rights as set forth in the Declaration of Human Rights. It shall refrain from any action which may be regarded as violations of such rights unless in the interest and for the preservation of national security. 2. Up hold the power and independence of

15 *Elections in Thailand*, Department of Interior, Thailand, 1958.

16 *Thai News Bulletin* Royal Thai Embassy, London, November 12th, 1958.

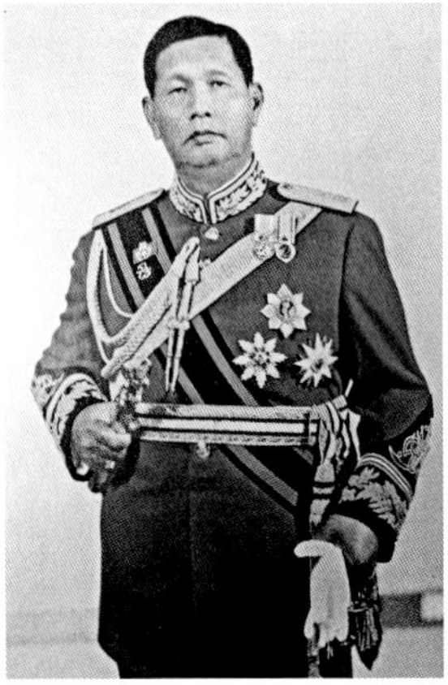

Field-Marshal Sarit Thanarat. (Paisarn Piemmettawat)

the Courts of Justice which shall not be subjected to any influence or intervention by the Revolutionary Party. 3. Abide by the international obligations binding on Thailand by virtue of the treaties and conventions, strictly observe the principles of International Law both in the form of written statutes and time-honoured customs and practices among the nations. Furthermore, it shall carry out the duties and obligations binding on Thailand as a member of S.E.A.T.O. 4. Above all, strictly adhere to the principle that the sovereign and the Thai nation are one and the same inseparable entity. Thai history is founded on the conception that the sovereign is the symbol of the nation and the palladium of the Thai people. The Revolutionary Party shall do all in its power to uphold and cherish this institution and to see to it that the sovereign is held in the deepest veneration and that no sacrilege is perpetrated on the sovereign, the royal family, and the royal Traditions."[17]

Field-Marshal Sarit, as Leader of the Revolutionary Party, addressed His Majesty the King directly in an official note, pledging to uphold the constitutional monarchy system of government. His Majesty graciously replied through his Principal Secretary as follows:-

"His Majesty the King has graciously observed that the Revolutionary Party's objective of protecting the people, safeguarding national welfare and interest and promoting the prosperity of the country is a noble one. Having set yourself a noble objective, you are expected to proceed with your work with loyalty and uprightness, placing the interest of the nation above all. All future actions should be pondered over carefully to ensure the attainment of the said objective. You should be constantly mindful of the pledges made in the declarations. You will have His Majesty's full blessing if all this is carried out."[18]

All observers, Thai and foreign, have generally agreed that Field-Marshal Sarit had the support of the vast majority of the Thai people. On January 28th, 1959, a Provisional Constitution was proclaimed and members of a Constituent Assembly appointed. Field-Marshal Sarit was made premier by the king on February 9th. On February 23rd he underwent another serious and successful operation, this time in Bangkok by U.S. surgeons.

Thus far is the history of Thailand. Her future rests in the hands of the Thai people, from generation to generation.

17 *Ibid.*
18 *Ibid.*

King Bhumibol in full dress uniform at the beginning of his reign. (Paisarn Piemmettawat)

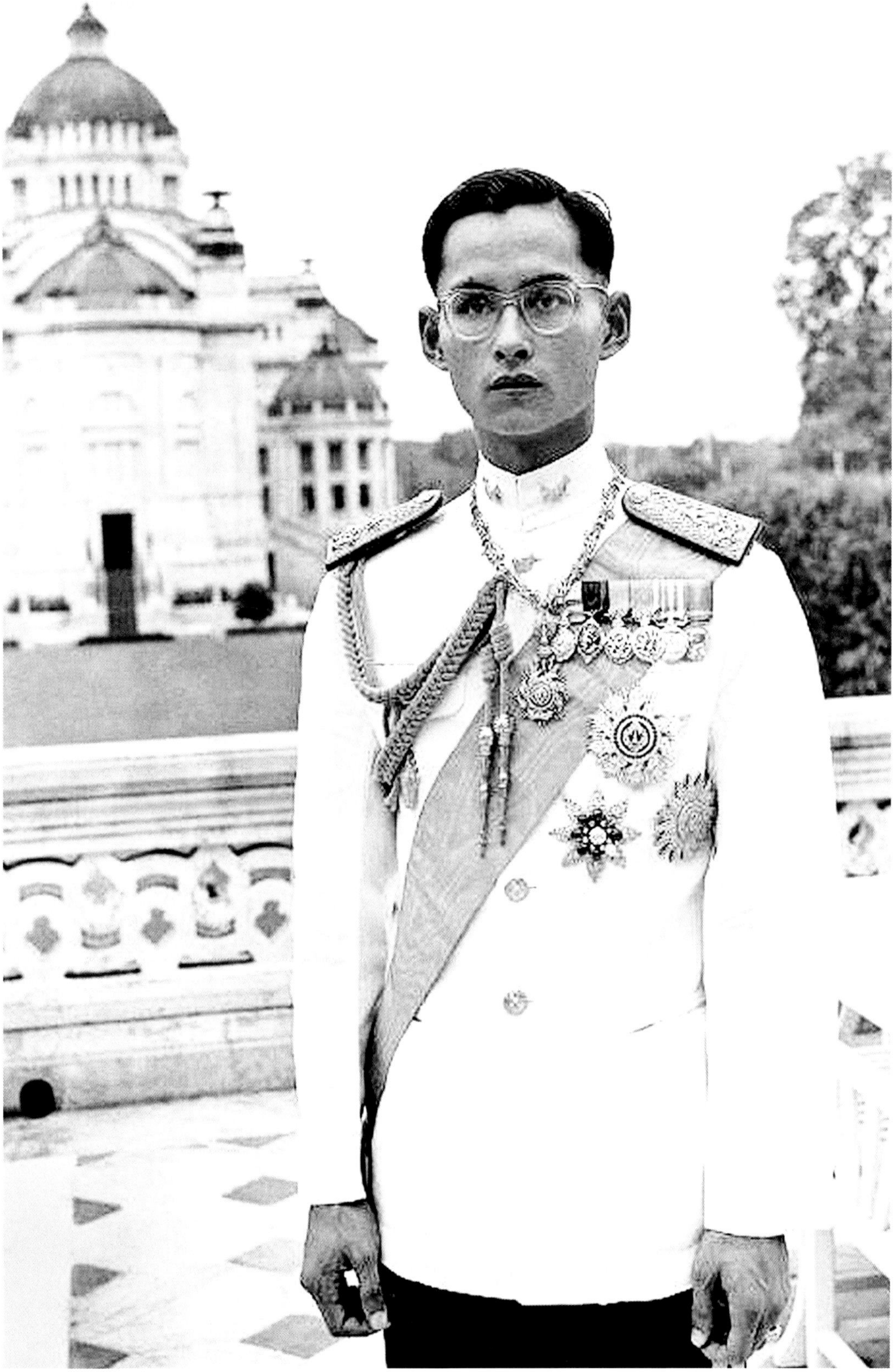

Afterword

Barend J. Terwiel

Prince Chula's book ends in the year 1959. Two years earlier an election had taken place, but it had not resulted in the formation of a stable government. This, Prince Chula tells us, motivated General Sarit Thanarat on 20 October 1958 to stage a coup d'état. Three months later a new provisional constitution was proclaimed.

This sequence – an election, a period of democracy, tensions rising, a coup d'état followed by a recasting of the constitution – was to occur repeatedly in the following decades. During the more than eighty years that have passed since the first successful coup in 1932 that ended the absolute monarchy, political scientists have counted eighteen more coups, during which time no less than thirteen prime ministers were removed from office. The interim constitution of 2014 is the nineteenth draft of that key document, indicating that Thai lawmakers still are struggling with the formulation of a stable set of rules. It is not here the place to present the array of prime ministers that led the country after 1959. Neither is this the place to note the differences between the various constitutions. Some constitutions attempted to construct a viable democratic framework, others tried to uphold the innate inequality of the traditional Thai hierarchical system and protect privileges of the ruling elite. A balancing act between popular democracy and Praetorianism.

Instead, the main theme of *Lords of Life* – the developments surrounding the monarchy – will be followed in broad outline. This afterword ends on October 13, 2016 with the demise of the ninth monarch of the Chakri dynasty on October 13, 2016 and the beginning of the reign of his son Vajiralongkorn.

The relationship between King Bhumibol and General Sarit was mutually supportive. The king provided legitimacy to the Field Marshal and Sarit encouraged the king to play a greater public role. Sarit's successor Thanom Kittikachorn also encouraged the popularization of the throne.

Old rituals, such as the royal *kathin* ceremony with a spectacular barge procession were reenacted. School textbooks were rewritten in order to stress the prominent role of the king in maintaining the nation. In 1960, the king's birthday was proclaimed as a national holiday. Daily announcements of the king's activities were broadcast on the radio and TV, invariably using the elaborate royal vocabulary. A visit to Vietnam in December 1959 by the royal couple proved a great success. During the following five years, the king and queen made more than twenty goodwill visits – to Indonesia, Burma, the United States, many European countries Australia, Japan and the Philippines. Invariably, the young king and his stylish wife proved to be major hits with the media.

At home the king officiated over countless ceremonies. In the 1960s, a number of agricultural projects were placed under the king's patronage and test projects with new food crops, the opening up of new agricultural areas, water management, and opium eradication, were launched while in the spacious palace grounds, the monarch established an experimental farm. Over the years, the king became a much admired head of state, a caring, frugal and gentle monarch.

The nationalist slogan Nation, Religion and Royalty (*chat, sasana, phramahakasat*), first propagated by Rama VI, was revived and featured prominently in the government's efforts to suppress and combat communism. Not only did the king cut many ribbons, inaugurating new bridges, irrigation projects and hospitals, but from 1961 onwards, King Bhumibol personally officiated at degree ceremonies of higher institutes of learning. The successful candidate was given the opportunity of having a photograph made of the moment when the monarch handed over the diploma. Over time, thousands of Thai households and offices proudly displayed this magic moment when the graduate was directly in contact with the king.

Political tensions rose dramatically in the early 1970s, culminating in October 1973 with a mass protest in Bangkok which went out of control. Widespread rioting caused the army to intervene leaving a toll of

77 dead and more than 800 wounded. The king then directly intervened by ordering the gates to Chitralada Palace to be opened so that demonstrators could find refuge. On October 16 the ruling military clique fled the country and King Bhumibol appointed a civilian to form an interim government.

The student leaders who had hoped that a liberal democratic system would now transform Thailand soon ran into difficulties. However, it was the Americans withdrawal from Southern Vietnam in 1975 that alarmed the king's major advisers. In quick succession Cambodia and Laos fell to the communists whilst the democratic experiment in Thailand appeared not decisive enough to large sections of the military. The royal family then decided to support the village scout movement, whereby hundreds of thousands of rural adults swore an oath to protect king and country.

Student protests in October 1976 once more led to a massacre; officially 46 people were killed and hundreds wounded, but probably the toll was much larger. The king again intervened, this time siding with the conservative forces and a return of the old elite

In 1980 General Prem Tinsulanonda became prime minister; and soon developed a close cooperation between him and the king, who sided with those anti-democratic forces in his country that combated the threat of communism. A year later a faction of the army attempted a coup d'état causing Prem to flee to Khorat in northeastern Thailand. Immediately the king also went to Khorat, a gesture which sufficed to make the coup fail. In the following eight years the king and Prem continued to guide Thailand and in 1988 when Prem retired he became member of the Privy Council, and ten years later President of that body. In later years when Bhumibol became frail, Prem became his trusted agent.

Another crisis took place in May 1992 when a large demonstration against Prime Minister Suchinda Kraprayoon was dispersed by the army causing the death of hundreds of citizens. On May 20th the king once more intervened, ordering both the Prime Minister and the leader of the opposition Chamlong Srimuang to appear before him. During the audience, broadcast live, Suchinda promised to stop the military crackdown and announced an amnesty for protesters. He also agreed to an amendment to the constitution, requiring the prime minister to be elected. The opposition leader asked the demonstrators to disperse, which they did. Four days later Suchinda resigned and the king chose a neutral politician, Anand Panyarachun as the new leader of the government, who began preparing a new, more liberal constitution. The king was widely praised for defusing the situation.

The business tycoon Thaksin Shinawatra who had won the 2001 election on a populist platform was a political outsider and the first premier who took it upon himself to diminish the influence of the establishment. Unusually, the king occasionally uttered a veiled criticism, for example by mentioning the increased ruthlessness with which the separatist movement in the south was being suppressed. Early in 2005 Thaksin was re-elected winning more than fifty per cent of the vote, and many members of the establishment feared losing their historic privileges. The judiciary declared the election void, but before a new election took place, in September 2006 the army staged a coup.

Massive unrest broke out in the capital with pro- and contra-Thaksin demonstrations, but the king was less able to use his influence. For some years the king, who in 2006 had celebrated the 60th anniversary of his coronation, had been ailing. In 2009 he was transferred to Siriraj hospital to be treated for pneumonia and, apart from a few short interludes he remained in a special wing of the building for almost four years. In 2013, now 85 years old, the frail monarch visited his seaside resort in Hua Hin. On June 9th 2015, the 69th anniversary of his coronation he held his final audience in Bangkok. More than sixteen months later, on October 13th 2016, now aged 88, he passed away in Siriraj hospital as a result of kidney failure and pneumonia.

He was succeeded by Crown Prince Maha Vajiralongkorn.

King Bhumibol's cremation took place almost a year later, on 26th October 2017. For five days, hundreds of thousands of mourners had attended the accompanying ceremonies, many in tears bemoaning the loss of the king who had occupied such a special place in their hearts.

BIBLIOGRAPHY

In Thai

Chao Phraya Dibakarawongse: *History of the First Reign,* Bangkok, 1869. Edited by Prince Damrong in 1901 and reprinted in 1935.

Prince Damrong: *History of the Reign of Rama II,* Bangkok, 1916.

Luang Udom Sombat: *Journals* 2nd Edition, Bangkok, 1916.

Phra Nala Kamluang, poem by King Rama VI, Bangkok, 1917.

King Chulalongkorn's Letters to Queen Saowabha during his European tour of 1897, Bangkok, 1919.

King Rama VI: Preface to *History of Warfare,* by Prince Chakrabongse, 2nd Edition, Bangkok, 1920.

American Envoys in the Third Reign, Bangkok, 1923.

Klai Ban (Far from Home). King Chulalongkorn's Letters to his daughter, Bangkok, 1924.

Phra Pinklao: *Manual of the Artillery,* Bangkok, 1924.

King Rama III: *Collected Works,* Bangkok, 1929.

Prince Damrong: *King Chulalongkom before his accession,* Bangkok, 1929.

Collected History No. 52 "Death of King Mongkut", Bangkok, 1929.

News of the beginning of the Fourth Reign in a Singapore newspaper (in Thai and English), Bangkok, 1932.

Chao Phraya Dibakarawongse: *History of the Reign of Rama III,* Bangkok, 1934.

Chao Phraya Dibakarawongse: *History of the Fourth Reign,* Bangkok 1935.

Luang Vichitra Vadhakam: *Siam and the Golden Land,* Bangkok, 1936.

Collected History Part 62 "Farang Envoys to Bangkok", Bangkok, 1937.

List of Names of Princes and Princesses of the Chakri House, Bangkok, 6th Edition, 1938.

King Chulalongkorn: *Text for a sermon in honour of Rama III,* Bangkok 1939.

Royal Daily Life, Bangkok, 1946.

Captain Leng Srichandra: *The Revolution of 1912,* (R.S. 130) Bangkok, 2nd Edition, 1946.

Prince Damrong: *Memoirs,* Bangkok, 1946.

M.R. Seni Pramoj: *King Mongkut as Legislator,* Bangkok, 1949.

Queen Sukumala to Her Son, Bangkok, 1950.

Collected Royal Writings (Partly in English') Bangkok, 1951.

Prince Damrong: *Tales of Ancient Times,* Bangkok, 1954.

The Abolition of Serfdom in the Fifth Reign, Bangkok, 1956.

Princess Prasong Paribatra: *Memoirs,* Bangkok, 1956.

Prince Dhani: *An Enlarged Thai version of The Reconstruction of Rama I,* Bangkok, 1957.

History of Ayudhya, Bangkok, 1958.

Prince Damrong and Prince Naris: *Letters of Princes,* Part 49, Bangkok, 1959.

M.R. S. Navaratana: *Thai Heroes,* Bangkok, undated.

General Prince Alongkot: *Notes for his unpublished book.*

Siam Samai (Weekly Thai Journal) Vol. 9 No. 444, November 15th 1955.

In English

John Crawfurd: *A Journal of an Embassy from the Governor-General of India to the Courts of Siam and Cochin-China,* London, 1828.

Edmund Roberts: *Embassy to the Eastern Courts of Cochin-China, Siam and Muscat,* New York, 1837.

Sir John Bowring: *The Kingdom and People of Siam,* London, 1857.

Anna Leonowens: *The English Governess at the Siamese Court, Boston,* U.S.A., 1871.

Spencer St. John: *The Life of Sir James Brooke, Rajah of Sarawak,* etc., London, 1879.

J. G. D. Campbell: *Siam in the Twentieth Century,* London, 1902.

Siam's Case for Revision of Obsolete Treaty Obligations, etc., 1919.

W. A. Graham: *Siam,* 3rd Edition, 1924.

O. P. Gilbert: *Men in Women's Clothes.* (English translation from the French by R. B. Douglas). London, 1926.

W. A. R. Wood: *A History of Siam,* Bangkok, 1933 Edition.

H. G. Quaritch Wales: *Ancient Siamese Government and Administration,* London, 1934.

K. P. Landon: *Siam in Transition,* London, 1939.

E. V. G. Kierman: *British Diplomacy in China,* 1880-1885, Cambridge, 1939.

E. W. Hutchinson: *Adventurers in Siam in the Seventeeth Century,* London, 1940.

Virginia Thomson: *Thailand, the New Siam,* New York, 1941.

Margaret Landon: *Anna and the King of Siam,* New York, 1944.

Sir Josiah Crosby: *Siam: The Crossroads,* London, 1945.

Dr. Malcolm Smith: *A Physician at the Court of Siam,* London, 1947.

Phra Sarasas: "My Country: Thailand." *Japan, 1940.* Bangkok Edition, 1950.

D. G. E. Hall: *A History of South-East Asia,* London, 1955.

Prince Chula Chakrabongse: *The Twain Have Met, or An Eastern Prince Came West,* London, 1956.

Walter F. Vella: *Siam under Rama III,* New York, 1957.

G. William Skinner: *Chinese Society in Thailand,* New York, 1957.

Sir Geoffrey Thomson: *Front Line Diplorriat,* London, 1959.

Ripley: *Believe It or Not,* London, 6th Impression.

The Ceremonies to be observed at the Royal Coronation of Their Majesties King George V and Queen Mary, etc., 1911.

Reports of the Financial Adviser, 1913-1914, W. J. F. Williamson.

Reports of the Financial Adviser, 1917-1918, W. J. F. Williamson.

Reports of the Financial Adviser, 1925-1926, Sir Edward M. Cook.

Reports of the Financial Adviser, 1936-1937, William Doll.

Reports of the Financial Adviser, 1937-1938, William Doll.

Reports of the Financial Adviser, 1938-1939, William Doll.

Prince Damrong: "Records of Siamese History". *J.O.S.S.,* Vol. XI, Part 2.

Prince Damrong: "The Introduction of Western Culture in Siam". *J.O.S.S.,* Vol. XX, Part 2.

J. Burney and G. Cœdès: "The Origins of the Sukhodaya Script". *J.O.S.S,* Vol. XXI Part 2.

M.R. Seni Pramoj: "King Mongkut as Legislator", *J.O.S.S.,* Vol. XXXVIII.

Prince Dhani: "The Reconstruction of Rama I of the Chakri Dynasty". *J.O.S.S.,* Vol. XLIII Part 1, August 1955.

Prince Dhani: Review of "Anna and the King of Siam", by Margaret Landon, *Standard,* Bangkok, 1946.

A. B. Griswold: "King Mongkut in Perspective". *J.O.S.S.,* Vol. XLV, Part 1, April, 1957.

Prince Dhani: Review of Prince Chula's "The Twain Have Met, etc.", in *J.O.S.S.,* Vol. XLVI, Part 1, June, 1958.

Professor Silpa Birasri (C. Feroci): "The Buddhist Sculpture". *Thailand Culture Series,* No. *17,* Bangkok, 1954.

Phraya Anuman Rajadhon: "Thai Language". *Thailand Culture Series,* No. 47, Bangkok, 1954.

Alexander B. Griswold: "The Real King Mongkut of Siam". *Eastern World,* London, 1955.

K. A. Lawson: "Thailand or Siam, Which is Correct?" *Samaggi Sara,* London, February. 1956, Vol. 27, No. 1.

The Honourable Sir Steven Runciman: *The Writing of History,* March 20th, 1957. (A lecture in Kuching).

Report of the Ninth Pacific Congress, Section on Anthropology, November, 1957.

M. L. Boonlua Kunjara and Dr. Bunchob Bandhumedha: Paper presented at the Round Table Conference of South-East Asian Experts. *Bangkok Post,* November 18th, 1957.

Elections in Thailand, Department of Interior, Thailand, 1958.

Thai News Bulletin. Royal Thai Embassy, London, November 12th, 1958.

Eric Beresford: Talk to the Malvern Branch of the China Inland Mission. *Malvern Gazette,* May 29th 1959.

D. J. Enright: Review of "The Mask of Siam ", by David Barnett. *The Spectator,* August 14th, 1959.

M.R. Kukrit Pramoj: The *King of Siam Speaks,* unpublished MS. in English.

In French

L'Abbé de Choisy: *Journal du Voyage de Siam fait en* 1685-1686, Paris, 1687.

Nicolas Gervaise: *Histoire naturelle et politique du Royaume de Siam,* Paris, 1688.

M. de la Loubère: *Description du Royaume de Siam,* 2 Vols., Paris, 1691.

Mgr. Pallegoix: *Description du Royaume Thai ou Siam, Paris,* 1854.

Capitaine Seauve: *Les Relations de la France et du Siam,* Paris, 1908.

A. Leclerc: *Histoire de Camhodge,* Paris, 1914.

Leopold Robert-Martignan: *La Monarchie Absolue Siamoise de 1350 à 1925,* Paris, undated, but sometime after 1926.

R. Lingat: "Note sur la revision des lois siamoise en 1808". *J.O.S.S.,* Vol. XIII, Part I.

Vachet as recorded in Adrian Launay "Histoire de la Mission de Siam". *Documents Historiques,* Paris, Vol. I.

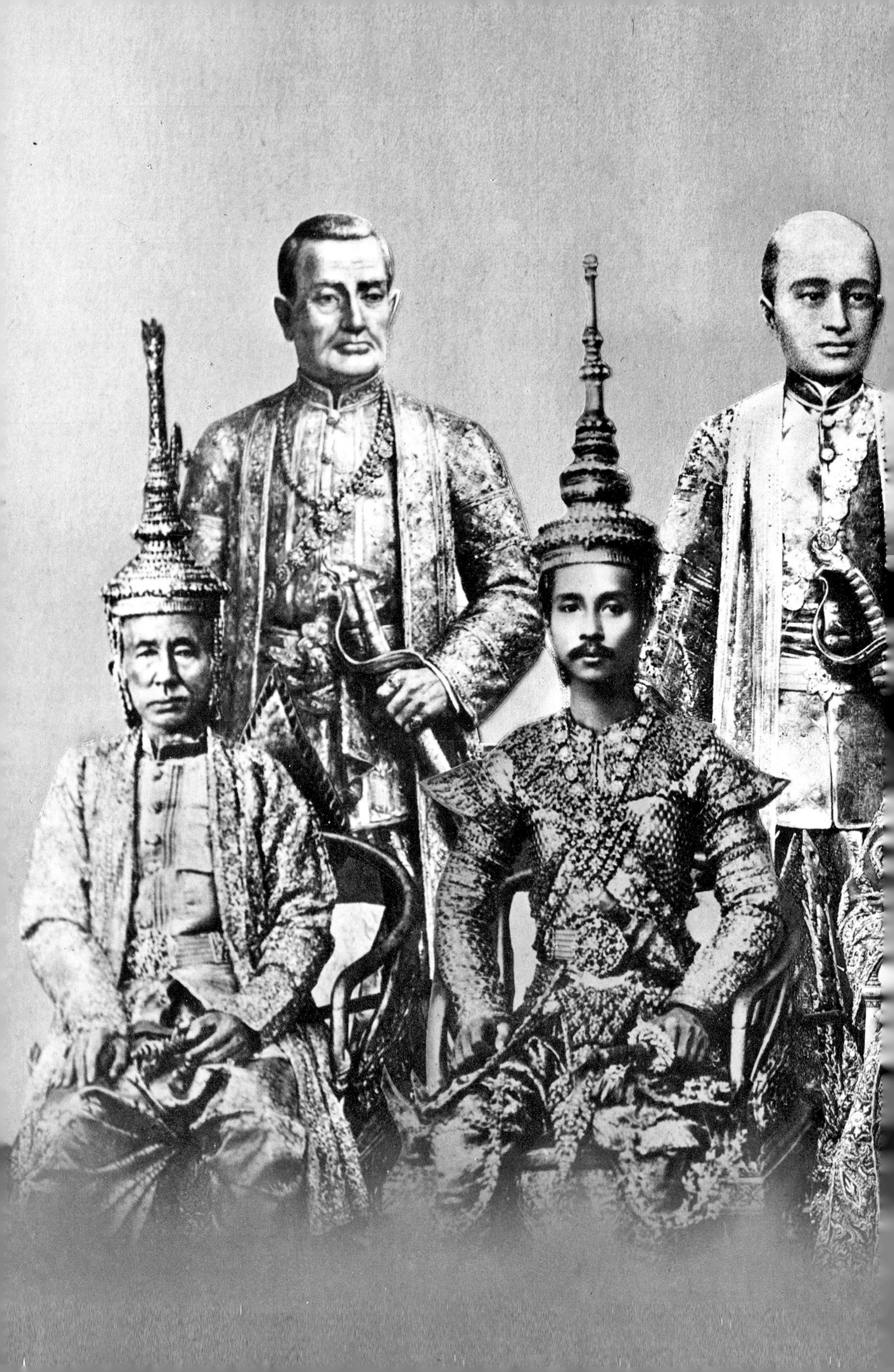

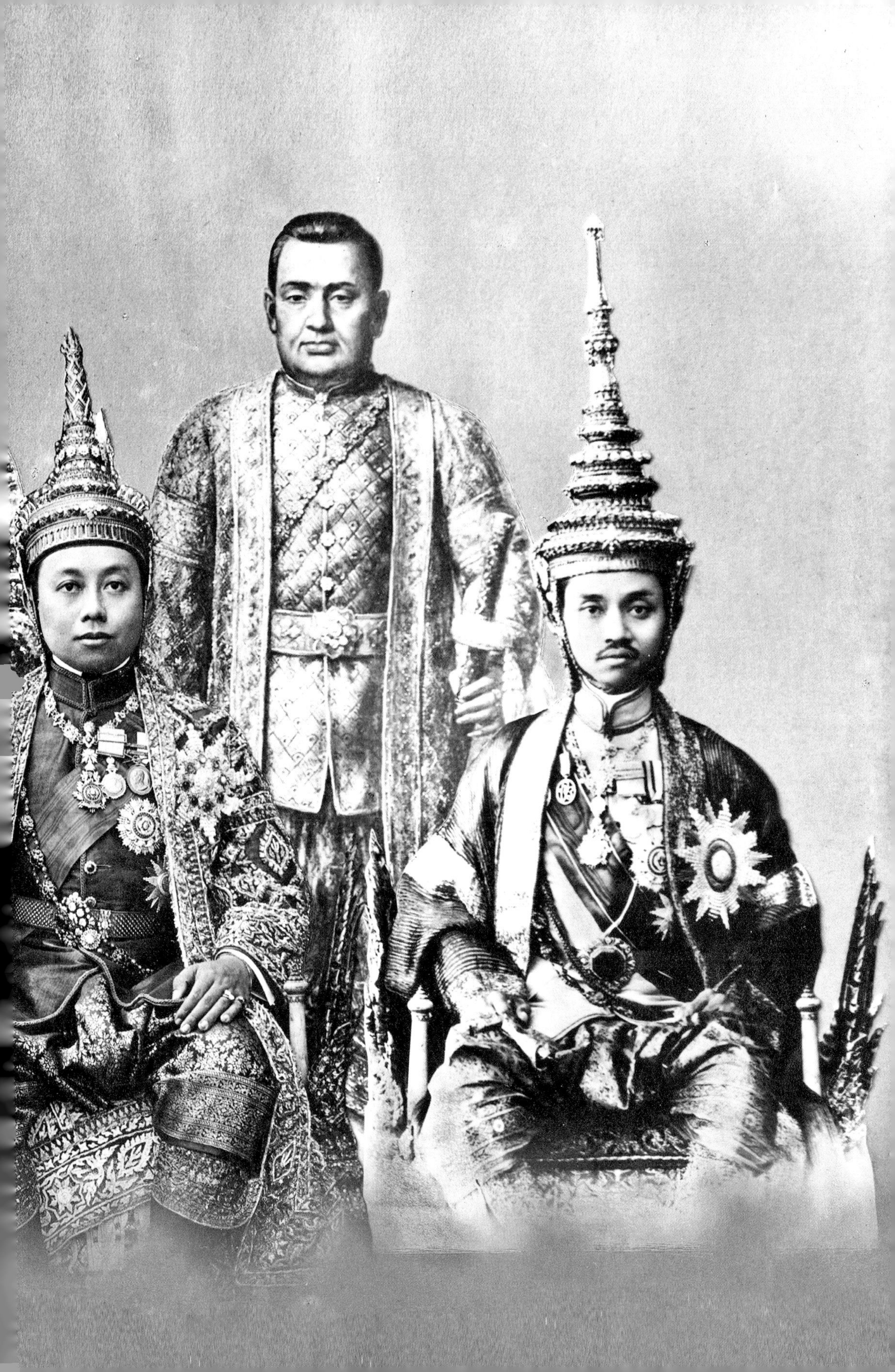

INDEX

Numbers in bold denote illustrations